The Leader Manager

The Leader Manager

John N. Williamson, Ed.D.

Wilson Learning Corporation

Editor

JOHN WILEY & SONS

New York   Chichester   Brisbane   Toronto   Singapore

Copyright © 1984, 1986 by Wilson Learning Corporation.
Published by John Wiley & Sons, Inc.

All rights reserved. Published simultaneously in Canada.

Reproduction or translation of any part of this work
beyond that permitted by Section 107 or 108 of the
1976 United States Copyright Act without the permission
of the copyright owner is unlawful. Requests for
permission or further information should be addressed to
the Permissions Department, John Wiley & Sons, Inc.

ISBN 0-471-83693-1

Printed in the United States of America

10 9 8 7 6 5 4 3 2 1

In Memory of
Tom Utne

CONTRIBUTORS

George Ainsworth-Land
Wilson Learning Corporation
Eden Prairie, Minnesota

Anthony Athos
Author, Consultant, and Lecturer
Gloucester, Massachusetts

Lloyd Baird
Boston University
Boston, Massachusetts

Louis B. Barnes
Harvard University
Cambridge, Massachusetts

Warren Bennis
University of Southern California
Los Angeles, California

David E. Berlew
Massachusetts Institute of Technology*
Cambridge, Massachusetts

David L. Bradford
Stanford University
Palo Alto, California

Allan R. Cohen
Babson College
Babson Park, Massachusetts

Cortlandt Cammann
University of Michigan
Ann Arbor, Michigan

Stanley M. Davis
Boston University
Boston, Massachusetts

John Enright
Pro Telos
Los Altos, California

John A. Fairbank
VA Medical Center and
University of Mississippi
Medical Center
Jackson, Mississippi

Andrew S. Grove
Intel Corporation
Santa Clara, California

Larry E. Greiner
University of Southern California
Los Angeles, California

Roger Harrison
Harrison Associates
Berkeley, California

Frederick Herzberg
University of Utah
Salt Lake City, Utah

John Immerwahr
University of Villanova
Villanova, Pennsylvania

Rosabeth Moss Kanter
Yale University
New Haven, Connecticut

Kathy E. Kram
Boston University
Boston, Massachusetts

Allan A. Kennedy
Selkirk Associates, Inc.
Boston, Massachusetts

Steven Kerr
University of Southern California
Los Angeles, California

William B. Lashbrook
Wilson Learning Corporation
Eden Prairie, Minnesota

Edward E. Lawler III
University of Southern California
Los Angeles, California

Rensis Likert (d. 1981)
University of Michigan
Director Emeritus
Ann Arbor, Michigan

Jane Gibson Likert
University of Michigan*
Ann Arbor, Michigan

Donald N. Michael
Author and Lecturer
Berkeley, California

David A. Nadler
Columbia University*
New York, New York

Richard Tanner Pascale
Stanford University
Palo Alto, California

Julien R. Phillips
McKinsey & Company
San Francisco, California

Donald M. Prue
VA Medical Center
and University of Mississippi
Medical Center
Jackson, Mississippi

Donald A. Schon
Massachusetts Institute of Technology
Cambridge, Massachusetts

R. Roosevelt Thomas, Jr.
R. Thomas and Associates
Decatur, Georgia

Alvin Toffler
Author and Lecturer
New York, New York

Daniel Yankelovich
Yankelovich, Skelly, and White
Washington, D.C.

*Affiliation at the time of original publication.

PREFACE

Wilson Learning has been involved in helping business organizations plan their futures for many years. Increasingly, we observe that the vast majority of our client companies find themselves at critical times of transition — a transition triggered by dramatic changes in their competitive environments and the realization that the management strategies of the past are no longer working. Consequently, over the last five years, Wilson Learning has directed much of its attention to the development of conceptual models and learning systems that assist our client organizations and their managers make this difficult transition.

One of the principal hallmarks of the new environment we are entering as a society is the elevation of *people* as businesses' key leverageable asset. Consequently, managers must come to view their leadership responsibilities toward their people with every bit as much respect, discipline, and sophistication as they do their fields of functional expertise. The days of viewing people management as a tangential issue to the "real" business of management are over. As Peter Drucker observes, leveraging the creative and productive potential of people is fast becoming *the* business of business today.

Five years ago I challenged our research department to examine closely the parts of our client organizations that continued to be high performing despite the dramatic changes the organizations were confronting. What are their characteristics? How are they managed? Why are they effective? This ongoing inquiry has resulted in the five factor performance system model described by Dr. William B. Lashbrook in the Leadership section of this volume.

About the same time, Wilson Learning attracted George Ainsworth-Land, our Vice-Chairman for Advanced R & D. He is a noted general systems theorist whose insights into the principles governing change in organizations and society have tremendously expanded Wilson Learning's ability to assist our clients in understanding the change they are experiencing and chart a path through it. George also has contributed to this volume. His systems framework for the phases of change is presented in the Growth section.

A third member of Wilson Learning's professional staff making significant contributions to both our performance systems and growth models is Dr. John R. Wenburg, Wilson's Senior Vice-President for Strategic Business Services. John not only informed the models conceptually, but also has been one of their major translators to the business environment.

The two frameworks I have mentioned here are synthesized and serve as the theoretical basis for Wilson Learning's *Leadership-Management* program. I truly believe that *Leadership-Management* will prove to be the most outstanding management program ever developed.

It will play a significant role in leading our clients into the twenty-first century.

This collection of outstanding readings, while part of Wilson's *Leadership-Management* program materials, has been developed also to be of independent value to experienced managers who want to develop as leader-managers in their changing organizations. It is a remarkable volume. I commend it to your personal enjoyment and professional growth.

W. Mathew Juechter
President and CEO
Wilson Learning Corporation
September, 1984

CONTENTS

SECTION SEVEN — REWARDS

SECTION EIGHT — SUPPORT

The Leader~Manager

INTRODUCTION
John N. Williamson

The contributions in this collection are each outstanding statements of a facet of the emerging task facing experienced business managers today. This task centers around the necessity to fundamentally shift their point of view regarding their role in a dramatically different and rapidly approaching new business environment.

The volume necessarily focuses on change. Unfortunately, the current popularity of concern about the accelerating pace of change has made its discussion all too often a cliché. What is threatened by all of the popular attention is our understanding and appreciation of the fundamental implications that the ground swell of change will increasingly have on the lives of today's managers and the people they are responsible for "managing."

Together, the contributions to this volume provide readers with a new lens through which to view the management of people. This new perspective will, I hope, prove to be more powerful, more useful, and more appropriate to the business environment that is rapidly coming into focus. It is a perspective that requires the manager to play a more complex, diverse, and adaptable role — a role that may also prove to be richer, more human, and ultimately more fulfilling.

The overriding conclusion of these readings is that the emerging business environment is transforming the essential ordering of the assets of the business. People rather than materials, machines, facilities, or money are becoming the critical asset that must be managed and leveraged in business today.

Traditionally, except for a select executive group or a core of "fast-track" managers, businesses have tended to view their people as an expense item rather than an asset and relegated responsibility for people development to relatively low-level staff departments. Yet in an environment increasingly characterized by unpredictability and uncertainty, "demassification" of customer value, radical technological changes, continual shifts in competitive forces, and an increasingly complex level of social and economic influences on decision making, people, at all levels of the business, become the essential leverageable asset — the source of the required creativity, diversity, and adaptability.

People are the essential assets to be leveraged today. That is a drastic perceptual shift indeed. The readings that follow address how we must learn to manage, to lead, to leader-manage in response to this new point of view.

The readings follow a logical order. Since *change* itself has catalyzed the need for managers to alter their mindset about their jobs, this book begins with a series of readings that describe change today in terms of its overall social implications, its meaning in the business context, and its consequences for the individual.

3

The second section focuses on the essential importance of *leadership* today and builds the case for the requirement to synthesize one's notions of leader with those of manager into what is called the Leader-Manager.

The remainder of the volume provides a two-dimensional framework for exploring the role of the new Leader-Manager. The first dimension is that of growth and development. The readings in the *Growth* section provide the reader with an understanding of the underlying principles that govern change in any developing system. Together, the readings in this section argue that similar principles apply whether the readers are concerned with understanding what is happening to their organizations as a whole, to the work units they are responsible for managing, or to individuals (including themselves) within their work units.

The remaining five sections — *Mission, Goals, Feedback, Rewards,* and *Support* — focus on the second dimension of the Leader-Manager framework: the set of essential factors that have emerged from Wilson Learning's work with over 50,000 managers, as essential to "leveraging the human asset" and to producing work unit cultures that are both highly productive and personally fulfilling in a changing environment.

Together, these contributions document a powerful trend in management theory, a trend that recognizes the leadership and management of people not as a tangential human-relations problem, but as the central issue of business today.

SECTION ONE
CHANGE
Overview

For the past quarter century, all industrial nations have been buffeted by a radical pattern of change that has grown increasingly complex. Almost without our awareness this pattern of change is transforming the fundamental structures, relationships, and essential metaphors of industrial society. It is also threatening the long-term economic leadership of the United States, and undermining many of the personal habits and assumptions with which we have been coping with change. The three articles in this section focus on the impact and implications of this continuing period of radical change for our society, our businesses, and for ourselves and co-workers.

In "Beyond the Break-Up of Industrial Society," Alvin Toffler describes the change impacting the industrialized world as an economic "earthquake" which will alter and restructure our entire social, economic, and political system. Toffler argues that, despite apparent cultural differences, the industrialized nations share far more profound similarities. All have *massified* their societies through mass production, mass distribution, mass communication, and mass education.

All industrial societies tend to *standardize* everything from lifestyle to time. All *synchronize* activity, *centralize* power, and *concentrate* their capital into large organizations and their people into cities. Despite the different curriculum content in their schools, all industrial nations share the same "covert curriculum" — of punctuality, obedience, and tolerance for repetitive work. Such an education prepares the young for useful work in the production-line factories and classical bureaucracies that are the inevitable organizational forms of industrialized society.

Despite the growing economic and political dominance of the industrialized (or what Toffler refers to as Second Wave) societies over the past 300 years, Toffler argues persuasively that the underpinnings of the Second Wave are well on their way to being crushed by the mutually-reinforcing complex of changes that are transforming our entire way of life.

In Toffler's eyes, the break-up of Second Wave society is not a cause of despair. The transition to a Third Wave civilization is likely to be difficult and even problematic in its particulars. Yet, we are in a period of profound opportunity — we have an opportunity to renew the significant social and economic advances of the Second Wave while reversing many of its dehumanizing qualities. The matrix of change producing the Third Wave will inevitably shift the governing characteristics of the industrialized nations toward demassification, increased diversity, and decentralization. In turn, it will force a parallel shift in the rigid hierarchical

5

bureaucratic institutional form that dominated the Second Wave, a shift toward the increased flexibility of smaller, more fluid internal units, greater participation in decision making, and more diversity of values and work styles.

Experienced managers are well aware of the initial signs of this shift of organizational form. In many organizations, these early efforts, for example: to increase worker participation, to develop more adaptive and less hierarchical reporting structures, or to institute more flexible work rules, are the center of significant tension — a clash of world views between those who wish to return to the "successful" practices of the past and those who realize that these are necessary first steps if their organization is to remain successful and make the transition to a viable Third Phase business.

In "Transformations in the American Corporate Environment, 1960s-1980s," Rosabeth Moss Kanter echoes Toffler's theme of the transforming implications of recent change by tracing its impact on U.S. business organizations.

Kanter details the disturbing consequences of the relative failure of American companies to adapt to these changes over the past two decades. What is required, according to the author, for American businesses to remain successful is innovation at every level of organizational life. Innovation not just in new products and services, but also in the way organizations operate, in the way they engage and allocate resources, and even in the way they view themselves.

The characteristics of the required new organizational forms must, above all, center on increasing flexibility. Businesses must learn to bring resources together quickly to respond effectively to changes in their fluid markets, to the multiple requirements of their diverse stakeholders, and to the increasingly unpredictable shifts in their competitive environment. To do so, business organizations must develop more "surface" or interactive contacts with their various environments, create better environment-sensing mechanisms and organizational-response procedures, and above all, learn to manage a diverse and educated work force that is empowered to engage in the response-making process. In short, according to Kanter, business is moving from an era of *control* to an era of *responsiveness*.

These organizational shifts will necessarily require major changes in the manager's task. The days of the infallibility of management, the certainty of management tasks, and the predictability of management careers are numbered. There will be less and less clarity about the distinction between manager and subordinate as workers become more professional, sophisticated, and are asked to contribute their expertise at all decision-making levels. Managers will be persuaders and bargainers, and will influence work performance indirectly by managing the contextual parameters of the work unit.

Kanter concludes her analysis by observing that many managers today feel dislocated, disoriented, and anxious about the changes that are taking place in their businesses. What is slipping away is their sense of control and security; they are unprepared for change and feel at its mercy. They view change as their enemy rather than their friend or companion. As Kanter observes, "The corporations that will succeed and flourish in the times ahead will be those that have mastered the art of change . . . and the individuals who will succeed and flourish will also be masters of change."

The requirement for managers to be personal masters of change is what John Enright addresses in "Change and Resilience." According to Enright, change itself is not the real issue affecting managers today, rather it is their fundamental assumptions and perceptions of change that make the mastery of change such a complex issue.

For example, most experienced managers grew up during a period when a "Newtonian" world view pervaded popular perception. Within that point of view, the context of interpreting change rests on the assumption that the things in life are essentially stable. Consequently, change is the unusual occurrence and, therefore, the more change there is the more difficult it will be to cope with. From this point of view, we expect the circumstances surrounding us to remain pretty much the same or at least to be predictable if not controllable. Personal security rests with the maintenance of external "forms" or things we have accumulated and the anticipation that these forms will continue.

As Enright points out, however, there is an alternative frame of reference which is reemerging as this century's advances in elementary particle physics begin to seep into the popular consciousness. That frame of reference sees continual change — not stability — as the appropriate context for perceiving life. From this perspective, security rests not with the maintenance of external forms but with internal flexibility, with the ability to continually adapt and find new forms to promote the substantive ends we desire in life.

Enright parallels these alternative world views with contrasting approaches for coping with change. First is the approach of maintaining *solidity*, of responding to change through attempts to preserve the threatened forms that one has associated with satisfaction or success. These forms might include material objects, certain relationships, or one's current job and responsibilities. Enright calls the second approach to deal with change *resilience* or *versatility*. This second approach involves focusing on the substance of what is desired rather than the particular means that one may have assumed are required to achieve it.

Everyone has both of these approaches in their personal repertoire. Generally *solidity* is the more developed one. But Enright argues that, as change increasingly becomes the dominant characteristic of business life, the underdeveloped skills of *resilience* or *versatility* need to become paramount. He concludes his article with a discussion of specific tools

7

managers can use to improve their mastery of change and to develop the ability in the members of their work units.

Together the three articles in this section provide a contemporary framework for managers to understand the significance of the changing environment that is transforming their businesses and the tasks required of them to remain healthy and effective in that new environment.

BEYOND THE BREAK-UP OF INDUSTRIAL SOCIETY: POLITICAL AND ECONOMIC STRATEGIES IN THE CONTEXT OF UPHEAVAL

Alvin Toffler

"The future is being colonized all the time by people who have the resources, who do spend time thinking about it, planning for it and trying to shape it in their direction."

Let me begin with a few disclaimers. First, I don't have a crystal ball, and no futurist with a brain in his or her head would claim to know what the future holds. Futurism is not a science, and nobody should pretend to make it one. The best we can do is look at the world around us, collect as much information as we can, and run it through some models. There is no science to it, although it can be dressed up with computer numbers, more formal quantitative modeling and so forth.

Second, it is easy to talk about the long range when you are not struggling for survival. I recognize that people who have their backs against the wall must think about the immediate.

But I also recognize that the failure to devote some attention to the long range presses your back against the wall even more. Such failure means that decisions made are frequently counterproductive and chosen strategies frequently lead to disaster.

As hard as it is, I think some attention to the long-range future is absolutely critical for any organization or any group in society trying to fight for a better place in that future. The future is being colonized all the time by people who have the resources, who do spend time thinking about it, planning for it and trying to shape it in their direction.

Finally, since I said that I do not deliver a set of prophecies or predictions, what's the use of this exercise? One of the uses is to provide an unconventional framework; to look at what is happening today through lenses which are different from those we normally use; and to see if that alternative structuring of the information around us might not yield some interesting ideas for action today.

With that introduction in mind, I would like to address the mounting economic crisis we find ourselves in. This crisis is characterized by racing inflation, by high levels of unemployment, by pressure to reduce social spending, by rising attacks upon women and minorities, by outbreaks of racial conflict, and one could go on.

Much has been written about this economic crisis. The traditional right talks about the decline of productivity. The neoconservatives lash out at "entitlements," the code word for non-market redistribution. The liberals talk about bad management and betrayal by the president. The Marxists talk about the general crisis of capitalism. I believe that none of these views explain what is happening to us today.

What is happening today is not a recession or a depression. Rather, we are passing through a total restructuring, not merely of our economy, but of our whole society and way of life. To think of the phenomenon as *only* economic or *only* something which is happening in the United States is to totally misunderstand what we are now experiencing.

As I look about the world, I see a breakup of the system. However, the system which is breaking is not capitalism, nor is it communism or socialism. Rather, it is the world industrial system of which capitalism and communism are the children. I believe we are witnessing the general crisis of world industrial society, rather than the crisis of capitalism which the Marxists forecast. And it is one of the great turning points in human history.

One can look at history any number of ways and divide it into any number of pieces. At the risk of oversimplification, I find it useful to point out that the first historic wave of change began to move across the planet some ten thousand years ago after the invention of agriculture. Some three hundred years ago, the Industrial Revolution in Britain launched a second wave of historic change. Today I think we are feeling the third wave of change, a world-transforming event. And this transformation is not a purely American phenomenon.

If we stand back and look at the world, we find an industrial belt, some two dozen or so industrial nations, beginning with some 250 million people in the United States and Canada who live under industrial circumstances. In Western Europe, from Scandinavia in the north to Italy in the south, another 250 million people live in industrial societies. In Eastern Europe and the western part of the Soviet Union, approximately another 250 million people are living under industrial conditions. And finally in Asia, the youngest of the world's industrial regions — Japan, Singapore, Hong Kong, Australia, part of mainland China — there are another quarter of a billion human beings. Altogether a billion human beings live in the civilization created by the Industrial Revolution; and for all practical purposes, they have dominated the remaining three billion people on the planet for the past couple of hundred years.

If we look at these various industrial countries, we are immediately struck by the tremendous differences among them. The Soviet system is hardly our own, and I couldn't speak or write freely in the Soviet Union. There are also differences of culture. The Japanese culture is certainly radically different from the Swedish or the American cultures. There are differences of history and tradition. And yet, if we look beneath the surface in all of these industrial societies, we find some remarkable parallels.

All industrial societies utilize and are dependent upon fossil fuels. All industrial societies engage in mass production. All industrial societies are based on certain classical industries — steel, rail, textile, auto, coal. All of them require high capital, high energy inputs, and all of them produce huge amounts of pollution. All industrial societies, communist or capitalist, develop systems of mass distribution; because if you don't have a system of mass distribution, mass production makes no sense.

All industrial societies develop systems of mass education, and, on the surface, there are differences in education systems in various countries. If you look at the *visible* curriculum, you see big differences. The Russians teach Marxist economics and we teach classical or neoclassical economics. The French teach French literature and we teach English literature. But beneath that *overt* curriculum, there is a *covert* curriculum in all of these countries. And if we look at the covert curriculum, we once again find startling similarities. Virtually all children in all the industrial societies study three fundamental hidden courses.

First, they study a course in *punctuality.* Kids are required to show up on time and to march down the corridors of the school when the bell rings because it is expected that in adulthood they will show up at the factory gate when the whistle blows. They will be expected to pay attention to time and not to be late.

In all of these industrial societies, kids study a second course in *obedience.* They are taught not to ask certain questions; and even in the places where they are encouraged to ask questions, the smart ones know which ones you don't ask. In industrial societies (or what I call "Second Wave" societies), a disciplined industrial labor force is expected to be essentially obedient.

The third course which is taught in all industrial societies is a course in *rote* and *repetitive* work. Kids are exposed to rote and repetitive work year-after-year because it is the function of the system to get them to resign themselves to performing rote and repetitive work for the rest of their lives. That is what Second Wave production systems require.

All industrial societies also develop systems of mass communication, along with mass production, mass distribution, and mass education.

Furthermore, all industrial societies rely on certain fundamental principles. They all engage in *standardization.* We all know about the standardization of products, so that one item coming off the assembly line looks exactly like the next one. But the second wave of change launched by the Industrial Revolution did a lot more than merely to standardize products. It standardized even such subtle and profound things as time.

Before the Industrial Revolution, people did not use the same system for telling time, even though they lived in neighboring villages. A day might consist of 24 hours in one village and 10 hours in the village next door. There was a patchwork of systems of time measurement in society. The Second Wave standardized time — and today we even speak of

"Standard Time." (As early as 1790, when the Industrial Revolution dawned and the first factories cropped up, watches began to be mass-produced in England and Switzerland; because time took on new meaning in the factory. If you are late, you disrupt production down-stream in an interdependent work situation.)

All industrial societies also developed standard currencies. Money used to be issued in the form of script by local banks and by local communities. Then the nation-state monopolized the power to issue and to standardize currency in each society. We standardize political ideas and we standardize values. We have eliminated regional dialects and regional cuisines. We standardized lifestyles as the steamroller of industrialization rolled across the landscape. Standardization is a key principle of all Second Wave societies, capitalist or socialist.

All Second Wave societies also engaged in *synchronization.* It is not just the standardization of time but also the synchronization of activity. In Warsaw, Moscow, Tokyo or Detroit, people get up at a certain time in the morning, eat their breakfasts at the same time, get in their cars or on their bicycles and commute at the same time, get to the factory or the office pretty much at the same time, and they leave, go home, eat, watch television and maybe even do other things at the same time. There is a synchronization which runs through the system.

All Second Wave societies engaged in the *centralization* of political power, and they became *concentrated* societies. Before the Industrial Revolution, the energy required to run the society was in the form of the sun, water power, animal power, human muscle power, forms of energy that were distributed all over the planet — wherever there were people and animals. After the second wave of change, we became dependent upon highly concentrated deposits of energy and created huge cen-tralized generating facilities to turn that energy into a useful form.

Not only did we concentrate energy, we also created the corporation. In the socialist countries, it is called the "socialist production enterprise," which, like the corporation, has the function of concentrating capital for the purpose of supporting technological development.

We concentrated money and we also concentrated people. We took them out of the countrysides and concentrated them in the big cities. That was called "urbanization." Within the cities, we concentrated sub-populations. We took children out of the streets and homes and put them in special locations called "schools." We took sick people and con-centrated them in "hospitals." All industrial societies made use of the principle of concentration.

All industrial societies also embraced the principle of *maximization.* Europeans used to kid Americans for believing that "bigger is better." Americans in general would tease Texans for their obsession with bigness. But it is not an American or a Texan characteristic. It is an industrial characteristic.

Back in the 1930s, when Stalin was still the ruler of the Soviet empire, he would call in his planners and ask, "What's the biggest steel mill in the world?" After he had received his answer, Stalin would order, "Build me a bigger one!" He gave the same orders for the biggest copper smelting plant, the biggest hydro-electric dam, and so on. Finally, the Russian planners and economists literally took their lives in their own hands and dared to criticize the government for what they called "gigantamania." Nevertheless, today the Soviet Union still proudly boasts that it is building the biggest truck manufacturing facility in the world which covers some 43 square miles.

If you take these various principles and put them together — standardization, synchronization, centralization, concentration, maximization — and you apply them in an organization, the result is a certain kind of organization; namely, a classical bureaucracy. And the classical bureaucracy became the dominant organizational form in all the industrial societies — capitalist, communist, eastern, western, northern, southern.

There are many other similarities in the industrial societies. For example, all industrial societies standardized on the nuclear family as a particular kind of family that became the dominant model. Before the Industrial Revolution, most families were large, with lots of kids and several generations living under the same roof, and the whole family working together as a production team in the fields or in the village. When the first factories sprang up, the family began to adapt to the new character of production in the society. Fathers would take their entire families — the old folks and the kids — into the factory and put them to work. The father was the labor contractor, the "straw boss," and the members of the family were the workers.

But this form of organization, which was highly efficient in the fields for ten thousand years, was soon discovered to be not very efficient in a factory. The old folks couldn't keep up. Sometimes the kids were too small even to reach the levers on the machines. They tried everything; standing the children on boxes, tying them to the machines, and literally hanging them from the rafters. But the kids were not really good, efficient workers. Gradually, a smaller family unit, with the father going into work and the wife and kids staying home, turned out to be more malleable, more disciplined and more appropriate to the new form of production required in a factory.

Moreover, a mobile labor force was needed. When layoffs occurred in one town, those who were laid off would look for work in the next town. Such mobility is much more difficult when a large family must be moved. In every industrial society, family size began to shrink, taking on the characteristics of the nuclear family which became the basic standard model. Even in Japan, the nuclearization of the family occurred, although it took much longer.

13

But there are even more parallels among Second Wave societies. All industrial societies became part of the nation-state system. All of them became dependent upon Big Government, Big Corporations, Big Cities. In effect, the Industrial Revolution created a chain of *mass societies* which emphasized the uniformities rather than the differences among people.

When we look at the principles, the technologies, the institutions, the energy systems and so forth, they form an interactive social system — a civilization. And when I say that the system is breaking, I mean that the parts of this system are no longer interfacing and interacting the way they used to.

As we look around the world, we find that the subsystems of all the industrial societies are in deep trouble. There are crises in the energy systems, the health-delivery systems, the welfare systems, the family systems, the urban systems, the value systems. We see wild oscillations in the world industrial economy, with currencies swinging up and down, the emergence of a huge bubble of Eurodollars, money and credit unregulated by any central bank, inflation, unemployment and so on. And I would argue that we are also seeing signs of political crisis in country after country. The governments find themselves increasingly helpless to cope with their multiple crises.

This breakdown of industrial society can be viewed as bad news. But there is another way to look at the same phenomenon.

At the very same time we see the crumbling of many of the institutions of this society, we are also beginning to see the emergence of what might be called a new "civilization," with its own new systems. This new civilization (which I call "Third Wave" civilization) is not merely a straight line extension of the old industrial civilization, but is, in fact, based on new technologies and new principles, even contradictory principles.

We see a shift at the level of energy, economics, technology and industry; a shift from the traditional mass production industries to a new stage of technological development based upon information, computers, electronics, communications, genetics, oceans, space and so on. There is a new breed of technology beginning to appear on the horizon.

Nor is it only technology and energy which are changing. Third Wave civilization will have radically different social structures which operate on new principles. For example, instead of synchronization, we are beginning to see a movement away in the demands for decentralization and destandardization. Instead of maximization, we now hear talk about "small is beautiful."

We are seeing many movements challenging the principles of industrial society. Such movements are leading to new kinds of organizational structures — matrix organizations and ad hoc forms — which are no longer the traditional monolithic bureaucratic structure. None of these tiny elements are significant in and of themselves. But taken together, they begin to form a self-reinforcing pattern; the beginning, I believe, of a

14

new way of life, a new social system, based upon new principles. This presents new problems and new opportunities for us — for business, organized labor, women and minorities, and for *all* of us.

* * *

One key difference between the emerging system and the past has to do with diversity. Second Wave societies were mass societies in which all of the cultural, political, social and psychological pressures seemed to go in the direction of uniformity. In the United States, it took the form of the melting pot. Forget your national origin and melt. If you were black, the push was for integration. In every case, the push was to assimilate and become part of the whole.

The Third Wave society, I would argue, is no longer a mass society but rather a demassified society in which diversity rules rather than uniformity. And I believe that demassification of our society is taking place at every level simultaneously in self-reinforcing and powerful ways.

For example, we are moving from an energy system based primarily on a single source to an energy system based upon a multiplicity of sources and technologies. Not only are we moving from a nonrenewable to a renewable energy system, but we are moving also toward an energy system based on high diversity — one much less vulnerable than the systems we use now. We are going to see a thousand different technologies and combinations of technologies come into place.

For example, there are people looking at the relationship of solar electricity generation, through the use of photovoltaic cells, to extracting the hydrogen out of water and then using the water to power automobiles. Others are looking at the waste steam coming out of industrial plants. Until now, steam was used to create the heat necessary for various industrial processes and then was vented into the air as thermo-pollution. Thought is now being given to using the waste steam to power turbo-charged windmills. There are scores of combinations of technologies emerging on the horizon.

Demassification is occurring in the field of communications. Take magazines, for example. Back in the 1950s and 1960s, magazines with very large circulations fell one after another like trees chopped down in a forest. The giant magazines collapsed, although some of them came back. But they came back with a small circulation rather than the seven or eight millions they used to enjoy.

Some people predicted that this signaled the end of reading; that Americans just don't read anymore. But the publishers know better; because the magazine industry is now booming. Rather than a few magazines with huge circulations, the industry is now based on scores, hundreds and even thousands of magazines with miniature circulations, each of them targeted for special groups in the public. A fundamental shift has occurred in the print media.

In the television industry, too, a demassification of the mass media is taking place. For the first time, the three networks are losing audiences. They are getting competition — Ted Turner's Cable News Network, the qube system in Columbus, all kinds of experimental cable systems and interactive systems.

Some of these systems reverse the fundamental principles of industrial communications. During the Second Wave period, a mass media (a newspaper, a magazine or a television station) was a factory which created the image at one place and distributed it to the millions of consumers at the other end. It was a one-way communication from producer to consumer.

Now we are beginning to get interactive communications. In Columbus, Ohio, my wife and I appeared on the qube system, which makes it possible for viewers to get a high diversity of information: thirty channels of television offering everything from courses in accounting or anthropology to sports to concerts to porno films to every conceivable variety of programming. In addition it is possible for viewers to send information back into the studio. No longer is the information conveyed one way from the microphone or camera to the listener or viewer but rather it flows the other way as well.

In Japan, we visited a system outside Osaka. Homes have been wired so that viewers not only have a hand-held device for sending "yes" or "no" responses to the studio but every subscriber also has a television camera and microphone of their own. As we were being interviewed in the studio, the monitor clicked on and a Japanese woman in her own kitchen, with her child running around in the background, was saying, "Welcome to Japan, Mr. Toffler. And pardon me for my poor English, but next year it will be better because we housewives are going to communicate with each other through this television system and learn English together." Such systems of two-way, high-diversity communication challenge the fundamental principles of the mass media.

In the field of economics, the same shift toward diversity is evident. For example, I believe that we no longer have a uniform national economy, although I am not an economist and I don't have the figures to prove it. The Industrial Revolution created consolidated national markets and that, in combination with a consolidated political system, became the modern nation-state. Today, in many parts of the rich world, regional economies have grown as large and complicated as national economies were thirty or forty years ago, and this is the reason for a rising sectionalism, regionalism and divergence. Economies in different parts of a country are no longer becoming more massified, but rather becoming more diverse and more demassified, requiring different kinds of policies for each one. And that creates enormous difficulties for those who try to manage the economy from the nation-state center, whether through monetary policy, fiscal measures, or central planning.

The rise of regionalism is not merely economic but also cultural; the insistence upon linguistic autonomy, the rise of regional poetry magazines, and other kinds of regional magazines — *New West, New York, Big D* in Dallas, and so on. On the political scene, it is reflected in its extreme form as separatism.

Ten years ago, in Canada, anyone who talked about separatism or secession was regarded as some kind of "flake." As recently as five years ago, in England, the suggestion that Scotland or Wales should be viewed as separate regions with their own requirements and demands was laughed off. But nobody is laughing now. The French aren't laughing about Britany, or Corsica, or Alsace-Lorraine. And when you drive through Belgium, you see slogans along the highway proclaiming, "Power to the provinces." Such expressions of separatism and localism are seen throughout Europe, throughout Canada, and, I believe, may very well appear throughout the United States, as well, before very long.

For good or for ill, all of this represents the emergence of a new level of diversity in the society. The society is becoming more differentiated and more complex. Part of our difficulty arises from the fact that many of our institutions, corporations, or governments were not designed to handle the level of complexity and diversity that is now common around us.

The emerging Third Wave society is no longer a mass society. The emergence of a new demassified society leads to a collision between those who would encourage diversity and demassification and those committed either to massifying the society or remassifying it. There are people who like diversity and there are people who are terribly afraid of it. We are beginning to see a battle between the massifiers and the demassifiers.

*   *   *

In the social institutions, I think we see exactly the same process of demassification taking place. In the family situation, we see a collision between Second and Third Wave attitudes. In my judgment, we are not witnessing the much-heralded "breakdown" of the family. I don't think the family is being destroyed, and certainly not by some evil, immoral forces. Rather, a family system dominated by the nuclear family form, which was appropriate during a Second Wave period, may no longer be appropriate to a Third Wave society. We are not seeing the death of the family, or even the death of the nuclear family, but rather we are witnessing the emergence of a much more complicated and diverse family structure — and the nuclear family is just one of many family styles and forms.

We are seeing solos, single parents, live-togethers, childless couples, career couples, remarrieds, and an emergence of a new kind of kinship form which I call the "aggregate family." (A husband and wife start a family and then get divorced. Then they remarry to another two persons, each of whom also has children by previous marriages. All of the children get to know each other, and suddenly there is a small tribe of children who sometimes get along better than the parents do.) We don't know what long-range effects these relationships among tribes of children will have. Will they help each other get jobs when they grow up? Will there be an "old boy" or "old girl" network?

So we are shifting away from a unitary family system, in which it was expected that most people would be part of a nuclear family, where the husband goes to work and the wife stays home to raise two under-18 age children. That "traditional" family model now accounts for only seven percent of America's population. Just as powerful forces caused the shift from the multi-generational farm family household to the nuclear family form, so again we see powerful pressures converging on the family to create new forms.

One of those forms may well turn out to be what I call "the electronic cottage." The electronic cottage is a throwback into the past and a fragment of the future at the same time.

The Industrial Revolution separated work from home, and it split work from life in general, creating the phenomenon known as "commuting." Today, as gasoline prices skyrocket, the average worker in the United States travels 18.8 miles to and from work every day. The higher up the management scale a person is the more miles he or she travels. In a California survey, it was found that employees were traveling about twenty miles and management was traveling about thirty-three miles. The "commuting costs" to society are going out of control — time wasted, vast indirect transportation expenditures and the huge additional energy losses resulting from peak-loading the system at certain hours.

This commuting cost must be contrasted with what is happening simultaneously as a result of the communications revolution. Not only are we seeing video cassettes, video discs and video recorders suddenly popping into the society, but we are also beginning to see word processors, home computers (an estimated 300,000 to 500,000 computers sitting in homes already), and all kinds of new equipment beginning to turn up in people's kitchens and living rooms.

As the costs of gasoline and transportation zoom, the costs of telecommunications go down. Says an ad in *Computer World* magazine, "If the auto industry had done what the computer industry has done in the last thirty years, a Rolls Royce would cost $2.50 and get two million miles to the gallon."

We are seeing a convergence of forces, and I believe that the high cost of commuting and the low cost of communication is going to begin to shift some work back into the home. It doesn't mean everybody, and it doesn't mean full time. But it does mean that a lot of work which has been done in offices and factories, in fact, can be done in the home.

When we are traveling, my wife and I make it a habit to visit factories, since we worked as blue-collar workers for many years. Other people go to the cathedrals and museums, but we usually wind up on a factory floor. We try to visit factories which use the most advanced technological equipment. During these visits, we began asking the chief engineers, "How many of your workers could be doing their work at home, given today's technology and work force?" I expected to get an answer of three percent to five percent. I was surprised when the numbers I started getting back were more like twenty-five and thirty-five percent, with the added comment that with real motivation it could be fifty percent in five years. Even in factories today, most people are no longer handling materials goods. At least half of the factory population is handling symbols and pieces of paper. And much of that "handling" can be done from the home.

On all the major newspapers in this country, reporters now use text-editing machines. You can take an electronic typewriter out to cover a story in the street. You can write a story and plug it into a telephone line and it comes out in the editorial office; eventually it will go right from the street into the printing machines. Now if you can write a story on the street, it seems to me not impossible to type a memo in your living room!

We are going to begin to see a significant fraction of the work force doing a significant fraction of its work at home, with consequent changes in the character of family life. We may possibly even see the emergence of a new kind of family, which will — lo and behold — be a production unit again as was the case during First Wave civilization. Husband and wife may be working together with the kids pitching in a little bit also. In the Second Wave system, old folks are cast aside and told that they are nonproductive. If work is brought back into the home, there may well also be a role for old folks too. They can help with child-rearing and pitch in to the degree they are able. Suddenly, the whole relationship of family changes.

If this were to develop, it has implications for education in the home, enormous implications for the central cities, for tax structure, for work force organization, for the size of work units, for free enterprise forms of organization, for co-ops, and a whole variety of other phenomena. No one knows whether or not this will happen; but changes in family structure and changes in work arrangements could transform the society.

*   *   *

In the corporation, we also see a collision between Second Wave and Third Wave ways of doing things.

If we look at the economy, there is a conflict beginning to develop. It is not merely a conflict between sunbelt and frostbelt, but rather between the industries on which those regions are based. Steel, rail, auto and textile versus computers, electronics, information and genetics. I believe that we are going to see Second Wave industries decline and the new Third Wave industries gain. It is not inevitable, but I think it is likely.

Moreover, I think we will have to begin to move towards renewable energy forms, recyclable resources and the use of a wider variety of technologies. Compare Chrysler with any one of the semi-conductor companies. At any rate, look at the difference between Chrysler's struggle to stay afloat and how any one of the semi-conductor companies seem to be booming. Look at the difference between Detroit and Dallas. Compare the regions — Northeast and Southwest. And for that matter, compare the performance of Second Wave companies as opposed to Third Wave companies in the stock market.

The future depends upon our understanding of what these changes imply. I believe that the corporation itself is going to begin to change as a result of fundamentally changed conditions of production in society; that a new frame or matrix of forces is beginning to impinge upon corporations. The corporation stands in a new relationship to multiple environments.

The first environment which has changed radically over the last twenty years is the biosphere. So-called "crazy" environmentalists and ecologists aren't the only ones telling Hooker Chemical to clean up its act. Fanatical romantics are not the only ones calling for cleaning up pollution. Mother Nature is saying it, too. Twenty or thirty years ago, we had roughly half the present global population, resource use was much lower, pollution was less, and it was easier to dump, strip, rip or gouge as nature tended to heal itself because it was less overloaded.

Now we are getting warning signals, and not just from people writing reports on the "limits to growth." The biological systems themselves are overloaded, and I therefore believe that corporations will find it increasingly impossible to ignore environmental imperatives. It will take action and struggle but eventually corporations are going to pay attention. There is no way that we can continue to function in the old manner with respect to the biosphere.

A second environment which has changed is the geo-political environment outside the United States. We are witnessing a shift in power from the nation-state upward to some trans-national or multi-national institutions and downward to regions and communities. The dominance of the world industrial system is beginning to decline, because tightly wired advanced economies are easily disrupted from the outside and not only by OPEC embargoes. Furthermore, industrial countries are in the business of selling arms to the rest of the world and we are thereby arming many little countries that have legitimate complaints against the big super-powers. Like the six-gun in the Old West, which was the "Great Equalizer" among participants in a shoot-out, we are going to pay attention when the little countries of the world begin to sport nuclear or other high-powered weapons which the rich countries, capitalist and communist alike, are only too happy to provide.

We are, in fact, witnessing the withdrawal of the two fundamental subsidies which accelerated the process of industrial development in the rich countries. For generations, the rich countries have lived off of cheap energy and cheap resources; these were hidden subsidies for the system. Those two subsidies are now being withdrawn and it is a new ball game.

It cannot be said that rich countries would not have developed industrially without those two subsidies, but it surely would have taken a lot more time. Without these subventions, we would not be enjoying the amenities and technologies of 1980. Rather, we would probably still be at the stage of industrialization we were at in about 1920. The change in the world geo-political environment is as important as the change in the biosphere.

A third environment which is changing has to do with the socio-sphere or, for short, the social system. Today the society is densely organized, and not merely into trade unions. In the United States, there are 100,000 schools and colleges, 300,000 churches, 12,000 national organizations with countless local branches. In addition, there are any number of nonnational organizations devoted to environmental and consumer purposes — racial, religious, sexual, educational, recreational, political and so on. The country is honey-combed with organization. Practically everyone is organized, and 150,000 law firms are required to sort out all the relationships.

Corporations' actions, therefore, no longer impinge upon isolated, powerless individuals. Every action or decision impacts upon a network or organization, and these organizations frequently have Ph.D.s, Xerox machines, lobbyists, and ways of exercising a certain degree of sophisticated influence within the system. Of course, there are people who are not organized and people who are still entirely left out; but the society as a whole is now densely organized and the corporation now finds itself surrounded by organizations. The corporation cannot ignore public and social pressures the way it used to. The socio-sphere, too, has been transformed.

A fourth environment which has changed might be called "the people-sphere."

People themselves are changing, and again there is an emerging conflict between Second Wave people and Third Wave people. We are beginning to see people demanding desynchronization, flex-time, and personalization of their schedules, decentralization and de-standardization.

Take fringe benefits, for example. The Second Wave way of dealing with the issue is for the union to negotiate a contract which provides uniform benefits for all workers in the same class. But at TRW, the aerospace company, employees are given a menu. They can choose the particular fringe benefits they want. Younger employees, less interested in pensions, may opt for a pension reduction in favor of more holidays. An older employee who wants more pension benefits may choose the option of working a few more days each year. Employees can switch and trade and custom-tailor a fringe benefit package to their own requirements. It is a smorgasbord offering rather than an ultimatum. This humanization or

21

individualization of treatment custom-tailors working conditions, just as the new technologies increasingly custom-tailor products.

We are witnessing, then, an emerging difference of temperament, values, and style among people. Second Wave people, to the degree they reflect industrial culture, tend to be more uniform in lifestyle — ethnically, sexually and politically — and they accept routine and monotony. They have been brought up to accept it as their life's lot. They accept authority, and look to one boss for their orders. They accept synchronization, uniform treatment and they trust the experts. They work primarily for economic reward. They seek fulfillment outside the job — in family life, leisure or religion — but not in work. They expect permanence.

On the other hand, Third Wave people, to the degree they reflect the emerging culture, fight against routine. They hate routine work and despise boredom. They see life as rounded, with work being only a small part of it. They seek other satisfactions. They are big on "do-it-yourself." They are diverse — ethnically, sexually and in terms of family structure, preference and in lifestyle.

They also demand a revolution in the character of work itself. They want challenge, meaning and participation. They improvise and mistrust experts and authority. They are more educated and sophisticated. They are accustomed to more complex forms of organization. Many of them are used to working for several bosses rather than one boss as they move through the organization doing different things. Above all, they expect change. These "people changes" converge with the changes in biosphere, geo-politics, and social organization.

For this reason, I believe that we are going to see the emergence of new corporate forms which take these various new environmental forces into account. We are seeing the emergence of pressures to create a new kind of production organization which we can call a Third Wave corporation. These pressures come from the government, interest groups and elsewhere, and will begin to form and shape the corporation despite its enormous power.

The new corporation will be based on Third Wave principles. It will be compelled to use new energy forms and recycle its by-products. It will produce multiple customized products rather than a single standardized product. It will essentially react to "multiple bottom lines." Instead of measuring the individual and corporate performance according to a single number on the bottom of the page, they will also be measured in terms of social and environmental performance and so forth. Within these new corporations, we will see more diverse and smaller internal organizational units, new organizational forms and longer planning horizons with participation in the planning process.

Perhaps such projections are utopian. They may not happen. Yet there are strong pressures moving in these directions. These are healthy, good pressures. Therefore, we may see the emergence of a corporation which is more responsive to society and more adapted to high-speed change; a corporation not built for a traditional, industrial mass society but rather for a rapidly changing, demassified society.

* * *

The third institution which is facing rapid, almost explosive change is the political system itself, including government and the political parties. In the last presidential election, millions of people were disillusioned by party politics; millions felt that the choices were nauseating; millions stayed home; and a popular joke suggested that we are no longer being asked to vote for the lesser of two evils but rather for the evil of two lessers.

I would argue that the breakdown of the political system is not only an American phenomenon. People are disaffected from their governments all across the industrial world. Our governments are malfunctioning. They cannot control inflation with simple Second Wave measures, such as monetary policy or tax manipulation. Governments cannot get themselves organized to deal with the energy crisis, technological change, family structure transformation, or the breakdown of community, nor with the problems of welfare, health, education.

In the United States, the paralysis is incredible. It is now seven years since the OPEC embargo, and yet we still do not have anything which passes for a comprehensive, comprehensible or intelligent energy policy, let alone a technological policy or a transition policy to move from one stage of industrial development to another.

I would argue that the key issue is not government controls versus no controls, or Republicans versus Democrats, or liberals versus conservatives. I believe that *all* the existing political parties, whatever their other differences, share an overriding concern — they are all parties of the Second Wave.

Their underlying fundamental commitment is to the preservation of industrial mass society and to prevent the changes which are moving us toward a new kind of society. This analysis does not imply that these parties are evil; it merely observes that the political parties themselves are an historical product of the Second Wave.

Therefore, I believe that the old labels no longer matter. The key issue is the issue of *obsolescence.*

Just as the arrival of the Third Wave makes it necessary for family structures and business structures to change, so also does it make our elections largely a farce and our government institutions obsolete. Changing the faces of "leaders" matters less than changing the institutions. In my judgment, even saints and geniuses elected to office today would be unable to carry out decisive, intelligent, humane policies, so long as they attempt to operate with the existing government institutions.

We are attempting to govern with institutions which were designed for an agrarian age and not even an industrial age. Our Constitution was written to govern a country of four million people, rather than 225 million;

23

a society in which most people were farmers with a low level of education and no contact with the outside world; a society of low complexity and low speed. Compare that with the society itself. Governmental institutions, whether in Japan, Germany, Great Britain, the Soviet Union or the United States, are essentially trying to govern with political technologies that are a couple of centuries old. We wouldn't try to do anything else with technologies that old. And I use the term "political technology" advisedly. If you listen closely to our language and political vocabulary, you begin to realize that the forms of government we have created were designed for a machine age. They are an outgrowth of Newton and Descartes, and they are based on assumptions which have long been challenged in physics and are now being challenged in the culture.

The Founding Fathers talked about "checks and balances." You can almost hear the gears grinding! Madison spoke of "successive filtrations." More recently, we talk about "steamrollering a bill," or "railroading legislation," or "engineering consent," and the Marxists talk about "capturing the state machine."

Such political vocabulary does not come about by accident. Each civilization creates political institutions appropriate to its time. The institutions with which we are now governing were appropriate to another age. They were brilliant and stunning advances in their time. I believe we are going to have to restructure our political institutions, just as we are restructuring our family life, our corporations and our other systems.

If we look at the political system, what is the implication of a demassified society? We see the implications all around us. We are witnessing the breakup of consensus, the growth of single-issue groups, the splintering of regions and ethnic groups. Such splinterings and divisions are occurring at high speed in country after country. This part of the historic process of political demassification parallels the changes in energy, production, communications and family life.

*   *   *

Energy, technology, information, culture, science, and cities are all impacted by the Third Wave. We see a social order reeling under the impact of an historic transformation and a wave of change. We also see a collision of the forces committed to preserving Second Wave institutions and the emerging forces committed to the necessary restructuring of our way of life. This is the "super-struggle" raging around us. And I believe that this is the most important event taking place on the planet.

The arrival of the Third Wave does not mean the automatic substitution of a new society for the old one. Rather, it means that simultaneous waves of change are moving through various societies. In Brazil, for example, you will find people who are not yet agricultural. They are stone age, primitive, tribal peoples who are being hit by bulldozers as the

Amazon is agriculturalized. They are feeling the impact of the First Wave of change.

A few hundred miles away, in a city called Santos, you see a classical Second Wave industrial development — steel mills and refineries belching smoke into the air, looking like the Pittsburgh of an earlier day. The Second Wave is also rolling across Brazil. But elsewhere in Brazil, satellites are being used to map resources, computers to adjust the ecology and so on. We see the very beginnings of the Third Wave. In the same society, there are multiple waves of change, each with its associated political and economic forces. It is the conflict among these forces that determines political life in Brazil. And I think something similar is happening in the United States as well. Advocates of the Second Wave past are trying to hold back vital changes in energy, communications, environment, family life, work and the economy.

*   *   *

What strategies are suggested by this analysis? We need different strategies for different countries. We hear a lot about Japan. We are told that the Japanese know what they are doing; that the Japanese are highly productive, while we are unproductive. But that is an overly simple picture of what is happening.

Japan in general does have a kind of strategy. The Japanese government and the Japanese corporations do not rule Japan all by themselves. Japan is a complicated society with consumer groups, environmentalists and even racial minorities. We never hear about them in the United States, but Japan is a very rich, complex, bubbling system filled with diverse opinions and political groupings.

Nevertheless, there is a general strategy. The Japanese talk about moving to the information society. It is a strategy which the entire public has been educated about for ten years. They speak of shedding their old Second Wave industries and encouraging Third Wave industries while protecting the workers against unemployment. They speak about reducing their energy and food dependency.

The United States does not have a coherent strategy for this transition. We seem more confused and torn by the arrival of the Third Wave. Yet the U.S. still has many advantages which other countries lack. The United States is more decentralized than most other industrial countries, and I think that makes us more flexible and potentially responsive. We have more natural resources, a better education base, and a better scientific base. What is missing is a consciousness of the need for some kind of strategy to get through the turbulence of the years ahead. What is needed is a grasp of the broad meaning of the term "Third Wave."

What we are offered in place of an intelligent strategy for change is "reindustrialization." The Carter Administration and Second Wave ele-

25

ments of the business community have concocted a so-called policy for economic survival. But it is a fraud.

First, reindustrialization points in the wrong direction with regard to time. It is oriented toward the past rather than the future. It is a political sop to the dying, Second Wave industries and their associated trade unions. The very prefix "re" indicates the direction! Reindustrialization seeks not a transition toward the new society, but rather a restoration of the old society as though it could somehow continue to work. John Nesheim of National Semiconductor put it in a nutshell: "What I find most distressing is that taxpayer dollars are directed toward dying things rather than growing things."

Secondly, reindustrialization is wrong because it focuses almost exclusively on economics and so-called "growth." It is "econocentric." We are not just faced with an economic problem, and the attempt to deal with our crisis as though it were simply a matter of economics will get us into deeper trouble. The corrosion of family life, the rise of sectionalism, the need for political restructuring, the fundamental role of information are all interrelated with energy problems and many other issues, and we cannot solve the crisis with a few essentially economic decisions.

Third, the whole level of analysis of the reindustrialization debate is wrong as I see it. It focuses on surface, first-order effects rather than on complicated secondary and tertiary impacts. It ignores conflict. It assumes that no one will be hurt and that everyone will simply fall nicely into line. With a few crumbs for laid-off workers and minority groups, mass support will materialize for the policy. But conflict, while it should be contained and constructive, is essential to change.

Finally the vision of the reindustrializers is narrow, paternalist and politically dangerous. Despite much rhetoric about bringing blacks and other minorities "into the system," it envisions a basically corporatist America, run by Big Government and Big Companies with Big Labor as a junior partner. It calls for a new social contract based on consensus. But it is not the image of a future society, but rather the image of a perfected, Second Wave, industrial society, the old mass society and run from the top down.

The whole idea is inherently centralist. The advocates of reindustrialization recognize this fact and try to offset it by talking about indicative planning rather than central planning, and about involving citizens in the process. But they plan to involve citizens through three institutions in which nobody any longer has confidence — Big Government, Big Labor and Big Companies, as though these institutions would adequately represent the diversity of interests of the society as a whole.

I believe it will be impossible to manufacture the national consensus of purpose which the reindustrializers think is necessary. The very forces who until now have been unable or unwilling to open the system to minorities, women, young people and the elderly are now telling us that reindustrialization is the way to create a better society for everybody.

With the Reagan Administration in place, the debate over reindustrialization will undoubtedly take new forms. But the fundamental crisis of industrial society will not disappear. We will be compelled to face an accelerating sequence of crises and to cope with these over a long time frame.

*　*　*

To focus on the whole picture, rather than one isolated element of it, we may need to create what might be called a "Third Wave coalition." I do not picture this as a mass movement, but as a loose, fluid, continually shifting aggregation of largely local groups.

Such a coalition, for example, should not support indiscriminate investment incentives but rather selective ones; should not offer blind support to bankrupt Chrysler, but should support efforts to convert dying industry into new lines of socially desirable production. Such a coalition should not support centralized welfare programs but decentralized job creation and training. It should not try to block the new technologies, but rather fight for more control over them and for more of an awareness of the political and social implications of these technologies.

This coalition needs support from those who have been frozen out of Second Wave society and who can be brought back in only through a transition to a Third Wave America. It doesn't need a bland kind of universal support.

Such a coalition can be built with a broad range of citizens' groups, including environmentalists, who will discover that Third Wave industry tends to be clean while Second Wave industry tends to be filthy. Such a coalition will find support from consumers, women, blacks and Hispanics as well, once they too recognize that real solutions are possible when we step outside the mind-paralyzing traditional framework of Second Wave economics and politics.

I do not think that such a coalition should offer indiscriminate support for organized labor. Some unions are your enemies and some are your friends. Nor should the coalition take the form of an indiscriminate crusade against the corporations. Some corporations are doing excellent things and others are doing things that are destructive. Rather, I think that a coalition for a Third Wave America should take advantage of the emerging cleavage between Second Wave and Third Wave industries. Some companies are potentially powerful allies for a Third Wave coalition.

Finally, we need to eliminate knee-jerk reactions to both public and private sectors. The old antagonisms between industry and government, Right and Left, liberals and conservatives, labor and capital are increasingly obsolete in the new framework.

We need a strategy for renewing America and making a peaceful transition to the new society. We are on the edge of a new civilization. If

27

we do not understand the Third Wave and participate in shaping it from the start, the future will leave us behind as casualties of change.

But if we stop relying on yesterday's strategies, labels, concepts and ideologies, we can begin to make a peaceful transition to a more humane tomorrow and take part in *creating* that Third Wave civilization.

TRANSFORMATIONS IN THE AMERICAN CORPORATE ENVIRONMENT, 1960s-1980s

Rosabeth Moss Kanter

But I'm coming to believe that all of us are ghosts . . . . It's not just what we inherit from our mothers and fathers. It's also the shadows of dead ideas and opinions and convictions. They're no longer alive, but they grip us all the same, and hold on to us against our will. All I have to do is open a newspaper to see ghosts hovering between the lines. They are haunting the whole country, those stubborn phantoms — so many of them, so thick, they're like an impenetrable dark mist. And here we are, all of us, so abjectly terrified of the light.

— Henrik Ibsen, *Ghosts*

We thought they could never catch up, but they tried harder, and here we are — to paraphrase an old American slogan, a Sony in every house and two Toyotas in every garage.

— George A. Keyworth II,
Director of the Federal
Office of Science and
Technology Policy

Business organizations are facing a change more extensive, more far-reaching in its implications, and more fundamental in its transforming quality than anything since the "modern" industrial system took shape in the years between roughly 1890 and 1920.[1] These changes in the American business environment come from several sources: the labor force, patterns of world trade, technology, and political sensibilities. Each of these by itself has changed significantly at other times. The present situation is unusual not only in that each is undergoing transforming changes, but that the changes are profound, and that they are occurring together.

In this second transforming era, between 1960 and 1990, American business organizations will need to learn to operate in a wholly new mode. Those organizations which recognize the immensity and the scope of these forces, and carry out the required organizational changes, will probably survive; many, indeed, will prosper enormously. Those organizations which either fail to understand the need for the change or are inept in their ability to deal with it will fade and fall behind, if they survive at all. It is already clear, from the record of the past decade, that a few farsighted organizations have begun to make the necessary changes; these few are signposts to the future. Others have already failed; they are memorials to the past.

Recent business history is filled with the skeletons of companies that failed to innovate or even to recognize the need to adapt to obvious change. International Harvester's financial woes — in 1981, it predicted a $302-million profit for 1982; by the middle of 1982, the prediction was for a $518-million *loss*, and at the end of the 1982 fiscal year the total loss was $1.64 *billion* — are often traced to its inability to control its environment, as interest rates skyrocketed and product demand slumped. But Caterpillar Tractor, almost a line-by-line competitor, faced exactly the same situation. Unlike Harvester, however, it has not only been holding its own, but even improving a bit. Its strategy involves concentrating on quality and service, building and maintaining long-term relationships with customers, innovative products and services (such as a willingness to support dealers by buying back unsold parts), and, perhaps most important, a continued and long-standing tradition of investment in manufacturing technology and development of people at all levels.

AM International (previously Addressograph-Multigraph) seems to be rapidly disappearing as it sells off divisions, lurches from one "strategy" to another without clear or consistent direction, and demonstrates an evident inability to adapt to the changing environment.[2] In 1981, it sold its U.S. operation of the Addressograph Division, the business that started the company in 1893, along with its credit card recorders — perhaps its one "modern" product line. By that point, it had already sold off four other businesses, and two more were up for sale. Since 1967, AM had had three CEOs; its headquarters had been relocated twice in four years. Roy Ash, who took over in 1976 after a legendary career building Litton Industries, tried to mesmerize Wall Street by creating an effective image, a strategy that worked well in the go-go years of the early 1960s, but was out of touch with the new realities of later times.

There are also examples of American companies' almost literally handing a market over to the Japanese by failing to respond quickly or adapt to change. By 1981, Kyocera International, Inc., had 70 percent of the U.S. market for ceramic semiconductor housings, and its parent, Kyocera Company, had a similar worldwide market share, having taken the market completely away from the U.S. companies that pioneered this critical high-technology component.[3] Kyocera opened its first U.S. sales office in 1968, bought a Fairchild Camera (another loser) plant in 1971, and acquired Honeywell's San Diego ceramics plant shortly thereafter. Finally, in 1975, Du Pont stopped its ceramics production because Kyocera was the overwhelming leader.

Customers who switched from American producers to Kyocera faulted American companies for noninnovativeness, resistance to change, inability to adapt to fluctuations in demand, and slow response time compared with the Japanese producer's. The manager of raw-materials purchasing for Signetics Corporation complained: "We would go to American Lava with a request to quote a price on packages for us, and typically they would come back with two sheets of exceptions — all the things we required that they said we couldn't do." American Microsystem's materials manager echoed this: "If you called the president of an American company, you wouldn't hear from that company for three months. A salesman might finally come by and say, 'I understand you have a problem.' "

It was not just the legendary Japanese quality consciousness that paid off for Kyocera, but also a greater flexibility in the use of its people compared with its American rivals', and thus a greater ability to regroup to handle change. Kyocera's American marketing vice-president, who left a U.S. competitor to come to Kyocera, commented about his previous employer: "When they hit a deep valley, they simply disband things — like most of the U.S. companies. They shut off machinery, tear it up, and send people away because there is no work." Kyocera, in contrast, finds something else for its people to do to get ready for the next set of changes: executives might go on the road to market; production people might do forward planning.[4]

Over the last two decades, we have also witnessed a dramatic change in America's world position. Foreign competition, which used to be brushed off lightly, like dandruff, is now overtaking many of our major industries. (And the success of countries like Japan lies in some measure, ironically, in their use of models of "workplace democracy" or "team organization" well known in the United States, models that we have never fully implemented.) Not only does America have a different position in the world society than twenty years ago, but foreign nations also control critical supplies that our country needs — petroleum, and other raw materials. This too changes the context in which our organizations operate.

For example, during the period from 1960 to 1980, sales of Japanese autos in the United States went from one-quarter of 1 percent to 22 percent of the market — a hundredfold increase. The results for the American automobile industry are well known. During the same period, consumer prices went up by 180 percent; that is, nearly tripled. In manufacturing, American output per labor hour rose 3.4 percent per year between 1970 and 1975; the equivalent figure for 1975 to 1980 was 1.6 percent. Compare these figures with Japan's: 6.7 percent and 7.9 percent — output increasing while America's dropped precipitously. Japan, of course, is a well-known economic miracle; but look at France (4.6 percent and 5.1 percent), or Italy (4.6 percent and 4.9 percent), or the Netherlands (6.2 percent and 6.6 percent). Overall, the United States lost 23 percent of its share of world markets in the 1970s, according to Commerce Department calculations.[5]

Even in innovation — America's classic strength — there are signs of decline. After leading the world in percentage of Gross National Product spent on R&D, American companies' average yearly expenditure on industrial R&D (excluding our high military R&D expense) fell to 1.5 percent of GNP, trailing both West Germany (at an average of 2.0 percent) and Japan (at an average of 1.9 percent). Meanwhile, West Germany had been doubling its proportional spending, and Japan had increased its proportion by 20 percent. Furthermore, the American edge in invention was also declining. In the 1950s, according to Stanford Research Institute figures, the United States initiated more than 80 percent of the world's major innovations; today it is close to 50 percent, and foreigners are acquiring a larger share of U.S. patents. American firms' share of U.S.-issued patents dropped from 78 percent to 63 percent between 1967 and 1977, whereas Japan's share increased from 2 percent to 10 percent and West Germany's from 6 percent to 8 percent.[6]

Business failures have also been going up steadily. By June of 1982, U.S. business failures had reached the highest level since the Great Depression of the 1930s.[7] This is simply one indication of a set of wholesale shifts in industrial adaptation — or lack of it. The financial-services industries are, of course, in turmoil. Some organizations, however, are taking great advantage of the potential opportunities by innovative and even revolutionary changes in products, services, and market orientation. Brokerage firms, for example, have been branching out into insurance, broader financial services, investment alternatives and — except in name — banking. Banks themselves are reciprocating. Those which are innovative and are able to transcend their traditions are doing very well; for example, Bank One of Columbus, Ohio, an otherwise obscure regional bank, has leapfrogged its competitors by sewing on a vehicle for credit-card services.

Even though big companies can still ride out downturns better than smaller ones, size is no longer guaranteed protection against decline and either closing or — more likely — acquisition by another firm.

The total scope of what needs to be done is, of course, highly variable, in large part because it depends on the particular organization and industry. What *is* clear, however, is the need for innovation at every level — innovation not merely in the traditional sense of new products and services, but in the very ways that organizations operate, in their view of themselves, and in the mechanisms that can develop and engage their resources to the maximum extent possible. Most important, organizations need innovation to shift from the present tendency to deal with their tasks in a relatively single-minded, top-directed way and to a capacity to respond innovatively, locally, and promptly to a whole variety of organizational contingencies — to change shape, so to speak.

The organizations now emerging as successful will be, above all, flexible; they will need to be able to bring particular resources together quickly, on the basis of short-term recognition of new requirements and the necessary capacities to deal with them. They will be organizations with more "surface" exposed to the environment and with a whole host of sensing mechanisms for recognizing emerging changes and their implications. In such an organization, more people with greater skills than ever before will link the organization to its environment.

Until now, most organizations have attempted to deal with forthcoming change and with environmental contingencies by ever-more-elaborate mechanisms for strategic planning — essentially designed to help organizations feel in control of their futures. There will always be a need for this, of course, but the balance between planning — which reduces the need for effective reaction — and structural flexibility — which increases the capacity for effective reaction — needs to shift toward the latter. The era of strategic planning (control) may be over; we are entering an era of tactical planning (response).

And just as the economic challenges facing American business seem to demand more flexible, responsive people and sensitive practices, so do the accumulating social challenges indicate that a new era is at hand.

SIGNALS OF A TRANSFORMING ERA: FACTORS IN ORGANIZATION DESIGN

There are a few periods in history that deserve the label of "transforming eras," when circumstances change sufficiently to warrant a major shift of assumptions. Thomas Kuhn, the historian of science, has pointed out that major change takes place only occasionally, in what he called paradigm shifts, when the working assumptions on which people have depended become so inappropriate that they break down, to be replaced by a more appropriate set.[8] Thus, social or economic history is intrinsically characterized by long periods of stability in paradigm, punctuated by relatively short periods of high instability: history as staircase, rather than ramp. This model fits the changing world of the corporation very well.

Look at the differences between the factors bearing on the design of an organization in the 1890s-1920s, the formative era for the traditional industrial corporation, and those emerging in the environment of the 1960s-1980s. The turn-of-the-century labor force was largely uneducated (in the formal sense), less skilled, often immigrant, with high turnover and high labor conflict.[9] The distinction between workers and managers was one not only of task but also often of language and social class. Production tasks were quite straightforward: moving objects, assembling mechanical devices, adjusting machinery, and using sheer physical energy. Contrast this with the emerging organization design factors.

TRADITIONAL ORGANIZATION DESIGN FACTORS (1890s-1920s)	EMERGING ORGANIZATION DESIGN FACTORS (1960s-1980s)
Uneducated, unskilled temporary workers	Educated, sophisticated career employees
Simple and physical tasks	Complex and intellectual tasks
Mechanical technology	Electronic and biological technologies
Mechanistic views, direct cause and effect	Organic views, multiple causes and effects
Stable markets and supplies	Fluid markets and supplies
Sharp distinction between workers and managers	Overlap between workers and managers

Clearly, we cannot use the organization of the 1890s to solve the problems of the 1980s.

Ironically, many of the new organization design factors were themselves created by companies barely out of their infancy in 1960: Digital Equipment and Control Data were three-year-old toddlers, Hewlett-Packard was a still-gawky adolescent, and Apple Computers was not even a gleam in its founders' eyes. Today their competition, and others', has moved giant IBM into personal computers, robotics, and the glimmerings of a more entrepreneurial stance.

There has also been enormous change in the context shaping organizational realities. In less than twenty years, a number of powerful social movements have changed the very ways in which we think about our organizations. The civil rights and women's movements, the environmental and consumer movements not only have given new people a stronger voice in our institutions, bringing new interest groups to political bargaining tables, but have also brought in their wake the "heavy hand" of government regulation — heavy in terms of litigation and paperwork requirements if not the substance of compliance. Here are some of the striking things that have happened to us as a working society in the last twenty years:[10]

- The proportion of married women who work doubled, now including more than half of all wives.

- The proportion of families with at least two wage earners passed the 50-percent mark.

- The median amount of schooling of the whole labor force moved past a year of college, and for employed blacks it went from tenth grade to some college. Clerical workers (by 1970) replaced operatives as the single largest occupational category, and professional jobs continued to grow rapidly.

- Unions began to bargain for reduced work weeks or flextime, and the number of employees on flexible work hours or staggered hours grew to around the 10-percent mark.

- Corporate collective bargaining agreements began to contain provisions for joint labor-management committees for special production problems; in 1973 General Motors and the United Auto Workers consummated the first major agreement on "quality of work life" cooperation.

- Monitoring of job safety through OSHA and state action grew, and federal and state legislation barring employment discrimination was created.

- Employee health benefits grew in level and kind — from cash alone to services, from medical only to dental, and with ever-greater employer contribution.

And in national surveys, more men complained about inconvenient schedules, more women complained about sex discrimination, more union members complained about union leadership, and more employees, in general, questioned the fairness of their companies' policies and expressed concerns about advancement.[11] In this context, how organizations treat their people has to change.

It is harder to document changes in American corporate "culture" than to examine statistical indicators of labor trends, but I can try to provide an approximation. One rough estimate of what preoccupies the business community can come from looking at changes in the topics emphasized in the business press. David Summers and I analyzed the *Business Periodicals Index* for 1959-61, 1964-66, 1969-71, 1974-76, and 1979-80, measuring the amount of space devoted to the most prominent topics and counting the number of citations of articles on all topics concerned with the culture, environment, and human systems of business (e.g., tasks and roles of top managers, compensation/reward systems, economic environment, firings and resignations, laws, leadership, organizational change, relative attention to categories of workers, technology, treatment of people, types of structure, and union-management issues). In total, this study covered 7,297 pages of listings and 246 separate topics.

Appropriately, most space in the business press is devoted to reporting business news, and by far the largest categories are industry groups such as insurance, advertising, or autos. (For example, in 1959-60 advertising had 23 *pages* of citations, compared with about 11 *inches* for employment management — which was one of the biggest of my "cultural" topics.) Not surprisingly, a large number of topics remained relatively stable during the twenty-year period. And a few fads flew by during these two decades. Peaking around 1970 and then virtually disappearing were these topics, many of which have a 1960s "counterculture" flavor: drug problems in industry; group relations and sensitivity training; labor supply; government ownership; attention to engineers as an occupational category; general discussions about minority employment; debates about automation and its social aspects (but note that *office* automation expanded in 1980 as a topic); and social aspects of business.

But there were also a number of illuminating changes in *Business Periodicals'* listings, changes which highlight the differences between the corporate environment of 1960 and that of 1980. The topics that declined or disappeared over the two decades spoke of a traditional style of management, dominating and monitoring employees in an adversary relationship: e.g., management rights, work measurement, work sampling, and collective bargaining. The topics that grew in prominence showed corporations struggling with a changing environment with increasing external pressures; more employee rights; an uncertain economy focusing more attention on selection, training, and motivation; and a "new" management style involving teamwork and participation. Overall, there has been more self-conscious attention in the business press in recent years to the quality of management and to management actions as a factor in corporate success, and human resource management has moved from backstage to center stage.

Although the themes that increased in visibility through these two decades included several broad business concerns — for example, regulatory affairs, general economic conditions, planning, and office automation — the majority of the issues growing in importance concerned human resources. They included compensation and incentives, dismissal, outplacement and resignation, employee counseling and appraisal, job analysis and satisfaction, employee rights, and a host of issues concerning labor, its costs, its productivity, and its turnover. There was also considerable attention to executive training and management development, affirmative-action issues generally, and women and minority groups in particular.

A few issues changed names, in a linguistic reorientation of corporate culture: "employment management" became "personnel management" and then "human resources." There was visible and increasing concern with "participative management," a phrase that grew out of "employee participation and management" and then became, strikingly rapidly, almost a slogan.

Some of these concerns had always existed in some small way; they simply became much more significant during this period. Others, however, appeared for the first time and thereafter grew in importance. Some can be associated fairly closely with specific dates. Business-school graduates, "M.B.A.s," first appeared as a significant topic in *Business Periodicals'* listings about 1965. In about 1969 and 1970, such topics as decision making, obsolescence of personnel, executive ability, management research and organizational change, government regulations, sex discrimination and equal employment appeared for the first time. These years also saw the first mention of work councils, alternative work schedules such as staggered hours and flextime, and matrix and group or project management — all reflective of new ways of organizing work.

Five years later, between 1974 and 1976, "affirmative action" (as against equal employment opportunity) became visible along with "equal pay for equal work" and "family life" — something not previously evident in business literature. At the same time, job enrichment became significant. Management by objectives and management information systems also appeared then, as did executive-search consultants, teamwork, group decision making, and middle managers. Finally, at the close of the decade, in 1979 and 1980, business and employee communication appeared, along with employee motivation, quality of work life (QWL), and industrial productivity.

These dates tell us nothing, of course, about the origins and first introduction of these concepts — many of them were "invented" much earlier — but they *do* tell us when the concepts became firmly enough embedded in corporate culture to receive sufficient attention in the business press to in turn earn their own listing in an index. This lag between invention and attention makes me even more confident in concluding that the world of the American corporation has changed dramatically since 1960 and that we are indeed in a transforming era. Our practices may not yet have caught up with our ideas about what those systems should be; but there is no doubt that our ideas have changed, toward a greater concern for people and a new range of organization designs.

Examination of the rhetoric of corporate leaders also confirms these shifts of cultural emphasis. To see what top business people were saying over these last two decades, David Summers and I did an informal content analysis of fifty-two speeches recorded in *Vital Speeches* by executives such as Thomas Watson of IBM and Walter Wriston of Citicorp. We read speeches made in 1960, 1965, 1970, 1975, and 1980, and we noted the major themes as well as the changes.

During 1960-80, business leaders were continuously concerned with just what we would expect: the existence of the free-enterprise system, the benefits of technology, and what they called excessive federal government regulation of domestic business and foreign trade. They defended profit making, complained about problems with unions (demanding too much), argued that "big is beautiful" in terms of corporate size, and worried about foreign competition, a concern growing stronger throughout the 1970s. They also asked for U.S. "national goals," but argued that national economic planning by government is bad for business. They agreed that business needs ethical standards, felt that internal organizational communication and planning could be improved, and expressed concern over the bad image of business.

But some changes also crept in. Whereas a 1965 theme was the desirability of organizational loyalty — managers who are "married" to the organization — by 1975, leaders were calling for new hours of work and rewards systems and acknowledging their responsibilities to employees. By 1980, motivating employees was a major concern. The bold statement that, in effect, "Workers can go somewhere else if not satisfied with the organization" (1960) gave way to an interest in more effective management of human resources (1970). Look at these shifts in views: from employees in unions considered hungry for power (1960); to calls to develop job-retraining programs, special bargaining committees, and more direct communication with employees (1965) and better human resource programs (1970); to arguments for hiring, training, and promoting more women and minorities and to developing better reward systems (1975); and finally, interest in employee motivation (1980).

An air of humility and awareness of responsibilities began to replace *laissez-faire* arrogance in the rhetoric of business leaders. This shows up in other ways, too: from "fighting Communism" (1960) to "coexistence with Communism" (1970); from organizations' *causing* changes in their environment (1965) to organizations' needing to *sense* changes in their environment (1970). By 1980, corporate leaders were publicly acknowledging the defects in their own systems: too much occupational specialization, poor employee communication and incentives, and not enough concern for long-run health. Julius Heldman, a vice-president of Shell, talked about business's unavoidable role in public policy; Kenneth Dayton, chairman of the executive committee of Dayton Hudson, told Houston business people about the "5% club" — Twin Cities businesses contributing 5 percent of their pretax profits to charity. Reginald Jones, the highly respected ex-CEO of General Electric, commented on behalf of the Business Roundtable that "Public policy and social issues are no longer adjuncts to business planning and management. They are in the mainstream of it. The concern must be pervasive in companies today, from boardroom to factory floor."[12] And Roger Smith, the chairman-elect of General Motors, commenting on the "remarkable diffusion of economic power" in the last decade, expounded to the National Foreign Trade Commission in New York on GM's "long-term interest in helping developing countries become more competitive and prosperous" as General Motors is increasingly one worldwide company.

TRANSFORMING MANAGEMENT: WHAT IT IS, WHAT IT WAS, AND WHAT IT MUST BE TO SURVIVE

The changing corporate environment, and the emergence of new models, is also reflected in the critical management tasks inside organizations, the context in which people do their work.

The infallibility of management, the certainty of management tasks, and the predictability of management careers have declined; but the potential of the rest of the work force for contributing to the solution of organizational problems has increased. As uncertainties and interdependencies rise, the past is an increasingly less appropriate guide to the future. For example, the sharp distinction between "management" and "workers" possible in the old organizational era is no longer as clear in the new one.

In the new environment, people at all levels of the organization are affected by the power or the control or the interests others have in their area. And so the unquestioned authority of managers in the corporation of the past has been replaced by the need for negotiations and relationships outside the immediate managerial domain, by the need for managers to *persuade* rather than *order*, and by the need to acknowledge the expertise of those below.[13] In short, regardless of organizational level, managers must take other people, outside as well as inside their areas, into account in order to do their work, and they must learn, in this new environment, how both to acquire and to share power.

One of the main results of this profound shift is an equally profound need for managers at all levels to shift their traditional emphases and to occupy new organizational roles involving very different tasks from those with which they were originally involved. It is not simply that organizations need to use their conventional capacity to attack different problems, rather, the very management structure of the organization and the roles of managers at all levels need to change because these new pressures systematically strain each of those levels.

External Pressures on Corporate Leaders: Environmental Responsiveness or Strategic Blindness?

Top executives of large corporations may be less "powerful" today than ever before.[14] They are certainly *privileged,* and they can make or influence decisions with life-changing consequences for employees — in that sense they are very powerful — but in terms of the models that best explain their choices, they are now operating in open systems facing multiple constraints — retaining their jobs as long as they reflect the interests they are in place to serve, and as long as they can manage a wide variety of demands "external" to the organization.

At the top, limitations from the environment can inhibit action. The environment is increasingly activated, meaning that more stakeholder groups and interest groups identify themselves, feeling that they have a stake in their organizations' operations. They want representation, and they are willing to withhold their resources (material or symbolic) until they get it. Rather than simply assuming, as in the old models, that supply is certain and inevitable — that American corporations can get anything they want, whenever they want, from whomever they want — organizations now must develop strategies of bargaining for resources and of influencing the environment.

As one indicator of how much this recognition is now a mainstream part of elite corporate thought, the Business Roundtable, leading lobby for America's largest corporations, issued a new statement on corporate responsibility in 1981, which declared: "More than ever, managers of corporations are expected to serve the public interest as well as private profit." Four "constituencies" were identified — customers, employees, communities and society at large, and shareholders — and the needs of each delineated — e.g., for employees, financial security, personal privacy, freedom of expression, and concern for the quality of life, as well as fair pay. (Some progressive companies add a fifth constituency: vendors.) A leading economist pointed out, with disapproval, the shift of focus that this statement reveals:

> The Roundtable concerns itself with the expectations of constituencies of the corporation. This implies that the large corporation is a political entity subject to the votes of interest groups, rather than an economic organization subject to the market test for efficient use of resources . . . . Giving space to every group trying to politicize the corporation so as to make it the source of a gift or grant . . . must be the result of corporate executives not managing their companies, but rather becoming politicians.[15]

And "politicians" they are. Management of critical boundary-spanning issues is the task of the top: developing strategies, tactics, and structural mechanisms for functioning and triumphing in a turbulent and highly politicized environment. It is less and less possible to confine external interest to markets and competitors. The political tasks of top executives and the amount of time spent on them have grown enormously. Charles Burck commented in *Fortune* in 1975 that the political environment of the modern corporation was rapidly changing; an entirely new network of activist organizations and regulatory agencies confronts the top executive, leading to an increased public relations emphasis. A recent *Fortune* article pointed out that:

> Few executives on the way up can fail to note that companies are putting a premium on people who are adept at handling corporate relations with the public — and the government . . . .
> Like ambitious politicians, ambitious executives today are campaigning for higher office so to speak, by projecting a "vote-getting" image.[16]

Top corporate leaders are apparently spending a higher and higher proportion of their time outside their organizations, developing relationships and alliances. Boundary tasks and institution building were always important, of course, but they now seem to dominate. Reginald Jones, the well-regarded chairman of General Electric, reported to *Business Week* that he devoted only about half his time to managing his company's operations and the rest to "externalities," making speeches on such political and macroeconomic issues as tax reform, capital formation, and inflation.[17] When Thomas Murphy and Elliot Estes ran General Motors as chairman and president, "Mr. Inside" (Estes) gave "only" about thirty speeches in 1979, while "Mr. Outside" (Murphy) gave more than ninety. At a recent lunch meeting with thirty CEOs from companies, universities, and hospitals in Pittsburgh, I learned that most of them had just had breakfast together to meet a political candidate, and a high proportion of them had also had lunch together the day before to talk about community action. The meeting convener joked, "I think I'll tell all of you where I'm having dinner tonight, so you can join me." In short, these CEOs were spending virtually no time inside their organizations; they were spending time allying themselves and bargaining outside.

The CEO, of course, has always been largely focused on boundary-spanning issues. But these now seem to be an increasing preoccupation of other top corporate executives, especially with the proliferation of staff and staff organization in every sector. Some have commented that this has grown far beyond any reasonable rationale for the importance of planning. Even a *Wall Street Journal* columnist, a vice-president of McKinsey & Company, which specializes in strategic planning, wrote that perhaps planning has become a "fetish." "Fetish" in this context means a task providing an illusion of control in an environment that is clearly out of control: at least one can forecast, gather statistics, write reports, and hold meetings to provide the illusion of activity and control.

A turning away over the last decades from a concern with the technical side of an organization's functioning (the actual work process and product) to a concern with the environment is reinforced by the changing backgrounds of chief executives of major U.S. corporations. This has several aspects: education is one. Heidrick and Struggles, a leading executive-recruiting firm, noted in a recent survey of 971 top executives that only 16 percent of those over 50 years old had an M.B.A., rising to 31 percent of those between 40 and 49, and to an astonishing 48.7 percent of those under 40.[18] Another aspect is the shift to functional experience. It has been years since production and R&D dominated any but the newest high-tech industries (but those, after all, are largely still run by the founding generation). In the 1960s major corporations tended, by and large, to become market-driven and thus also market-run; but in the 1970s, executives with financial and legal backgrounds became preeminent.[19]

The impact of this kind of change is profound, so much so that an increasing number of analysts hold it in large part responsible for declining productivity in U.S. industry.[20] But it is not hard to see other implications: a stepwise move away from any interest in products (marketing, after all, is only one step away from production and closely linked to it) or even the industry in which the organization is located, and toward the freedom to make or break alliances with any other profit-making corporation to secure financial advantage: in short, mergers and acquisitions as the preferred investment strategy. We used to think, naively perhaps, that a university produced knowledge, not real estate holdings; that a steel company produced steel, not money; and that an airline moved people, not assets. But a shift away from product or market orientation at the top can also shift how the company conceives of itself.

The view of a corporation as merely a bundle of movable assets (a "portfolio") turns attention away from long-term productivity and innovation, both of which require internal investment. Faced with increased uncertainties and with "political" tasks in a politicized environment, chief executives sometimes find it easier to imagine shedding what is *not* working and acquiring what *is* working elsewhere than to undertake the longer, more tedious, more difficult, and less glamorous task of reorienting — changing — their own core company.

Moreover, decisions based on portfolio analysis tend to stress the benefits of broad diversification — distributing the eggs among as many baskets as possible. Especially in turbulent environments, such as the present one, this is argued to be the best way to reduce the risk of major loss. But it is *also* very much the *least* likely way to generate substantial benefits in any new area, and it is a complete reversal of the traditional entrepreneurial function, away from investment and innovation and toward conservation and fiduciary responsibility. Moreover, it probably doesn't even reduce the risk. As the recent set of events in the "merger wars" initiated by William Agee of Bendix Corporation demonstrated, Bendix' attempt to acquire Martin Marietta resulted in the swallowing up of Bendix by Allied Corporation, an increase in Marietta's debt, enormous fees to lawyers and investment bankers, and *no* net gain in the development of productive resources. At the very time when our leading banks are looking for opportunities for innovative programs and services, many of our formerly leading industrials (for example, in steel) are behaving more like banks.

The "New Politics" of Middle Management

For middle managers, some significant new pressures are also visible. Together, these require a very considerable reorientation of such managers, their development and their skills. For middle managers and professionals alike, changing times and new environments create a new set of pressures that need new insights, new skills, new orientations, and new roles.

One of the driving forces is direct career pressure, stemming from trends in the labor market, on both the demand side and the supply side. On the demand side, declining productivity and foreign competition have helped increase career insecurity and reduce the meaningfulness of formal tenure (e.g., university and civil service) or informal corporate tenure. On the supply side, the dramatic increase in jobholding women has increased the competition for lower-management jobs, as has the almost equally dramatic increase in years of schooling, which tends to be associated with increased ambition as well as a larger pool of competitors.[21] More young people have entered the work force recently than ever before in history, and they are not going to rise as fast as their seniors, just because there are so many of them. And now the whole population is

42

aging, creating a bulge of middle-aged employees wanting better jobs and in the near future fewer younger people for entry jobs. Demographic shifts shape how all of us do our work. Whereas previously there was a limited pool of the "traditional" employees who sought opportunity, the pool is now growing: younger people, the baby-boom bulge, who want opportunity; women and minorities pushing for a fair share of the better jobs and for upward mobility; and the larger educated population that no longer seems content to accept limited jobs, except as a temporary expedient when unemployment is high.

Career anxiety affects organizational functioning. In the organizational arena, it is interdepartmental power rather than merely individual power that is at stake. While peers in the same work unit may be direct competitors for better jobs, they are also collaborators in the larger struggle to improve the entire unit's bargaining position in the organization. Resource scarcities increase internal bargaining for resources, which affect daily quality of life as well as ability to produce accomplishments that net career advantages. Turbulent environments keep shifting the focus of relevance and make whole functions or departments relatively essential or inessential, depending on their control over critical issues, as those issues themselves shift. Thus, the critical issues being managed at the top — from changing market conditions to regulatory pressures — shift the ways functions and units line up with respect to each other. And that affects both the opportunity structure (what career paths are likely to be significant, what fields will be included in dominant coalitions) and the power structure (who has access to resources, information, and support, as manifested in discretion, visibility, and relevance in job activities).[22]

The traditional struggle for power in the middle ranks of the organization concerned individuals *vis-à-vis* each other and sets of tasks. For managers, it used to take the form of career competition: succeeding in winning over their peers in the competition to take on ever-more-important sets of responsibilities. For professionals, it used to take the form of struggles over job control: succeeding in gaining desired degrees of autonomy and control over the conditions and standards for their work. But now the terms of the power struggle have grown to include departments as well as individuals.[23] Just as adversity can bind together the members of a collectivity as they struggle for joint survival, while prosperity may drive them to compete, and a "lean" environment causes organizations to form resource-sharing networks, so can the new environment for middle-echelon employees drive them to jointly seek to elevate and protect their own unit of the organization, while continuing to compete for advantage within it. It has long been well known that subunits suboptimize, and that differentiation creates dramatically different outlooks as well as conflicts the organization must manage.[24]

Thus, added to individual career issues is a struggle for survival between departments or functions: whether the individual gets "ahead" becomes a function of whether his or her department stays in existence in a time of scarce resources. In the middle, allies in the same field strive to prove the importance of their field to the survival of an organization that has limited resources.

But one also acquires power by struggling to control those new issues which preoccupy the top of the organization, the new issues that crosscut old territories, such as issues of regulation, of political control, and of resource certainty, including human resources. Who should "own" those issues? Where should they go in the system? Management of an active, turbulent, changing environment poses a continuing series of new issues for organizations, issues that must be located in the structure. The middle-level power struggle is in part over "ownership" of new ideas, which by definition cannot be fitted into existing functional boxes and which throws the meaning of functional distinctions up in the air to be renegotiated.

For example, who should handle new issues in government relations — existing staff or a new department? At what level should productivity-improvement programs be designed and managed, and who should be included in their management? Where should the EEO function be put? If the latter decision seems obvious, remember that all the legal mandate entails is that an EEO officer be identified and consider this finding: In thirty-two corporations, I found six different departments housing the EEO office: legal, administration, personnel, labor and industrial relations, operations, and division management. In many cases, the EEO office had moved several times. In one not untypical case, the formal EEO officer was in the industrial-relations function, but the primary "champion" of the issue reported to the vice-president of personnel, who had a working charter from the top to do something about EEO; there was a great deal of political maneuvering around who "owned" EEO, and how credit or blame would be distributed. The "blame" part should not be ignored, either. While some new issues seem highly desirable and therefore are candidates for power plays, others may seem risky, and those who are assigned to them may engage in a series of self-protective political maneuverings.

With the new issues, in short, have also come new staff departments to handle them, ranging from the more "defensive" positions, such as those handling regulation, to the more "offensive" roles, such as planning, forecasting, or market research. Staff or stafflike roles are proliferating in the corporation. Internal consulting positions have also grown, as demonstrated by the growth of "organization development" activities and the increasing membership in professional associations concerned with these matters. Furthermore, some companies routinely appoint "problem solvers" with stafflike roles in line departments. All of these jobs, considered middle management in status and privileges even though they do not fit the traditional definition of a manager, reinforce the burden on middle managers to operate by persuasion and bargaining rather than by formal authority. These staff professionals may have a small group of subordinates reporting to them, but the bulk of their impact comes from the work they do with and through line managers, perhaps attaching themselves temporarily to the line organization or simply influencing the actions of the line.

Staff-line conflicts are classic and well known. My point here is that a larger proportion of middle managers may find themselves, during some part of their careers, needing to act in staff capacities. Their mastery of political skills is essential.

Finally, new and more appropriate organizational structures also tend to make power issues more salient at the middle and put pressure on middle managers to adopt new styles. In these turbulent times, and particularly for fast-growing high-technology industries (as well as for those which are following "fashion" by adopting new structures whether or not they are optimal), new forms of organization structure need to be designed to maximize responsiveness. But adding responsiveness may mean minimizing traditional line authority, thus increasing conflict and ensuring that power struggles dominate much of the life of the middle of the organization. It is no accident, of course, that the new organization structures were invented in, or largely carried by, companies in post-World War II industries, such as aerospace and electronics.

In matrix organizations, for example, which grew out of aerospace firms, employees or managers may combine two or more dimensions in their jobs: a functional specialty (such as sales) and a responsibility to a particular product line or market area. This combination is reflected in reporting to two or more bosses, e.g., one for the function, and one or more for the product areas. Thus, whereas in the classic unitary chain of command authority could be directly and relatively easily exercised, in the matrix influence down the line must substitute for authority to gain compliance, since neither boss has complete control over the employee. Traditional authority virtually disappears; managers must instead persuade, influence, or convince. The subordinate is expected to be the resolver of conflict, integrating the demands of these two dimensions of the organization. Conflict is thus built into the matrix. Depending on the design of the particular job and the coalitions that form, the balance of power may be held by the matrixed manager, who plays bosses off against one another, or by one or another of his bosses.

Other new forms of organization also make influence — or informal power struggles — more prominent than traditional line authority. "Parallel organizations" add a series of temporary, rotating task forces managed by a steering committee to the conventional line organization, and "ad-hocracies" may encompass similar fluid nonhierarchical structures, including project teams and other professional or quasi-professional self-managed work teams.[25] In these situations, people are brought together from many levels in new groupings that are highly participatory. Leadership may be independent of level; participation may be based on skills independent of formal position or formal authority. Such designs also undercut traditional authority because, as in the matrix, people cannot fall back on functional authority, on the traditional line, on the chain of command, or on the reasons for compliance that come from the rules of the organization. Instead, they have to bargain for influence and status; they struggle for power enough to have some impact on ever-more-confusing systems.

Thus, for middle managers subject to any of these "new" forms of organization, authority and career success are not granted automatically. Old sources of security are disappearing, and middle managers too find their positions shaped by the trends of the last two decades. But this is a "problem" for those trying to operate segmentally, acting as though they alone controlled the resources they need.

Reducing the Authority of First-Line Supervisors

First-line managers and supervisors — those who supervise direct production and service workers — have always had a difficult job: exhorting workers to live up to standards and demands thrust upon them by higher levels. The new corporate era, which has brought new work systems, only increases the pressures on them.

One of the reasons for new work systems at the bottom of the wage and supervision hierarchy is the changing labor market. Some have argued that more and more people today are "knowledge workers" who cannot be closely supervised and controlled, because the organization counts on their knowledge and internal commitment to get the work done. Through developments in microcomputers, 1973 can be singled out as a watershed in which even shop-floor factory workers may have started to become knowledge workers because of new technologies. And one key to managing knowledge workers is to let them alone to use their knowledge.

This is related to the educational changes in the work force. In the last twenty years, there has been a great increase in the number of working Americans who are college educated.[26] While forty years ago only 5 percent of the whole work force had graduated from college, today 25 percent of all people who work are college graduates, and that is rising quickly. Whatever else people learn in college, they learn attitudes about dignity, entitlement, and using their skills. One cannot manage this educated work force in the same way that seemed acceptable for a low-skilled, largely immigrant labor pool. Thus, education creates another pressure for autonomy, flexibility, and freedom — even at the lowest levels of organizations, since education is growing in blue-collar jobs as well. Now 20 percent of all crafts workers are also college graduates, leading one giant American manufacturing corporation to engage in "blueblooding," their informal name for a process to retrain all of its production supervisors to deal with this more educated population — changing a supervisory style known as "knocking heads together" to a new style stressing freedom and flexibility for the newly educated workers on the shop floor.

Overall, through increasing sophistication on a number of fronts, forms of authority in many companies have moved away from the "direct controls" involved in close supervision (issuing orders and monitoring behavior) to what is sometimes called "bureaucratic controls," or indirect authority.[27] Instead of direct order giving, the organization sets a context making it inevitable that people do the right thing, via the setting of targets and standards and long periods of training. Then employees are left freer to do their work as they see fit. Managers design the organization to make sure that performance is as predictable as possible, and then they leave people free to make a large number of more immediate decisions on their own, measuring results out the other end through performance appraisals and other devices.

A part of this shift to indirect controls is the growth of explicit "internal labor markets," as economists call them, or career-development systems. The motivation for performance under these systems is not the hope of immediate punishment avoidance or reward, but the long-term expectation of a "career." Such career systems are moving downward, further augmenting the atmosphere of choice at the bottom — and limiting the power of supervisors. Indeed, "bureaucratic controls" often serve to protect the interests of the worker against the manager. New performance-appraisal systems, with ratings that both supervisor and employee must sign, and with third-party review (perhaps by a personnel staffer), protect the worker against an arbitrary exercise of hidden authority by the boss. And leave the boss who does not understand participative management out in left field.

At the same time, greater participation in workplace decisions is creeping into the American system, and it seems to be gaining momentum. In forms such as quality circles, there is increasing evidence that it works to raise productivity, a clear incentive for executives. Fad and fashion also play a role in extending more participative work systems. Organizations can be just as "fashion-conscious" as individual consumers, and when a few leading ones start adopting reforms, often the rest quickly follow because they want to be "modern" too. (Indeed, concerns about "image" are a driving force for executives in the new, more political and more public corporate environment.)

Furthermore, trends in unions contribute to reinforcing these changes. The growing edge of organized labor in America has been among white-collar workers, especially in the public sector, who think of themselves as knowledgeable, are better educated, and also want freedom from close supervision (to be let alone to manage their own work in the way they know best). Whereas all unions emphasize traditional bread-and-butter demands of pay and benefits, white-collar unions have generally been the leaders in bringing quality-of-work-life demands to the bargaining table; white-collar unions have pushed for such options as flextime, and the public-sector unions have contributed the lion's share of joint labor-management committees.[28] In short, many important interest groups may be converging in their acceptance of more participation at the shop-floor level.

Other forces also affect those managing the "bottom" of the organization. There are a growing number of innovations and reforms permitting time flexibility and schedule control for lower-echelon employees. Within some predetermined limits, workers under these programs can come and go as they please. In addition, there are growing numbers of third-party rights advocates ready to protect the rights of individuals in the workplace. There has been a dramatic increase since 1970 in the number of decisions in the federal and state courts supporting new employee rights, such as rights to privacy, rights to due process in termination, rights to conscientious objection to some employer demands, and rights to a variety of new freedoms and new aspects of flexibility at work.[29] (Malcolm Forbes, Jr., the son of the founder of *Forbes* magazine, recently told a group of executives, "If you don't support these new rights for your employees, you're only going to make a lot of work for lawyers, politicians, and management consultants.")

All these trends dramatically change the meaning of supervision and limit the authority of the first tier of management. This is happening at a time when the career prospects for first-line supervisors are also declining; more and more companies are hiring directly into the levels above, limiting the chances for supervisors to move up. It is no wonder that many firms find it difficult to get workers to take supervisory positions. Here too, these things create problems in the context of traditional assumptions. There can be "solutions" only as part of more systematic and extensive shifts toward new assumptions.

THE NECESSARY SHIFT FROM SEGMENTALIST TO INTEGRATIVE ASSUMPTIONS

Only a few decades ago, before the transforming era began, ideas about the American corporation were dominated by four common assumptions of a segmentalist model, ideas embedded in the law, in management practice, and in organization theory.[30]

Old assumption 1. Organizations and their subunits can operate as closed systems, controlling whatever is needed for their operation. They can be understood on their own terms, according to their internal dynamics, without much reference to their environment, their location in a larger social structure, or their links to other organizations or individuals.

Old assumption 2. Social entities, whether collective or individual, have relatively free choice, limited only by their own abilities. But since there is also consensus about the means as well as the ends of these entities, there is clarity and singularity of purpose. Thus, organizations can have a clear goal; for the corporation, this is profit maximization.

Old assumption 3. The individual, taken alone, is the critical unit as well as the ultimate actor. Problems in social life therefore stem from three individual characteristics: *failures of will*, or inadequate motivation; *incompetence*, or differences in talent; and *greed*, or the single-minded pursuit of self-interest. There is therefore little need to look beyond these individual characteristics, abilities, or motives to understand why the coordinated social activities we call institutional patterns do not always produce the desired social goods.

Old assumption 4. Differentiation of organizations and their units is not only possible but necessary. Specialization is desirable, for both individuals and organizations; neither should be asked to go beyond their primary purposes. (Thus, in Milton Friedman's terms, corporations should pursue only profits and forget about social responsibilities.) The ideal organization is divided into functional specialties clearly bounded from one another, and managers develop by moving up within a functional area. As a corollary, it is not necessary for specialized individuals or organizations to know much about the actions of others in different areas. Coordination is itself a specialty, and the coordinators (whether markets, managers, or integrating disciplines) will ensure that activities fit together in a coherent and beneficial way.

Of course, many of these assumptions have been under revision or attack for many years. The notion of the corporation as an individual actor writ large once informed much legal thought, but there has been increasing acknowledgment that such social organizations are too complex to make the analogy to an individual appropriate. Beginning in the 1960s, the academic study of organizations, as well as managerial practice, moved away from closed-system assumptions, especially as it became increasingly clear that organizations are highly dependent upon and sometimes shaped by turbulent and uncertain environments. Tracing social problems back to individual characteristics has similarly been challenged, and neither "blame the victim" nor "blame the leader" arguments have been nearly as prominent in American social thought over the last few decades as previously. Consensus about the proper conduct of social actors and the proper ends of institutions, if it ever existed, has been undermined by events. It is no longer possible to talk about *the* American family or *the* American community, for example, as though there were only one type rather than a diverse and pluralistic group. In today's view, organizational goals are not "natural" and "given," but defined by an organization's "dominant coalition" as the result of a bargaining process that favors some interests over others.

Moreover, segmentalist models themselves arise under certain predictable social circumstances: they are a response to particular situations. These situations include economic expansion, where opportunity and power seem limitless, and where it thus appears that only individual limitations prevent success. They include circumstances in which one's own social group is dominant over forces in the environment, and is able to control its activities by predicting and therefore mastering all the elements needed to operate. Furthermore, in such times, opposing forces or groups are unorganized, unactivated, or quiescent. The environment is stable rather than turbulent, permitting the illusion that differences in the effectiveness of individuals or organizations are based largely on the quality of their own decisions. (This is an illusion because under these circumstances it is difficult to see the conditions in the environment that make such success possible; they are so predictable and so taken for granted that they simply become part of the background.) And consensus appears natural because clear challenging groups have not arisen.

Most of these conditions no longer apply to American society. Despite periodic longings for the establishment of simple and bounded "perfect communities" which can wall themselves off from the outside and operate consensually but mechanically, we must reconcile ourselves to a world that is contradictory and puzzling rather than orderly and controlled. No single social group or set of organizations dominates, and America no longer controls those who supply the resources it needs to carry out its activities. Even the best leader may not be able to control an organization, or accomplish all its objectives, in a turbulent environment in which the organization's success may depend less on its *own* decisions than on decisions made elsewhere, by others, according to different criteria.

We may not *like* the external pressures on corporations, from foreign competition to government regulations to activist groups to changing employee attitudes. We may not find them necessary or appropriate. But we cannot fail to notice that they exist.

And so these old assumptions need to be replaced by a set of new, more integrative assumptions, stressing the relationships between organizations and their environments, as well as the interdependence of an organization's parts:

New assumption 1. Organizations and their parts are in fact open systems, necessarily depending on others to supply much of what is needed for their operations. Their behavior can best be understood in terms of their relationships to their context, their connections — or nonconnections — with other organizations or other units.

New assumption 2. The choices of social entities, whether collective or individual, are constrained by the decisions of others. Consensus about both means and ends is unlikely; there will be multiple views reflecting the many others trying to shape organizational purposes. Thus, singular and clear goals are impossible; goals are themselves the result of bargaining processes.

New assumption 3. The individual may still be the ultimate — or really, the only — actor, but the actions often stem from the context in which the individual operates rather than from factors purely internal to the individual. Individual actions occur in response to the expectations of others with whom they are involved. Leadership therefore consists increasingly of the design of settings which provide tools for and stimulate constructive, productive individual actions.

New assumption 4. Differentiation of activities and their assignment to specialists is important, but coordination is perhaps even more critical a problem, and thus it is important to avoid overspecialization and to find ways to connect specialists and help them to communicate. Furthermore, beyond whatever specialized roles organizations or the units in them play, they also have a responsibility for the consequences of their actions beyond their own borders. They need to learn about and stay informed about what is happening elsewhere, and they need to honor their social responsibilities to act for the larger good. These tasks call for managers with general perspectives and with experience in more than one function.

In short, our transforming era requires not only that we change our practices in response but also that we change the way we *think* about what we do.

RESPONDING TO TRANSFORMING TIMES: CHANGE AS THREAT VERSUS CHANGE AS OPPORTUNITY

Historians wisely try to refrain from the writing of history until well after the events to be explored have passed and a decent perspective can be gained. It is always extremely risky to talk about the historical significance of the present, one's own times. But I believe from all the evidence that American industrial organizations stand today at a critical watershed. Their response to the new environment, for better or for worse, is likely to determine the path of our economic system over the next several decades.

If, faced with these changes and transformations, American organizations use their strength, accept the challenge, take the risks of which they were once proud masters, and extend the capacity of their organizations to innovate, we may yet emerge strengthened and prepared to capitalize on the future.

If, on the other hand, our organizations continue to operate as if, in Marshall McLuhan's memorable phrase, they were driving into the future while looking out of the rearview mirror, we will probably see, at best, a stagnation of American capacity, and at worst, a continuing decline in our competitive abilities.

The more optimistic path is clearly within our grasp; some companies have tried — and are continuing to try — to deal with these issues. But innovation cannot flourish where segmentalism prevails. Under segmentalism, change is a threat. It is perhaps because there has been so much segmentalism in large American corporations that so many of the managers I talk with seem to feel dislocated, disoriented by the changes

51

that have taken place in the American economy in recent years. What has slipped away for many managers and executives is not just a sense of supremacy ("America as #2") but a sense of control. That is what they find so unsettling, so frightening, so frustrating, so intolerable. They feel at the mercy of change or the threat of change in a world marked by turbulence, uncertainty, and instability, because their comfort, let alone their success, is dependent on many decisions of many players they can barely, if at all, influence. Where segmentalism has prevailed, security comes in the form of control, and loss of control is the supreme threat.

Thus, the sight of some corporations seeking government and union concessions in order to avoid cutbacks or closings is disturbing to those who are control-oriented. How far the mighty American corporation has fallen, the headlines seem to imply, when management symbolically wraps itself in rags and goes begging. Management turns its pockets inside out to show that they are empty, pleading poverty in order to gain wage concessions from the union, agreeing to profit sharing in return. A bargain is struck: financial assistance in exchange for a share of control.

Then the management experts tell executives to give up still more control — or so it seems to many of them. One message of the "how to manage like the Japanese" books is that companies should provide employment security, in effect losing control over layoffs and terminations as a smoothing strategy, while increasing consensual or participatory decision making — in effect relinquishing exclusive managerial control over decisions, and taking more time to boot. Interpreters of labor-force trends — myself included — report that employees want more rights, a greater voice in decisions.

And so it goes. Those in the corporate drivers' seats must sometimes feel that they are being asked to share the steering wheel while the vehicle is skidding on icy roads.

I do not mean to exaggerate the disturbing quality of contemporary lives in organizations. For many people and companies, daily life goes on as usual, there are numerous sources of security, and external pressures seem minimal or distant. Some of them find security as individuals in the rhythms of family or personal life; others feel they have relatively predictable careers.

But while individuals can try to wall themselves off from the effects of change in the private sphere, corporations do not have that luxury. Interdependence — and hence dependence — is even clearer in the world of organizations than it is in the world of individuals. The long arm of economic slowdowns, for example, reaches far down the raw-materials-to-market chain. Problems in the American auto industry not only affect the Big Three and smaller Fourth, not only threaten to board up the entire state of Michigan, but affect legions of other partsmakers, suppliers, and dealers. When Xerox and Polaroid, two of the reputedly most progressive companies in the United States, known for their *de facto* lifetime employment policies, begin laying people off, then the reverberations are felt more broadly: another security barrier knocked down by the winds of change.

This is the downside of change: feelings of loss of control and helplessness in the face of decline, change as "enemy." It implies loss when people are unprepared for it, when they have nothing in reserve, when their current capital fund of assets and skills is rendered obsolete, when no resources are available to help them make the transition to a new state — and they cannot even envision what the new state might be. Change brings pain when it comes as a jolt, when it is seemingly abrupt and shocking. The threat of change arouses anxiety when it is still just a threat and not an actuality, while too many possibilities are still open, and before people can experience themselves in the new state.

But not all change is negative, even though it may create uncertainty. Not all sharing of power implies loss; it can also lead to bigger gains. Not all turbulence is a mere distraction from business; it may lead to useful new inventions. There is, in other words, an upside to change. Change can be exhilarating, refreshing — a chance to meet challenges, a chance to clean house. It means excitement when it is considered normal, when people expect it routinely, like a daily visit from the mail carrier — known — bringing a set of new messages — unknown. Change brings opportunities when people have been planning for it, are ready for it, and have just the thing in mind to do when the new state comes into being. And it hardly needs pointing out that change also provides a chance for entrepreneurs to offer "change-management" products and services — turning other people's confusion into profitable businesses.

In short, change can be either friend or foe, depending on the resources available to cope with it and master it by innovating. It is disturbing when it is done *to* us, exhilarating when it is done *by* us.[31] It is considered positive when we are active contributors to bringing about something that we desire, or at least to making something valuable out of what is inevitable — lemonade from the economy's lemons.

Staying ahead of change means anticipating the new actions that external events will eventually require and taking them early, before others, before being forced, while there is still time to exercise choice about how and when and what — and time to influence, shape or redirect the external events themselves. But this does not mean turning into wild-eyed futurists or believing science fiction. In a practical sense, it means "leading the pack" without getting too "far out." I am reminded of a Woody Allen short story about an advanced civilization. Usually when we think about advanced civilizations, he recounted, we have in mind one that is thousands or millions of years ahead of us. But what worried Allen in the story was a civilization that was just *fifteen minutes* ahead: Its members would always be first in line at the movies, and they would never be late for an appointment. In short, a little lead time might be all the competitive advantage one needs!

I argue that tools already exist to "save the American corporation" or to "meet the Japanese challenge."[32] Along with the disruptions of the last twenty years, a proliferating number of social and organizational inventions have been developed, with demonstrated impact on productivity and motivation. Furthermore, the experience of growing numbers of companies with participative employee problem solving has shown that employees themselves more often than not know what needs to be done to improve operations.

Thus, *the problem before us is not to invent more tools, but to use the ones we have.* In many cases, segmentalist companies are not even taking advantage of their own successful innovations, letting them disappear or confining them to narrow uses.

Living with change need not imply insecurity but, rather, developing new forms of security. In the traditional corporation, security was based on control. It was based on knowing where everyone and everything belonged, on having categories into which to place jobs (tidy boxes on organization charts) or people ("woman's place") or events (guidance by precedent).

In an innovating organization, in contrast, security will come not from domination but from flexibility. It will come not from having everything under control but from quick reaction time, being able to cut across categories to get the best combinations of people for the job. For their people, security will come not from staying in the same field or department or area but from identification with the whole company, with its unity of effort. The new security will be based on pride in individuals and their talents — reawakening or reinforcing the spirit of enterprise in all employees at all organizational levels.

The corporations that will succeed and flourish in the times ahead will be those that have mastered the art of change: creating a climate encouraging the introduction of new procedures and new possibilities, encouraging anticipation of and response to external pressures, encouraging and listening to new ideas from inside the organization.

The individuals who will succeed and flourish will also be masters of change: adept at reorienting their own and others' activities in untried directions to bring about higher levels of achievement. They will be able to acquire and use power to produce innovation.

REFERENCES

1. Daniel Nelson, *Managers and Workers: Origins of the New Factory System in the United States 1880-1920,* Madison, Wis.: University of Wisconsin Press, 1975.

2. *Fortune,* January 25, 1982, and *Wall Street Journal,* December 8, 1981.

3. Gene Bylinsky, "The Japanese Score on a U.S. Fumble," *Fortune,* June 1, 1981, pp. 68-72.

4. *Ibid.*

5. *Statistical Annual of the United States,* 1981.

6. National Science Foundation and Stanford Research Institute figures; reported in Hunter Lewis and Donald Allison, *The Real World War,* New York: Coward, McCann & Geoghegan, 1982.

7. UPI release, June 24, 1982.

8. Thomas S. Kuhn, *The Structure of Scientific Revolutions,* Chicago: University of Chicago Press, 1962.

9. Nelson, *Managers and Workers.*

10. Rosabeth Moss Kanter, "Work in a New America," *Daedalus: Journal of the American Academy of Arts and Sciences,* 107 (Winter 1978): 47-48.

11. Michael R. Cooper *et al.,* "Changing Employee Values: Deepening Discontent?" *Harvard Business Review,* 56 (January-February 1979); Daniel Yankelovich, "We Need New Motivational Tools," *Industry Week,* August 6, 1979; D. Quinn Mills, "Human Relations in the 1980s," *Harvard Business Review,* 56 (July-August 1979).

12. *The New York Times,* December 27, 1981.

13. Increases in technical knowledge embedded in tasks means that managers cannot simply concentrate on getting the work out, because they are often less knowledgeable about the work process than those with whom they interact, including their subordinates. As Victor Thompson wrote: "Authority is centralized, but ability is inherently decentralized, because it comes from practice and training rather than from definition. Whereas the boss retails his full *rights* to make all decisions, he has less and less *ability* to do so because of the advance of science and technology"; *Modern Organizations,* New York: Knopf, 1961, p. 47. Thus, managers are increasingly less able to exercise the authority of command, and it is increasingly less appropriate to what their organizations need. They need instead to have "political" skills such as identifying issues, persuading, building coalitions, campaigning for points of view, and servicing constituencies, including subordinates.

14. Rosabeth Moss Kanter, "Power Failure in Management Circuits," *Harvard Business Review,* 57 (July-August 1979): 65-75.

15. Paul W. MacAvoy, "The Business Lobby's Wrong Business," *The New York Times,* December 20, 1981.

16. R. Kelly Hancock, "The Social Life of the Modern Corporation: Changing Resources and Forms," *Journal of Applied Behavioral Science,* 16 (July 1980): 279-98. Also H. E. Meyer, "Remodeling the Executive for the Corporate Climb," *Fortune,* July 16, 1979, pp. 82-92.

17. "The Corporate Image: PR to the Rescue," *Business Week,* January 22, 1979.

18. Heidrick and Struggles survey, reported in *Wall Street Journal,* December 8, 1981.

19. Robert H. Hayes and William J. Abernathy, "Managing Our Way to Economic Decline," *Harvard Business Review,* 58 (July-August 1980): 67-77.

20. Hayes and Abernathy, *ibid.,* are leading exponents of this view.

21. Kanter, "Work in a New America."

22. Rosabeth Moss Kanter, *Men and Women of the Corporation,* New York: Basic Books, 1977, Chapter 7.

23. This is a focus barely realized in the organizational literature, with a few exceptions: C. R. Hinings. D. J. Hickson, J. M. Pennings, and R. E. Schneck, "Structural Conditions of Intraorganizational Power," *Administrative Science Quarterly,* 19 (1974): 22-44; Andrew M. Pettigrew, *The Politics of Organizational Decision-Making,* London: Tavistock, 1973; Henry Mintzberg, *The Structuring of Organizations,* Englewood Cliffs, N.J.: Prentice-Hall, 1979.

24. On adversity's binding organization members together: Rosabeth Moss Kanter, *Commitment and Community,* Cambridge, Mass.: Harvard University Press, 1972. On resource sharing in lean environments: Howard Aldrich, *Organizations and Environments,* Englewood Cliffs, N.J.: Prentice-Hall, 1979. On differentiation of organizational parts creating different outlooks: Paul R. Lawrence and Jay Lorsch, *Organization and Environment,* Boston: Harvard Business School, 1967.

25. Barry A. Stein and Rosabeth Moss Kanter, "Building the Parallel Organization: Toward Mechanisms for Permanent Quality of Work Life," *Journal of Applied Behavioral Science,* 16 (July 1980): 371-88. Mintzberg, *Structuring,* uses the less specific term "adhocracy" in his lengthy discussion of this form, a term coined by Warren Bennis and subsequently picked up by Alvin Toffler.

26. Kanter, "Work in a New America."

27. Richard Edwards, *Contested Terrain: The Transformation of the Workplace in the Twentieth Century,* New York: Basic Books, 1979.

28. Kanter, "Work in a New America."

29. Allan R. Cohen and Herman Gadon, *Alternative Work Schedules,* Reading, Mass.: Addison-Wesley, 1978. Alan Westin, ed., *Individual Rights in the Corporation,* New York: Pantheon, 1980. David Ewing, *Freedom Inside the Organization,* New York: Dutton, 1977.

30. Rosabeth Moss Kanter, "Power and Change: Toward New Intellectual Directions for Organizational Analysis," Plenary Address, American Sociological Association Annual Meeting, 1980; and "Contemporary Organizations," in *Common Learning,* Washington: Carnegie Foundation for the Advancement of Teaching, 1981, pp. 75-94. Credit for first recognizing the shift goes to a number of analysts, including Arthur Stinchcombe, James Thompson, Paul Lawrence and Jay Lorsch, William Evan, Eric Trist, and others who wrote major papers or books in the 1970s. I summarize the shift of models as follows:

Old Model Assumptions	New ("Political") Model Assumptions
• Organizations and their participants have: choice freedom of contract limits set only by own abilities and capacities	• Organizations and their participants face: environmental constraints resource limits conflict and unequal power
• Organizations as tending toward "closed system" (rational focus and economic models)	• Organizations as tending toward "open system" ("institutional" focus and political-economy models)
• Organizations as having limited purposes (and therefore able to stay bounded because they produce bounded and identifiable outputs)	• Organizations as having multiple activities and impacts ("uses") any one of which is subject to scrutiny by other groups; bargaining by stakeholders to set organizations' "official goals"
• Key management problems: control (internal and external) coordination of isolated segments reducing friction around the work process	• Key management problems: "strategic decisions" issue management external political relations

Old Model Assumptions	New ("Political") Model Assumptions
• Internal, micro-focus primacy of leadership and interpersonal issues	• External, macro-focus
• Need to study static or relatively invariant properties of the organization — e.g., how size or formal structure affects "success"	• Need to study bargaining, competition, and mutual adjustment
• Organizational effectiveness as a technical matter, based on objective standards and relatively universal human and organizational requirements	• Organizational effectiveness as a political matter, based on standards set by an organization's "dominant coalition" after bargaining among constituencies

31. Paul R. Lawrence, "How to Deal with Resistance to Change," *Harvard Business Review,* 46 (January-February 1969): 4-13.

32. Of course, government actions and public policies play a role too; I am confining myself to the actions companies themselves can take.

CHANGE AND RESILIENCE

John Enright

THE NATURE OF CHANGE, AND STYLES OF RESPONSE TO IT

Changes in life and work are coming faster and faster, with every indication that the pace of change will continue to increase. Change is rendering obsolete not only the equipment, tools, and technology in the organizations that managers manage, and the skills associated with that technology, but also the managing skills and attitudes which the manager so laboriously learned. With changes and this obsolescence come, for many, increasing pain and anxiety.

Our beliefs, perceptions, and strategies about change itself are also becoming obsolete. Our once comfortable and familiar attitudes are now becoming barriers to easy and effective adaptation. Strategies for dealing with change that have been reasonably effective in the past are no longer working; we need new attitudes and strategies that allow us to move through this world of changing forms (objects, concepts, events) with ease and effectiveness. This article presents a new view of change and suggests strategies for dealing with change, applicable to both personal and business life.

What — and Where — is Change?

Many of us grew up in the stable world of Newtonian physics. In this world, change was something that happened occasionally to solid things. We existed in a stable framework of space and time. Reality essentially stood still, as the background; change happened in the foreground. Now, physicists describe a profoundly different world. Startling as some of the following assertions may sound, they are conservative compared to many theories seriously expounded in physics today.

In this world of the new physics, "solid matter" is seen as really nothing more than energy temporarily bound together in a relative and shifting space and time. Rather than "solid matter," this "reality" is more like an ocean of energy. Just as icebergs freeze out of the Arctic ocean, hold their identity for a while, then melt back into it, so do objects, entities, endlessly coalesce out of this ocean of energy, and dissolve back into it. Some of these entities, like a bolt of lightening, might exist very briefly. Some, like a written contract or a human being, persist a little longer; and some, like the Great Wall of China, might seem fairly permanent, but the essential nature of these "objects" is all the same. They are transitory. In the new physics, change is not the foreground which exists and is visible against the background of stable matter; rather, apparently stable matter is the foreground standing out against the background of endless change.

The physical process of objects emerging from and fading back into the energy-ocean is not itself change, it is just the way things are. The experience called change is the interaction of that physical process with our habits of perception and interpretation. Not only the way we respond to change, but the very way we see and experience it is largely learned habit. In fact, the physical process described above is only seen and experienced as "change" if it is resisted.

Thus, a branch floats peacefully down a river whose waters are high with the spring run-off. Although the branch is floating rapidly and occasionally bumps gently into a rock, it is almost effortlessly motionless in relation to the water it floats in. A similar branch has become wedged between some rocks, and is thus resisting the swift flow of water around it. This branch is buffeted, whipped, and battered by the water and debris floating past it, and will soon be broken by the pressure against it. If branches could experience, the one wedged into the rocks would be experiencing change with intense pain and distress; the floating one would experience ease and, paradoxically, comfortable stability even in the midst of rapid motion.

Change, Pain, and Attachment to Forms

Forms — objects, concepts, events — endlessly emerge and disappear in the world. We move through that world seeking gratification and fulfillment of a few basic needs and desires. We seek such experiences as intimacy, self-esteem, safety, meaning, joy and delight, mastery (knowledge, understanding, skill), and a chance to contribute to others and the world. In fact, each of these basic desires could be satisfied in any number of ways, but a fact about human learning intrudes, and trouble begins.

As we grow up, our experiences of fulfillment of our basic desires inevitably become associated with particular people, objects, and events — with specific forms. We eat our favorite food, for example, and associate the pleasure of taste and contentment with it. A friend comforts us or rescues us from pain and we feel safe in that friend's presence. We are acknowledged for a skill or contribution, and have a good feeling about ourselves thinking of that skill.

Soon, we think we need that specific form — that particular substance, that special person, that specific skill — to achieve the desired experience of safety, intimacy, worth, or whatever. We begin to think that of all the great varieties of food, people, and skills in the world, only these specific ones can give us the experience. Then, as the endless changes of reality make that particular substance unavailable, remove that special person, or make that particular skill obsolete, we feel loss of the certainty of achieving that experience again.

Very simply, change is experienced as painful because it is easier to see what is going than what is coming. Seeing the good we are losing is easier than seeing the good we will gain as a result of the change. The feelings of fulfillment, which could just as well have been connected with any of a countless number of possible forms, did happen to get attached to a certain, specific form. When that specific form becomes unavailable, we wrongly assume that fulfillment itself is unavailable, and we experience pain.

It is as if an Eskimo, moving off the ice onto land for the summer, should decide that only this particular iceberg could be home for him next winter. During the summer, that iceberg melts back into the sea. Next winter another, equally suitable one emerges and is available. But if the Eskimo has become attached to some feature of the specific iceberg, he will experience loss and pain as he searches for it. This is the essential source of pain in change. We fix our attention on a specific form. In chasing that form, we forget that the essential point of the search is not the form for itself, but the experience of fulfillment we hope to get from it — an experience we could easily obtain in many other ways if we were open to them.

Styles of Reaction to Change: Solidity versus Resilience

When change threatens to remove a source of satisfaction in life, there are two possible strategies we can use to try to insure the continuity of satisfaction. If an earthquake strikes, and the world shakes around us, we can hold onto a pillar or wall for support, or stand in the open, trusting our own sense of balance. The first of these, the "strategy of solidity," is to re-double efforts to hold onto the particular form that has been successful so far in delivering the desired satisfaction.

This strategy makes a certain amount of sense. After all, the wall has been standing a long time; the form that is passing out of our life did work, and it's hard to argue with success. The passing form has the weight of history on its side. No matter how good the form that is coming may be, it is still only a maybe. The new form is only an image, a hope, a mere possibility, which does not carry the weight of remembered reality. Maybe we ought to give the old form one more try . . .

Varieties of this argument are endless. "We've always done it this way." "This product has been a winner; let's not change it." "Joe's good at this kind of thing; let's give him the assignment." The decision a family makes to buy a summer home rather than travel freely each year represents this strategy in action. There is nothing wrong with this strategy, which is often useful in keeping us in our "comfort zones." In an earlier, more stable, time it was generally quite successful.

The alternative strategy is to let go of specific forms or means and concentrate on ends or the deeper purpose that the form was designed to serve. As an old form disappears, this style is to watch it go with equanimity and ask "Let's see; what was the point of that form, what purpose was it serving, and in the world right now, what alternative, available form might satisfactorily replace or improve upon it?" Obviously, this style requires some tolerance for anxiety and high versatility and flexibility. No single term captures the essence of this strategic style. "Resilience" catches some of it, and "versatility" some; so, both terms will be used almost interchangeably to refer to this strategy. This stance toward life is also the basis of creative thinking and behavior.

When we are resilient, we expect we are as likely to gain as lose in a situation when forms must change. We are more likely to be excited by opportunities in change than saddened by lóss. Everyone has had experiences which seemed like disasters at the time, yet later turned out to be blessings in disguise. When we are resilient, we remember this.

We have all hung onto familiar external forms of security or gratification at some times in some contexts, and have experienced the exhilaration of letting go of the familiar in other situations. Individual people (and individual companies) do have preferred styles which they employ most naturally; these modes or styles can be found in everyone's experience.

When in the "solidity" mode, we locate security and the source of good feeling in forms that are essentially external — bank accounts, degrees, licenses, long-term contracts, etc. We are more comfortable in stable environments doing familiar tasks. We are concerned with doing things the right, approved, and traditional way. Boundaries and "turf" are important; we don't want to encroach on others' jobs, or be encroached on. Given a range of jobs to do, we will choose the most familiar one, and thus get better and better at a narrower range of functions. We tend, when functioning in this mode, to be good at planning — laying out all steps before beginning a project.

When functioning in the "resilient" or "versatile" mode, we are more likely to locate the source of security and fulfillment inside, preferring to depend on our own resources rather than leaning on external ones. If we can do a job, we'll do it with or without the appropriate degree or license. And if we can't do a job, we're likely to assume we can learn it. In the resilient mode, we tend to like the challenge of new tasks, and if asked to do a familiar job we are likely to try to do it in a new way. We keep our attention on the essential point of what we are doing, on results rather than process. We'd rather succeed in a task by doing it the wrong way than fail at it doing it right. We will plunge into a project and improvise without elaborate planning — "ready, fire, aim!" We thus make many small mistakes, but are good at "course correction" — at cleaning up the small mistakes before they become large and troublesome. Creativity and innovation flow easily out of this mode.

Living life in the versatile mode is like maneuvering a sail boat. We can decide where we will go in our voyage — the end-point, or ultimate goal — but we cannot plot in advance the exact course we will steer to get there — the means or forms used. To be successful in a sailing voyage, we have to be simultaneously aware of our ultimate destination and the vagaries of the wind from moment to moment.

The "Plan" Model and the "Opportunity" Model

One more contrast can help differentiate life in the "solidity" mode and the "versatility" mode. The primary tools of a person in the solidity mode are planning and control. The planner makes predictable changes happen, instead of being caught by unpredictable changes. Since chance hunting and gathering was replaced by somewhat more predictable agriculture 10,000 years ago, we have been steadily increasing our ability to seize the reins of change and make things come out in planned ways.

Both in personal and business life, we are tempted to continue this quest for more and more controlled, deliberate change and shield ourselves from the change that is thrust upon us. If we wish to retain a familiar mode of gratification, we can often take significant control of the process and insure the survival of a preferred form. In many businesses, "planning" departments have significant power and access to resources and energy.

While obviously our ability to predict and control events is useful and desirable, "too much of a good thing" is possible. One drawback is that deliberate, controllable change tends to be limited to *quantitative* change, that is, to change within already known frames of reference. Deliberate, predictable change can only project slightly altered versions of the past onto the future. The more profound, *qualitative* change that transcends familiar frames of reference cannot be planned. Both individuals and organizations find it hard to go beyond their known "comfort zones." A planning department may have difficulty planning for other than more or better of the preexisting forms. Generals tend to start fighting each new war with improved weapons of the past one. Left to their own devices, caterpillars would generally produce fatter caterpillars — quantitative change — rather than butterflies — qualitative change! Rosabeth Moss Kanter, author of *The Change Masters* (1983), suggests a distinction between *incremental* and *innovative* change that is parallel to this distinction between quantitative and qualitative change. She also comments that planning is used to provide "an illusion of control in an environment that is clearly out of control."

An observation by Thomas Peters, co-author of *In Search of Excellence*, supports this point. In a talk at "Tarrytown," he asserted that essentially no "breakthrough" products in two major companies had ever come out of planning departments. All came from the field, customers, and unplanned sources. Qualitative, innovative change is not likely to come from careful planning, which can only incrementally extend what is already known. Many of the great innovations in our history, such as the telephone, steamship, and motor car, were met with assurances that they couldn't possibly work, and no one would want them if they did. Planning is good for fine-tuning, but not for writing symphonies!

The other negative consequence of excessive reliance on planning and control is the loss of resilience — the loss of the capacity to respond quickly and creatively to the new and unexpected. Fixed external forms quickly penetrate fixed internal habits to reduce flexibility and creativity, in both individuals and organizations. The time of maximum stability and predictability in our culture has probably passed. Try as we might, we can never be rid of unpredictable change, we can only reduce our capacity to respond flexibly to it!

The alternative to the "plan and control" model looks at first glance almost like a step backward. The planner develops clarity and pursues some selected possibilities in the situation, but the price for this selectivity is reduced clarity about options. The people who live by the alternative, "opportunity" model remain equally open to all possibilities in a situation. They concentrate on staying clear about their purpose, and constantly scan the situation for opportunities to fulfill that purpose. In a rapidly changing situation, these people have an advantage. When an unexpected opportunity presents itself, they will see it and improvise the exact steps to take.

Peters and Waterman (1982) suggest that one attribute of successful companies is a simultaneous "loose/tight" stance. Successful companies are "tight" — very firm — on ends, their basic values and goals, but "loose" — very flexible — on means for achieving these goals and values. This is a very precise statement of the "opportunity" model suggested here as the versatility-supporting alternative to planning and control.

This section briefly presents a physical and psychological model of change, and suggests why change is often experienced as painful. There are two different styles of response to change. One, the "solidity" model, attempts to achieve security by clinging to familiar forms of satisfaction that have been successful in the past. Planning and the attempt to control change are derived from this model. The alternative style emphasizes resilience or versatility, maintaining satisfaction by letting go of past forms and being open to new forms. People in this style live by the "opportunity" model — remaining clear on basic purposes while being open to a variety of means as they present themselves.

Both of these modes have been useful in the past, but the increasing rate of change is tipping the balance decisively in favor of less dependence on planning and old forms in favor of more versatility and reliance on seizing opportunities as they emerge.

This section concludes with Exhibit 1 which contrasts the cultures of Solidity and Resilience. The next section will outline ways of increasing versatility in oneself and others.

EXHIBIT 1

The Cultures of Solidity and Resilience

There are clusters of attitudes and values that are more supportive of resilience/versatility and others more supportive of the tendency to look for security in outside, solid forms.

	Culture of Solidity	Culture of Resilience
Some Primary Virtues and Values:	Polished, finished Predictable Specialized skills Values clarity Elaborate planning	Room for more development Versatile General abilities Values scope Skill at improvising
In education:	Values degrees, certificates, licenses	Values *substance* of education and training
Prefers:	Formal arrangements (contracts, tenure) Familiar environments	Informal arrangements (independent consultant) New environments
Emphasis:	Means and procedures Process (means) Letter of the law Power through hierarchy Control reality People should fit jobs Turf and jurisdiction	Values and mission Results (ends) Spirit of the law Influence through networks Accept reality Jobs should fit people Relevance and convenience
Slogans:	"Polish and perfect it." "Let's do it right!"	"Master it and move on." "Let's get it to work!"
Lives in:	Tradition and past	Present
View of Mistake:	It's bad; things must be going wrong. It means failure.	Necessary sign that chances are being taken. "Failure is incomplete learning."
View of Success:	Good sign that things are going well. Desired state.	Mixed blessing. Not enough chances being taken. "Success is a missed opportunity to learn something new."

MANAGING OURSELVES FOR VERSATILITY

Each day, the plates on which the land masses of the earth rest shift slightly. In some places, this movement immediately manifests as a tiny, scarcely noticeable tremor. In other places, where the plates for some reason do not succeed in moving each day, the tension builds, and eventually a major earthquake results. The personal strategy of solidity, of resisting small changes as they try to happen, seems to work momentarily in avoiding change — while the pressure builds up to a personal earthquake. The strategy of resilience, or versatility, is to allow each tiny shift to happen when it happens. With each small change, there is anxiety and insecurity, but no potential earthquake builds up.

When the rate of change in life was relatively slow, the "solidity" strategy worked reasonably well, even with its occasional earthquake of change. The thesis of this article is that, with the rate of change increasing steadily, the strategy of solidity will no longer serve. Major — and often painful — earthquakes of change will come more and more frequently if we do not become more versatile in both our personal and business lives. This section raises the possibility of increasing versatility/resilience in ourselves and others.

Increasing our own versatility begins with truly accepting the need for it. Since versatility comes from living on the edge of the unknown, we are encouraged to recall times when we have been more resilient, and remember the excitement and rewards of living closer to that edge. The primary enemy of versatility is habit — thinking and acting in familiar and comfortable ways. (The very word "familiar" means "like one's family" —the place in which most deeply engrained habits were first learned and practiced.)

Some habits are of action — the route we usually drive to work, the newspaper we read, even such little things as how we roll or don't roll the toothpaste tube. We can try to change these intentionally — especially the ones that seem resistant to change. I once noticed my tendency to avoid meeting new people in an organization by seeking friends during the social hour. To get past this limiting habit, I assigned numbers to each table in the coffee shop, then at the social hour I would pick a number at random and go to that table. Some awkward and uncomfortable times, and some new and different friends, resulted.

Habits are engrained in thought, speech, and self-concept. The way we think and talk about ourselves ("I'm the kind of person who . . . ") and situations ("I've never liked . . . ") hold the habits of action in place. We can watch for repeated phrases or "jargon" in our speech, and set for ourselves the exercise of rephrasing such hackneyed phrases into fresh statements that truly mean what we want to say. If we are having difficulty solving a problem, we can start by re-phrasing, re-stating the problem, making it into a new and less familiar one. Familiarity breeds blindness, the tendency to overlook the obvious.

Generally, when there are several tasks to be done and several people to do them, we will each volunteer for the task with which we are most practiced and familiar. (This fits the "culture of solidity's" emphasis on specialization — doing a few things well.) Inevitably, we get better and better at what we are already good at, and become narrow and bored experts instead of excited and broad generalists. In such a situation, we can let our self-concept go and volunteer for a less familiar task.

Contemplating this possibility, we almost always think "But what if I fail! I'd better stick with what I know!" On the path of resilience, we realize that failure is a necessary and desirable step. There will be a high proportion of "failures" on that path — but each failure indicates we are stepping out into the unknown. Developing versatility is a little like learning any skill: no one expects to learn how to ski well without taking a few falls.

To be more exact, a fall in skiing and not doing well on a particular job are not even failures; they are steps in a learning process. Anyone who gets it all right the first time is not learning as fast as she might. If failure is an incomplete learning situation, then constant success can be seen as a missed opportunity to learn something new! The goal, the "end-point," in learning a simple skill is definable. *There is no definable, fixed end-point in learning resilience*. Success in one step in learning a simple skill suggests that we should continue what we are doing. A success in learning resilience is likely to mean "time to change, and do something different!" This is the meaning behind the motto occasionally heard in personnel circles, "Never hire someone for a job he is completely prepared to do." Similarly, in ordinary learning, the feeling of comfort is a sign we are on the right track. In developing resilience/versatility, comfort is likely to be a sign we are on the dead-end, and it is time to change!

In short, we need to put ourselves in the way of change wherever and however that is possible. Each time we do that, there will be the mini-tremor of anxiety — "maybe I can't do it, I'll do it wrong, people will laugh" — and each time we will gain in resilience and not save up tension for the earthquake.

A second major barrier to developing resilience will come from our friends, co-workers, and those close to us. We are all Pygmalions to each other, holding each other in set patterns by our interactions. Acting out of our fear of change, we are quick to put the lid on others' changes, lest their changes upset and force us into change! Groups of friends and co-workers are awesomely narrow and repetitive in their behavior with each other, talking and acting in very narrow ways with each other, and literally punishing each other for straying out of narrow ranges of behavior. There is little we can do to stop our friends from such narrow and limiting behavior, but we can make ourselves a little less controlled by their restrictions and we can release them from some of our limiting thoughts and judgments.

Since the essence of versatility is to be surprised, we can use friends to help us in the process of developing it. Food habits are among the most engrained and hardest to break, so I will occasionally, when out to lunch with a friend, ask the friend to order! When we notice ourselves about to do something in a familiar way, we can think of a friend we respect but frequently disagree with, and ask ourselves what she would do in this situation.

The largest barriers to the development of versatility are the structures of society and organizations — the formalized rules and procedures. These are to the group what habits are to the individual — unconsciously repeated ways of doing things. There is little we can do immediately to change them, but learning to see them as arbitrary and unnecessary begins to help. These "structural habits" can seem incredibly reasonable.

For example, it seems reasonable and obvious to fill a position that has been vacated in an organization. In one organization which used internal movement of people for its training and development, however, this was never routinely done. When one person left a position, that position was abolished. When a new employee arrived, he participated in creating a new job, with a new title, which carried out most of the functions of the old one. While this new position was often quite similar to the one it replaced, it was never quite identical. The new person, rather than being a "replacement," was the co-creator of a new job — and the first to hold it.

The culture message of "replacement" is: jobs are fixed and static and people must fit into them. The culture message of the second approach described above is: people and their interests and creativity are of primary importance, and "jobs" and "positions," like the world, must keep changing to fit people. Awkward and inefficient as the second approach must seem to an efficient planner, something like it will be crucial to support the culture of resilience.

Developing resilience/versatility is a life-long, never-ending process. It may be useful to realize that it is really not a process of doing, but of un-doing. Children are highly versatile, and in a way we are trying to "be as little children," keeping the resilience and flexibility we naturally had then, rather than developing something new.

MANAGING OTHERS FOR VERSATILITY

To increase our own versatility in a world committed to habit and comfort, and interpersonal and organizational rigidity, seems difficult. Is it possible at all to assist another person in such development, especially when a power relationship such as "manager-employee" exists?

There are two absolute requirements in assisting another to develop greater resilience, more versatility, and fluidity of response in thought and action. The first is that the manager must be convinced of the possibility of living with greater resilience, and committed to developing it herself. The second is that the employee, the "managee," must be committed to the goal of developing greater resilience, to at least some degree.

In addition, it would be very helpful if the company were supportive of this goal, but that support is not crucial. If two individuals agree on the goal, they need not wait for support from the company. One essential aspect of resilience is reliance on ourselves, not dependence on outside forms; to wait for circumstances to be just right would not do at all! Development of resilience can begin whenever one person is ready, and assisting another can begin whenever those two are ready. Support from "the system" might be very helpful, but cannot be considered necessary.

Since resilience is the capacity to respond in novel, innovative ways, it cannot be taught by means of a formal, preset training program. The details of assisting another must be according to the "opportunity model" — improvised in the situation. This article will conclude with some guidelines and some examples of the kinds of attitudes and activities that might assist.

The manager's primary contribution to employee versatility is to help the employee stay on purpose. The nature of humans, particularly in organizations, is to "go on automatic" — to develop fixed and nonresilient repeating patterns. The greatest assistance one can be to another is to remind him frequently of his purpose, and call attention to any automaticity so that he can begin again to respond in fresh and creative ways.

Beyond continued inspiration and help in "staying off automatic," the manager can provide help and support to someone developing resilience in three practical ways by:

1. Helping to set *specific goals* — ("What shall I do?")
2. Supporting progress toward these goals with good *feedback* — ("How am I doing?")
3. Supporting achievement of these goals with *rewards* — ("You're doing great!")

Goals

Specialization — "segmentalism" — is widely accepted as the norm in the business world, but the goal of anyone seeking greater versatility must constantly go counter to this norm by seeking a wider range of skills and responsibilities. An employee committed to developing versatility would expect to continually branch out beyond her job, learning other jobs that those around her were performing. As an ideal, everyone in a department would know and, if necessary, be able to perform every job in the department.

Some of the new airlines that have sprouted since deregulation emphasize multi-function, multi-trained people who can carry out many of the job-roles required. Though done primarily for economy and convenience, this practice also serves to keep people versatile and knowledgeable about the work of others. Nissan, in one of its U.S. plants, pays people to learn all the jobs in their section, in addition to their own.

Ideally, we should be learning not skills that exist now, but skills that will be needed soon. The manager committed to developing versatility will stay alert to opportunities for people to expand themselves into new competencies. Even at the risk of taking a little longer on a job, or making some mistakes, we should be trying new things, new aspects of a project. We should be setting such goals as discovering what technology is becoming relevant to our industry, or visiting other companies.

Feedback

Versatility is more difficult to assess and evaluate than a simple skill, so informing people of how they are doing in developing it is harder. A person who failed to learn a specific skill might actually receive high marks on versatility for having stretched himself to try it, while a person who succeeded in a project might get low marks on versatility for not having attempted an appropriately difficult jump in skill!

Peters and Waterman (1982) mention a company that awarded the "failure of the week" award, given to someone who had unsuccessfully attempted a project, which was, however, appropriately challenging and possibly rewarding. The *project* may have failed, but, recognizing that many such projects must be tried for a few to succeed, the *fact of trying* was rewarded. Managers who wish to develop resilience in themselves and others will have to learn that distinction, and apply it in managing.

The other side of the "failure of the week" concept will be the need to see that someone who regularly succeeds at attempted projects may not be taking enough chances, not stretching herself enough! In giving feedback to such an employee, the manager must be able to acknowledge and reward the successes, while pointing out the failure to stretch.

There is no reason why a manager and employee who have a contract to enhance versatility should not design an additional "performance evaluation" form to supplement whatever form is in use in the company. (And, of course, a versatile manager would be working to upgrade and improve the company's standard performance evaluation.) On this revised performance evaluation form would appear such items as "Is initiating a satisfactory number of new ventures," "Has added a sufficient number of new skills to his repertoire," "Has an adequate number of failures — that is, has attempted to achieve appropriately difficult new skills," and "Meets emergencies with creative solutions."

Rewards

Behavior that is most likely to be rewarded now in a company is not innovative steps, but "doing things right," the safe and familiar way. To reward something not yet tried and proven, but that will have to be done, is risky and frightening. "Better safe than sorry" will no longer work as a guide to plan and reward behavior.

In addition, not only will *what is rewarded* have to change to support versatility, but also *what is considered rewarding*. Our cultural views of "rewards" are holdovers from an earlier time and culture, in which fear and scarcity were far more widespread than now. These views are archaic and mechanical — much more supportive of automatic behavior than of versatility. In our present way of thinking, rewards are largely *extrinsic* — e.g., financial or status. To serve creative and versatile people, we need to shift to *intrinsic* rewards in which the reward fits the act rewarded.

Tracy Kidder, in *The Soul of a New Machine* (1981), suggests the "pinball game" image for such a reward. Just as the reward for winning at "pac-man" is the opportunity to play a more challenging, faster version of the game again, so to a creative person, an appropriate reward for successful completion of a project may be an opportunity to participate in another, more challenging project! A creative person becomes excited by having a new idea. That excitement would be best rewarded by support for carrying the idea into action, rather than an extrinsic, less relevant reward of money or status. Such a reward is forward-looking in time to what may work, not backward-looking at what did work. The versatile and creative manager will discover in her own life and experience what is truly rewarding for innovative work, and use this knowledge in training others.

Ultimately, the entire structure of feedback, reward, and support will have to change to encourage versatility. Some of Kanter's early chapters in *The Changemasters* contain horror stories of how corporations now in fact do *not* support creative versatility. Seeing what structures we produce as we take up this challenge will be interesting. But creative managers cannot wait for that heaven on earth; they will have to do the best they can right now with their own experience. Down the line, there may even be a "department of change and creativity" in every company, analogous to the department of quality. And when there is, we can rest assured that the most creative innovations will be popping out from somewhere else in the system!

SUMMARY

Change is not just something that happens every now and then; it is the basic nature of reality. Apparently stable forms — concepts, objects, structures — have always emerged from and faded back into the flux of reality, but now they are doing so faster and faster.

The deeply ingrained human habit of attaching our feelings of satisfaction and fulfillment to stable external forms has meant that change is usually feared as a source of pain instead of welcomed as an opportunity for new and more satisfying fulfillment. With the stepping-up of the pace of change, we must either prepare for ever-increasing pain, or change how we deal with change. The development of personal resilience/versatility as an alternative to reliance on external solidity is suggested as a solution to the problem of fearing and avoiding change.

Habits (of thought and speech, as well as action), fixed interpersonal relations, and organizational structures are the three major barriers to developing resilience. Changing our own habits of thought and action is the primary route to developing resilience in ourselves. A manager who values and is developing versatility himself can assist employees in their goal of developing versatility by inspiration and by modifying present systems of feedback and rewards.

REFERENCES

Kanter, Rosabeth Moss. *The Changemasters*. Simon and Schuster, New York, 1983.

Kidder, Tracy. *The Soul of a New Machine*. Atlantic-Little, Brown, Boston, 1981.

Peters, Thomas J., and Waterman, Robert H. Jr. *In Search of Excellence*. Harper and Row, New York, 1982.

SECTION TWO

LEADERSHIP

Overview

Warren Bennis is fond of making a deceptively simple but insightful distinction between managers and leaders. A manager does things right; a leader does the right things. Both functions clearly are essential in any successful business organization. But, as Bennis observes, American businesses have come to be dangerously overmanaged and underled. Determining the right things for the business to do has become progressively more complex and ambiguous. Furthermore, discretionary decisions regarding the right things to do are being made today, not just by top executives, but by managers throughout the organization. Leadership is fast becoming a critical dimension of interpersonal influence that must come to permeate the management of any company that intends to remain successful in the new business environment. Consequently, managers must grow to embrace leadership as a central component of their self-concepts and roles. In the vocabulary of this volume, managers must grow to become *Leader-Managers*.

Together, the four articles in this section identify two essential qualities of leadership today. The first quality is the capacity of a leader to engage people and draw them to a compelling *vision* of what is possible, to empower people to commit their highest efforts toward the achievement of a worthy end. The second quality is the leader's focus on shaping the *context* of the work environment, on the underlying assumptions and frames of reference through which people in their organizations perceive and interpret what they do.

Warren Bennis, in "Four Traits of Leadership," derives his insights about the renewed opportunity for leadership today from an in-depth study of ninety of the most effective and successful leaders in the nation. Bennis' central question was, How do outstanding leaders empower their people and reap the harvest of human effort? How do they leverage their human asset? While Bennis found more differences than similarities in management style among his subjects, he came to realize that they all are grounded in a powerful personal vision of what they intend to accomplish, and all manifest their visions through their people by being exemplary managers of:

Attention — They draw people through the strength of their intentions. They live their visions with a passionate focus.

Meaning — They have an extraordinary, though not necessarily charismatic, ability to communicate their vision in a way that allows their people to make it their own and give it personal meaning.

75

Trust — They are totally reliable and congruent. Their actions have integrity and embody a consistent interpretation of their vision.

Self — They have high personal self-regard and have similar attitudes toward others. They view failure as impossible and error as mistake, a necessary opportunity to learn.

Collectively these four leadership traits have the effect of empowering people by: (1) making them feel significant, (2) focusing on their developing competence rather than failure, (3) creating a shared sense of community, and (4) making work exciting and worthy of dedicated commitment.

David Berlew emphasizes this latter result in "Leadership and Organizational Excitement." His concern in this article is with a failure of large, mature organizations in the United States to attract and hold highly talented young people. Berlew argues that much of the failure results from the inherent inadequacy of current management theory. Most theories currently in vogue focus on two variables: (1) the manager's task-related behavior and (2) the manager's relationship behavior. From Berlew's point of view, these theories are seriously incomplete. They do not anticipate the new worker or the new business environment. They can neither explain why the new worker who is productive and treated respectfully is not committed or fulfilled, nor why some organizations are "turned on" while most others are not. As Berlew observes, two-factor management theories tell us more about management than they do about leadership.

Berlew's insights about how to extend management theory to incorporate the dimension of leadership focus on the central importance of *vision*. Berlew proposes three aspects of vision-centered leadership.

1. The ability to *discover* and articulate the common vision that will propel and excite the organization.

2. The ability to create value-related opportunities for people to act in behalf of the vision.

3. The ability to empower people, to make organizational members feel stronger and in control of their own destinies.

Berlew ends his article with a number of questions regarding the conditions and circumstances under which a leadership-oriented management style is appropriate and effective. These are important questions and ones which the growth perspective developed in the next section of this volume will address.

In "Transforming Organizations: The Key to Strategy is Context," Stanley M. Davis makes a bold attempt to articulate a perspective toward leadership that will be foreign territory to most managers. While parts of this article may be difficult, the persevering reader will find its message valuable.

Davis is concerned with the possibility of organizational transformation and the growing need to develop a technology of transformation as businesses are increasingly required to radically renew themselves and make profound adaptive responses to their shifting business circumstances.

The author makes an important distinction when he contrasts *change* and *transformation*. Change is any incremental adjustment in a situation. For example, change might result from producing *more* of something, making a situation *better* in certain respects, or doing something *different*. Incremental change is not contextual since actions that lead to more, better, and different modifications do not necessarily challenge the implicit underlying assumptions or frame of reference governing how a situation is perceived and interpreted. Consequently, Davis views change as properly the domain of management since it is primarily an issue of efficiency.

Transformation, in contrast, requires and accompanies a shift of context. For example, the movement that Alvin Toffler describes in his contribution to the previous section, from an Industrial to a Third Wave society, is transformational since it causes and results from a shift in the underlying assumptions of the society (e.g., from massification to demassification). Only through such transformation or contextual shift can an individual, a work unit, an organization, or a society break the self-limiting barriers imposed by the old frame of reference and open up to the possibility of renewal.

The shaping and reshaping of the *context* of work, argues Davis, is the proper domain of leadership, a domain that is possibly the most critical frontier of management theory today.

In the final article of the section, "Management as a Performance System," William B. Lashbrook suggests a conceptual framework for viewing the manager's task as a performance system. Research that Lashbrook and his colleagues have conducted at Wilson Learning Corporation suggests that the central task of management in a performance environment is to shape the work unit culture. The influence of the work unit culture, not particular management actions, is the principal determinant of work unit performance. Furthermore, Lashbrook argues, the effectiveness of the work unit culture is largely dependent upon how well the members of the work unit can answer the following five questions: (1) Why are we here? (2) Where are we going? (3) How are we doing? (4) What's in it for us? and (5) What happens when we need help?

In other words, from a performance system perspective, the leader-manager's primary role is to shape the context of work by focusing attention on influencing the work unit's perceptions with respect to: mission, goals, feedback, rewards, and support.

These five contextual factors will each be explored in depth as they provide the organizing framework for the last five sections of this volume.

FOUR TRAITS OF LEADERSHIP

Warren Bennis

For nearly five years, I have been researching a new book on leadership. In this period, I have traveled around the country and spent a lot of time with 90 of the most effective, successful leaders in the nation: 60 from the corporate side and 30 from the public sector. (More about the people in the sample later.)

My goal was simple and straightforward: to find common traits in all these leaders, a task that has taken much more digging than expected. For a while, I sensed much more diversity than commonality. In the group are both "left brain" and "right brain" thinkers; some dressed for success and some were not so dressed; they were well-spoken and articulate leaders, as well as laconic and inarticulate ones; John Wayne types and definitely not John Wayne types. Interestingly, the stereotypically charismatic leader does not show up very often in the group — although there are a few.

The people in the study are of every type and style. But, despite the differences and diversity (which are profound and must not be underestimated), I was lucky enough to find certain areas of competence *shared by all* 90. Before presenting those findings, though, I believe it is important to place this study in context, to review what had been happening in America — just before and during the research.

CONTEXT: DECLINE AND MALAISE

When I left the University of Cincinnati late in 1977, our country was experiencing what former President Carter called a kind of "despair" or "malaise" in our society. From 1960 to 1980, there had been a steady erosion of the trust and credibility of institutions. In fact, I wrote an article about that time called "Where Have All the Leaders Gone," in which I described how difficult the times were for leaders — including university presidents like myself. I argued that, because of the complexity of the times, leaders were feeling impotent. Added to that was the effect of the assassinations, the war in Vietnam, Watergate, the Iranian hostages . . . all of it leading to a loss of trust in our leadership and institutions.

In a time when bumper stickers said "Impeach Someone," I resolved to seek out leaders who managed to be effective and successful, even under these adverse conditions.

The end of the 1970s was a hard time for America. And, even though my reading of the polls leads me to believe that we "bottomed out" in 1980

"Four Traits of Leadership," by Warren Bennis. The Hay Group lecture, October 1983. Reprinted by permission of Dr. Warren Bennis, Los Angeles, California.

and are on the road back to confidence and credibility, none of us knew then that the end was in sight. Indeed, during my work I came across an apt quotation in a letter from Abigail Adams to Thomas Jefferson; in 1790 she wrote, "These are the hard times in which a genius would wish to live." If, as she believed, great necessities call forth great leaders, I wanted to get to know the leaders called forth by the current malaise.

At the same time that America was suffering from this "leadership gap," it was also suffering from a "productivity gap." Consider these trends:

- In the '60s, the average growth in the GNP was 4.1%; in the '70s it was 2.9%; in 1982 it was negative.

- The U.S. standard of living, which was the highest in the world in 1972, is now ranked fifth.

- In 1960, when the economies of Europe and Japan had been rebuilt, the U.S. accounted for 25% of the manufacturing exports of the industrial nations and supplied 98% of its own domestic markets. Now, the U.S. has less than a 20% share of the world market, and that share is declining.

- In 1960, U.S. automobiles had a 96% market share and today we have about 71%. The same holds true for consumer electronics; in 1960 it was 94.4% and in 1980 it was only 49%. And that was before Sony introduced the Walkman!

So, it seems right now that one of our few growth industries is the publishing of books dealing with our declining productivity and how to remedy it. Most of these books, unfortunately, recommend economic fixes, none of which seems to be very reliable. In fact, it seems that none is working and, if it is, the economist cannot really consign to any particular economic theory an account of what is causing the present economic recovery.

When we hear the economic nostrums, then, we must treat them with a very big grain of salt. In fact, there is one current danger, which I think some of the best selling books partly reflect: namely, in our thirst, in our zeal to become more productive, we may just grab for the instant fixes, for the quick remedies, for the buzz words. We see some sign of this these days when, for the last several months, three books on management either headed the best seller list or were in the top ten. And when management books surpass the sales for Garfield's cats and Jane Fonda's exercises, there is a risk that we will look too quickly, or grab too zealously, for the instant solution, the Theory Z, the Japanese management, even "organizational culture," as a panacea.

In addition to the "leadership gap" and the "productivity gap," there was also a subtler "commitment gap." That is, a reluctance to commit to one's work or employer.

The Public Agenda's recent survey of a national cross section of working Americans shows the following key statistics. Of this sample of almost a thousand people, it was learned that less than one out of four jobholders, 23%, say they are currently working at their full potential. Nearly half of all jobholders say they do not put much effort into their jobs, over what is required of them. For them the slogan is: "I only work here." The overwhelming majority, 75%, say they could be significantly more effective on their job than they are now. And, perhaps even more disturbing, the tendency to withhold effort from the job may be increasing; nearly 6 out of 10 working Americans believe that "most people do not work as hard as they used to."

Now, a number of observers have pointed out that a considerable gap has existed, and continues to exist, between the number of hours that people are paid to work and the number of hours that they actually spend on productive labor. Evidence has just been developed by the University of Michigan that indicates the gap may be widening. They found the difference between paid hours and actual working hours grew by 10% over the ten years from 1970 to 1980.

This decline, this increasing "commitment gap," leads me to raise what I think is the central question. How can we *empower the workforce* and reap the harvest of human effort?

And if there is anything I have learned over the last four or five years, it is that the key answer, the pivotal one, the factor that empowers the workforce and ultimately makes the difference between winning and losing organizations, is the *leadership of those organizations*.

My research reveals that even when strategies, processes, or cultures change, the real key to improvement is the leadership of the institution.

THE SAMPLE: 90 LEADERS

For my study, I was interested in finding 90 successful, effective people with proven track records. The resultant group contains 60 corporate leaders, most, but not all, in the Fortune 500, and 30 from the public sector. My goal was to find people that really had what I would consider *leadership ability*, as contrasted with just being "good managers" — true leaders of people who really affect the culture, who are the social architects of their organizations and who create and maintain values.

Leaders are people who do the right thing and managers are people who do things right. There is a profound difference between those two roles, and both are crucial — to do the right thing *and* to do things right. But I have often seen people in top positions continue to do the *wrong* thing and do it well. In fact, given my definition, one of the key problems facing organizations in American society (and probably other parts of the industrialized world) is that they are *underled and overmanaged*. They are not paying enough attention to doing the right thing, while paying too much attention to doing things right. Part of this is the fault of our schools of management; we do very well at teaching people how to be good technicians and good staff people, but I doubt that we are training people for leadership.

The group of 60 corporate leaders was not particularly different from any profile done of top leadership in America. Their median age was 56, most white males; there were six black men and six women in the group. The only surprising thing I found was that all of the CEOs were not only married to their first spouse, but also seemed to be enthusiastic about the institution of marriage.

Examples of some of the CEOs are Bill Kieschnick, Chairman and CEO of Arco, Ray Kroc, who was, at the time I interviewed him, head of McDonalds. In the public sector the group included such people as Harold Williams, who was then Chairman of the SEC, one genuine all-American hero who happened to be at the University of Cincinnati, Neil Armstrong, three elected officials, two orchestra conductors, and two winning coaches. (I wanted conductors and coaches because I thought that these were the last roles in our society where the leader had the ultimate and complete control over the constituents; that turned out to be untrue.)

Again, my first sense of this group was that there was much more diversity than commonality. But, after years of observation and conversation, I have defined four traits that are evident, to some extent, in every member of the group. These traits, in no particular order, are:

- Management of Attention
- Management of Meaning
- Management of Trust
- Management of Self

MANAGEMENT OF ATTENTION

One of the most apparent traits of the leaders in this group is that they are the kinds of people to whom other people are really *drawn* — not because of their personalities but because they have a vision, a dream, a set of intentions, an agenda, a frame of reference. Clearly, when you are with these individuals, you sense an extraordinary focus of commitment, which attracts people to them. It was said of one of these leaders that he is a guy who makes you want to just *join* in with him; he enrolls you in this vision.

Leaders, then, manage attention through a compelling vision that can bring people to a place they have not been before through any of a variety of means. I came about this understanding in a sort of back door way. Let me explain with an anecdote.

One of the people I most wanted to interview was one of the few people I thought I couldn't get to; he refused to answer my letters and phone calls. I even went so far as to get in touch with the members of his board. The man was Leon Fleischer — a well-known child prodigy who grew up to become a well-known pianist, conductor, and musicologist.

Leon Fleischer had been on a concert stage as a child, but, what I did not know about him was that he had lost the use of his right hand and was no longer performing. When I called him originally to see if I could entreat him to join the University of Cincinnati, he declined and told me he was working with some orthopods from Johns Hopkins Medical School trying to regain the use of his right hand, so that he could once again start playing. He did visit our campus, and I did get to know him, and I was very impressed with the will that he had to learn. But I was also impressed with the fact that he was staying where he was in Baltimore because he was so committed to the future of what he might learn from this therapy.

Fleischer was the only person who kept turning me down for an interview and, finally, I gave up. A couple of summers later, though, I was visiting in Aspen, Colorado, and Fleischer was conducting the Aspen Music Festival.

So, I tried again, even going to his dressing room behind the Aspen tent and leaving a note on his door — but getting no answer.

I gave up again until one day when I was in downtown Aspen about three miles from the music tent; I saw two perspiring young musicians carrying their cellos and asked them if they wanted a ride to the music tent. They hopped in the back of my open jeep and I questioned them about Fleischer. Now, unlike most musicians I know, they seemed to be very inarticulate; they mumbled, and I could not hear them over the noise of the muffler. Finally, though, at the music tent, one of them looked at me and said, "I'll tell you why he is so great." I waited expectantly. And he said, "He doesn't waste our time." I thought to myself, "I drive three miles out of my way to hear that brand of response: He doesn't waste our time."

Later, I thought about the remark, and, then, I got to know Fleischer. He did submit, finally, not only to some interviews but to letting me watch him rehearse and conduct music classes. I put together the way I saw him perform and that very simple sentence, "He doesn't waste our time." Every moment Fleischer was before the orchestra, he knew exactly what sound he wanted. Clearly, the reason he didn't waste time was because his intentions were always out there, always evident. What united him with all these individuals was their concern with intention and outcome.

When I reflected on my own experience, when I thought about being effective and ineffective, it struck me that when I was most effective, it was because I *knew what I wanted* from a meeting or from an interaction. And when I was ineffective, it was because I was murky or unclear about it.

So, the first point I want to emphasize is the *management of attention* through a set of intentions or vision, not in a mystical or religious sense, but in the sense of outcome, goal and direction.

There is a slogan in front of the American pavillion at Disneyworld's EPCOT, which reads:

If you can dream it, you can do it.

Leaders make their dreams apparent and enroll others in making them happen.

MANAGEMENT OF MEANING

To make dreams apparent to others, leaders must communicate their vision to align people with it. Communication and alignment go together.

Consider, for example, the national political scene: contrast the presidencies of Reagan and Carter in this one area. Now, it is said of Ronald Reagan that he is the "great communicator." One of his staff speech writers said Reagan can read the phone book and make it interesting. And the *reason* he makes it interesting is that he can use certain metaphors or references that people can identify with. In Reagan's first budget message, for example, he showed the world what a trillion dollars might be like by comparing it to piling up dollar bills beside the Empire State Building. Most people think they have a good notion of how tall the Empire State Building is and Reagan — to use one of Alexander Haig's interesting words — "tangibilitated" the idea, meaning to make it tangible. Leaders make ideas tangible and real to other people, so they can get behind them. For, no matter how marvelous the vision, the effective leader must use a metaphor, a word, or a model to make that vision clear to others.

Not all the leaders in my group were articulate; they were not all word masters. But they all had a variety of ways of getting people to understand where they wanted to go and where they wanted help — and getting people to line up with the help they needed.

In contrast, it was said about President Carter that his problem as a president was that he was *boring*. Actually that is not quite the point. Ironically, Carter was one of our best informed presidents; he probably had more facts at his fingertips than almost any other president has ever had and, certainly, in many areas was better informed about details than Reagan. But his problem was that the *meaning* never came through the facts.

One of the people I interviewed — an Assistant Secretary of Commerce under Carter, a loyal Democrat appointed by him — said to me that after four years of being in his administration, she still did not know what Jimmy Carter stood for. She said that working for him was like looking through the wrong side of a tapestry, all blurry and indistinct.

What I'm really talking about is not just explanation or clarification but the *creation* of meaning, as in my favorite baseball joke. An umpire hesitates a split second in a key playoff game; it's the ninth inning, with a count of 3 and 2 on the batter, and the batter angrily turns around and says, "Well, what was it?" And the umpire says, "It ain't *nothing* until I call it!"

And the more far-flung and complicated the organization, the more critically important is this ability. The effective leader has a way of communicating ideas through several layers of the organization, across great distances, even through the jamming signals from special interest groups and opponents.

In this connection, I am reminded again of my experience as a university president. A group of us — vice presidents, administrative staff, and I — would hatch what we knew was a great idea. Then, we would do the right thing: delegate, delegate, delegate. Naturally, when the "idea" finally appeared on the scene, it scarcely resembled what we had "dreamed up."

The problem was that we had not communicated well. In fact, this process happened so often that I gave it a name: the Pinocchio Effect. (Because I am sure that Geppetto the puppeteer had no idea how Pinocchio would look when he finished carving him.) The Pinocchio Effect leaves us surprised. Because of our inadequate communication, the result rarely resembles our expectations.

We read and hear so much these days about *information* that we tend to overlook the importance of *meaning*. Actually, the more bombarded a society or organization, the more deluged with facts and images, the greater its thirst for meaning. And that is what leadership provides; it integrates facts, concepts, and anecdotes into meaning for the public.

Contrast again the examples of Reagan and Carter. Regardless of your political preferences, when you are talking about communication, you are talking about the management of *meaning*, and that is what creates alignment; that is what creates team spirit. Indeed, that is what our American hockey team possessed in 1980, enabling it to outplay both the Finnish teams and the Russian teams (both of which had better personnel and more experience). Yet this *team* was aligned and felt what should almost be called a *passion* to realize that goal.

This ability to manage attention and meaning comes from the whole person. It is not enough to say the right buzz word or use cute techniques or hire a public relations person to write the speeches. That is not leadership. No, as a true example of leadership, consider another man in my group, Frank Dale, publisher of the afternoon newspaper in Los Angeles, *The Herald Examiner*. Dale's charge was to cut into the market share of its morning competitor, *The L.A. Times*. When he first came there a few years ago, he created a campaign, with posters all over the place, showing the *Herald Examiner* behind and slightly above the *L.A. Times*, which looked as if it would be overtaken. The whole campaign was based on this message and how the *Herald Examiner* was going to overtake the *L.A. Times*.

When I finished my first interview with him, we made another appointment for *his* office, and when he got into his chair, he fastened around him a *safety belt* like those on an airplane. I could hardly suppress a smile; in fact, I don't think I did suppress a smile. He did it to remind me and everybody else what business he was in. His *whole person* was developed, and it was not just some theory he espoused; it was a *practice*, and he was deeply involved.

Now, I don't think there are any people more cynical than newspaper reporters. You can imagine some of the cynical reactions that went

85

through the hall of the *Herald Examiner* building. But, at the same time, *nobody ever forgot what Frank Dale was trying to communicate*. And that is the management of meaning.

MANAGEMENT OF TRUST

Trust is essential to all organizations. Without it, no organization can work. None.

And the main determinant of trust is reliability, or what I prefer to call *constancy*. When I talk to the board members or staffs of the leaders in this group, I hear certain phrases again and again. "He (or she) is all of a piece." "Whether you like it or not, you always know where he (or she) is coming from, what they stand for."

When John Paul II visited this country, he gave one press conference. He was asked *one negative question*: how could he account for allocating funds to build a swimming pool at the Papal Summer Palace? And Pope John Paul II responded very quickly; he said, "I like to swim. Next question." There was something remarkably refreshing about that; he did not go through rationalizations about health or claim he got the money from another source. He was just simply straightforward, and it was plain refreshing.

Or consider a recent study done of a national sample indicating that people would much rather follow individuals they can count on, even when they disagree with their viewpoint, than people whose viewpoint they agree with, who flip-flop in getting there or who might change at any time. I cannot emphasize enough the significance of constancy and focus and, if you will, staying the course.

Margaret Thatcher's re-election in Great Britain is another excellent example. When she won office in 1979, all the pundits said that she would do a U-turn and would revert to those defunct Labor Party policies. Well, Ms. Thatcher did not! In fact, there was an article not long ago in the London *Times* which headlined (parodying Christopher Fry's play) "The Lady's Not for Returning." She has not turned; she has stayed the course; she has been constant and focused and all of a piece.

MANAGEMENT OF SELF

The fourth leadership trait is management of *self*, knowing one's skills and deploying them effectively. Management of self is critical; without it, leaders and managers can do more harm than good. Like incompetent doctors, incompetent managers can make life worse, make people sicker and less vital. (The term "iatrogenic," by the way, refers to illness *caused* by doctors and hospitals.) Some managers give themselves heart attacks and nervous breakdowns; still worse, many are "carriers" — they give them to their employees.

Management of self is the appropriate deployment of one's own capacities. Leaders know themselves; they know what they are good at and they nurture those skills and competencies. Part of it is positive self-regard, where people know their talents, nurture them, and discern their strengths within an organization. They also have a faculty I think of as the "Wallenda Factor."

Many people have heard of the Flying Wallendas, perhaps the greatest family of aerialists and tightrope walkers that ever lived. I was fascinated when in the early '70s Karl Wallenda said on a TV talk show that, for him, living is walking the tightrope, that everything else is waiting. I was struck with that, his capacity for concentration on the intention, the task, the decision. "Life is walking the tightrope." The only time he felt truly alive was walking the tightrope.

I was fascinated and intrigued, even more so, when several months later he fell to his death, in San Juan, Puerto Rico, at the age of 71, trying to walk between two high office buildings. Without that proverbial safety net, Karl Wallenda fell to his death — still, by the way, clutching onto his balancing pole, which he always warned his family never to drop, lest it hurt somebody below!

Later, his daughter and wife were on a similar talk show, and his wife said that before her husband fell to his death in San Juan, for the first time since she had known him, for the first time in his life, he was thinking about *falling*, not walking the tightrope. He began to put all of his energies into falling, not walking; in fact, he personally supervised the attachment of the guide wires, which he had never done before. It was as if he envisioned himself falling and not being alive on the tightrope.

Like Wallenda, *before* his fall, the leaders in my group seemed unacquainted with the concept of failure. What you or I might call a failure, they would refer to as a *mistake*. In fact, I began collecting synonyms for the word failure and came up with over 20, including *mistake, error, false start, bloop, flop, loss, miss, foul-up, stumble, botch, bungle* . . . but not failure.

One CEO said to me that if she had a knack for leadership, it was the capacity to make as many mistakes as she could, as soon as possible, and thus, to get them out of the way. Another said that a mistake is simply "another way of doing things."

We all must appreciate how these people construe the idea of a mistake, of something going wrong. They have a capacity to learn, to *use* something that doesn't go well; what the rest of us call a failure is simply the next step.

Harry Truman once said that if he ever made a bum decision, he just wouldn't make another one. He did not dwell on it.

Or consider Harold Williams, now president of the Getty Foundation. When I asked him what was the most formative experience that shaped him as a leader, he said it was when he was *passed over* for the presidency of Norton Simon. When it happened, he was furious and demanded reasons, most of which he considered idiotic. Finally, though, he spoke to a friend who said that if some of the reasons were true, he could make some *corrections*. Williams made some changes and, about a yeer and a half later, became president.

Or consider coach Ray Meyer at DePaul University, whose team had lost its first home game after winning 29 straight home games. I called him to ask how he felt. He said, "Great. Now we can start to concentrate on winning, not *not losing*."

The "Wallenda Factor" is really an approach to life; it goes beyond leadership and power in organizations. It has to do with how one approaches a relationship, or how one approaches moving into a new neighborhood, or how one approaches life. These leaders, somehow or other, all have it. Consider Harold Prince, who calls a press conference for the morning right after his show opens, without reading the reviews, to announce his next play. Or Harold Williams, who learned a great deal from the "mistakes" that temporarily cost him the presidency of Norton Simon. Or Ray Meyer who says, "Great," when he loses. Or Susan Anthony who said, "Failure is impossible." Or Fletcher Byrum who, after 22 years as president of Coopers, was asked his hardest decision. He replied that he did not know what a hard decision is; that he never worried, that he accepted the possibility of being wrong. Byrum said that worry is an obstacle to clear thinking.

EMPOWERMENT: THE EFFECTS OF LEADERSHIP

Leadership can be felt throughout an organization. It gives pace and energy to the work and *empowerment* to the workforce.

Empowerment is a central idea in my research; it is the collective effect of leadership. In organizations with effective leaders, the empowerment is most evident in four themes or feelings.

1. *People feel significant*. Everyone in the organization, at least in some small way, feels that he or she makes a difference to the success of the organization. Whether it is delivering potato chips to a small mom and pop store in western Colorado or developing a small but essential part for an airplane . . . where there is empowerment, people feel that their work is connected to the world, that what they do has meaning and significance.

2. *Learning and competence matter*. Leaders value learning and mastery. Leon Fleischer turned down my offer to be Dean of the School of Music because he wanted to stay with his orthopedic therapy, to learn what he needed to learn to regain the use of his hand. And, as most people know, he succeeded and returned to the concert stage.

So, leaders value learning and so do people who work for leaders.

Leaders make it clear that there is no failure — only mistakes that give us feedback and tell us what to do next.

3. *People are part of a community*. Where there is leadership, there is a team, a family, a unity. Even people who do not especially like each other feel the sense of community. When Neil Armstrong talks about the Apollo explorations of the moon, he tells you how an almost unimaginably complex set of interdependent tasks was carried out by a team. And the team worked beautifully. Until there were women astronauts, the men referred to this feeling as "brotherhood." I suggest they rename it "family."

4. *Work is exciting*. Where there are leaders, the work is stimulating, challenging, fascinating . . . fun.

An essential ingredient in organizational leadership is that the leader *pulls* rather than *pushes* people along. A pull style of influence works by attracting and energizing people to enroll in an exciting vision of the future. It motivates through our identification, rather than through rewards and punishments. The leaders in an organization articulate and, if possible, embody the ideals toward which the organizations strive. They enroll themselves in a vision of that idea, as attainable as their behavior, and exemplify the idea in action.

It is also apparent that organization members cannot be expected to enroll in just *any* kind of exciting vision. Some visions and concepts have more staying power and are more deeply rooted in our human hungers than others. I believe that the lack of two such concepts in modern organizational life is in large part responsible for the alienation and lack of meaning that so many managers and workers are likely to experience in their work.

One of these is the idea of *quality*. Modern, industrial society has been oriented to *quantity*: providing *more* goods and services for everyone. In this preoccupation, we have inevitably failed to keep quality in the forefront. Quantity is measured in money; we become a money-oriented society. Quality is often not measured at all, but is appreciated intuitively. Our response to quality is a feeling; feelings of quality are intimately connected with our experience of meaning and beauty and value in our lives.

Closely linked to the concept of quality is that of *dedication*, even love, of quality and organization. And this dedication is evoked by quality and is the attracting force that energizes high performing systems. When we love our work, when it has quality, we do not have to be managed by hopes of reward or fears of punishment. We can create systems that facilitate our work, rather than being preoccupied with checks and controls of people who want to beat or to exploit the system.

And that is what the human resources profession should care about most.

LEADERSHIP AND ORGANIZATIONAL EXCITEMENT

David E. Berlew

In the past several years, an increasing number of individuals — often new graduates and professionals — have rejected secure positions in apparently well-managed organizations in favor of working alone or joining up with a few friends in a new organization. Usually they are not protesting, but searching for "something more." The nature of this "something more" is the subject of this article.

Many executives have blamed this disenchantment with established organizations on changes in Western society which have made an increasing number of people unsuited for organizational life. They often express the view that changes in child-rearing practices and the breakdown of discipline in the family and in our schools has produced a generation which cannot or will not exercise the self-discipline and acceptance of legitimate authority required for bureaucratic organizations.

Because it has been so acceptable to fault society, the leadership of most organizations has felt little need to look inward for the source of the problem and to analyze their own and their organization's failure to attract and hold some of the best-trained people our society produces.

Those organizations which have tried to change to keep pace with society have often been frustrated. In analyzing our failure to stem the tide of increasing alienation in the workplace, Richard Walton describes "a parade of organization development, personnel, and labor relations programs that promised to revitalize organizations,"[1] such as job enrichment, participative decision-making, management by objectives, sensitivity training or encounter groups, and productivity bargaining. He argues that while each application is often based on a correct diagnosis, it is only a partial remedy, and therefore the organizational system soon returns to an earlier equilibrium. His prescription is a systematic approach leading to comprehensive organization design or redesign.

Whether we are concerned with organizations that have viewed the problem as outside of their control or those that have been frustrated in their attempts to change, one factor which has not been adequately explored and understood is that of effective organization leadership. Only an organization with strong leadership will look within itself for causes of problems that can be blamed easily on outside forces. Exceptional leadership is required to plan and initiate significant change in organizations, whether it is one of Walton's partial remedies or comprehensive organization redesign. Short-term benefits from change projects often result from leadership behavior which excites members of an organization about the *potential* for change rather than actual change introduced.

CURRENT LEADERSHIP MODELS

Almost without exception, theories of managerial leadership currently in vogue postulate two major dimensions of leadership behavior.[2] One dimension concerns the manager's or leader's efforts to accomplish organizational tasks. Various writers have given this dimension different names, including task or instrumental leadership behavior, job-centered leadership, initiating structure, and concern for production. The second dimension is concerned with the leader's relations with his subordinates; it has been labelled social-emotional leadership behavior, consideration, concern for people, and employee-centered leadership. Measures of the effects of leadership also usually fall into two categories: indices of productivity and of worker satisfaction. A leader or manager who is good at organizing to get work done and who relates well to his subordinates should have a highly productive group and satisfied workers.

There is nothing wrong with two-factor models of managerial leadership as far as they go, but they are incomplete. They grew out of a period in history when the goal was to combine the task efficiency associated with scientific management with the respect for human dignity emphasized by the human relations movement. They did not anticipate a time when people would not be fulfilled even when they were treated with respect, were productive, and derived achievement satisfaction from their jobs. As a result, two-factor theories of managerial leadership tell us more about management than about leadership. They deal with relationships between man and his work, and between men and other men, but they do not tell us why some organizations are excited or "turned-on" and others are not. They do not help us understand that quality of leadership which can " . . . lift people out of their petty preoccupations . . . and unify them in pursuit of objectives worthy of their best efforts."[3]

LEADERSHIP AND EMOTION IN ORGANIZATIONS

In an effort to help fill that void, the outline of a model relating types of leadership to the emotional tone in organizations is presented in Exhibit 1. Stages 1 and 2 of the model are derived from familiar theories of work motivation[4] and the two-factor models of leadership discussed earlier. Angry or resentful workers (Stage 1) are primarily concerned with satisfying basic needs for food, shelter, security, safety, and respect. Organizations in Stage 1 try to improve these situations by eliminating

EXHIBIT 1

Organizational Emotions and Modes of Leadership

	Stage 1	Stage 2		Stage 3
Emotional Tone:	Anger or Resentment	Neutrality	Satisfaction	Excitement
Leadership Mode:	CUSTODIAL	MANAGERIAL		CHARISMATIC
Focal Needs or Values:	Food Shelter Security Fair treatment Human dignity	Membership Achievement Recognition		Meaningful work Self-reliance Community Excellence Service Social Responsibility
Focal Changes or Improvements:	Working conditions Compensation Fringe benefits Equal opportunity Decent supervision Grievance procedures	Job enrichment Job enlargement Job rotation Participative management Management by objectives Effective supervision		Common vision Value-related opportunities and activities Supervision which strengthens subordinates

"dissatisfiers" through improved working conditions, compensation, and fringe benefits, and by providing fair or "decent" supervision. The type of leadership associated with a change from an angry or resentful emotional tone to one of neutrality, or from Stage 1 to Stage 2, has been labelled *custodial*. The workers are neutral, lacking either strong positive or negative feelings about their work or the organization.

In the absence of "dissatisfiers," they tend to become increasingly concerned with group membership or "belonging" and opportunities to do inherently satisfying work and to receive recognition. In order to increase employee satisfaction organizations at Stage 2 introduce improvements such as job enrichment, job enlargement, job rotation, participative management, and effective (as opposed to decent) supervision. Changes are oriented toward providing work that is less routine and more interesting or challenging, building cohesive work teams, and giving employees more say in decisions that directly affect them. The type of leadership associated with this movement from neutral to satisfied workers, or from Stage 2 to Stage 3, has been labelled *managerial.*

Most of the advances in organization theory and management practice in the past few decades have related to Stage 2: defining and controlling the elements of supervision and the organizational environment that result in high productivity with high satisfaction. While these advances have been substantial and have led, in most cases, to healthier, more effective organizations, they have not prevented the increasing alienation of professional employees.

The addition of Stage 3 to the model to extend the emotional tone continuum to include *organizational excitement* is an attempt to deal with a phenomenon of the '70s — the increasing number of professionals and new graduates who are rejecting secure positions in established organizations. The model suggests that for this small but growing element of the population, the satisfaction of needs for membership, achievement, and recognition is no longer enough. The meaning they seek has less to do with the specific tasks they perform as individuals than the impact of their individual and collective efforts — channelled through the organization — on their environment. The feelings of potency which accompany "shaping" rather than being shaped or giving up (and dropping out) are a source of excitement. So, too, are the feelings that stem from commitment to an organization that has a value-related mission and thus takes on some of the characteristics of a cause or a movement. At the extreme, this can lead to total involvement or total *identification* — the breaking down of boundaries between the self and the organization so that the "individual becomes the organization" and the "organization becomes the individual."

STAGE 3 LEADERSHIP

Although Stage 3 leadership must involve elements of both custodial and managerial leadership, the dominant mode is charismatic leadership. The word "charisma" has been used in many ways with many meanings. Here we will define it in terms of three different types or classes of leadership behavior which provide meaning to work and generate organizational excitement. These are:

- the development of a "common vision" for the organization related to values shared by the organization's members;

- the discovery or creation of value-related opportunities and activities within the framework of the mission and goals of the organization; and

- making organization members feel stronger and more in control of their own destinies, both individually and collectively.

The first requirement for Stage 3 or charismatic leadership is a common or shared vision of what the future *could* be. To provide meaning and generate excitement, such a common vision must reflect goals or a future state of affairs that is valued by the organization's members and is thus important to them to bring about.

That men do not live by bread alone has been recognized for centuries by religious and political leaders. All inspirational speeches or writings have the common element of some vision or dream of a better existence which will inspire or excite those who share the author's values. This basic wisdom too often has been ignored by managers.

A vision, no matter how well articulated, will not excite or provide meaning for individuals whose values are different from those implied by the vision. Thus, the corporate executive who dreams only of higher return on investment and earnings per share may find his vision of the future rejected and even resented by members of his organization. Indeed, he may even find his vision of a profitable corporate future questioned by stockholders concerned with the social responsibility of corporations. Progressive military leaders may articulate a vision or mission congruent with the needs and values of the young people they are trying to attract to an all volunteer service, only to discover that the same vision conflicts with the values of their senior officers.

An important lesson from group theory and research is that informal groups tend to select as leader the individual who is most representative of the group's needs and values. Thus his hopes and aspirations, and the goals toward which he will lead the group, are automatically shared by the group's members.

One problem for heads of complex organizations is that if they are to function as leaders (as opposed to custodians or managers) they must represent and articulate the hopes and goals of many different groups —the young and the old, the unskilled and the professional, the employee and the stockholder, the minority and the majority, union, and management. Only the exceptional leader can instinctively identify and articulate the common vision relevant to such diverse groups. But to fail to provide some kind of vision of the future, particularly for employees who demand meaning and excitement in their work, is to make the fatal assumption that man *can* live by bread alone.

There are dangers as well as advantages to a common vision. If top management does not sincerely believe in the desirability of the vision they articulate, they are involved in an attempt to manipulate which will probably backfire. Another danger might be called the "Camelot phenomenon": the articulation of a shared vision that is both meaningful and exciting, but so unrealistic that people must inevitably be disillusioned. Whether the responsibility in such cases lies with the seducer or the seduced is difficult to say, but the end result is a step backward into cynicism.

Finally, the effectiveness of the common vision depends upon the leader's ability to "walk the talk": to behave in ways both small and large that are consistent with the values and goals he is articulating. In this regard, my experience in the Peace Corps taught me that the quickest way to destroy or erode the power of a common vision is for the leader to allow himself to be sidetracked into bargaining over details instead of concentrating all of his attention on identifying, tracking, and talking to the value issue involved. For example, at a meeting where Volunteers are reacting negatively to a proposed reduction in their living allowance, the Peace Corps Director or leader cannot afford to get involved in a discussion of whether or not female Volunteers will be able to afford pantyhose with their reduced allowance. The role of the leader is to keep alive the common vision which attracted Volunteers to the Peace Corps in the first place: in this case, the idea of a group of Americans whose help will be more readily accepted if they live at about the same standard as their local co-workers.

Value-Related Opportunities and Activities

It is a mistake to assume that individuals who desert or reject established organizations are basically loners. In fact, many start or join new organizations, often at considerable personal sacrifice in terms of income, security, and working conditions. It is revealing to analyze these "new" organizations for sources of meaning or excitement which may be lacking in more mature organizations. A list of opportunities present in many of the younger organizations in our society are presented in Exhibit 2, along with values related to those opportunities.

EXHIBIT 2

Sources of Meaning in Organizations: Opportunities and Related Values

Type of Opportunity	Related Need or Value
1. A chance to be tested; to make it on one's own	Self-reliance Self-actualization
2. A social experiment, to combine work, family, and play in some new way	Community Integration of life
3. A chance to do something *well* — for instance, return to real craftsmanship; to be really creative	Excellence Unique accomplishment
4. A chance to do something *good* — for instance, run an honest, no "rip-off" business, or a youth counselling center	Consideration Service
5. A chance to change the way things are — for instance, from Republican to Democrat or Socialist, from war to peace, from unjust to just	Activism Social responsibility Citizenship

A Chance to Be Tested. — Many of us go through life wondering what we could accomplish if given the opportunity. Our Walter Mitty fantasies place us in situations of extreme challenge and we come through gloriously. Few of us, however, have an opportunity to test the reality of our fantasies, as society increasingly protects us from getting in over our heads where we might fail and thus hurt the organization or ourselves. This is especially true of corporations where managers are moved along slowly, and only after they have had sufficient training and experience to practically insure that they will not have too much difficulty with their next assignment.

As a Peace Corps Country Director in the mid-sixties, I was struck by the necessity of having to place many Volunteers without adequate training or experience in extremely difficult situations, and the readiness — even eagerness — of most Volunteers to be tested in this way. Some

Volunteers rose to the challenge in remarkable ways, others held their own, and some could not handle the stress. Volunteers who were severely tested and succeeded were spoiled for the lock-step progression from challenge to slightly more difficult challenge which most established organizations favor to protect both themselves and the individual from failure. The same thing happens in wars and other emergency situations where planned development and promotion systems break down.

The point is that many people want an opportunity to be tested by an extraordinary challenge, and such opportunities rarely exist in established organizations. As a result, some who are most able and most confident leave the shelter of the established organization to measure themselves against a value of independence and self-reliance.

Social Experimentation. — A great deal has been written about the increasing superficiality of personal relationships in our society and the resulting loneliness and alienation. Organizations have responded with efforts to build cohesive work teams and to provide individuals doing routine, independent work with opportunities to talk with co-workers on the job. These gestures have not begun to meet the needs of persons who have been influenced by the counter-culture's emphasis on authentic relationships as opposed to role-regulated relationships, and the need to reduce social fragmentation by carrying out more of life's functions —working, child-rearing, playing, loving — with the same group of people.

Established organizations do not provide these kinds of opportunities. Many prohibit husbands and wives from working together. Child-care centers, if they exist, are separate from the parents' workplace, and the workplace is geographically and psychologically separated from the home. As a result, individuals who desire more integrated lives often leave established organizations and form new organizations, such as businesses in which wives and children can play a role and professional firms whose members live as well as work together.

A Chance To Do Something Well. — Established organizations fight a continual battle between controlling costs and maintaining standards of excellence; and standards are usually compromised. This is not cynicism: a group of skilled metal workers, machinists and mechanics can nearly always produce a better automobile than General Motors if cost is no object. The opportunity to seek true excellence, to produce the very best of something, is a strong attraction, even though the market may be extremely limited and the economic viability of the venture questionable. Individuals frustrated by the need to cut corners in established organizations find the alternative of a new organization committed to excellence an attractive one, and they will work long hours at low pay to make it financially viable.

A Chance To Do Good. — Still others desert established organizations in the belief that they are compromising standards of honesty and consideration in their struggle to survive in "the capitalistic jungle." They form organizations to do *good*: to provide honest, no "rip-off" services or products, or services which they believe a "good" community should have, such as free schools, legal, medical, and counselling services for the deprived, or low-income housing.

A Chance To Change Things. — Finally, many thoughtful individuals leave established organizations because they view them as too interwoven with or dependent upon the system to be an effective force for change. So they form new organizations as vehicles for bringing about change, whether it is to increase our appreciation of art, eliminate discrimination, or protect the environment.

The critical difference between these new organizations and established organizations is that the newer ones provide opportunities and activities closely related to the value of their members within the framework of the mission and goals of the organization. This is true even when the organization is as intent on making money as any established corporation (as they often are), and when they resemble a modern version of a nineteenth-century sweatshop (as they often do). Members of these organizations are not against profit-making *per se* or hard work, or putting the organization before the individual. But there must be a reason for doing these things; they are not ends in themselves. The reason comes from a common vision of what they are trying to create together, as well as opportunities to behave in a value-congruent manner. These factors justify and even make desirable those characteristics of organizations which otherwise would be rejected as unnecessary or exploitative.

Few, if any, progressive executives will find the types of opportunities and values noted above distasteful or undesirable. Many, however, will conclude that it is simply unrealistic to expect to find such opportunities in a large corporation or government agency under pressure from stockholders or the voting public to maximize profits or minimize expenditures.

However, such opportunities *do* exist in large, established organizations, and where they do not, they can often be created. For example, established organizations do not have to be tied to a step-by-careful-step advancement ladder. AT&T, for example, has experimented with a system whereby potential new hires for management positions are offered exceptionally challenging year-long assignments, and are told that depending on their performance, they will either leapfrog ahead or be asked to leave the company. It provides confident individuals with a series of opportunities to test themselves. If implemented successfully, it benefits the organization by attracting and developing self-reliant managers while quickly weeding out security seekers and poor performers.

While it takes managerial leadership to introduce such changes, it takes charismatic leadership to recognize the value relevance of such a program and to integrate it with the organization's mission in such a way that it creates and sustains excitement. Too often such programs go unrecognized or unexploited as sources of increased organizational excitement simply because of a limited conception of leadership.

Our organizations and institutions have, for the most part, been quite uncreative about countering or controlling the increasing fragmentation of work and family life, and the many problems that result. I know from my relationships with my wife and children now that I work at home a few days a week compared to when I spent fifty to eighty hours at the office or out of town and came home tired and irritable, often with homework. I doubt if I am much different from most other professionals in this regard. Why not actively recruit husbands and wives as work teams when possible, with child-care facilities nearby? Or, where possible, encourage employees to work at home on individual projects when they may have fewer interruptions than at the office?

Many organizations have a manifest commitment to excellence in their products and services, and to carrying out their corporate responsibilities toward the community. Occasionally they are in a position to spearhead social change. Too frequently, however, the value-relevant message seems directed toward customers or stockholders and only secondarily toward organization members. When it is directed toward members, it usually comes from a staff department such as corporate relations or the house organ rather than directly from the senior-line officers. This is public relations, not leadership, and whereas charisma might substitute for public relations, public relations, no matter how good, cannot substitute for charisma.

MAKING OTHERS FEEL STRONGER

The effective Stage 3 leader must lead in such a way as to make members of his organization feel stronger. To achieve the organization's goals as well as to meet the needs of his more confident and able employees, his leadership must encourage or enable employees to be Origins rather than Pawns.

Richard deCharms has described Origins and Pawns in the following terms:

> An Origin is a person who feels that he is director of his life. He feels that what he is doing is the result of his own free choice; he is doing it because he wants to do it, and the consequences of his activity will be valuable to him. He thinks carefully about what he wants in this world, now and in the future, and chooses the most important goals ruling out those that are for him too easy or too risky . . . he is genuinely self-confident because he has determined how to reach his goals through his own efforts . . . he is aware of his abilities and limitations. In short, an Origin is master of his own fate.

A Pawn is a person who feels that someone, or something else, is in control of his fate. He feels that what he is doing has been imposed on him by others. He is doing it because he is forced to, and the consequences of his activity will not be a source of pride to him. Since he feels that external factors determine his fate, the Pawn does not consider carefully his goals in life, nor does he concern himself about what he himself can do to further his cause. Rather he hopes for Lady Luck to smile on him.[5]

Clearly, there may only be a few people in the real world of human beings who are *always* guiding their own fate, checking their own skill, and choosing their own goals, but some people act and feel like Origins more of the time than do other people. Similarly, there are only a few people who *always* feel pushed around like Pawns. Some individuals —parents, teachers, managers — have the ability to relate on a one-on-one basis in ways that make another person feel and behave more like an Origin and less like a Pawn. Certain types of leaders can apparently affect entire groups of people the same way.

In an experiment conducted at Harvard University,[6] a group of business school students were shown a film of John F. Kennedy delivering his inaugural address. After viewing the film, samples of the students' thoughts or fantasies were collected by asking them to write short imaginative stories to a series of somewhat ambiguous pictures. The thoughts of students exposed to the Kennedy film reflected more concern with having an impact on others and being able to influence their future and their environment than the thought samples of students exposed to a neutral control film. J.F.K. made them feel like Origins.

Replicating this experiment in a number of leadership training sessions, I have found the same thing: exposure to a certain type of leader — such as John F. Kennedy — leaves people feeling stronger, more confident of being able to determine their own destinies and have an impact on the world. It was this type of reaction to J.F.K. that attracted many young people to the Peace Corps to "change the world" during the early and mid-sixties.

It is difficult to assess precisely what it was about Kennedy's leadership that had this strengthening effect. We do know that he articulated a vision of what could be which struck a resonant chord, particularly in young people and citizens of developing nations. He also projected extremely high expectations of what young people could do to remake their country, if not the world.

Although most organization leaders cannot count on such dramatic moments as a presidential inauguration, or perhaps on their oratorical powers, they nevertheless do have a powerful effect on whether those around them feel and behave like Origins or Pawns. A number of factors determine the effect they have on others in this critical area.

Beliefs about Human Nature. — One important factor is the manager's beliefs or assumptions about human nature. If he believes that the average human being has an inherent dislike of work and will avoid it if he can, that most people must be coerced or controlled to get them to put forth effort toward the achievement of organizational objectives, and that he wishes to avoid responsibility, has relatively little ambition and wants security above all, then the manager will organize and manage people as if they were Pawns, and they will tend to behave as Pawns. If, on the other hand, the manager believes that the expenditure of physical and mental effort in work is as natural as play or rest, that individuals will exercise self-direction and self-control in the service of objectives to which they are committed, and that commitment to objectives is a function of the rewards associated with their achievement, including psychological rewards, then he will organize and manage people in quite a different way, with the result that they will tend to behave more like Origins than like Pawns.[7]

High Expectations. — Another important factor is the expectations a manager has about the performance of his subordinates. To some extent, all of us are what others expect us to be, particularly if the others in question are people we respect or love. A dramatic demonstration of this phenomenon is the strong positive relationship between a teacher's expectations of how well a student will do and the student's actual performance, a relationship which persists even when the teacher's positive expectations are based on invalid information.[8] A second study, done in a corporate setting, demonstrated that new managers who were challenged by their initial assignments were better performers after five years than new managers who were initially assigned to relatively unchallenging tasks, despite the fact that the potential of the two groups was about the same.[9]

Reward Versus Punishment. — Some managers tend to focus their attention on mistakes — to intervene when there are problems, and to remain uninvolved when things are going well. Other managers look for opportunities to reward good performance. An overbalance in the direction of punishing mistakes as opposed to rewarding excellence lowers self-confidence and is relatively ineffective in improving performance. Rewarding examples of effective action, however, both increases self-confidence and improves performance.

Encouraging Collaboration. — Americans have a tendency to compete when the situation does not demand it, and even sometimes when competition is self-defeating (as when individuals or units within the same organization compete). Diagnosing a situation as win-lose, and competing, insures that there are losers; and losing is a weakening process. If a situation is *in fact* win-lose in the sense that the more reward one party gets the less the other gets, competition and the use of competitive strategies is appropriate. This is usually the situation that exists between athletic teams or different companies operating in the same market. Diagnosing a situation as win-win and collaborating is a strengthening process because it allows both parties to win. A situation is *in fact* win-win when both parties may win or one can win only if the other succeeds, as is usually the case *within* a company or a team.

The leader who is effective in making people feel stronger recognizes collaborative opportunities where they exist and does not allow them to be misdiagnosed as competitive. When he identifies instances of unnecessary competition within his organization, he uses his influence to change the reward system to induce collaborative rather than competitive behavior. If confronted with a competitive situation which he cannot or does not want to alter, however, he does not hesitate to use competitive strategies.

Helping Only When Asked. — It is extremely difficult to help someone without making them feel weaker, since the act of helping makes evident the fact that you are more knowledgeable, powerful, wise, or rich than the person you are trying to help. Those familiar with this dynamic are not surprised that some of the nations that the U.S. has most "helped" through our foreign aid resent us the greatest, particularly if we have rubbed their noses in their dependence by placing plaques on all the buildings we have helped them build, the vehicles we have provided, and the public works projects we have sponsored.

Yet the fact remains that there are real differences between individuals and groups in an organization, and help-giving is a real requirement. The effective Stage 3 leader gives his subordinates as much control over the type and amount of help they want as he can without taking untenable risks. He makes his help readily available to those who might come looking for it, and he gives it in such a way as to minimize their dependence upon him. Perhaps most important, he is sensitive to situations where he himself can use help and he asks for it, knowing that giving help will strengthen the other person and make him better able to receive help.

Creating Success Experiences. — A leader can make others feel stronger, more like Origins, by attempting to design situations where people can succeed, and where they can feel responsible and receive full credit for their success. People, whether as individuals or organizations, come to believe in their ability to control their destiny only as they accumulate successful experiences in making future events occur — in setting and reaching goals. The leader's role is to help individuals and units within his organization accumulate such experiences.

When an organization, through its leadership, can create an environment which has a strengthening effect on its members, it leads to the belief that, collectively, through the organization, they can determine or change the course of events. This, in turn, generates organizational excitement. It also becomes an *organization* which has all the characteristics of an Origin.

SOME UNANSWERED QUESTIONS

In this article, I have tried to analyze one aspect of the problem of alienation in the workplace: the increasing attrition of professionals and new graduates from established organizations. I have tried to suggest the nature and source of the meaning and excitement they are seeking in their work, and the type of organizational leadership required to meet their needs. However, a number of questions have been left unasked which must be explored before any conclusions can be drawn.

One question concerns the relationship between organizational excitement and productivity. We know there are many productive organizations — some of our major corporations, for example — which cannot be called excited or "turned-on." We have also seen excited organizations expending tremendous amounts of energy accomplishing very little. In the case of excited but unproductive organizations, it is clear that they are overbalanced in the direction of Stage 3 leadership and need effective *custodial* and *managerial leadership* to get organized and production-oriented rather than solely impact-oriented. The case of efficient and productive organizations that are not excited is more complex. Would General Motors or ITT be better off if they could create a higher level of organizational excitement? Would they attract or hold better people, or are they better off without those who would be attracted by the change? Are such corporations headed for problems which can only be dealt with by an emphasis on Stage 3 leadership, or have we overstated the magnitude of the social change that is taking place?

A second question concerns the relevance of the model to different types of organizations. There is little question of the relevance of charismatic leadership and organizational excitement to such as the Peace Corps, the United Nations, religious organizations, political groups, community action organizations, unions, and the military. The same is true of start ups where new industrial or business organizations are competing against heavy odds to carve out a piece of the market. What is not so clear is whether it is any less relevant to large, established corporations and government bureaucracies. Quite possibly, it is precisely the element that is missing from some government agencies, and one of the key elements that give one great corporation the edge over another.

While more questions have been raised than answered, there should be no confusion about one point: just as man cannot live by bread alone, neither can he live by spirit alone. Organizations must have elements of custodial and managerial leadership to achieve the necessary level of efficiency to survive. It is not proposed that Stage 3 or charismatic leadership increases efficiency; indeed, it may reduce the orderly, professional, totally rational approach to work which managerial leadership tries to foster. However, it does affect motivation and commitment, and organizations will face heavy challenges in these areas in the coming decade.

REFERENCES

1. Richard E. Walton, "How to Counter Alienation in the Plant," *Harvard Business Review*, Nov.-Dec. 1972.

2. Robert J. House, "A Path Goal Theory of Leader Effectiveness," *Administrative Science Quarterly*, 16, No. 3 (1971), pp. 321-338; and Abraham K. Korman, "Consideration, Initiating Structure, and Organizational Criteria — A Review," *Personnel Psychology*, 1966, Vol. 19, pp. 349-361.

3. John W. Gardner, "The Antileadership Vaccine," *Annual Report of the Carnegie Corporation of New York*, 1965.

4. Frederick Herzberg, *Work and the Nature of Man* (Cleveland: The World Publishing Company, 1966); Abraham H. Maslow, *Toward a Psychology of Being*, 2nd ed. (New York: D. Van Nostrand Company, Inc., 1968); and Douglas McGregor, *The Professional Manager* (New York: McGraw-Hill Book Company, 1967).

5. Richard deCharms, *Personal Causation* (New York: Academic Press, 1968); and Richard deCharms, "Origins, Pawns, and Educational Practice," in G. S. Lessor (ed.) *Psychology and the Educational Process* (Glenview, Ill.: Scott, Foresman and Co., 1969).

6. David G. Winter, *Power Motivation in Thought and Action* (Ph.D. dissertation, Harvard University, Department of Social Relations, January 1967).

7. Douglas McGregor, *The Human Side of Enterprise* (New York: McGraw-Hill Book Company, 1960).

8. Robert Rosenthal and Lenore Jacobson, *Pygmalion in the Classroom* (New York: Holt, Rinehart and Winston, Inc., 1968).

9. David E. Berlew and Douglas T. Hall, "The Socialization of Managers: Effects of Expectations on Performances," *Administrative Science Quarterly*, 11, No. 2 (1966), pp. 207-223.

TRANSFORMING ORGANIZATIONS:
THE KEY TO STRATEGY IS CONTEXT

Stanley M. Davis

"Is there any other point to which you would wish to draw my attention?"

"To the curious incident of the dog in the night-time."

"The dog did nothing in the night-time."

"That was the curious incident," remarked Sherlock Holmes.

> — Arthur Conan Doyle in
> "The Adventure of Silver Blaze"
> From *Adventures of Sherlock Holmes*

I once asked an executive vice-president who was responsible for the future development of a very large corporation, "What is the thing you worry about most on your job?" His answer was startling. "I worry most about what my people don't know that they don't know. What they know that they don't know, they are able to work on and find the answers to. But they can't do that if they don't know that they don't know."

What does it mean not to know that you don't know? In some ways, this is the condition of "Ignorance is bliss." It is only when a problem is identified and defined that people can go to work resolving it. Before that time, there is no problem. The same events may have occurred long before the identification of the phenomenon as an issue, but they are meaningful only because meaning has been attached to them.

The way in which people perceive a problem, a question, an event determines what they will be able to know about it. The newborn, for example, is not able to distinguish itself from its environment; it must sense the environment as "not me" before it can develop any distinct sense of "me." The infant moves from not knowing that it doesn't know there is a difference to knowing that it doesn't know what is "out there" beyond itself. Initially, this is frightening and confusing. There is both terror and exhilaration in being on the existential edge. From this new place, knowing that it doesn't know, the infant then goes on to knowing. Exploration, growth, mastery, and maturation all therefore involve a three-step process, moving from: (1) not knowing that you don't know to (2) knowing that you don't know to (3) knowing.

In the world of business, knowing is the realm of daily activities, the operating company, today's job; and "knowing that you don't know" is represented in the corporate planning and research and development functions. Most people and organizations pay attention to the move from (2) to (3). Very few consider the shift from (1) to (2) — and quite naturally, for you cannot consider what you don't even know that you don't know.

The shift from (1) to (2) is generally referred to as "a major breakthrough." This shift raises more questions than it answers. That is its purpose. Before this shift, no one ever thought of asking such questions. The questions raised in the first shift are then answered in the second shift, from knowing that we don't know (2) to knowing (3). The second shift gives us the *content* that was missing. The first shift transforms the *context*. A shift in the content of anything will be referred to herein as *change*. A shift of the *context* will be referred to as *transformation*. This article focuses more on how to manage the transformation of an organization than on managing the changes within it.

Here are some examples of transformations of context:

- *From physics*: When Einstein theorized that mass and energy are the same thing expressed differently ($E = mc2$), he transformed the context in which we understood reality. Mass and energy are *content*, the relationship expressed by the equation is *context*.

- *From psychology*: Freud's work on the unconscious transformed the *context* in which one must examine the mind. What goes on in the unconscious is part of the *content* of the mind.

- *From economics*: Financial intermediaries *transform* the liabilities that investors wish to incur into assets that savers wish to hold. Financial intermediation is a transformation of *context*. All the products and services of banks, insurance companies, trusts, and underwriters are the *content*.

TRANSFORMING CONTEXTS

Context, itself, has no meaning. The word is not the thing. To make the word the thing is to reify it — to treat an abstraction as having a substantial existence when it doesn't. Roosevelt conveyed this message to depression-ridden America: "There is nothing to fear but fear itself." Anyone who was able to experience the depression in that context was no longer governed by the depression. Poverty, unemployment, hunger, and anxiety were consequences; they were not the thing itself. Roosevelt's greatness as a leader was that he redefined the context in which people experienced their poverty. Though they were poor, their poverty was not they themselves. From that new space they could eliminate some of the unwanted consequences.

Contexts are the unquestioned assumptions through which all experience is filtered. Context has no meaning — yet it provides, in Paul

Tillich's phrase, the "ground of being" from which content derives. An elementary example of this might well be useful here.

EXHIBIT 1

Contexts for Two (I)

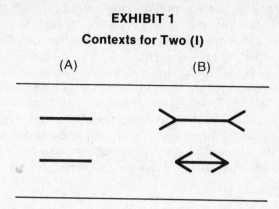

(A)   (B)

A context for "two" is illustrated in Section A of Exhibit 1, where two lines of equal length are shown. Another context for "two" is shown in Section B of Exhibit 1. Again, two lines are shown, only now one looks longer than the other. Actually they are the same length — but presented in a different context, they are not perceived as equal.

Other examples of context are given in Exhibit 2. In Section A, we see two squares, two circles, and two crosses. "Twoness" is the context for "two." The same content seen in a different context of "twoness" is shown in Section B of Exhibit 2. The content is the same, but the context has changed. Another example of the same content in yet another context is shown in Section C of the same exhibit.

EXHIBIT 2

Contexts for Two (II)

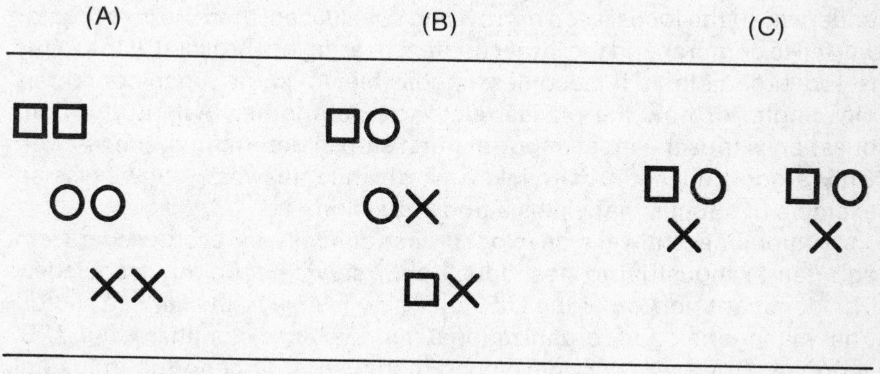

(A)   (B)   (C)

□□   □O

OO   OX   □O   □O
                          X   X
XX   □X

Context creates a reality, and the reality it creates is the content. Most managers manage the content, and only during a major strategic shift is the context brought into question. An operating budget or a two-year plan mainly provides content within a given and unquestioned context. The function of a ten-year plan is to provide the context. An organization's leadership will have implemented a long-range strategic plan when they manage the *context*, not the content.

Effectiveness and *efficiency* are the salt-and-pepper terms of management; we rarely see or use one without the other. The two are very distinct, however, and help clarify the difference between context and content. Effectiveness may be thought of as doing the right thing, and efficiency as doing that "thing" in the right way. The person who manages content can only improve the efficiency of the organization, and can never make it more effective. In this article, I will be focusing on how to make the context effective.

ASKING THE RIGHT QUESTIONS

How are contexts created? Leaders should spend as much time posing questions as they do attempting to answer them. Perhaps they should spend even more time on framing them.

Context is created by the drawing of a boundary — the frame. What lies within the boundary becomes content. The reason that asking the right question is so important is that it determines the boundaries of the inquiry that is to follow. A question focuses attention, provides direction, and tells people where to look for the answer. Given that the boundary of inquiry is determined by the formulation of the question, what is inside that boundary becomes what we know that we don't know, and what we focus our attention on. What is outside the boundary of the question is, in effect, what we don't know that we don't know and therefore pay no attention to.

If the wrong question is posed, then the inquiry will focus on the wrong data, and the outcome is sidetracked even before the search gets underway. If the focus is too narrow and specialized, then the investigator will fail to comprehend the larger context bearing on the issue. If the focus is too broad, then it becomes impossible to know what content is meaningful or how the pieces relate to one another. Asking the right question is thus the most important first step in determining the answer. Only a good question can yield a worthwhile answer. Following is an example of a focus that yields a good question.

Nations have always developed economically by progressing from agrarian to industrial to postindustrial or service economies/societies. The dominant portion of the U.S. economy is now in the service sector. The managerial and organizational models that dominate the U.S. economy, however, were developed in industrial firms for an industrial economy. Most corporations in the service sector use the models developed in and for the industrial sector as the basis for their design and management. For example, the product-division structure developed in General Motors in the 1920s and 1930s came from this industrial giant, and has been used by the nonindustrial giants in the service sector of the economy.

Industrial models of management and organization are probably as inappropriate for service economies and their corporations as agrarian models are inappropriate for industrial economies. What, then, are the appropriate models specifically suited for corporations in the service economy? This is a question that transforms the context for developing models of management and organization.

The implementation phase of a strategic plan first must re-create this new context in each employee. Only after this is done will each employee be able to provide the appropriate methods (content) for carrying out his or her job as an element in fulfilling the strategic plan.

STRATEGY AND ORGANIZATION

You have to know what you want to do before you can do it. The two elements of this statement — knowing what to do and knowing how to do it — are definitions of strategy and organization, respectively. Organization, here, refers to the culture, structure, systems, and people in the corporation.

Strategy is the plan for future survival. Organization is the current arrangement for day-to-day living. In principle the relation between the two is that a team, company, army, or nation should be organized in the manner that will best implement the strategy. A good strategy with poor organization is a thoroughbred without a rider, trainer, stable, or track. In principle, strategy precedes organization. Also in principle, the two are closely related; in practice, often they are not.

The proposition is that, by definition, *organization always lags behind strategy*. You have to know what it is you want to do before you can know how to do it. According to this logic, unless there are no changes in the environment or in the strategy, all organizations are created for businesses that either no longer exist or are in the process of going out of existence!

That is a terrible state of affairs. The inherent weakness of the model is that no organization can ever be totally appropriate for carrying out its mission or purpose. The mission, objectives, and strategy of the firm will always come first; they will always be ahead of the structure and organization. The lag between formulating a strategic plan and implementing it may be thought of as the distance between a strategy and its appropriate form of organization.

Organizations can do no better than catch up to the present, and there is even a Catch-22 to catching up: When you get there, "there" isn't there any more. Strategy is always focused on the future; organization may focus on the future, but it is rooted in the present, or even in the past if management is inefficient.

The name of the game, managerially and organizationally, is to catch up as quickly as possible. The shorter the lag between strategy and organization, the more efficient is the firm. Reduce the lag by which organization follows strategy and, all else being equal, you will increase your success by whatever measurements you choose.

This is a very inert conception of organization. Organization does not have to be *pulled* along by the strategy. Organization can be used to *push* the strategy toward its realization. An organization's culture, structure, systems, and people can implement a strategic plan without the lag.

FROM EXTRAPOLATION TO INTERPOLATION

When strategic planning was in its infancy, it was little more than extrapolation of the past into the future, as shown in Exhibit 3. As the field became more sophisticated, practitioners engaged in various assessments of that likely future, as in the environmental scans and future scenarios. From these tools a clearer statement of strategy emerged: "This is what our company is going to look like at time (3)." Thus interpolation replaced extrapolation in strategic planning. "If this (2) is what our firm looks like today, and this (3) is what we intend it to look like X years from now, then we can know *what* changes must be made to become that newly described entity."

EXHIBIT 3

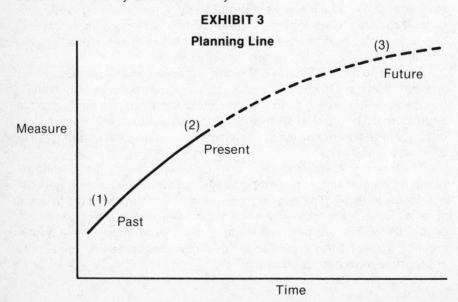

110

This is one way of describing what has since become the very sophisticated area of strategic planning and the formulation of strategy. Organization planning, or the implementation of strategy, however, is still not that sophisticated. Remember the logic: Organization lags behind strategy. There is a lag in the evolution between strategic planning and organization planning just as there is a lag between strategy and organization. Organization planning, to the extent that it exists at all, is still largely extrapolative:

Our sales have grown at X percent for the past ten years, and the number of our employees has grown at 80 percent of X during that same period. Given our expected size at time (3), we will therefore have to hire _____ people during the next _____ years.

Planning the future organization should be accomplished in the same way that the strategy for the future is determined — interpolatively. Each element of organization that will be appropriate for the future should be spelled out in detail. They should say, for example:

Given the kind of business that we intend to be, what is the appropriate structure for *that* business? How does it differ from the current structure? What steps are necessary to move it from here to there?

Is organizational lag necessary? Theoretically, there must be some; practically, there should be as little as possible. Remember, strategy is the allocation of future resources to anticipated demand. Strategy tells you what the business is going to look like; organization tells you how you are going to get it to be that way. Once the organization is "that" way, it has implemented the strategy; and when this has occurred, "that" is no longer the strategy. By definition there is no organization whose culture, structure, systems, and people are completely appropriate for its strategy. If all components of the organization were completely appropriate, the strategy would be realized; that is to say, it would be operational and no longer strategic. Successful strategy self-destructs. An objective, once accomplished, is no longer an objective. The realization of strategy is always futuristic. Because organization is the mechanism for implementing strategy, it is therefore the mechanism for realizing the future.

This is the appropriate orientation to take. Organization is too often taken to be the current framework, at best, or the inadequate and unresponsive framework, at worst. Literature on organization, organization consultants, and most personnel, for example, deal with organization from a remedial point of view: how to cure what is wrong with it, how to make it better, how to get it to somewhere that it is not. The organization is thought of as some lethargic giant that never quite does what you want it to do, and you have to pull and tug at it to get it to go where you want it to be. Those who focus on organization in each case have a sense of what it should be, and when they look at what the current organization is, their conclusion is, "This is not it."

From this viewpoint, the organization retards the implementation of strategy. The valence is always negative; it is only a question of how much. Reduce the negatives, remove the impediments, improve the organization, and you will reduce the lag between the formulation of strategy and its realization. Most restructurings, management development programs, reward systems, information processing techniques, and other elements of organization are aimed at such improvements.

STARTING FROM THE CONTEXT

What generally is not appreciated is that any improvement is premised on the supposition that what exists is what is not wanted. Even though individual executives may not lean toward philosophy, this is nevertheless a philosophical anchorage point from which most tend to proceed. Millions of dollars are then spent improving the organization to move it in the direction of the announced strategy. And success is always measured by degree — more or less, never complete.

The context in which we usually view organization is therefore a context in which we always have the wrong organization — maybe only a little bit wrong; maybe only a very, very little bit wrong; but never, "This is it." All effort, whether it be good works in religion or outstanding achievement in business, is an overlay on the fundamental belief that "This is not it."

A corollary of the context "This is not it" is that the desired organization does not exist. Ever! If it existed, no effort would be necessary. Can any executive imagine running an organization based on such a context? Probably not. Is effort necessary? Probably so. But it is not an effort needed to create an organization that, once created, will be appropriate to the strategy. This does not work. Rather, it is the effort needed to demonstrate that such an organization already is — that it currently exists. The effort lies in enlightening the members of the organization to that fact.

This is comparable to Michaelangelo's approach to sculpture. The lesser artist carves a figure out of stone. He believes that the figure did not exist before he created it. He approaches the stone from the context that the figure is not there. Michaelangelo began with the assumption that the figure was in the stone before he touched it. His job was to uncover the figure that was already there. His statues of the slaves, alongside his David in Florence, are the best examples of this approach. Only part of the figures are visible; the rest are enslaved by the stone. His genius is that anyone looking at the statues knows that the rest of each body is there within the encumbering rock.

The effective organization, particularly its leadership, understands that it has already succeeded ("This is it"). The only problem is that not everybody in the organization knows this. If we assume, for example, that the new culture is out there to be gotten, then we don't have it, and in fact we never will. If we start from the context, "The way we behave is inappropriate; instead we must learn how to behave like . . . , " then the message we are putting out is that we are not implementing the strategy.

If, on the other hand, we start from the context, "The way we behave is appropriate to the strategy," then the membership in the organization will know that their goals are being accomplished each moment. Each meeting, each decision, each activity is confirmation that the new culture "is." It already exists.

Those who lead an organization from this context are powerful because they already have what they want. By contrast, executives who lead from an orientation that what they want for the organization lies "out there" can be as powerful only in the never-realized future. That is to say, they are less powerful.

Notable examples come from major political and religious leaders. Lenin and Mao knew that the revolution had already taken place in Russia and in China, respectively. A transformed context is revolutionary; and you can't invent revolution. Long before these men reached the pinnacle of organizational power, while they were still considered fugitives by those who ruled, they knew they had succeeded. All that remained, however great the task and whatever the cost, was to execute whatever steps were necessary for others to accept the new reality. From the position that the revolution has already occurred, and that a return to the previous context is impossible, no hardship is unbearable. In fact, paradoxically, hardships are taken as tests and signs that strengthen rather than diminish the new order.

ON PROBLEM SOLVERS

A key to creating an organization that accomplishes strategy is the ability of the leadership to transform the context in which the task is held. When an organization is "at risk," there is sometimes a tendency to view the task as a problem. In banking, to take a current example, there is a tendency to see the task (that is, intermediation — or acting as a financial intermediary) as a problem (that is, disintermediation — or bypassing the intermediary). People who identify problems generally identify themselves as problem solvers. By transforming the context, they have created a role for themselves. The irony is that they then have a stake in having the problem stay identified and unsolved. Once they have identified it, the posture taken is that the problem is so large that the best they can do is whittle away at it.

Socially meaningful lives can be devoted to curbing crime, disease, poverty, addiction, and the like. In banking, meaningful lives can be devoted to curbing disintermediation. What all these people share in common, however, is a baseline that starts with the presumption that the problem cannot be totally eliminated. The problems are so great that totally eliminating them is treated as absurd and ridiculous. If you are beginning to penetrate, you are treated as dangerous and subversive. And it is subversive. It subverts the context on which the problem solver has built a career, on which the professionals have built their organizations, and on which the society has built its institutions.

If the problem is actually eliminated, totally, then the need for the services of the problem solver is also eliminated. How low does the crime rate have to get before it is a threat to law enforcement agencies? How many people have to get jobs and come off the welfare rolls before they are a threat to social work agencies?

Medical doctors are another good example of the need to change the context in which they hold their task. The context of modern medicine is the cure of sicknesses. The overwhelming majority of time, money, and personnel is therefore devoted to remedial medicine rather than preventive medicine. This is why doctors know so much about illness and so little about health. In fact, the only way we have to define health is in terms of the absence of illness. Anyone who can identify health can transform the context of medicine.

Personnel officers in corporations often share the same problems. The most perceptive statement I've heard about the context in which personnel managers usually hold their jobs came from one such personnel figure, a senior vice-president in a *Fortune* 500 company. He said, "Personnel people can be the conscience of the corporation; they can say, 'The king has no clothes'; they can call bluffs, speak truths, speak out for good against evil, and care for people. They can do all of this with support and impunity because, even though they don't acknowledge it to themselves, they have made a psychological contract with the corporation that they will never win."

What would the personnel function look like if those who occupy the role transformed the context? How would it affect people's behavior? One function for which a personnel department is responsible is the organization's reward system. Reward systems in almost all organizations are built on the context of "what is not" — if you do better you will get more. Rewards in such a system are accumulated; they are earned, as in salaries; and they are taken away, as in cutbacks and demotions. As one management psychologist once put it, most are based on the carrot-and-stick mentality, and what stands between the carrot and the stick is the jackass that the system is designed for.

What would a reward system look like that was built on "what is"? It would begin with the mission, objectives, and strategy of the corporation, related to each business unit. Every organization member — not just the leadership — would be very clear about how his or her job implements that strategy.

Currently, how many employees carry out their jobs every day with a clear idea of the organization's fundamental purpose? How much stronger would an organization be if they had this perception, and what would the organization look like? One thing is certain, it would reduce an emphasis on hierarchy. Each job is of equal importance, both to the organization and to all individuals in it. Put another way, the most important job is the one that is not being done. Doing the job is the reward in such a system. The more this is so, the more powerful is that organization. That is a system whose reward is wisdom. Few reward systems are premised on this context.

AFTERMATH AND BEFOREMATH: TIME AND IMPLEMENTATION OF THE PLAN

The term *strategy* as used here means a plan for the allocation of future resources to anticipated demand, and *organization* is a way of integrating existing resources to current demand. This corresponds, in many senses, to the two periods of formulating and implementing a long-range strategic plan.

We have seen from the classic paradigm that organization therefore lags behind strategy, and that it is impossible to have the desired organization with a remedial, catch-up approach. To reiterate — by the time you get there, "there" isn't there anymore. "Getting there" —realizing a strategy — requires using a new paradigm, one that has a different conception of time. Put differently, by the time the desire is realized, it is no longer desired because it is no longer appropriate or needed.

How can this be avoided? How can an organization implement its strategic plan with actions that are appropriate to the present-future rather than with ones that are catching up with the past-present? The past, present, and future have to do, of course, with our traditional concept of time. A key element in implementing strategy involves a very different *sense of time* that has to do with managing from the new context. The difference is akin to shifting from a Newtonian sense of time as absolute, to an Einsteinian sense of time's relativity. Initially this requires a rather abstract presentation of some fundamentals, which are necessary to state if we are to apply them in implementing strategic plans.

The sense of time that executives employ with the classic model is to use the present organization as the vehicle for getting to the future, to the objective. At first glance this is logical. "What other organization can we use? It's the only one we've got." In the context of the classic model, that is true. In the new context, leaders operate from a different tense — from a different place in time. Implementing a strategic plan in the new context will require operating with a different concept of time.

The only way that an organization's leaders can get there (the objectives of the strategy) from here (the current organization) is *to lead from a place in time that assumes you are already there, and that is determined even though it hasn't happened yet.* This sounds bizarre or obscure only at first reading.

To explain this different sense of time requires a brief entry into the world of phenomenology and of semantics. Here, I will be drawing on the work of George Herbert Mead, Gordon Allport, B. F. Skinner, A. Schutz, and Karl Weick. They hold that "an action can become an object of attention only *after* it has occurred. While it is occurring, it cannot be noticed." If everything is retrospective, then how are we to account for the fact that people and organizations plan and guide their actions according to their plans? Weick says that "even though a plan appears to be something oriented solely to the future, in fact it also has about it the quality of an act that has already been accomplished . . . . The actor visualizes the completed act, not the component actions that will bring about the completion." This last sentence may be restated to read, "The manager visualizes the completed strategy before visualizing the component actions that will bring about the completion."

Schutz names this sense of time explicitly in Karl Weick's *The Social Psychology of Organizing* (Addison-Wesley, 1969):

> . . . The actor projects this action as if it were already over and done with and lying in the past . . . Strangely enough, therefore, because it is pictured as completed, the planned act bears the temporal character of pastness . . . . The fact that it is thus pictured as if it were simultaneously past and future can be taken care of by saying that it is thought of in the future-perfect tense.

The implementation of a strategy has to be considered in the future-perfect tense. Using this time perspective, *the present is the past of the future.* Also from this perspective, all meaning is retrospective. This formulation is very comfortable to the existentialist. It is, however, at odds with the Aristotelian and Hegelian bases used in the formulation of the concepts of context and content. Because our purpose is to establish the grounds for successfully implementing a strategy — initially through establishing the philosophical conceptions for implementing change — it is worth pointing out this dilemma. Does existence precede essence, or follow it? I am comfortable leaving us with the seemingly irreconcilable foundations, however, because we are more concerned with action than with philosophy. I suggest that how the egg becomes a chicken that can lay another egg is more important than which comes first.

Two additional points flow from this, and although they will be developed further, they are worth connecting now.

- "Visualizing the completed act" means, first, that the breakthrough quality of a plan lies in its totality. It cannot be appreciated and implemented fully — any more than it could have been conceived — if it is approached incrementally. "The component actions," the steps individuals will take in carrying out a plan, will be suboptimal unless each individual first apprehends the completed totality.

Being comfortable with contradictory formulations (thesis and anti-thesis) is the only path to resolution in a large synthesis. Subcultures in an organization, for example, generally are held as contradictory formulations by the membership. Trying to blend subcultures will not lead to a synthesis, because it tries to eliminate or deny the contradictions. The prelude to synthesis, and the emergence of a unified culture that is appropriate for a new strategy, will only occur by allowing the paradox to be. Leaders have to take this approach consistently, even though to do so will be very confusing in the early stages.

Of Strategy and Time

To return to the discussion of time, strategic planning in the context of the classical paradigm is approached incrementally and in the future tense. A strategic plan that transforms the context of the business and of the organization is conceived with the use of a different paradigm. The successful delivery of a strategy means that its implementation also will have used (note the future-perfect tense) that same new model. I want to take the imagery from conception through delivery a bit further, for the perspective is equally appropriate whether we are speaking of a human baby or a corporate plan.

Most parents have dreams for their children. Some want their children to be doctors, some musicians, and all want them to be healthy, wealthy, and wise. These are parents who raise their children by focusing on content. Following in father's footsteps, or in the footsteps father never had and therefore wants for his son, are well-known examples of this approach. Other parents, however, raise their children by focusing on context. In Helen Keller's famous phrase, their dream is, "Be all you can be." The orientation here is to "parent" the context and let the child discover the content.

This same process later takes place in reverse, that is, with the now-adult child accepting the now-elderly parents as they are and are not —moving past rebellion. One teenager who heard about this distinction grasped the point immediately — saying, "I'd much rather discover my boyfriend than invent him." Similarly, human beings discover their humanity; they don't invent it.

The same distinctions can be made in a corporation. To reiterate, an operating budget or a two-year plan mainly provides content within a given and unquestioned context. *The function of a ten-year or other long-range plan is to provide the context.* Managers will have implemented a long-range plan if they manage the context, not the content. When this is done, every action taken is both discovery and implementation of the content. It is management as source, not as outcome. Another way of expressing this is to ask yourself the question, "Would I rather work for a boss who discovers me or one who invents me?" This is central to a transformed leadership in the new organization's culture. Also, managing this way takes place with a mental orientation in the future-perfect tense.

EXHIBIT 4
Time-Line Context

Before decision is made.	The decision is made and not yet implemented.	After the decision is implemented.

| (1) Resources are allocated. | | (2) Resources are expended. | Time |

These different orientations toward time can be understood better if we differentiate between two points (see Exhibit 4):

1. The point that separates the time before and after the decision has been *made* and the resources have been allocated.

2. The point that separates the time before and after the decision has been *implemented*.

It is between these two points in time that management seems to have the greatest difficulty: between (1) an effective decision and (2) its efficient implementation. The context in which most managers hold this middle span in time makes it very difficult for them to get from (1) to (2).

Operating managers generally begin in the present with the already-made decision (1) and work toward the future (2). Managing from a different context, they would mentally operate from point (2), working to realize what they know is already so, even though it hasn't happened yet.

To understand this transformed notion of time, let's take examples from the physical world: sound and light traveling through time. Sound travels at the speed of about 660 miles per hour. Think of two airplanes, one subsonic and the other supersonic, traveling from points (1) to (2). The sound emitted from the subsonic plane reaches point (2) at the same time the plane does. The supersonic plane, however, reaches point (2) before its sound does.

Imagine arriving in a plane at (2) and then waiting for the arrival of your own sound. In this context, you are there before the fact. You have created a phenomenon, gotten ahead of it after it was created, and observed it catch up with you.

In this example of sound traveling through time, the lag between the two points in time is so brief that there is not much more one can do than observe the occurrence. But if one takes the essence of the act, it is possible to conceive of the lag as an indefinite period of time. During this extended period of being someplace that has not yet happened, the pilot/leader can be very busy preparing for the arrival of the sound. Similarly, the leader can be very busy managing the arrival of the organization that will be appropriate for the time when it arrives.

Light traveling through time operates by the same principles, even though our experience of it is different because of its speed. Light travels at 186,000 miles per second. Einstein's principle of relativity enables us to comprehend what it means for light to get ahead of itself. We know that the starlight we see is the light of stars that no longer exist. It is leftover light, aftermath. Relativity, the Big Bang, and black holes now cause astronomers to talk of "leftover starlight from a future universe, its time flowing in the opposite direction from ours," according to Lance Morrow's "In the Beginning: God and Science," (*Time* Essay, February 5, 1979).

If the leftover starlight of dead stars reaches us as aftermath, perhaps we can speak of the starlight of stars yet to be born reaching us as *beforemath*. Aftermath is the effect of past actions. Beforemath is the effect of actions that have not yet occurred. Anxiety about a forthcoming event is a familiar example of beforemath. Implementing a strategy involves managing the future-perfect tense — that is, managing the beforemath. Surely, if science can renew a dialogue with religion that was unattended for centuries, then management can derive benefit from the farthest horizons of science as much as from science's more familiar territories.

We need not go galaxies away, however, to find examples of these different perspectives for managing time. People considering several alternative jobs in pursuit of successful careers have not yet committed their resources. Their options are open. At Point (1) (in Exhibit 4) they choose a job and commit their resources to a particular course of action. During the time between (1) and (2), when they consider that they have "successful careers," they employ different mental perspectives toward realizing their objectives. Some will view the initial job choice as the first step of a journey toward the goal, while others will take the new job as the first piece of evidence that their careers are already successful.

In one sense the difference is simply in the perspective you take; in another sense the difference in perspective makes all the difference. Operating from the latter perspective is comparable to starting from the position that the organization we currently have is the one it should be. Operating from the former perspective is comparable to starting from a perspective that the current organization is somehow not right for the needs, and should be improved. From this more classic context, one "takes steps" to improve it; one uses an incremental approach to reach the desired state. In this context, as in Zeno's paradox, however, it is *impossible to get there (2) from here (1)*; each move may be so great as to halve the distance between (1) and (2), yet there is always distance remaining.

CONTEXTS DO NOT SHIFT INCREMENTALLY

Contexts shift by redefining the nature of the inquiry, by redrawing the boundary. Simply moving the boundary "more or less," however, will not shift the context. Contexts do not shift incrementally. One problem with current wisdom on the subject of policy formulation is the preference for incrementalism. The distinction between incremental and nonincremental shifts is analogous to the mathematician's distinction between continuous and discrete data. The boundaries of discrete data are identifiable, while the boundaries of continuous data are not. That water boils at 100° C and freezes at 0° C are examples of discrete data. In continuous data, everyone can name a small number and a large number, but no one can state the point where the shift from small to large occurs.

Contexts exist in the realm of the nondiscrete. Everyone can acknowledge the difference between a previous and a current context, yet the crossover point cannot be measured or invented, as the points in a Celsius scale. The shift from a 10 percent to a 15 percent growth target changes the content and strategic goal, not the context of the goal itself. AT&T's shift from a government-regulated utility to a market-oriented service organization in the communications business is a transformed context. The shift from a domestic commercial bank in an industrial economy to a universal financial intermediary in agrarian, industrial, and postindustrial economies is a transformed context.

The shifts seem to occur in a flash of insight. Of course, many preliminary steps are taken that move the inquirer closer to the discovery, but the moment of discovery is not simply the last of these steps, nor is it the sum of them. It is as though the solution "pops" into the person's mind.

Archimedes sits in his bathtub and yells "Eureka!" because he discovers that a body immersed in fluid loses in weight proportionate to an amount equal to that of the fluid displaced. An apple falls on Newton's head and in a flash he realizes the universal law of gravitation. These are what we popularly call the "Ahaaa" experience. Eastern religious philosophy calls it enlightenment. When Christ, or another questioner, wanders in the desert seeking enlightenment, the hundreds of steps that are taken are a necessary prerequisite to what is then experienced as the sudden awakening. The awakening is outcome; it does not occur along the way.

Education, in contrast to enlightenment, *is* incremental and discrete. As students accumulate the necessary 120 credits for a college degree, for example, they become more and more educated. Completion of education, at least in the formal sense, is determined by an arbitrary boundary that says, "Now there is enough content." Education occurs along the way; it is not outcome. People are more or less educated; they are not more or less enlightened.

Similarly, education may be viewed as the acquisition of knowledge, whereas enlightenment is to be possessed of wisdom. Knowledge is accumulated in discrete bits; wisdom is not divisible and cumulative. Because knowledge is incremental, it is also measurable; wisdom is not. What would happen to our institutions of higher learning if the focus of the instructors were on wisdom through enlightenment rather than on knowledge through education? What would happen in business corporations if strategic planning or any other organizational task were approached from the perspective of an enlightened shift in context rather than as an educated change in content?

In this new context, formulation of a strategy is not the first step in its implementation; rather, it is the first piece of evidence that it already has been implemented. Each succeeding step is not then built on the ones preceding. One does not, for example, build an organization's new culture by spreading, replicating, and extending desirable behavior. That desired behavior can be re-created. Each re-creation is evidence of the presence of the new culture, just as each undesirable action is evidence of the continuation of the old conflicting subcultures. More of the new and less of the old will have represented a shift in content. In each individual, at some point in time, that leap will have occurred and the organization's context and his or her behavior in it will be altered forever.

The occurrence of transformation is not dependent upon the relative mix of old and new behavior (content). For the first ones to apprehend this transformed context, there may be only a scintilla of evidence of the new culture; for the last ones to come to it, it may be as aftermath. Somewhere between is probably an irrelevant and unidentifiable moment when the body corporate will have been transformed. Working on a new plan, both as formulation (strategy) and as implementation (structure, people, systems, and culture — that is, organization), I have often been asked and have often asked myself, "How do you know when you're there?" The answer, it appears, is "When you don't have to ask the question any more." When this occurs, people have moved from confusion (knowing that they don't know) to composure (knowing).

DISCOVERY AND INVENTION

Another important element in the determination of a context comes from a basic distinction that is made between discovery and invention. Discovery is the finding out of something that existed previously, yet was unseen or unknown. Invention is the act of creating or producing by exercise of the imagination. That which is discovered certainly existed prior to its "discovery." The laws of gravity existed before Newton discovered them; the genetic basis of heredity existed before Mendel's discovery; and rivers, islands, and continents existed long before the explorers discovered them. By contrast, inventions have no prior existence. Their conceptions are each original acts.

Now let us ask the following:

- How would strategy formulation and the management of organizations differ if they were premised on the act of discovery vs. the act of invention?
- Is a new organization to be discovered or invented?

Let's take strategy first. Strategy involves formulating a plan for accomplishing certain objectives. The objectives are specified by determining the relationship of purpose (mission) to the conditions in the environment.

If one approaches this strategy as the act of discovery, then the appropriate strategy for carrying the organization into the future already exists. The problem is that no one knows yet what the strategy is, and the job of the corporate strategist is to uncover and then promulgate it. Speaking of the dynamics of innovation, Peter Drucker writes that an innovative opportunity is "the exploitation of the consequences of events that have already happened but have not yet had their economic impacts." Techniques such as environmental scans, demographic projections, and future scenarios tell us what the relevant world will look like when we get there, and the strategist as discoverer behaves like an archeologist of the future. He wants to find the artifacts that give the answers before anyone else finds them. For him, the answers are already there; he does not have to create them. There is a key to the puzzle. As with Michaelangelo, the figure already exists within the stone; the strategy already exists within the future environment; and the organization already exists within the strategy.

Discovery is not to be confused with the "power of positive thinking," which is invention. I am speaking only about what exists; if it doesn't, it can't be created by the power of will.

To perceive strategy as the art or science of discovery is powerful. To perceive it as invention, however, is to presume that there is, as yet, no answer. The strategist as inventor is the engineer of the future. He constructs the answers; he carves the figure (strategy) into the stone (future environment).

Scarcity and Abundance

Most of us are familiar with the maxim, "Necessity is the mother of invention." Necessity bespeaks need, survival, and scarcity. To premise a strategic plan or a corporation's culture on invention is to create within a framework of scarcity. If, however, necessity is the mother of invention, then abundance is the mother of discovery. A long-range strategic plan for a declining business has to be created in the framework of abundance. That framework is not the context of increased competition and declining profit margins. Rather, it is the context that whatever is replacing the dominance of the past has an abundance that needs to be discovered and linked up with.

In the same sense, the culture of an organization cannot be invented — it can only be discovered. Inventing the culture would mean operating in a context of scarcity. It would be the presumption, "We don't have what we need, and we need to develop it." This is quite a powerless position to start from; it is also a costly one because it assumes that enormous resources will have to be expended to eliminate the scarcity.

With respect to the relative costs involved, it may also be useful to think of basic research as taking place in the context of discovery, whereas applied research is focused on inventing. We know that basic research typically takes place in small groups and does not thrive in large, bureaucratic organizations. Applied research efforts, however, seem to accumulate large organizational underpinnings, and they expend far more money in the process. Some large corporations such as Exxon and 3M have set up independent entrepreneurial ventures in which people work on fundamentally innovative ideas for just the above reasoning. It would be wise to assure that people in entrepreneurial units operate in a context of discovering, and that it is the fruits of their labors that are then developed through the invention of products and services in the larger organization.

Another way of representing scarcity or abundance is through the life-cycle curve. A business or an industry that is seen as being in decline is approaching the end of the life-cycle curve. Operating within the current (declining) context, most managers in such situations plan ways to keep the curve up, in order to prevent further erosion of their position.

This is done by culling out the product line, jockeying for share, and extending the life-cycle curve as long as possible. Managing and planning within this frame of reference is to do so within the perspective of scarcity. What is not appreciated widely enough is that to the extent the curve declines, there is something above the line taking its place. The decline does not take place in a vacuum. The greater the decline of the old context, the more abundant is the new context. It does not have to be invented or created. It does, however, have to be perceived, discovered, and then made operational.

In the same way, the new culture of an organization will never be in abundance if it is held as something to be invented — as a scarce good that must be created and then imitated. The only relative scarcity with regard to discovery is that the first-in reaps the largest share of the rewards. The rewards are derivatives of the discovery, not the discovery itself. Thus the appropriate strategy existed long before it was discovered; similarly, the appropriate culture is also around, "waiting" to be discovered. Once it is discovered by one organization in a particular field, it will likely be discovered by others, in turn. There is no scarcity involved, although there are headstarts.

If invention is conceived in scarcity, it is raised in secrecy. Its value often lies in its possession, measured as an absolute — hoarded and protected. This orientation would be inimical to spreading a new strategy, a new culture, a new context.

Competitors can imitate inventions, they cannot imitate discoveries. Each competing institution will have to make the same discovery for it to have the same power.

In the beginning, most people will ignore the discovery when it is made known to them. Again, they will not know that they don't know. The first-in will have to keep communicating the discovery until more and more members discover the new context. And one institution, as leader, will have to keep communicating the discovery until more and more institutions discover the new context. Inventions can be kept secret more readily than can discoveries. Keeping the discovery a secret is not the problem, for you can have its power and use only by letting go of it. Making it known, transforming the individuals, will be a problem.

Product and Market Foci

Before concluding this section on invention and discovery, I want to show that the two are related to a product and a market focus, respectively.

Patent law applies to invention, not to discovery. This is why the Wright Brothers had such difficulty patenting their airplane; was it an invention or a discovery? Invention, according to patent law, is the conception of an idea and the means or apparatus by which the result is attained. Invention, then, has connotations of tangibility and concreteness. It is product-related. So, too, invention-strategy tends to be product-focused. The greatest discoveries of mankind are the laws of the universe. The greatest inventions of mankind are machines. Social principles are invented; moral principles are held as discoveries.

I wish to return here, briefly, to basic philosophical abstractions. Transformation, in the psychology of individuals, is a process of uncovering or discovering what is inside; of knowing oneself. Knowing oneself through discovery is different from creating oneself through invention. Here, again, we are in the realm of the essence-versus-existence dilemma. Essence, or context, has a certain intangibility. It is not a thing or an event. It is a space in which things and events come into existence. The power of a strategic plan lies in the context it uncovers, in its essence-ness.

If we understand discovery as redefining the context, and invention as the outcome of a redefined context, then we come close to a marketing orientation for strategic planning. In the same way that content is a consequence of the context, products are a consequence of the marketing effort in a marketing-focused business.

MANAGEMENT AS A PERFORMANCE SYSTEM

William B. Lashbrook

Management training is a hot item in organizational development circles. A brief examination of the recent trade literature shows that skills training for managers has become a dominant concern for those advocating adult, business-oriented education. Almost all of the ads for the various management seminars stress a supposed relationship between the attributes taught and an increase in the productivity of employees. Thus, management training is being offered as a solution to problems of worker productivity.

Two particular themes or approaches seem highly popular (Welch 1981). The first is built around teaching managers to use the techniques of behavior modification in order to increase the productivity of individual members of their work units. The second approach centers on training a manager to share his/her functions with subordinates in some type of participative mode (like "participative management" and "quality circles"). Certainly behavior modification has a good track record in terms of getting individuals to change their behaviors (Luthans and Kraitner 1975). If the behavior that is modified is a factor of employee performance, then productivity should be affected by managerial involvement. The use of a participative mode of management has less going for it, at least in the American society (Likert 1967). The assumption of this mode of operation is that employee productivity is tied to the amount of responsibility he/she is prepared to take for productivity issues, particularly for solving problems which, if left unresolved, result in low performance (Hersey and Blanchard 1977). In this context, the manager becomes the leader of a group of equals who, together, solve productivity problems in the work unit. Given this context, it is not surprising that advocates of the participative mode of management would become concerned about leadership style and techniques of group interaction (Lorsch 1979, Welch 1981).

The point is not to argue against either approach to management training per se but, instead, to offer a model that makes the manager an important element of a performance system that encourages and supports high productivity. This model is unique in that it suggests work culture as a mediator of managerial effectiveness when unit productivity is the bottom-line issue. Further, it suggests that a major concern of managers should be their impact on the work culture as it affects productivity. In other words, managers should not just settle for increasing the productivity levels of individual employees, nor be content to limit their roles to being the leaders of groups. Within a performance system, management is an important dynamic that has a significant impact on that which directly influences productivity: the work culture. Managers can be trained to positively impact the work culture within the operational constraints imposed by any organization.

CONCEPTUALIZING THE WORK CULTURE

Terms like *culture* have long been talked about by people interested in organizational development (Herzberg 1966, 1974). The problem is that the talk has been difficult to translate into theoretical terms. From a sociological perspective, terms like *culture* tend to reference norms about how people with specific demographics behave in such a way as to set themselves apart from others (Lincoln, Hanada, and Olson 1981). From a psychological perspective, "culture" encompasses a set of values on which there is consensus and because of this consensus, exerts influence on individual judgment and choice. Recent concerns about the culture of an organization tend to blend these two perspectives (Lincoln, Hanada, and Olson 1981). The "culture of an organization" refers to the standards of behaviors that will be tolerated as one goes about doing one's job. The "culture of an organization" also refers to the value to be placed on meeting such standards.

For empirical reasons, we would like to offer a slightly different paradigm than those alluded to above. Let us start first with the reference. In a series of studies, employees were asked which unit within their organization most influenced their productivity (Lashbrook 1979, 1980). The most common unit referenced was composed of "themselves, their job, their co-workers, their manager, and their manager's manager." This turned out to be the case regardless of where the employee was in the organizational hierarchy. These responses suggested to us that the term "culture" could be given more specificity if, rather than referencing an entire organization, it applied to a work unit whose members could realistically be expected to interact on the job. Subsequent research led us to drop the manager's manager as a work unit parameter because of infrequent interaction between that person and the subordinates of a given manager. To make sure we were not misleading people, we decided to call our conceptualization the "work unit culture."

More substantively, we decided to build our conceptualization around perceptions that could be held about one's job. That is, when productivity is the issue, the perceptions held by the employee of a unit could be taken as his/her meaning for the work culture. Again, by simply asking people, we came up with two general classifications of cultural perceptions. The first category was "levels of satisfaction." Workers tend to look at satisfaction multidimensionally (Elizur and Tziner 1977; Smith, Kendall, and Hulin 1969). Our research (Lashbrook 1981b) suggested the following levels of satisfaction to be conceptually related to work culture:

1. Satisfaction with self on the job

2. Satisfaction with the job itself

3. Satisfaction with co-workers

4. Satisfaction with the way one is managed

The second category of perceptions that seem to be conceptually related to the work culture has to do with norms of behavior. Again, wanting to be specific rather than general, we chose to concentrate on the things that workers perceive they can talk about on the job. It turned out that the things that they report they can talk about are the very same things they use to rationalize their levels of satisfaction (Lashbrook 1981b). These include:

1. Recognition and *rewards* they receive

2. Managerial *support* they receive

3. Employee involvement in setting work *goals*

4. The importance of their jobs (*mission*)

In other words, we are suggesting that when employees of a work unit are asked to rationalize their levels of satisfaction, they will do so by referencing how they and their co-workers talk about mission, goals, feedback, rewards, and support. Thus, a positive work unit culture is characterized by members of a work unit perceiving themselves to be satisfied with themselves, their jobs, their co-workers, and the way they are managed, and by using as evidence for their levels of satisfaction the norms of the work unit with respect to communication about mission, goals, feedback, rewards, and support.

MANAGEMENT FACTORS

Isolating the factors that contribute to effective management is a difficult task. Part of the difficulty stems from not having a realistic, even empirical, consequence to measure effectiveness against. We think that the conceptualization of the "work unit culture" represents an interesting context in which to discuss managerial effectiveness.

Let us begin by laying out some basic contextual parameters:

1. Work unit performance is, at best, an indirect consequence of managerial effectiveness.

2. The perceptual characteristics of an effectively managed employee are valid measures of managerial influence.

3. Effectively managed employees come from units that have positive work cultures.

The notion that work unit performance is an indirect consequence of managerial effectiveness is a somewhat controversial position. Certainly, one-on-one encounters between a manager and a subordinate built around techniques like behavior modification have resulted in increased job performance (Luthans and Kraitner 1975). The problem with using behavior modification techniques is that they must be individualized to be effective (Hersey and Blanchard 1977). Seldom will even one contingency apply to more than one member of a work unit unless, by consensus, the work unit members make the contingency a norm. Under this condition, the work culture mediates the contingency. The point is, if a particular contingency, or set of contingencies, is to be effective for everyone in a work unit, it must be incorporated within the existing work culture. Individual contingencies, while proving effective for the employees who form the work unit, run the risk of introducing inequity into the culture, thus rendering it less positive. We maintain that regardless of how increased performance is achieved, it will be sustained only when the production levels desired become part of the work culture. A manager, to really affect productivity, must do so within the context of the work culture. He/She is only an indirect influence on job performance. He/She can set the expectations, but how and if they are met depends on the work culture into which they are introduced. Thus, managerial effectiveness should be judged in terms of how it directly affects perceptions of the work unit culture rather than its indirect effect on productivity. Productivity will be increased when the culture of the work unit allows it to be, not when simply mandated by a manager.

The qualities of an effectively managed employee relate to his/her ability to answer for himself/herself and others, five basic job-related questions:

1. Why am I here?

2. Where am I going?

3. How am I doing?

4. What is in it for me?

5. What happens when I need help?

We believe that effectively managed employees can readily answer the previous questions for themselves (intrapersonal communication) and for others (interpersonal communication). Let us take a look at what employees can mean by their responses to each question.

The "Why am I here" question, whether asked by oneself or someone else, seeks to determine the degree to which an employee identifies himself/herself with his or her job within the organization (Keller 1975). What we are talking about here is a sense of mission — a reason for belonging to a work unit — a sense of both pride and affiliation with work unit membership. We believe that, operationally, "sense of mission" equates to perceptions of job importance (Herzberg 1974). That is, a job is perceived to be important to the degree to which it is seen as relating to something more than just the accomplishment of some task (i.e., goal/objective). Employees with a "sense of mission" can relate to something outside their immediate environment to establish their job worth (Morrisey 1977). Thus, an employee may relate to the servicing of client needs by an organization even though he/she may have, on the job, no client contact. An employee may relate to landing a man on the moon though he/she will never set a foot in a spaceship. Sense of mission also has a transfer quality. An employee may see his/her job as essential to the accomplishment of a task by another department within the organization. If the employee senses that the other department's function is important, he/she will transfer the same sense of mission to his/her own job. We believe that a manager can help an employee acquire a "sense of mission" by stressing the importance of specific jobs in the work unit to something outside its immediate parameters.

The "Where am I going" question, whether asked by oneself or someone else, seeks to determine the degree of meaning and under-standing that an employee has for the goals of a work unit (the objectives that a work unit must meet if the unit is to be a functional element of an organizational system). The degree to which an employee sees himself/herself contributing to reaching such objectives is really a measure of job interest. Note that we are suggesting that an individual employee needs to see the accomplishment of his/her job as vital to the attainment of an objective that is commonly held by the members of a work unit. The point is, the meeting of a work unit objective/goal is not just an individual responsibility in a positive work culture — it is a unifying force (Morrisey 1977). The manager of a work unit is accountable for seeing to it that his/her subordinates clearly understand what is expected of them if the work unit goals are to be met. Further, the manager must provide an environment that allows for the tying of job performance to the meeting of commonly held goals. Thus, when an employee talks about where he/she is going, it is in reference to a clearly articulated goal, understood by oneself and understandable to others, and one that is commonny held by the members of a work unit. It is this lexicon that distinguishes one work unit from another within an organization. This lexicon must be mastered and influenced by a manager. In this respect, the manager needs to function as a group leader.

The "How am I doing" question, whether asked by oneself or someone else, seeks to determine the valence of the information the employee receives as an indication of his/her progress toward a goal. We want to clearly differentiate this notion of "feedback as information" from "rewards as reinforcement." Rewards are the consequences for exhibit-ing a specific kind of behavior. Feedback is information about how one is progressing toward a goal, the attainment of which may result in a reward. The point is that feedback precedes reinforcement in our model. Feedback need not be tied to a specific behavior unless simply "making progress" is the goal of a work unit. Think of feedback as a set of indications about how close one is to receiving reinforcement. We feel that with respect to management, there is a lot of confusion associated with the term *feedback* (Argyris 1971). We would like to reserve the term for use as an antecedent to the reinforcement process. Reinforcement demands a consequence; feedback does not. Simply put, feedback is information about how one is doing (Steers 1976). Its value depends on its accuracy, its relevance, and the fidelity of its giver. In many respects, the giving of feedback and support by a manager to the members of a work unit are parallel processes. It is probably not unusual for the feedback to indicate that one is in need of help.

Our dimensions of feedback, namely its accuracy, its relevance, and the fidelity of its giver, come from the fact that feedback is informational. The requirement that feedback be accurate is an interesting thing for which to hold a manager responsible. We maintain that in the absence of managerial feedback about how a subordinate is doing his/her job, it will be invented. Further, that invented feedback will often be unrealistic and distorted (Habegger and Lashbrook 1981). A manager needs to provide feedback in sufficient quantities so as to prevent it from being made up by his/her employees. Feedback also needs to be accurate — that is, verifiable. The more data-based the feedback given by the manager, the better (Beatty and Schneier 1977). Feedback also needs to be relevant. We suggest that feedback must be tied to a goal the employee wants to achieve in order to be relevant. Finally, feedback needs to be perceived as coming from a trusted and knowledgeable source. Feedback needs to be consistent, clear, and deliverable on demand. An employee, in a positive work culture, is entitled to receive feedback from his/her manager whenever he/she wants an estimate of his/her progress toward a goal. In a positive work culture, a manager feels free to give feedback whenever he/she feels that it is necessary to correct a problem or to motivate an employee. Most importantly, feedback in a positive work culture is not a punishing experience for either its giver or receiver.

In a positive work culture, there are many sources of feedback: the manager, co-workers, even the employee himself/herself. The characteristics of the feedback, regardless of its source, are its accuracy, its relevance, and the fidelity of its giver. In fact, multisources of feedback should be encouraged because of the potential for cross-modality checking.

The "What's in it for me" question, whether asked by oneself or someone else, seeks to determine what an employee/subordinate finds to be rewarding. It is extremely important that within the constraints of an organization, managers find out what they can do to reinforce the employees for doing good work (Greene 1975). Note that we are putting a lot of stress on what the managers can do. There is no doubt that traditional reward systems (like salary) and changing values about "why work" present to most managers dilemmas about how to manage. What we are suggesting is that managers need to consider the reinforcement aspects of reward giving (Beatty and Schneier 1977). In a reinforcement model, rewards become things that are personal, social, immediate, and tied to specific behaviors, which, when they are exhibited, are desired to be maintained (Hersey and Blanchard 1977). The process of delivering rewards becomes more important than the reward itself. People (employees included) have a not-so-strange habit of repeating those behaviors which are reinforced. What needs to be clear is that whatever reward is offered for doing good work be seen as a reinforcement for doing a specific kind of behavior. A manager can define, for his/her subordinates, what rewards he/she can give within a specific context. Then he/she needs to make sure that the employee sees the rewards as part of a reinforcement process. For example, if a manager can smile and if the employee finds a smile from his/her manager to be rewarding, then the manager, when the employee does something that is desired, needs to smile. The point is that smiling becomes something more than just self-expressing or a personality disposition. It becomes a tool to be used to reinforce behavior.

While our example may seem somewhat trivial, the point remains the same: rewards, to be reinforcing, must be tied to behaviors. Rewards are not really part of how they are used to affect behavior. It is important that a manager makes sure that what he/she uses as rewards are capable of reinforcing behaviors. The best way to find out what rewards an employee finds reinforcing is simply to ask. If money is not a reward for good performance, then throwing money at a performance problem will have little to no effect.

There is an interesting subtlety to the use of rewards by a manager that relates to a trust issue within a work culture. Employees want to be treated with equity — perhaps "fairly" would be a better word. The point is that to be fair, a manager and his/her subordinates need to come to some agreement as to *how much* of something needs to be given in order for the reinforcement process to take effect. A manager who gives a disproportionate amount of reinforcement to one subordinate runs the risk of being perceived as unfair — someone who is inconsistent, unfair, and not to be trusted. Most subordinates can tolerate differential benefits, but they have trouble with disproportionate use of reinforcement processes (Habegger and Lashbrook 1981). It is interesting that high performers probably need as much reinforcement to sustain their behaviors as low performers need to change theirs. In a positive work culture, the members of a work unit sense what they are being rewarded for when they behave in a specific way. In fact, in a positive work culture, members can learn to model the delivery of reinforcement and actually assist the manager in doing his/her job. Here the point is that a manager needs to provide an environment in which people can reinforce each other for doing good work. Such an environment is what we call a positive work culture.

The "What happens when I need help" question, whether asked by oneself or someone else, seeks to determine both the knowledge level and the amount of trust that exists within a work unit. Employees need to know that when something goes wrong on the job, they can legitimately seek help from someone else (Scanlan 1976). Further, they must know that the seeking of such help will not be cited as an admission of fault or guilt. Finally, employees need to know that the seeking of help is the responsible thing to do if the goals of the work unit are to be achieved. Note what we are saying: where the help comes from is not as significant an issue as that it is provided within a context that is nonthreatening. Seeking help is not just something one does when his/her wits have failed, but rather is a common behavioral response to a problem that, if left unsolved, could mean that a work unit would fall short of its goals. We believe that the behaviors of a manager in response to the seeking of help by his/her subordinates have a significant impact on their perceptions of the work culture (Muchinsky 1977). Two common responses of managers show how this impact can be less than positive. Many managers have gained their position by being productive employees. Thus, when someone asks for help, they respond with:

1. "Here's how I used to do it."

2. "Let me do it for you."

Both of these responses, no matter how sincerely given, run the risk of threatening the self-esteem of the seeker of the help. We want to be clear in our association of the response that managers make when subordinates request help. Even our two examples could be acceptable if the work culture allowed the seeker to trust the helper (Timbers 1974). This would be true even if the helper were a co-worker. In a positive work culture, members (including managers) can seek help without the seeking having a negative consequence. We suggest managers can, through their behaviors, minimize the negative consequences of seeking help by maintaining a supportive climate in their work units. Further, that in doing such, they will effect a positive work culture for those they manage and reap the advantage when it turns out that it is management that needs the help (Greene 1975).

THE PERFORMANCE SYSTEM MODEL

All of the preceding comments point to the work culture as a significant mediator of work unit performance. It does this mediation in three ways. First, the work culture provides the context for job performance. The work culture must support high performance if high performance levels are to be achieved and sustained. If the work culture does not support high performance, then its attainment, regardless of what is tried to produce it, is unlikely. To put the point even more succinctly, an intervention (training, for example) aimed at increasing the productivity levels of members of a work unit will likely fail if the culture of the work unit does not support a higher level of productivity. Given this position, it is not surprising to find examples where the best of training fails to have any real or lasting effect on productivity.

Second, what can be said about interventions and their potential influence on job performance can also be said about management. That is, the *effectiveness* of a given manager is also mediated by the work culture in which he/she operates. A manager, via the use of missions, goals, rewards, feedback, and support, can impact the positiveness of the work culture. The work culture exists regardless of the actions of management. It exists as a mediator; however, the degree to which that culture has a positive effect on some desired outcome is largely determined by the behavior of managers and how those behaviors are perceived by subordinates. The consequence of effective management is in terms of the *positiveness* of the work culture. It is the positiveness of the work culture that gives value to such things as high productivity. Those things which a manager does (management factors) to impact the work culture in a positive way have a significant influence on the job performance level of the work unit he/she manages.

The third point to be made is that there are nonmanager factors (non-MGR) that have some influence on job performance. This influence is also mediated by the work culture. Here we are talking about such factors as the work environment, the availability of resources, personal concerns of employees, and so on. Our position is that these nonmanager factors provide a metaperspective for looking at the effects of management. Managerial effectiveness can take a broad range of values within this metaperspective. For example, within any organizational environment there are effective and ineffective managers who impact the work culture in varying ways. Another way of saying the same thing is to suggest that the relationship between a manager and the work culture is orthogonal to the relationship between a manager and the organizational environment in which he/she operates. Likewise, the relationship between the job performance and the work culture tends to be orthogonal to its relationship to the organizational environment. The direct relationships hold between the manager and the work culture, the job performance and the work culture, and the nonmanager concerns and the same work culture.

Exhibit 1 represents a graphic representation of our performance system model. The solid lines link the relationships we feel are important to the consideration of management as part of a total performance system.

EXHIBIT 1

Performance System Model

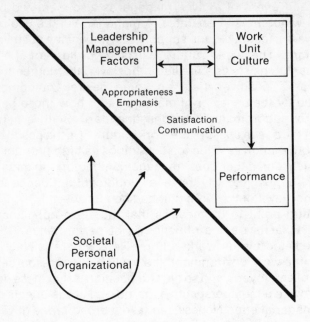

CONCLUSIONS

Needless to say, all the data needed to support or reject the idea of considering management to represent a performance system are not currently available. What exists, to date, tends to support the model. The model suggests a unique context in which to view both manager behaviors and job performance — the work culture. The model also suggests that within any organization, a manager can maximize his/her influence on job performance by impacting the work culture. It seems clear to us, but still deserving of emphasis, to suggest that the impact that a manager has on the work culture involves his/her communication behavior (what is talked about on the job). When that behavior is directed toward providing answers to five basic questions that employees have, then the manager is taking his/her proper role in a performance system.

REFERENCES

Argyris, C. 1971. *Management and organizational development: The path from XA to YB*. New York: McGraw-Hill.

Beatty, R. W., and C. E. Schneier. 1977. A case for positive reinforcement. In *Organizational design, development, and behavior*, ed. K. Magnuson. Glenview, Ill.: Scott, Foresman.

Drucker, P. F. 1967. *The effective executive*. New York: Harper & Row.

Elizur, D., and A. Tziner. 1977. Vocational needs, job rewards, and satisfaction: A canonical analysis. *Journal of Vocational Behavior.* 10:205-11.

French, W. L., and R. W. Hollman. 1977. Management by objectives: The team approach. In *Organizational design, development, and behavior*, ed. K. Magnuson. Glenview, Ill.: Scott, Foresman.

Greene, C. N. 1975. The reciprocal nature of influence between leader and subordinate. *Journal of Applied Psychology.* 60:187-93.

Greene, C. N., and D. W. Organ. 1973. An evaluation of causal models linking the received role with job satisfaction. *Administrative Science Quarterly.* 18:94-100.

Habegger, P. J., and William B. Lashbrook. 1981. *An empirical examination of perceptual differences/similarities for managers and their subordinates concerning job satisfaction*. Eden Prairie, Minn.: Wilson Learning Corp.

Hersey, P., and K. H. Blanchard. 1977. *Management of organizational behavior: Utilizing human resources*. 3d ed. Englewood Cliffs, N.J.: Prentice-Hall.

Herzberg, F. 1966. *Work and the nature of man*. New York: World.

Herzberg, F. 1974. The wise old turk. *Harvard Business Review.* 52:70-80.

Keller, R. T. 1975. Role conflict and ambiguity: Correlates with job satisfaction and values. *Personnel Psychology.* 23:57-64.

Koehler, J. W., K.W.E. Anatol, and R. L. Applebaum. 1976. *Organizational communication: Behavioral perspectives*. New York: Holt, Rinehart & Winston.

Lashbrook, William B. 1979. *ManCom phase I alpha report for Finning Tractor*. Eden Prairie, Minn.: Wilson Learning Corp.

Lashbrook, William B. 1980. *ManCom phase II alpha report for Mountain Bell*. Eden Prairie, Minn.: Wilson Learning Corp.

Lashbrook, William B. 1981a. *The management performance inventory: revised*. Eden Prairie, Minn.: Wilson Learning Corp.

Lashbrook, William B. 1981b. *The statistical adequacy of the management performance inventory*. Eden Prairie, Minn.: Wilson Learning Corp.

Likert, R. 1967. *The human organization*. New York: McGraw-Hill.

Lincoln, J. R., M. Hanada, and J. Olson. 1981. Cultural orientations and individual reactions to organizations: A study of employees of Japanese-owned firms. *Administrative Science Quarterly*. 26:93-115.

Luthans, F., and P. Kraitner. 1975. *Organizational behavior modification*. Glenview, Ill.: Scott, Foresman.

McFillen, J. M., and J. R. New. 1979. Situational determinants of supervisor attributions and behaviors. *Academy of Management Journal*. 22:793-809.

Morrisey, G. L. 1977. *Management by objectives and results for business and industry*. 2d ed. Reading, Mass.: Addison-Wesley.

Muchinsky, P. M. 1977. Organizational communication: Relationships to organizational climate and job satisfaction. *Academy of Management Journal*. 20:592-607.

Odiorne, G. S. 1979. *MBO II — A system of managerial leadership for the 80s*. Belmont, Calif.: Fearon Pitman.

Scanlan, B. K. 1976. Determinates of job satisfaction and productivity. *Personnel Journal*. 55:12-14.

Smircich, L., and R. J. Chesser. 1981. Superiors' and subordinates' perceptions of performance: Beyond disagreement. *Academy of Management Journal*. 24:198-205.

Smith, P. C., L. M. Kendall, and C. L. Hulin. 1969. *Measurement of satisfaction in work and retirement*. Chicago: Rand-McNally.

Steers, R. M. 1976. Factors affecting job attitude in goal-setting environments. *Academy of Management Journal*. 19:6-16.

Timbers, E. 1974. Strengthening motivation through communication. In *Readings in interpersonal and organizational communication*, ed. R. Huseman, C. Logue, and D. Freshley. 2d ed. Boston: Holbrook Press.

Welch, P. L. 1981. Relationships among management style, communication, and leadership style: An instrument validation. Master's thesis, San Jose State University.

Wren, S. 1980. Motivation is the key to reducing turnover. *ABA Banking Journal*. 72:28, 31.

SECTION THREE
GROWTH
Overview

One of the most perplexing dilemmas facing management theorists over the last several decades has been the difficulty of establishing a modern science of management behavior. Equally compelling evidence can be garnered to support the efficacy of highly directive management styles, of participative strategies, or virtually any combination in between. Trends in management theory often seem to be more a matter of following social fashion than the evolution of a disciplined science.

During the past two decades, the search for a single, optimal management style has begun to give way to an understanding that the needs of workers are situational and that managers must begin to adapt their actions to be appropriate for particular circumstances. Until recently, however, there has not been a sufficiently clear understanding of the underlying dynamics of change in organizations or their people to make the notion of "appropriate management" either palatable or particularly helpful in penetrating the needs of the new worker in the new business environment.

The four contributions in this section are each insightful efforts to describe the changing requirements of management in terms of a generalizable pattern of growth. While each of these essays describes the pattern in slightly different ways with somewhat different emphasis, together they present a picture of an emerging approach to managing in a changing environment that opens the door to the prospect of a truly coherent science of managing people.

In "New Rules for Growth and Change," George Ainsworth-Land looks at management through the eyes of a general systems theorist. General systems is the disciplined study of the common properties of any complex system, whether it be a single-celled animal, a business corporation, or a society. From a general systems point of view, changes in any developing system can be understood in terms of distinct phases or stages. Ainsworth-Land proposes three such phases.

Phase I:	The *formative* phase of development is one in which the system is searching for a workable pattern of survival.
Phase II:	During the *normative* phase, the system is focused on extending, elaborating, and improving the basic pattern within established limits.
Phase III:	The *integrative* phase is characterized by a new collaborative relationship with the environment. The old pattern is opened up and integrated with the new

137

or different that was intentionally excluded during the previous phases.

As the author points out, once the common phase change nature of any developing system is truly understood, one can easily see why "all management theories are correct." Each theory refers implicitly to a different phase of an organization's or an individual's development. A highly directive style of management, for example, is most appropriate during Phase I of a work unit or an individual's job skill development when the principles of predictability, security, and dependency are in line with the needs and interests of the unit or individual. In contrast, a highly participative approach is most appropriate once Phase II is well established and the work unit or individual is more skilled and confident. From this perspective, it becomes self-evident why certain management styles may be effective in one setting and fail miserably in another.

Ainsworth-Land focuses the remainder of his article on the implications of his growth model for managing in today's business environment. According to Ainsworth-Land, the rules are dramatically changing in business. For the first time, society as a whole and with it many of its major corporations are entering a period when they must learn to manage all three phases at once. This will be an inherently complex time, one that will require what Ainsworth-Land calls Phase III leadership. Phase III leadership is largely uncharted territory in management theory but one toward which this volume will, I hope, make a significant contribution.

Larry E. Greiner offers us the second contribution to this section, "Evolution and Revolution as Organizations Grow." In this article, he is concerned with the characteristic pattern of issues and crises facing organizations as they develop. Like Ainsworth-Land, Greiner proposes a phase change model for interpreting organizational growth. His five-phase model consists of:[*]

Phase I (Creativity): In this birth stage, the organization must create a product and a market.

Phase II (Direction): Here the organization formalizes its direction and basic procedures.

Phase III (Delegation): In this phase, the organization must decentralize to sustain growth and take advantage of diverse opportunities.

Phase IV (Coordination): During this phase, growth is starting to slow and the organization attempts to continue to sustain momentum through more efficient allocation of limited resources.

---

[*]Greiner's five phases can be made to parallel Ainsworth-Land's general systems model by grouping phases II through IV and interpreting them as sub-phases of Ainsworth-Land's second phase.

138

Phase V (Collaboration): Here the organization breaks from the logic of rigid efficiency and becomes more spontaneous and innovative.

One of Greiner's important insights is his observation that within each phase the range of viable management alternatives is inherently limited. Furthermore, management's success in a particular organizational phase will inevitably generate a crisis that is peculiar to the end of that phase and which must be effectively resolved before the organization can successfully make a transition to its next phase of development.

Andrew Grove, the CEO of Intel Corporation, arrives at similar conclusions about the dynamic relationship that must exist between management style and growth phases. In his article "Task-Relevant Maturity," Grove focuses on the individual worker and the evolution of management styles that is appropriate to individuals as they grow in their jobs.

Grove proposes three levels of task-relevant maturity and discusses the characteristics of the most appropriate management style for each level. These levels and styles are:

Low: Structured; task-oriented; tell "what," "when," "how."

Medium: Individual-oriented; emphasis on two-way communication, support, mutual reasoning.

High: Involvement by manager minimal: establishing objectives and monitoring.

Grove's three growth phases roughly parallel Ainsworth-Land's Phases I and II. This fact reveals one of the primary advantages of viewing management theory through the lens of a general systems model of growth. While Grove's observations are excellent and practical, he does not address the emerging needs of Phase III. Here managers are faced with a combination of experienced and increasingly values-oriented professionals in organizations requiring unprecedented collaboration and ongoing innovation. In such situations, a management style of minimal involvement and the delegation of independent authority does not adequately serve the integrative needs of either the individuals or the organization. As Ainsworth-Land observes, the domain of Phase III leadership is where management theory faces its biggest challenge.

The final contribution to this section, "Career Dynamics: Managing the Superior/Subordinate Relationship," takes a growth perspective to a management issue that is generally ignored — the reciprocal nature of any superior/subordinate relationship. In their article, Lloyd Baird and Kathy Kram discuss the phases of a career and explore the changing task and personal needs that must be served on both sides of the relationship as both manager and subordinate progress through their careers.

This article will be particularly valuable in helping managers place their own evolving needs into the equation for identifying the appropriate management strategy for themselves in their work units. The authors propose that a productive, ongoing superior/subordinate relationship be based on the following principles:

1. A recognition that the relationship is an exchange.
2. A clear and continuing identification of one's own and the other party's needs.
3. A recognition that the relationship must necessarily evolve and change.
4. An understanding of the constraints under which the manager operates.
5. The establishment of a process for continuously assessing the relationship.

As Baird and Kram observe, superior/subordinate relationships often fail not out of lack of interpersonal skills or good will, but because one or both parties fail to understand and serve their own and the other person's evolving needs.

NEW RULES FOR GROWTH AND CHANGE

George Ainsworth-Land

"The only constant is change."
— Heraclitus, circa 400 B.C.

We can no longer remain blind to the radical and difficult form of change besieging our era. The manifestations of today's change that was predicted by Peter Drucker in his book *Age of Discontinuity* have also been described by a host of other authors, including Alvin Toffler in *Future Shock* and *The Third Wave,* Daniel Yankelovich in *New Rules,* and John Naisbitt in *Megatrends.* Today, we are on the brink of a "new paradigm" that will help the manager of today's business enterprise develop ways of more effectively dealing with change.

MANAGEMENT "SCIENCE"

Since Machiavellian days, management has come under more and more scrutiny in the hope of someday transforming the *art* of managing into a *science*. In the past few decades, even the most arcane of disciplines have advanced beyond the "rule of thumb" stage to the point where fundamental, scientific principles become apparent. The art of managing, however, stemmed from practical managerial experience that only yielded further practical guidelines for managing. The underlying basic rules or theories that would begin to establish management as a science remained hidden. Now, with a new grasp of the processes of change, management can finally begin to mature into its own "discipline." To grasp the scope of this giant step in understanding organizational growth and success, we need to step back to see what has happened in science and how the scientific revolution has impacted our ability to develop a science of management.

WHAT IS CHANGE?

For decades, change has been an elusive subject, as modern dictionaries testify. Their definitions of change range from "small differences" to "major revolutions." We can say "Things are changing," and imply many very different meanings. The secret to understanding what change really is and how it works laid buried for centuries by orthodox scientific method. Only recently has an entirely different view of change emerged —a view full of surprises and deep insights, one that can finally shed some fresh light on the current problems that managers face in attempting to guide change in productive directions.

THE PROBLEM WITH CHANGE

Science's past inability to understand the process of change had its roots in the nature of the scientific revolution itself. Although the concept of a scientific grasp of nature came from the ancient study of natural philosophy, modern science substantially revised the game by shifting its viewpoint of inquiry from the question "What is nature?" to those of "How does nature work?" and "How much?" At the same time, science moved from overall "philosophic" views to a very partial, practical focussing on smaller pieces of nature. Each division of nature could then be studied independently. The scientific tendency of looking at "snapshots" of isolated phenomena gave us a multitude of useful tools, which continue to serve us, but at the same time presented an insurmountable obstacle to asking questions about change.

The "scientific objectivism" introduced by Galileo additionally obfuscated change by demanding that "truth" be not only reasonable and logical, but that it also be reproducible. Science became defined as the understanding, prediction, and control of nature. This kind of thinking required a perspective that severely inhibited any attempt to probe processes of change; many fundamental change processes are neither predictable nor reproducible.

THE REVOLUTION

By the second decade of the twentieth century, the scientific community confronted a series of problems and paradoxes that are only now beginning to be studied and resolved. From 1875 to 1925, one by one, each of the sciences discovered that it had to live with evolving rules. Absolutes and certainty were no longer the operating principles: relativism and probability comprised a new paradigm. Einstein, Freud, Escher, Mendel, Heisenberg, and others of that era conclusively demonstrated that nature did not operate in the straightforward, logical, and linear way that everyone had assumed. Science faced another frontier — the challenge of understanding change.

DIFFERENT KINDS OF CHANGE

The most obvious kinds of changes, like the acceleration of a falling object, the heating of liquids, and the effects of friction, had been considered as part of the logical scientific framework. The most difficult and enigmatic change to study was the radically different kind of change called "phase change." An example of phase change is the different states of water: water can change from a solid, to a liquid, to a vapor —and back again. The changes between these states are *phase changes*. Dealing with the issues stemming from a phase change would be like learning to live in a liquid water environment, getting comfortable and at home with the ways things work, and then suddenly, having to live in a world of water *vapor*. None of the old rules would apply, even though we were still living in water. A phase change brings on very radical changes.

PHASE CHANGES AND SYSTEMS

In the 1930s, simultaneously with the emerging studies of change, a discipline called "general systems" began to develop in the scientific world. Scientists began to note that despite the great gulfs among the various divisions that had been made of nature, very different kinds of things often acted in very similar ways. For example, the mechanism of jet engines copied the propulsion systems of a octopus. The structure and operation of heart and mechanical valves were identical, and highways took the form of blood circulation systems. In response to these observations, scientists created a type of study that attempted to look across various fields and find the general principles that might apply to all of them. With the advent of general systems, the question of "Why?" began to emerge as a complement of the traditional "What?" and "How?"

After almost four decades of research, one particular aspect of the study of general systems stood out as a possible clue to a new view of nature: parallels kept cropping up in the areas of phase changes. A chemical transition in state looked very much the same as a biological change; the growth of nerve networks took the same form as telephone exchanges; a cell colony developed the same functions as a growing city. Growth processes stood out especially in these comparisons; developmental growth appeared to be nothing more than a series of phase changes.

A NEW SCIENCE

During this period, science advanced from its single-frame, "snapshot" perspective of nature's elements to continuous, "moving picture" panorama of nature's overall parallel processes. Science became increasingly aware of the implicit rules that guided the processes of evolution, growth, development, and cycles of change throughout all of nature. In the early seventies, a master pattern of developmental phase changes and cyclical changes started to take shape. These rules have begun to form a "science of change."

A NEW MANAGEMENT PARADIGM

This viewpoint or new "paradigm" can at last begin to provide some guidance for those attempting to deal with change in a more effective way. In the last decade, the science of change has begun to make inroads on the art of management, and to resolve some of the most basic enigmas facing growing companies in changing environments. The old paradigm resulted in many confusions: as a prime example, research studies now show that practically every management theory that has been expounded can be shown to be correct. This leaves a manager without much help or direction. Now, it is becoming clear that if we *understand* the processes of change, we can utilize the different management approaches that are appropriate to and effective at different points in the change process.

To get a basic feel for managing today's and tomorrow's ongoing changes in individuals, companies, and markets, and to see how we can use this recent knowledge in a productive way, we need to return to the findings of general systems and phase changes. Although at first it may appear far afield of the problems facing a manager, we gain enormously instructive insights from watching the growth and development of a simple biological organism. So, let's take a brief look at the "life of a simple flatworm."

The young worm, growing in a small dish of nutrient solution, at first exhibits extraordinarily creative behavior as it pokes and prods around in its environment. It darts this way and that, forming and reforming itself, finding out what its environment is made of and how it might be able to grow in this particular situation. Suddenly, we see the initial cells begin to stabilize their form and enter an entirely new kind of activity. Not only do they grow larger, but they also begin to rapidly divide and grow. After the first spurt of growth, we can almost predict the rate at which it will continue to grow. This rapid development continues for some time, depending on the food in the environment it inhabits. As we watch the worm, suddenly it once more begins to change — in a different way. Some cells on the outside of the growing mass of cells start to toughen and thicken; other cells from the inside begin to form new organizations, and linkages between these various parts begin to crop up. Before our very eyes, we see a complete flatworm taking shape. This organism has undergone a cycle of phase changes — a series of changes that tells us how the whole world of change works.

THE MASTER PATTERN OF CHANGE

What was the pattern of change going on during the development of our flatworm? At first, we saw the "forming" first phase of the organism's development. This period is characterized by high levels of creative activity, geared to discovering what the environment is like and what kind

Phases of Change

of a pattern might be successful. It is hard to tell during this first phase what that pattern might end up being, as even the embryonic cells themselves do not know how they will ultimately organize themselves. If the exploration is successful though, once it has found a pattern, it will shift gears into a very new kind of behavior.

The second phase of the creature's life follows the ancient wisdom, "When you find something that works, stick with it." The flatworm enters a normative phase of development. Now instead of exploring and forming, it is intent on repeating its successful pattern; as it grows, it improves its efficiencies of reproduction and extends itself further and further into the environment. During this phase its behavior is very predictable, routine, and organized; we can even measure its success by calculating its rate of growth. If it's successful in this phase, its own growth will ultimately cause it to shift to another level of behavior. The flatworm will have changed its environment so much, used so much of its resources, and put such a degree of pressure on the other parts of the environment that it will enter a period of diminishing returns. As we watch it, we notice that it goes through a short spurt of growth — sort of testing the ultimate limits of its environment — and then shifts to a different kind of activity.

In this third phase — the integrative phase — the organism, rather than continuing to just grow larger, starts to shift its relationships, both internal and external. Internally, various parts of the creature that previously competed among themselves for the available nutrition start to "mutualize," that is, they shift to a cooperative kind of relationship. They create lines of communication and channels of resource sharing that previously did not exist.

145

Through all of this, the flatworm also begins to dramatically alter its relationship with the environment. It becomes much more sensitive to the environment and begins to mutualize with it in an "ecological dynamic." Instead of trying to eat up the environment to make it more of itself, the creature enters a period of cooperative activity with the rest of the environment. In the third phase, cell growth becomes qualitative rather than quantitative. These cells begin to mutualize, share resources and information. Because the flatworm is organized in a very different way in the third phase, it can respond to changes in the environment in dynamic and innovative ways, rather than following the competitive, predictable, and limited behavior of the second phase.

A MANAGEMENT SCIENCE AT LAST

Our little flatworm has given us a microcosmic view of the series of phase changes that go on not only in the biological and physical world, but also in the world of individuals, organizations, and cultures. Everything we know of in nature follows the same cycle of three phases: forming, norming, and integrating. The process that business enterprises go through, from entrepreneurship to production to diversification, represents precisely the same three phases of natural growth and development. Likewise, departments within organizations go through these same processes, and just so, every individual in the organization will relate to his/her job in a developmental cycle. The laws of change can now inform us about what these changes really mean and what we can do as managers in a changing and growing world.

We can now see why "all management theories are correct": every past theory that has been studied refers to a *different period* in an organization's and an individual's life cycle. Theory X, for example, is very appropriate during the first and early second phase of an organization's development. The management concept of "plan, organize, direct, and measure" makes good sense during the early phase of any organization or person, when the ideas of security, predictability, and measurability are in tune with the natural dynamic and motivation of the system, or persons in it. When an organization reaches mid-second phase, its needs to change significantly.

Theory Y, an approach that concentrates on participative relationships, is very appropriate during an individual's or organization's late second phase. Thus, we can see why traditional forms of management work well in an early second phase situation, but fail later. Organizations and managers in these changing times must know that management techniques need to be appropriate to the different kinds of developmental levels of their people, their organizations, and their environments.

Today, as we enter an uncharted phase of development, we need to learn dramatically different rules. Unfortunately, the guidelines for success today completely differ from those that have worked so well in the past. We are moving not just from a "liquid" to a "vapor" phase of management but to one that incorporates *all three* phases! A natural parallel that can give us some idea of what we face is "weather," the complex system of relationships among air currents, water currents, and clouds, which are themselves complex combinations of water, ice, and vapor. As we all know, taken together, the behavior of these elements, "weather," is unpredictable at best. So, as managers facing elements in complex combinations of developmental levels, we are starting to have a lot of weather out there.

WHY NOW?

Our Western-developed societies have just recently begun to make the broad shift into a third phase. What we know of as Western civilization had its forming period of cultural village experimentation from about 16,000 B.C. to approximately 8,000 B.C. The emergence of the Sumerian-Babylonian-Egyptian cities established the pattern for our culture and its institutions. That pattern's extensions and improvements have brought our societies and businesses to their current level of success. Now, just like the flatworm whose successful growth began to exhaust its environment, Western organizations have grown so well that they now put pressures beyond their knowledge and experience on their environments, on their resources, and on each other. They have prepared the ground for the flowering of a new form of growth.

Large systems tend to affect the developmental behavior of the small systems that form their parts. In our example of the flatworm, while each cell had the capacity or potential for developing into a third-phase type of behavior at any time, the individual cells did not do so until the larger organism made that change. This is exactly what we face in our business enterprises today. As our society and culture starts to move into a third phase, our organizations and our people follow along (and often lead us, as well). Behaviors and expectations are changing in completely novel ways.

We need to look carefully at what makes the third phase so different. Remember that the most important aspect of the first to second phase change, that is, pattern forming, depends on the system's setting *limits* for itself. The organism (the business, and so on) makes decisions based not so much on what it will be or what it will become, but on what it will not do. The entrepreneur, for example, decides that certain things, businesses, markets, practices, and so on, will not be part of the pattern. This allows for the development of stability and norms. The organization lives successfully within those boundaries, establishing rules, procedures, and practices that extend and improve the basic pattern. Ideas, people, and markets that are "different" are rejected.

In the third phase everything changes. Those things that lay outside of the limits, things that were previously out of bounds, begin to be integrated into the system. The untried and unfamiliar, rather than being rejected, now become the most important resource for continuing development. This combining of the novel with the traditional, the strange with the familiar, represents the most significant change in the rules for any growing organization in the world we now live in.

THIRD-PHASE INNOVATION

We face an era in which we will continuously destructure and restructure the norms and patterns of the past. Instead of looking the other way, or setting aside those things that are different, we will need to adopt a viewpoint that allows us to not only become aware of the things outside of our blinders, but also invite them in to cooperate with us in a creative and innovative way. Therefore, we need to shift from a repetitive pattern of predictable and measurable growth to an interactive mode of continual *innovation*.

In a mature and innovating phase three, the organization and the individuals operate by taking the old, opening it up for examination, redefining it, and combining it with the new. The result yields something that is beyond either. A + B does not equal AB, as it would in the second phase. The result is C, something both different from and better than either of its predecessors. Phase three produces not just win-win, but both/*and*. Based on the past, the "and" part of the transaction is unpredictable: it is a real innovation.

Thus, when individuals, departments, or organizations enter into empowering and creative partnerships, the results strikingly differ from anything we have seen before. In the world of biology, this is referred to as "hybrid vigor." Plant and animal breeders have long known that this process of combining differentness is a very practical way of "improving the species." That empirical wisdom of "outbreeding" now makes sense in the light of the new science of managing change.

RE-CREATING AND TRANSFORMING

An organization entering its third phase has yet another task to consider. Essentially, it is not only "maturing" in a third phase, but it is also beginning to re-create itself through a self-generated first phase. The dotted line on the S curve of growth shows this process. The main organization, department, etc., provides a "cocoon" for an internal "intrapreneurship" function. Under this protection, people and resources have an opportunity to completely rethink the business — to figure out a way to put us out of business.

A successful, mature business today needs to spawn its own second generation. This begins during the third phase, not after it. It starts when the organization is healthy, growing, and creative. To a great extent, this is a direct replica of how biological organisms create offspring and shelter them with their accumulated resources, so that they have a better chance of getting off to a good start.

In American industry, companies (even whole industries) are replaced not by themselves but by outside forces — railroads did not create the airlines, hardcover publishers did not create paperback books, and the steel industry is not creating the structural plastics industry. Today's businesses are learning from the science of change that they must re-create themselves even when they would like to believe that the old business will go on forever. As Peter Drucker put it, "The best way to predict the future is to create it."

MANAGING GROWTH AND CHANGE

All of us must accept the simple fact that an individual or organization that has entered the third phase is "unmanageable" — just like third-phase "weather." If we examine the central ideas behind second-phase management, we find that planning, organizing, directing, and measuring have to do with *limiting* an organization or an individual's performance, while maintaining the boundaries of the normative system. That works very well in a second-phase, predictable, stable situation. In a third phase, management must shift to what we now see as "leadership."

Leadership-management empowers individuals and organizations. It evokes the power latent and constrained by normal limits. A company growing in a third phase certainly needs some form of guidance, but that process must be one that allows the people and organizations within the system to respond to the dynamics of continuing innovation and change. Traditional, second-phase limits circumscribe people by a past that will never return. Today, "limits" allow for the creation and re-creation of the future. The mechanism for contemporary organizations is encompassed in the idea of "mission."

Within the mission-directed framework, individuals and managers in organizations can make the day-to-day decisions and create the continuing innovations that will provide perpetual success — success beyond the normative boundaries. This is very different from that of "directing the attainment of objectives."

The organization changes from "input," planned and managed, direction to "outcome" directed. In other words, it "self-organizes" in order to reach a destination. The organization is internally *navigated*.

APPROPRIATE MANAGEMENT

What we have learned and are learning from the science of change requires a "context" shift in our managerial functions. Instead of following external directives and applying rigid theories, we need, more than anything perhaps, to be more thoughtful about where we, our organizations, our people, our markets, our society, our products and services are — and where they are going. We're learning that the guidance mechanisms for effective management and leadership are actually those that are natural, intuitive, and "in sync" with people's needs.

The intuitive manager knows that a person just beginning a job needs both the freedom to explore and learn the tasks and well-understood limits. That manager knows that as a person learns, he/she takes more responsibility and needs objectives and measurements. As the employee progresses, we sense the need for independence and participation. Good managers try to be appropriate to the developmental processes of their people. Beyond first-phase control and second-phase influence, we emerge into an era when more and more of our people can become creative third-phase contributors — just what we need to deal with our current problems and opportunities.

The modern manager will take advantage of rapidly expanding knowledge about change and growth to clarify those internal signals. He or she will be able to shift not only to the traditional levels of management style and culture, but will be able to incorporate the very new rules of our emerging third phase. This is our challenge and opportunity.

EVOLUTION AND REVOLUTION
AS ORGANIZATIONS GROW

Larry E. Greiner

A small research company chooses too complicated and formalized an organization structure for its young age and limited size. It flounders in rigidity and bureaucracy for several years and is finally acquired by a larger company.

Key executives of a retail store chain hold on to an organization structure long after it has served its purpose, because their power is derived from this structure. The company eventually goes into bankruptcy.

A large bank disciplines a "rebellious" manager who is blamed for current control problems, when the underlying cause is centralized procedures that are holding back expansion into new markets. Many younger managers subsequently leave the bank, competition moves in, and profits are still declining.

The problems of these companies, like those of many others, are rooted more in past decisions than in present events or outside market dynamics. Historical forces do indeed shape the future growth of organizations. Yet management, in its haste to grow, often overlooks such critical developmental questions as: Where has our organization been? Where is it now? And what do the answers to these questions mean for where we are going? Instead, its gaze is fixed outward toward the environment and the future — as if more precise market projections will provide a new organizational identity.

Companies fail to see that many clues to their future success lie within their own organizations and their evolving states of development. Moreover, the inability of management to understand its organization development problems can result in a company becoming "frozen" in its present stage of evolution or, ultimately, in failure, regardless of market opportunities.

My position in this article is that the future of an organization may be less determined by outside forces than it is by the organization's history. In stressing the force of history on an organization, I have drawn from the legacies of European psychologists (their thesis being that individual behavior is determined primarily by previous events and experiences, not by what lies ahead). Extending this analogy of individual development to the problems of organization development, I shall discuss a series of developmental phases through which growing companies tend to pass. But, first, let me provide two definitions:

1. The term *evolution* is used to describe prolonged periods of growth where no major upheaval occurs in organization practices.

2. The term *revolution* is used to describe those periods of substantial turmoil in organization life.

As a company progresses through developmental phases, each evolutionary period creates its own revolution. For instance, centralized practices eventually lead to demands for decentralization. Moreover, the nature of management's solution to each revolutionary period determines whether a company will move forward into its next stage of evolutionary growth. As I shall show later, there are at least five phases of organization development, each characterized by both an evolution and a revolution.

KEY FORCES IN DEVELOPMENT

During the past few years a small amount of research knowledge about the phases of organization development has been building. Some of this research is very quantitative, such as time-series analyses that reveal patterns of economic performance over time.[1] The majority of studies, however, are case-oriented and use company records and interviews to reconstruct a rich picture of corporate development.[2] Yet both types of research tend to be heavily empirical without attempting more generalized statements about the overall process of development.

A notable exception is the historical work of Alfred D. Chandler, Jr., in his book *Strategy and Structure*.[3] This study depicts four very broad and general phases in the lives of four large U.S. companies. It proposes that outside market opportunities determine a company's strategy, which in turn determines the company's organization structure. This thesis has a valid ring for the four companies examined by Chandler, largely because they developed in a time of explosive markets and technological advances. But more recent evidence suggests that organization structure may be less malleable than Chandler assumed; in fact, structure can play a critical role in influencing corporate strategy. It is this reverse emphasis on how organization structure affects future growth which is highlighted in the model presented in this article.

[1]See, for example, William H. Starbuck, "Organizational Metamorphosis," in *Promising Research Directions*, edited by R. W. Millman and M. P. Hottenstein (Tempe, Arizona, Academy of Management, 1968), p. 113.

[2]See, for example, the *Grangesberg* case series, prepared by C. Roland Christensen and Bruce R. Scott, Case Clearing House, Harvard Business School.

[3]*Strategy and Structure: Chapters in the History of the American Industrial Enterprise* (Cambridge, Massachusetts, The M.I.T. Press, 1962).

From an analysis of recent studies,[4] five key dimensions emerge as essential for building a model of organization development:

1. Age of the organization.
2. Size of the organization.
3. Stages of evolution.
4. Stages of revolution.
5. Growth rate of the industry.

I shall describe each of these elements separately, but first note their combined effect as illustrated in *Exhibit 1*. Note especially how each

EXHIBIT 1

Model of Organization Development

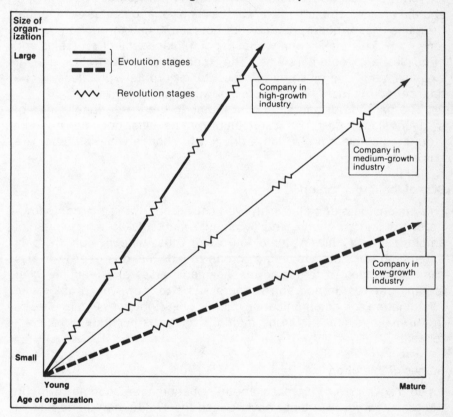

[4] I have drawn on many sources for evidence: (a) numerous cases collected at the Harvard Business School; (b) *Organization Growth and Development*, edited by William H. Starbuck (Middlesex, England, Penguin Books, Ltd., 1971), where several studies are cited; and (c) articles published in journals, such as Lawrence E. Fouraker and John M. Stopford, "Organization Structure and the Multinational Strategy," *Administrative Science Quarterly*, Vol. 13, No. 1, 1968, p. 47; and Malcolm S. Salter, "Management Appraisal and Reward Systems," *Journal of Business Policy*, Vol. 1, No. 4, 1971.

dimension influences the other over time; when all five elements begin to interact, a more complete and dynamic picture of organizational growth emerges.

After describing these dimensions and their interconnections, I shall discuss each evolutionary/revolutionary phase of development and show (a) how each stage of evolution breeds its own revolution, and (b) how management solutions to each revolution determine the next stage of evolution.

Age of the Organization

The most obvious and essential dimension for any model of development is the life span of an organization (represented as the horizontal axis in *Exhibit 1*). All historical studies gather data from various points in time and then make comparisons. From these observations, it is evident that the same organization practices are not maintained throughout a long time span. This makes a most basic point: management problems and principles are rooted in time. The concept of decentralization, for example, can have meaning for describing corporate practices at one time period but loses its descriptive power at another.

The passage of time also contributes to the institutionalization of managerial attitudes. As a result, employee behavior becomes not only more predictable but also more difficult to change when attitudes are outdated.

Size of the Organization

This dimension is depicted as the vertical axis in *Exhibit 1*. A company's problems and solutions tend to change markedly as the number of employees and sales volume increase. Thus, time is not the only determinant of structure; in fact, organizations that do not grow in size can retain many of the same management issues and practices over lengthy periods. In addition to increased size, however, problems of coordination and communication magnify, new functions emerge, levels in the management hierarchy multiply, and jobs become more inter-related.

Stages of Evolution

As both age and size increase, another phenomenon becomes evident: the prolonged growth that I have termed the evolutionary period. Most growing organizations do not expand for two years and then retreat for one year; rather, those that survive a crisis usually enjoy four to eight years of continuous growth without a major economic setback or severe internal disruption. The term evolution seems appropriate for describing these quieter periods because only modest adjustments appear necessary for maintaining growth under the same overall pattern of management.

Stages of Revolution

Smooth evolution is not inevitable; it cannot be assumed that organization growth is linear. *Fortune's* "500" list, for example, has had significant turnover during the last 50 years. Thus we find evidence from numerous case histories which reveals periods of substantial turbulence spaced between smoother periods of evolution.

I have termed these turbulent times the periods of revolution because they typically exhibit a serious upheaval of management practices. Traditional management practices, which were appropriate for a smaller size and earlier time, are brought under scrutiny by frustrated top managers and disillusioned lower-level managers. During such periods of crisis, a number of companies fail — those unable to abandon past practices and effect major organization changes are likely either to fold or to level off in their growth rates.

The critical task for management in each revolutionary period is to find a new set of organization practices that will become the basis for managing the next period of evolutionary growth. Interestingly enough, these new practices eventually sow their own seeds of decay and lead to another period of revolution. Companies therefore experience the irony of seeing a major solution in one time period become a major problem at a latter date.

Growth Rate of the Industry

The speed at which an organization experiences phases of evolution and revolution is closely related to the market environment of its industry. For example, a company in a rapidly expanding market will have to add employees rapidly; hence, the need for new organization structures to accommodate large staff increases is accelerated. While evolutionary periods tend to be relatively short in fast-growing industries, much longer evolutionary periods occur in mature or slowly growing industries.

Evolution can also be prolonged, and revolutions delayed, when profits come easily. For instance, companies that make grievous errors in a rewarding industry can still look good on their profit and loss statements; thus they can avoid a change in management practices for a longer period. The aerospace industry in its infancy is an example. Yet revolutionary periods still occur, as one did in aerospace when profit opportunities began to dry up. Revolutions seem to be much more severe and difficult to resolve when the market environment is poor.

PHASES OF GROWTH

With the foregoing framework in mind, let us now examine in depth the five specific phases of evolution and revolution. As shown in *Exhibit 2*, each evolutionary period is characterized by the dominant *management style* used to achieve growth, while each revolutionary period is characterized by the dominant *management problem* that must be solved before growth can continue. The patterns presented in *Exhibit 2* seem to be typical for companies in industries with moderate growth over a long time period; companies in faster growing industries tend to experience all five phases more rapidly, while those in slower growing industries encounter only two or three phases over many years.

It is important to note that *each phase is both an effect of the previous phase and a cause for the next phase*. For example, the evolutionary management style in Phase 3 of the exhibit is "delegation," which grows out of, and becomes the solution to, demands for greater "autonomy" in the preceding Phase 2 revolution. The style of delegation used in Phase

EXHIBIT 2

The Five Phases of Growth

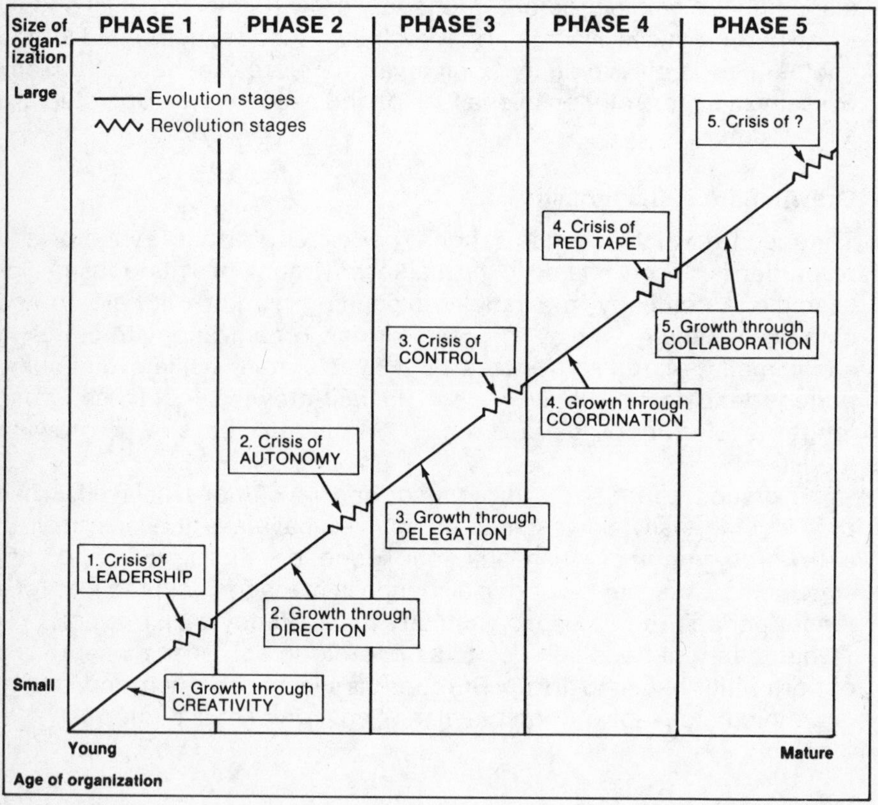

3, however, eventually provokes a major revolutionary crisis that is characterized by attempts to regain control over the diversity created through increased delegation.

The principal implication of each phase is that management actions are narrowly prescribed if growth is to occur. For example, a company experiencing an autonomy crisis in Phase 2 cannot return to directive management for a solution — it must adopt a new style of delegation in order to move ahead.

Phase 1: Creativity . . .

In the birth stage of an organization, the emphasis is on creating both a product and a market. Here are the characteristics of the period of creative evolution:

- The company's founders are usually technically or entrepreneurially oriented, and they disdain management activities; their physical and mental energies are absorbed entirely in making and selling a new product.
- Communication among employees is frequent and informal.
- Long hours of work are rewarded by modest salaries and the promise of ownership benefits.
- Control of activities comes from immediate marketplace feedback; the management acts as the customers react.

. . . the leadership crisis: All of the foregoing individualistic and creative activities are essential for the company to get off the ground. But therein lies the problem. As the company grows, larger production runs require knowledge about the efficiencies of manufacturing. Increased numbers of employees cannot be managed exclusively through informal communication; new employees are not motivated by an intense dedication to the product or organization. Additional capital must be secured, and new accounting procedures are needed for financial control.

Thus the founders find themselves burdened with unwanted management responsibilities. So they long for the "good old days," still trying to act as they did in the past. And conflicts between the harried leaders grow more intense.

At this point a crisis of leadership occurs, which is the onset of the first revolution. Who is to lead the company out of confusion and solve the managerial problems confronting it? Quite obviously, a strong manager is needed who has the necessary knowledge and skill to introduce new business techniques. But this is easier said than done. The founders often hate to step aside even though they are probably temperamentally unsuited to be managers. So here is the first critical developmental choice — to locate and install a strong business manager who is acceptable to the founders and who can pull the organization together.

Phase 2: Direction . . .

Those companies that survive the first phase by installing a capable business manager usually embark on a period of sustained growth under able and directive leadership. Here are the characteristics of this evolutionary period:

- A functional organization structure is introduced to separate manufacturing from marketing activities, and job assignments become more specialized.
- Accounting systems for inventory and purchasing are introduced.
- Incentives, budgets, and work standards are adopted.
- Communication becomes more formal and impersonal as a hierarchy of titles and positions builds.
- The new manager and his key supervisors take most of the responsibility for instituting direction, while lower-level supervisors are treated more as functional specialists than as autonomous decision-making managers.

. . . the autonomy crisis: Although the new directive techniques channel employee energy more efficiently into growth, they eventually become inappropriate for controlling a larger, more diverse and complex organization. Lower-level employees find themselves restricted by a cumbersome and centralized hierarchy. They have come to possess more direct knowledge about markets and machinery than do the leaders at the top; consequently, they feel torn between following procedures and taking initiative on their own.

Thus the second revolution is imminent as a crisis develops from demands for greater autonomy on the part of lower-level managers. The solution adopted by most companies is to move toward greater delegation. Yet it is difficult for top managers who were previously successful at being directive to give up responsibility. Moreover, lower-level managers are not accustomed to making decisions for themselves. As a result, numerous companies flounder during this revolutionary period, adhering to centralized methods while lower-level employees grow more disenchanted and leave the organization.

Phase 3: Delegation . . .

The next era of growth evolves from the successful application of a decentralized organization structure. It exhibits these characteristics:

- Much greater responsibility is given to the managers of plants and market territories.
- Profit centers and bonuses are used to stimulate motivation.
- The top executives at headquarters restrain themselves to managing by exception, based on periodic reports from the field.

- Management often concentrates on making new acquisitions which can be lined up beside other decentralized units.

- Communication from the top is infrequent, usually by correspondence, telephone, or brief visits to field locations.

The delegation stage proves useful for gaining expansion through heightened motivation at lower levels. Decentralized managers with greater authority and incentive are able to penetrate larger markets, respond faster to customers, and develop new products.

. . . the control crisis: A serious problem eventually evolves, however, as top executives sense that they are losing control over a highly diversified field operation. Autonomous field managers prefer to run their own shows without coordinating plans, money, technology, and manpower with the rest of the organization. Freedom breeds a parochial attitude.

Hence, the Phase 3 revolution is under way when top management seeks to regain control over the total company. Some top managements attempt a return to centralized management, which usually fails because of the vast scope of operations. Those companies that move ahead find a new solution in the use of special coordination techniques.

Phase 4: Coordination . . .

During this phase, the evolutionary period is characterized by the use of formal systems for achieving greater coordination and by top executives taking responsibility for the initiation and administration of these new systems. For example:

- Decentralized units are merged into product groups.

- Formal planning procedures are established and intensively reviewed.

- Numerous staff personnel are hired and located at headquarters to initiate companywide programs of control and review for line managers.

- Capital expenditures are carefully weighed and parceled out across the organization.

- Each product group is treated as an investment center where return on invested capital is an important criterion used in allocating funds.

- Certain technical functions, such as data processing, are centralized at headquarters, while daily operating decisions remain decentralized.

- Stock options and companywide profit sharing are used to encourage identity with the firm as a whole.

All of these new coordination systems prove useful for achieving growth through more efficient allocation of a company's limited resources. They prompt field managers to look beyond the needs of their local units. While these managers still have much decision-making responsibility, they learn to justify their actions more carefully to a "watchdog" audience at headquarters.

. . . the red-tape crisis: But a lack of confidence gradually builds between line and staff, and between headquarters and the field. The proliferation of systems and programs begins to exceed its utility; a red-tape crisis is created. Line managers, for example, increasingly resent heavy staff direction from those who are not familiar with local conditions. Staff people, on the other hand, complain about un-cooperative and uninformed line managers. Together both groups criticize the bureaucratic paper system that has evolved. Procedures take precedence over problem solving, and innovation is dampened. In short, the organization has become too large and complex to be managed through formal programs and rigid systems. The Phase 4 revolution is under way.

Phase 5: Collaboration . . .

The last observable phase in previous studies emphasizes strong interpersonal collaboration in an attempt to overcome the red-tape crisis. Where Phase 4 was managed more through formal systems and pro-cedures, Phase 5 emphasizes greater spontaneity in management action through teams and the skillful confrontation of interpersonal differences. Social control and self-discipline take over from formal control. This transition is especially difficult for those experts who created the old systems as well as for those line managers who relied on formal methods for answers.

The Phase 5 evolution, then, builds around a more flexible and behavioral approach to management. Here are its characteristics:

- The focus is on solving problems quickly through team action.
- Teams are combined across functions for task-group activity.
- Headquarters staff experts are reduced in number, reassigned, and combined in interdisciplinary teams to consult with, not to direct, field units.
- A matrix-type structure is frequently used to assemble the right teams for the appropriate problems.
- Previous formal systems are simplified and combined into single multipurpose systems.
- Conferences of key managers are held frequently to focus on major problem issues.
- Educational programs are utilized to train managers in behavioral skills for achieving better teamwork and conflict resolution.

- Real-time information systems are integrated into daily decision making.

- Economic rewards are geared more to team performance than to individual achievement.

- Experiments in new practices are encouraged throughout the organization.

. . . the ? crisis: What will be the revolution in response to this stage of evolution? Many large U.S. companies are now in the Phase 5 evolutionary stage, so the answers are critical. While there is little clear evidence, I imagine the revolution will center around the "psychological saturation" of employees who grow emotionally and physically exhausted by the intensity of teamwork and the heavy pressure for innovative solutions.

My hunch is that the Phase 5 revolution will be solved through new structures and programs that allow employees to periodically rest, reflect, and revitalize themselves. We may even see companies with dual organization structures: a "habit" structure for getting the daily work done, and a "reflective" structure for stimulating perspective and personal enrichment. Employees could then move back and forth between the two structures as their energies are dissipated and refueled.

One European organization has implemented just such a structure. Five reflective groups have been established outside the regular structure for the purpose of continuously evaluating five task activities basic to the organization. They report directly to the managing director, although their reports are made public throughout the organization. Membership in each group includes all levels and functions, and employees are rotated through these groups on a six-month basis.

Other concrete examples now in practice include providing sabbaticals for employees, moving managers in and out of "hot spot" jobs, establishing a four-day workweek, assuring job security, building physical facilities for relaxation *during* the working day, making jobs more interchangeable, creating an extra team on the assembly line so that one team is always off for reeducation, and switching to longer vacations and more flexible working hours.

The Chinese practice of requiring executives to spend time periodically on lower-level jobs may also be worth a nonideological evaluation. For too long U.S. management has assumed that career progress should be equated with an upward path toward title, salary, and power. Could it be that some vice presidents of marketing might just long for, and even benefit from, temporary duty in the field sales organization?

IMPLICATIONS OF HISTORY

Let me now summarize some important implications for practicing managers. First, the main features of this discussion are depicted in *Exhibit 3*, which shows the specific management actions that characterize each growth phase. These actions are also the solutions which ended each preceding revolutionary period.

EXHIBIT 3

Organization Practices During Evolution in the Five Phases of Growth

Category	PHASE 1	PHASE 2	PHASE 3	PHASE 4	PHASE 5
MANAGEMENT FOCUS	Make & sell	Efficiency of operations	Expansion of market	Consolidation of organization	Problem solving & innovation
ORGANIZATION STRUCTURE	Informal	Centralized & functional	Decentralized & geographical	Line-staff & product groups	Matrix of teams
TOP MANAGEMENT STYLE	Individualistic & entrepreneurial	Directive	Delegative	Watchdog	Participative
CONTROL SYSTEM	Market results	Standards & cost centers	Reports & profit centers	Plans & investment centers	Mutual goal setting
MANAGEMENT REWARD EMPHASIS	Ownership	Salary & merit increases	Individual bonus	Profit sharing & stock options	Team bonus

In one sense, I hope that many readers will react to my model by calling it obvious and natural for depicting the growth of an organization. To me this type of reaction is a useful test of the model's validity.

But at a more reflective level I imagine some of these reactions are more hindsight than foresight. Those experienced managers who have been through a developmental sequence can empathize with it now, but how did they react when in the middle of a stage of evolution or revolution? They can probably recall the limits of their own developmental understanding at that time. Perhaps they resisted desirable changes or were even swept emotionally into a revolution without being able to propose constructive solutions. So let me offer some explicit guidelines for managers of growing organizations to keep in mind.

Know where you are in the developmental sequence. Every organization and its component parts are at different stages of development. The task of top management is to be aware of these stages; otherwise, it may not recognize when the time for change has come, or it may act to impose the wrong solution.

Top leaders should be ready to work with the flow of the tide rather than against it; yet they should be cautious, since it is tempting to skip phases out of impatience. Each phase results in certain strengths and learning experiences in the organization that will be essential for success

162

in subsequent phases. A child prodigy, for example, may be able to read like a teenager, but he cannot behave like one until he ages through a sequence of experiences.

I also doubt that managers can or should act to avoid revolutions. Rather, these periods of tension provide the pressure, ideas, and awareness that afford a platform for change and the introduction of new practices.

Recognize the limited range of solutions. In each revolutionary stage it becomes evident that this stage can be ended only by certain specific solutions; moreover, these solutions are different from those which were applied to the problems of the preceding revolution. Too often it is tempting to choose solutions that were tried before, which makes it impossible for a new phase of growth to evolve.

Management must be prepared to dismantle current structures before the revolutionary stage becomes too turbulent. Top managers, realizing that their own managerial styles are no longer appropriate, may even have to take themselves out of leadership positions. A good Phase 2 manager facing Phase 3 might be wise to find another Phase 2 organization that better fits his talents, either outside the company or with one of its newer subsidiaries.

Finally, evolution is not an automatic affair; it is a contest for survival. To move ahead, companies must consciously introduce planned structures that not only are solutions to a current crisis but also are fitted to the *next* phase of growth. This requires considerable self-awareness on the part of top management, as well as great interpersonal skill in persuading other managers that change is needed.

Realize that solutions breed new problems. Managers often fail to realize that organizational solutions create problems for the future (i.e., a decision to delegate eventually causes a problem of control). Historical actions are very much determinants of what happens to the company at a much later date.

An awareness of this effect should help managers to evaluate company problems with greater historical understanding instead of "pinning the blame" on a current development. Better yet, managers should be in a position to *predict* future problems, and thereby to prepare solutions and coping strategies before a revolution gets out of hand.

A management that is aware of the problems ahead could well decide *not* to grow. Top managers may, for instance, prefer to retain the informal practices of a small company, knowing that this way of life is inherent in the organization's limited size, not in their congenial personalities. If they choose to grow, they may do themselves out of a job and a way of life they enjoy.

And what about the managements of very large organizations? Can they find new solutions for continued phases of evolution? Or are they reaching a stage where the government will act to break them up because they are too large?

CONCLUDING NOTE

Clearly, there is still much to learn about processes of development in organizations. The phases outlined here are only five in number and are still only approximations. Researchers are just beginning to study the specific developmental problems of structure, control, rewards, and management style in different industries and in a variety of cultures.

One should not, however, wait for conclusive evidence before educating managers to think and act from a developmental perspective. The critical dimension of time has been missing for too long from our management theories and practices. The intriguing paradox is that by learning more about history we may do a better job in the future.

TASK-RELEVANT MATURITY

Andrew S. Grove

A manager's most important responsibility is to elicit top performance from his subordinates. Assuming we understand what motivates an employee, the question becomes: Is there a single best management style, one approach that will work better than all others?

Many have looked for that optimum. Considering the issue historically, the management style most in favor seems to have changed to parallel the theory of motivation espoused at the time. At the turn of the century, ideas about work were simple. People were told what to do, and if they did it, they were paid; if they did not, they were fired. The corresponding leadership style was crisp and hierarchical: there were those who gave orders and those who took orders and executed them without question. In the 1950s, management theory shifted toward a humanistic set of beliefs that held that there was a nicer way to get people to work. The favored leadership style changed accordingly. Finally, as university behavioral science departments developed and grew, the theories of motivation and leadership became subjects of carefully controlled experiments. Surprisingly, none of the early intuitive pre-sumptions could be borne out: the hard findings simply would not show that one style of leadership was better than another. It was hard to escape the conclusion that no optimal management style existed.

My own observations bear this out. At Intel we frequently rotate middle managers from one group to another in order to broaden their experience. These groups tend to be similar in background and in the type of work that they do, although their output tends to vary greatly. Some managers and their groups demonstrate themselves to be higher producers; others do not. The result of moving the managers about is often surprising. Neither the managers nor the groups maintain the characteristic of being either high-producing or low-producing as the managers are switched around. The inevitable conclusion is that high output is associated with particular *combinations* of certain managers and certain groups of workers. This also suggests that a given man-agerial approach is not equally effective under all conditions.

Some researchers in this field argue that there is a fundamental variable that tells you what the best management style is in a particular situation. That variable is the task-relevant maturity (TRM) of the subordinates, which is a combination of the degree of their achievement orientation and readiness to take responsibility, as well as their education, training, and experience. Moreover, all this is very specific to the task at hand, and it is entirely possible for a person or a group of people to have a TRM that is high in one job but low in another.

Let me give you an example of what I mean. We recently moved an extremely productive sales manager from the field into the plant, where he was placed in charge of a factory unit. The size and scope of the two jobs were comparable, yet the performance of the seasoned manager deteriorated, and he started to show the signs of someone overwhelmed by his work. What happened was that while the personal maturity of the manager obviously did not change, his task-relevant maturity in the new job was extremely low, since its environment, content, and tasks were all new to him. In time he learned to cope, and his TRM gradually increased. With that, his performance began to approach the outstanding levels he had exhibited earlier, which was why we promoted him in the first place. What happened here should have been totally predictable, yet we were surprised: we confused the manager's general competence and maturity with his task-relevant maturity.

Similarly, a person's TRM can be very high given a certain level of complexity, uncertainty, and ambiguity, but if the pace of the job accelerates or if the job itself abruptly changes, the TRM of that individual will drop. It's a bit like a person with many years' experience driving on small country roads being suddenly asked to drive on a crowded metropolitan freeway. His TRM driving his own car will drop precipitously.

The conclusion is that varying management styles are needed as task-relevant maturity varies. Specifically, when the TRM is low, the most effective approach is one that offers very precise and detailed in- structions, wherein the supervisor tells the subordinate what needs to be done, when, and how: in other words, a highly structured approach. As the TRM of the subordinate grows, the most effective style moves from the structured to one more given to communication, emotional support, and encouragement, in which the manager pays more attention to the subordinate as an individual than to the task at hand. As the TRM becomes even greater, the effective management style changes again. Here the manager's involvement should be kept to a minimum, and should primarily consist of making sure that the objectives toward which the subordinate is working are mutually agreed upon. But regardless of what the TRM may be, the manager should always monitor a sub- ordinate's work closely enough to avoid surprises. The presence or absence of monitoring, as we've said before, is the difference between a supervisor's *delegating* a task and *abdicating* it. The characteristics of the effective management style for the supervisor given the varying degrees of TRM are summarized in the table below.

A word of caution is in order: do not make a value judgment and consider a structured management style less worthy than a communi- cation-oriented one. What is "nice" or "not nice" should have no place in how you think or what you do. Remember, we are after what is most *effective.*

TASK-RELEVANT MATURITY OF SUBORDINATE	CHARACTERISTICS OF THE EFFECTIVE MANAGEMENT STYLE
low	Structured; task-oriented; tell "what," "when," "how"
medium	Individual-oriented; emphasis on two-way communication, support, mutual reasoning
high	Involvement by manager minimal: establishing objectives and monitoring

The fundamental variable that determines the effective management style is the task-relevant maturity of the subordinate.

The theory here parallels the development of the relationship between a parent and child. As the child matures, the most effective parental style changes, varying with the "life-relevant maturity" — or age — of the child. A parent needs to tell a toddler not to touch things that he might break or that might hurt him. The child cannot understand that the vase he wants to play with is an irreplaceable heirloom, but he can understand "no." As he grows older, he begins to do things on his own initiative, something the parent wants to encourage while still trying to keep him from injuring himself. A parent might suggest, for example, that his child give up his tricycle for his first two-wheeler. The parent will not simply send him out on his own, but will accompany him to keep the bicycle from tipping over while talking to him about safety on the streets. As the child's maturity continues to grow, the parent can cut back on specific instruction. When the child goes out to ride his bicycle, the parent no longer has to recite the litany of safety rules. Finally, when the life-relevant maturity of the child is high enough, he leaves home and perhaps goes away to college. At this point the relationship between parent and child will change again as the parent merely monitors the child's progress.

Should the child's environment suddenly change to one where his life-relevant maturity is inadequate (for example, if he runs into severe academic trouble), the parent may have to revert to a style used earlier.

As parental (or managerial) supervision moves from structured to communicating to monitoring, the degree of structure governing the behavior of the child (or the subordinate) does not really change. A teenager *knows* it is not safe to cross a busy interstate highway on his bicycle, and the parent no longer has to tell him not to do it. Structure moves from being *externally imposed* to being *internally given*.

If the parent (or supervisor) imparted early on to the child (or subordinate) the right way to do things (the correct operational values), later the child would be likely to make decisions the way the parent would. In fact, commonality of operational values, priorities, and preferences — how an organization works together — is a must if the progression in managerial style is to occur.

Without that commonality, an organization can become easily confused and lose its sense of purpose. Accordingly, the responsibility for transmitting common values rests squarely with the supervisor. He is, after all, accountable for the output of the people who report to him; then, too, without a shared set of values a supervisor cannot effectively delegate. An associate of mine who had always done an outstanding job hired a junior person to handle some old tasks, while he himself took on some new ones. The subordinate did poor work. My associate's reaction: "He has to make his own mistakes. That's how he learns!" The problem with this is that the subordinate's tuition is paid by his customers. And that is absolutely wrong. The responsibility for teaching the subordinate must be assumed by his supervisor, and not paid for by the customers of his organization, internal or external.

MANAGEMENT STYLE AND MANAGERIAL LEVERAGE

As supervisors, we should try to raise the task-relevant maturity of our subordinates as rapidly as possible for obvious pragmatic reasons. The appropriate management style for an employee with high TRM takes less time than detailed, structured supervision requires. Moreover, once operational values are learned and TRM is high enough, the supervisor can delegate tasks to the subordinate, thus increasing his *managerial leverage*. Finally, at the highest levels of TRM, the subordinate's training is presumably complete, and motivation is likely to come from within, from self-actualization, which is the most powerful source of energy and effort a manager can harness.

As we've learned, a person's TRM depends on a specific working environment. When that changes, so will his TRM, as will his supervisor's most effective management style. Let's consider an army encampment where nothing ever happens. The sergeant in command has come to know each of his soldiers very well, and by and large maintains an informal relationship with them. The routines are so well established that he rarely has to tell anyone what to do; appropriate to the high TRM of the group, the sergeant contents himself with merely monitoring their activity. One day a jeepload of the enemy suddenly appears, coming over the hill and shooting at the camp. Instantly the sergeant reverts to a structured, task-oriented leadership style, barking orders at everyone, telling each of his soldiers what to do, when, and how. . . . After a while, if these skirmishes continue and the group keeps on fighting from the same place for a couple of months, this too will eventually become routine. With that, the TRM of the group for the new task — fighting — will increase. The sergeant can then gradually ease off telling everybody what to do.

Put another way, a manager's ability to operate in a style based on communication and mutual understanding depends on there being enough time for it. Though monitoring is on paper a manager's most productive approach, we have to work our way up to it in the real world. Even if we achieve it, if things suddenly change, we have to revert quickly to the what-when-how mode.

That mode is one that we don't think an enlightened manager should use. As a result, we often don't take it up until it is too late and events overwhelm us. We managers must learn to fight such prejudices and regard any management mode not as either good or bad but rather as effective or not effective, given the TRM of our subordinates within a specific working environment. This is why researchers cannot find the single best way for a manager to work. It changes day by day and sometimes hour by hour.

IT'S NOT EASY TO BE A GOOD MANAGER

Deciding the TRM of your subordinates is not easy. Moreover, even if a manager knows what the TRM is, his personal preferences tend to override the logical and proper choice of management style. For instance, even if a manager sees that his subordinate's TRM is "medium" (see table), in the real world the manager will likely opt for either the "structured" or "minimal" style. In other words, we want either to be fully immersed in the work of our subordinates, making their decisions, or to leave them completely alone, not wanting to be bothered.

Another problem here is a manager's perception of himself. We tend to see ourselves more as communicators and delegators than we really are, certainly much more than do our subordinates. I tested this conclusion by asking a group of managers to assess the management style of their supervisors, and then by asking those supervisors what they thought their style was. Some 90 percent of the supervisors saw their style as more communicating or delegating than their subordinates' view. What accounts for the large discrepancy? It is partly because managers think of themselves as perfect delegators. But also, sometimes a manager throws out suggestions to a subordinate who receives them as marching orders — furthering the difference in perceptions.

A manager once told me that his supervisor definitely practiced an effective communicating style with him because they skied and drank together. He was wrong. There is a huge distinction between a social relationship and a communicating *management* style, which is a caring involvement in the *work* of the subordinate. Close relationships off the job may help to create an equivalent relationship on the job, but they should not be confused. Two people I knew had a supervisor-subordinate relationship. They spent one week each year by themselves, fishing in a remote area. When fishing, they never talked about work — it being tacitly understood that work was off conversational limits. Oddly enough, their work relationship remained distant, their personal friendship having no effect on it.

This brings us to the age-old question of whether friendship between supervisor and subordinate is a good thing. Some managers unhesitatingly assert that they never permit social relationships to develop with people they work with. In fact, there are pluses and minuses here. If the subordinate is a personal friend, the supervisor can move into a communicating management style quite easily, but the what-when-how mode becomes harder to revert to when necessary. It's unpleasant to give orders to a friend. I've seen several instances where a supervisor had to make a subordinate-friend toe a disciplinary line. In one case, a friendship was destroyed; in another, the supervisor's action worked out because the subordinate felt, thanks to the strength of the social relationship, that the supervisor was looking out for his (the subordinate's) professional interests.

Everyone must decide for himself what is professional and appropriate here. A test might be to imagine yourself delivering a tough performance review to your friend. Do you cringe at the thought? If so, don't make friends at work. If your stomach remains unaffected, you are likely to be someone whose personal relationships will strengthen work relationships.

CAREER DYNAMICS: MANAGING THE SUPERIOR/SUBORDINATE RELATIONSHIP

Lloyd Baird
Kathy Kram

"I don't know what's wrong with my boss. When we came to the data center together three years ago, we knew our job was to decentralize and over a two-year period put ourselves out of a job. We used to work well together. We've done what we came to do, and we should be looking for new jobs. I have been thinking about switching from data processing to human resources. Trouble is, my boss is no help at all. I can't even get any leads from him or help in deciding what to do."

— Bill

"When I joined the organization three months ago I had high hopes. I liked the group I'd be working with and I particularly liked the person I would be reporting to directly. He had been on the job only three months and had lots of enthusiasm and drive. He seemed like a fast-rising star that it would be good to link up with. But nothing has worked out. He just doesn't seem to have the time or interest to help me get established and learn this job."

— Sue

Most of us have, at some time, faced frustration and failure when working with a superior. No matter what we do, the relationship just doesn't work. Like Bill and Sue, we don't understand why it is not working and because we don't know how to manage the relationship, we give up and withdraw. Many times superior/subordinate relationships don't work right from the start because we don't recognize the different needs each of us brings to the relationship. Other times, relationships start well and then go sour as our needs change and the relationship doesn't change to match them.

In this article we draw from recent research on career development to develop a model for understanding what is happening in superior/subordinate relationships and how such relationships can be managed. We begin by reviewing how career stages affect the superior/subordinate relationship, make some comments and give some examples of how to manage the relationship, and then provide some suggestions on what people in organizations can do to improve the way in which superiors and subordinates work together.

HOW CAREER STAGES AFFECT PERSONAL NEEDS

A superior/subordinate relationship is affected by the particular needs that each person brings to it. To effectively manage the relationship, it is essential to understand not only these needs at any given point but also how they change over time. What each subordinate needs from his or her boss, and vice versa, is different now from what it will be next month, in two months, or next year. What each individual needs to get his or her work done, and what each needs as a person will change with time.

Research on the careers of engineers, scientists, and professional managers has found that what one wants and needs from a job will depend on the person's career stage — that is, the jobs they have held, their current position, and the direction in which they are moving. This research has also found that individuals progress through particular career stages, each of which is characterized by unique dilemmas, concerns, needs, and challenges. Because experience and maturing cause people to go through these career stages, and what they need from each other changes as they move through successive career stages, it is important that they maintain a dynamic perspective on their superior/subordinate relationships.

Career development research suggests that individuals generally go through an establishment stage, an advancement stage, a maintenance stage, and a withdrawal stage. At each stage, a person will face characteristic psychological adjustments, work responsibilities, relationships, and needs. Adult development research broadens this understanding by suggesting that other spheres of life will also affect an individual's concerns and dilemmas at each career stage and that to understand particular career stage needs, one must consider the person's broader life structure.

The Establishment Stage

During the establishment phase, at the outset of a career, people are most likely to need guidance and support to launch their careers. It is generally a period of great uncertainty about one's competence and performance potential. The person who is in the establishment phase is dependent on others for learning, support, and guidance, and at the same time is likely to resist dependence as attempts to establish competence are made. It is a period of building new roles both at work and in one's personal life. Questions about competence, whether to commit oneself to a particular organization, and what kind of family relationships to develop are primary concerns at this stage.

In *The Seasons of a Man's Life* (Knopf, 1978), Daniel J. Levinson and his coauthors describe the major tasks of early adulthood as forming a dream, forming an occupational identity, forming intimacy, and forming a mentor relationship. This is the apprentice stage when the individual's primary role is learning, when she or he must confront and manage dependence, and when she or he is preparing to become an independent contributor. Sue is a good example of a person at this career stage. Having been with the organization for only three months, she faces the challenge of learning the ropes, proving her competence, and building new relationships. She needs coaching, sponsorship, and opportunities to learn from her new boss.

The Advancement Stage

During the advancement stage, people become fully independent contributors. Needing less guidance, they know the ropes of organizational life and are most concerned with exposure and advancement through continued demonstration of competence. While people need close supervision and guidance when they're in the establishment stage, collegial and peer relationships become more important in the advancement stage. To learn to operate autonomously at this point in one's career is a major psychological adjustment. If an individual's career is launched in his or her twenties, then the advancement stage is likely to occur in the person's thirties, when concerns about self and family are related to settling down, building a family, and/or radically changing important aspects of the life structure. It is likely to be a period of making commitments — a period that is less prescribed than the establishment stage. A person in this stage is likely to be most concerned about advancing and about appropriate commitments at work and in the family. Thus coaching and exposure are important aids to advancement, while counseling, role models, and friendship are important aids for resolving important dilemmas at this stage.

The Maintenance Stage

At the maintenance stage, people are likely to have achieved the greatest advancement opportunities of their careers, and they are now investing greater energies in helping and developing less-experienced subordinates. For those who feel satisfied with their organizational accomplishments, it becomes a period of guiding others and finding satisfaction in contributing to the development of human and organizational resources. For those who are dissatisfied with their accomplishments and/or face blocked opportunities, it can be a difficult period of coming to terms with disappointments and losses. The latter are likely to be ineffective supervisors and unable to help other people develop as long as they are plagued with personal dissatisfaction. The maintenance stage frequently commences with midlife — a time when people also face concerns about the family structure's changing as children leave home, as well as the realities of aging and disappointment over what one has accomplished in contrast with earlier dreams and expectations. Concerns about self, career, and family are likely to stimulate a period of reassessment and redirection. Some of this reassessment may lead

173

supervisors in this stage to devote greater effort to developing subordinates.

The Withdrawal Stage

Eventually careers do end as people retire or move on to new careers. As they begin to anticipate leaving an organizational career, the withdrawal stage begins. At this stage one can still make contributions. The experienced worker has invaluable perspectives based on experience and history that can be shared with other organization members. Outside of work, concerns about self and family are likely to involve adjusting to greater leisure time and future retirement and to the reality of aging and mortality. Letting go of a highly involving work identity is a major task of the withdrawal stage.

Other Concerns at Various Stages

Career stages are affected by outside work concerns, as well as by particular features of the organizational context. Thus there are variations in how individuals progress through these major stages. It is not uncommon, for example, to see individuals launching new careers at midlife, or individuals moving through the four stages several times during a lifetime. In other instances, the particular needs of the individual will be unique. The progression from advancement to maintenance and on to withdrawal identifies in general the concerns people have as they move through a career.

However, we must attend to the life circumstances and organizational circumstances involved to develop an accurate picture of the unique needs and concerns of a boss or a subordinate. Consider, for example, Mary, who is launching a new career in a manufacturing firm at midlife. She has developed confidence and a sense of competence in other life endeavors, but comes to an organizational career with concerns about establishing herself in the new setting. At an older age, however, the experience of being an apprentice dependent on superiors for information, coaching, and support presents a challenge. In addition, her superior is much younger, and yet more knowledgeable and established in the profession. In this situation both Mary and her boss must adapt to a unique set of circumstances. How the boss feels about having an older subordinate and how the subordinate feels about being a novice will affect the quality of their relationship. These concerns evolve directly from previous life and career histories.

The organization can also affect the concerns people have at the various career stages. For example, John is an entry-level manager in a fast-growing, high-technology firm; movement and advancement are generally rapid. John will not have long to launch his career and get established before he will be moved to a new position with greater responsibility. The opportunity to build a supportive relationship with his boss is confined to a short period of time. Yet it is essential to build a good relationship so that he can learn as much as quickly as possible from the position. Not only will his career stages be compressed into a much shorter time, but the challenges in managing the relationship are greater because individuals and positions are changing so rapidly.

It is also true that individuals will go through the four stages on a minor scale with each new position. There are always periods of establishment, advancement, maintenance, and withdrawal as one begins a new job, experiences the learning curve, works easily as a result of completing the learning required to do the job effectively, and finally withdraws to move on to something new. So beyond understanding where an individual is in a broad career and life cycle perspective, another source of insight can be found by looking at his or her tenure in a current position.

When assessing the needs each party brings to a superior/subordinate relationship, it is useful to begin with a look at each party's career stage. One can predict what concerns about self, career, and family are likely to be salient and how these concerns may be shaped by the current organizational context or the individual's particular life history. This diagnosis of needs based on career stage is a critical first step toward effectively managing a superior/subordinate relationship. Let's examine, respectively, what subordinates and their superiors need at each stage.

WHAT DOES THE SUBORDINATE NEED FROM THE BOSS?

The subordinate will have both task and personal needs on the job that his or her boss can help fulfill. Task needs relate to accomplishing job responsibilities and personal needs relate to the person's own adjustment, coping, and learning. Let's look at how subordinates' needs from their bosses change as they progress through their careers.

Task Needs

Accomplishing job responsibilities happens in three phases: deciding what is to be accomplished (the goal), how it is to be accomplished (activities), and how progress will be measured (evaluation and feedback). Subordinates need help from the boss in each of these phases.

The Objectives (Where Are We Going?)

In order to get the job done, people need to know what their jobs are and what they are expected to accomplish. The boss has a key role in defining those expectations. He or she translates the organization's objectives into job responsibilities. The boss identifies not only the job responsibilities, but the constraints within which each subordinate works to accomplish them.

In the best case, the subordinate's responsibilities and objectives are clearly defined and understood by both boss and employee; moreover, they fit the boss's goals. In some cases, however, resources aren't available, or the organization's objectives aren't clear — or, if they are, they conflict with the superior's objectives. Subordinates need to know where the areas of conflict are and what resources are limited. They need to know what areas are flexible, what is uncertain, and what is likely to change.

The Plans (How Are We Going to Get There?)

To get the job done well, subordinates need help in determining appropriate activities. What should they do and how should they do it? They need the resources and assistance necessary to get the job done. To be motivated, they need challenging work that is properly directed towards the desired results.

Feedback (How Do You Know When You Have Arrived?)

To change and improve, people need feedback on their accomplishments. This feedback will allow them to know what they have accomplished, how well they've done, and what adjustments are appropriate to improve future performance. They need coaching and counseling on how to proceed. Without it, there is no guidance. This feedback may come from the superior, or it may come from systems and procedures that are built into the job by the subordinate and the supervisor. Wherever feedback comes from, it must be related to performance on the job and as specific as possible.

These task-related needs remain fairly fixed, with some slight variations as people move through their careers. During the early stages people will need more attention to all the components, particularly setting goals and learning how to do the job. As they gain experience they will be able to develop realistic goals. They will know how to do the job and assess their own accomplishments. The superior will still be involved, but not nearly as much as at the beginning.

Personal Needs

Even though the task needs won't change much through the career stages — except to be reduced — personal needs really change. Personal needs arise from concerns about self, career, and family. Let's look at the four major career stages and consider how person-related needs change.

During the establishment stage, when people are newcomers to an organization, there are a variety of ways in which the boss can help them learn the ropes of organizational life and develop competence and comfort in their new roles. During this period of building a professional identity in a new setting, people may have concerns about how to get the work done, who the players are, whether they are performing up to expectations, and whether they are building the required skills for future advancement. A boss can serve a critical function by providing on-the-job training, coaching, and feedback on performance. Ostensibly these are task-related functions that enable people to get the job done. At the same time, however, they are directly responsive to the developmental needs of the establishment stage.

In this early stage of a career, as people are learning a great deal about their competence, career interests, and potential in the organization, a boss can also serve as a role model — someone to emulate and to identify with as one searches for one's own professional niche. The boss can also provide protection in high-risk situations when people may be putting themselves in difficult situations unlike anything they've experienced before. Exposure to such situations can also have high payoffs. The boss's support in these contexts will enable the subordinate to gain from the exposure without risking his or her newly emerging reputation as a competent professional. Finally, because self-confidence may be tenuous during this stage of a career, ongoing acceptance and confirmation by the boss of the person in the new role can be critical. Consistent support and encouragement from a boss, while desirable at every career stage, is particularly important in the earliest years of a new career.

During the advancement stage of a new career, person-related needs are likely to shift somewhat. With their greater self-confidence and knowledge of the organization, people are more likely to be concerned about promotion, advancement, and growth than about basic competence and ability to get the work done. With a track record developing, they will be looking ahead with questions about whether to stay and advance, and how to balance promotional opportunities with outside work interests and responsibilities; they will be interested in clarifying the range of possible long-term options available.

The most useful thing a boss can offer at this stage is the opportunity to do challenging work that gives the person a chance to develop skills, to demonstrate potential, and to gain visibility in the organization. Challenging work alone, however, won't provide as much mileage without exposure to those who can judge the person's potential and will be making promotional decisions in the future. Thus both *challenging work assignments* and *exposure and visibility* will be central to paving the way for advancement. Finally, *sponsorship* ensures that the person's hard work and competence will benefit him or her by creating actual opportunities for promotion. A boss can greatly facilitate career development during this stage by speaking highly of the person in places where it counts — to his or her own superior, for example.

While the primary concern during this stage is with advancement possibilities, career stage theory also clarifies concerns about self and family that coincide with these career-related concerns that are intimately intertwined with work experiences. The decision to accept a promotion and the possible costs to one's personal life are likely to be of concern. Whether to stay with the organization and become increasingly committed to it may also surface. What kind of relationships to nurture in the organization with peers, superiors, and subordinates will also arise because the person is no longer a newcomer, but rather one with a history in the organization. The opportunity to discuss these concerns with a good listener and sounding board will greatly aid work on these concerns and free the person's energies for productive work. This *counseling* function is valuable at every career stage, but particularly important during the advancement stage.

By the time people reach the maintenance stage of their careers, many of their person-related needs of earlier career years have been addressed. They may no longer need coaching, protection, training, or frequent counseling, but as subordinates they are likely to need autonomy and the opportunity to develop younger subordinates. Passing on their own experience and knowledge to those in newcomer positions enhances self-esteem at midcareer. The opportunity to guide others will enrich their worklife. Thus a boss who encourages autonomous action and rewards a subordinate's attempts to support less-experienced employees will be most supportive of career development in the maintenance stage.

Finally, as an individual approaches retirement and enters the stage of withdrawal, a boss will be most helpful by conveying the message that one's tenure and experience in the organization is still valued. The opportunity to continue to develop others and to serve in consultation to others counteracts any fears of becoming useless in one's work role. A boss who assigns consultative roles acknowledges the person's experience and provides a vehicle for utilizing the person's talents in productive ways — both as an individual and for the organization.

People's personal needs at each major career stage are summarized in Exhibit 1. Ideally, many of these functions would be provided by the boss. However, that likelihood depends on each person's ability to know what he or she needs and to negotiate for it, and on the boss's willingness and capacity to provide it. Assessment of one's own needs and assessment of one's boss's needs must be accomplished before successful negotiation can occur.

EXHIBIT 1

What People Need From Their Bosses:
A Checklist of Personal Needs

Career Stage	Personal Needs
Establishment	Coaching
	Feedback
	Training
	Role-modeling
	Acceptance and confirmation
	Protection
Advancement	Exposure
	Challenging work
	Sponsorship
	Counseling
Maintenance	Autonomy
	Opportunities to develop others
Withdrawal	Consultative roles

WHAT DOES THE BOSS NEED FROM THE SUBORDINATE?

Any relationship is an exchange. Knowing the boss's career stage can greatly enhance the subordinate's ability to manage their relationship effectively. The better subordinates understand their superiors' concerns and needs that arise from a particular career stage, the better prepared they are to offer support in exchange for what the superior can provide. Because every relationship involves give and take, this understanding enables the subordinate to predict what he or she can offer to develop a mutually enhancing relationship. While it is difficult to know someone else's career stage exactly, it is possible to make some educated guesses on the basis of the perspective offered in the previous sections.

When the boss is in the establishment stage, it is quite likely that she or he will be primarily concerned with demonstrating supervisory competence, with learning the ropes, and with developing a positive reputation in the organization. While it is unlikely that people in this stage will be bosses (because they are relative newcomers), that can happen in at least two types of situations. An individual may come from another organization or department, and although he or she may have been established in another job, in this new position establishment-stage concerns will surface. Alternatively, competent technicians who are assigned supervisory responsibilities may be well established in their technical competence but just beginning their supervisory careers.

While it is unlikely that a boss who is in the establishment stage will be assigned subordinates who are in either an establishment or advancement stage, such a situation is the most difficult for all concerned. Supervisors in the establishment stage themselves need guidance, support, visibility, and sponsorship, just as subordinates do. Because of their own uncertainties about their own performance and potential, such supervisors may not have the energy or inclination to provide support to subordinates. And they may also have competitive feelings that interfere with giving such support. What such a boss is likely to need from subordinates at this stage of his or her career is technical and psychological support. This is something that subordinates frequently don't think of, but it is something that can enable a boss to provide some of what subordinates need as well.

During the advancement stage of a boss's career, what she or he will need most from subordinates is loyal followship that can reflect well on his or her competence as a boss. A subordinate who actively supports a boss by producing good work and by using his or her expertise to make the department and the boss look good will be valued. When a boss in the advancement stage is confident of this followship, she or he will be more likely to provide coaching, challenging work, sponsorship, and the other functions that subordinates may need.

It is not until the maintenance stage, however, that a boss is psychologically prepared to provide the range of support that subordinates need in their early career stages. It is at this stage that a boss is prepared and inclined to be a mentor to others, particularly if he or she is self-confident about his or her own accomplishments. Becoming a mentor to others can be intrinsically rewarding at midcareer. The superior needs a vehicle for redirecting creative energies away from rapid advancement concerns towards developing others. She or he can share valued wisdom and experience with less experienced subordinates. It is the individual at this stage who has the greatest potential to be the ideal boss for someone in the establishment or advancement stage.

Finally, a boss in the withdrawal stage needs, most of all, the opportunity to be in a consultative role to others. With a positive reputation in the organization, she or he can continue to provide a subordinate with sponsorship, exposure, coaching, and other functions needed through the advancement stage. However, because such a person is now looking toward retirement — most likely with some ambivalence — the opportunity to feel like a valued resource because of, rather than in spite of, his or her age and experience is critical at this late career stage. The subordinate who solicits such consultation and demonstrates respect for what is offered will find a receptive boss who can provide a variety of the type of help needed in earlier career stages.

From these descriptions it is obvious that there are matches of boss and subordinate that are likely to work better than others. The boss in an establishment stage will not be of great value to a subordinate in the advancement stage, for example. The reality is, however, that more often than not, a subordinate has no choice as to who his or her boss will be. The next best thing is for the subordinate to diagnose what the boss's situation is, and to make some assessment about what they can give each other. In this way, the subordinate increases the likelihood of developing an exchange that supports both parties. These assessments must extend beyond the normally considered task needs into personal needs. When only task-related needs are considered, it is likely that opportunities will be missed and problems created. Exhibit 2 presents a checklist of the boss's personal needs from subordinates.

EXHIBIT 2
What The Boss Needs From Subordinates:
A Checklist of Personal Needs

Career Stage	Salient Personal Needs
Establishment	Technical support Psychological support
Advancement	Loyal followship
Maintenance	Opportunities to mentor
Withdrawal	Consultative roles

THE RELATIONSHIP AS AN EXCHANGE

The relationship between a boss and a subordinate involves two people, each of whom is in a particular career stage characterized by unique challenges and psychological adjustments. In some instances there will be a good fit, and the needs of each will be complementary. In other instances there will be a mismatch, and their needs will conflict. In general a relationship is most effective, contributing to both productivity and individual development, when it responds to both individuals' most salient concerns; it becomes troublesome when it is unresponsive to one or both people.

For example, if the subordinate is in the establishment phase and the boss is in the maintenance stage, it is likely that needs will be complementary. (See Exhibit 3, Time 1). At that point, the subordinate needs guidance, coaching, training, feedback, and protection in high-risk situations, and the boss is inclined to want to develop and support younger employees. Both will find satisfaction and support in the

181

EXHIBIT 3
Career Dynamics

(Bill)

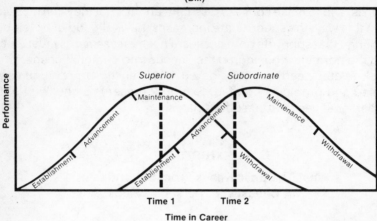

Time in Career

relationship. Either individual can initiate a useful exchange of resources that will be responsive to both individuals' needs. More often than not in this situation, the exchange emerges naturally; it is equally feasible for the subordinate to initiate the exchange by soliciting coaching and advice from his or her boss.

On the other hand, there are many situations when the fit is not good. For example, consider a case such as Sue's, which is represented graphically in Exhibit 4, Time 1. Here both superior and subordinate are

EXHIBIT 4
Career Dynamics

(Sue)

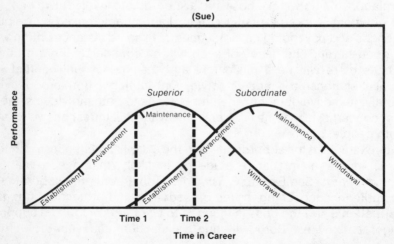

Time in Career

in the early stages of their careers at the same time. It is not likely that the boss will be able to provide the kind of attention and guidance that the subordinate needs, and competition for advancement may interfere with potential collaboration and mutual assistance.

The most complex thing about the superior/subordinate relationship is that it changes. The needs of both boss and subordinate change as each moves to different stages of their careers. What was once a productive relationship may become unproductive unless adjustments are made. Similarly, unproductive relationships can become productive. Consider the examples in Exhibits 3 and 4. In a case like Bill's (represented in Exhibit 3) the relationship may have been productive early on (at Time 1), but as Bill begins to look for advancement and possibly a new career (Time 2), he finds that his boss doesn't have the time or the interest to provide guidance and assistance. A boss who is entering a declining period in his or her career is unlikely to be available to offer critical support.

On the other hand, relationships like Sue's may work in reverse, moving from bad to good. As her superior gains more experience and security (Exhibit 4, Time 2), he should be better able to provide the support and sponsorship that Sue needs.

The moral of these shifts is clear. The boss can't provide everything, and whatever the relationship is now, it will change. It is a wise subordinate that recognizes his or her own needs, understands clearly what the boss can provide now and in the future, and finds and prepares alternatives to the boss's support.

HOW DO PEOPLE GET WHAT THEY NEED?

We have identified what subordinates need to manage their jobs and themselves, how those needs change as they progress through their careers, and how they and their supervisors relate to each other. Here are some suggestions for both parties on how to manage the superior/subordinate relationship so it can be as productive as possible.

1. *Recognize that "the relationship" is an exchange.* Clarifying what each party needs from the other is a critical first step towards managing the relationship. Both parties must realize that this is a two-way process through which both parties try to meet their own personal objectives.

Most work relationships involve an exchange of technical, psychological, and/or organizational resources. For example, the boss can provide technical guidance and information, and support and encouragement, and/or she or he can open doors for advancement and success. Similarly, a subordinate can support his or her boss by producing quality work on a timely basis that supports departmental objectives, by listening to his or her concerns and frustrations, and by making the boss look good to other departments. By recognizing the relationship as an exchange, both parties improve the chances of getting what they need by fulfilling the other's needs.

2. *Clearly identify your own and the other party's needs*. It is critical that subordinates and bosses identify their own needs, as well as each other's needs, so they can ask for, and provide, the resources that will be most meaningful to both. We have identified two broad categories of needs: task needs and personal needs. The better that bosses and subordinates understand the needs that each has in these two categories, the more likely it is that they will cultivate a productive relationship.

Task needs are shaped by organizational objectives and constraints. Both bosses and subordinates have formal business objectives, and will need technical assistance, psychological support, and organizational support to further these objectives. So, for example, if a subordinate needs access to information at higher levels of the organization to complete a task, the boss may have to get it or the subordinate may need advice on how to get it on his or her own. The variety of possible task needs is very broad. Once they are identified and understood, it is possible to develop an exchange that is mutually beneficial.

As we've discussed, everyone has personal needs as well. These are shaped by life and career history, and current circumstances. Thus, in addition to considering task needs, bosses and subordinates must assess the personal needs they bring to the relationship.

Age and experience shape personal needs a great deal. A subordinate who is launching a career and attempting to learn the ropes of the organization is likely to need guidance, coaching, feedback, sponsorship, and support. It is not unusual to need and want these from one's supervisor; and knowing what is needed is a first step towards making them a part of the exchange of technical, psychological, and organizational resources.

At the same time, however, it is necessary to assess what personal needs the boss brings to the relationship. Boss and subordinate may have complementary needs; in which case they can work together to meet each other's needs. For example, a boss who is at midcareer and relatively satisfied with his or her accomplishments to date is likely to be willing to provide support, guidance, and opportunities for growth to a subordinate. In fact the opportunity to help a subordinate grow and develop is likely to meet the needs of a superior in midlife and midcareer who wants to pass on his or her experience and wisdom.

On the other hand, the subordinate and the boss may have competitive needs — in which case both will have to learn how to work together and meet their needs from other sources. A boss who is launching a career, for example, may be so concerned by his or her own quest for knowledge and support, that she or he may not be able to provide the resources the subordinate needs at the beginning of his or her career. Because both need support and guidance, maybe they can work together to find what they need.

Ultimately it is likely that task and personal needs will never be entirely complementary because people are always changing. More often than not, in fact, some needs may be complementary while others are competitive. Because of the complexity of relationships it is necessary for people to periodically assess (1) when their needs are complementary (for instance, when the boss wants to be a mentor and the subordinate wants to be coached), (2) when the boss's and subordinate's needs are shared (for example, when both boss and subordinate are concerned about advancement and both want to produce a high quality departmental record), and (3) when their needs are competitive (for example, when a subordinate wants exposure while the boss wants to take all the credit for the department's good performance). When needs are shared or complementary, a positive exchange of technical, psychological, and organizational resources is possible. When needs conflict, it is most fruitful for the parties to recognize the conflict, not to expect mutual support, and to find ways of minimizing conflict by finding the resources they need elsewhere.

3. *Understand how the two of you fit together now and recognize that the relationship is likely to change.* It is unrealistic to expect that any relationship can provide a satisfactory exchange forever. Indeed, research on mentor relationships has indicated that most such relationships progress through predictable phases of initiation, cultivation, separation, and redefinition. During the initiation phase both individuals discover the value of relating to the other, and it is this discovery that sets the relationship in motion. During the cultivation phase, a broad exchange of resources is established and maintained as each person discovers what he or she has to offer and to gain from the relationship. During the separation phase, needs and/or organizational circumstances change, and the relationship established during the cultivation phase is disrupted. The individuals come to the painful realization that the relationship is no longer meeting their needs, and they begin to withdraw from each other. Finally, as new relationships are formed and needs are met elsewhere, the relationship reaches a point of redefinition that is generally characterized by a minimum expectation of resource exchanges beyond ongoing friendship and mutual respect.

These phases of a relationship apply to superior/subordinate relationships. During the initiation phase, both parties must discover what kinds of resource exchange will be mutually beneficial. During the cultivation phase, each can provide technical, psychological, and organizational resources that make it possible for both to attain individual and organizational goals. During the separation phase, a subordinate may simply move on to a new boss or may have to look to others for resources and support. Finally, at some time it is likely that both parties will no longer expect or need resources from each other, but because they have worked together, some kind of ongoing friendship and mutual respect remains. The key then is to recognize that the relationship will change, that the needs of both parties vary, and that they must continually monitor the relationship and recognize changes in it. One key to managing superior/subordinate relationships successfully would be for both parties to recognize their future needs and find and prepare the resources to fill them.

4. *Understand the constraints under which the boss operates*. Realism about what a boss can provide in terms of technical, psychological, and organizational resources is critical. Clearly there are constraints that make it impossible for the boss to provide all of the resources the subordinate needs. Once subordinates understand these constraints, they can identify which resources the boss can provide. So, for example, the boss may not be able to allocate more technical resources to the subordinate because of budget constraints, but he or she may be able to sponsor the subordinate in an effort to make a lateral move. While organizational constraints may prevent the subordinate's obtaining some important resources, the boss's personal needs may make it possible for him or her to give the subordinate other equally important resources. The time and attention that a boss spends helping the subordinate to learn may be far more important than the desk and office he or she cannot provide. Not receiving resources because the boss can't provide them is truly frustrating. But it is even more frustrating when the subordinate focuses on the resources that the boss just can't provide rather than on those she or he can provide.

The cultivation phase of a relationship begins when task and personal needs have been clearly identified, and both boss and subordinate are exchanging resources. Actively managing the superior/subordinate relationship is an attempt to get the relationship to the cultivation phase as quickly as possible. This can happen when the subordinate has realistic expectations about the boss and him- or herself.

5. *Establish a feedback and evaluation system for continuously assessing the relationship*. Finally, to monitor the quality of the superior/subordinate relationship, periodic feedback is needed. As needs and organizational constraints change, it will be necessary to make adjustments; some resources may become less available; others may become more necessary. Periodic dialogue about the relationship provides an opportunity to renegotiate when necessary. Just as performance is reviewed regularly, so should the quality of the relationship between superior and subordinate be assessed so that it can be cultivated and maintained to the benefit of both parties. Exhibit 5 provides a list of questions for the subordinate to use in assessing the superior/subordinate relationship. These can be adapted so the supervisor can also assess the relationship.

EXHIBIT 5

Assessment of the Superior/Subordinate
Relationship by the Subordinate

1. What is your current career stage? What will it be three to five years from now?

2. What is your boss's current career stage? What will it be three to five years from now?

3. What job and career needs do you have now? What will you need in three to five years?

4. What job and career needs does your boss have now? What will he or she need in three to five years?

5. How do you and your boss fit together?

   a. What resources can your boss provide you?

   b. What resources can you provide to the boss?

   c. Which needs are complementary? Shared? Conflicting?

   d. At what stage is your relationship? Initiation? Cultivation? Separation? Redefinition? Where should it be?

6. What preparations can you make for your future job and career needs?

7. What alternative sources do you have for the needs that your boss can't fill? Can you help provide alternative sources for your boss for the needs that you can't fill?

OTHER SOURCES OF SUPPORT

What if, in spite of all that the parties do, the relationship doesn't work? The last question in the assessment asks about other sources of support. There will be times when active management of the relationship does not result in a mutually satisfying exchange. Both personal and organizational factors can contribute to a situation in which it is not possible to achieve a productive relationship. If, after attempting to define goals, develop strategies for meeting goals, and design feedback systems, the subordinate finds that the boss is not providing the job and career resources that the subordinate needs, it is quite likely that the boss cannot do so.

Whether resources had been provided earlier and the relationship has moved into a separation phase or resources have never been provided — indicating failure to establish the relationship at all — this is a time for subordinates to consider other sources of support to help them meet their task and personal needs. The first step is for the subordinate to make sure he or she has clear goals, because that is the only way to determine if the relationship is working. Then he or she must determine what is needed from the relationship to make it productive. Certainly, it is preferable for the boss to be the subordinate's primary source of organizational resources, but if active management of the superior/subordinate relationship doesn't yield the appropriate results, it is time to seek other sources.

Relationships with other superiors and peers offer important alternatives. The immediate supervisor is not the only one who can provide critical resources. Others can coach, counsel, and provide exposure and sponsorship. By assessing one's own and one's co-workers' task and personal needs, it is possible to create mutually beneficial exchanges with a variety of people within the organization. By cultivating several relationships that provide a range of resources, each person is less likely to become dependent on any one relationship and may be able to establish a much wider resource base to draw on.

Peer relationships provide a unique opportunity to develop mutual problem-solving and counseling arrangements. Because it is likely that peers share common concerns and dilemmas, empathy and mutual understanding is relatively easy to achieve. Peers can learn from each other's experiences.

Peer relationships are uniquely suited to foster growth and mutual support because neither party is responsible for evaluating the performance of the other. However, the competition inherent in organizational life often prevents people from realizing the full potential of peer relationships. Competition among peers tends to create barriers to effective sharing and mutual problem solving. It is possible, however, to compete and collaborate simultaneously. Actively managing peer relationships will identify areas in which mutual support is possible. So, for example, a person might decide to share strategies for managing work and family pressures with one peer, but not discuss a particular job opportunity to which both aspire. Here again, identifying shared and complementary needs as opposed to competitive needs is a crucial step in the process of forming a relationship — in this case, between peers.

The option of developing relationships with individuals who are not in the organization is another possibility. This alternative eliminates the competition inherent within the organization and provides an opportunity to gain from an outsider's perspective on an insider's dilemmas. When needs are not met by active management of the superior/subordinate relationship or other internal relationships, external relationships can prove valuable.

Because relationships are constantly changing, it is necessary for people to periodically review their current networks of relationships. Active management of these networks involves periodic assessment and renegotiation in the same way as managing the superior/subordinate relationship requires such attention.

If none of these approaches works, it may be time to think about moving on. There is nothing worse for a person than to get stuck in an absolutely unproductive position. Notice, however, that this may not happen as often as most people anticipate. People can actively manage relationships in such a way that what at first appeared unproductive may prove to be beneficial. The key is active management of the superior/subordinate relationship.

SUMMARY

Superior/subordinate relationships often fail to work because both parties lack realistic expectations about what they can provide for each other. If people critically analyze and understand the needs of themselves, their bosses, and their subordinates, they will be in a much better position to take advantage of superior/subordinate relationships. Bosses can't provide everything. Many times their ability to provide resources is limited by the organization. They can, however, often provide such important personal needs as training, counseling, exposure, and sponsorship.

Two critical characteristics of a superior/subordinate relationship make managing it important. First, the relationship is an exchange. The subordinate gives the boss support and resources in the same way that he or she supports the subordinate. The relationship will be productive only if it is mutually beneficial. So, in analyzing and managing the relationship, both boss and subordinate must consider what they can do for each other. Second, inevitably this relationship will change. Both parties must anticipate and plan for the change and must actively manage the superior/subordinate relationship.

SELECTED BIBLIOGRAPHY

The literature on adult and career development encouraged us to look at how life and/or career stages affect relationships with bosses and subordinates. Adult development perspectives suggest that individuals are likely to encounter characteristic concerns about self, career, and family at every life stage. For an indepth look at a model of adult life stages see *Seasons of A Man's Life*, by Daniel Levinson et al. (Knopf Publishing, 1978), and *Transformations: Growth and Change in Adult Life*, by R. Gould (Simon & Schuster Publishing, 1978). Career development perspectives focus more specifically on the professional and personal concerns that are faced as one advances in a career. Several of these works illustrate how both career stage and life stage affect individuals' experiences in a work setting. The most prominent of these books include: *Careers in Organizations*, by Douglas T. Hall (Goodyear Publishing Company, 1976), and *Career Dynamics: Matching Individual and Organizational Needs*, by E. H. Schein (Addison-Wesley Publishing Co., 1978).

Our particular interest in superior/subordinate relationships was supported by an important study of the careers of engineers and scientists. "The Four Stages of Professional Careers: A New Look At Performance By Professionals," by Gene W. Dalton et al. (in *Organizational Dynamics,* Summer 1977) highlighted the psychological adjustments, changes in role, and changes in relationships that one is likely to encounter at each major career stage. This work illustrated how the nature of relationships would shift significantly with career advancement, suggesting the need to further understand how superior/subordinate relationships are affected by the career stage of each individual. In addition, several works have emphasized the important role that supervisors play in the new careers of young managers. The most prominent are: "The Socialization of Managers: Effects of Expectations of Performance," by David E. Berlew and Douglas T. Hall (in *Administrative Sciences Quarterly,* November 1966), and "Pygmalion in Management," by J. S. Livingston (in *Harvard Business Review,* July-August, 1969).

Recent work on mentoring relationships has identified a range of developmental functions that are provided in this type of relationship to support career advancement and personal development. See "Mentoring In Managerial Careers" by James Clawson (in *Work, Family and Career*, edited by C. Brooklyn Derr; Praeger, 1980), "Much Ado About Mentors," by G. R. Roche (*Harvard Business Review*, January-February, 1979), "Everyone Who Makes It Has a Mentor," by E. Collins and P. Scott (in *Harvard Business Review*, July-August, 1978). Some studies also suggest that mentoring relationships are not readily available and that when they do exist, they last only a few years until the career stage of either individual changes or organizational circumstances change. These findings reinforce the importance of encouraging the boss to provide mentoring functions. For a comprehensive view of mentoring relationships and how they affect personal and professional development see *Mentoring at Work*, by Kathy Kram, to be published by Scott, Foresman, & Company in 1984.

There are a number of references on interpersonal communications that can provide practical guidance on the skills required to build supportive work relationships. For a review of the important concepts see *Essays in Interpersonal Dynamics*, by Warren Bennis et al. (The Dorsey Press, 1979), and *Interpersonal Behavior*, by A. G. Athos and J. J. Gabarro (Prentice-Hall, Inc., 1978).

For a look at the more concrete skills needed to accomplish what we suggest in the article see "Barriers and Gateways to Communication," by Carl Rogers and Fritz Roethlisberger (in *Harvard Business Review*, July-August, 1952). "Active Listening," by Carl Rogers and R. Farson, and "Defensive Communication," by J. Gibb, both printed in *Organizational Psychology: A Book of Readings*, edited by David A. Kolb and James M. McIntyre et al. (Prentice-Hall, 1979).

Finally, we recognize that boss/subordinate relationships are influenced by the organizational context in which they are imbedded. The structure, norms, and culture of an organization will affect which developmental functions are provided, and how a particular relationship evolves over time. To date there has not been much published on how organizations affect relationships. However, a very interesting case study of an organization that considers this in some depth is *Men and Women of the Corporation,* which was written by Rosabeth Moss Kanter (Basic Books, 1977).

SECTION FOUR

MISSION

Overview

Several years ago Peter Drucker observed, "Every one of the great business builders we know of . . . had a definite idea, had, indeed, a clear theory of the business which informed his actions and decisions." Drucker's observation aside, few managers today are prepared or particularly inclined to address the question, "Why are we here?" either for themselves or for their people.

Until recently such issues as higher purpose, overarching goals, or basic values have not been viewed as central to the real business concerns facing managers — aims and values are not the "hard-stuff" of budgets, plans, or procedures.

This perspective is perfectly understandable from the frame of reference that has dominated American business most of this century. When principal markets and competition are assumed to be predictable, where the relevant causal factors are assumed to be under the control of management, and where employees both view themselves and are viewed as filling simple, prescribed, essentially straightforward roles, the central management issues must necessarily revolve around controlling established structures and procedures, and executing a prescribed plan of action.

In such an environment, efforts to achieve work unit alignment around "Why are we here?", "What is our purpose?", or "What do we stand for?" would naturally seem to be irrelevant and possibly disruptive. The real issue under such conditions was to insure that people understood how to do what was required of them.

All this has changed dramatically in recent years as managers are faced with increasingly complex and unpredictable situations — situations where a common sense of direction rather than prescribed procedures is a more reliable compass for decision making. In addition, managers find themselves responsible for and to the "new worker" who is educated, sophisticated, and demanding; who has job alternatives; and who insists that work has meaning and significance beyond a paycheck and career ladder.

Possibly the clearest indication of the shift toward a recognition of mission as a critical management factor has been the rash of recent studies of high performing organizations. These studies all point to the fact that one of the most significant common characteristics of consistently high performing companies today is that there is a simple, clearly articulated sense of purpose and values that permeates these organizations.

In their article, "Shaping and Managing Shared Values," Julien R. Phillips and Allan A. Kennedy reinforce this conclusion as they reflect on the efforts of McKinsey & Company to understand the role that shared values play in highly successful corporations. According to Phillips and Kennedy, values serve the manager in three principal ways: (1) They focus attention, (2) They guide decision making, and (3) They are a primary source of dedication and commitment. The authors stress that value-oriented companies are ones in which managers recognize their continuing responsibility to shape and reinforce desired values through a variety of channels. These channels include, for example, the processes through which the company assimilates new hires, the strategies for rewarding and recognizing workers, the means by which company folklore is perpetuated, and the formal company structures and procedures.

Value-oriented leadership, while essential in today's business environment, is not without its risks and pitfalls. For example, Phillips and Kennedy observe that shared values are the social glue of an organization and consequently extremely difficult to change. This poses serious problems for managers during periods when the old values have become obsolete and continued success requires new dominant values.

Pascale and Athos extend and deepen our understanding of the role of mission in their article, "Great Companies Make Meaning." Through a number of excellent case examples from both the United States and Japan, the authors sensitively develop the perspective that the "superordinate goals" of the firm must ultimately be linked to higher human values and that this linkage is growing in importance.

Pascale and Athos acknowledge that such a linkage between corporate purposes and deep human concern runs counter to the cultural norm in the West of separating a person's spiritual and institutional lives. Over the last twenty years, the business community has greatly expanded its understanding of goals to parallel the growing ranks and influence of the "legitimate" stakeholders of major corporations (e.g., environmental groups, minorities). However, the role of business organizations in serving higher human values is still not totally accepted.

"What is needed in the West," according to the authors, "is a nondeified, nonreligious 'spiritualism' that enables a firm's superordinate goals to respond truly to the inner meanings that many people seek in their work or, alternatively, seek in their lives and could find at work if only that were more culturally acceptable."

The third contribution to this section expands our understanding of managing mission by exploring managers' tendencies to try to control the systems they desire to improve. In "Strategies for the New Age," Roger Harrison observes that in complex organizations, attempts to exert effective influence through greater control generally exacerbate the problems a manager is attempting to solve. The expectation that such will not be the case is due to the "analytical trap," the illusion that the

194

organization is autonomous and not fundamentally interconnected within itself and within its environment.

In his efforts to find an alternative to control, Harrison also appeals to the central importance of leading through vision and values. But he goes further than the previous authors by exploring the potential "shadow" or "daimonic" side of an overly zealous attachment to managing mission. In this regard, Harrison draws an important distinction between the force of *alignment* and the counterbalancing force of *attunement* in organizations. Alignment is the voluntary commitment of people to serve the purposes of the organization. Attunement is the support that people share as a result of their mutual caring and love. The effective management of mission requires that these two forces be kept in a dynamic balance. An unbalanced emphasis on alignment may increase objective performance, but at the almost inevitable cost of exploiting and disregarding the individual. On the other hand, a failure to balance attunement results in a flawed sense of community — one that is nonproductive.

With this framework as a base, Harrison goes on to explore in some detail the role of intuition in leadership, the proper meaning of strategic thinking, and high performance as a function of organizational and personal balance and harmony.

David Bradford and Allan Cohen's article, "Overarching Goals," is an appropriate conclusion to this section. It is highly practical and directed to the middle manager who is charged with managing mission at the level of the work unit. The authors argue very persuasively that "even when the company as a whole has a clear mission (overarching goal) that is supported through the organization's actions, each work unit must have a parallel mission that serves the unit membership the way the corporate mission serves the organization as a whole."

In addition to clearly describing the essential characteristics of an effective work unit mission and the functions such a mission serve, the authors outline a straightforward approach to assist readers to formulate a mission with their work units and gain its acceptance by work unit members.

SHAPING AND MANAGING SHARED VALUES

Julien R. Phillips
Allan A. Kennedy

Every organization has shared values. The values may be grand in scope ("Progress is our most important product") or narrowly focused ("Excellence in underwriting"). They can capture the imagination: "The first Irish multinational." Or they can simply drive: "15 percent period-to-period sales and earnings growth." If they are strong, they can command everyone's attention: "What people really care about around here is quality." If they are weak, they may often be ignored: "It's not the same company since the old man stepped down. Nowadays everyone around here is just more or less doing his own thing."

Tough-minded managers and consultants rarely pay much attention to the value system of an organization. Values are not "hard," like organization structures, policies and procedures, strategies, or budgets. Often they are not even written down. And when someone does try to set them down in a formal statement of corporate philosophy or values, the product often bears an uncomfortable resemblance to the Biblical beatitudes — good and true and broadly constructive, but not all that relevant to Monday morning.

Yet "hard" or not, shared organizational values powerfully influence what people in an organization actually do. They ought therefore to be a matter of concern to managers and consultants alike.

We find compelling support for these assertions in our own professional experience. Excellent performers among the organizations we know seem commonly to (a) have highly focused and widely shared values, and (b) work hard at keeping these shared values intact. This suggests to us that senior managers who aim for outstanding performance can ill afford to neglect the task of shaping and sustaining the values of their organizations.

SHARED VALUES MAKE A DIFFERENCE

Some time ago a number of McKinsey consultants were discussing differences in the basic organizational effectiveness of companies we knew reasonably well. One of us, characterizing one of his favorite high-performance companies, remarked, "They're just turned on, up and down the line." The phrase rang a bell: all of us had at some time seen this phenomenon. Most people in each "turned-on" company, we noted, shared a common belief about the distinctiveness of their organization.

We were particularly impressed with the case of Jefferson-Smurfit, "the first Irish multinational," which has grown 200-fold in sales and 100-fold in earnings in the last 11 years. Smurfit's chairman articulates a guiding belief that is deeply imbedded in the minds of the young Irish businessmen who run the company: "For too long we gave our brains away . . . we lost our brightest jewels. Now we are trying to make the country richer, to end poverty and emigration. If chaps like me don't change it, then who will?"

But the range of examples cited was diverse:

- **International Business Machines**: "IBM means service," a succinct statement of the primacy of satisfying the customer.
- **General Electric**: "Progress is our most important product," an implicit faith in the value of tinkering by engineers that dominated the corporate culture for better than half a century.
- **Caterpillar**: "24-hour parts service anywhere in the world," again symbolizing an extraordinary commitment to meeting customers' needs.
- **Leo Burnett**: "Make great ads," commitment to a particular concept of excellence.
- **American Telephone & Telegraph**: "Universal service," an historical orientation toward standardized, highly reliable service to all possible users, now being reshaped into values more relevant to a newly competitive marketplace.
- **Du Pont**: "Better things for better living through chemistry," a belief that product innovation, arising out of chemical engineering, is Du Pont's most distinctive value.
- **Sears, Roebuck**: "Quality at a good price — the mass merchandiser for Middle America."
- **Rouse Company**: "Create the best environment for people," a dominating concern to develop healthy and pleasant residential communities, not just build subdivisions.
- **Continental Bank**: "We'll find a way" (to meet customer needs).
- **Dana Corporation**: "Productivity through people," enlisting the ideas and commitment of employees at every level in support of Dana's strategy of competing largely on cost and dependability rather than product differentiation.
- **Chubb Insurance Company**: "Underwriting excellence," an overriding commitment to top-quality service.
- **Price Waterhouse**: "Strive for technical perfection" in accounting.
- **McKinsey & Company,** our own firm: "professionalism" and "top-management problem solving."

Most of these phrases sound utterly platitudinous to the outsider. Within an organization, however, they take on rich and concrete meaning. More, they often determine what people do.

Take IBM. Years ago one of us, then an IBM salesman, was called out on a customer's problem. Thirty hours later, with the problem apparently fixed, and testing and retesting already under way, he left the customer's premises to catch a few hours' sleep. A minor bug developed in his absence. Despite an otherwise excellent record, he was very nearly fired. "IBM means service" never seemed abstract after that.

Or take Dana Corporation. As a competitor in the long-established auto-parts manufacturing business, it has virtually doubled its productivity over the past 7 years, a period when overall U.S. productivity growth has been slowing. It did not accomplish this record with massive capital investment, with sophisticated industrial engineering studies, or with management-imposed speed-up measures. Instead, it relied on its people, right down to the shop-floor level. Management continually stressed the importance of productivity to company success. It created a multitude of task forces and other special activities; gave its people practical opportunities to generate productivity-improving ideas and then implemented them; and consistently, visibly, and frequently rewarded success. "Productivity through people" is no mere advertising phrase to the employees of Dana Corporation.

Mediocre organizations present a different picture. Although their senior managers often point to values they regard as characteristic of their companies, one finds that these values are less strongly held, and that the sharing is confined to a limited executive group. There is no real sense of everyone pulling together, no clear evidence of managerially established patterns in the flow of decisions and action. Below the executive suite, motivation and identification with the company are relatively low.

SHARED VALUES: THE UNDERLYING THEORY

Reviewing the shared values of outstanding companies that we know well, we come to a simple, central insight: For those who hold them, shared values define the fundamental character of their organization —the attitude that distinguishes it from all others. In this way, they create a special sense of identity for those in the organization, giving meaning to work as something more than simply earning a living. They are a reality in the minds of most people throughout the company. Sometimes managers refer explicitly to one or another of these values in providing guidance to subordinates. They are embodied in company folklore: new people may be told stories about the company's past that underline the importance of these values to the company. People interpret these values in the context of their own jobs. The values really guide behavior.

As we have already seen, shared values define a company's view of itself in relation to the outside world — notably to customers and competitors. But they do not deal only with an organization's relationship with the outside world. Within an organization, they also govern "the way we do things around here." For example, they indicate what matters are to be attended to most assiduously — current operations in one company, external relations in a second, longer-term strategy in a third. They suggest what kind of information is taken most seriously for decision-making purposes — experienced judgment of "old hands" in one organization, detailed "number-crunching" in another. They define what kind of people are most respected — engineers vs. marketing men vs. financial types. "The way we do things around here" is also part of the distinctive character of an organization.

Other shared values may be less directly linked to the basic concept of the business. For example, some companies are ardently committed to equal opportunity for employment and advancement, while others place little value on it; some seek industry leadership in environmental protection while others consciously defer compliance until the last possible moment. These too are shared values so long as they really do influence behavior in the organization — especially managerial behavior.

Shared values, when strongly held, tend to establish the strategic ground that the company will occupy. This gives a lot of room for initiatives, as IBM, Du Pont, GE, Dana, and others illustrate. But it also sets the bounds of the strategic alternatives that a company is likely to generate, and of those that its people are likely to implement success- fully. Deeply held shared values are hard to change. Hence, although they provide a source of clear common understanding in a business, they also constitute a constraint. When a company with strongly held values finds that it has lost marketplace or economic relevance, it generally has great difficulty adjusting successfully. Witness AT&T's current difficulty in adapting to a newly competitive marketplace.

While shared organizational values have obvious economic impli- cations, they are — significantly — rarely if ever financial in character. As a matter of fact, the paramount shared value (sometimes the super- ordinate goal) in virtually every outstanding organization we have surveyed centers on a key business function such as customer service or product innovation, or an ideal such as "the first Irish multinational," rather than a financially oriented goal, such as growth or profitability. Three explanations suggest themselves. First, it is probably easier for most organizations to identify with qualitative dimensions of excellence than with abstract financial goals. Second, a value that focuses attention on a means to successful performance — e.g., customer service — provides managers with more practical guidance than one concerned only with end results — e.g., a simple dictum to make more money or grow. (There is an intriguing parallel finding from another area: MBO systems focused on completion of a few key actions are apparently more effective than those focused on financials.) Third, it may be that financial goals, being totally abstract, are less effective in capturing the imagination of people throughout the organization.

How do shared values actually help to determine organizational performance? In broad terms, they act as an informal control system that tells people what is expected of them. At Dana Corporation, Rene McPherson actually threw out piles of policy manuals when he became CEO, preferring to rely on the guidance of shared values. More specifically, we hypothesize that shared values affect organizational performance in three main ways:

1. *Managers and others throughout the organization give extraordinary attention to whatever matters are stressed in the corporate value system* — and this in turn tends to produce extraordinary results. An oil company we know produces crude and petroleum products much more efficiently than others because efficient operation is what it values and what its managers concentrate on. One of this company's principal competitors values trading and financial management most highly; accordingly, its managers worry less about production operations and concentrate instead on squeezing every cent of potential revenue from their sales.

2. *Down-the-line managers make marginally better decisions, on average, because they are guided by their perception of the shared values.* When a manager at Dana is confronted by a close question — e.g., making a particular investment in increased productivity versus one in new-product development — he is likely to opt for productivity.

3. *People simply work a little harder because they are dedicated to the cause.* "I'm sorry I'm so late getting home, but the customer had a problem and we never leave a customer with a problem."

THE ROLE OF LEADERSHIP

Shared values are not timeless. They do not come into being spontaneously, and though durable they are not immutable; on the contrary, they are perpetually subject to modification or reinforcement. As unfashionable as it may be to say so, the driving force behind their creation and maintenance, and change, seems to be nothing other than top-management leadership. This is clearest in the case of origins.

Creating and Instilling Values

A strong set of shared values seems always to come initially from a forceful leader who is bent on their establishment. Our model for this conclusion is close to home.

Marvin Bower built McKinsey & Company into the institution it is today. His mark is on virtually everything that we do. As a lawyer, he brought to the Firm the concept of professionalism that became the distinctive stamp of our approach to clients. He articulated most clearly our concept of top-management consulting, and he was the first to document many elements of our problem-solving approaches — approaches that can still be found in Firm training guides. He formalized elements of our style, ranging from nonhierarchical internal structure to standard report formats to our conservative dress code.

It was above all through remarkable persistence that Marvin Bower put his mark on McKinsey. In all his own consulting work, in his relations with his colleagues, and in his community service roles, he reflected the values that he believed should characterize the Firm. Moreover, far from being embarrassed to talk about something as subjective as values, he took every possible opportunity in open meetings and private conversations to relate the values he thought we should share to some current concern within the Firm. During his tenure as Managing Director and since, he has made a point of meeting consultants at all levels in order to communicate his concepts of outstanding problem solving and professional dedication to client interests. He has written hundreds if not thousands of individual memos to individual consultants or teams, praising or criticizing their work — always reinforcing at least one of the Firm's shared values.

Although long retired in a formal sense, Marvin Bower still addresses groups of new associates in our Introductory Training Program. He still catches airplanes to Milwaukee and Cleveland to counsel top managers on problems of transition — and to contribute, by example and instruction, to the continuing professional development of the consultants working with each client. He still writes frequent memos to convey his views. And he still prowls the halls of McKinsey looking for things that are out of whack.

Marvin Bower is to us the living symbol of how value systems are located and instilled. But stories from other companies support the same model. Tom Watson, Jr., is legendary for his commitment to the value system that should characterize IBM. To symbolize his concern with customer service, he continued to answer a number of customer complaints personally as long as he served as CEO. Like stories are told of men such as General Wood at Sears, Roebuck, Alfred J. Sloan at General Motors, Adolph Ochs at *The New York Times* — and, more recently, of J. Willard Marriott, of Bill Hewlett and David Packard, and of Ray Kroc at McDonald's. None of these men was content simply to be a manager. None shrank from articulating the values that he believed should guide his organization and insisting on their rightness in the face of "do your own thing" countertendencies. All, unmistakably, were leaders.

Their success in instilling values, however, appears to have had little to do with charismatic personality. Rather, it derived from obvious, sincere, sustained personal commitment to the values they sought to implant, coupled with extraordinary persistence in reinforcing those values. None of these men relied on personal magnetism. All *made* themselves into effective leaders.

Sustaining and Modifying Values

Given that shared values stem from a leader's initiative, what keeps them fresh and vital in an organization over long periods of time? Certainly one key is continuing, explicit management attention. Here is Tom Watson, Jr., writing to all IBM managers in 1971:

> My associates, without exception, have told me that I should never write to you about business attire or personal appearance because my comments would be subject to misinterpretation and run the risk of appearing arbitrary. But I have noticed a trend recently which, if not corrected, could eventually affect the performance of this corporation in a negative way, and having been around IBM now for 34 years without having had much success with the indirect approach, I am going to tell you candidly about my concern and ask your help in getting us back on the right track. I think that too many of our people are beginning to exceed the bounds of good common sense in their business attire . . . .

What in the world was the CEO of a multibillion-dollar industrial giant up to with such a communication? As Watson himself explained in a different context, he was reinforcing a set of beliefs — everything from "IBM means service" to conservative dress — that had built the company:

> Undoubtedly the principal reason these beliefs have worked well is that they fit together and support one another. If you hire good people and treat them well, they will try to do a good job. They will stimulate one another by their vigor and example. They will set a fast pace for themselves. Then if they understand what the company is trying to do and know they will share in its success, they will contribute in a major way. The customer will get the superior service he is looking for. The result is profit to employees, customers, and shareholders.

In general, the primary stimulus and example for constant reinforcement of values continues to come from the chief executive. People pay attention to what he says, and even more attention to what he does. They read the patterns of business decisions emanating from the executive floor to figure out what *really* counts with top management. When the chief executive's statements and his actions remain consistent with the established values of the company, people remain oriented to those values. When the pattern of his actions begins to diverge from those values, people become confused, their own focus dissolves, and the drive born of the sense of shared values may simply evaporate.

Other senior managers as well, of course, help to reinforce (or weaken) the shared values of the organization through their words and actions. It could be said, in fact, that the mark of a senior-management team, as opposed to a disparate collection of individuals, is coherent support for common values — despite possible differences over policy and practice.

ORGANIZATIONAL SUPPORTS

More than persistent senior-management attention is needed, however, to sustain a strong set of shared values in a large and complex corporation. In addition, the values must be reflected in several other key features of organizational life. Perhaps the most important of these is the process of assimilation or "socialization" of new employees.

Assimilating New Hires

The first 1 or 2 years on the job are crucial for the instilling of value systems in new employees. In *Japan as Number One,* Ezra Vogel[1] reports that Japanese companies take elaborate steps to develop a tightly shared philosophical framework for their new employees:

> They provide elaborate annual ceremonies for inducting the new employees, who enter as a group shortly after the end of the school year. The official training program can be anywhere from a few weeks to years, and includes not only useful background information but emotional accounts of company history and purposes. For spiritual and disciplinary training, the employees may go on retreats, visit temples, or endure special hardship . . . . Companies commonly have their own uniforms, badges, songs, and mottos. Each company has a special lore about the spirit of a "Matsushita person" or a "Sumitomo person."

All of this, Vogel argues, is what enables them later on to give so much autonomy to their working groups at all levels.

Although the ritualistic elements of the Japanese system would be unlikely to go over well in America, U.S. companies with strongly held and tightly focused value systems work almost as hard to manage the early process of socialization. For example, virtually all of General Electric's engineers start out in "trainee" jobs in line functions. There they learn "the way we do things around here" and begin to understand, through exposure to managers up the line, the traits that lead to success in GE. During the early stages of their careers, they also form strong

---

[1] Ezra Vogel, *Japan As Number One: Lessons for America,* Harvard University Press, Cambridge, 1979.

204

peer-group bonds, based on engineering competence, that sustain them and the company in later years. Even the most senior managers continue to socialize with lower-level colleagues in the field with whom they share bonds of mutual respect and friendship dating back to their earliest days in the company.

Other companies use similar approaches to achieve early and thorough assimilation of new managers and technical people. Hewlett-Packard's current CEO, John Young, says, "I don't care if they do come from the Stanford Business School. They've got to get their hands dirty, or we're not interested." (In H-P, that generally means starting in marketing and sales, participating in the introduction of a new product.) These typical first job assignments tell future managers something basic about the shared values of the organization they are joining — and, at the same time, enable them to demonstrate both their own basic competence in a key discipline and their ability to internalize the organization's value system. Without these attributes they are unlikely to last very long. With them, they may in effect be signed on for life. As at GE, the first jobs also help create the peer-group networks that build loyalty — and in so doing — implicitly enforce the company's shared values.

Rewards and Recognition

In outstanding companies, personnel systems typically support the shared values in several ways. Virtually all promotion is from within; this minimizes dilution of the company's value system and enables it to guide communication and behavior throughout the company. Promotions tend to go to those with outstanding achievements of the sorts prized by the company's value system. Fast-track people are often channeled into jobs that make them proselytizers for the value system, and thereby deepen their commitment to it. At IBM, for example, "fast-trackers" become assistants to vice presidents with the sole responsibility of ensuring prompt and full response to customer complaints.

Informal personnel rewards are equally important. It is natural that top managers should more readily lend an ear to people whose behavior is attuned to the corporate value system. These are the people whose accomplishments are most likely to be publicly recognized, and who are most likely to be favored with privileges such as attendance at conventions or personal use of executive facilities. Many companies even structure these informal rewards — providing special titles, on-the-spot bonuses, and various other kinds of recognition. To the outsider such rewards may appear hollow, but those on the inside really aspire to win them.

Company Folklore

People in the organization are consistently trying to interpret why it is the way it is. One of the commonest ways of doing this is by telling stories that capture important aspects of its character.

Everyone in General Electric, for example, knows the story of how Thomas Edison developed the vehicle for simultaneous two-way telegraphic communication. He spent 22 straight nights inventing and testing 23 different duplexes until he found one that worked. Within the GE culture, this story serves to reinforce the understanding that the company's success is based on engineers tinkering away in their laboratories until they finally develop the next useful product. GE has always understood the value of such stories. One of the authors, who grew up in a GE company town, remembers the booklets that the company distributed in order to disseminate the legends of Thomas Edison, Charles Steinmetz, and other great inventors of the company. All of those booklets were about inventors; none was about managers, salesmen, or other kinds of employees. Inventing was what GE was all about: "Progress is our most important product."

In conspicuously value-driven companies, senior management seizes opportunities to create legends that will reinforce shared values. Consider a recent incident in a leading graduate school, where the administration discovered to its embarrassment that a young assistant professor, already under contract, had misrepresented a relevant item in his personal background on applying for the appointment. The administration decided that the offense was too minor to warrant ruining the man's career by a public dismissal, but it would have flown in the face of academic ideals to let it go unpunished. Accordingly, the administration quietly reassigned the young professor from teaching to solo research and banned him from seeing any students for a full academic year. The story spread like wildfire through the academic community, as the administration had intended it should, and bids fair to become legendary. As an example of the conscious creation of value-reinforcing folklore, this is very much in the same vein as the action of Tom Watson of IBM when he fired one of his leading salesmen in that sales-driven company for overselling a customer.

The thesis that folklore makes an important contribution to a company's shared values is supported by recent academic research.[2] A study contrasting two companies found employee commitment higher in the one in which employees could tell a lot of organizational stories.

Structure and Systems

Companies that are guided by strong shared values also tend to reflect these values in the design of their formal organization. The most readily recognizable case is the company oriented to tight control of costs. Generally, its financial vice president and controller will be leading members of the top-management group, and very frequently the divisional controllers will report directly to the corporate controller —

[2]Alan Wilkins, *Organizational Stories as an Expression of Management Philosophy*, unpublished doctoral dissertation, Stanford University, 1978.

rather than to the division head. Almost always, its dominant management systems will be those for budget development and operation control, and even its longer-range planning will be geared to the needs of financial control.

To take a second example, a company with values geared primarily to the external marketplace is likely to have at least one very senior marketing vice president in its top-management structure, and it is likely to rely on some version of product managers or brand managers to handle product marketing. It will surely have rather elaborate systems for gathering and sifting data on customer tastes, response to its products, and initiatives by its competitors.

IMPLICATIONS FOR SENIOR MANAGERS

A fashionable school of thought characterizes decision making and control, rather than leadership, as the essence of the managerial job. Heavily influenced by management science models, this school of thought argues that modern corporations are so enormously complex, and so vulnerable to diverse external and internal forces and pressures that they present only a very limited scope for managerial initiative.

The argument is plausible but our observations fail to support it. By and large, the most successful managers we know are precisely those who strive to make a mark through creating a guiding vision, shaping shared values, and otherwise providing leadership for the people with whom they work. More generally, the companies cited earlier in this article all seem to have dealt more successfully than most with external and internal pressures, precisely because their shared values have provided a sense of common direction.

Risks and Pitfalls

The power of values is that people — at least some people — care about them. This power can be a problem as well as a source of strength. If a manager chooses to build or reinforce the shared values of the group of people he works with, he had better recognize the risks he is assuming:

1. *The risk of obsolescence: What if the environment changes?* One of the most serious risks of a potent system of shared values is that economic circumstances can change while shared values continue to guide behavior in ways no longer helpful to the organization's success. This risk has affected some of the companies we mentioned earlier.

   Consider the case of "The World's Most Experienced Airline." When Pan Am was young and a vast market awaited an introduction to air travel, the airline's slogan and sense of itself served it well. But times have changed. Travelers no longer need persuasion to fly; their only

207

concerns are service and fare. In addition, new competitors — many financed by their governments for reasons of national prestige — have emerged. In this new environment it was only a question of time until Pan Am, still conducting itself as the world's most experienced airline, got into trouble.

Again, consider the Bell System: With a monopoly franchise, a paramount goal of "Universal Service" made sense and worked. (The United States does have the best telephone system in the world, in case you hadn't noticed.) But it also fostered a preoccupation with total system integrity that has inhibited AT&T's ability to identify and meet the needs of particular market segments — a serious limitation now that competitors have been allowed to enter the marketplace. Senior management perceives the threat very clearly and understands what must be done, but the mentality and work practices of down-the-line employees are so strongly tied to the obsolete value system that it will take years for the company to adapt itself fully to the new circumstances.

The consequences of obsolescence are serious enough to give some managers pause in their pursuit of shared values. But they should look at the other side of the coin as well: Would AT&T or Pan Am have been as successful in the past had they lacked such strongly held values? Almost certainly not.

2. *The risk of resistance to change: Barring an environmental upheaval that forces everyone to adapt or perish, can an institution of true believers ever change?* Look at Sears, Roebuck. It faced no fundamental transformation in its environment like that in telecommunications, but its management nonetheless saw an opportunity to become an up-scale merchandiser on the department store model. The market was large and growing rapidly, and margins were undoubtedly fatter.

Yet no sooner had Sears set out on this road than it fell flat on its face. Its army of loyal employees, who had cut their eyeteeth on delivering value to Middle American consumers, simply did not know how to run a Macy's-style operation. As a result, performance lagged and the appealing strategy had to be abandoned.

Sears is by no means an isolated example. In a glamour growth company, one of the authors spent 2 years trying to help the CEO in a determined effort to cut out excessive overhead, in the face of increasingly strong cost competition. Overall, fewer than 1,000 overhead positions were eliminated, and many of those were soon added back. Because of the powerful growth mentality that persisted in the company, cost reduction simply would not fly.

3. *The risk of inconsistency: What if managerial behavior contradicts professed values?* In one company we know, the CEO speaks

frequently and eloquently about the value of serving customers better. But when year-end approaches, he demands financial performance — the customer be hanged. Given the demonstrated primacy of clearly articulated financial objectives, it is no wonder that very few people in the organization buy into the customer service rhetoric.

In a second company, a large bank, top management talks constantly about the need to become more entrepreneurial in response to the changing regulatory and competitive environment. When budget time comes around, however, new ventures are held to the same targets of financial return and cost growth as established divisions. Not surprisingly, evidence of real entrepreneurship is very hard to find.

In order to avoid the risk of contradiction, top management must be convinced that it can adhere faithfully and visibly to the values it intends to promote.

Although there are serious risks in tampering with the shared-value system of an institution, there are also rewards if it is done right. Companies with strong shared values seem universally to be outstanding performers as long as the values are relevant to environmental conditions. Those with the strongest track records, in fact, seem to be just the companies whose operative values are most directly relevant to the performance of key competitive functions. When the environment changes and the objectives of the key functions change, the shared values can get in the way until they are reshaped.

Deciding Priorities

If shared values influence behavior as powerfully as we have asserted, then managers can hardly afford not to be concerned with them. Nowhere do shared values matter more than in the giant corporations that characterize modern economies today. The top managers of these companies are highly dependent upon the the ability of a large number of subordinates to appraise situations correctly and take the actions that will best serve the corporation. There can hardly be a more important job for the top manager than shaping shared values that will guide those down-the-line managers in their day-to-day work.

All the same, it is clear that the task of shaping shared values can't always head the top manager's agenda. When should it get special priority? Our experience suggests at least four situations in which top management should consider the shaping of shared values as something close to its most important mission:

1. *When the environment is undergoing fundamental change, and the company has always been highly value driven.* This is the case of AT&T and Pan Am. In both instances, it is absolutely clear that the traditional values will lead to serious decline, if not disaster. These values must be changed. Xerox is in a similar situation.

209

2. *When the industry is highly competitive.* Why is Digital Equipment so successful as a company? Or Intel? Or McDonald's in another arena? One answer is that they are serving rapidly growing and highly profitable markets. Another is that each has a clear vision of its sustainable competitive advantage. But the analysis does not end there. What each has done, as well, is to convert its corporate vision — basically an intellectual construct that people can understand — into a set of common expectations about everyday behavior that people can feel. The case of Dana demonstrates that a strong and appropriate set of shared values can enable a company to achieve extraordinary success even when the market is neither fast growing nor unusually profitable.

3. *When the company is mediocre, or worse.* Only a few years ago, when Frank Borman took over as chief executive, Eastern Airlines was on the ropes financially and beleaguered by its own discontented employees. Borman threw himself into the task of rebuilding a sense of shared commitment to the company's welfare, linked to an overriding orientation toward customer service. Today, Eastern — like most of the airline industry — is still in a difficult financial position but it has succeeded in stabilizing its performance and is poised for an upswing.

4. *When the company is truly on the threshold of becoming a Fortune 500-scale corporate giant.* Corporate character, we would hypothesize, is forged relatively early; IBM, for example, had total sales of only about $100 million when Tom Watson, Sr., retired from management. The shared values of many of today's leading companies in electronics, consumer services, and retailing likewise seem to have taken shape long before these organizations attained their present size and competitive clout. This is not surprising; strongly held shared values do tend to keep people moving in roughly the same direction even in a company's early days when formal policies and systems have yet to be developed. Later on, however, the process of bureaucratization begins to take hold. At this point the values are often seriously threatened and may require conscious support if they are to survive the transition.

Pursuing a Value-Shaping Program

If a top manager decides to place the value-shaping task high on his list of priorities, how should he pursue it? Today's manager knows how to control operations, how to evaluate a capital investment proposal, how to recruit fresh executive talent, how to deal with regulatory agencies. But what does he do to shape values?

To begin with, he gives it as much attention as he gives any other truly top-priority task, which is to say, a lot. He puts shared values at the center of his agenda and consciousness, not in the "get to it as soon as possible" category. This is not mere exhortation; it is an empirical conclusion from the careers of men like Marvin Bower, the two Tom Watsons, Alfred Sloan, and from our own observation of a large number of other chief executives who have been effective value shapers in industries as diverse as oil, electronics, scientific instruments, engineering services, and government.

Often the first step a top manager takes to shape shared values is to begin talking about them with his closest colleagues. He explores with them the role shared values can play in an excellent company, the state of the company's current values, and the ways in which they need to be reinforced, reinterpreted, or revised. These conversations have two aims: to gain collective commitment to the idea that a strong set of shared values is to be a principal legacy of this particular top team, and to forge a common understanding of the specific values to be pursued.

Soon after taking this first step, value-shaping top managers look for ways to reach down into their organizations to establish the importance of the chosen values. Almost invariably they spend an unusually high proportion of their time "in the field," making contact with as many people as possible in the organization. In addition, many look for relatively structured devices for focusing attention on shared values. For example, the chairman and the president of an engineering service company we know conduct a series of seminars for down-the-line managers — several levels down — on the basics of their business as they see them. They demonstrate the economics underlying the overriding need for cost control — particularly as expressed in high staff utilization and low overhead — and for cultivating continuing business with a relative handful of customers, and describe the implications of these values for everyday management practice and for the tough one-off decisions. Other top managers arrange regular lunches or dinners at which they find occasions to talk with high-potential junior managers about "what made this company great," or "what's going to be distinctive about this company," or create "events" to highlight further the importance of key values. Examples:

- "Kick-off meetings" for managerial programs aimed, perhaps, at serving a new group of customers better, taking excess costs out, or developing more strategically-oriented middle managers.

- Special contests and awards aimed at giving public recognition to those who have done something to serve a key value, and for stimulating others to do likewise.

- Specially appointed ad hoc working groups with responsibility for short-term projects related to key values.

Special management initiatives such as these go a long way toward dramatizing the values that a management team aims at establishing or reinforcing, but they are not enough unless the day-to-day behavior of the value-shaping manager reflects his concern — indeed, very frequently his near obsession — with the importance of key values. People are interested by what a man says he values, but they are only really convinced by what he does. What counts is rarely the single dramatic act (managerial life is seldom like that, nor should it be), but the consistency of pattern of behavior over time.

Down-the-line managers are constantly analyzing the behavior of their superiors, and their peers for that matter, to figure out what they really care about, what they really expect, and what they really will accept. The manager who would shape values turns this reality to his advantage. Particularly in the case of "close calls," when an important value is the "tie-breaker," he consciously explains the decisions that he makes — new hires, investment projects, plan approvals, operating redirections, and all the rest — in terms of their relevance to key values. He develops questioning routines rooted in important values. The questions he asks when a subordinate makes a proposal, gives a presentation, or talks about his work, tell that subordinate — and others listening — what expectations must be met to secure his approval. The value-shaping manager also develops something close to a reward routine; that is, he actively seeks ways to provide frequent and visible praise, or other recognition, for even modest contributions to the service of important values. He seeks to use each contact with another member of the organization — a meeting, a phone call, a chance encounter in the hall, a memorandum in the in-box — to send a message reinforcing a value theme. In fact, he organizes his calendar so that he will be seen to spend a lot of time on matters visibly related to the values he preaches. Even in dealing with outsiders he neglects no opportunity to reinforce the theme. What is said to customers, to investors, or to journalists can often have a powerful impact on people inside the organization. It provides further evidence that management's commitment to the shared values is "for real."

All this is to say that top managers who would shape values must consistently and continuously regard themselves not only as deciders, controllers, or doers, but also as symbolic leaders, sending signals by their behavior. This view of the manager's job flies in the face of much current management mythology, but it is consistent with the realities we have observed: the reality of followers who continuously scrutinize and interpret top-management behavior, and the reality of successful value-shaping leaders.

At first, the senior manager who lays no claim to personal charisma may be unsettled by the suggestions that he should manage his symbolic behavior so as to reinforce important values. On reflection, however, he should be encouraged by the message that mere mortals can be value-shaping leaders. Charisma has little to do with it; it may even be a long-run liability if the source of strength is in the leader's personality rather than the values he espouses. Attention, commitment, persistence, and perhaps a measure of risk taking are required — but no magic.

Even if the reader accepts our theses that shared values are powerful influencers of organizational performance, and that determined manager-leaders can shape and reinforce them in important ways, one reservation may remain. Our society today suffers from a pervasive uncertainty about values, a relativism that undermines leadership and commitment alike. Who today really does know what is right? On the philosophical level, we find ourselves without convincing responses. But the everyday business world is quite different. Even if ultimate values are chimerical, particular values do clearly make sense for specific organizations operating in specific circumstances. Choices must be made, and values are an indispensable guide in making them. Moreover, it is equally clear that actual organizations have, in fact, gained great strength from shared values — with emphasis on the "shared." Perhaps because ultimate values seem so elusive, people do respond positively to practical values that give life in the organization some sense of meaning. And that considerably eases the task of value-shaping managers as they strive to "make meaning" for the employees and the organization. Instead of encountering resistance, they can usually expect to meet with respect and support as contributors in some distinctive way to the larger society.

GREAT COMPANIES MAKE MEANING

Richard Tanner Pascale
Anthony G. Athos

In management, as in music, there is a base clef as well as a treble. The treble generally carries the melody in music, and melody's equivalent in management is the manager's style. A manager's style—the way he focuses his attention and interacts with people—sets the "tune" for his subordinates and communicates at the *operational* level what his expectations are and how he wants business conducted. Beneath these messages is a deeper rhythm that communicates more fundamentally. The bass in music—whether hard rock or a classical symphony—often contains much of what moves the listener. So, too, the "bass" of management conveys meanings at a deeper level and communicates what management *really* cares about. These messages can influence an organization profoundly. In Japanese organizations, a great deal of managerial attention is devoted to ensuring the continuity and consistency of these "bass clef" messages.

In our book, *The Art of Japanese Management*, we have variously referred to these "bass" clef messages as an organization's "significant meanings," "shared values," and "spiritual fabric." For clarity, we will adopt one all inclusive term to describe these characterizations: *superordinate goals*—the goals above all others.[1] Superordinate goals provide the glue that holds an organization's strategy, structure, systems, style, staff, and skills together. When all are fitted together, organizations tend to become more internally unified and self-sustaining over time.

Superordinate goals play a pragmatic role by influencing implementation at the operational level. Because an executive cannot be everywhere at once, many decisions are made without his knowledge. What superordinate goals do, in effect, is provide employees with a "compass" and point their footsteps in the right direction.[2] For example, at IBM that translates into never sacrificing customer service; at Matsushita it means never cheating a customer by knowingly producing or selling defective merchandise. These values permit the CEOs to influence the actions of their employees, to help the employees make correct independent

---

[1] There is a substantial literature on organizational values (superordinate goals). See Henry Mintzberg, *The Nature of Managerial Work* (New York: Harper & Row, 1973), p. 73; Michel Crozier, *The Bureaucratic Phenomenon* (Chicago: University of Chicago Press, 1964), pp. 180f.; Thomas J. Peters, "The Case for Getting Things Done," unpublished paper, May 5, 1976, pp. 16-21; Phillip Selznik, *TVA and the Grass Roots* (Berkeley: University of California Press, 1949).

[2] This imagery was proposed by Allan Kennedy, partner, McKinsey & Company, Evian, France, March 20, 1980.

decisions. These value systems act as "tie breakers" in close cases, those in which decisions otherwise might be made the wrong way.[3]

Year after year, decade after decade, Delta Air Lines has been the most consistent money-maker in the airline industry. Undoubtedly, its route structure, concentrated in the fast-growing South, has contributed to its success. But route structure alone cannot explain Delta's performance—for neither United Airlines (with its dominant position in America's busiest air terminal, Chicago) nor American Airlines (with the lion's share of the market in fast-growing Dallas/Fort Worth) has been able to match Delta's performance over the long term.

Delta considers its key to success in the highly competitive and largely undifferentiated airline industry to be *service*. Delta considers service to be the direct result of a motivated and friendly work force. Delta's approach, which includes virtually open-door access for all of its 36,500 employees, has enabled the airline to maintain its esprit de corps and remain non-union in an industry plagued by labor-management strife. Delta's management *style* and strongly reinforced *superordinate goals* are largely responsible for this achievement.[4]

At the heart of Delta's philosophy is "the Delta family feeling." More than a slogan, it is what makes Delta different. This "family" emphasis was introduced and nurtured by the airline's founder and has been carefully institutionalized. "It's just a feeling of caring within the company," says Delta's current chairman, W. Thomas Beebe.[5]

It's difficult to find workers with serious complaints at Delta. The firm promotes from within, pays better than most airlines and rarely lays off workers. These policies are what makes the "family feeling" real. When other airlines were slashing employment during the 1973 oil embargo, Mr. Beebe told senior management: "Now the time has come for the stockholders to pay a little penalty for keeping the team together."[6] Notice how the superordinate goal of preserving the "family feeling" took precedence over near-term profits and return on investment.

Like Matsushita, Delta pays attention to the socialization of new employees. It makes sure employees embrace the "family" concept by emphasizing it in training programs and at meetings. It also carefully screens job applicants. Stewardess candidates, for example, are culled from thousands of applicants, interviewed twice and then sent to Delta's psychologist, Dr. Sidney Janus. "I try to determine their sense of cooperativeness or sense of teamwork," he says. At Delta, "you don't just join a company, you join an objective."[7]

[3]Ibid.

[4]Janet Guyon, "Family Feeling at Delta Creates Loyal Workers, Enmity of Unions," *Wall Street Journal*, Monday, July 17, 1980, p. 13.

[5]Ibid., p. 13.

[6]Ibid., p. 13.

[7]Ibid., p. 13.

The Delta example sheds light on several features of effective superordinate goals. First, they need to tie into higher-order human values. Second, they need to be consistent with the other six S's, especially the firm's *style* and *staffing* and *systems* practices. Third, management needs to be meticulous in respecting these values (even if it means sacrificing short-term profits) or they will be seen as empty slogans.

KINDS OF SUPERORDINATE GOALS

Effective superordinate goals should be (1) significant, (2) durable, and (3) achievable. Most tend to fall into one or more of the following categories:

1. *The company as an entity:*
   Here the whole organization is reinforced as an entity one lives within and should identify with and belong to, and which is deserving of admiration and approval from employees and society (e.g., Delta's belief in the "family feeling").

2. *The company's external markets:*
   Here the emphasis is on the value of the company's products or services to humanity, and on those factors important in maintaining this value—that is, quality, delivery, service, and customers' needs (e.g., Matsushita's belief in advancing the standard of living in Japan by distributing reliable and affordable electrical products).

3. *The company's internal operations:*
   Here attention is focused on such things as efficiency, cost, productivity, inventiveness, problem solving, and customer attention (e.g., Delta's emphasis on "service" and Matsushita's dedication to first-class production engineering).

4. *The company's employees:*
   Here attention is paid to the needs of groups of people in reference to their productive function, and to individual employees as valued human beings in a larger context—that is, human resource systems, growth and development, opportunity and rewards, individual attention and exceptions (e.g., Matsushita's commitment to developing employees not only for the firm's benefit but to contribute to each employee's personal growth over a lifetime).

5. *The company's relation to society and the state:*
   Here the values, expectations, and legal requirements of the surrounding larger community are explicitly honored, such as beliefs in competition, meritocracy, the necessity of obeying the law, or being sensitive to other nations' customs (e.g., Matsushita sees itself as a major contributor in restoring Japanese status and prestige).

6. *The company's relation to culture (including religion):*
   Here the underlying beliefs about "the good" in the culture are honored—beliefs in our own case largely derived from Judeo-Christian tradition, and including such things as honesty, and fairness (e.g., the strong influence of religion in shaping the Matsushita philosophy—which reinforces many Confucian and Buddhist values including harmony, solidarity, discipline, and dedication).

IBM, THEN AND NOW

IBM has for many years been one of our most successful and effective U.S. corporations. It is known for its remarkable development of strategy, structure, systems, style, skill, and staff, and the fit among them, *and* for its equally advanced development of superordinate goals.

In a 1940 *Fortune* article describing the company and its president (Thomas John Watson), the author's imagery is initially surprising. For example, he describes the young Mr. Watson as having the appearance and behavior of a "somewhat puzzled divinity student" who "began to confect the aphoristic rules of thumb that have since guided his life and policies. 'Ever onward,' he told himself. 'Aim high and think in big figures; serve and sell; he who stops being better stops being good.' . . . Mr. Watson caused the work THINK to be hung all over the factory and offices . . . . Generally it is framed, sometimes graven on pediments in imperishable granite or marble, again embossed in brass, yet again lettered in gold on a purple banner, but always and everywhere it is there . . . . Whether you particularly agree with [what Mr. Watson is saying] you listen . . . . Mr. Watson's monumental simplicity compels you to do so . . . . Let him discourse on the manifest destiny of I.B.M., and you are ready to join the company for life. Let him retail plain homilies on the value of Vision, and a complex and terrifying world becomes transparent and simple. Let him expound the necessity for giving religion the preference over everything else, and you *could not help falling to your knees* . . . . Everybody in the organization is expected to find the ubiquitous THINK sign a constant source of inspiration, as the weary travelers of old found new strength in the wayside crucifixes."[8]

That the author found such images useful to *his* purpose does not necessarily mean, of course, that such images captured an important truth about the company. They could have been useful mostly in capturing the writer's *reaction* to IBM and Mr. Watson. But three senior executives quoted in the article add weight to the "religious" impression. One said: "Mr. Watson has spread his benign influence over the earth, and everywhere it has touched, people have gained, mentally and morally,

[8]Gil Burck, "International Business Machines," *Fortune*, January 1940, pp. 36-40.

materially and spiritually."[9] Another remarked:"I think that we do not always count our blessings. Every so often we should all of us stop and think of the many things that have been done for each member of this organization."[10] A third echoes a similar theme: "Mr. Watson gave me something I lacked—the vision and the foresight to carry on in this business, which from that day forward I have never had any thought of leaving."[11]

There is an implied reference to cultural values of gratitude, faith, and commitment. There is repeated reference to the beneficial impact of Mr. Watson on *individuals*. The tone is evangelical. In the 1930s, society's acceptance of various absolutes was not yet much undermined by existential beliefs and moral relativism, and there was still widespread acceptance of the use in business of explicit, usually Christian, religious metaphors.

It was then not uncommon, and even recently not unheard of, for secular enterprises to express their organizational fervor in fundamentalist religious ways. The development of "creeds" which employees were expected to hold, of "cults" of membership differentiating employees from outsiders and identifying them with insiders, and of "codes" of behavior that reduced uncertainty and prescribed right action and attitudes was an important part of the early years of some companies. The use of company songs, dress codes, sales meetings that Elmer Gantry might have staged, ubiquitous displays of "the leader" in photographs, oils, and bronze statues, slogans presented in expensive and long-lasting materials, an often-referred-to book of the leader's speeches and essays (Mr. Watson's was *Men, Minutes, and Money*), and a house organ to reinforce values and educate were all part of early IBM. The rah-rah sales orientation of that time reminds us of the zealous proselytizing of some churches, and the ways of reinforcing the developing creeds, cults, and codes also seem similar. (It is not accidental, we think, that pushing a new product line is often referred to as "missionary work" by businessmen.)

But Mr. Watson's role certainly was not confined to devising those methods. He also created superordinate goals based on the beliefs of his society. The average person's belief in the Horatio Alger story, and in the dream of "getting ahead," probably accounted for the following remark from the same article:

There is a careful selection of all employees, whether for the factory or the sales department. Mr. Watson never hires an office boy, but always a potential leader, or at any rate a potential assistant. Everyone addresses every man as "Mr." The company publications never refer to any man without prefixing a "Mr." to his name.[12]

[9]Ibid., p. 43.

[10]Ibid., p. 43.

[11]Ibid., p. 43.

[12]Ibid., p. 40.

That attention to selecting employees, the respect expressed by the prefix "Mr.," the numerous employee programs, as well as efforts to assist employees in growth and development, indicate that Mr. Watson was aware of the power of honoring within his organization the values and beliefs of the surrounding society.

In addition, Mr. Watson attended to the developing conflict in Europe by having PEACE join THINK all over the company; he also commissioned a symphony on an important company occasion to express the longing for international cooperation, and gave and reprinted speeches on that theme. IBM was aligned with the *world* situation in employees' minds. (War was dangerous to mankind, as it was to IBM's developing international business.)[13]

The article includes far more than attention to what we call superordinate goals. It includes fascinating and detailed descriptions of all the Seven S's. But for our purposes here, it is interesting to note how the great corporation IBM has become is related in part to conscious attention over time to superordinate goals as well as the other elements.

In the years since 1940, IBM's expression of its beliefs, and its ways of honoring them, has become what seems fair to call "more sophisticated." The approach is much more analogous to the best functioning of some of our established formal religions. There is less obvious conformity required, more subtlety in technique, more complexity acknowledged in goals, and thus more skill required to behave "well." Yet the more recent statements of IBM's superordinate goals, the basic beliefs reinforced within the present firm, can be seen as having evolved from the first Mr. Watson's original efforts. And that IBM has been at it so long gives the present beliefs the enormous advantage of a successful and shared history. A recent statement of IBM's basic beliefs is as follows:[14]

Basic Beliefs

A sense of accomplishment and pride in our work often go hand in hand with a basic understanding of what we're all about, both as individuals and as a company. IBM is fortunate to have a timeless statement of its purpose—in its basic beliefs.

The underlying meaning of these beliefs was best expressed by Tom Watson, Jr., in his McKinsey Foundation Lectures at Columbia University in New York in 1962, when he said:[15]

I firmly believe that any organization, in order to survive and achieve success, must have a sound set of beliefs on which it premises all its policies and actions.

---

[13]Ibid., pp. 40, 43.

[14]"IBM's Basic Beliefs," *IBM Orientation Booklet*, updated, p. 11.

[15]Thomas Watson, Jr., "A Business and Its Beliefs," *McKinsey Foundation Lecture* (New York: McGraw-Hill, 1963).

Next, I believe that the most important factor in corporate success is faithful adherence to those beliefs.

And finally, I believe that if an organization is to meet the challenges of a changing world, it must be prepared to change everything about itself except those beliefs as it moves through corporate life.

In other words, the basic philosophy, spirit, and drive of an organization have far more to do with its relative achievements than do technological or economic resources, organizational structure, innovation, and timing. All these things weigh heavily in success. But they are, I think, transcended by how strongly the people in the organization believe in its basic precepts and how faithfully they carry them out.

What is this set of beliefs Watson was talking about? There are three:

- Respect for the individual. Respect for the dignity and the rights of each person in the organization.

- Customer service. To give the best customer service of any company in the world.

- Excellence. The conviction that an organization should pursue all tasks with the objective of accomplishing them in a superior way.

In addition to these basic beliefs, there is a set of fundamental principles which guide IBM management in the conduct of the business. They are:

- To give intelligent, responsible, and capable direction to the business.

- To serve our customers as efficiently and as effectively as we can.

- To advance our technology, improve our products, and develop new ones.

- To enlarge the capabilities of our people through job development and give them the opportunity to find satisfaction in their tasks.

- To provide equal opportunity to all our people.

- To recognize our obligation to stockholders by providing adequate return on their investment.

- To do our part in furthering the well-being of those communities in which our facilities are located.

- To accept our responsibilities as a corporate citizen of the U.S. and in all the countries in which we operate throughout the world.

Note that Mr. Watson, Jr., says he believes that a corporation's survival and success are dependent upon beliefs, sound beliefs, from which it acts, and to which it is faithful. He says everything else may change, but not the beliefs. They remain "absolutes." Given that last

221

observation, the basic beliefs are naturally stated at high levels of abstraction, and in "high-minded" language. Respect for the dignity and rights of the individual; the best customer service in the world; accomplishing tasks in a superior way. The individual, the customer, the *ways* of working. At least the first and third are not likely ever to require altering, although the ways they are applied may well change.

Notice, too, the statements of fundamental principles, expressed at lower levels of abstraction, and in somewhat less high-minded language. They refer to:

management competence

customer service

technical progress

employee opportunity development

stockholders' return

community well-being

national and international responsibilities

It will be clear immediately that, over time, the tradeoffs and balance will require a lot of managerial skill applied constantly in order to confirm these principles and their modes of application in the minds of thousands of people. If one assumes, as we do, that IBM really works at living up to its basic beliefs and principles, and if one assumes, as we do, that such effort has a powerful effect on the company's success, then it becomes possible to set aside the skepticism often reserved for high-minded pronouncements of top executives. If it is *not* just fluff, then it is a powerful and positive force indeed. One signal that IBM has been practicing what it preaches is the criticism it has received in the past related to employee "commitment and conformity." Those white-shirted, polite, competent, hard-working employees of twenty years ago were often regarded as corporate "fanatics," or even corporate "fascists," because they appeared not to display in superficial ways their "American individuality." White shirts were mistaken for laundered minds. The shirts are now colored, but it appears that their wearers are still politely service oriented, highly competent, and hard working (everything may change but the beliefs). And in our culture, any evidence of a reduction in obvious "individuality," which naturally accompanies increases in organizational commitment, will produce criticism from those who *overvalue* individuality. We have a suspicion that IBM executives in the early 1960s recognized the criticism for what it was, and smiled politely on their way to the bank. In any event, it seems to us that IBM has long attended explicitly to its superordinate goals, and that they have played an important part in its being a remarkably successful, self-renewing, profitable company with a very strong internal culture.

Mr. Matsushita may have been quick to grasp the value of strategy, structure, and systems, but the Watsons were not naive about the "soft"

S's and "the arts of Japanese management." (In the 1930s, Mr. Watson, Sr., visited Mr. Matsushita in Japan and presumably was influenced by what he saw there.) In the forties, IBM was functioning very much like Matsushita. From company songs to employee recreation, from careful selection and indoctrination to employee "uniforms," from pictures of the CEO everywhere to slogans, the two companies seemed more alike than different. Each has continued to fashion its internal culture to reflect changes in the society outside, but both still pay a lot of attention to articulating and honoring superordinate goals.

SUPERORDINATE GOALS AND CHANGING EMPLOYEE VALUES

As noted, superordinate goals tie the purposes of the firm (e.g., goods, services, profits) to human values. We believe that this linkage to human values is growing in importance. The vast majority of Americans who work today do not view their jobs as "the only alternative." Fifteen percent of all people who work are in skilled blue-collar occupations; 45 percent are white collar. Sixty percent are employed by firms with over 1,000 employees, and 47 percent work for organizations with over 10,000 employees.[16] What these statistics tell us is that most people who work today are highly skilled and/or white collar, and employed in relatively large institutions. In these kinds of environments, all sorts of factors cushion employees against the occupational hazards that plagued those employed only three or four decades ago. First, the job market itself, while never as hungry as we might wish, offers backup employment opportunities for most people with qualifications who wish to work. In addition, there are financial cushions of various kinds—unemployment insurance, a spouse's income, the opportunity to moonlight, and the capacity to save enough over a period of time to handle a transition between jobs.

These factors have moved us a long way from the circumstances that shaped employment attitudes in the nineteenth and the first half of the twentieth century. The implications of these changes are profound. The majority of people who work don't have to for economic *survival* in the short term. Increasingly, they seek, *in addition* to pay and career opportunities, other kinds of income from their jobs, including work they enjoy, colleagues they like working with, and *meaning*. Far too many generalizations are made about work on the basis of the automobile assembly-line stereotype. For the vast majority, work is a far different and far more fulfilling experience. For people in these new circumstances to be satisfied, it helps enormously if they can see the link between what they do and a higher purpose.

When the linkage between human values and a firm's objectives is unclear, employees often seek to create meanings of their own which

[16]Rosabeth Moss Kanter, *Men and Women of the Corporation* (New York: Basic Books, 1977), pp. 15-16.

reconcile what they do on the job to higher purposes. Curiously, we may have seen some evidence of this at ITT.

Geneen inculcated in his organization a belief in the importance of "unshakeable facts" in the service of "bottom-line results." These narrowly envisioned meanings were reinforced constantly and few managers failed to internalize them. Yet there are indications that some of Geneen's executives were unwilling to view their endeavors exclusively in terms of such bottom-line results. Their comments suggest that they created larger meanings. They told us they took pride in being a part of such a demanding, fast-moving, successful company, that they saw themselves as stimulated, accomplished, fast-track executives, a kind of corporate pro ball team. In short, they created a *larger meaning* to give value and dignity to their work lives. They were the outstanding, hard-ball pros in an economic game, no quarter given or taken. Tough, lean, mean. A winning-is-the-only-thing, best-of-their-kind elite.

Like ITT, many Western organizations pride themselves on having made a virtue of bottom-line results and other similar measures of "efficiency." If anything, the emphasis has intensified in recent years as companies have sought to produce profits during a period of slowed growth and world economic uncertainty. The problem with efficiency is that it is a little like white bread and refined sugar: Taken in isolation, it becomes bland and vaguely unhealthful—all the life-supporting nutrients seem to get refined out. Obviously, organizations need to be somewhat efficient in order to accomplish their tasks. But the problem is that people can end up performing instrumental functions as if they were truly interchangeable parts in a great machine.

SUPERORDINATE GOALS FOCUSING ON EMPLOYEES

In *The Art of Japanese Management* we listed six kinds of superordinate goals. One category, of particular interest, focuses on the firm's relations with its employees. Generally speaking, people want to identify with their organization; they want to trust and depend on those they work with and invest through their labor in the organization's success. But, as we have seen, the tendency of Western organizations to deal at arm's length, to neglect coaching and mentoring of subordinates, to abruptly transfer (rather than carefully *transplant*) people from one job to the next, to reorganize by decree and provide brutally direct feedback without regard for the grace and pace necessary for successful change—all these things teach employees to be wary. Most American executives think only in macroterms about "morale." They do indeed worry about massive layoffs, or gross inequities in pay or major contradictions in policy. Many far more subtle things are equally important and commonly neglected.

Employment involves a psychological contract as well as a contract involving the exchange of labor for capital. In many Western organizations, that psychological contract, while never explicit, often assumes little trust by either party in the other. If the only basis for the relation of company and employee is an instrumental one, it should not be surprising that many people in our organizations do what they must do to get their paycheck but little more. While there can be all kinds of superordinate goals, those that concern themselves with the development and well-being of employees can play a particularly important role in establishing the moral context for this psychological contract. If such superordinate values are consistently honored (as we saw at Delta during the 1973 oil embargo), then employees tend to identify more fully with the company. They see the firm's interest and their own as more congruent and tend to invest themselves more fully in the organization—including looking for ways to improve how they do their job.

Most consultants will confirm that they have been called in to solve a client's problem only to discover in the course of conducting interviews that someone in the client organization already had the solution. But because communication channels were blocked, or, more often, because the individual with the good idea was "turned off" and convinced that the organization wouldn't listen, no initiative was taken. The potential initiator hesitated to invest himself, in the last analysis because trying is linked to caring and history had taught him that the firm was not worth caring that much about.

Without a doubt, the most significant outcome of the way Japanese organizations manage themselves is that to a far greater extent than in the United States they get everyone in the organization to be alert, to look for opportunities to do things better, and to strive by virtue of each small contribution to make the company succeed. It is like building a pyramid or watching a colony of ants: thousands of "little people" doing "little" things, *all with the same basic purpose*, can move mountains.

A recent study of product innovation in the scientific instruments and tool machinery industries indicates that 80 percent of all product innovations are initiated by the customer.[17] The majority of ideas doesn't flow from R&D labs down but from the customer up. To be sure, customers don't do the actual inventing, but their inquiries and complaints plant the seeds for improvements. Given these statistics, it matters a lot whether a company's sales force and others operating out at the tentacles of its field system are vigilant. They need to be open to new ideas *and* willing to initiate within their organization. Here is a key to success of many Japanese companies. We saw this at Matsushita, where they rarely originated it but had an unerring ability to do it better. This formula is not inconsistent with most of the major corporate success stories in the United States. Careful scrutiny reveals that despite the exalted status of "strategy" in the lexicon of American management, few great successes stem from one bold-stroke strategic thrust. More often,

[17]Eric von Hippel, "Users as Innovators," *Technology Review,* January 1978, pp. 31-39.

225

they result from one half-good idea that is improved upon incrementally. These improvements are invariably the result of a lot of "little people" paying attention to the product, the customer, and the marketplace.

To be sure, the case for superordinate goals can be overstated. Innovative firms tend to have a *style* of management that is open to new ideas, ways of handling *staff* that encourage innovation, *systems* that are customer focused and which reward innovation, *skills* at translating ideas into action and so forth. But the ideas don't flow unless the employee *believes* in the corporation and identifies enough with its purposes to "give up" his good ideas. Further, any of us who work in organizations knows how hard they are to move. One has to really believe an organization *cares* in order to invest the energy and effort needed to help it change. Such commitment derives from superordinate goals. And if we look at outstanding American firms that have a sustained track record of innovation, we see this to be the case. Texas Instruments, Procter & Gamble, 3M, and IBM, for example, all pay close attention to the customer and each has a highly developed value system that causes its employees to identify strongly with the firm.[18] Perhaps the intense loyalty that these firms inspire is just an interesting idiosyncrasy. But we believe, on the contrary, that this bond of shared values is fundamental to all of the rest. In our view, this is probably the most underpublicized "secret weapon" of great companies.

As we noted with Matsushita, Japanese firms, despite their evident success in adopting Western technology and their skill at devising aggressive strategies, innovative organizational structure and comprehensive systems, have not followed the West in deemphasizing the "soft" S's. They do not trade off human relationships for impersonal efficiency. Almost all of the American employees of the twelve Japanese subsidiaries in the United States whom we interviewed in this study remarked on the personal concern of these companies toward employees.[19] This concern was manifested in two ways. First, invariably, the Japanese firms made a big deal about "meaning." Whether Toyota, Sony, or YKK (a manufacturer of zippers), the senior managers stressed the importance of developing their employees and the contribution of their product to society as a whole. These were not just "ad slogan" values, but something that management deeply believed in.

We call attention to the Japanese companies' commitment to people. One Japanese manager said, "Anyone who works for a company seeks approval for what he does and acceptance for who he is." "Almost all firms give approval through the normal reward system, but providing acceptance of each individual as a unique person requires a lot more effort."

[18]See, for example, John A. Prestbo, "At Procter and Gamble Success Is Largely Due to Heeding Customers," *Wall Street Journal*, April 29, 1980, p. 1.

[19]Richard T. Pascale, "Personnel Practices and Employee Attitudes: A Study of Japanese and American Managed Firms in the United States," *Human Relations*, Vol. 31, No. 7 (1978), pp. 597-615.

Japanese firms in the United States institutionalized "acceptance" in two ways. One was by increasing the contact between boss and subordinate. Even on the shop floor, Japanese firms fostered twice as much contact between workers and their foremen as was usual elsewhere. (Fifteen employees reported to each first-line supervisor as compared to a 30:1 ratio at American firms.)[20] One manager said, "If you're striving to give employees a sense of being recognized for their unique contributions, you have to have enough supervisors to listen." Supervisors at Japanese-managed firms more frequently worked alongside their subordinates, were more extensively engaged in personal counseling, and permitted more interaction among workers than those of the American companies did. In an effort to express their commitment to people, the Japanese subsidiaries also spent an average of nearly three times as much per employee on social and recreational programs as did their American control companies ($58.49/employee/year vs. $20.79 for American companies).[21] All of these programs were presumably symbolic; but that's not all they were. Employees often commented that the programs also fostered increased off-the-job contact among employees, had the effect of personalizing the firm, and reinforced the superordinate goal that "people mattered."

WESTERN HISTORY AND SUPERORDINATE GOALS

By an accident of history, we in the West have evolved a culture that separates man's spiritual life from his institutional life. This turn of events has had a far-reaching impact on modern Western organizations. Our companies freely lay claim to mind and muscle, but they are culturally discouraged from intruding upon our personal lives and deeper beliefs.

The dilemma for modern Western organizations is that, like it or not, they play a very central role in the lives of many who work for them. Employees in all ranks of the hierarchy not only "work" at their jobs, but (1) derive much of their daily social contact there, and (2) often locate themselves in social relations outside the firm through their association with their company and occupation. (One of the first questions we are asked when we meet a person for the first time is: "What do you do for a living?") Splitting man into separate "personal" and "productive" beings makes somewhat artificial parts of what is the whole of his character. When we do so, our cultural heritage not only too strictly enforces this artificial dichotomization, but deprives us of two rather important ingredients for building employee commitment. First, companies are denied access to higher-order human values, which are among the best known mechanisms for reconciling one's working life with one's inner

[20]Ibid., p. 604.
[21]Ibid., p. 609.

life. Second, the firm itself is denied a meaning-making role in society, and thus pays excessive attention to instrumental values, such as profit, market share, and technological innovation.

If we trace the history of goal setting in U.S. organizations, we find that over the past twenty years management's understanding of goals has greatly expanded—from mere monetary goals (e.g., profit and return on investment) to stockholder and constituency goals (such as environmental objectives and minority hiring). The trend has been toward expanding the notion of corporate purpose. Nevertheless, recognition of an organization's role in serving higher-order human values still awaits full-scale acceptance.

We recognize that some readers will resist the specter of a merger between "the Church and the corporation." But that is not what we are proposing. There is an important difference between religiosity and spiritualism. In the West, because of the Church's monopoly on the spiritual side of man, all spiritualism was religious. That is not so in Japan, and it need not be so in the West.

There are no strong imperatives in Japan for an individual to choose among religious beliefs. People there commonly have several religions—believing in Confucianism, Buddhism, and Shintoism simultaneously. Likewise, Japanese firms can take a general spiritual position without seeming insincere or superficial. Such firms are able to work with each employee to help him flow with the ups and downs of a career and to find deeper meanings in his own development. In the West, many managers feel both the employee and the organization are culturally conditioned to an arm's-length relationship. This causes the firm to let the employee fend for himself in adversity and draw upon the problematic spiritual resources available to him from friends, family, and religious affiliations.

What is needed in the West is a nondeified, nonreligious "spiritualism" that enables a firm's superordinate goals to respond truly to the inner meanings that many people seek in their work—or, alternatively, seek in their lives and could find at work if only that were more culturally acceptable.

Western institutions are, in fact, backing into this role. Two forces are at work: employees seeking more meaning from their jobs and demanding more concern from the corporation, and legislative pressures enforcing a broad range of personal services, including employee rights to counseling. In response to these forces, most major firms now describe these activities as "Human Resource Management" instead of "Personnel"—it is to be hoped, the first step in adopting a larger perspective. Most larger firms also provide assistance to employees dealing with chronic personal problems, such as divorce, alcoholism, and stress. And, as noted earlier, some of our most outstanding companies have long acknowledged a larger role in the lives of their employees and foster greater interdependence among them. All are remarkably "Japanese" when we look at them closely. Their success may have important implications for Western organizations of the future.

SUPERORDINATE GOALS AND DIVERSIFICATION

One problem inherent in diversification is that it becomes more and more difficult to establish *one* set of superordinate goals that provides useful guidance within a particular industry, yet is general enough to be relevant across many industries. Conglomerates, in particular, face this dilemma. Most tend to conclude that it is unnecessary or impossible to fashion unifying meanings for multiproduct, multimarket portfolios. Their method of growth through acquisition tends to encourage this. They acquire successful companies and are dedicated to making them even more successful. But they often overlook the fact that a conglomerate's meanings (which are almost always largely limited to the impersonal and financial) undermine the older meanings that gave the acquired firm its former sense of purpose. Most conglomerates stress their desire to be supportive, to avoid interfering. But the absence of positive new meanings, or, at least, the impetus for continually reinterpreting existing meanings, inevitably results in atrophy and empty slogans. Subtly, the new financial control system, the corporate emphasis on profit, or ROI, visits by the controllers, and messages conveyed at quarterly review meetings erode the earlier "faith." Is it any wonder that vibrancy and sense of commitment frequently disappear from subsidiaries within a year or two after they are acquired? One thinks of the change at Avis. Once a spirited company that was "Trying Harder," Avis today seems just another enterprise. The meanings lost through acquisition are rarely offset by gains through superior resources and more "scientific" management.

TRADEOFFS

In any particular situation requiring a decision, it is entirely possible that an executive may have to choose to affirm one superordinate goal rather than others. Let's say a firm has effectively developed goals which include "service," as well as one related to the "professional development" of managers. If an important customer's need for delivery requires a particular manager to stay on the job when he has been scheduled for a lengthy outside executive program—to which he has been unable to go twice previously—a choice may have to be made between goals. In any particular situation, it may not be possible to honor all the important superordinate goals simultaneously. They may have to be met sequentially. There are days when we need to sin bravely and make tradeoffs between one goal and the other. A "separate and related" way of thinking about superordinate goals enables us to "fire (or transfer) an employee on Thursday" in order to attain higher levels of service, successive phases in a dynamic cycle. The issue is the *balance over time* of such decisions. If delivery-installation *always* comes first, even when a specific situation may not support such primacy, then people will come to see the goals related to managerial development as mostly noise.

It seems true that top executives measure, or try to monitor, what they care about. No measurement equals no real caring in most companies, and most managers know that early in their careers. In short, effectively honoring superordinate goals requires not only managerial skill and appropriate system development but also CEO reinforcement through style. Too little skill, or inappropriate systems, or CEO indifference, leads rapidly to cynicism. And cynicism is the enemy of the trusting commitment most CEOs sincerely want from their employees. The moral: Don't claim you care about it unless you are prepared to act accordingly, for you don't get goodwill from subordinates by promising what you do not deliver, anymore than they do from you.

STRATEGIC ERAS AND SUPERORDINATE GOALS

An organization's superordinate goals emerge, in part, from leadership which instills values through clarity and obsessive focus. A firm's history also contributes to its enduring value system. Organizations tend to grow through stages, face and surmount crises, and along the way learn lessons and draw morals that shape values and future actions. Usually these developments influence assumptions and the way people behave. Often key episodes are recounted in "war stories" that convey lessons about the firm's origins and transformations in dramatic form.[22] Eventually, this lore provides a consistent background for action. New members are exposed to the common history and acquire insight into some of the subtle aspects of their company. Matsushita made a considerable effort to pass on his company's legacy to each new recruit.

Superordinate goals are immensely helpful at the beginning of a strategic era.[23] Setting out to build a fast-food empire, not only did McDonald's stress price, quality, profit, and market share, but they believed they were performing a real service to Americans living on limited means. This "social mission" gave a larger meaning to operational objectives. The cooks and order takers in McDonald's franchises found higher-order goals helpful in accepting the company's rigorous quality control system. Strict standards could be met more readily when seen in the context of "helping society." As one manager put it, "the lower down you go in an organization, the more difficult it is for employees to identify with the firm's business objectives. A firm's social and humanitarian

[22]John J. Leach of the University of Chicago was one of the first to investigate organizational history as a diagnostic tool in consulting. See John J. Leach, "The Organizational History," Thirty-Eighth Annual Academy of Management *Proceedings*, 1978.

[23]The term "strategic era" was coined by Thomas J. Peters, consultant, McKinsey & Company. The notion that superordinate goals impede the shift from one strategic era to the next was first introduced by McKinsey director Lee Walton, Ventura, Calif., December 5, 1979.

objectives are far more tangible to a dishwasher or janitor than is its goal of market share."[24]

Toward the end of a strategic era, a firm's past meanings can get in the way. In fact, this invisible force has undone late-in-an-era executives who sought to change things. Case studies of incumbents whose terms of office spanned the time periods when their organizations were moving from one era to another seem to indicate that they "failed" more often than they "succeeded." Organizational meanings can be so deeply ingrained, so fundamental to what people think and feel, and so important to their beliefs about their jobs and themselves, that when initially these meanings are challenged, there is often resistance and later dismay and a great sense of loss.

One recent example is the current transition at AT&T.[25] That company's deeper meanings were built on providing *reliable* and *inexpensive* telephone *service* to America. The firm's superordinate goal uniting managers, workers, and even stockholders has been the "social mission" of providing a reliable, low-cost phone system to America. Bell Labs and Western Electric further enshrined AT&T's pride as the "World's Best Telephone Company." But in the early 1970s competitive data processing applications began to spill over into AT&T's traditional domain. It became increasingly clear that the telecommunications fields and computer fields were overlapping. The result: AT&T was increasingly facing competitors in the computer industry; it would have to broaden its focus, change its strategy and become more of a marketing-oriented company in order to meet that competition. Ideally, its superordinate goal needed to shift to being a "marketer and innovator in telecommunications." In competing with firms like IBM, AT&T has to tailor its products and respond more rapidly to shifting market needs—in short, to make significant changes in all Seven S's.

Two of AT&T's chief executive officers saw this happening and began to move to change the company's direction. Their names are not likely to be enshrined as "great leaders" in AT&T's legends. They attempted to realign the strategy, but all of AT&T's systems were oriented toward tight operational controls—the sort that keep track of costs, operator errors and equipment reliability in the traditional phone service. They also encountered a staff of employees whose middle and senior managers had come up through the ranks as managers of telephone switching offices and repair facilities. With backgrounds in engineering and accounting, this management cadre lacked strong instincts for sales and marketing. In short, there were formidable barriers to change. Perhaps this helps us understand why the current chairman of AT&T believes that the shift to a true marketing orientation will require twenty years.

---

[24]Interview with middle management, McDonald's, San Jose, Calif., June 6, 1974.

[25]This example is based upon R.H. Waterman, T.J. Peters, and J.R. Phillips, "Structure Is Not Organization," *Business Horizons*, No. 80302, June 1980, p. 23.

Transitional times are periods in which older meanings and behaviors are slowly and painfully relinquished, and leaders who anticipate future threat when things are still apparently going well make an important contribution that is not often widely recognized at the time or, for that matter, honored later. Not until this painful and difficult process has run its course will the readiness for new meanings permit a "great leader" to articulate them convincingly. Strategic eras impose their own destiny on organizations and their leaders.

There are, to be sure, numerous tales of CEOs who have taken an ailing company, revitalized it, and achieved great success and recognition for doing so. The key word is "ailing." When a firm is widely seen as being in deep difficulty, as Memorex was in 1971, for example, there is an obvious imperative for change and a general recognition by employees of the need to alter older beliefs and ways of doing things. With Memorex at the brink of bankruptcy, its former beliefs in "rapid growth" and "free form entrepreneurialism" were in disgrace.[26] Not only was Bob Wilson free to move forcefully, the organization was ready to receive him. The mourning for past meanings had already largely taken place. Many of the entrepreneurial figures connected with the earlier era had already departed. Dissatisfaction with the way things were, and fears for the future, were strong. Wilson was thus in a position to build from the near-ruins. In contrast, his contemporaries at AT&T were having first to tear down monuments still standing *before* problems were clearly evident to all concerned and the costs of changing accepted.

Superordinate goals affect nations as profoundly as they do companies. Without such goals, around which a nation can rally, each constituency is out for itself and each citizen is more on his own. It appears as if the same late-in-the-era malaise is currently at work in our country. We have gone through a string of Presidents, each roundly criticized in his time, each dropping low in the polls during his tenure, and each facing great difficulty in building a consensus as to what America is all about, what it is for, where it is going, how it can get there, and what its priorities should be. The heart of these difficulties, we think, is not just the quality of leadership, but the angry resistance of a nation that is still mourning the accumulating losses of more of its earlier beliefs than it is prepared to relinquish. Perhaps a new President will be able to fashion a compelling expression of an adjustment of our nation's superordinate goals and begin anew.

MISUSE OF SUPERORDINATE GOALS

Having made the case for the importance of superordinate goals in motivating employees and sustaining an organization over time, we must

[26]These comments on Memorex based on the trial transcript, *Memorex v. IBM*, C-73-2239-SC, U.S. District Court, Northern District of California, August 11, 1978.

note that a skillful grasp of the use of all of our seven variables *can* be directed toward truly tragic outcomes. The staggering horror of the Third Reich and the mass suicides in Guyana come to mind. It is not hard to imagine an indoctrination of people into some kind of corporate Hitler Youth Corps. Indeed, fascist imagery is often used to express our unease with enterprises that succeed in fashioning intense commitment, and our fear of the fanatical is certainly not paranoid. We have seen enough of it in our Western history to be wary. There is no reason to rest assured that we are safe from pathology, madness, or evil in leaders or social systems at any level of enterprise, from small corporations to larger religious movements to nation states.

Yet, if our fear of the totalitarian of either the right or the left keeps us from struggling to encourage meanings that are between those extremes, that move men's hearts and compel action within ranges acceptable to our society and culture, we risk creating the kind of corporate emptiness which invites the extremists to fill the void. We cannot protect ourselves against such threats, either nationally or in a corporate context, by preferring a kind of pseudo-innocence (which suggests that our ignorance or naiveté about such meanings is acceptable, since others are "assigned" the function of dealing with extremists in our society). Rather, we must accept that owning up to our power to influence meanings imposes responsibilities to guard against the risks of its misuse. In this, we have some advantages built into our society. The still large separation of the state, the corporation, and the church from one another, and of the media from all three, provides at least reasonable assurance that checks exist to achieve balance in the distribution of power and its uses. But, nonetheless, it needs to be said that increasing our understanding of executive manipulation of superordinate goals does not necessarily ensure benign outcomes. Indeed, as the power and responsibilities of businessmen continue to expand, it is appropriate that they be subjected to the kind of scrutiny and limitations that our constitution imposed on the leaders of the nation. And if they are wise, these businessmen will not complain too much at these constraints, for in the long run history suggests they are useful and even necessary, even if they seem a damned nuisance a lot of the time.

STRATEGIES FOR A NEW AGE

Roger Harrison

During the last few years of my career as a management consultant, I have been impressed with the apparent intractability of organization problems. I ask myself why our attempted solutions so often produce no effect, or else exacerbate the problems they are designed to solve.

As we look around at business organizations, we see that decades of human relations training have made managers and supervisors more skillful and sophisticated about relationships. Why is it that we do not, therefore, have committed and happy workers? We have better information systems than ever. But do we make decisions more easily — or significantly better? We have sophisticated models and programs for planning and strategizing, and yet the environment seems more turbulent and out of control than ever. How is it that organizations seem so unmanageable just when we have learned so much about the arts and sciences of management?

As ever, hope is just over the horizon. The Japanese seem to have solved vexatious problems of productivity and quality. In this country, new plant experiments have shown that workers are able to manage themselves and produce superior quality and quantity with less supervision that we used to think necessary.

Peters and Waterman have made "excellent companies" a national catch-phrase for the 1980s that perhaps rivals the evocative power of Sputnik in the 1960s. The word "leadership" is back in favor, even among the academics who consigned it to oblivion for its vagueness and softness a few decades ago. Recent interest in "high performance" at both the individual and the organizational levels has produced considerable insight into the ways in which high-performing systems differ from their more mediocre competitors.

Where should we look for the key to improving organizations and management? Should we emulate the Japanese? Do we study "excellent" companies and try to be more like them? Should we start anew so as to do it right at the beginning, leaving existing organizations to limp along or decline?

I do not know. An ancient story tells of a man who sees his neighbor looking under the streetlamp. The seeker says he dropped the key to his door and is trying to recover it. Asked if he dropped it under the streetlamp, he replies, "No, I dropped it while trying to open my door, but there's more light here." This article is written for those managers,

"Strategies for a New Age" by Roger Harrison. HUMAN RESOURCES MANAGEMENT, Fa! 1983. Reprinted by permission of John Wiley and Sons, Inc.

consultants, and academics who feel that in our efforts to improve organizations we have perhaps made some basic error which dooms us to repeat both our mistakes and our successes, but not move beyond them. It is an attempt to move beyond the circle of light given by our current concepts and methods.

Faced with a plethora of choices, I find myself drawn toward an ideal of *balance* and *harmony*. For a couple of hundred years we as a nation have been in the forefront of progress, of improvement, and of innovation. As managers and consultants we have focused on fixing problems and making things better. We have ignored the Hippocratic maxim, "First do no harm," and we have created organizations which are chronically unbalanced, internally and externally. In consequence, we face increasing difficulty in maintaining control and autonomy. We shall explore how attempts to achieve desired levels of control destabilize and unbalance the systems we are endeavoring to improve. By endeavoring to maintain an *illusion* of autonomy and control, we exacerbate the problems we are trying to solve and find ourselves running ever faster just to stay even.

We shall consider two approaches to the integration of organizations other than direct control: *alignment* and *attunement*. By the first is meant the voluntary "joining up" of individual members of the organization, finding fulfillment in the larger purpose of the organization. By attunement is meant the support of the individuals by one another and by the larger whole which comes about through a sense of mutual responsibility, caring, and love. Organizations which become and remain healthy, vital, and productive over long periods of time embody both alignment and attunement in their values and cultures, and in their structures and systems. Building and maintaining alignment and attunement in healthy tension is a major function of leadership. When either becomes dominant, organizations become unbalanced and destructive.

The effective leader keeps the forces of attunement and alignment in balance within the organization and also within him or herself. According to this concept, the "new age leader" is both visionary and steward: visionary in the forging of the dream and in keeping the flame alight; steward in caring for and nurturing the organization and its human parts.

Among leadership tasks a special place is reserved for vision and the power of thought. We shall explore the part which intuition has to play in organization learning and decision making. We shall also consider what sorts of management tasks and activities might constitute the beginnings of a "technology of attunement."

Finally, we shall look at strategic planning in the light of our concepts of attunement and alignment. We shall attempt to apply the concepts of harmony and balance to the relationships of the organization with its environment: customers, suppliers, competitors, and communities.

LEADERSHIP AND ORGANIZATION ALIGNMENT

Interest has been awakening in the concept of leadership through vision, purpose, and intention. We are becoming aware that trying to improve productivity and quality through systems of rules, regulations, checks, and controls is not only costly but ineffective. The low trust and depersonalization that are engendered by ever more elaborate attempts at control further reduce the voluntary motivation to contribute, and a vicious circle of control and alienation perpetuates itself.

There is hope that the visionary leader (as opposed to the mere manager) can revitalize organizations through giving people meaning, purpose, and a sense of higher values in their work. By articulating common purpose and exciting future possibilities, the leader lines up the organization members behind a shared dream or vision, and they all march forward into the future.

Both within the organizations and in our private lives, many of us hunger for purposes higher than mere career success, and seek a nobler vision in which we can enroll. We await the emergence of charismatic figures who will lift us from our apathy. The concept of "organization alignment" expresses our wish for meaning and purpose and tells us how we may achieve them in our work settings.

Alignment occurs when organization members act as parts of an integrated whole, each finding the opportunity to express his or her true purpose through the organization's purpose. According to Kiefer and Senge (1982), the individual expands his or her purpose to include the organization's purpose. An organization is "aligned" when the parts choose voluntarily to act fully as members of the whole.

Organization alignment is seen by its advocates as different from the situation where an individual sacrifices his or her own identity to the organization. It is rather the *expansion* of the individual's identity and sense of purpose to include the organization and its purpose. I believe, however, that there is a shadow side to the benefits.

Organization alignment behind visionary leadership must involve the merging of the individual's strength and will with that of the collectivity, along with a willingness to be directed by the leadership. In high-performing organizations animated by noble purpose this may not feel like much of a sacrifice. It is a bit like being a member of a fine symphony orchestra. Instead of playing in their own tempo, volume, and style, the members "line up" behind the conductor in the service of his vision of the ideal rendition of the noble and aesthetic qualities of the piece being played. By doing so, each is able to be part of an achievement which no one could aspire to alone. Much of the time it must be a satisfying experience.

The trouble is that even organizations animated by noble purposes have their inhumanities. The symphony conductor may inspire the orchestra to perform at its best, but he may also be dictatorial, may humiliate members who fail to perform to his standards, may have scant regard for the personal needs of orchestra members, and so on. Nobility of aim is no guarantee of an open heart.

Nor is the inhumanity of high-performing organizations confined to the leadership. In my own work with plant startup (Harrison, 1981), I have documented how peer pressures develop that cause people to exploit themselves in the service of the cause. People burn themselves out; they sacrifice their personal lives and family relationships; and they ostracize those who do not share their commitment. Tracy Kidder's *The Soul of a New Machine* (1981) describes both the light and the dark sides of the aligned organization in fascinating detail. It illustrates the tendency of aligned organizations to demand and receive total commitment of their members toward purposes that are actually rather narrow.

It is not inevitable that alignment must be exploitative of individual members. But the tendency is there. It is no accident that many of our most exciting tales of high-performing, closely aligned organizations are referred to as "war stories." War is the ultimate expression of unbridled will in the pursuit of ends believed to be noble.

ORGANIZATIONS AND THE DAIMONIC

Rollo May's (1969) concept of the *daimonic* is extremely useful in seeking to understand the tendencies of organizations of all sorts to become unbalanced and inhumane. The daimonic is that aspect of man that seeks to express itself no matter what the cost or consequences. May describes it as follows:

> The daimonic is *any natural function which has the power to take over the whole person.* Sex and eros, anger and rage, and the craving for power are examples. The daimonic can be either creative or destructive and is normally both. The daimonic is the urge in every being to affirm itself, assert itself, perpetuate and increase itself. The daimonic becomes evil when it usurps the total self without regard to the integration of that self, or to the unique forms and desires of others and their need for integration. It then appears as excessive aggression, hostility, cruelty — the things about ourselves which horrify us most, and which we repress . . . or, more likely, project on others. But these are the reverse side of the same assertion which empowers our creativity. All life is a flux between these two aspects of the daimonic.

Our hopes for finding meaning and purpose in the workplace easily blind us to the daimonic dark side of aligned organizations and charismatic leadership. In our enthusiasms and hopes for a new order or renaissance in business, it is easy to create daimonic organizations. Business and government are full of examples of the daimonic: the narrow paternalism of a Henry Ford; the expansive dreams of an entrepreneur like John DeLorean; the limitless personal ambition of a Richard Nixon; the zealous invasions of privacy of the "sensitivity trainers"; and the shortsighted dedication to the "bottom line" of the dedicated careerist or "Gamesman" (Maccoby, 1976).

We must remind ourselves that an organization need not be dull, hidebound, and bureaucratic in order to be inhuman. High ideals and disregard of the individual frequently go hand in hand. Witness Hitler's SS, the Japanese kamikaze squadrons, the elite troops of every nation, willingly sacrificing every moderating human value to the nation, to brotherhood, and to victory. In our pursuit of the ideals of high performance and control, it is easy to forget that in a balanced system, neither the whole nor the parts dominate. The idea that we can achieve perfect integration between the needs of the people and the purposes of the organization is fatally flawed.

HIGH PERFORMANCE AND THE ILLUSION OF CONTROL

In our attempts to manage and improve organizations, we have overlooked the fundamental connectedness of things. Charles Perrow's new book (forthcoming) tells how minor and unimagined errors in tightly coupled complex systems combine in unpredictable ways to create major catastrophes, which he calls normal accidents. These result because we try to fix the parts of systems in isolation from one another, without appreciating their interdependencies.

This article is not the place for an essay on the ultimate interconnections of all to all, but it is important to illustrate by a few examples what happens when we enter into illusions of autonomy and control.

THE ILLUSION OF AUTONOMY AND CONTROL

The implicit belief in autonomy is so pervasive in our society that it is difficult to step outside of it. It is, however, fundamentally wrong. A friend described a conversation with her Japanese host in Tokyo. Noticing the throngs of unlocked bicycles parked on the streets, my friend asked if theft were a problem. "Of course not," responded her host. "Anyone would know that to steal a bicycle would be the same as taking it from himself." If we somehow came to believe that we were so totally dependent on others, and they on us, that we experienced our actions as reflexive, how would we behave differently?

When we disposed of our waste products and pollutants, we would experience them as landing in *our* environment, not someone else's. When we "leaned down" our organizations by "getting rid of dead wood" we would experience the unused human resources, the decline in living standards, and the hopelessness and despair of those who lost their jobs as our own loss. When we put shoddy merchandise on the market or cut a sharp and not too honest deal, we would feel the disappointment and diminished trust as our own. When we acquired the best and brightest employees for our own department and found a way to transfer out the less competent and motivated ones, we would experience the decrement in performance of the receiving department as our own. When we negotiated a fat and juicy budget for ourselves, and another group had to limp along on meagre resources as a consequence, we would experience their shortage of resources as well as our surplus. In short, we would know and believe that a part cannot remain healthy in a system which is sick, and that the whole cannot thrive when its parts are suffering.

Most of us realize that we are more intimately interconnected than we allow for in our plans and actions. Because we share a mechanical, atomistic view of the world, it is hard for any of us to live our daily lives in continuous appreciation of our dependence on others and theirs on us. We cannot take into account our connections with other individuals, groups, organizations, nations, and global systems because we do not experience them directly and continuously. We are in a real sense prisoners of our perceptual frames. In a curious way our illusion of autonomy only frees us to wander in the dark, tripping over the unseen bonds which connect us to others.

The illusion of autonomy causes us to ignore our connections with others. The illusion of *control* leads us often to do violence to the systems of which we are parts, in our attempts to manage, repair, and improve them. We love to experiment, to tinker with things, to fix them when they are broken and improve them when they are not. We are driven to produce, to create, to innovate, to build, and to expand. We want the good things of life.

To build, to create, and to solve problems so that they stay solved for a while requires that we have *control*, that we be able reliably to produce the consequences we intend, and that the unintended consequences of our actions do not nullify our gains. We do not always realize that without autonomy we cannot have control; we can only have reciprocal inter- action in which we are as much acted upon and affected as we are impacting on others. Our lack of appreciation of the interconnectedness of things leads us to attempt to solve many problems which we cannot solve, because we cannot know and manage the connections of the parts we act upon with the larger systems of which they are members.

At global and national levels our failures are glaring and obvious: attempts to manage the economy, to stamp out poverty, to solve population problems, to rid ourselves of insect pests, all have been more or less undone by unanticipated consequences of our actions, or by unappreciated connections which stabilized the systems we tried to change. Many, viewing recent history, argue for a "return" to *laissez faire*. These, however, have not really given up the illusion of control; they still believe that, freed of interference, business organizations can be controlled by their managers, and individuals can be autonomous in their own lives.

When we turn our attention to the organization, we have not far to look for examples of unanticipated consequences of attempts at control and problem solving. General Motors established a highly automated plant at Lordstown at least partly to gain greater control over the human element in production. Lordstown suffered from crippling wildcat strikes because people hated working there.

Banks have turned to automatic data processing in an attempt to reduce errors and cut costs. But partly because the job of teller is now both deskilled and low paying, teller turnover has become and remained a serious problem.

"Sociotechnical" and "open systems planning" approaches to plant design have succeeded in creating with large organizations "islands" of high performance, productivity, motivation, and worker satisfaction. After the startup phase, when the new plant becomes more closely integrated into the host organization, the productivity often suffers. Attempts to redesign existing plants along the lines of the experimental facilities have generally been unsuccessful.

It would be easy to overstate my case. There are indeed many counterexamples of organizations that have been changed and improved significantly, of problems that have been solved successfully, and of companies that have been well managed consistently over many years. We have become ingenious in diagnosing difficulties and solving problems during the years in which capitalism and science have flowered hand in hand. Most of us would agree, though, that it is not getting easier. It requires more knowledge, more information provided more rapidly, more management attention and skill, and more hard work to manage organizations successfully than it used to. The proliferation of training programs in stress reduction, negotiation, and conflict management tell us what we knew already: that stress, tension, and disagreement are on the increase within organizations, and between them and their environments.

The point of this review is not to sound another note of doom and gloom; it is to suggest that we are unlikely to find the key to our dilemmas by continuing to search in the circle of light cast by management science, analytical problem solving, job design, operations research, management information systems, strategic planning, and the like.

We should not just abandon these tools for newer methods, but rather we must do something much harder: change our minds, expanding and altering the mindsets of perceptual frames that produced the tools that are now diminishing in effectiveness. We need to stretch in two directions. The first is to move beyond the realm of facts and analytical thinking into that of vision and intuition. The second, more difficult one will be to move beyond our preoccupations with purpose and action into a realm of being and harmony.

THE NEED FOR VISION, INTUITION, AND THE POWER OF THOUGHT

It is interesting that while the established core of business and bureau-cracy has been a bastion of rationality, ideas about the "power of positive thinking" have cropped up with great regularity in sales training and in books for some would-be entrepreneurs. Organizations as successful as Matsushita and Toyota in Japan and IBM, Tupperware, and Mary Kay Cosmetics in the U.S. have not been ashamed to motivate their employees by group singing and highly emotional celebrations. Successful entre-preneurs in business have often been known for their intuitive hunches and impulsive decision making, as have the "deal makers" who make the running in merchant banking.

Because of our rational-analytical bias, we do not support people in business organizations in learning to use such intuition and Pied Piper motivation. The chances are that we are only fractionally as powerful in intuitive thinking as we could be if we supported one another.

A major barrier to legitimizing intuitive thinking in organizations is that many of us have trouble distinguishing high-quality intuition from sloppy, wishful thinking. Obviously we would like to install the former in our "new age organizations" and avoid the latter. We should *add the power* of what we loosely call right brain thinking to our already formidable talents for assembling, organizing, and reasoning with data. Intuition is not a substitute for facts, for experience, or for logic. It is a way of building on and going beyond facts and experience.

Studies of high-performing individuals in many fields have shown that successful people tend to visualize the results they want in their lives and work, and to affirm to themselves that they can accomplish their goals. They create a clear and conscious *intention* as to the desired outcomes, and allow their actions to be guided by that frequently affirmed intention. Rather than planning in detail what they will do and how they will go about it, they start by creating an intensely alive mental represen-tation of the end state. That representation then works through the individual's intuition and subconscious perceptual processes as she or he makes the multitude of everyday decisions which bring the goal ever nearer.

Purpose and intention are far more powerful than plans. Never in my years as a consultant have I seen an organization changed in any fundamental way through rational planning. The leaders I have seen deeply influence their organization's characters and destinies have always operated out of intuition, guided by strongly held purposes and drawn on by a vision of a better future. They communicated their intentions verbally to others who could share their vision, and they communicated it daily to others through their "real time" actions and decisions. In due course, enough people shared the vision and the intention to reach "critical mass," and the dream became reality.

Some people believe that when we create our own future through vision and intention, we are tapping into spiritual powers and energies, that there is an almost supernatural quality to it. Louis Tice (1980), in his program "New Age Thinking," has a more rational explanation. Tice says that when we establish and affirm an intention and create a vision of the end state, we "program" our subconscious minds to selectively perceive anything which could help us achieve our purposes. Thus, although we may begin with no idea of how to achieve our goal, we will begin to see the means we need through the filter we have set up which will selectively bring to our attention events, people, and other resources which could be useful to us. Conversely, Tice cautions, we must avoid words and thoughts about failure, because these program us to see barriers and difficulties, and indeed to engage in actions which will bring about the negative ends we have visualized.

Warren Bennis tells a story that supports such a view. Observing that the successful leaders he has interviewed are more than ordinarily reluctant to talk about the possibility of failure, he links that trait to the superstition among high wire artists against speaking about the possibility of accident. Bennis goes on to describe how the great Kurt Wallenda upset his family a few days before his death by talking about falling, and then describes the missteps and hesitancies which later led to his fall from a high wire into a street in San Juan, Puerto Rico. Our visions, it would seem, program us for life and death, as well as for success and failure.

Sports psychologists report similar findings in their programming of athletes to concentrate on doing the right things instead of focusing on not doing the wrong things. Their experiences are supported by the literature on attribution — people who see themselves in a negative light attribute failure to themselves, but attribute success to outside forces beyond their personal control.

Louis Tice points out that our subconscious "programs" can be charted by observing our "self-talk," the commentary we make on ourselves and the world as we go about life. Negative self-talk includes, "It's not like me to do so well." "Some people have all the luck!" "I never seem to be able to . . . ." "That's not one of my strengths." Positive self-talk includes such affirmations as, "I'm specially good at . . . ." "I'm learning how to . . . ." "Every time I try this I do it better." "I'm going to find a way to . . . ."

Organizations have self-talk, too. It can be heard in the organization's myths and rituals, as Joanne Martin reports in cognitive social psychology. The "war stories" about heros and villains tell us where an organization has been *and where it's going*. They tell us whether it is programmed for success or decline. When leaders want to prepare the organization for levels of performance beyond its self-image, they have to create new stories, myths, and rituals which will program the organization's collective consciousness for success. As Peters says, they have to create a series of "small wins," each of which is a sign and signal of positive change. It is not enough to articulate a vision of a hoped-for future; that is necessary but not sufficient. Organization members have to be given new stories to tell, stories that point toward the successful achievement of the vision. The leadership's ability to conceive and create dramatic events, both large and small, is critical to changing the self-talk of an organization. A new achievement in quality, a promising innovation, a better safety record, these are the "small wins" that can be dramatized to form the basis for new stories. They lead to the big wins, such as Lee Iacocca's recent announcement that Chrysler has just paid off its government loans.

We may make fun of the group singing of Toyota and Tupperware, but they appear to sing all the way to the bank. Mottos such as "Better Things for Better Living, through Chemistry," and "Progress is Our Most Important Product" may seem a little dated to us now, but both the songs and the mottos have been important parts of the self-talk of highly successful organizations. Purpose, vision, intention: when we venture into the turbulent waters of the unknown future, it gives us heart to have songs to sing and stories to tell, and a talisman to guide us. Our mythmaking may not be rational, but neither are the hopes and dreams that spur us on to success. Both spring from the human spirit.

ATTUNEMENT: THE SEARCH FOR HARMONY IN ORGANIZATIONS

The concept of organization alignment speaks to us of human *will*, driving toward the fulfillment of vision and purpose. I believe that the counter-balancing force is to be found in the operation within organizations of human *love*, expressed as empathy, understanding, caring, nurturance, and support.

The potency of love in organizations is largely denied and repressed. We experience the same fear of it that we previously did with sex and power. Love has its daimonic side, and we are not wrong to be wary of it. There is a very real danger in encouraging people to look to the organization for the satisfaction of needs for nurturance which are frustrated due to the fragmentation of family and community. And there are real limits on how much trust we can permit ourselves in the competitive and conflict-ridden cultures of many organizations.

I propose only that we allow ourselves to become aware of the reality of love. We shall not get rid of love by ignoring its operation in organizations, any more than we can avoid power by looking the other way. By refusing to examine love in organizations, we only prevent ourselves from accessing its healing, supportive, and creative influences. And these we do need.

Love is made necessary by the fact that there is no such thing as independent life. It arises from the recognition of our fundamental connectedness. Thus, its denial is part of the illusion of autonomy, and makes us vulnerable to the daimonic side of our needs for power and control. An understanding and acceptance of the power of love in organizations makes healing possible. It does not end conflict and competition, but it can bring grace and restraint into the dance of the warriors, and bind the wounds of both victor and vanquished.

As Kahlil Gilbran wrote in *The Prophet* (1969), "Work is love made visible. And if you cannot work with love but only with distaste, it is better that you should leave your work and sit at the gate of the temple and take alms of those who work with joy."

Or, as a recent Delta Airlines ad put it, "When people love their work, it shows . . . . Our people are happy. Because they love what they do and who they do it for. When people feel that way, they simply have more to give."

Perhaps they do. They gave a Boeing 747 airliner to their company not long ago.

By the concept of attunement in organizations is meant a resonance or harmony among the parts of a system, and between the parts and the whole. When we are attuned, we become more receptive to the subtle energies that connect us with one another. We become open to one another's needs and to our own sense of what is worthy of reverence in the work we do. Where alignment channels high energy and creates excitement and drive, attunement tames and balances the daimonic qualities of our quest by opening us to each other and to the messages from our hearts.

If an aligned organization is like a symphony orchestra, then attunement is represented by a jazz combo improvising. The members are alert to what each other player is doing and they support and build upon one another. Space opens for those who have solos to play. There is a sense of flow between the players which is unforced and uncompetitive. The essence of attunement is that the purposes of the parts are served by the whole and by the other parts. Each member's individual needs are respected and served by the organization and by the other members.

Alignment and attunement are both processes for achieving integration and unity of effort among the differentiated parts of a system. We need more integration, because we have created a world in which many of us are highly oriented to meeting our personal needs, often at the expense of the maintenance of our organizations and institutions. We have a lot of personal freedom; it is difficult to obtain needed integration through coercion or through rules and systems.

Neither alignment nor attunement is sufficient by itself. Organizations that are aligned but not attuned tend to be high-performing systems, which exploit their members and which may expend vast quantities of human energy and economic resources for dubious ends. They become daimonic warriors, so busy fighting the good fight that they forget what the battle was about. Organizations that are attuned but not sufficiently aligned tend to enjoy and support one another but do not get much done. They may be so oriented to caring for one another's needs that they cannot make and implement task decisions. They are not viable in a highly competitive environment. The leaders we need now are those who have the balance, the vision, and the heart to create both alignment and attunement in their organizations.

In the past, leaders we call "great" have often been very strong, ruling through fear and respect, or very charismatic, releasing and focusing the daimonic for their followers. Neither is appropriate to the balance between purposive thrust and nurturing harmony which I believe makes for sustainable performance in organizations.

Michael Maccoby (1981) has looked at the emerging character of the workforce and has identified the leadership traits which fit the emerging culture. Maccoby's new leader is seen as having a caring, respectful, and positive attitude toward people, and a willingness to share power. S/he is open and nondefensive regarding his or her own faults and vulnerabilities and avoids the use of fear and domination. The picture is of a secure and mature individual who can articulate values and high principles that give organizational life meaning, but who is more receptive and self-aware than we normally expect visionary leaders to be.

The new leader shares the characteristics which Joseph Campbell (1949) discusses in *The Hero with A Thousand Faces*. He or she is *called* by a mission and accepts the sacrifices and hardships of the task because s/he must. The hero does not only overcome barriers and obstacles, but is personally transformed in the process. The hero follows his or her *daimon* but is humanized by the challenges and difficulties of the journey.

There is something of the hero in all of us. The hero is not always strong, but is tempted, attacked, often overcome. S/he responds to an inner call, but is not independent. S/he receives help along the way, without which the journey would end in failure. The hero is often torn between inner forces of love and will, and he or she embodies and expresses both.

The hero's journey purifies the individual to a degree from the passions of the ego. Thus liberated from the daimonic, the individual is able to approach his or her role in the spirit of *stewardship*: leadership as a trust exercised for the benefit of all. As a steward, the leader serves the followers, guided by a vision of the higher purposes of the organization.

The organization is animated by and aligned with the sense of its own higher purpose. The leader focuses the attention and consciousness of the members on those purposes. But the leader also knows that the parts have legitimate purposes of their own which are not completely expressed by the purposes of the whole, and s/he facilitates the attunement processes by which organization members can come to know, respect, and care for one another's needs and individual purposes. The flow of human energy is not one way, from the members to the organization, but the uniqueness of each part is also preserved and nourished by the whole.

Leaders such as those described above are not numerous. Most of us do not embody equally the forces of love and will, nor have we been so purified by our own hero's journey that we are able to act for long periods of time without selfish interest. Also, leaders are shaped by the organizational cultures in which they develop, socialized by the myths, war stories, and rituals of that culture. An organization of "gamesmen" is likely to produce winners and losers, not heroes.

Processes of social change always seem to have a spiral quality: The times and circumstances bring forth the leaders, and the leaders influence the times. If we wish to facilitate such a process, we can look for the leaders, and we can in part alter the circumstances in which they develop. Creating such a climate for the development of the hero-cum-steward involves two aspects: finding and strengthening the sense of higher purpose in the organization, and creating processes that harmonize and integrate through attunement.

STRATEGIC THINKING AND THE CREATION OF MEANING

We turn now to the leader's task in creating a sense of purpose and meaning in the organization. Partly, of course, this is a question of having values and acting consistently according to them. But that is a hallmark of integrity, not necessarily of leadership. It is in the creation of value-loaded *meaning* that leadership focuses and channels human energy.

As Peters and Waterman (1982) have argued so convincingly, effective leadership begins with action, followed by *labeling*. It is by labeling that we create meanings. The actions do not have to be large or dramatic in order to shape a sense of direction and purpose. Indeed, it is the series of "small wins" appropriately labeled and interpreted that weaves the fabric of stories, myths, and memories out of which we create the meaning in our organizational lives.

We usually think of strategy as the art of predicting the future, and then planning how to change the organization so that it will perform well in future time. It is a frustrating business, not least because the organization is thus always defined as wanting, when compared with the strategic ideal. Add to that the fact that the most dramatic events of the future are those which are least predictable. It is little wonder that some managers are losing their taste for strategic planning.

We seem to do more planning in organizations, as planning becomes less effective in a desperate attempt to make the future behave. It is, perhaps, an outgrowth of our preoccupation with maintaining the illusion of control. In fact, planning can only help us to deal with conditions and variables which we already know or suspect to be important. Planning defines what we know and don't know within a given context. Any future changes in context (variables and events not thought to be probable or important when the planning was carried out) will more or less invalidate our plans (Davis, 1982). Planning can estimate the risk of a downturn in the economy based on known historical factors such as inflation, interest rates, leading economic indicators, and so on. We can use that estimate to judge whether or not this is the right moment to launch a new product. But planning cannot tell us anything about either the likelihood or the impact on our marketing plans of unforeseen events such as the sudden rise of a new cult religion, the discovery of a major new oil field in China, or the development in Russia of a successful inoculation against cancer.

Most of us seem to be aware that unforeseen events are looming over our futures. We know that we do not know. We imagine wars, economic disasters, cataclysmic natural events, but we do not believe we can predict their likelihood by reference to historical data trends, so we cannot plan for them. If we could assign a probability to these events, we should still find it difficult to plan, because the events we imagine are so sharply discontinuous with our current experience as to paralyze both mind and will. Because we cannot plan for the future we fear and imagine, we plan instead for the future we hope for, one in which even the projected negative events possess a comfortable familiarity.

But how can such an approach best prepare our organizations and ourselves for the future? Barry Stein (1983) says that instead of relying on strategic planning, the organization must learn to *adapt* to a condition of continuous change. "The old managerial cry, 'I don't want any surprises' will have to give ground. Managers need to understand that they absolutely will have surprises and that they and their subordinates . . . will have to learn to handle them, and handle them well."

Peters and Waterman report that their "excellent companies" are animated by a strong set of cultural values that give meaning to events occurring in the environment and guide people at all levels in the organization in making decisions that are consistent with the thrust of policy and purpose. At the same time, these companies are in a dialog with their customers and are so oriented to the marketplace by their "appreciation systems" that they quickly find meaning in and take action on the feedback they receive.

In our terms, these organizations are aligned behind a sense of mission and purpose. They are also attuned, but not only in the sense that the individual is valued and supported: They are in resonance with the marketplace as well, engaged in a continuous process of mutual influence and support with their customers.

Effective as it has been, this concept of attunement to the environment must be radically expanded in order for organizations to remain excellent, or indeed viable, in the future. Being sensitive to the marketplace is simply too narrow a connection with the world. It implies a degree of autonomy from events in the wider environment that simply does not exist.

Seen from a global viewpoint, the organization exists only as part of a larger reality, supported and nurtured by the larger system on which it depends: the nation, its culture, and many interest groups, the world economic and political system, and the physical and biological planet itself. To the extent that an organization acts in ignorance of the connections that link it to other parts, and to the whole system of the global environment, it will tend to experience surprise and shock at unanticipated events originating in the larger system. It will experience such events as deficient in meaning, and hence as a threat to its sense of reality and its own identity.

Long-range and strategic planning are one approach which organizations have taken to predict and control events in the wider environment and so experience fewer surprises. Because the web of causality is so complex, and because the larger system is *evolving* rather than simply operating as a steady-state system, such efforts must be unsatisfying. The error is not so much in the operations we use as in a mistaken *definition* of the organization as an autonomous entity, and were we to approach strategy from the point of view of endeavoring to *discover* the place of the organization in the larger systems of which it is a part and on which it depends, we would do far better.

From such a viewpoint, organization purpose is not simply decided by its members, but is in large part "given" by its membership in the larger system. The process of discovery is partly internal to the organization, involving an inner search for values and meaning. It also has an external aspect, that of discovering meaning through the transactions of the organization with its environment. Viewed in this way, a primary task of the leadership is the discovery of the organization's place and purpose in the world. And every event in its history can be viewed as part of a lesson.

Adopting such a point of view requires a fundamental change in one's orientation to goals and to the success and failure of one's plans. Most business organizations strive to succeed, to win against their competitors, against the government, sometimes against their suppliers and customers as well. The tougher conditions become, the harder they strive. Since conditions are increasingly tough, there are a lot of people out there striving. They experience a lot of failure in the difficult conditions, and they experience blame from others and from themselves. They experience high stress, as can be seen from the ever-increasing popularity of alcohol, drugs, and stress management courses.

A lot of that stress comes from seeing ourselves and our organization as autonomous. We deny our dependency on larger systems and events, and then we blame ourselves when our inharmonious actions do not lead to the achievement of our goals.

When we are striving to achieve goals, our learning is oriented to *means*. We learn more and more about what to do or not do in order to achieve the goals we have chosen. The excitement and stress often prevent us from questioning the goals themselves, or from seeking to read the lessons that our successes and failures are sending us about our place and purposes in the larger system.

When goals become very difficult to achieve, and it begins to seem as though the environment is hostile and unsupportive, it is typical of our culture to engage in problem solving — to identify the barriers to success and to work and plan to overcome them. We can, however, take the point of view that our organization has an appropriate place in the larger system, and that our task as managers and leaders is to attune our organization to its environment in order to discover what our part is and play it. The difficulties we experience are interpreted as signs and signals from the environment that we are somehow out of resonance with our true role. We read events as messages, rather than as judgments. We shall then expend less energy striving, and we shall move in harmony with the ebb and flow of events. If at some point we find that there is no longer joy in the struggle, that we are burning ourselves out in the effort to survive and succeed, then that will stimulate us to reevaluate our purpose and the meaning of our work. According to this point of view it should not be *difficult* for an organization to survive and thrive, if it is attuned to its part in the larger system, any more than an organ in a healthy body has to work especially hard to survive. When it plays its part, it receives the nourishment it needs.

THE SEARCH FOR MEANING

From a systems point of view, then, strategic thinking is a search for meaning, rather than a search for advantage. It is rational in its search for signs and signals from the environment and in its intentional search for relevant feedback. It is intuitive in the process of *appreciating* events and examining the activities and goals of the organization against the criteria of the heart.

In approaching strategy from the point of view of purpose, our aim is differential rather than positional in a market domain. Our endeavor is to forge a shared view of reality that will serve the organization members as a base for day-to-day decision making and direct the leadership thrust of the dominant coalition.[1]

The activity is definitional in that we are attempting to penetrate the forms of the organization in its internal and external relationships in order to discover its essence. Our belief is that when the forms (systems and structures) and processes (doings) of the organization flow from its essential qualities (being), the organization will become energized and integrated, and will become attuned with its environment. Therefore, it will prosper.

The questions we ask in order to determine the essential qualities of the organization are simple, though the process of answering them may be difficult.

We may ask ourselves what we experience of *energy* and *meaning* in our work:

> Does the production of goods and services enliven us, giving value and meaning to life?

[1] I am indebted to my colleague, David Nicoll, for this view of the strategizing process.

Do we strive joyously, or with desperation?

Do we feel that we are net contributors of value in our work in the world?

We may ask questions about our organization's identity and special characteristics:

Who are we; how would we describe our core being?

What are our "gifts," our distinctive competences and resources; what have we to contribute which is unique and valuable?

What do we value and believe in? What constitutes integrity for our organization? Can we as organization members fully identify with the values?

We may ask what we are being "called" to do in the world:

What messages do we receive from customers about their needs?

What are we hearing from government, from the public, from financial markets, from special interest groups? What do these messages tell us about how we are positioned with our many stakeholders?

What do developments in technology and resource availability tell us about our mission and purposes?

As we look farther afield in the world, what messages do we read in global trends and events about our calling?

As we search within ourselves, what needs in the world do we want to meet? What activities and processes have "heart" for us? What are the ways in which we love to work? What is it like when we are performing at our best?

We may examine our "core processes," the technology and systems we use to transform inputs into outputs:

How do our core processes link us to the rest of the world and structure our relationships with our stakeholders?

Are the relationships created by our core processes consistent with our values and with what we see to be our mission in the world?

Do our core processes provide us with the degree and kind of "energy flow" we need to survive and thrive (money, natural resources, people, "strokes").

Such questions are difficult to answer and test the commitment of leaders to the strategizing process. However, such a strategizing process is not without precedent, and those wishing to undertake it need not proceed entirely without guidance. The questions we pose above are similar to those addressed by the Open Systems Planning processes introduced in the early 1970s by Will McWhinney, Charles Krone, and

James Clark (1983). Practitioners of the approach have developed techniques for leading organizations through a strategizing process, but for too long they have been communicated almost entirely through an oral tradition.

Work by Jerry Fletcher (1983) suggests another approach, equally compatible with our point of view. Fletcher works with individuals and groups to find their "high-performance pattern." He asks clients to recall a series of episodes, in each of which high performance came easily, flowing in harmony with inner purpose. In such a state, barriers in the environment are not experienced as limitations, but simply as part of the dance. Fletcher has found that everyone can recapture such experiences, and that a common pattern runs through all such experiences of a single individual.

Fletcher's approach embodies the idea that high performance does not flow simply from an inner sense of purpose. An essential part of each individual's high-performance pattern is a specification of the environmental conditions that must exist for the person to "catch fire" and jump to that level of performance in which he or she is perfectly in tune with and supported by the environment. The search for the key to high performance places an emphasis on harmony with the environment, which is as strong as the weight given to the skills and values of the individual.

Following Fletcher's approach, organizations can examine their memories, myths, and war stories to find their high-performance pattern, and to learn what constitutes the attunement to the environment which releases high performance for that organization or subunit.

This strategizing process may or may not result in specific plans. Fundamentally, it has two aspects: *focusing* and *appreciating*. The appreciating process results in internal and external "mapping" of the organization in its environment. It is an expression of the members' shared beliefs about the nature of reality. Focusing results in a statement of the mission or purpose of the organization, and of the values that underpin it. Together, the "reality maps" and the mission statement form the basis for a projection of the organization into the future.

David Nicoll refers to such a projection as the "willed future." It is a statement of the organization's state of being at a later time when its essence will have been realized in its structures and processes, and it will be making its maximum contribution to the common good.

A statement of the willed future becomes the basic policy document of the organization, to which all lesser plans and decisions are related, and upon which the *intentions* of the organization members are focused. In this way the power of thought to create reality is brought into play.

The statement of the willed future becomes a center of the self-talk of the organization. By consulting the willed future at points of uncertainty and endeavoring to keep plans and decisions in conformity with its statement of intentions, the organization aligns its efforts, its "doings" with the strategy.

EVALUATING THE STRATEGIZING APPROACH

How shall we evaluate our approach to strategy? We are told to know who we are, and to appreciate and understand our dependence on the environment. Out of these two flow both our sense of purpose and our high-performance pattern. Once so grounded, we can apparently "act according to our hearts, and trust in the Lord."

Many of our most successful enterprises were built by people who had just such a sense of who they were and what they were to contribute. Because such individuals did see more clearly than most their right relationship to the environment, they succeeded, and they put the stamp of their visions and values firmly on reality.

But of what utility is our approach in the established modern organization? There are real obstacles in most organizations to the establishment of a sense of common purpose, a unified appreciation of the meaning of events in the environment, and a vision of the willed future. If, as is common, it is difficult to keep coordinated planning going between, say, the production and marketing people, what shall we say of the chances of their agreeing on ultimate values and the meaning of organizational life?

The idea of establishing consensus around values with one's business associates implies a high degree of *mutual* commitment between the individual and the organization. The individual has to be there not just for what he or she can take, but for what he or she can create together with others to develop greater value. And the members must trust that their willingness to give will not be exploited or misused.

Then, too, there are questions of personal style. Sitting around and talking about our values and our relationship to the environment is exciting to those who like to think, but it can be exceedingly frustrating for those who prefer doing. Using one's intuition to go beyond the actual to a vision of the possible is a meaningful activity for those who trust their intuitions, but to more concrete, data-oriented people it can seem no more substantial than building castles in the air.

Whether we like it or not, we are being nudged by events to change our consciousness. Our old ways of seeing ourselves in relationship to the world no longer produce reliable satisfactions. We can struggle harder to change the world to accord with our perceptions, or we can allow ourselves to change internally.

The seeds of those changes are in all of us; we each need to experience conditions which support the growth of those seeds. One way to create those conditions is through the strategizing process. We need to stretch our whole brains if we are to live comfortably and competently in a world in which causal connections are increasingly tenuous, and in which data become dated almost as soon as they are collected. Becoming more intuitive does not mean becoming less rational. It means knowing the limits of rationality and being comfortable in venturing beyond the data.

MODEST BEGINNINGS

No matter how grand our flights of fancy, our visions of a New Age, we each have to start where we are. Usually that is in a situation of mixed threat and promise, our hopes approximately balanced by our cynicism and our fears. This final section is written for people who wish to make a start in such directions, but who wish to test the water before committing themselves in a very visible way. In the sections that follow are some suggestions for applying intuitive thinking and the idea of attunement in organizations.

Many of us mistrust intuition, because it seems not to be grounded on data. We see others parading their wishes as intuitive truths, and we do not wish to join them. There are two questions we may ask ourselves to ensure that we do not confuse our wishes and hopes with true intuition. Have we collected as much data as is practical in the situation? Are we showing respect for the data and using it to check our hunches and intuitions? By showing respect for the "negative case," we can often improve our intuitive performance.

If we can affirm that we are using intuition to both work with and go beyond the data, then we shall be able to benefit from the power of intuition, while avoiding its excesses. We can begin to introduce and make legitimate the use of intuition in organizations which pride themselves on being practical, realistic, and tough minded. A few suggestions follow.

In conducting meetings, distinguish explicitly between what Neil Rackham calls *filter* and *amplifier* meetings. A *filter* meeting is (much like a brainstorming session) conducted to sift through a number of options for action, and to choose the best one. An *amplifier* meeting is one in which divergent thinking is encouraged. The idea is to *generate* possibilities, not to choose among them. Appropriate behavior is supportive and stimulative: recognizing contributions and giving credit for ideas; building on the contributions of others; drawing others out; summarizing, and testing for understanding and agreement. Criticism is deliberately withheld or turned into a "how to?"

The supportive and free-flowing atmosphere of an amplifier meeting encourages intuitive thinking. The competitive and abrasive qualities of the more prevalent filter meetings discourage it.

Ask subordinates to go beyond the data. Ask them to stretch their imaginations and support them in doing so. Ask, "What might be going on here that we're missing? Are there possible explanations we haven't thought of?"

Imagine the future. With colleagues, use techniques of the futurists to build alternate scenarios for your business, your technology, your markets, the society we live in.

Show people the whole picture. It is hard to be creative and imaginative about one's small part unless you can see how it fits the whole. Ask people to be aware of and think about the whole enterprise. Encourage them to cross boundaries and use their imaginations on operations other than their own.

Value the results of imaginative activities. Separate the selection of ideas to be acted on from your appreciation of the effort and mind stretching which has gone into their development.

When it comes to the "technology of attunement," we will find useful precedents from Japanese management, from Quaker practice, and from our own early history.

LESSONS ALREADY LEARNED

The development by Japanese management of Quality Circles is clearly an example of the practice of attunement. When a team from Lockheed went to Japan in 1973 to study these small groups of employees who met on company time to discuss quality and other work-related problems, they reported two key factors in their success. One was the uniquely cooperative and participative attitude on the part of Japanese supervision, an attitude which has since become something of a legend. The other was that the emphasis is not on improving productivity, but on improving the quality of working life by making the job better for the employee. Subsequent attempts to apply the Quality Circles approach in the United States have consistently demonstrated that they do not work unless they are experienced by employees as a genuine expression of these attunement values. Workers have proven hard to fool in this regard.[2]

Early American communities provide us with many examples of the means of attunement: structures and customs that expressed the responsibility and caring of the community and of each member to each other. The town meeting was a forum in which the viewpoint and concern of each interested member could be heard on any issue of the day. The responsibility community members took for individual members is seen in the "raising bees" in which everyone pitched in and helped a family put up the frame of a barn or house. The practical expression of love can be seen in the practice of taking turns sitting with the sick of other families, and in the community participation in laying out the dead and providing for the funeral supper. These customs gave concrete expression to the basic value of attunement: that the whole community had the responsibility to take account of and respond to the viewpoint, the concerns, and the needs of each of its constituent parts. We may ask what are some of the ways in which we in modern organizations can and do actualize this same value.

At the heart of the process of organizations attunement is *knowing and being known*, not in the sense of exchanging mere information, but in

[2]I am indebted to Beverly Scott of Foremost-McKesson for this historical note.

255

the sense of what Geoffrey Vickers has called *appreciation* (the dictionary definition of which is "sensitive awareness," implying deep understanding rather than favorable evaluation). For attunement to occur, the parts of the organization must know and appreciate the whole and must be known and appreciated by it and by one another.

The innovative approaches to new plant design, which are variously called "sociotechnical," "open systems planning," and the like, all emphasize processes which result in knowing and being known. Process design and redesign may be conducted by creating a visual representation of the productive process, which is contributed to and revised by each member. The process invariably results in surprises to management, who have no idea of the multitude of modifications to the system and interconnections among the parts that have come into being over the system's life. Then, when changes are to be made to the system, all participate in mapping the connections and consequences that an alteration to one part will have for the others. The trust of all this communication is for the system to be known as a whole by its members, and for each member to be known as a unique individual.

Appreciation promotes trust. Workers in the new plants are frequently permitted unsupervised access to the plant site and are given a large measure of responsibility for the selection (and deselection) of their fellow workers. They exercise their freedom responsibly.

Sometimes attunement begins in stillness, as in the Quaker business meeting which begins with silence and returns to it whenever the discussion becomes confused or overly contentious. The result, according to a British colleague, David Megginson, is that an extraordinarily high proportion of Quaker meeting verbal behavior are "builds": that is, they take account of what the previous speaker has said, and add to it, rather than disagreeing or going off on an unrelated tangent.

Attunement may begin in discord, as in David Nicoll's use of the "discussion arena." Discussion arenas are like an organization town meeting, except that no decisions are taken. All parties interested in a problem or proposed change are invited to a meeting to present their viewpoints and hear those of the others. No decisions are taken at the meeting. Its purpose is solely to widen the appreciation by the participants of the concerns and needs of the various "stakeholders" in the problem, so "you don't have to fight if you don't want to."

Debriefing and "premortems" are attunement exercises if they are conducted in a "no fault" climate dedicated to increasing understanding and not to assigning blame. Both are used extensively in the military and defense establishments to bring to bear the accumulated experience and knowledge of both participants and experts around complex, expensive experiments such as space shots and nuclear tests. A "premortem" is a process whereby a proposed test procedure is reviewed exhaustively by a multidisciplinary group of specialists. The object is to predict in advance all the things that might go wrong.

The processes of iterative decision making that are widely used in Japanese management as well as in many of our own informal political systems, are also examples of attunement. A proposal is circulated; each recipient comments on it; it is revised by the originator to take account of the comments; it is recirculated, and so on.

The costs and requirements for attunement are time and the willingness to be responsible. No technique can work unless there is at least a wish on the part of the participants to take account of and give weight to one another's concerns and needs, and those of the organization. Where people are highly competitive, the requirement of responsibility is difficult to meet.

We have become a nation of time misers. We give our time grudgingly, and we seem more willing to give it to tasks than we are to people. The Japanese have shown that the investment of time in gaining commitment, understanding, and appreciation can pay economic dividends. We must become convinced that putting time into the development of connectedness will ultimately be of value, if the idea of organization attunement is ever to become more than an interesting theory. By making the required investment, we can develop "Organization Appreciation Systems" which will outperform the Management Information Systems on which we now rely in order to control organizations from the top.

In thinking about attunement, it is perhaps useful to make a historical link to a style of management which has nearly disappeared as a coherent philosophy in large organizations, benevolent autocracy. Though the style is no longer dominant, it still survives to a degree in the great enterprises where it once flourished, companies such as Procter & Gamble, Eastman Kodak, J. C. Penney, and Eli Lilly. The business leaders who articulated and practiced philosophies of benevolence toward their employees were moved by deep caring and a sense of personal responsibility. They did not take care of their employees primarily because they thought it was good business to do so; rather, it became good business because they did it with heart. Because the employees perceived love behind the policies, they responded with loyalty and commitment, building strong emotional ties between individuals and the organization which have proven remarkably resilient even in these latter days. The reaction against benevolent autocracy seems to have been part of a general drive in our society toward autonomy and personal power. It was the autocracy we were unhappy with, not the benevolence.

We shall not succeed through the use of techniques, in the absence of heart. We have learned that through years of experimentation with participation, with human relations training, and with Quality Circle. We shall not succeed in establishing a network of support and caring while we are engaged in internal power struggles and cut-throat competition. Attunement does not require equality any more than love does, but it does need a climate of mutual respect, and a measure of peace in which to grow.

What then is the role of competition in the attuned organization? Must we, as some new age thinkers contend, make an evolutionary leap into a new age of love and light, in which we shall no longer experience fear, anger, and the drive to power? Perhaps, but it is hard to imagine a world without fear and power. In the real world, we can see successful social groupings of all kinds and sizes: couples, families, work groups, organizations. In these organizations, as in all nature, there is a balance of love and will, of support and competition. In the best such social systems, each person is a valued part, no matter what place they occupy. People feel valued and cared for for themselves, not merely for their instrumental skills, abilities, and personal characteristics.

One can experience in such organizations the difference between personal competition and depersonalized conflict. It is the latter, not the former, which creates the horrors of war and of industrial and commercial exploitation. Then the daimonic which is so often repressed in our individual lives as members of organizations, communities, and families finds expression in corporate acts of callous inhumanity. Conflict that takes place within a framework of responsibility and mutual respect may be fierce, indeed, mortal, but the dance of the warriors is not inhuman. We can look to the rituals of combat among Native Americans, or those observed by the samurai and by chivalrous combatants in our own past, to see ways in which the competitive daimon can be bounded and given a human face. Concepts such as honor, responsibility, and integrity may have an old-fashioned ring to them, but without them in the foundation, our "new age leaders" will be unable to build anything lasting to contain and channel the daimonic forces of both love and will.

FIRST STEPS

We each need experiences that support the growth of understandings, especially when those understandings are new, uncertain, and somewhat countercultural. One way to create those experiences is through forming or joining a small discussion group. In small groups we can experience that combination of mutual support and forthright confrontation which we need in order to test our insights and visions. We all need to be reminded occasionally that reality is changing, and we also need to be understood and accepted in our struggles to come to terms with that change. A small group composed of people who basically respect and feel good will for one another can provide the right balance of conditions, nudging us to change through exposing us to differing views of reality, while creating a climate of mutual support, which transcends differences of belief and opinion.

For those who wish to explore applications of "new age thinking" to work, I suggest meeting regularly with a few others you trust and respect. Spend enough time at it to create the conditions for sharing your hopes and fears a little more deeply than you would ordinarily feel comfortable in doing. Here are some basic questions you might address:

Do we use intuition to make decisions? For what kinds of decisions? How can reason and intuition support one another in our decision making?

Can we change reality with thought? What is the rate of intention in bringing about the results we achieve? Do we visualize our desired results? What would happen if we shared a common vision?

Do we see love at work in our organization? What are the pros and cons of seeing and talking about it?

What "daimonic" tendencies and processes do we see in our organization or in our own work? How does it express itself? In what ways do we suppress the daimonic, and how does it then come out?

What does the idea of stewardship mean to us? Can we identify genuine heroes we have known as leaders? What kind of leadership does our business need? What kinds of leaders do we regard as worthy of following?

What is our organization's purpose? What is its driving thrust? What are its distinct competences? What are its values? How do these relate to our own purposes and values?

Of what larger systems is our organization a part? Can we intuit our organization's purpose from its place in these larger systems? Does such a concept as global or planetary purpose have any meaning for us in our work lives?

What messages do we attend to from the environment and what messages do we consistently ignore or consider illegitimate? What would happen if we listened to them?

With respect to goals, are we for the most part *pushed* by events, or *pulled* by our vision of a desirable future outcome? Do we experience more stress when we are reacting to events than we do when we are "on purpose"?

What is the relationship between our stated strategy and what we do? If our strategy doesn't determine our actions, what does?

As an organization, can we identify a "willed future"? How does it focus our efforts? If we don't have one, would it make a difference if we did?

What do we hope and fear from the future? Can vision, purpose, and attunement contribute to the realization of our hopes, and the avoidance of what we fear?

It is possible that if we give ourselves the opportunity to open our hearts and minds to one another, we will discover levels of attunement and common purpose that we didn't know existed. Perhaps together we will find our way home.

REFERENCES

Campbell, Joseph. *The Hero with A Thousand Faces*. Princeton, NJ: Princeton University Press, 1949.

Davis, S. M. Transforming Organizations: The Key to Strategy is Context. *Organizational Dynamics*, Winter 1982.

Fletcher, J. L. *Achieving Sustained High Performance*. Los Angeles, CA: J. P. Tarcher, Inc., 1983 (in press).

Gibran, Kahlil. *The Profit*. 85th ed. New York: Alfred A. Knopf, 1969.

Harrison, Roger. Startup: The Care and Feeding of Infant Systems. *Organizational Dynamics*, Summer 1981, 5-29.

Kiefer, Charles, and Senge, Peter M. "Metanoic Organizations in the Transition to a Stable Society." Paper presented at The Woodlands Conference, August 1982.

Kidder, Tracy. *The Soul of a New Machine*. Boston: Little, Brown, 1981.

Maccoby, M. *The Gamesman, the New Corporate Leaders*. New York: Simon and Schuster, 1976.

Maccoby, M. *The Leader*. New York: Simon and Schuster, 1981.

May, Rollo. *Love and Will*. New York: Norton, 1969.

McWhinney, W. The Transformative. Chapter 5 in *Resolving Complex Issues (A Work in Progress)*. Venice, CA: Enthusion, Inc., 1983.

Perrow, Charles. *The Normal Accident*. New York: Free Press, 1984.

Peters, T. J., and Waterman, R. H. *In Search of Excellence*. Yew York: Harper & Row, 1982.

Stein, Barry. *Goodmeasure Notes*. Cambridge, MA: Goodmeasure, Inc., Spring 1983.

Tice, Louis. *New Age Thinking For Achieving Your Potential*. Seattle, WA: The Pacific Institute, Inc., 1980.

OVERARCHING GOALS

David Bradford
Allan Cohen

If we are to renew, it's because we have a vision of something worth saving or worth doing.
— John Gardner

To tackle something mammoth and then to accomplish something of real consequence — that's the only thing that matters. Fame, money, position — none of that stuff comes near.

— Robert Irwin, quoted by Lawrence Wechsler

INTRODUCTION

One of the key components for the Manager-as-Developer in reaching excellence is the establishment of an overarching goal for the unit, which serves to give coherence, excitement, and meaning to the department's work. An overarching goal can motivate, provide direction, and serve as a focus for change in the department. To lead a unit to excel, rather than just to manage existing arrangements well, the Developer has to create an explicit goal to serve as a guiding star, to shape actions so that all parts of the organization reinforce one another and the goal. Without identifiable purpose, greatness cannot emerge.

The concept of the overarching goal is directly analogous to the concept of a superordinate goal or mission for the total organization (Pascale and Athos, 1981). Peters and Waterman (1982) found in their study of excellent companies that each had a chief executive officer who had articulated a goal that used only a few words to summarize what was unique and special about the company, what all employees could focus on and use as a guideline, what the company stood for. IBM, for example, has as its superordinate goal "customer service." Hewlett Packard's is "innovative people at all levels." Sears stands for "value at a decent price." AT&T has been guided by the idea of "universal service." Bechtel, a huge construction company, prides itself on "a fine feel for the doable." GE is known for its "progress is our most important product" theme. Although each of these goals or themes could be, and in many other companies are, treated as empty, meaningless slogans, the chief executives identified by Peters and Waterman not only believe and constantly talk about these goals, but work to reinforce them by their personal actions, reward systems, hiring practices, organizational structure, and other aspects of managing. Having adopted a goal that uniquely distinguishes the organization, the chief executive works to align all parts of the organization in support of the goal.

When well formulated and backed up with appropriate executive action and organizational support mechanisms, these superordinate goals help managers at all levels of the organization make better decisions and function in ways that advance the organization. But the organization's goal needs to be translated, or specifically formulated, for each department or unit. Exactly what is the goal that General Electric's CAT scanner service department should follow to be consistent with the idea of progress as a product? What is the goal of the finance department within IBM's office products division that supports "customer service"? How does the contract estimating department at Bechtel run itself to have "a fine feel for the doable"? Even when the organization as a whole has a clearly articulated and well-supported superordinate goal — an all-too-rare occurrence in American companies — each unit must also have an overarching goal that does specifically for the unit's members what the corporate goal does for the company at large. Even if the organization has nothing more explicit than its generalized purposes, a unit can be greatly aided by adopting a goal.

In our leadership training programs we have worked with more than 200 highly competent managers from some of America's premier organizations. They manage units that are important to their companies and to consumers, yet very few of them had ever translated their department's functions into a clear and exciting overarching goal. They were missing a significant opportunity for inspiring excellence, especially since we were able in a short time to help almost all of them develop a goal.

The unit's goal must be consistent with overall corporate goals, but it is more than a mere restatement of a company purpose. Instead, it must be distinctive and suited to the specific unit's purposes and competences. In organizations that have no superordinate goal beyond a vague mission statement that no one looks at, the unit's goal can still be distinctive and challenging, so long as it does not violate the implicit goals of top management. In either case, the first step toward excellent unit performance is the identification of a challenging, unifying, unique, and creditable overarching goal.

An overarching goal has several important effects. It builds a common frame of reference that allows people with different backgrounds and varying orientations to pull collectively toward the same ends. It is an important force for change; it describes what could be, what the department should strive for. Finally, it is highly motivational. It places individual tasks within a larger framework, thereby giving work greater significance. This motivational power is enhanced when the goal is stated as a challenge, a difficulty that is to be overcome.

Too often, the only time anything resembling an overarching goal appears is in a disaster or around the development of a new task or product. Only under conditions such as a plant closing or start-up, a unionization drive, or possible loss of a major consumer do people rally around a common issue, giving greater effort than ever before. Similarly, the struggle to meet deadlines in coming out with a state-of-the-art machine or service often galvanizes member effort. (One excellent example is the description in *The Soul of a New Machine* [Kidder, 1981] of how a group of engineers at Data General worked night and day to design a badly needed computer.) But such occasions occur irregularly; when they do occur, they are often out of the manager's control (although some leaders may manufacture crises to produce this outcome, even though this ruse is often transparent to subordinates). The challenge comes with trying to build that same common focus and collective effort in non-emergency, regular work conditions. We believe that most departments can set such an overarching goal. To determine an exciting and challenging goal, one must find out how this specific department achieves its mission in ways that are different from comparable departments faced with the same general purpose.

For example, 10 production departments in 10 different organizations may manufacture video terminals. Yet each can have a unique thrust. The production department in organization A defines its goal as "customized work to meet idiosyncratic customer demands." Organization B's production department prides itself on doing "state-of-the-art video terminal manufacturing." Organization C stresses reliability, the lowest failure rate. Organization D strives for responsiveness by shipping all customer orders within four working days. Organization E focuses on high-volume, low-cost styles; F on producing a design that can be easily serviced; G on simplifying design to speed installation; H on high-margin standard types, and so on. Each department can be successful, despite the differences, if its goal serves to unite the department while meeting market needs and being consistent with the thrust of the rest of the organization.

In some ways the overarching goal is the departmental parallel to a corporate strategic posture, in which a firm examines the environment and its opportunities, assesses its own capabilities, and then determines a market niche that will allow it to be successful. Just as the chief executive officer must lead the effort to formulate a strategy that can be encapsuled in an exciting, challenging, superordinate goal statement, the middle manager needs to work toward the formulation and dissemination of a departmental overarching goal.

CHARACTERISTICS OF AN OVERARCHING GOAL

An effective overarching goal has four essential characteristics:

1. *The goal reflects the core purpose of the department*. The human relations movement over the past few decades has sometimes caused

managers to forget the centrality and motivating potential of work. The very important need for appropriate relationships can sometimes be confused with, or even displace, the department's tasks as an objective. For example, if the goal is to focus member effort around task attainment, the goal must reflect that task; a departmental goal of "fielding the best volleyball team in the company" or "being the department where people have the most fun" may build esprit de corps, but it does not guarantee high work performance.

2. *The goal is feasible.* Feasibility has several measures. First, as suggested earlier, the goal must be consistent with the general purposes of the organization as a whole. Thus, it has to be compatible with the organization's superordinate goal. For example, if the organization aims to provide low-cost products on a mass basis, the research and development department can't define its goals as developing state-of-the-art, customized technology. Second, the departmental goal has to be compatible with what the other departments can deliver. The sales department can't work toward immediate turnaround time if the production department's technology requires continuous-process batches with a 10-day cycle. The goal also has to be feasible in terms of what subordinates within the department are capable of producing. The goal can't be "providing end-user training to all clients" if the salesmen aren't themselves highly skilled and knowledgeable or at least capable of acquiring needed skills. Finally, the goal has to be feasible in terms of the departmental manager's personal capacities. Bold, risky marketing approaches are not appropriate if the marketing manager's style doesn't include risk taking.

3. *The goal is challenging.* One of the most fundamental motivations for any employee, especially one who is basically competent and doing complex tasks, is challenge. Tasks that are stretching — difficult but achievable — will pull the best from most subordinates. Challenge creates the willingness to invest in work, high commitment, and pursuit of excellence (Kanter, 1977). The overarching goal must include a challenge — a way toward a future state of excellence: the department that is best, first, most, fastest, or some other superlative that fits with the core task.

4. *The goal has larger significance.* Work is a central aspect of most people's life, a way the person defines identity and self-worth. Thus, people will extend themselves for work that they can see is important. Though not all tasks can have earth-shattering significance, most work can be put in terms that highlight its meaning to others. Whether the unit produces outputs for external customers or for other units within the organization, an overarching goal that stresses benefits to other people or their objectives can put even routine work into a larger perspective.

Core purpose, feasibility, challenge, and larger significance help transcend the merely adequate performance that occurs when goals are only short-term financial targets or nebulous platitudes.

One example of a useful, although unusual, overarching goal, occurred in the maintenance and engineering department of a medium-size company. The leader saw his department as "the glue that holds the organization together." Normally, this opinion might be a bit presumptuous, but it was somewhat valid in this situation since the company was faced with stringent economic belt-tightening in order to survive. There would be no money in the foreseeable future for new equipment or major renovations. Engineering had to help other departments make do with what plant and equipment they had, so the department's ability to respond quickly to requests for repairs and refurbishing did much to boost morale in the struggling organization. Members of the department increasingly saw themselves as vital to the organization's survival rather than as the ones who had to do the dirty work. The manager found he needed far less time seeing that people actually put in their hours and more time jointly solving problems raised by subordinates who were eager to perform. When combined with challenge, a goal that underlines the larger organizational significance of everyday tasks can be highly motivating.

A Case of the Development of an Overarching Goal

The setting was a suburban office of a major bank that was experiencing low morale and lower productivity than had been forecast. One of the difficulties was that this office had been used as an informal "training center" for young managers. New hires who needed experience as loan officers or assistant branch managers were assigned here for training; when they reached a certain level of competence they were promoted out. Such a practice was demoralizing to the less mobile tellers and other assistants, who saw no personal reward in "training their boss" and instead felt exploited by the process.

After some checking with her boss and other people at corporate headquarters, a new branch manager concluded that it would be impossible to change this rotation procedure; her branch and several others were used as the backbone of executive development in this bank. During this exploratory period, she also got to know her subordinates, particularly those who were "solid citizens" and had been carrying the place while numerous superiors had rotated in and out. She found that many of them were quite capable and could do much more than they were presently doing, but they had never seen themselves as "going anywhere" in that bank.

The branch manager searched for what could be a unique thrust for this branch, one that would integrate an individual's needs with the bank's rotation objectives and in the process better serve the branch's customers. She formulated as a goal the desire to be "the branch in the organization that best develops managerial talent while still offering quality customer service." From this decision, a series of actions flowed. First, she declared that if the task is development, opportunities for growth would be open to all. She inaugurated a career development program for each of her employees. She and the other managers sat down with each of their subordinates to find out what aspirations they had. For those who did want to advance, she negotiated with the central training department of the bank for spaces in some of their programs. She negotiated with the personnel department to inform her regularly of job openings, which might interest some of her subordinates, and not just those assigned to the branch for "development." Next, she built rewards into the appraisal system for those who did help others learn, so that even those who did not personally aspire to advance would get some benefit from the new thrust. In order to provide adequate backup in service functions, she instituted cross-training so that people in one area could fulfill functions in another. Not only did this arrangement provide a reserve of assistance when one area was experiencing peak work and development demands, but interdepartmental cooperation increased as each area more fully understood the policies and procedures in other areas. The branch manager also used this practice with her own immediate subordinates; she frequently had the assistant branch manager run staff meetings, other subordinates represent the office at some of the central bank meetings downtown, and members of her staff carry out some of her other designated tasks.

These efforts resulted in major gains. By stressing and restressing these goals in words and actions, the branch manager gave the office a distinctive character. Members felt increased pride in their place and morale improved. Some of the old-timers acquired new aspirations, developed their skills, and moved into higher positions. Even those who remained at the branch office felt good about the advancement of others because they saw their role not as fulfilling thankless tasks but as crucial for individual and organizational success. The spirit of the place carried over to how customers were treated. Service also benefited from the cross-training, since there was now less shuffling of customers around to other employees.

Note how the formulation of an overarching goal also served as a guide to many aspects of operating the department. The goal functioned as both a reference point and a stimulus. It was not just an endlessly repeated slogan; a number of concrete actions reinforced the goal and built commitment to it. Though each of the changes the manager made —creating new opportunities, fitting them to individual aspirations, altering rewards, cross-training, delegating responsibilities — was in itself a useful device, collectively they were more potent because of the common theme. In addition, the theme's articulation suggested actions she otherwise might not have considered. The manager-as-developer has to sell the overarching goal, but any goal is likely to be believed, and therefore be impactful on excellence, only when it is backed with supporting actions.

THE IMPORTANCE OF AN OVERARCHING GOAL

The lack of an overarching goal represents a major loss of potential power on the part of the manager. In the absence of a challenging goal that sets high aspirations, the manager tends to fall into a maintenance role that at best produces a more efficient version of an existing situation. Developing toward potential is a necessary ingredient of excellence and also encourages a manager to assume a leadership role.

Thus, one major purpose of such a goal is as a *vehicle of change*. If the manager can articulate and gain member commitment to a vision of the future, the goal then serves as an important stimulus for change toward excellence. As occurred in Deborah Linke's department, subordinates' acceptance of the goal means that they too push for change. This mandate for change spreads to include not only what is to be done but how the unit is to operate.

For example, if a personnel department that is used to just making sure that all forms are properly filled in now redefines its role as "creating the conditions that will increase corporatewide managerial competence to meet the new goals the executive committee is setting," pressure inevitably develops for all sorts of improvement within the personnel department itself. Forms and procedures are reexamined: Are they only for the convenience of personnel, or do they really help the managers supervise better? Training has to be instituted that meets the managers' needs. Wage and salary policy, as well as the performance appraisal system and career development pathways, have to be improved so that subordinates get accurate and timely feedback and appropriate rewards for their performance. Finally, the skills and abilities of personnel department employees may need to be retrained so that they can deliver on these new tasks.

Use of a challenging goal *alters the nature of the Developer's relationships with subordinates*. The impetus for change becomes the need to meet the goal, not pressure from the leader. Depersonalization of justification for the change can make it easier for subordinates; they do not feel they have to subjugate themselves to a superior's grandiose, personal power play or ego trip in order to stay employed. Once the goal is articulated, it assumes a life of its own; influence seems more objective and impersonal. The demand is for commitment to the goal rather than to a person, which in turn means less coercion and a greater likelihood that joint problem solving will occur. Energy can go into finding the best solutions to achieve the goal, not into one person's "winning." Subordinates can be fully involved in deciding what barriers prevent goal attainment, what steps are needed, and how to implement action. A far more potent form of control is created than the traditional, close supervision that breeds resentment.

The acceptance of an overarching goal *provides a common vision*, a similar frame of reference for all. If members buy into the same goal, the likelihood is increased that they will act in compatible ways despite strong individual differences. Compatibility is an increasingly important issue as heterogeneity in background, experiences, knowledge, and values grows — contemporary organizations need to recruit diverse talents to deal with a changing, complex environment. The conventional practice of limiting access to management to those homogeneous in background, race, sex, and schooling severely limits organizational capacity to adapt to complexity. But with increased differences among members, a way must be found to achieve a common orientation if coordinated behavior is to occur, particularly important for shared responsibility. The advantage of using the overarching goal to achieve the commonality, rather than common social background, is that the goal is directly task related. People with diverse viewpoints can strive to achieve the same ends.

This objectification of the goal also allows for *better resolution of those conflicts that are inevitable* whenever people work together. Honest disagreements take the place of power plays. Differences can be productively explored rather than used to foster further divisiveness. Too many managers fear conflict so much that they prematurely stifle it. They worry that everything will fall apart if they allow conflicts to surface. Yet conflict is inherent in the nature of organizations; dividing tasks requires that each person have slightly differing goals to do his or her job well. Struggling over issues helps promote more creative resolution of issues.

Problems arise — impasse or fragmentation — when subordinates pursue their subgoals *only*. Acceptance of a clear, overarching goal can allow the manager to *promote* conflict, to encourage the expression of differences and full engagement among the subordinates, because the goal serves as an integrator. Reference to the common goal can help even a manager who is nervous about his or her personal ability to manage conflict; the goal is an objective standard to refer to when fur is flying.

In short, the existence of a common vision pushes subordinates and the superior to see the larger picture, the overall purpose for bringing subunits together. This understanding is crucial if subordinates are to share responsibility for the managing of the whole department.

An overarching goal helps *keep the leader and members focused on the larger issues*. Managers can easily be swamped by the day-to-day minutiae of procedures, rules, deadlines, and other annoyances and lose sight of the department's reasons for existence, but continued reference to the goal guards against tunnel vision.

Further, the overarching goal is important for its *motivational properties.* When the departmental task is defined in terms of a challenge that has a larger meaning, involvement goes up. As we have mentioned, most people need to believe in something that is larger than their day-to-day, often mundane, tasks. They are more likely to become committed to making things happen right if they believe in the significance of the unit's goal.

In fact, many people, even quite independent professionals, want a clear overarching goal almost apart from its specific advantages. They want to know that the organization has a clear direction; if they strongly disagree with it they will leave, but so long as it doesn't strongly violate their beliefs, they are more comfortable with clarity. For example, soon after an accounting firm chose a new managing director, one of the senior partners commented, "I have some questions about our new activities, but at least with Thomas we have a direction; we know where we are going and we are actually moving."

If any goal is better than none, how much more potent is a goal that also inspires! The leader who can excite subordinates about a larger vision is able to tap a vast pool of dedication and motivation. In most contemporary organizations, where mobility is high and allegiance is more frequently granted to each person's professional group than to the company, it is probably misguided to expect intense commitment to the leader as a person. There is natural reluctance to overcommit to a boss who may soon be moving or who might be arbitrary. It is less threatening and less dependency-creating to become excited about a specific goal. Therefore, an important leadership skill is the ability to articulate a superordinate goal that is congruent with organization requirements and member needs.

This is not to say there is no room for personal style or energy. Charisma can be inspirational. But the most organizationally relevant aspect of charisma is the ability to formulate and sell a goal that taps into member needs for belonging to a unit that does challenging and meaningful work. Not "charm," but showing subordinates how they can meet their needs for significant accomplishment is the key to being charismatic.

Finally, the overall goal helps to *sustain attention to excellence*. Even though most people want to work well, putting out the extra effort to share responsibility can be burdensome. There frequently comes a point in any task when the motivation is strong to "just get it done." There is reluctance to put in the final extra effort. The report is adequate, but it really could use going over one more time; procedures seem to be working, but the routine isn't quite smooth enough; the action plan to implement the solution really should get one more review to make sure all conditions are covered.

In all these situations, it is likely that the initial excitement of the project has long since worn off, the challenge from problem solving has already been answered, and the learning has been achieved; new tasks look appealing and returns are definitely diminishing with this final push. Managers often feel their only recourse for keeping up quality is to ride herd on the troops, which irritates everyone. Instead, an overarching goal that stresses excellence can be used by the leader (and by other members) as the standard by which tasks are to be judged. Excellence is a much more useful standard than "Will it get by?" or "Are we personally thrilled to continue working?" Pressure from the leader should be exercised in the pursuit of excellence, not because "work has to be done my way."

ESTABLISHING AN OVERARCHING GOAL

Establishing an operative overarching goal requires two distinctly different tasks of the leader: to *formulate* an appropriate overarching goal and to gain its *acceptance* by the members. Each task requires different sets of skills. The first task demands intuitive and analytic ability to sense what would excite subordinates, even though they themselves might not be able to; the second requires inspirational and selling ability. Common to both sets of skills is an ability to think beyond the daily routine, to see a greater vision that ties day-to-day activities to significant future goals.

Developing the Overarching Goal

A leader cannot discover a goal, as if it already existed and waited to be unearthed. Instead, it is more appropriate to think of a goal as being woven from many strands, including core purpose, feasibility, challenge, and larger significance. The process is dynamic, playing back and forth among ideas about who needs the department's services, what is exciting to members and to you, and what is feasible given the skills and resources likely to be available.

The following sequence has proved to be useful in our work with managers trying to develop an appropriate goal. First identify what the department does for its clients, the total organization, and society. Look at your own interests, skills, and areas of commitment, then at the department's internal resources. See what kind of match can be made between external service and internal capacities. Once you have formulated the goal, sell it by talking first about what it does for the larger good, then for the organization, for your clients, for you personally, and finally, for your subordinates. In general, identify a goal component and then clarify how all interested constituents will benefit. Initially, a leader should think externally, identifying the department's clients (either inside or outside the organization) and their needs. We encourage managers to assume that their units are central to the organization and that what they produce — documents, information, services, or goods — is crucial to people outside the unit, who are also performing crucial functions. Often managers have not concentrated on what their department activities do for the rest of the organization or end users.

For example, one manager in our workshop headed a unit that repaired circuit boards in a computer company. She was so caught up in the technology of her unit's function that she had lost sight of its significance. Repairing parts sent back by customers appeared to have little glamour — a necessary task perhaps, but not one that seemed crucial to the organization, which prided itself on producing state-of-the-art computers. Given the problem of setting a goal for her department, she realized that although customers may initially buy the hardware on the basis of what it could deliver, continued customer satisfaction could be insured by speedy return of repaired parts. She thus formulated this goal statement: "We're the ones who sustain the reputation of Compucorp for quality and reliability."

The process of looking at departmental activities to discover their larger significance often means that a manager has to see through layers of grimy routine that over years have obscured the department's function. In some situations, the manager may have to reinterpret or expand a department's purpose to have greater relevance. A manager must undertake goal exploration with clear criteria for the goal's relevance, practicality, and capacity to excite.

Clearly, one must first look at the nature of the department's task. If the department markets sows' ears, dreams of silk purses are wholly irrelevant; but it can be satisfying to find just those sows that are in need of ears! Besides the task itself, the technology, technical expertise of the members, abundance of resources, and so forth all affect the determination of a goal. The loan department of a small bank might be very excited about moving into international lending, but their gratification may be short-lived if members experience failure in assessing risks or collecting on loans. Finding a match between what the unit can deliver and external market needs is necessary, but by itself not sufficient. A manager must consider what he or she can personally believe in and be excited or challenged by. As salespeople know, it is very difficult to sell a product that the seller is not personally committed to. Without genuine personal excitement, expressions of enthusiasm about the goal will seem hollow. Furthermore, a manager must take account of subordinates and what would excite them. What could they find challenging in the department's activities? An overarching goal with larger significance might work in one situation, but not in another, because it doesn't fit with members' skills and interests.

The answers to these issues are seldom obvious. It is usually necessary to experiment back and forth, balancing among external needs and different sources of personal excitement. A promising lead in one dimension may not be supportable in another. A goal that seems to fit all criteria may not reflect the core purpose of the department or might not be feasible, given external reality. But in our experience helping managers, we have found that successful goal identification mostly depends on time and effort. The experiences of one manager illustrates how the process of identifying a useful overarching goal might begin.

Mark was head of personnel in a small company that manufactured machinery for the oil industry. In mulling over what might be a possible overarching goal, he was unclear about what would make his group unique from personnel departments in other organizations of a comparable size. He had three assistants, all responsible for developing appropriate personnel precedures and forms and for training. How could the task be defined as challenging and exciting?

The company had recently gone through change and stress. It had been known as a leader in its field in terms of quality products (which had been a source of pride to both management and workers). In the past, the company had employed slightly under a thousand people, which allowed for a high degree of informal and personalized contact between superiors and subordinates. In fact, employees talked about the family atmosphere of the place and the high degree of concern shown by management. Employees displayed high loyalty, low turnover, willingness to put in overtime, and a general commitment to quality work.

Much of this work atmosphere had deteriorated recently. The oil crisis in the 1970s had produced a dramatic increase in demand for the company's products, and in the last 18 months, employment had doubled. Increased size led to new procedures, which led to a more formal bureaucratized atmosphere. Employees complained that the friendly family feeling was gone and that the company was becoming "just like any other." Also, the new hires didn't have the same commitment and loyalty to the company of the older employees and tended to treat their jobs like "any other job."

Mark had received a lot of information about what his "clients" did and didn't want. Supervisors complained about unnecessary paperwork, about the personnel department not providing the sort of people who were "like our old employees," and about irrelevant training. Employees complained that it took too long to correct mistakes in benefits payments and that the personnel division was only interested in issuing rules and regulations.

Mark then started to think about what his department could do that would serve the needs of the consumers of his department's services. It didn't help just to think in terms of "better" services, because it wasn't clear just what that meant. Also, as a small department they were not able just to give "more"; instead, there had to be some way to prioritize services. After much thought, Mark had been able to formulate an exciting overarching goal for the personnel group: to provide the training and procedures that would enable managers to "manage humanely in a growing company." This goal might make it possible, Mark thought, to recapture the atmosphere of personal concern.

Mark believed that the goal reflected the key function of the personnel group and that it was feasible, given his skills and those of the three people reporting to him. It was certainly challenging, and it put their tasks into a larger framework that had great significance. The goal had fundamental implications for how the department operated. New personnel procedures would be judged not only on whether they got the job done; they had to prevent a bureaucratic atmosphere and foster a personalized one. New orientation programs would be needed to socialize recent hires into the past culture of the company. Training programs would have to be modified and new ones added that would help managers carry out leadership functions in a more humane way. This formulation of the goal would shape what was to be done *and* how the personnel group would go about it. Rather than just imposing decisions, the group would need to solicit actively user input in the development of new programs and procedures.

In this case, Mark worked in isolation to determine the goal; he saw the convergence of client needs and his and his subordinates' interests and abilities. In most cases, however, it is more productive to set up an interactive process between superior and subordinates to explore a range of possibilities before a decision is made. Usually a considerable amount of talking it over, "chewing on it," looking at what is initially a vaguely defined goal from different angles must occur before a definition firmly captures the interest and energy of the leader and the members. This informal approach also has the benefit that such discussions build commitment among subordinates while gathering data.

This initial discussion phase with subordinates enables the leader to collect information. The actual determination of the goal can be accomplished two ways: by the leader alone or, as Deborah Linke did, by group consensus. The latter option increases the likelihood that the goal will meet members' needs; the group struggling together often produces a more creative outcome (as Deborah found), and through the process of arriving at a decision much of the next stage (gaining commitment) is already achieved.

Nevertheless, quite often the determination of the overarching goal is a decision that ultimately the leader will have to make. Like any creative act, determining an exciting, galvanizing overarching goal is something that often can best be done by one person. Even though many variations are possible, a useful goal usually requires a creative blend of disparate elements. It may not be possible for group consensus on such a fundamental issue. After all, the selection of a specific goal generally is more to some members' liking than to others', depending on its fit with members' goals, aspirations, skills, and current status.

Thus, unless a group is highly homogeneous and already arrayed in just the right network of relationships, the chosen goal will increase the influence of some members at the expense of others. Those who would lose influence or who do not like the direction implied by the goal, have it in their best interest to block the group from reaching a decision. Any goal that all members would readily agree to, because it makes no one uncomfortable, is likely to be so general that it would have low potency for guiding departmental decisions. Goal statements that do not force choices may find easy acceptance, but their influence won't be worth the time it takes to say them.

It is also difficult for a group to achieve consensus because useful overarching goals have a stretch quality to them. They are intended to be challenging, which means that they postulate a higher standard of member performance than is current. Although the subordinates we have been discussing seek and are motivated by challenge, they often feel some ambivalence. The unknown raises fears of failure or at least gives pause to those who are comfortable now, even though they have longed for loftier goals. Sometimes those who have most pushed for changes are suddenly resistant when change is at hand; the security one felt from railing at the status quo is threatened. In the sense that social workers *need* the poor clients they are supposedly helping to overcome poverty, complainers often need the weak conditions about which they most complain. At any rate, research shows that the leader of a high performing department sets higher standards for members than members would set for themselves (Likert, 1961).

In the last analysis, it is the leader's responsibility to determine the overarching goal. If the goal can be developed and won by consensus, so much the better, but not all Developers may be as fortunate as Deborah and, might have to deal with the absence of a unanimously favorable reaction. But if there have been thorough and open discussions to assess members' interests and personal goals, and if preliminary versions of overarching goals have been shared with subordinates, a leader's selection of goal is likely to be acceptable and even inspiring to most members.

Gaining Member Commitment

Selecting an appropriate goal is only half the process. Equally important is what follows — gaining members' commitment, which is neither easily nor quickly done, especially if the goal was selected by the leader, not by the team. Subordinates will be justifiably skeptical and initially withhold acceptance. They will be asking themselves, "Is the boss really committed to this goal or is it a passing whim?" The last thing subordinates want is to give commitment and energy to a transitory goal.

Securing member acceptance must be viewed as a long-term effort that will require persistence and consistency. Without reinforcement, an initial lofty statement will sink largely unregarded. The goal must be recalled by repeated mentions on relevant occasions and backed by actions that give weight to the verbal statements. Subordinates need to see the overarching goal used as a basis for running the department and personally use it in helping to manage the department.

This stage of the goal process poses an interesting paradox. The aim is to gain member commitment to the overarching goal so that it will serve as a standard for their behavior. But one of the best avenues to such commitment is by using the goal as the basis for action, which demonstrates both your commitment and the goal's utility in building a more effective department. It's hard to build commitment without use, but difficult to get effective use without commitment! Perhaps the way out of this situation is first to acknowledge the dilemma, then to conceptualize implementation as a constantly alternating process, each part building on the other. But the leader must be willing to take the early risk of pushing the goal before support has been completely built.

Several methods can be used to further this process of commitment. As we mentioned, simply the persuasive articulating of the goal is important, with careful attention to the actual words used. The words don't have to be elegant but they must convey the core message. One of the best documented examples of a middle manager at work can be found in *The Soul of a New Machine.* Kidder (1981) shows how hard Tom West, the manager of Data General's project team on the Eagle computer, works to define the team's goal in an exciting way. At first, some of his key recruits refused to work on the machine, because they saw it merely as a variation of the existing 16-bit model with which it had to be compatible — "a bag on the side of the Eclipse," in the derogatory jargon of computer experts. West characteristically responded with "his little grin," saying, "It's more than that — we're really gonna build this f—— and it's gonna be fast as greased lightning. We're gonna do it by April." Though not exactly an elegant statement, West's goal was challenging and formulated in an effective way that directly tapped the key motivations of his subordinates.

Words do make a difference, and the way a goal is stated and then reinforced in frequent references has great impact. You do not have to be a gifted orator who can enthrall an audience, but you must be able to talk about your unit's work vividly and about its goal convincingly. Surprisingly, the ability to convey enthusiasm does not seem to be a natural managerial skill — or has been stamped out by organizational routine.

In our work with managers we have been struck by the blandness with which so many leaders convey their departmental goal. We have helped participants in our training programs improve their ability to gain subordinate commitment by having each one role-play a meeting with a recent hire. The boss's assignment is to convey the unit's overarching goal in a way that inspires the new employee and wins commitment.

Each participant works with several others to think through a possible goal statement for the real back-home department. Then, one at a time, each manager talks to another participant, who plays the role of new employee. We instruct the manager to "use this opportunity to be enthusiastic and convincing about your (newly formulated) overarching goal." We then videotape the manager's presentation.

After everybody has made a presentation, we play back the tapes and observe. The results have a dismal similarity; the manager's presentations of goal statements are almost universally unexciting. Managers have delivered their messages in a flat, colorless way, or they have buried the core message in a mound of trivia. After a few practice rounds, however, and after some coaching from fellow participants, most managers find ways to generate enthusiasm about their goal.

Are the difficulties these managers experience due to the emphasis on rationality held by professional organizations or to the belief that enthusiasm is somehow immature? Perhaps managerial sobriety is a carryover from Western heroic images, where taciturn understatement is the strongest emotion allowed. Action, not fancy words, is the hallmark of our cultural heroes; the picture of John Wayne punching out a villain is apparently worth a thousand sissified words. Whatever the cause, managers who bemoan the lack of subordinate commitment are often those who have difficulty showing their own enthusiasm to the department.

Peters and Waterman (1982) found that enthusiastic repetition of the goal, in many settings, was an important tool for chief executive officers who wished to gain organizational commitment to the superordinate goal. But even the best-delivered inspirational speeches have to be accompanied by actions that firmly plant the concept in the department's operations. For example, the goal can be reinforced every time an important decision is to be made by questioning how the solutions being discussed are consistent with the goal. The goal is thus seen as an action standard, not just pretty words. Departmental policies and practices can be examined to insure that they are consonant with the goal; espousing a goal of quality, for example, remains rhetorical if promotion policies are based on friendship or seniority. In this case, aligning practices with the department goal demands the introduction of a new, more open procedure for promotions.

To get maximum leverage from new actions, situations should be sought that would provide decisions that had symbolic value to demonstrate the centrality of the overarching goal. This could mean looking for subordinate actions that reflect the goal and giving public supporting to them, dramatically shifting the reward system to reflect new priorities, confronting a key resister who has consistently blocked progress, or finding some other way to signify in action that it is no longer business as usual.

The importance of the goal will be further demonstrated if it is visibly used to guide a decision under crisis conditions. When things are going well and resources are ample, it is relatively easy to espouse and enact a lofty goal. But the point will be more convincingly made when the goal is firmly maintained in problem times. For example, it is more difficult, but more persuasive, to hold fast to a goal of attention to customer service when a department is faced with a reduction in-force. Yet if the first departmental cut eliminates the extended service hours that were to ease customer access, while the departmental travel budget remains intact, goal credibility is lost. Adverse conditions can provide the perfect challenge to move people out of their routines. The bank branch manager mentioned earlier used adversity in such a way to turn around low morale and productivity.

In addition to selling the goal and using it for crisis decision making, you can work to build norms and standards that are consistent with it. For instance, if the goal focuses on quality, then quality must guide personnel decisions, the way meetings are run, how the offices are furnished, what people wear, the thoroughness and formatting of reports, and everything else. When a large automobile manufacturer decided to stress quality, the head of an assembly plant rejected a shipment of interior trim from a feeder plant because the color didn't match the model's metal interior color. On closer inspection, feeder plant personnel discovered that the problem was "only" that plastic takes the identical dye differently from metal. To their astonishment, the assembly plant manager still refused to assemble the desperately needed automobiles until the problem was corrected. Although his was an expensive — and gutsy — decision, everyone in his organization and in his suppliers' organizations got the message that quality was indeed important.

The building of an environment that reflects and reinforces the overarching goal does not always require such dramatic moves, although drama is helpful to broadcast intentions widely. Organizational culture is also built in countless small ways, on a daily basis. The manager's interactions with others — interested in problems or disinterested, caring or not, thoughtful or not, honest or not, helpful or not — all help establish the department's norms about what is valued and how things are done. When these interactions are consistent with the overarching goal, the goal is reinforced, intermeshed with operations.

You can also work to implement and reinforce the overarching goal by linking it to individual work tasks as they are assigned. Subordinates will place more value on their work if they see its relationship with larger departmental and organizational goals. Yet too frequently managers assume that such relationships are obvious and don't bother to elucidate the connections, or worse, they fall into the trap of believing that subordinates should just carry out orders without having to know how their parts fit into the larger structure. Even the organization itself can be severely damaged by such a situation.

The computer operators in the data processing department of a large insurance firm were told to do an analysis of premium and claims payment at the end of each day. The task was unpleasant, because of frequent errors in the submitted data that required correction. Completing the run often held the operators past closing time. Periodically, the operators would delay finishing the computer run until the next morning, which brought admonitions from management and excuses from the computer operators. During one of these failures the exasperated manager said, "Don't you realize how crucial this run is?" An operator replied, "Not really. You only told us that it was important and to do the job."

The operators had never been told that the information not only reported the company's cash flow position, but was used the next morning as the basis for short-term investments. Not having that information, even periodically, had resulted in the company's losing millions of dollars of investment potential over the years.

Thus, the importance of the task can be forcefully underlined by the act of establishing linkages between individual tasks and the larger departmental purpose. You may discover weak linkages, which can be strengthened by utilizing an overarching goal in redefining and enlarging individual tasks. If the data processing department described above had had as a component of its overarching goal the development of user sophistication around data processing, the task of the computer operators would not have been perceived as merely responding to client requests. The task would have included service and instructional components, and both company and operators would have tangibly benefited. The effects of an overarching goal are not hype or public relations; the goal often leads to the modifying of work assignments or departmental procedures, which in turn lead to increased work challenge and task significance. The resulting altered work performance is a concrete demonstration of the centrality of the goal and increases the likelihood of goal acceptance.

In many of these initiating situations, it is the Developer alone who will make the connections between day-to-day actions and the overarching goal. But even when the goal is determined by you and not by group consensus, more direct subordinate involvement in deciding *how* the goal is to be implemented is relatively easy to obtain. In effect, the Developer can say, "Given that this is our goal, what do we need to do to make sure it is fully integrated into our department?" A great deal of latitude can be given to subordinates in determining implementation steps. As time passes and subordinates see that the goal has actual impact, they will begin to apply the goal on their own initiative (as was the case in Deborah Linke's unit).

Finally, it is important that you let subordinates in on your own feelings about the goal, its impact on your own effectiveness and career. Operating only in a selling mode, focusing only on what adherence to the goal will do for the subordinate, may act as a barrier to subordinate commitment. Subordinates will inevitably wonder about "what's in it for the boss," whether or not they ask, so it might as well be dealt with openly. You can talk about your own commitment to the department, what hopes you have for recognition when excellence is achieved, your aspirations within the organization, and even about your likely time horizons for staying in the department.

This kind of openness, though difficult for many managers, can not only help foster commitment to the overarching goal, but it will also accelerate the kind of reciprocal honesty that is needed for the shared-responsibility team. Although we do not advocate that managers go around spilling their guts about everything all the time, it is helpful to work toward the time when all important and relevant feelings can be mutually expressed and acknowledged.

To summarize, for the overarching goal to assume a central part in the department, all elements have to be congruent. You must not only talk convincingly about the goal, your own behavior must embody the goal. The goal has to be evoked not only in times of plenty but in times of want, and it has to be used for major decisions as well as minor. This degree of congruency is both the goal's power and the source of problems. All parts build on and reinforce each other, but definite limits are placed on superior and subordinate behavior. Although the limits set by a good overarching goal are legitimate, they nevertheless are constraints and can be perceived as confining.

POTENTIAL DIFFICULTIES WITH THE CONCEPT OF AN OVERARCHING GOAL

Can All Departments Have an Overarching Goal?

Although all departments have purpose and can have a mission statement, it is probably not possible for every department to have an exciting, inspirational, overarching goal. Remember that the criteria for such a goal include that it be challenging and have a larger significance. Some departments necessarily perform work that is so routine and so mundane that it could not possibly excite most people. Perhaps the industry has the cynical motive of taking advantage of particular conditions or customer gullibility. Or the top management may be interested only in activities that milk the corporation's assets, which render the productive work of departments meaningless, as was true in a company described by Cohen, Gadon, and Miaoulis (1976). For a leader to try to espouse an exciting and challenging overarching goal under any of these, those conditions would be seen as a sham maneuver. Similarly, if top management has long accepted a manufacturing organization that turns out shoddy work, a service operation that consistently delivers less than it promises, or a sales group that can never deliver on time, subsequent development of a meaningful overarching goal is very difficult.

Nevertheless, we have almost never had a participant in our workshops who was unable to come up with at least a modestly challenging goal for his or her unit. Goal potential is probably more widespread than may be apparent at first.

Although we believe that most departments can have a useful overarching goal, many different variables determine how easy a goal is to develop. In some situations the goal is obvious and needs little leader persuasion to gain its acceptance. An example is the engineering modeling department of a large organization that works on America's space program. The ability of that department to respond quickly and accurately to scientists' requests for simulation tests is crucial to the success not only of that organization but to the entire space effort. On the other hand, for many other organizations, the relationship between individual work and larger significance is more obscure; greater leader effort is needed to make the connection.

We have seen many situations that would have been fertile grounds for the formulation and invocation of an overarching goal, but leadership was unable or unwilling to carry through such development. The production department of a major pharmaceutical company, for example, treated employees as extensions of the pill-forming equipment and never helped the employees see themselves as in the business of saving lives. The rehabilitation department of a major teaching hospital suffered from weak leadership and low status relative to other departments; no one helped its members think about the larger significance of the restorative work that built on the brilliant efforts of the higher status surgeons and radiologists. As a result, department members were depressed, low in energy, and unable to combine efforts or make a collective case for a reasonable share of the hospital's scarce resources.

These examples suggest failure of leadership imagination, not an inherent misfit between the department and an inspirational overarching goal. Of course, not all jobs or department work is easily placed in a wider context, but there is often more potential than managers realize. Even when top management pays little attention to wider purposes, a department head can often choose a challenging goal.

How Long Does it Take to Identify and Gain Commitment to a Workable Overarching Goal?

There is no fixed time for goal development, although a year is probably a closer estimate than a few months. The time needed depends in part on the extent to which an obvious connection exists between tasks and objective importance as well as the extent to which the goal is inherently exciting and challenging. The time varies as the level of leader commitment and effort to implement the goal. The strength of member resistance caused by the distance of the goal from member needs and the resultant necessary changes in orientation also affects the schedule of goal development. Peters and Waterman (1982) estimate that getting an entire large organization to accept a new superordinate goal takes five to ten years. Much less time, probably months, not years, is required, of course, to gain acceptance of one department's overarching goal. Fewer people are involved and the degree of change is likely to be less fundamental.

There is an important distinction between a goal's complete acceptance by most of the members in their day-to-day work and the impact of such a goal on the department. The former event may take a year's time, but the latter effect can occur almost immediately. If you fully believe in the goal, it will certainly affect your own behavior and that of others in your presence. Finally, we want to reiterate a previous point: One of the best ways to gain acceptance of the goal is to use it, which demonstrates both its value and your personal commitment to it.

How Easy is it to Change an Overarching Goal Once it is in Place? What Happens When Technology, Task, or External Conditions Necessitate a Shift?

Unfortunately, not much information exists on the circumstances of changing an established overarching goal. Our experience suggests that it is possible for the manager who created an overarching goal to modify it, but probably not fundamentally change it. Remember that a criterion for the goal is that it receive the manager's personal commitment. Because such commitment is difficult to build, it is equally difficult to abandon in a shift to a new objective. Although a goal certainly can be modified — changed somewhat in form and emphasis — even modified it remains the same basic goal. For example, if the overarching goal of a sales department had been to provide information and instruction to the customer so that the product could exactly fit their needs, it would subsequently be possible to modify the goal to emphasize semi-customized product development. But goal development would be seriously disrupted if the company decided to change its focus to the provision of a limited range of low-cost products.

Support for this notion is found in work by Pfeffer (1983), who argues that for organizations within a turbulent, changing business environment there is a better match between the organization's goals and the environmental requirements when there are also relatively frequent changes of leadership. Perhaps even when the leader has recognized the need for change and has overcome his or her own resistance against giving up something accomplished with great effort, subordinates may be reluctant to credit such a change in course. When the goal has to be changed fundamentally, it is probably expedient for the previous leader to move on and a new leader to come in.

Leadership transfer may not be a severe penalty for change. Even in rapidly changing situations, most change is evolutionary rather than revolutionary, and in most organizations successful managers are expected to move. Indeed, the problem in many companies is not too slow a change in management but too rapid a change, as managers are rotated in and out in 18-month cycles — just long enough to stir things up but not to work out significant, stabilized operations. The personnel in more innovative companies in Kanter's (1983) research had high career mobility, but generally two to three years between moves.

How Compatible are the Skills Needed by the Leader to Develop an Overarching Goal and the Skills Then to Gain Subordinates' Commitment to the Goal?

The question of complementary leadership skills for both steps of goal development is critical to the success of an overarching goal. Unfortunately, the set of skills needed to formulate a goal (that of being able to sense what would excite others) and the set needed to gain commitment (that of being persuasive) are often seen as contradictory. The former effort requires reflective behavior, taking in more than is given out and being highly responsive to others. The latter behavior, on the other hand, is frequently perceived as being more closed to outside influence and more certain of self-"rightness," so that the views and needs of others are ignored — at its extreme, the image of the hail-fellow-well-met salesperson whose enthusiasm overwhelms all opposition.

If both sets of skills are important, but by nature incompatible, how reasonable is it to expect that more than a few managers can successfully be ambidextrous with them? If the number is few, isn't doubt cast on the validity of this approach to managing complex organizations?

We agree that not many leaders are highly proficient in both skill areas, although the salesperson image may be more stereotype than reality. The highly successful salesperson probably succeeds by determining the customers' needs and then demonstrating the product's relevance. But even if few fully developed managers exist who fit the profile of our Developer model, we have observed that each set of skills can be learned. There are a multitude of training programs that develop listening skills.

Furthermore, we have found that in a relatively short time managers are able to learn how to redefine departmental purposes and missions in ways that produce exciting and challenging overarching goals. In our training exercise, when we ask managers to state the overarching goal to a new subordinate and few can generate enthusiasm on the first try — only a little coaching leads to great improvement. The problem seems to have been that managers had never conceived of the need for such goal statements, not that they were incapable of formulating them with some practice.

Goal formulation skills are more easily seen as teachable and learnable. What about the more persuasive, inspirational set of skills —can managers really learn charisma? We believe that almost any manager can learn the functional equivalent of charisma — inspiring high commitment — even if the manager does not become a magnetic personality. We are not saying that we can infuse all or even most managers with great oratorical powers, crowd-excitement talents, or personal charisma. But these extreme gifts are not necessary for the people we are talking about. Remember, we are focusing on middle and upper-middle managers who need to excite their departments — we are not talking about leaders who need to electrify a nation. The aim of the manager is not personally to be the source of excitement (that is, by producing adoration and commitment to oneself), but to attribute excitement to the departmental task. To the extent that the leader has done the job of defining an exciting goal, the goal will hold the power to excite. The goal should be based on untapped needs of the subordinates and should show how they can be larger than themselves by buying into it. If well formulated, the goal itself will carry a great deal of the excitement.

But the goal, no matter how well defined, still needs a conveyer who can represent the excitement in the message. We have found in working with managers that they can learn how to be truly enthusiastic about their goal and to convey their enthusiasm. Even those who initially appear quite bland — those whom the organization has made routine and bureaucratic — can learn to express effectively their personal commitment to the goal. With some coaching and practice, the manager becomes able to show involvement and commitment, without enormous effort and without recourse to a stereotypical rah-rah style. Each manager finds that he or she can generate excitement and commitment to an overarching goal in a personally comfortable style, consistent with his or her usual communication style. Some are fervent, some quietly intense, some witty and charming, while others are straightforward or blunt. Each can be effective.

As mentioned earlier, it's far easier to sell a product you personally believe in. For a departmental overarching goal to be accepted by subordinates as a central standard, you must be able to sell it through words and actions. You need to be able, at public occasions, during staff meetings, while meeting one-to-one, to convey the importance of the goal and your personal commitment to it. Enthusiasm, repetition, and brute attention can outperform flashy delivery and slickness.

If the Concept of an Overarching Goal is so Valuable and Possible for Most Departments, Why Isn't Its Use Widespread?

Only part of the reason for the underapplication of the concept of an overarching goal is that it is new. It is important to realize that this concept goes counter to the thrust of most management theory of the last 30 years. Past emphasis was on logical rationality, planning out all contingencies, and reducing the challenge in work (Athos and Pascale, 1981). The notion of a manager having the responsibility to inspire fell more into the domain of political leaders than organizational managers.

Furthermore, business was on the defensive throughout the 1960s and 1970s. Pollution concerns, the Vietnam war effort, discrimination policies, planned obsolescence, and other pressures created a business climate in which gung-ho enthusiasm seemed out of place, if not frankly misguided. And the heroic model didn't allow for much fancy talk.

But the answer must also be that developing skills to articulate well and to inspire subordinates is a difficult endeavor, not only because of the divergent efforts involved but also because of the demands it makes on the person. The Developer has to be able to "walk the talk" — that is, to be able to express the goal in all of his or her actions. If the overarching vision involves quality work, then the leader can't personally perform at a mediocre level. A manager can't stress performance and hire only friends, emphasize the importance of development and be defensive when receiving personal feedback. A department head can't say that people should take on challenging tasks and then reserve for personal use the pleasurable assignments.

Our basic observation about why so few departments have developed meaningful overarching goals is that many managers balk at taking on the added personal responsibility that living up to a goal requires. Yet we have seen the same longings in managers that we have noted in their subordinates: for challenge, something to believe in, significance. The creation of an overarching goal and the commitment to excellence make it possible for middle managers to take the initiative, to make their own work as meaningful as they would like.

REFERENCES

Cohen, A. R., Gadon, H., and Miaoulis, G. "Decision-Making in Firms: The Impact on Non-Economic Factors." *Journal of Economic Issues, 10*(2), (1976).

Kanter, R. M. *Men and Women of the Corporation.* New York: Basic Books, 1977.

Kanter, R. M. *The Change Masters: How People and Companies Succeed through Innovation in the New Corporate Era.* New York: Simon & Schuster, 1983.

Kidder, T. *Soul of a New Machine.* Boston: Little-Brown, 1981.

Likert, R. *New Patterns of Management.* New York: McGraw-Hill, 1961.

Pascale, R. T., and Athos, A. G. *The Art of Japanese Management.* New York: Simon & Schuster, 1981.

Peters, T. J., and Waterman, R. H., Jr. *In Search of Excellence.* New York: Harper & Row, 1982.

Pfeffer, J. "Organizational Demography." In L. L. Cummings and B. M. Staw (Eds.), *Research in Organizational Behavior,* Vol. 5. Greenwich, Conn.: JAI Press, 1983.

SECTION FIVE

GOALS

Overview

Not too long ago, the question "Where are we going?" was relatively straightforward for managers and their people to answer. A business's goals were simple and few. The economic health and growth of a company were sufficient ends. What was good for business was assumed to be good for the community. Employees, by and large, did not expect more from their work than a steady job, fair pay, and decent working conditions. A controllable or at least relatively predictable market environment allowed established goals to be a reliable basis for management action. Future goals were generally extrapolations of current objectives. The problem of managing goals was a matter of their specification, their communication, and the organization of resources to achieve them. At least that is the way we thought the world worked.

The world that business finds itself in today, however, does not work this way at all. The economic ends of business, while still central, have been joined by others either embraced by business or thrust upon it by increasingly active and powerful interest groups. On the same stage with economic goals are, for example, those of affirmative action, environmental stewardship, consumer safety, community responsibility, and even the political sensitivity of a business's investment portfolio. Employees, now educated and mobile, are demanding that their work fulfill their own personal needs and expectations. Work is playing a more important role in their lives, and they will hold their allegiance and commitment to their company hostage until they feel their needs are being met. The goals a manager must deal with today are multiple, complex, and generally conflicting. Furthermore, the continually changing competitive marketplace is forcing managers to disband the illusion of goal stability or even the relatively short-term reliability of goals as a guide to decision making. Goals are becoming fluid "hypotheses" that must be continually tested and altered in reference to changing conditions and the company's mission. As Rosabeth Moss Kanter observes in her book *The Change Masters,* "The era of strategic planning (control) may be over; we are entering an era of tactical planning (response)."

The two contributions to this section have been chosen to reflect this new environment of goal management. The first article, "Integrative Goals and Consensus in Problem Solving," by Rensis Likert and Jane Gibson Likert, addresses the issues involved in managing situations when confronted with multiple and conflicting goal demands. In the second article, "Managing Work Relationships Through the Psychological Contract," Roosevelt Thomas deals with the problems of managing the implicit contract that exists between managers and their work units where expectations and goals are reciprocal and changing.

The Likerts propose that managing goal conflict within an organization requires the discovery of common ground among the conflicting parties — what the authors call "integrative goals." Only when the process of resolving conflicting goals is guided by reference to such integrative goals will true consensus and commitment characterize the group. Consequently, the task of leadership in managing such goal conflict is to make integrative goals operationally effective — to see that the influence of integrative goals is used fully when these goals are known and to help bring potential or implicit integrative goals to awareness when they are not known.

The Likerts make a helpful distinction between *substantive conflict* (over ideas) and *affective conflict* (interpersonal) and discuss conditions under which goal consensus can be achieved when each of these types of conflict is dominant.

Finally, the authors outline strategies for the manager when complete consensus is impossible. For example, they refer to *pragmatic consensus* as reaching agreement to give a particular solution a trial run.

As the Likerts point out, managing goals in conflict situations is becoming more and more complex and typical. The requirement to develop dynamic consensus among conflicting parties is a difficult but essential management responsibility today.

Roosevelt Thomas examines the other domain where a dynamic consensus must be developed and sustained — the needs and expectations of employees versus the goals and objectives of the company. Thomas uses Harry Levinson's notion of the "psychological contract" as a framework for understanding, organizing, and managing this reciprocal relationship between employee expectations and company objectives. The psychological contract is the implicit understanding between employees and their managers regarding how personal and corporate expectations will be coordinated and jointly fulfilled. The expectations that make up the psychological contract can be verbalized or unverbalized; recognized or unrecognized. To the extent that managers are not aware of the unverbalized or unrecognized aspects of the contract, they tacitly agree to expectations of which they have no knowledge.

Thomas presents several case examples of the psychological contract in action. Through these cases, he shows how a psychological contract framework can provide valuable insight into diagnosing and resolving ambiguous performance problems. As Thomas points out, all managers have psychological contracts with their people regardless of whether they acknowledge it explicitly. Managers can either understand, manage, and utilize these contracts in their efforts to run more efficient and effective operations, or they can ignore them and experience surprises, conflict, and disappointment.

INTEGRATIVE GOALS AND CONSENSUS IN PROBLEM SOLVING

Rensis Likert
Jane Gibson Likert

The research on conflict and decision making clearly indicates the great importance of integrative goals, common values, and mutual interests in facilitating the constructive resolution of conflict (Blake et al., 1964; Maier, 1963; Sherif, 1962). These goals reflect more deep-seated, more overriding, more fundamental wants than those which either party would be able to obtain by "winning." For example, citizens and leaders of the United States and the U.S.S.R. share the goal of wishing to stay alive, of not being annihilated in a nuclear holocaust. It is hoped that this mutual goal will motivate both nations to keep the peace.

"Common values," "mutual interest," or "superordinate goals" are terms used by different writers to describe the powerful forces compelling conflicting parties to seek the "integrative solution" urged by Mary Parker Follett (Fox & Urwick, 1973). Following her lead, we have selected "integrative goals" as the most satisfactory term for our purposes. Integrative goals which express the deep-seated needs and desires of the conflicting parties will bring them to the conference table when all else fails and will keep them hard at work seeking to find or create mutually acceptable solutions. In the presence of integrative goals, conflicting groups attempt to solve the problem in terms of the best interests of all rather than in terms of the parochial goals of a few.

When individuals feel indifferent toward an organization or institution and do not see the relationship between their well-being and its success, they have little motivation to strive to reach agreement to serve its objectives. If the conflict between units is strong and becomes structured into a win-lose struggle, they may well seek to have their unit win even though it may seriously damage or even destroy the entire organization. When individuals are deeply committed to the objectives of an organization, they are not willing to sacrifice its well-being for the benefit of one of its parts. Stagner (1956) found, for example, that union members were loyal to their union, but they also were loyal to the company. They felt that they needed the union to protect their interests but that the company had to succeed if they were to have interests to protect.

The task of leadership to make integrative goals operationally effective in helping to resolve a particular conflict varies with the extent to which these goals are clearly present and accepted or must be developed from potential sources. In some conflicts, these integrative goals are clearly present and accepted by everyone. The role of the leader in such conflicts is to see that the influence of shared goals is used fully. In other situations, the integrative goals may exist but may not yet have been explicitly recognized. In still others, nothing more is present than the potential for creating goals. Leadership is responsible for seeing that the integrative goals that are potentially or implicitly present become explicitly and fully recognized and accepted.

This task of leadership varies, of course, from one conflict situation to another and also is affected by the character of the integrative goals. Integrative goals, for example, can derive from basic human motive sources, such as the desire for physical security and survival. They also can be based on the situational requirements (i.e., the hard facts of life). Common problems can be a source of integrative goals. Regardless of [the problems'] source or character, leadership has an extremely important role to play in any conflict in helping to make all potentially integrative goals as clear and operationally effective as possible.

In field experiments in a boy's camp, Sherif (1962) demonstrated the great power of integrative goals in resolving conflicts (Sherif uses the term "superordinate goals"). He found that: "When groups in a state of friction come into contact under conditions embodying superordinate goals, they tend to cooperate toward the common goal" (p. 11). In one experiment with two groups of boys, the superordinate or integrative goals included preparing for an outing much desired by all, overcoming a threatened water shortage, and repairing a truck. Both of the latter two provided resources greatly needed by both groups. These integrative goals required greater efforts than either of the conflicting groups could provide by itself. These goals brought about highly effective cooperation in a situation in which there had been bitter hostility and conflict between the two groups (Sherif et al., 1961).

An example of excellent leadership in making explicit an integrative goal and of using it in decision making is the following (*National Civic Review,* October, 1959):

"I dislike contentiousness," our (National Municipal League) former president, Lawson Purdy, used to say. "It doesn't accomplish anything; it only tightens snarls."

But then in 1916 he faced an official commission organized to consider regulating the heights and bulks of buildings in New York City. The real estate fraternity was hostile to governmental interference with any man's right to build what he pleased on his own plot. Socialism! Ruination! It was well represented on the commission. Contention was waiting to explode. Purdy, the city's esteemed tax gatherer, looked around the lion's den, waited for the right moment and obtained quiet attention. "Let's all agree," he said, "to propose no regulations that do not enhance the values of the properties affected."

"*Enhance* values? Do you mean it?" "Yes," said Purdy. "It will, for instance, enhance residential neighborhood values to protect them from ruinous invasions by filling stations or shops . . . . Let's begin that way and see if we don't get somewhere on that principle!"

Down the table faces changed. Fiery speeches, constitutional doubts, conservative scorn faded out unspoken. Well, they'd try it. The talk turned creative and amiable. Within the hour, constructive work began. Eventually as their interest grew in their task, members did diverge where necessary from Purdy's proposed standard. The outcome was the first zoning ordinance in America, pioneer of a practice that is now all but universal in our cities, profoundly stabilizing the tax bases and reducing the hazards of home ownership. An era started by one wise phrase! (p. 452)

Serious problems faced by both parties to a conflict can become integrative goals. The Scanlon Plan, for example, came into being as a result of such integrative goals. As Clinton Golden[1] describes it:

It was my good fortune to have known and worked with Joe Scanlon for twenty years prior to his untimely death a little more than a year ago. He was one of the millions who suffered cruelly as a result of the depression of the Thirties. He did not become embittered as a result of these trying experiences. Indeed, while unemployed and without enough food and fuel for his family, he took the leadership among the workers in his community in securing unused land, in borrowing tractors and other equipment, in literally begging seed and fertilizer so that he and his fellow workers could raise food and get wood for fuel to meet their basic needs.

Perhaps it was out of these experiences in cooperative effort to assure simple survival that he first became aware of the capacity of people to work together. As the depression lifted and he was able to get back to work in the local mill, the friendships created in the common struggle for survival encouraged a continuation of cooperative endeavor.

Even before the Steel Worker's Organizing Committee was formed in 1936, and the organizing campaign was launched, a local union had been formed among the employees of the company he worked for. Wages were low, employment was uncertain, and competition for a share in the limited market was keen.

[1]Reprinted from *The Scanlon Plan,* edited by F. G. Lesieur, by permission of The M.I.T. Press, Cambridge, Massachusetts, © 1958.

The company had but recently emerged from bankruptcy, equipment was obsolete, and costs were high. Then came the union demands for higher wages and improved conditions of employment to compound the difficulties of management. If the demands were granted, it would threaten the survival of the company.

Joe took the leadership again in this period of adversity. He induced the president of the company to come with a committee of the union employees to the Pittsburgh office of the International Union to seek advice and help if possible. It was at this point my acquaintance with him began.

I have told the story of subsequent events so many times I am reluctant to repeat it. Suffice it to say that I suggested that the group return to the mill and arrange to interview every employee in an effort to enlist his aid and familiarity with work processes in eliminating waste, improving efficiency, reducing cost, and improving the quality of the products in order to keep assured of the survival of the company.

My advice was accepted; they returned to the mill and under Joe's leadership and with the full cooperation of management, set about in a most thorough and systematic manner to do just what I had suggested.

The local union did not immediately press requests for higher wages and other improvements. Within a few months, as a result of the sustained cooperative efforts of the workers and management, costs were reduced noticeably, and the quality of products improved. Even with its obsolete equipment, the company survived and was able to grant the wage increases and improved conditions of employment already granted by their more prosperous competitors.

The employees were rightfully proud of their part in this effort to assure the survival of the company and so to preserve their jobs. Management was equally proud of the dramatic but practical result of the teamwork. Thus was the foundation laid for building what has since come to be known as the Scanlon Plan.

Unless hostilities are so deeply ingrained as to preclude any cooperation, leaders can help conflicting parties recognize that their common problems can be integrative goals by having them examine the benefits both parties would experience if these problems were solved.

A company which needs to merchandise new products attractive to customers in order to survive is another example. If the company fails, there will be no jobs. The explicit recognition of this situational requirement can establish a strong integrative goal among the production, sales, and research and development departments of the firm. This will facilitate cooperative group problem solving focused on how to improve cooperation among the departments and on how to accelerate the successful development, production, and marketing of new products.

As this example indicates, situational requirements often can be powerful integrative goals. Not all situational requirements, however, are integrative goals. For example, time or budgetary limitations set boundaries within which a solution must fall to be acceptable. These serve as constraints and usually do not provide strong motivational forces in the parties to a conflict to find a mutually acceptable solution.

A leader can help a group recognize which situational requirements can become powerful integrative goals by having the group list all these requirements and select from among the total list those situational requirements which are integrative in character. This process usually will result in the discovery of several important integrative goals.

Basic human needs often are important integrative goals. Since their presence in a particular conflict situation may go unrecognized, the leader plays a crucial role in helping a group state them explicitly. All human beings, for example, seek to achieve and maintain a sense of personal worth and importance but do not ordinarily think in these terms. This is equally true of many of the motives or needs derived from the sense of personal worth and importance, including such needs as those for achievement, self-fulfillment, recognition, and self-actualization.

Many persons who recognize the existence of their own basic needs do not mention them because of the "of course" phenomenon. They feel that "of course" everyone recognizes the existence of these needs, and hence there is no point in mentioning them. By means of questions and even direct statements, the leader can help the conflicting parties recognize that they hold *in common* many of these basic human wants which will be satisfied more fully if their differences can be resolved.

Integrative goals can be used in a bitter conflict to mitigate the adverse effect of hostile attitudes on problem solving. When hostile attitudes are both pervasive and intense, they create strong forces in the persons holding them. These forces influence the behavior of those persons at every step in the problem-solving process. It is difficult to behave supportively toward persons for whom one feels a strong hostility. It is equally difficult to accept at face value their statements concerning the essential conditions that a solution must meet to be acceptable. Prejudices and hostile attitudes often seriously limit creativity in the search for new solutions.

Recording and analyzing the problem-solving process of the conflicting parties as they seek an innovative, mutually acceptable solution is a useful device in assisting them to recognize clearly the adverse influence of their hostile attitudes and the need to reduce the hostility by bringing into play the integrative goals. Tape recorders or videoscopes can be used to record the problem-solving behavior. In addition to the analysis of these tapes, each person can examine his or her own behavior by listening to the tapes and learning how well that person has been able to be objective and productive in the various steps of the problem-solving process. When recording equipment is not readily available, observers can be used to help the group be objective and productive in its problem solving.

THE NEED FOR CONSENSUS

If win-lose confrontation is used in resolving a conflict, the winning party, whether a nation, organization, or an individual, imposes its preferred solution on the other. Victory brings elation for the winner. Defeat brings feelings of rejection, failure, and impotence and is accompanied by bitterness and hostile attitudes. The losing party may be forced to accept the solution imposed on it, but it will continue the conflict, at least subversively, and sooner or later seek to achieve an outcome more acceptable to it.

Win-lose always means that the solution fails to give one party the minimum it needs for the solution to be acceptable. If all parties are to accept the outcome of a dispute willingly, the conditions that each feels are essential for a satisfactory solution must be met. Each party must win, at least to that extent. To bring this about, the conflict must be resolved with a win-win approach rather than a win-lose.

The use of consensus is essential at each step in the decision-making process and especially in the selection of the final agreement if the solution is to be win-win. Consensus, in Quaker terms, is "the sense of the meeting," a willing acceptance of the group's conclusions. The process of arriving at consensus is a free and open exchange of ideas which continues until agreement has been reached. This process assures that each individual's concerns are heard and understood and that a sincere attempt has been made to take them into consideration in the search for and the formulation of a conclusion. This conclusion may not reflect the exact wishes of each member, but since it does not violate the deep concerns of anyone, it can be agreed upon by all.

Consensus, then, is a cooperative effort to find a sound solution acceptable to everyone rather than a competitive struggle in which an unacceptable solution is forced on the losers. With consensus as the pattern of interaction, members need not fear being outsmarted or outmaneuvered. They can be frank, candid, and authentic in their interactions at all steps in the decision-making process. Win-win problem solving is being used increasingly in corporations, governmental agencies, and other organizations. The top committees or work groups of several of America's most successful corporations habitually use win-win problem solving and reach decisions with consensus.

In the League of Women Voters, a highly effective voluntary organization, most decisions are made by members of the various local Leagues in small groups by consensus. The national program also is developed in this way with suggestions going back and forth from local and state Leagues to the National Board and back and between local Leagues and between state Leagues. The resulting proposed national program is then presented to the representatives from all the local and state Leagues in the country at a national convention, held every two years. Changes may be made from the floor in the wording of items and sometimes a proposed item is rejected and another substituted, but since there has been thorough preliminary discussion and substantial agreement prior to the convention, radical changes at the convention are the exception rather than the rule. Although the final determination of the program is made by this large body using parliamentary procedures and majority rule, its use has a minimum of the win-lose consequences that often accompany such procedures. The prior give and take of ideas throughout the membership, the substantial agreement reached by consensus before the convention opens, and the conviction by the members of the value of using consensus whenever possible all contribute to a problem-solving attitude and not to a win-lose confrontation. Of great importance, too, is the membership's dedication to a common cause. The League's super-ordinate, integrative goals override differences about specifics.

Since the parliamentary procedure and *Robert's Rules of Order* are widely used today in dealing with conflict, their capacity to achieve consensus and win-win solutions deserve to be examined. As a rule, parliamentary procedures structure an interaction into a win-lose relationship. The rigidity of a formal motion with changes possible only by amendment makes the orderly problem-solving steps required for the search and discovery of a mutually acceptable solution difficult if not impossible. The parliamentary struggle is a confrontation between alternative solutions already formulated. Arguing from a fixed position rules out the possibility of innovative ideas generated by the systematic search for them in a free and open manner. Ruses such as tabling the motion in an attempt to defeat an opposing position or the maneuvering of countermotions and amendments are devices that can transform a group of well-intentioned and intelligent persons into warring camps. In the heat of argument, bruising statements may be made which never are entirely forgotten or forgiven. Parliamentary procedures typically yield a win-lose rather than a win-win outcome.

ACHIEVING CONSENSUS

The material in this article on problem solving proposes principles and procedures for facilitating the achievement of consensus. Evidence confirming the effectiveness of these principles and procedures is reported by Guetzkow and Gyr (1954). Their paper was a part of a larger project concerned with problem-solving conferences (Marquis, Guetzkow, & Heyns, 1951). The groups studied ranged in size from 5 to 20 persons and were called together to make policy and staff decisions. Only one session of each group was observed and analyzed.

The main headings in the material quoted below from Guetzkow and Gyr (1954) are taken from their summary of their findings. Under the headings are quotations from their paper which amplify the summary statement:

Study of the conflict itself revealed it not as a single characteristic, but rather consisting of two relatively unrelated traits. "Substantive conflict" is associated with intellectual opposition among participants, deriving from the content of the agenda. "Affective conflict" is tension generated by emotional clashes aroused during the interpersonal struggle involved in solving the group's agenda problems.

Certain conditions existing within the conference in either type of conflict are associated with the conference ending in high consensus.

A. Conditions associated with High Consensus in Groups in either Substantive or Affective Conflict.

  (i) When there is little expression of personal, self-oriented needs.

  (ii) When whatever self-needs are expressed tend to be satisfied during the course of the meeting.

  It is found that the expression of many self-oriented or personal needs by the conference participants is detrimental to the reaching of consensus. This is true under high as well as under low conflict conditions. The self- or ego-oriented needs of a participant express themselves in many ways in the social interaction which constitutes a conference. Some persons express such needs by verbally arguing with others; some need to dominate the scene. Expression of these needs in a conference, either in an overt fashion or in more subtle, hidden ways, does not promote consensus. With reference to the expression of ego-needs it is interesting to note that when self-needs are satisfied through rewarding personal interrelations within the conference itself, there is a significant tendency for the group to achieve consensus, especially when intense conflict prevails.

  (iii) When there is a generally pleasant atmosphere and the participants recognized the need for unified action.

  (iv) When the group's problem-solving activity is understandable, orderly, and focused on one issue at a time.

  Those meetings in which discussion is orderly in its treatment of topics, and without backward references to previously discussed issues, tended to end in more consensus, despite large amounts of substantive or affective conflict. When participants discussed but one issue at a time, instead of simultaneously dabbling in two or three, it was more possible for the group to reach consensus. The ability of the members to understand what each said led to agreement. When participants knew the vocabulary the others were using, when they talked on a common conceptual level, then high conflict tended to end in consensus.

B. Conditions associated with High Consensus in Groups in Substantive Conflict. (These conditions do not hold for groups in affective conflict.)

(i)   When facts are available and used.

Comparison of the high consensus and low consensus groups reveals that facts resolve substantive conflict. Those groups that have more expertise available and that utilize this knowledge are those whose substantive conflict ends in more consensus. The utilization of expertise does not significantly influence affective conflict, however, except in low conflict groups.

These results are made more understandable by analyzing the behavior of the leader. Chairmen of groups in high substantive conflict which ended in consensus did three times as much seeking for information of an objective factual nature from members of their groups as did chairmen in groups which did not end in consensus.

(ii) When chairman, through much solution-proposing, aids the group in penetrating its agenda-problems.

(iii) When the participants feel warm and friendly toward each other in a personal way.

When the members of the group seem to like each other personally, substantive conflict tends to be more easily resolved. The attractions of the participants towards each other on the basis of personal characteristics, help to achieve consensus. This friendliness permeates their problem-solving activities. The participants are warm and supportive of each other and encourage the full expression of personal opinions, without restrictions. (pp. 378-382)

Samuel (1971, p. 36) found a sizable relationship (r = +.74) between managerial support scores and consensus when consensus was measured both by the "distance" between the views among the members of a group and the extent of agreement. He also found that supportive behavior among the members of a group, i.e., peer support, showed a marked relationship to his two measures of consensus ($r = +.69$).

These findings show that the probability of resolving substantive conflicts by consensus is enhanced substantially by the orderly group problem solving undertaken in a supportive atmosphere. This research demonstrates again the importance of the principle of supportive relationships in contributing to the successful management of conflict.

PRAGMATIC CONSENSUS: AGREEING TO COOPERATE

In some situations where a conflict is extremely bitter and of long duration and where attitudes between the parties are very hostile, it is unrealistic to expect that consensus will be reached in the early efforts to resolve the conflict by problem solving. Even though the initial efforts focus on those aspects of the conflict which can be most easily resolved, it still may be impossible to achieve full consensus. When this occurs, it may be possible to reach a useful form of working relationships which we will call "pragmatic consensus." Pragmatic consensus is a willingness to give a particular solution a trial run. It represents an agreement to try out a solution for a period of time even though some members of the group still have reservations concerning it. The solution on trial may deal with only a part of the problem, but, even so, the willingness to agree to try a part often represents an important step toward ultimately achieving a solution to the total conflict.

A leader should seek to use pragmatic consensus when a group is unable to reach full consensus. When the reluctant persons agree to "go along" with a trial run of the proposed course of action, it is extremely important that the effort be accompanied by special attention to their expressed interests and concerns. The principle of supportive relationships needs to be applied fully in these attempts since its use will increase greatly the likelihood of success.

Every successful use of pragmatic consensus in dealing with some aspect of a major conflict yields more favorable attitudes and greater confidence and trust among the parties to the conflict and strengthens the interaction-influence network between them. This improvement in the interaction-influence network makes it more capable of dealing successfully with the more serious aspects of the conflict. The likelihood of reaching full consensus in dealing with them is increased.

THE BACKUP, RECYCLING TECHNIQUE

When it is impossible to reach full consensus or even some simple form of pragmatic consensus, it is advantageous for the leader to use the "backup, recycling technique." The group starts over and repeats all the steps in the problem-solving process. In essence the group says, "Since we have not reached consensus, we must not have done the problem solving well. Let's try again." The group starts by reexamining the statement of the problem to be sure that it is considering the real problem and that the problem is stated well and clearly. It would be well to examine the conditions that were originally thought to be essential to see if any of these conditions can be classified as desirable but not essential. Two steps, in particular, need intensive effort when trying to do a better job the second time. These are (1) searching for both additional and stronger integrative goals and relevant situational requirements, and (2) seeking to create or discover an innovative solution which will meet all of the essential conditions and, consequently, be acceptable to all.

When the conflict is intense and bitter, it may be necessary for the group to use the backup, recycling technique more than once. This technique is likely to be most effective when the parties to the conflict recognize that the well-being of all will suffer serious consequences if a constructive solution is not reached.

ACTION WITHOUT CONSENSUS

At times, a problem will be so difficult or the hostilities will be so great that even with able leadership and the use of the backup, recycling procedure, the group is unable to reach consensus on a final solution within the time available for its deliberation. When this occurs, the leader may face situational requirements which necessitate that something be done by a given time and be compelled to take action.

There are several courses open. If the group is a unit in a hierarchical organization, the leader can select the solution that best meets the essential conditions and that is least detrimental to any of these conditions. Another alternative, which may be less damaging to the group, is for the leader to suggest that, since they have not reached consensus and yet action must be taken, they proceed with the solution favored by the persons who have the major responsibility for implementing the decisions since it is up to them to make it work. This procedure usually meets with a favorable response providing that the solution does not seriously violate any of the conditions felt to be essential by the group or some of its members.

When consensus is not reached and a solution which does not meet all the essential conditions stated by the group is put into effect by hierarchical pressure, some members of the group will be displeased. When this occurs, the attitudes of the members toward each other tend to become less favorable. The same will be true of the loyalty of members to the group and of the confidence and trust which the members have in each other and in the leader. These developments are apt to result in a general deterioration in the problem-solving and performance capability of the group. Leaders can permit this to occur occasionally, but not often.

The loyalty and cohesiveness of groups need to be rebuilt and sustained by successful problem solving, or leaders will find that they and their groups have overdrawn their goodwill bank account.

The failure to reach consensus is much more serious when the group is a unit in an interorganizational linkage structure between two organizations in conflict. In this situation, leaders can make little use of hierarchical authority. They must rely on the skillful use of situational requirements, common values, and integrative goals, and the sensitive and skillful use of the principle of supportive relationships. One procedure for arriving at a course of action is to encourage the group to review its problem-solving activity, step by step, and to ask each member whether that member feels that the rest of the group understands his or her position, needs, goals, and point of view. If members feel that they are understood, the leader may be able to obtain action by suggesting that, since everyone has been heard fully and with empathetic understanding, the group should adopt for action, on a pragmatic consensus basis, that solution which appears to meet the essential conditions best. This procedure is likely to result in action when the group recognizes the existence of compelling situational requirements and strong common values and integrative goals.

INDUSTRIAL RELATIONS EXPERIENCE SUPPORTS THE USE OF CONSENSUS

Many leaders in industrial relations recognize the superiority of consensus over win-lose procedures. In his presidential address to the Industrial Relations Research Association, Dunlop (1960) emphasized the substantial advantages achieved from the greater use of consensus.

> The theme of the preceding three sections [of this paper] has been that our national industrial relations system suffers from seeking solutions to problems in terms of legislation and litigation, formal arbitration and public pronouncements. This malady afflicts alike national governmental policy, the labor federation, and the confederation level of management. The common difficulty in its essence is a failure to develop a consensus within government, the labor movement, or management. The consequence is resort to partisan legislation and litigation and the ascendency of the politicians in national industrial relations policy. An alternative policy is reliance, to a greater degree, upon the development of consensus.
>
> Greater reliance upon consensus is particularly appropriate since the range of industrial relations problems has become increasingly technical, and uniform rules across wide reaches of the economy are impractical in many cases. Moreover, in our society, rules and policies which have been formulated by those

directly affected are likely to receive greater respect and compliance than when imposed by fiat. The rapidly changing circumstances of technology and markets require greater reliance on consensus since those most directly affected are more sensitive to such change, and adaptation can be more gradual than that imposed belatedly from without. Consensus develops habits of mind which encourage continuing adaptation to new circumstances.

The method of consensus is admittedly difficult to apply; it is so much easier simply to pass another law, or issue another decision or another resolution. The achievement of consensus is often a frustrating process since it must triumph over inertia, suspicion, and the warpath. It is slow to build. But it is clearly the most satisfying and enduring solution to problems. It always has significant by-products in improved understanding in many other spheres than those related to the consensus . . . .

An industrial society requires a considerably greater measure of consensus on industrial relations problems than we have. The present course is set toward an unending sequence of legislative regulation, litigation, and political pronouncement. The community has a right to expect more from organized labor, confederation levels of management, and governmental agencies. Indeed, a shift in the method of national policy-making in the industrial relations area is required if labor and management are to make their potential contributions to the larger problems facing the community. The place to begin is to resolve that the method of consensus will be used internally in reaching decisions within the federation and confederation levels of management and in the formulation and administration of governmental policies. This is the fundamental challenge —in my view — of the next four to ten years in industrial relations in the United States. (pp. 14-15)

CONSENSUS DOES NOT MEAN COMPLACENCY

Employing consensus does not mean that the group is to settle into sweet, complacent unanimity. If it does, the leader is failing in his role. There should be full recognition of genuine differences, and the problem solving should be done in an atmosphere of "no nonsense." The existing differences should be used to stimulate the search for innovative solutions. Moreover, if the disagreements are significant and important to the group members, they, themselves, will help maintain the "no-

nonsense" orientation. Complacent unanimity will occur only when the problems are inconsequential, the disagreements of no significance, or the leadership incompetent and the problem solving done poorly.

CONSENSUS DOES NOT MEAN LEVELING TO MEDIOCRITY

A criticism of consensus voiced by some is that it leads to mediocre decisions since the decision must always represent the average of the views held by the problem-solving group. This criticism is based on the assumption that each person's opinion carries equal weight in arriving at a consensual decision. Nothing is farther from reality in a group skilled in problem solving. The influence exercised by each person reflects the group's estimate of the significance of that person's contribution. Those persons who customarily make the more important contributions tend to be the more influential. This is true concerning both the process of decision making and the content of the decision being dealt with. On highly technical problems, the persons best informed on that problem tend to be more influential. In discussing the concept of consensus, the chief executive officer of a large corporation said, "Although we use consensus in our top finance and operating committees, this does not mean each member of a committee exercises the same amount of influence from decision to decision. Those who do their 'homework' well, who come fully informed and fully prepared to discuss all aspects of the problem are the influential members."

Decisions reached by consensus are distinctly different from those reached by voting, particularly when each person's vote carries equal weight.

Farris (1969) has found that, among engineers and scientists, those who exert more influence on decisions are those persons who have demonstrated that they are better performers. Those who accomplish more exert more influence than do others on decisions related to their area of competence.

When consensus is used, each member of the group has the opportunity to exert influence on the decision. The magnitude of this influence depends upon such variables as the level of the member's technical knowledge related to the problem, the member's knowledge of the problem and the situation, the importance of the issue to the member, how strongly the member feels about it, how well the member knows and adheres to the group problem-solving process, how much the member contributes to building group loyalty, how innovative-minded the member is, the member's competence, judgment, and strengths as demonstrated in previous decision making, and the member's sincerity, integrity, and supportive treatment of others.

SYSTEM 4 LEADERSHIP IS *NOT* "PERMISSIVE"

The principle of supportive relationships which emphasizes the importance of aiding each person to achieve and maintain a sense of personal worth had led some persons to conclude that leaders should be "permissive," i.e., exert no influence, but let each member of the group go his or her own independent way. This is a serious misinterpretation. In a System 4 interaction-influence network, leaders first must see that a multiple overlapping structure is built whereby each person can exert significant influence upon decisions and, in turn, be *influenced by the system*. There is a *reciprocal* relationship in a System 4 social system: each person can influence the system and each accepts influence from it. This is basically different from being subjected to relatively little influence which would be the case if the leadership were permissive. *System 4 is participative, not permissive.* *Permissiveness is a characteristic of System 0 and is laissez faire.*

FREEDOM MAY NOT BE MOTIVATING

Some persons hold the view that freeing an individual from influence by managers, or even by peers, will bring substantial improvement in performance. This view holds that each person knows exactly what to do and how to do it, can and will provide his or her own direction, will be more highly motivated, and will accomplish more if freed from the influence of the organization. Experience as well as quantitative research shows that this is not the case. Over the centuries, artists and scholars who experience long periods of isolation have been less productive than those who were members of "schools" and "colleges." Extensive research shows that persons who are entirely or substantially on their own and do not experience the stimulation from structured interaction with others tend to be less motivated and less productive than persons who are an integral part of a highly effective interaction-influence network. Persons in a System 4 interaction-influence network are much more highly motivated and productive than persons in a System 0, laissez-faire organization (Likert, 1961; Pelz, 1957; Pelz & Andrews, 1966; White and Lippitt, 1960).

This same confusion exists concerning self-actualization. This motive, like all the others which derive their strength from the desire to achieve and maintain a sense of personal worth and importance, is powerful. But the values one embraces, the goals one sets in terms of which self-actualization is sought, and the level of motivation to achieve these goals are all determined by the individual's social environment. The isolated person derives far less motivation from self-actualization than does the person who is an integral part of a System 4 interaction-influence network.

Any attempt to create highly motivated behavior in a conflict situation by relying on permissive leadership or self-actualization isolated from an effective interaction-influence network will yield highly disappointing results. Permissive leadership which frees persons from all constraints is likely to yield irresponsible behavior and to fail to achieve the co-ordinated, motivated behavior that membership in an effective interaction-influence network attains. Permissive leadership is ineffective in resolving conflicts.

REFERENCES

Blake, R. R., Shepard, H. A., and Mouton, J. S. *Managing intergroup conflict in industry.* Houston: Gulf Publishing, 1964.

Dunlop, J. T. *Consensus and national labor policy,* IRRA Presidential Address, 1960, pp. 14-15.

Farris, G. F. Organizational factors and individual performance. *Journal Applied Psychology,* 1969, *53,* 87-92.

Fox, E. M., and Urwick, L. *Dynamic administration: The collected papers of May Parker Follett* (2nd ed.). London: Pitman Publishing, 1973. (Page citations from 1st ed., Metcalf, H. C., and Urwick, L., eds., New York: Harper, 1940.)

Guetzkow, H., and Gyr, J. An analysis of conflict in decision-making groups. *Human Relations,* 1954, *7,* 367-382.

Likert, R. *New patterns of management.* New York: McGraw-Hill, 1961.

Maier, N. R. F. *Problem solving discussions and conferences: Leadership methods and skills.* New York: McGraw-Hill, 1963.

Marquis, D. G., Guetzkow, H., and Heyns, R. W. A social psychological study of the decision-making conference. In H. Guetzkow (Ed.), *Groups, leadership, and men: Research in human relations.* Pittsburgh: Carnegie Press, 1951, pp. 55-67.

National Civic Review. October 1959, p. 452.

Pelz, D. C. *Motivation of the engineering and research specialist.* New York: American Management Association, General Management Series #186, 1957, pp. 25-46.

Pelz, D., and Andrews, F. *Scientists in organizations: Productive climates for research and development.* New York: Wiley, 1966.

Samuel, Y. *The role of social consensus as a conditioner in organizational planned change,* (Technical Report). Ann Arbor: University of Michigan Institute for Social Research, 1971.

Sherif, M. (Ed.). *Intergroup relations and leadership: Approaches and research in industrial, ethnic, cultural, and political areas.* New York: Wiley, 1962.

Sherif, M., Harvey, O. J., White, B. J., Hood, W. R., and Sherif, C. W. *Intergroup conflict and cooperation: the robbers cave experiment.* Norman, Okla.: University of Oklahoma Book Exchange, 1961.

Stagner, R. *The psychology of industrial conflict.* New York: Wiley, 1956.

White, R. K. and Lippitt, R. O. *Autocracy and democracy: Experiments in group leadership.* New York: Harper, 1960.

MANAGING WORK RELATIONSHIPS THROUGH THE PSYCHOLOGICAL CONTRACT

R. Roosevelt Thomas, Jr.

To make intelligent choices from among various approaches to managing people, the manager needs a framework that will highlight the central issues. This article suggests that the psychological contract concept can facilitate the selection and design of systems for managing work relationships between the organization and its employees.

As representatives of the enterprise, managers are charged with developing and maintaining viable and effective work relationships. This means that management must ensure that organization participants are willing to cooperate in fulfilling task requirements. To secure individual cooperation, the manager must make certain that the employee is sufficiently rewarded for contributing; that is, that the person receives sufficient and appropriate benefits to enhance the likelihood of continued effective participation. In sum, the manager must endeavor to facilitate fulfillment of both the organization's and the individual's expectations.

In deciding how to go about meeting this responsibility, the manager must make explicit or implicit choices with respect to managerial style, structural arrangements, control systems, performance appraisal processes, recruitment and hiring procedures, and reward practices.

The manager also must be able to evaluate and select from a variety of contemporary managerial approaches; for example, Management by Objectives (MBO); Planning, Programming, and Budgeting System (PPBS); Zero Budgeting; Job Enlargement; Job Enrichment; Participatory Management; Centralization; Decentralization; and Autonomous Work Groups — just to name a few. The point of this article is that an awareness and understanding of the organization's psychological contract with its people can facilitate the design of effective systems for managing human behavior.

THE CONCEPT

Before proceeding to examples of how the psychological contract can be useful in decision making around managerial approaches, the concept will be defined and illustrated.

The Concept Defined

When an individual joins an organization, he does so because of his expectations of what he can get in exchange for his services. Similarly, when a manager hires a person, he does so because of expectations of what the individual can contribute toward the accomplishment of the organization's objectives and, in exchange for this contribution, the manager expects to provide the employee with certain benefits to enhance the likelihood of continued membership. To sum the relationship, each party expects to receive value for value given. These expectations, which can be verbalized or unverbalized, constitute what some organizational writers have called the psychological contract.[1,2]

The offering and acceptance of employment implies tacit agreement on the part of the manager and the individual to each other's expectations —verbalized and unverbalized. By hiring an individual, the manager as the organization's representative establishes a reciprocal relationship based on the psychological contract consisting of each party's expectations of what will be given and received. To the extent that the manager is not aware of the unverbalized aspects of the contract, he agrees to expectations of which he has no knowledge.

A number of reasons exist to explain why some important parts of the psychological contract are unverbalized.

- Both parties may not be entirely clear about their own expectations and how they wish them fulfilled. They may wish to avoid detailing the contract until they have a better feel for their own needs. Thus managers and prospective employees describe their expectations in very general terms; the manager may see himself "buying brains" which will adapt to some poorly defined position, while the individual may endeavor to maintain as much latitude as possible in specifying his job interests.

- The individual and the manager may not be aware of some of their expectations of the other. Managers frequently are not aware explicitly of how much loyalty they demand of their employees. Similarly, individuals are not always aware of the extent to which social interactions on the job are important to them. Being unaware of these needs does not make them any less real, for if they are not fulfilled, both parties will quickly become aware of their reality.

- The individual and the manager may perceive some expectations as so natural and basic that they do not feel the need to express them. Two examples would be the expectations of "no stealing" and "an honest day's work for a day's pay."

[1] Harry Levinson, Charlton R. Price, Kenneth J. Munden, Harold J. Mandl, Charles M. Salley, *Men, Management and Mental Health* (Cambridge: Harvard University Press, 1966), pp. 22-38.

[2] Edgar Schein, *Organizational Psychology* (Englewood Cliffs, New Jersey: Prentice-Hall, 1970), pp. 50-79.

- Cultural norms may inhibit verbalization. A desire to be perceived as an "Horatio Alger" type of self-starter may prevent an applicant for employment from probing too deeply into the manager's expectations. Norms against violations of an individual's privacy may cause a manager to be careful in expressing his expectations of loyalty on and off the job.

- Some aspects of the contract are unverbalized because they are derived from articulated expectations. Each party assigns its own meanings and priorities to the verbalized parts of the psychological contract; consequently, both parties have a set of unverbalized expectations derived from their interpretations of those verbalized.

Psychological contracts may vary in an infinite number of ways. Below are some examples.

- **Fast-Track Contract**. The manager seeks an individual capable of rapidly rising through the ranks. He desires potential and ambition which can easily be converted into achievements. In exchange, the manager agrees to grant promotions as quickly as they are earned and to provide a track of positions with increasing responsibilities and rewards. Typically, the fast-track path operates separately from the regular career paths.

- **Factory Contract**. While contracts in manufacturing operations vary, the relationship described here is probably among the more typical.

    The manufacturing manager in one company offered the workers high wages, good fringe benefits, and a broad program of social activities including sports and parties. In exchange, management expected the employees to follow orders, satisfy work standards, observe safety procedures, and to perform repetitive, noisy, and dirty tasks. Though these expectations were not explicitly stated, they were real to both managers and workers.[3]

- **Paternalistic Contract.** The manager offers a contract in which the company promises "to take care" of its people in many ways. Not only is job security provided, but the organization assumes responsibility for other needs of its "family." Listen to one manager talk about the paternalistic practices of his company.

    There is a sense of family here. An expectation exists that if you are loyal to the company, it will be loyal to you; that if you have a problem you can take it to Papa President and he will seriously consider your situation. Twenty years ago, a tornado came through and fiercely hit the town. The company stepped in and gave considerable aid. Those houses you see along the river are a result of the company's generous response.

[3]Paul R. Lawrence and J. D. Donnell, Empire Glass Co. (B), 9-109-044. Boston: Harvard Business School, 1964.

I could go on and on. Our fringe benefits reflect how the company takes care of its people. The whole fringe benefit package is oriented toward taking care of the employee's family. We were the first to ensure the education of a worker's children should he die. We continually upgrade retirement benefits to offset inflation. The company's hiring and promotional practices are also paternalistic. The offspring of employees always have first shot at openings — if they are qualified. Further, the company has a strong policy of promoting from within. Rare is the case of someone being hired from the outside for a top position.

What more is there to say. This is a darn good company.[4]

The paternalistic contract is largely unstated and the result of an evolutionary process. Typically, the manager's paternalistic expectations are signaled through actions and reflected in traditions and myths. For example, if management over the years sponsors educational programs, pays for therapeutic treatment of its people with alcoholic and psychological problems, ensures that retirement benefits keep pace with cost of living increases, and develops a comprehensive system for facilitating the growth of employees, organization members could perceive these actions repeated over a period of time as signals of a paternalistic contract. If nothing happens to contradict their interpretation, employee perception of a paternalistic attitude gradually will grow stronger.

In some instances, the organization participants' beliefs about paternalism may not reflect the actual attitude of management; specifically, management can perform the activities described previously for reasons other than a desire to be paternalistic. However, regardless of the manager's true attitude, if subordinates perceive the existence of a paternalistic contract, they will behave accordingly and expect fulfillment. Any violation would likely produce dissatisfaction.

- **Loyalty Contract**. Managers have expectations concerning loyalty. This contract prescribes the extent to which "dirty organization linen" can be washed and where it can be aired. A frequent prescription is that it be washed internally — if at all, but definitely not outside with the press or regulatory bodies.

  This contract is usually implicit in the norms of the enterprise and is often not verbalized. Violations typically bring a penalty of dismissal from the organization.[5]

[4]R. Roosevelt Thomas, Webster Industries (A), 9-476-110. Boston: Harvard Business school, 1976.

[5]For example of violations of the "Loyalty Contract," see David W. Ewing, "Employee Rights: Taking the Gag Off," *Civil Liberties Review,* Fall, 1974, pp. 54-61.

- **Prestige Contract**. Some managers pay low wages, but offer considerable organization prestige. Here, the assumption is that the employee will receive some satisfaction in saying that he or she works for the prestigious enterprise. At one time, bank managers were perceived as offering this type of contract to bankers. Similarly, some establishments seek "prestige" relationships with secretaries. When this contract falters, it usually leads to signs reading, "We can't eat prestige."

The contracts described above are a few of the more common alternatives. Once the manager and the individual have established a relationship based on verbalized *and* nonverbalized expectations, the managerial task becomes that of facilitating fulfillment. If the manager is successful in fostering contract compliance, each party will realize its expectations while simultaneously fulfilling those of the other.

A FRAMEWORK FOR MANAGING WORK RELATIONSHIPS

This section will demonstrate the power of the psychological contract concept as a way of thinking about managerial issues and a tool for facilitating decision-making. Illustrations in the areas of leadership style, performance appraisal, employee attitudes and the management of change will be presented and discussed in the context of the psychological contract.

Leadership Style

Ralph Langley managed a production department comprised of eight women and two men. While each of the eight women had specialities, they rotated considerably among the various production tasks. Because the women were flexible in their skills, it was not uncommon for several women at different times, and occasionally simultaneously, to perform the same operation. The women were augmented by two men, one who worked part time in the department and another who served as the maintenance person.

When Langley assumed responsibility for the department, he came with explicit assumptions about management and motivation. One was a strong belief that individuals needed to feel as though they were part of the company, that they were working for the company, and not their supervisor. In this context, his job as a manager was to help his workers. Another of his beliefs was that an individual's job should represent the greatest source of satisfaction experienced. The individual, in Langley's view, should feel that life at work was worthwhile and full of accomplishments. Finally, Langley felt that employees were most productive when they were doing what they wanted to do, rather than what was prescribed for them.

Operationally, Langley's assumptions about management and people led him to adopt some interesting managerial practices. First, he emphasized to his people that they were working for the company, and that he desired to help them, rather than to tell them what to do. He stressed that they were on their own as far as getting out production, scheduling work, pacing themselves, and monitoring their wastes. Consequently, he did not position a supervisor in the room with the employees. Second, he was open with the workers in sharing his technical knowledge and information about company matters. Whenever an employee approached Langley with a problem, as he encouraged them to do, he was always careful to "give his knowledge." Thirdly, during regular visits to the production room, he always spoke to the workers about whatever was of interest to them. To foster a sense of fairness, he practiced speaking to a different person first whenever entering the room. Finally, he urged his workers to use budgets and standards as guideposts, rather than as controlling devices. He advised his people that, "You should be taking your incentives from yourselves."

Prior to Langley's assuming responsibility for the department, its members had acquired a reputation for being agitators, hotheads, and persistent troublemakers. Production was down, costs were out of control, and deliveries were unpredictable. Since Langley had taken over, circumstances had improved considerably.

Between January of the previous year and March of the current one, the department had realized a 53% improvement in the dollar output per man-hour of work; also, direct labor efficiency had increased by approximately 24%. Raw material utilization had improved by about 12%, while expenses had averaged 81% of budget. In sum, Langley's workers were very profitable and successful.

With respect to Langley, the group was very pleased with their new boss. Among their sentiments were the following:

- Ralph is fair, and knows what he is doing.

- ...That guy made our work something it had never been before . . . . And it's not only respect I feel for Ralph. Ralph is my friend. I look forward to work every morning. Now, this is just a small department here, and I'm not over anyone, but I feel important. I feel there's a purpose in my life . . . .

- It's how Ralph and people like him can make you feel about [your job]. I know I'm not very bright and it doesn't take much for anyone to make me feel stupid, but Ralph has never done that. He's always made me feel that I've got ideas that are useful . . . every time I talk over a problem with him I feel as though I'm learning something. And I am learning!

- . . . Ralph has a way of using his knowledge to help a person build up her own knowledge. He gives it to you — he doesn't use it on you.

That's how I feel about Ralph as a friend and as the best boss I've ever had.[6]

Discussion. Why was Langley successful with a group which previously had been a problem for its supervisors? One explanation can be developed by looking at the situation in the context of the psychological contract. Specifically, Langley's unverbalized assumptions about management along with his managerial practices matched the unverbalized expectations of the workers' psychological contract. Implicit in Langley's managerial beliefs was the psychological contract outlined in Exhibit 1. That Langley's views were on target was indicated by the increase in the unit's productivity and profitability and the remarks of praise offered by the employees.

EXHIBIT 1
Langley's Implicit View of the Psychological Contract

	Expectations		
	By Manager	**By Workers**	
TO RECEIVE	• Cooperative effort • Problem solving by the workers • Considerable self-management • Production beyond minimum required • Improvements in overall group performance • Open communications of any unresolved problems	• Cooperative effort • Some problem solving • Some self-management • Service beyond the minimum • Performance as required	**TO GIVE**
TO GIVE *	• Adequate compensation • Sense of belonging to company • Sense of importance • Sense of accomplishment • Sense of purpose • Training and knowledge • Sense of fulfillment through autonomy to do what they want to do	• Adequate compensation • Sense of belonging • Sense of importance • Sense of accomplishment • Sense of being valued	**TO RECEIVE**

*In this instance, "to give" should read as "to facilitate realization of."

[6]Cyrus R. Gibson and John Darman, The Nuclear Tube Assembly Room (B), 9-476-004. Boston: Harvard Business School, 1975.

313

Two observations are in order. One, the agreement between Langley's philosophy of management and the unverbalized expectations of his workers apparently was based on his intuitive judgment, rather than on a formal or systematic assessment of the workers' needs and dissatisfactions. In other words, one could argue that Langley and his beliefs happened to be in the right place at the right time. Two, what turned out to be critical aspects of the contract — sense of importance, purpose, accomplishment, belonging, etc. — were unverbalized, but yet very real to Langley and the members of his unit.

Performance Appraisal

Baines Electronics Corporation was a medium-sized company with annual sales of about $280 million. The company had developed a climate intended to minimize status differentials and to foster a team or cooperative spirit. This goal was facilitated by an "open door" policy to the president's office and "fair treatment of employees." Baines offered its engineers a variety of fringe benefits along with stable employment. Also, there existed numerous company sponsored athletic teams. The net result of this climate was a non-union organization characterized by friendly relations and unanimity of purpose.

Baines' merit performance appraisal system was based on three salary curves plotted against experience. For every level of experience there was a 100% (maximum), a 50% (mid-point), and a 0% (minimum) salary point. Depending on his or her rating, each engineer would fall somewhere between the minimum and maximum points for the relevant experience level. Only evaluators and the salary administration staff group had knowledge of the ratings given to individuals. Further, no individual knew his or her own rating. Under this system raises (good and average) were given randomly throughout the year.

In November, 1961, Baines' president became concerned that the company's merit system had evolved into a "cost of living" scheme. He believed that the relationship between salary increases and performance was not as clear as it should be. Consequently, he recommended a new merit-performance appraisal scheme.

Under the new arrangements, the timing and amount of raises were to be tied more significantly to performance. The new system had three key features:

1. High performers were to be given raises earlier than low performers.

2. The granting of raises was to be accomplished by a public gesture of commendation.

3. The dollar amount set aside for raises was double the previous year's percent.

The plan was received enthusiastically by managers and engineers. All agreed that changes were needed.

Implementation began in January, 1962. Typical of the experiences with the system were those of Paul Jefferson, a project manager at Baines. As Jefferson began use of the system, his people quickly deduced that individuals called to his office on Friday mornings were being granted raises. After about a month with the system in operation, a stream of complaining engineers began a continuous flow through Jefferson's office. The complaints varied from inquiries as to why certain people received raises before others to a respected senior engineer's embarrassment that his raise would be among the last given. The "old-time" engineer had made some valuable contributions in the early years of the company, but had plateaued about five years ago and thus was not viewed as one of the top professionals — though he had displayed spirit and loyalty down through the years. The net result of the complaints presented to Jefferson was a decline in morale.

Because Jefferson's engineers were not unique, the company's president decided that the system had to be modified.[7]

Discussion. Why did Baines' new performance appraisal-compensation system fail? The failure can be attributed to the fact that it did not fit well with the psychological contract existing between Baines and its engineers. True, the system was congruent with the employees' expectation that salary adjustments be based on performance, but it also violated other key aspects of the contract. See Exhibit 2 for an outline of the contract.

The new system conflicted with three important areas of the contract. First, it violated the engineers' expectations of fair treatment. Some individuals felt that they had not been treated fairly under the new system. This did not mean necessarily that the new system was any less fair than the old, but rather that the inequities of the new system were much more visible than those of the old. In the past, it was more or less assumed by the engineers that the system was fair. Now, the "public" features of the new system made this assumption more difficult.

Second, the engineers' expectation that each individual would be held in equal esteem and granted equal respect was violated. In reality, this expectation probably never was fully met, but the organizational climate and practices operated to minimize respect and esteem differentials. By publicly tying raises more closely to performance the new system signaled clearly that the company valued and respected high performers more than low performers. Though this no doubt had always been the case, the new system raised the esteem and respect differentials to a higher level of consciousness.

Finally, the engineers' expectation of rewards for experience and past service was violated. Under the old system, the company had developed a practice of recognizing service and loyalty, while the new approach

[7] Jay W. Lorsch and Jeanne Deschamps, Baines Electronics Corp. (A), 9-470-065. Boston: Harvard Business School, 1969.

315

EXHIBIT 2

Baines' Psychological Contract with Its Engineers

Expectations		
By Managers	**By Engineers**	
T O R E C E I V E • Good team effort — success of project depended on ability of project personnel to work as a team • Loyalty and commitment • Cooperative spirit • Professional excellence and professional development	• Good team effort • Loyalty and commitment • Cooperative spirit • Professional excellence and professional development	**T O G I V E**

T O G I V E
 • Good working conditions:
  • fringe benefits
  • stable employment
  • adequate compensation
 • Cooperative and friendly climate
 • Collegial relations between management and engineers:
  • open-door policy
  • give and take with engineers
 • Fair treatment
 • Recognition for service and loyalty
 • Reward for performance
	• Good working conditions:
	  • fringe benefits
	  • stable employment
	  • adequate compensation
	 • Cooperative and friendly climate
	 • Collegial relations between engineers and management:
	  • open-door policy
	  • give and take with management
	 • Fair treatment
	 • Recognition for service and loyalty
	 • Reward for performance
	 • Collegial relations with engineering peers — expected minimization of formal status differentials among engineers
		T O R E C E I V E

down-played their importance and actually could result in some old-timers feeling unappreciated. To the extent that the situation of the old-timer described earlier was typical, loyalty and experience counted for little under the new arrangements.

Given these conflicts with verbal and non-verbal expectations, it is not surprising that the new approach worked poorly. The Baines case demonstrates the importance of having a fit between a system and the psychological contract it is intended to facilitate. A fit with one key aspect of the contract does not guarantee success; instead, Baines' experience suggests that the more extensive the fit, the greater the likelihood of an effective system.

Employee Attitudes

The top management of a bank was concerned that its employees did not have the "right attitudes," despite the fact that the organization had one of the best salary scales in the industry. Specifically, the officers were disturbed that their people were not sufficiently aggressive to meet the demands of the increasing competition in the loan and trust business. They hypothesized that the attitudes could be explained by the following observations.

- Employees lacked a sense of loyalty to the bank.
- The status of bank work had declined in the eyes of the employees.
- Employees were too preoccupied with money.
- Employees, especially the younger ones, held unrealistic aspirations for advancement.
- Employees lacked interest in their work.
- High national employment had spoiled people. They desired "something for nothing."

Perplexed as to exactly what was happening with its employees, the bank brought in a researcher to look at the problem.

His research, in essence, revealed the psychological contract displayed in Exhibit 3. Of particular interest is the gap between what top management expected to receive and what the employees expected to give. This mismatch is the source of the bank's difficulty with employee attitudes.[8]

Discussion. How can this gap be explained? This example represents a situation where the employee has sent *verbal* signals of a desire to change the contract, while the organizational arrangements continue to send *unverbalized* signals that the old contract is still valid. To a considerable extent the contract in Exhibit 3 has never been verbalized; instead, it has evolved over a period of time and has been based largely on

[8]Example is based on data in Chris Argyris, "Human Relations In A Bank," *Harvard Business Review*. September-October, 1954, pp. 63-72.

EXHIBIT 3

The Psychological Contract Between the Bank and Its Employees

Expectations				
By Managers		**By Employees**		
T O R E C E I V E	• Aggressiveness • "Go-getting" attitude • Maximum effort • Obedience • Passivity • Cautious behavior • No "rocking of the boat" • Some "bootlicking" • Courteous behavior to customers and to peers **GAP**	• No aggressiveness • Little "go-getting" • Less than maximum effort • Obedience • Passivity • Cautious behavior • No "rocking of the boat" • Some "bootlicking" • Courteous behavior to customers and to peers	**T O G I V E**
T O G I V E	• High industry pay • Low pay relative to non-banking alternatives • Job security • Little direct supervision	• High industry pay • Low pay relative to non-banking alternatives • Job security • Little direct supervision	**T O R E C E I V E**

signals emanating from the organizational practices. Consider the following examples.

That passivity, courteous behavior, and obedience were desirable was never articulated explicitly, but was signaled very clearly by the selection process. In screening applicants, the bank sought the "right type" of candidate. Specifically, the officers assessed dress, poise, cleanliness, manners, grammar, and the extent to which the application had been completed correctly. One manager reported,

I usually like a certain kind of youngster — a quiet youngster, slightly on the nervous side. Oh, I don't mean that he or she should be completely upset, but I think that's the kind of person we are looking for. They should have a certain amount of poise and should not do too much talking.[9]

Similarly, no one articulated the expectation that "bootlicking" was necessary to facilitate receiving a promotion. Instead, the promotion process signaled that this was appropriate and essential behavior.

Another example of how organizational practices influenced the psychological contract was the expectation of less than maximum effort. Until the increase in competition, both parties agreed on this aspect of the contract. It, however, was not verbally articulated, but was signaled as acceptable by the lack of complaints by management. The employees, motivated by their sense of fairness, came to feel that less than maximum effort was an appropriate exchange for relatively low pay and slow advancement. The absence of reprimands by management indicated that this behavior was acceptable.

To close the gap, or to realize a contract appropriate for a marketplace characterized by increased competition, the bank must seek to bring the *unverbalized* signals of its organizational practices into alignment with its *verbalized* desires for a new psychological contract. The closing of the gap, however, may require other changes in the contract; for example, higher pay and more rapid advancement may become necessary. In any event, management must examine the implications of its organizational practices.

What appeared at first glance to be a problem of employee attitudes really was a case of ineffective management of the psychological contract.

Management of Change

In 1941, Richard Hicks served as manager of one of Sussex Oil's district sales offices. Hicks had joined Sussex primarily because of the company's reputation as a "class organization." Sussex enjoyed an image of being a desirable and prestigious place to work, and indeed, had attracted many of its employees from competitors. More specifically, the company was perceived as "willing to spend money to make money."

However, in 1941, the Sussex management became concerned that growth in profits was not keeping abreast with increases in expenses. As a result the corporate officers exerted pressures for better cost control. Hicks found this stress on expenses distasteful and expressed fears that Sussex was becoming like the large oil company he had left. Hicks and his people were especially displeased with management's suggestions that their district office be moved from its downtown central location to a frame building located at the company's storage tank. Sussex officers reasoned that the shift in locations would save at least $30,000 per year.

Hicks' office was located in the center of the city, in the vicinity of the better hotels, shops, and theaters. This site was attractive and pres-

9Argyris, p. 66.

tigious, especially when compared to Sussex storage and pumping facilities situated in a waterfront area of docks, shipyards, warehouses, factories, and other oil terminals. Although Hicks and his employees were emphatic and vocal in their opposition to the move, the company's top officials insisted. In preparation for the move, the waterfront building was painted, soundproofed and thoroughly renovated. The shift took place in March, 1941.

Approximately six weeks after the change, a noticeable unrest developed among Hicks' workers. The new work situation was characterized by "strained relations, repressed spirits, and lack of enthusiasm," and was totally different from the previous climate. The performance of the whole group appeared lackluster and lethargic. Further, there were complaints about the time wasted in driving to work, the noise and dirt, and the inconvenience of having to eat at lunch counters around the plant area.

As Hicks pondered the complaints, he discounted many of them. The new offices, because of the soundproofing, were not nearly as noisy as the old. While there were transportation problems, the office workers were granted free parking; before they had paid a $10 parking fee. Also, the arrival and departure of the office force had been scheduled so that they would miss the heavy traffic as the refinery shifts changed. Although the climate at "Mammy's" was not that of the mid-town restaurants, Hicks considered the service and food excellent.

Nevertheless, the complaints continued along with increasing demands for wage and salary increases. Hicks resisted because he was not convinced of the validity of the complaints, and also because the company already paid competitive scales. On the other hand, he did not wish to risk losing good people, so he secured a raise.

The raise resulted in less talk about money, but a continuation of complaints about working conditions and "the company." Statements like the following were made: "The company is on the down-grade; we are no longer pushing ahead; it's all retrenchment." "The company is losing its spirit of competitive aggressiveness and is going to the dogs." Morale degenerated so much so that the managers at the refinery reported that the office force's discontent was spreading to the factory workers.

Hicks was perplexed as to what action should be taken.[10]

Discussion. Why did Sussex have difficulty in implementing the change in location? The problems can be attributed to a gap between the *unverbalized* expectations of the employees and those of management. Had Sussex management recognized this gap, it would have been in a better position to anticipate and understand the resistance stemming from violations of the office force's psychological contract (Exhibit 4).

The employees' version of the psychological contract was largely unverbalized and based primarily on Sussex's *reputation*. At no time did

[10] E. P. Learned, J. D. Glover, and G. F. F. Lombard, Sussex Oil Co., 9-446-002. Boston: Harvard Business School, 1947.

management express a desire to be a "classy" organization, but by not refuting the signals of its reputation Sussex managers *implicitly* agreed to the contract expectations implied in its reputation. Individuals joined the company because of its reputation and the organization welcomed them — especially those who were skilled and experienced in the industry. In this manner, Sussex entered into the implicit contract outlined in Exhibit 4.

The difficulty with the change in location was that it conflicted with the "classy" expectations of the office workers. Had management recognized its implicit contract with the employees, it probably would have realized that the change would violate the relationship. Faced with

EXHIBIT 4

Sussex's Contract with the Office Force
(From the Employees' Perspective)

Expectations			
	By Managers	By Workers	
T O R E C E I V E	• Good performance • Loyalty and commitment • Pride in Sussex • Concern with what is best for company	• Good performance • Loyalty and commitment • Pride in Sussex	T O G I V E

T O G I V E	• A "classy" work environment:
	  • better than average pay
	  • office in a "better" section of town
	  • "better" treatment of white collar workers
	  • liberal spending to ensure success; no penny-pinching
	• Job security for satisfactory performance
		• "Classy" working conditions:
		  • better than average pay
		  • office in "classy" location
		  • better treatment of white collar workers
		  • liberal spending; no penny-pinching
		• Job security for satisfactory performance
			T O R E C E I V E

this possibility, the company could have either cancelled the move, taken steps to develop alternative means of satisfying the "classy" expectations, or commenced contingency planning in the event that the dissatisfied workers quit. Any of these actions would have been better than trying to pacify the employees' symptoms (demands for more money) of a deeper unrest.

IMPLICATIONS

Each manager has a psychological contract with his workers regardless of whether he has acknowledged it explicitly. The manager can either understand, manage, and utilize the contract in his efforts to run a more efficient and effective operation, or can ignore it and experience surprises and disappointments. Drawn from the previous discussions and presented below are some implications for managing the psychological contract and implementing change.

Managing the Psychological Contract

Successful management of the psychological contract can result in a mutually satisfying relationship for the manager and the employee. Guidelines are offered for facilitating successful fulfillment of such contracts.

One, the manager should know the contract that he desires to establish and implement. Specifically, the manager should know the answer to the following questions:

- What are my objectives?
- What are the relevant tasks?
- What behavior must my people emit if objectives are to be realized?
- What expectations am I able and/or willing to fulfill to ensure that my people behave in the desired ways? (What am I willing and/or able to provide my people in exchange for their working toward my managerial objectives?)

Responses to these questions will help the manager understand the nature of the contract needed to realize his objectives. This is an essential and crucial first step.

Two, the manager must select a set of managerial tools appropriate for the contract he wishes to establish and implement. A fit must be sought between the tools and the contract. Among the tools available to the manager are interpersonal skills, group skills, leadership style, structural arrangements, selection and recruitment practices, control systems, performance appraisal procedures, rewards, and planning systems. In deciding from among specific alternatives the manager must ask, "What does this tool contribute to the fulfillment of my psychological contract with people who work with me?" "Given my psychological contract with the employees, will this tool do more good or harm?" Each tool must be subjected to these questions and related ones. If a tool threatens to violate the psychological contract, or does not fit with the contract, then the manager should not use it.

Over a period of time the manager is hit with a barrage of contemporary managerial approaches. Recent examples would be Management by Objectives (MBO); Management by Exception; Theory X vs. Theory Y, vs. Theory Z; Authoritarian vs. Democratic; Planning, Programming, and Budgeting System (PPBS); Zero Budgeting; Centralization vs. Decentralization; the Managerial Grid; Sensitivity Group; and Job Enrichment. The manager's task is to sift through these approaches and utilize only those that make sense in his particular setting. The psychological contract concept can be useful in sifting. The test is the same as described earlier, "What does the approach contribute to the fulfillment of my psychological contract?" Any approach, regardless of how popular or unpopular, that does not contribute to contract fulfillment should not be used.

Three, the manager should establish only contracts he is able and willing to honor. The framework of the psychological contract is developed in the recruitment and selection processes. These activities should reflect reality in the organization. It makes little sense to recruit and make false promises to a bright chemist, if you are unable to fulfill such a contract. Specifically, it is being implied here that the characteristics of a "good applicant" are relative to the particular situation for which he or she is being considered. There is no such creature as a "good applicant." "Good" is not absolute, the question is "good for what?" If a manager does not have a contract for an extremely bright, ambitious, articulate, and polished marketing specialist, then these characteristics are not "good" in light of the company's needs. On the other hand, if the organization has an ideal spot for a *reasonably* bright, ambitious, articulate, and polished marketing specialist, the candidate with these traits would be an *excellent* applicant *for that particular position*. Many problems in managing psychological contracts can be traced to the establishment of unfulfillable expectations.

Four, after development of the framework in the recruitment, selection, and hiring processes, management must take care in operationalizing the psychological contract. As manager and employee work together, the contract takes on life — ambiguities are clarified, some unverbalized expectations are verbalized, and conflicts are recognized and possibly resolved. In working together, each party gives off explicit and implicit signals concerning its understanding of the contract. Key signaling devices for the manager are his managerial tools, especially structural arrangements, selection and recruitment processes, reward practices and performance appraisal procedures. These tools in operation provide employees with indications of what is expected or desired behavior. (Remember the case of the bank described earlier.) Consequently, the manager must subject his tools to periodic operational tests. This is crucial, for an organizational system might conceptually offer a good fit with the psychological contract, and yet fail to work in practice. The operational test should include at least the following two questions:

- What signals does this tool send to employees?
- Are these signals compatible with the psychological contract that I wish to maintain?

Five, once established, the contract must be monitored. Expectations change as the manager and employee develop new values and objectives. As the individual goes from one stage in his life to another, he may desire a different contract. Similarly, as the manager functions within the organizational context, his values, priorities, and objectives may change and thus necessitate a new contract. Further, even if the contract were relatively stable, monitoring could pay dividends in the knowledge that it can provide on the extent to which the contract is being fulfilled. The manager needs to know his people's views on whether their expectations are being realized. Also, the employees need data on whether management expectations are being fulfilled. This feedback process can take place in many ways; for example, informal conversation and observation, performance appraisal sessions, surveys and accompanying discussion, and problem solving sessions. One final advantage in monitoring is that it can produce additional data on unverbalized expectations.

Six, the manager must pay special attention to unverbalized expectations. As our previous illustrations demonstrated, they are just as important and real as those verbalized. In the hiring and recruitment processes, management should attempt to verbalize and clarify its important expectations, while being sensitive to those of the applicant. Similarly, when monitoring the contract, the manager should look for evidence of the unverbalized expectations. In addition to the means identified for receiving and providing information on the extent of contract fulfillment, another way of getting at the unverbalized is through an examination of the organization's traditions, myths, and reputation. Employee perceptions of these three areas can furnish considerable information on unstated expectations and assumptions. Further, it is legitimate for the manager to hold "assumption testing" sessions. Here, he can raise his views of the implicit contract and bounce them off employees as a means of securing some indication of their reality. Success in identifying unverbalized expectations can be the difference between an effective and ineffective enterprise.

Seven, myths, traditions, and reputation must be managed. They are powerful determinants of behavior and signals of expectations. A manager who fails to monitor these organizational features may find it difficult to live with some of the implicit psychological contracts that they can foster. The goal should be to ensure that myths, traditions, and reputation are as close to reality as possible.

Eight, and related to five, the manager must legitimize contract renegotiation. If the manager recognizes that expectations do change, then he should realize that both parties need a legitimate opportunity to renegotiate the contract either because of grievances or changes in expectations.

Sometimes this may involve time off to reflect and to regroup. This need at least partially explains the growing practice of sabbaticals for business persons. Frequently, these periods are used to reflect on the past and to develop ideas for changing their psychological contract with the organization. Indeed, some sabbaticals result in expectations that can only be filled by seeking employment in a new setting. In brief, it is unrealistic to expect a contract to remain valid indefinitely. Management by Objectives (MBO), in theory, provides an opportunity for renegotiations in its provision for a goal-setting session between manager and employee.

The message of the guidelines is that successful management of the psychological contract will not just happen, but will require a deliberate and systematic endeavor. Yet, the potential rewards are great. An enterprise with both parties realizing their expectations has the greatest chance for attaining efficiency and effectiveness.

Implementation of Change

Managers constantly find themselves implementing change and dealing with accompanying resistance. The psychological contract can provide a useful framework for facilitating implementation.

When an employee learns of a change, he or she implicitly or explicitly asks, "What impact will the proposed change have on my psychological contract with my manager?" "Will the change threaten or increase my present level of fulfillment?" If the individual reaches a negative conclusion or is uncertain about the impact, he is likely to resist the change. Consequently, resistance to change can be viewed as evidence of the individual's concern that the present contract is threatened. The person will resist until assured that the contract is not threatened or a new and acceptable one is established. Thus, the manager wishing to understand, anticipate, and cope with potential resistance to a proposed change must ask, "What impact will the change have on the existing psychological contract?"

After identifying the possible consequences and the likely areas of resistance, the manager has at least two options. One, steps can be taken to ensure that the employee expectations can be reached under the new conditions. He then must communicate successfully to the employee that the psychological contract is not threatened by the change. Two, he can arrange a new contract with the employee. Here, the manager admits that changes will require a different relationship and engages in a renegotiation process with the individual. Assuming the parties are able to develop a replacement contract, the individual will cease his resistance. This option is exercised usually when the manager is not disturbed by the possible resignation of those resisting, or when he thinks the resistance will subside.

Frequently, managers believe that resistance to change is almost automatic. This may be true to an extent. The psychological contract concept, however, suggests that much of the resistance to change can be traced to legitimate concerns of the employee about the relationship with the organization. An understanding and recognition of the potential and source of resistance should enhance the manager's ability to manage implementation.

SECTION SIX

FEEDBACK

Overview

In a business environment where the central management issues are related to refining and extending a proven business pattern within well understood operating limits and predictable market conditions, it was generally appropriate to view the primary functions of performance feedback to be that of *control* and *constraint.*

In principle, at least, goals regarding future performance requirements could be well defined, objectively measured, and assumed to remain reasonably stable. Current performance could be assessed unambiguously against those goals. Errors could be detected and control reasserted through the communication of corrective feedback to the appropriate individuals and groups.

In the business environment that is now ending, answering the question "How are we doing?" was *simple* in principle although it was not always *easy* to accomplish.

In the emerging business environment dominated by unpredictability, complex internal and external interrelationships, ambiguity, and change, it is too limited to view feedback as merely information for assisting a manager to get from a well defined "here" to an established "there" efficiently. The concept of performance feedback must be extended to include information that assists managers to reassess their working assumptions about the very business itself. To paraphrase Donald Michael in his contribution to this section, feedback must become a tool for assisting managers and their people continually to determine what "here" now means as conditions change and whether "there" is where they still want to go. In other words, today's Leader-Managers must expand the role of feedback to include the additional functions of *reconnaissance* and *learning.*

The articles in this section explore this expanded range of functions required of feedback in the new business environment.

In "Developing Performance Feedback Systems," John A. Fairbank and Donald M. Prue provide an excellent synthesis of the traditional research literature on performance feedback. The authors offer a number of practical insights and propose a framework for developing and implementing more effective feedback systems. In their discussion of why performance feedback appears to be such an effective intervention tool for improving performance, Fairbank and Prue conclude that feedback:

1. Serves to reinforce desired behavior,

2. Helps instruct employees in the behavioral requirements of their jobs,

3. Provides information about what the manager feels is important,

4. Influences the content and quality of work-related communications,

5. Can increase job satisfaction.

In addition, the article examines such issues as: feedback as an appropriate performance intervention; selection of appropriate performance measures; characteristics of outcome versus process feedback; and guidelines for developing performance feedback systems.

This is a perspective toward feedback that will be familiar to most experienced managers. The article serves as a solid launch pad for the rest of the section. The remaining three articles progressively move into less familiar territory and begin to explore the additional new requirements of feedback for the manager.

"Fit Control Systems to Your Managerial Style," by Cortlandt Cammann and David A. Nadler, also conceives of feedback within the traditional framework of organizational control. Yet the authors extend the discussion of the previous article by recognizing that the purposes and appropriate strategies for managing feedback are situational.

The authors note, for example, that control systems often have very unintended consequences. While they successfully influence the amount of energy subordinates put into an area, they do not guarantee how that energy will be used. Subordinates may be motivated by the system to direct their energies toward producing more or higher quality results, but not necessarily. The system may also produce "game playing" attempts to "beat the system." For example, subordinates may begin to reduce the level of their objectives, manipulate data to their advantage, or censor crucial negative information.

Cammann and Nadler compare the relative benefits and risks of highly directive (external control) systems with highly participative (internal motivation oriented) feedback systems. They argue that the choice of an appropriate feedback control system will depend upon how the system relates to the following factors:

1. The management style of the work unit manager.

2. The reliability of the measures.

3. The needs, climate, and structure of the organization.

4. The various needs among the work unit members.

While the authors do not explicitly mention the changing needs of the organization and individuals in their discussion of the latter two factors, the reader who is familiar with the perspective developed in the Growth section of this volume will recognize the implied importance of these changes in the manager's choice of feedback strategies.

Donald A. Schon's article, "Deutero-Learning in Organizations: Learning for Increased Effectiveness," argues the case for a significant expansion of the organization's meaning of feedback to reflect the changing decision-making context facing businesses today. Schon traces the evolution of the primary question on organizational effectiveness since World War I. Between World War I and World War II the dominant question was "Is the firm well organized?" From World War II to the late 1950s, the issue became "Does the organization foster sufficient individual creativity" to insure the development of new products and services? From the late 1950s through the mid-60s, the concern was with innovation in general but still within the implied constraints of secure assumptions about the nature and future of the business. Since the mid-60s, however, the question that has become increasingly dominant is "Can the organization manage discontinuous change?"

According to Schon, this current period is characterized by the realization of:

1. Broad-scale shifts in the nature of business and the business environment.

2. The requirement to focus on *purpose* rather than *objectives* which have become increasingly ambiguous, conflicting, and shifting.

3. The inadequacy of the model of "rational purpose" for organizational action — a challenge to the notion that the proper action is to adapt means to ends.

In this new environment, managers can no longer assume that there are clear rules for making valid inferences from past experience. There is no longer the assurance of another stable or even predictable state to which the economy or a particular company will return. Consequently, Schon argues that the competence and feedback systems to insure on-line *learning* become crucial requirements.

Here, *learning* refers to the process of "continuing redesign in response to changing values and a changing context for action." The most central kind of learning, what Schon refers to as deutero-learning, is that which leads to change in the assumptions and governing values underlying an individual's or an organization's strategies.

Such a learning capacity requires the development of feedback and information systems that:

1. Include intelligence and reconnaissance functions that sense the environment.

2. Involve a new generation of cost-benefit analysis tools that are congruent with an environment of changing assumptions.

3. Encourage the development of an "ecological" relationship with the environment and the recognition, therefore, that information is inherently limited and prejudiced.

4. Facilitate inquiry and learning about situations we are in while we are in them.

5. Reinforce a commitment to overarching values rather than temporary objections.

Donald N. Michael, in "On the Importance of Feedback and the Resistances to It," shares Schon's conclusions regarding the expanded learning role that feedback must come to play in organizations. Michael is writing for a public-sector audience, but his arguments hold equally well for any large-scale company. In this article, Michael is concerned with what he calls long-range social planning (lrsp) systems that are appropriate in a time of radical social change. In particular, he is interested in the fact that, despite its obvious necessity today, attempts to implement learning-oriented feedback systems will likely meet with significant individual and organizational resistance.

Some of these resistances stem from the fact that there remain deep technical and conceptual inadequacies in feedback systems that serve learning purposes. More importantly, however, are other sources of resistance; most notably, social psychological factors related to the need of people to be protected from uncertainty, error, ambiguity, and instability. There are deep social psychological benefits for avoiding feedback. Until these benefits can be attended to and overcome, feedback systems are likely to remain minimal and ineffective.

Michael also points out that there are strong structural resistances to feedback built into most complex organizations. Organizations are structured to avoid unfamiliar or disruptive information and have elaborate ways to declare such information illegitimate. Furthermore, organizations already suffering from information overload find it increasingly difficult to know what to pay attention to, thus reinforcing their tendency to withdraw. Finally, unless sensitively handled, opening up more diverse sources of feedback to an organization may serve to exacerbate conflict over goals, values, and priorities.

Michael proposes two capacities that need to be developed to lessen resistance to feedback. The first capacity, within the organization, is to reduce fears and anxieties about threats to competence, purpose, and status by replacing present organizational norms and procedures with ones that will reward learning. The second capacity lies outside the organization. That is to encourage outside stakeholders groups to become more sophisticated in forcing greater openness and responsiveness in the organizations they want to influence.

DEVELOPING PERFORMANCE FEEDBACK SYSTEMS

John A. Fairbank
Donald M. Prue

Ms. Jones, the general manager of the photofinishing division of a large newspaper and magazine publishing company, had been advised by corporate cost-efficiency analysts that, due to sudden unanticipated increases in the market value of silver, the cost of photographic paper coated with silver nitrate had increased dramatically. They warned that, at the rate at which the photofinishing division currently used silver nitrate photographic paper, the company stood to suffer a reduction in their annual profits of hundreds of thousands of dollars.

Determined to find a solution to this problem, Ms. Jones instructed her assistant to carefully monitor quantities of silver nitrate paper used by the division's three shifts of photofinishers. Results indicated that during a one-week period a total of 30 thousand sheets were used, but only 10 thousand pictures were printed, an unacceptably high waste-to-use ratio of photographic paper. Ms. Jones instructed her assistant to identify the specific factors responsible for high rates of waste. This analysis indicated that waste resulted from (1) repetitive and careless mistakes in exposure time, (2) unnecessary duplication of prints, and (3) loss due to soiling and spoilage as a function of improper handling or storage of paper. At a scheduled intradivisional management meeting, Ms. Jones informed her production manager and operations supervisors of the details of this problem. She instructed them to meet with each shift of photofinishers in order to encourage them to decrease current levels of photographic paper waste and to provide them with specific procedures for doing so. Subsequently, rates of paper waste decreased significantly, but several weeks later they returned to previous high levels.

Disappointed but undaunted, Ms. Jones began to meet with her production manager and operations supervisors on a biweekly basis for the purpose of providing them with feedback on the amount of paper wasted during the preceding two-week period. Waste decreased progressively over the next few weeks with no adverse side effects on photofinishing productivity rate or quality. After six months of regularly scheduled biweekly feedback meetings, Ms. Jones found that she could maintain low rates of waste by scheduling performance feedback meetings with her management staff at monthly intervals. Eventually Ms. Jones transferred responsibility for the waste-reduction performance feedback program to her administrative assistant with no loss in program effectiveness.

The above vignette describes an effective, relatively uncomplicated, and increasingly popular procedure for modifying behavior in organizational settings, performance feedback. Feedback intervention strategies, designed to provide information to individuals or groups about the quantity or quality of their performance, have been impressively effective in producing organizational change. Organizational problems such as waste (Eldridge, Lemasters, and Szypot, 1978), employee productivity (Parsons, 1974), absenteeism (Kempen and Hall, 1977), and supervisor effectiveness (Bourdon, 1977), to name but a few examples, have all been effectively modified using performance feedback techniques.

The goal of this article is to provide a framework for developing and implementing more comprehensive and effective performance feedback systems in organizational settings. An overview of performance feedback will first be presented, to be followed by a set of guidelines for evaluating the suitability of feedback techniques for organizational performance problems. Next, five parameters of feedback that require careful consideration when planning a performance feedback system will be discussed. Specific guidelines for developing feedback systems from among the numerous options available will then be offered. Finally, a summary section will discuss the implications of this article for future development of performance feedback systems.

OVERVIEW OF PERFORMANCE FEEDBACK INTERVENTION TECHNIQUES

Advantages of Feedback

Besides effectiveness, performance feedback systems have a number of other characteristics that make them attractive. One of the primary advantages has been their relatively low economic costs to organizations. Feedback techniques have been reported to be less expensive to implement than other productivity-enhancement techniques (cf. At Emery Airfreight: Positive Reinforcement Boosts Performance, 1973). Significant investments of organizational resources into expensive accounting, legal, or other support systems are usually not required to implement and maintain effective performance feedback programs. Also organizations employing performance feedback systems do not have to rely upon often expensive employee incentive or reward programs.

Another advantage of performance feedback programs is simplicity of implementation. First, prolonged, cumbersome, and sophisticated training programs are seldom required to change target behavior (Sulzer-Azaroff and deSantamaria, 1980). Although managerial personnel sometimes receive detailed training in the technology of behavior analysis (Bourdon, 1977), simple instruction on how to provide positive feedback to employees is more often sufficient for managerial personnel to successfully implement feedback interventions. Second, although feedback interventions occasionally require the development of mechanisms to collect performance information, it is more often the case that organizations have existing information or accounting systems that offer easy access to performance data (Hall, 1979; Stoerzinger, Johnston, Pisor, and Monroe, 1978). In these latter cases the behavior analyst simply identifies relevant sources of performance information and then instructs organizational personnel on the use of extant sources to provide feedback.

Still another advantage of performance feedback techniques is decreased use of punishment procedures, such as unsystematic criticism, docked time, warnings, or other disciplinary action. Skinner (1953) has observed that punishment, or the threat of punishment, is the typical "control" procedure employed within organizations. For example, employees typically arrive at work on time to avoid the immediate aversive consequence of being fired from their jobs, not to earn the more distant positive consequence of their paychecks. In contrast, informal observations of the behavior and comments of workers in organizations that have employed performance feedback systems suggest that changes in worker behavior can be initiated and maintained without reliance upon the use of disciplinary procedures (Komaki, Barwick, and Scott, 1978).

Lastly, performance feedback techniques are attractive in organizations that may not have access to other intervention strategies. Many organizations find their ability to use monetary incentives or rewards for increased productivity restricted by factors such as union constraints. These organizations find that feedback techniques are one of the few options available to change employee behavior.

In summary, characteristics such as effectiveness, low cost, simplicity of implementation, and positive emphasis make performance feedback an attractive intervention technique for organizations. These advantages have permitted performance feedback programs to be implemented in organizations with varying resources, from small, owner-operated retail businesses with few employees (Komaki, Waddell, and Pearce, 1977) to large multidivisional corporations (Runnion, Watson, and McWhorter, 1978) and institutions with numerous employees (Prue, Krapfl, Noah, Cannon, and Maley, 1980).

Why Is Performance Feedback Effective?

Historically, changes in employee behavior that follow feedback intervention have been attributed to the effects of feedback as a reinforcer. A reinforcer is defined as any event that increases the probability of occurrence of behavior that it follows. The following example illustrates how performance feedback might be considered a reinforcer. The accounting department of a large metropolitan utility employs two shifts of keypunch operators. Although the personnel profiles (e.g., average age, sex, level of training, and experience) for employees on each shift are comparable in every way, the second shift makes significantly more programming errors than the first shift. In an attempt to increase the quality of performance of the second shift, management begins to publicly post a chart that compares the weekly percentage of correctly typed programs for each shift. After one month percentages of correctly typed programs increase for both shifts, with no significant difference between the two. Since increased production quality followed the feedback intervention, management might then consider feedback as a reinforcer. Yet, as straightforward as a reinforcement interpretation of feedback effects seems to be, it merely describes the more obvious changes in performance that follow feedback intervention. Elsewhere (Prue and Fairbank, 1981) we have argued that feedback intervention often produces additional subtle changes in organizational behavior that might contribute to the dramatic success of performance feedback systems, but have been neglected in prior interpretations of feedback.

One such effect occurs when performance feedback instructs employees in the behavioral requirements of their position. When a supervisor provides verbal feedback to an employee — "Tom, the mileage on your truck this week was over 10 m.p.g. That is 2 m.p.g. above our goal. Keep up the good work" — he or she is informing employees of job-related behavior of concern to the organization. These feedback-based "instructions" presumably specify job performance procedures or standards of importance to the organization. The instruction function of feedback may act much like a more formal change in an employee's job description or contract. Also, since feedback sessions typically are repeated over time, they continue to notify the employee of what their supervisors consider to be critical features of organizational functioning. The overall impact is to inform individuals or groups of workers at all levels of the expected or "now to be enforced" performance criteria operating within an organization. Evidence for this point has been provided by Locke and his colleagues (Locke, Cartledge, and Koeppel, 1968), who have argued that performance feedback always implicitly states a performance standard.

Another explanation of feedback effects, and one that appears to be especially important in organizations that rely upon public display of performance information, occurs when performance within an organization is below standard. Instruction regarding the feedback intervention, as well as the intervention itself, may lead individuals or groups within an organization to meet performance standards in order to avoid potentially aversive consequences associated with the public posting of low levels of performance. The aversive consequences may take the form of embarrassment over low productivity, or they may involve more tangible consequences such as supervisor or co-worker disfavor. For example, public posting of number of work days missed might act as an impetus for employees to decrease absenteeism to avoid supervisor or co-worker disfavor resulting from the perception that the individual is not doing a fair share of the work.

Performance feedback interactions may lead to other changes in the organizational environment that could account for some of the effects of feedback on behavior. One possible change would be modification of the manner in which people interact in an organization during a feedback intervention. For example, supervisors may begin to interact more, or perhaps differently, with workers as a function of feedback intervention. In addition, the quality of interpersonal interactions within levels of an organization may also change. For example, Prue et al. (1980) noted that the topic of conversation among employees seemed to increasingly center on job-related issues and activities during and following feedback intervention. Prue et al. (1980) suggested that some of the behavioral changes that followed the feedback intervention might have been related to these feedback-associated changes in the way organizational members interacted. Others (Parsons, 1974; Pedalino and Gamboa, 1974) have noted that competition, another form of interpersonal interaction often associated with performance feedback intervention, can play a significant role in motivating employee behavior change.

Finally, the effectiveness of feedback systems upon performance may be enhanced by increased job satisfaction during feedback intervention. For example, Sims and Szilagyi (1975) found that employees are more satisfied and report being more productive when they receive information based upon objective evaluations of their performance. Since the latter is the hallmark of feedback intervention, it is likely that feedback techniques are accompanied by increased employee satisfaction that might enhance performance apart from effects associated with reinforcement or other environmental changes.

The relative contributions of each of the above effects to the dramatic success of feedback intervention remain unclear at this time. However, the fact that feedback can play an instrumental role in organizational change, and that there are a number of likely interpretations of its effects, suggests that future feedback interventions should attempt to maximize both instructional and reinforcement effects of feedback.

DETERMINING THE SUITABILITY OF PERFORMANCE FEEDBACK INTERVENTIONS FOR ORGANIZATIONAL PROBLEMS

A careful analysis of organizational performance problems is mandatory when considering the application of performance feedback techniques. In point of fact, several authors (Ellsworth, 1973; Nadler, Mirvis, and Cammann, 1976; Oberg, 1972) have warned that performance feedback intervention can inadvertently boomerang, producing negative consequences such as low worker morale, when applied without an adequate a priori analysis of the organizational performance problem. Quite simply, not every organizational problem that results in a performance decrement represents an appropriate intervention for performance feedback. One situation in which feedback may not be appropriate is poor performance due to inadequate job skills. If workers have not received the specialized training required for adequate performance, then performance feedback intervention alone is not likely to lead to acceptable levels of performance. More subtly, when an employee lacks information on how to improve performance, feedback is unlikely to help him or her solve performance problems.

Another situation in which feedback might be inappropriate would be when structural characteristics of a task are at the root of the performance problem. For instance, extended restaurant turnaround time between when an order is received and when preparation of the meal is completed may be only partially related to the cook's performance. A more important factor might be the length of time it takes to cook food.

Finally, unknown, ambiguous, or unreasonable standards of performance also set the occasion for low rates of performance within organizations. Several investigators (Kim and Hamner, 1976; Locke, Cartledge, and Koeppel, 1968; Nemeroff and Cosentino, 1979) have shown that unspecified or unknown performance standards diminish the effect of feedback intervention. Consequently, when individuals at various levels within an organization fail to agree upon standards of performance, the effects of a feedback intervention upon performance are less likely to be predictable and positive.

The outcome of all these situations is generally a failure to improve performance with feedback alone. Additionally, extended periods of feedback on poor levels of performance may be aversive and lead to a number of unintended side effects, such as employees leaving the organization. The following are offered as task analysis guidelines for determining the suitability of performance feedback techniques for modification of organizational performance problems.

1. Determine if individuals within the organization possess the requisite skills for adequate job performance.

2. If workers do not possess the necessary skills for adequate job performance, implement appropriate training programs, personnel actions, etc.

3. After teaching the necessary job skills, reassess the need for performance feedback.

4. If lack of skills or knowledge was not a component of the performance problem, assess reasons for unacceptable performance. Identify the relative contributions of worker behavior and other factors (e.g., structural characteristics of the task) to the low performance level.

5. Determine the performance standards operating within an organization and their clarity. If performance standards are ambiguous or unreasonable, set new standards upon which an organizational consensus can be reached.

6. After performance standards are established, reassess the need for a performance feedback intervention.

SELECTING PERFORMANCE MEASURES

Once the suitability of performance feedback as an intervention technique has been established, the question of which measures of performance should be targeted for feedback can be addressed. For performance problems that are circumscribed to a specific individual or group within an organization, often a single measure of performance is sufficient to document an intervention effect. However, when performance problems are complex, or when they involve individuals or groups from diverse levels within an organization, multiple measures of performance are often more appropriate. The two types of performance measures that should be considered for inclusion in any feedback intervention are outcome and process measures (Gilbert, 1978; Nadler, 1979; Nadler et al., 1976). In general, outcome measures of performance refer to organizationally valued accomplishments of individuals or groups. Outcome factors are usually measures of individual or group performance that are directly related to the ultimate success or failure of the organization. Typical examples of organizational outcome measures include number of objects assembled per hour by line operators, total dollar amounts of sales by franchised dealers, and number of extended service warranty contracts issued by sales personnel. Many measurable outcome factors can be identified by using existing organizational data that document quantity, quality, time, or cost of performance. Examination of inventory control mechanisms, sales records, accounting practices, and so forth often provides a wealth of important organizational outcome data. In contrast to outcome measures, process factors refer to measures of compliance with organizational procedures, rules, or guidelines considered essential for the accomplishment of organizational goals. Process factors may also include measures of any other activities engaged in by workers during performance of their jobs (Mollenhoff, 1977). Common examples of organizational process measures are latency of report filing, numbers of telephone solicitations of potential customers, hours worked, frequency of intragroup communications, absenteeism, and orderliness of work areas.

In selecting between outcome or process measures of performance the primary requirement is to identify the important parameters of the organizational problem in question, as well as ways to measure these parameters. Generally it is more desirable to provide feedback on outcome measures. Results are what matter most to organizations, and therefore they should be the basis for performance measures. However, process measures are sometimes easier to obtain and are typically selected for use in feedback systems when results occur infrequently (e.g., number of industrial safety accidents) or are not easily measured (e.g., number of clients who show improved psychological functioning at the end of treatment), or when process measures relate directly to the attainment of important organizational results (e.g., number of suggestions for improvements in productivity).

337

PARAMETERS OF FEEDBACK INTERVENTIONS

Feedback systems can be implemented in a variety of different ways. Five parameters on which feedback interventions can vary are discussed in this section:

1. Recipients.
2. Content.
3. Temporal characteristics.
4. Mechanism.
5. Source.

The discussion of each parameter includes a brief description of possible variations.

Recipients of Feedback

An initial consideration in feedback intervention in organizational settings is to identify the intended recipients of the performance information. Studies in the feedback literature have provided information to both individuals and groups about their performance. Information distributed to groups has been further divided into data about the performance of individuals within the group, or about the performance of the group as a unit. Feedback can also be delivered either privately, when performance information is shared only with a targeted individual or group, or publicly, when performance information is shared with the targeted individual and also provided to other individuals. Factors to consider when choosing appropriate recipients of feedback include the generally greater success of public feedback (Welsh, Ludwig, Radiker, and Krapfl, 1973), the amount of resources available for the intervention (e.g., private feedback sessions are labor intensive), and the ability of organizational members to carry out the intervention (e.g., private feedback requires socially skilled managers to conduct sessions).

Content of Feedback

Another important parameter of feedback intervention systems is the specific content of the information provided to recipients. As noted above, feedback can focus on output or process measures of performance (Nadler, 1979; Nadler et al., 1976). The content can also vary with respect to how the performance measures are derived from available data. That is, feedback may include (1) comparison of an individual's performance with his or her previous performance; (2) comparison of an individual's performance with a standard performance, which is determined by the performance of a large number of individuals; (3) comparison of a group's performance (performance of individuals not important) with its previous performance; (4) comparison of a group's performance with a standard

338

group performance; and (5) presentation of an individual's performance as a percentage of group's performance. The determination of which of the above should be employed is based on several considerations. One is the type of information available. Are data available on individual employee productivity, or do data represent a group effort? Another consideration is comparability of performance of different groups or individuals, e.g., are tasks similar enough to allow meaningful comparisons? Another factor is the specific type of information to be included in the feedback message, e.g., praise for appropriate performance, statements of goals, constructive criticism, and so forth.

Temporal Characteristics of Feedback

The third parameter of feedback involves the question of when and how often feedback should be provided. There are two major temporal characteristics of feedback. The first is the total duration of the feedback interaction. Duration is clearly a function of the content of as well as the mechanism employed to deliver the performance information. It may range from a short glance at a printout counter to an extensive performance analysis interview. In most cases duration plays an interdependent role with other feedback parameters, and thus is not a significant factor in and of itself in the overall effectiveness of an intervention.

The second and more significant temporal characteristic is the contiguity between performance and feedback, that is, the length of time between performance and feedback. Feedback may be provided immediately after performance of a targeted behavior or after a delay. In the latter case feedback, delivered on daily (Shook, Johnson, and Uhlman, 1978), semiweekly (Sulzer-Azaroff and deSantamaria, 1980), weekly (Andrasik and McNamara, 1977), bi- and triweekly (Komaki et al., 1977) and monthly (Miller, 1977) schedules, has been reported to be effective in changing employee target behavior. Important considerations regarding the contiguity of feedback with performance include task complexity (e.g., is feedback provided for relatively simple or complex tasks?), rate of feedback (e.g., is performance feedback scheduled as a relatively frequent or infrequent event?) and the content of feedback (e.g., outcome versus process feedback). With respect to the latter dimension, Tosti and Jackson (1981) suggest that feedback provided to change the topography of an employee's performance, a process feedback system, should only be provided when an individual has the opportunity to immediately practice or try out the new performance. For example, feedback on how to load pallets should be provided sometime during the actual working day rather than at the end of the day when employees would not have the opportunity to modify their performance based upon the feedback.

Feedback Mechanisms

Another characteristic of feedback is the type of mechanism used to deliver the performance data. Four basic feedback mechanisms (verbal, written, mechanical, and self-recorded) have been used in the organizational behavior management literature.

Verbal feedback. Perhaps the most common method of providing feedback within organizations has been verbal feedback in one-to-one interpersonal interactions. The following statement, cited by Eldridge, Lemasters, and Szypot (1978), describes a simple face-to-face verbal feedback interaction from a supervisor to an employee. "Today your piece yield is at 60 percent. That's higher than yesterday." As this brief example shows, the advantages of face-to-face verbal performance feedback include short duration and contiguity of feedback with performance. Yet the simplicity of verbal feedback may be deceptive. Verbal feedback intervention must take into account the interpersonal skills of individuals delivering the feedback, the past history of interpersonal interactions between the providers and recipients of feedback, and the physical proximity of recipients to providers.

Written feedback. Another mechanism commonly used to provide performance data to employees has been written feedback. Written feedback has been provided in a variety of ways, including written personal communications (Weitz, Antoinetti, and Wallace, 1954); memos (Kreitner, Reif, and Morris, 1977), newsletters (Patterson, Cooke, and Liberman, 1972); and public posting of performance information (Quilitch, 1975). Traditional written evaluations, typically placed in employees' files, are also a form of written feedback. Typically, publicly posted performance feedback is provided in terms of a graphical display in which quantifiable performance measures (e.g., number of days absent, total sales in dollars) are charted over time. All forms of written feedback, however, must take into account the potential advantages (e.g., employees have a record of performance to show co-workers, friends or spouses for additional reinforcement) and disadvantages (e.g., employee embarrassment and anger over public posting of low rates of performance) of permanent documentation of performance.

Mechanical feedback. Still another method of providing performance feedback has been the delivery of performance data via mechanical devices. Examples of this type of delivery include videotape feedback (Bricker, Morgan, and Grabowski, 1972; Walter, 1975) and electro-mechanically operated tape printouts (Parsons, 1974). For instance, Parsons noted that the Hawthorne data demonstrated that simply providing employees with a continuous, electromechanical record of their daily output increased productivity. Although the application of mechanical devices to deliver feedback has not received much research attention, the future for mechanical feedback systems looks particularly bright. The low cost, usually continuous and immediate nature of delivery and the fact that once mechanical devices are established they are likely to be maintained are potential benefits of mechanical feedback mechanisms.

Self-recorded feedback. Another feedback delivery mechanism is to have employees generate their own feedback by self-recording their performance (Komaki, Blood, and Holder, 1980). This feedback mechanism, commonly called self-monitoring, has been applied to a wide range of clinical problems, but has received less attention in organizational intervention. A number of recent studies, however, have demonstrated the utility of this feedback mechanism in organizational intervention. Komaki, Blood, and Holder (1980) used a self-monitoring procedure to increase smiling and conversation between a fast food restaurant's employees and customers by having workers self-monitor their performance. Lamal and Benfield (1978) increased the punctuality and on-task behavior of an employee with self-monitoring. Prue et al. (1980) combined self-monitoring with three different types of feedback to increase employee treatment activities in a hospital. Potential advantages of self-recorded feedback include the high level of employee participation in the intervention, and its applicability to situations in which employees are not closely supervised. It's also useful when there are no physical products of the behavior of concern (e.g., number of positive comments to employees by supervisors), or when process variables play an important role in the employees' overall productivity (e.g., effective use of time). These advantages must be weighed against potential disadvantages such as employee subversion of the system, and cost of devising an independent procedure for assessing the reliability of self-report data.

Source of Feedback

The final parameter of performance feedback intervention is the source of feedback. The organizational behavior management (OBM) literature reveals that performance feedback has been effectively provided by supervisors of varying rank (Chandler, 1977; Sulzer-Azaroff and deSantamaria, 1980). Feedback has been provided by subordinates (Hegarty, 1974), co-workers (Greller, 1980), outside consultants (Komaki et al., 1977), the targeted employees themselves (Lamal and Benfield, 1978), and a variety of mechanical devices (Ford, 1980; Parsons, 1974). Unfortunately, there have been no reports in the OBM literature of well-controlled studies comparing the outcome effectiveness and cost-efficiency of these sources of feedback upon performance measures. Further, the effects of different sources may interact with the status and power of the provider of feedback and the history of interactions between the recipients and providers of feedback.

GUIDELINES FOR DEVELOPING PERFORMANCE FEEDBACK SYSTEMS

The preceding section introduced five parameters of feedback systems and briefly described the alternatives within each. Since no single procedure for developing effective performance feedback systems exists, the purpose of this section will be to provide guidelines for designing a system that takes into account the numerous options available. This will be a best-guess effort, since very few studies have compared different feedback systems in organizational settings. References from the organizational behavior management literature will be cited to provide distinctions on the effects of the different options.

1. Feedback messages should be precise and objective (Brethower and Rummler, 1966; Hamner and Hamner, 1976). Effective feedback messages need only to convey information specific to targeted performance measures. Externally verifiable quantitative or qualitative aspects of performance, exclusive of subjective standards or bias, should always be emphasized.

2. Insure that organizational performance goals are specified and understood by feedback providers and recipients prior to implementation of any feedback system. This is important, since feedback systems have been reported to be more effective when accompanied by goal setting, a procedure for specifying performance standards whereby employees are assigned specific amounts of work to be accomplished (Kim and Hamner, 1976; Nemeroff and Cosentino, 1979).

3. Whenever possible, feedback systems should be yoked to the compensation system, i.e., pay and incentive formats, of the organization to enhance the effects of both the feedback and compensation systems.

4. Prior to developing performance feedback systems, consider the potential of specific components to produce detrimental side effects within the organization. For example, individual feedback provided to group members often produces competition as a side effect. If interdependence exists between individual performance and the behavior of others, carefully weigh the potentially negative long-term side effects of intragroup competition against the long-term positive effects of the overall feedback program. Similarly, group feedback may have undesirable side effects. For instance, before providing group feedback to individuals with diverse but interrelated jobs, consider the potentially disadvantageous effects of groups making an individual a scapegoat for inadequate group performance. Regarding private and public dimensions of feedback intervention, consider: (1) the potential for negative employee response to public feedback (e.g., public posting) especially when baseline performance

levels are low; (2) the costs to the work force of private feedback systems upon organizational resources (e.g., supervisor time); and (3) the problems involved in attempting to implement private feedback programs in organizations where feedback providers lack good interpersonal skills.

5. Provide feedback on several relevant outcome or process measures of performance when possible. If only a single performance measure is employed in a feedback system, recipients may fail to attend to other important aspects of their jobs. This may have detrimental effects upon organizational functioning. Also, when process feedback is employed to improve the performance of work tasks, employees should be queried regarding how *they* think their performance should change. This should facilitate employee cooperation with implementation of feedback systems.

6. Utilize multiple sources of feedback at varying levels of the organizational structure (Sulzer-Azaroff and deSantamaria, 1980). This will decrease the likelihood of feedback drift, i.e., the tendency to drift from feedback based upon objective performance standards to feedback based upon subjective bias. Participation of individuals and groups at multiple levels of the organizational structure is also likely to increase the probability of program maintenance.

7. Whenever possible use multiple feedback mechanisms. This may increase the durability (maintenance) of feedback programs, since recipients are less likely to become overly accustomed, or habituated, to one particular feedback mechanism. For example, include both written and verbal feedback on performance. Whenever possible, use feedback mechanisms that fit within the organizational structure, e.g., feedback during regularly scheduled planning meetings, since these feedback systems are more likely to be maintained. The limitations of various approaches to delivering feedback must be taken into account when developing performance feedback systems. For example, personal individual verbal feedback may not be the feedback mechanism of choice in organizations in which supervisors and workers have little opportunity for daily face-to-face contact (e.g., truck drivers).

8. Basic experimental literature suggests that contiguous feedback is best for increasing performance proficiency on complex tasks (Hall, 1966). For simple tasks, however, delayed feedback appears to be effective using a variety of interval schedules, e.g., semiweekly, weekly, or monthly.

9. Provide individual feedback when a situation calls for an individual to initiate a behavior, and when the individual has the opportunity to immediately practice the new behavior. Individual feedback appears to be especially effective in shaping new rates of performance. Also,

rely on individual feedback when baseline rates of behavior are low or when providing criticism of past performance.

10. Provide group feedback when organizational goals require co-operation or there is an interdependent function to individuals' performance. Group feedback is also the procedure of choice when it is difficult to distinguish any one individual's contribution to the total performance, and when total performance is greater than the sum of differentiated individual performances. Also, use group feedback when group affiliation, often a process measure of performance, is an important organizational consideration.

11. Feedback should be delivered frequently, i.e., daily or semiweekly, when implementing a performance feedback system. Frequent performance feedback is recommended in order to familiarize targeted individuals and groups with the system, and more importantly, to expose them to the relationship between their performance and feedback content. As performance stabilizes at acceptable levels, the frequency of feedback often may be decreased. In point of fact, satisfactory steady-state performance may often be maintained with relatively long interfeedback intervals, e.g., monthly or bimonthly.

The following case study illustrates how these guidelines may be used to develop an effective feedback intervention system for an organizational performance problem.

Mr. Smith is the owner of a fleet of taxicabs that operate in the suburbs of a major northeastern city. He employs more than 200 drivers, many of whom work part-time afternoons, nights, and on weekends to supplement their incomes. During a recent 10-month period an increasing number of Mr. Smith's drivers were assaulted or robbed while on duty. As a result, his business had experienced a greater than usual employee turnover rate. Concurrently, he began to have problems recruiting adequate numbers of replacement drivers, which resulted in idle cabs and decreased company profits. Termination interviews with several drivers who had resigned indicated that they quit primarily out of concern for their safety. These events alarmed Mr. Smith, as he was genuinely concerned about the safety of his employees, and he knew that the success of his business depended upon maintaining a large pool of experienced part-time drivers.

Analysis of the situation by a consultant indicated that the frequency of assaults and robberies of drivers could be reduced if driver-operated safety devices were installed in each cab. At a meeting with driver representatives it was agreed that if Mr. Smith installed protective equipment in the cabs, the drivers would use them as part of their routine operating procedure. Following this agreement, he had a number of expensive safety features and protective devices installed in each of his cabs. These included a driver-operated door locking system, an impact-resistant safety glass divider between the driver and passenger compartments, a locked cash deposit box that could not be opened by the driver or removed from the cab, and a two-way intercom system for driver and passenger communication. In addition, he arranged for each driver to be trained to properly use the safety equipment. Then Mr. Smith and representatives of his drivers drafted standards and regulations for use of safety equipment by drivers.

Several months after installation of the safety devices, completion of training, and adoption of safety regulations, Mr. Smith was disappointed to learn that neither the rate of assaults upon drivers nor driver turnover rate had decreased substantially. An analysis of the circumstances surrounding each robbery or assault revealed that most of the drivers had, at the time of the robbery, failed to comply with one or more of the rules governing use of safety equipment. Although company regulations required drivers to use the devices, threats and implementation of punitive measures for violations of safety standards, such as suspension or dismissal, had little effect upon employee compliance with safety regulations. At this point, faced with seemingly interrelated problems of low rates of driver adherence to regulations regarding use of safety equipment in company cabs, high rates of assault and robbery upon drivers, and high driver attrition rates, Mr. Smith decided to consider developing and implementing an intervention program based upon the principles of performance feedback presented in this article.

His initial step in developing a performance feedback program was to specifically assess the suitability of this type of intervention for the organizational problems with which he was concerned. To rule out the possibility that performance decrements were primarily due to drivers' skills deficits, to structural characteristics of the job, or to misunderstood, unreasonable, or ambiguous performance goals, he followed the task analysis steps outlined earlier in this article. Only after determining that (1) his drivers had indeed acquired the necessary skills to utilize safety devices effectively, (2) structural characteristics of cab driving itself did not interfere with the proper use of safety devices, and (3) organizational standards and goals were clearly stated and understood by drivers, did he begin to devise a performance feedback system. His first decision involved choosing appropriate measures of performance. Specifically, he had to decide which process or outcome measures of the organizational performance problem to use in the intervention. He elected to primarily rely on a process measure of driver performance, rate of adherence to company safety regulations in the intervention. He felt strongly that the rate of adherence to safety regulations was directly related to each of the outcome measures in which he was ultimately interested. Also the outcome measures, robberies or assaults and turnover rate, occurred less frequently than the process measure of performance. However, to provide his drivers with additional relevant measures of their performance, he also gave feedback on these outcome measures.

Mr. Smith's next decision involved choosing a feedback mechanism. Should he provide performance information to his drivers using verbal, written, self-recorded, or mechanical feedback? In answering this question, he considered his proximity to the intended recipients of feedback messages, the drivers. Since he realized that he would have little opportunity for daily face-to-face contact with many of his drivers, he decided against using personal verbal feedback as the primary mechanism for his feedback system. Because his employees were generally unsupervised when driving their cabs, he decided to provide feedback on adherence to safety regulations by using a system that included both self-recorded and written feedback mechanisms. Regarding the former type of feedback mechanism, he designed an easy and quick "safety equipment checklist" that was completed by the driver each time a customer entered the cab. This checklist provided drivers with immediate feedback on their performance. The reliability of this self-monitoring feedback mechanism was evaluated by having trained observers pose as customers and make intermittent checks of drivers' adherence to safety regulations. One week prior to implementation of this self-monitoring feedback procedure, drivers were informed that checks would be made throughout the course of intervention. In addition to self-monitored feedback, Mr. Smith also provided his drivers with written feedback by the public display of group performance rates for the selected outcome and process measures. The content of publicly posted group feedback was selected so that overall group performance was compared with both a company performance standard and the group's previous performance. The combination of self-monitored and written feedback insured that the content of feedback messages included precise and objective information that was specific to targeted employee behavior.

With respect to the temporal characteristics of feedback, drivers' self-monitoring provided feedback that was contiguous with performance of the tasks of interest, while written group feedback was provided on a weekly basis. Following the guidelines for developing performance feedback systems that were presented in this article. Mr. Smith began to experiment with thinner feedback schedules once performance rates stabilized.

He also tied his performance feedback program to an incentive plan in order to enhance the effects of each. Each week that drivers met the organizational standard for compliance with safety regulations, they received a cash bonus amounting to 5 percent of their earnings for the week.

The feedback program was implemented on a trial basis for a period of one month. At the end of this period the effectiveness of the program was evaluated, and necessary adjustments were made. Mr. Smith noted a steady increase in driver adherence to safety measures during the trial period, with performance levels meeting company standards by the third week. Thus he found that he had designed a flexible performance feedback program that could be adjusted to suit the various aspects of his employee performance problem. In addition, he was pleased to find that over a several month period, robbery and assault rates had declined significantly, and employee turnover rate had ceased to be a major problem for his company.

SUMMARY

This article has attempted to provide a framework for developing and implementing comprehensive and effective performance feedback systems designed to fit the administrative structure of organizations. The specific components of feedback systems were delineated, and guidelines for developing and implementing flexible, efficient, and effective feedback systems were presented. These guidelines emphasized general rules that can be successfully applied to specific organizational performance problems. However, due to a lack of definitive research on the relative effectiveness of various system options, some of these guidelines might most appropriately be viewed as best-guess recommendations. Hopefully, the present article will serve both as a guide for developing effective feedback systems and an impetus for initiating the systematic research required to determine the necessary and sufficient components of effective performance feedback systems.

REFERENCES

Andrasik, F., and McNamara, J. R. Optimizing staff performance in an institutional behavior change system. *Behavior Modification*, 1977, *1*, 235-248.

At Emery Air Freight: Positive reinforcement boosts performance. *Organizational Dynamics*, 1973, *1*, 41-50.

Bourdon, R. D. A token economy application to management performance improvement. *Journal of Organizational Behavior Management*, 1977, *1*, 23-38.

Brethower, D. M., and Rummler, G. A. For improved work performance: Accentuate the positive. *Personnel*, September-October 1966, 40-48.

Bricker, W. A., Morgan, D. G., and Grabowski, J. G. Development and maintenance of a behavior modification repertoire of cottage attendants through T.V. feedback. *American Journal of Mental Deficiency*, 1972, *77*, 128-136.

Chandler, A. B. Decreasing negative comments and increasing performance of a shift supervisor. *Journal of Organizational Behavior Management*, 1977, *1*, 99-103.

Eldridge, L., Lemasters, S., and Szypot, B. A performance feedback intervention to reduce waste: Performance data and participant responses. *Journal of Organizational Behavior Management*, 1978, *1*, 258-266.

Ellsworth, R. B. Feedback: Asset or liability in improving treatment effectiveness? *Journal of Consulting and Clinical Psychology*, 1973, *40*, 383-393.

Ford, J. E. A classification system for feedback procedures. *Journal of Organizational Behavior Management*, 1980, *2*, 183-191.

Gilbert, T. F. *Human competence: Engineering worthy performance*. New York: McGraw-Hill, 1978.

Greller, M. M. Evaluation of feedback sources as a function of role and organizational level. *Journal of Applied Psychology*, 1980, *65*, 24-27.

Hall, B. H. Issues in assessing an organization. Paper presented at the fifth annual meeting of the Association for Behavior Analysis, Dearborn, MI, 1979.

Hall, J. F. *The psychology of learning*. Philadelphia: J. B. Lippincott Co., 1966.

Hamner, W. C., and Hamner, E. P. Behavior modification and the bottom line. *Organizational Dynamics*, Spring 1976, 3-21.

Hegarty, W. H. Using subordinate ratings to elicit behavioral changes in supervisors. *Journal of Applied Psychology*, 1974, *59*, 764-766.

Kempen, R. W., and Hall, R. V. Reduction of industrial absenteeism: Results of a behavioral approach. *Journal of Organizational Behavior Management*, 1977, *1*, 1-21.

Kim, J. S., and Hamner, W. C. Effect of performance feedback and goal setting on productivity and satisfaction in an organizational setting. *Journal of Applied Psychology*, 1976, *61*, 48-57.

Komaki, J., Barwick, K. D., and Scott, L. R. A behavioral approach to occupational safety: Pinpointing and reinforcing safe performance in a food manufacturing plant. *Journal of Applied Psychology*, 1978, *63*, 434-445.

Komaki, J., Blood, M. R., and Holder, D. Fostering friendliness in a fast food franchise. *Journal of Organizational Behavior Management*, 1980, *2*, 151-164.

Komaki, J., Waddell, W. M., and Pearce, J. G. The applied behavior analysis approach and individual employees: Improving performance in two small businesses. *Organizational Behavior and Human Performance*, 1977, *19*, 337-352.

Kreitner, R., Reif, W. E., and Morris, M. Measuring the impact of feedback on the performance of mental health technicians. *Journal of Organizational Behavior Management*, 1977, *1*, 105-109.

Lamal, P. A., and Benfield, A. The effect of self-monitoring on job tardiness and percentage of time spent working. *Journal of Organizational Behavior Management*, 1978, *1*, 142-149.

Locke, E. A., Cartledge, N., and Koeppel, J. Motivational effects of knowledge of results: A goal-setting phenomenon. *Psychological Bulletin*, 1968, *7*, 474-485.

Miller, L. M. Improving sales and forecast accuracy in a nationwide sales organization. *Journal of Organizational Behavior Management*, 1977, *1*, 39-51.

Mollenhoff, C. V. How to measure work by professionals. *Management Review*, November 1977, 39-43.

Nadler, D. A. The effects of feedback on task group behavior: A review of the experimental research. *Organizational Behavior and Human Performance*, 1979, *23*, 309-338.

Nadler, D., Mirvis, P., and Cammann, C. The ongoing feedback system: Experimenting with a new managerial tool. *Organizational Dynamics*, 1976, *4*, 63-80.

Nemeroff, W. F., and Cosentino, J. Utilizing feedback and goal setting to increase performance appraisal interview skills of managers. *Academy of Management Journal*, 1979, *22*, 566-576.

Oberg, W. Make performance appraisal relevant. *Harvard Business Review*, 1972, 50, 61-67.

Parsons, H. M. What happened at Hawthorne? *Science*, 1974, *183*, 922-932.

Patterson, R., Cooke, C., and Liberman, R. P. Reinforcing the reinforcers: A method of supplying feedback to nursing personnel. *Behavior Therapy,* 1972, *3*, 444-446.

Pedalino, E., and Gamboa, V. U. Behavior modification and absenteeism: Intervention in one industrial setting. *Journal of Applied Psychology*, 1974, *59*, 694-698.

Prue, D. M., and Fairbank, J. A. Performance feedback in organizational behavior management: A review. *Journal of Organizational Behavior Management*, 1981, *3*, 1-16.

Prue, D. M., Krapfl, J. E., Noah, J. C., Cannon, S., and Maley, R. F. Managing the treatment activities of state hospital staff. *Journal of Organizational Behavior Management*, 1980, *2*, 165-181.

Quilitch, H. R. A comparison of three staff-management procedures. *Journal of Applied Behavior Analysis*, 1975, *8*, 59-66.

Runnion, A., Johnson, T., and McWhorter, J. The effects of feedback and reinforcement on truck turnaround time in materials transportation. *Journal of Organizational Behavior Management*, 1978, *1*, 110-117.

Shook, G. L., Johnson, C. M., and Uhlman, W. F. The effects of response effort reduction, instructions, group and individual feedback, and reinforcement on staff performance. *Journal of Organizational Behavior Management*, 1978, *1*, 206-215.

Sims, H. P., and Szilagyi, A. D. Leader reward behavior and subordinate satisfaction and performance. *Organizational Behavior and Human Performance*, 1975, *14*, 426-438.

Skinner, B. F. *Science and human behavior,* New York: MacMillan, 1953.

Stoerzinger, A., Johnston, J. M., Pisor, K., and Monroe, C. Implementation and evaluation of a feedback system for employees on a salvage operation. *Journal of Organizational Behavior Management*, 1978, *1*, 268-280.

Sulzer-Azaroff, B., and deSantamaria, M. C. Industrial safety hazard reduction through performance feedback. *Journal of Applied Behavior Analysis*, 1980, *13*, 287-295.

Tosti, D., and Jackson, S. Formative and summative feedback. Paper presented at the seventh annual meeting of the Association for Behavior Analysis, Milwaukee, WI, 1981.

Walter, G. A. Effects of videotape feedback and modeling on the behaviors of task group members. *Human Relations*, 1975, *28*, 121-138.

Weitz, J., Antoinetti, J., and Wallace, S. R. The effect of home office contact on sales performance. *Personnel Psychology*, 1954, *1*, 381-384.

Welsch, W. V., Ludwig, C., Radiker, J. E., and Krapfl, J. E. Effects of feedback on daily completion of behavior modification projects. *Mental Retardation*, 1973, *11*, 24-46.

FIT CONTROL SYSTEMS
TO YOUR MANAGERIAL STYLE

Cortlandt Cammann
David A. Nadler

Not long ago, the Boy Scouts of America revealed that membership figures coming in from the field had been falsified. In response to the pressures of a national membership drive, people within the organization had vastly overstated the number of new Boy Scouts. To their chargrin, the leaders found something that other managers have also discovered: organizational control systems often produce unintended consequences. The drive to increase membership had motivated people to increase the number of new members reported, but it had not motivated them to increase the number of Boy Scouts actually enrolled.

The case of the Boy Scouts is a clear example of a widespread problem. Organizations spend large amounts of money, time, and effort in designing and maintaining control systems. These systems are intended to enhance an organization's ability to coordinate the actions of its members and to identify problems as they arise. Often, however, instead of increasing organizational control these systems reduce the amount of effective control that the organization exercises.

Why does this happen? Our research and the research of others indicate that the problem often lies with the ways that managers use control systems.[1] Most control systems, including budgetary, management information, and financial accounting systems, are essentially measurements. They regularly collect information about specific aspects of organizational performance.

The systems themselves are not capable of directly controlling organizational performance. Rather, they provide information to the managers who are in a position to exercise control. If managers use the information well, the control system works. If they use it poorly, the system may produce unintended effects.

Significantly, organizations seldom invest much effort in training managers to use control systems. Instead, most spend a lot of time designing, constructing, refining, and improving the technical aspects of their systems. The result is that while organizational control systems continually become more precise, accurate, and technologically sophisticated, two questions are often overlooked:

[1]Studies such as Chris Argyris's *The Impact of Budgets on People* (Ithaca, New York: Cornell University, 1952) and Frank J. Jasinsky's "Use and Misuse of Efficiency Controls," HBR July-August 1956, p. 105, provide concrete examples of the problems that can arise from poor use of feedback systems.

1. How effective is the system (and the way it is used) in doing what it is supposed to do?

2. How could the system be better used?

Recent research in a number of organizations has provided some answers to these questions.[2] First, control systems influence the way organization members direct their energies on the job; the members are more likely to put time and effort into those areas covered by the systems. Second, how members respond to control systems depends largely on the way managers use the systems. Third, different managers develop different strategies for using control systems. Finally, each strategy has certain drawbacks and benefits.

Only when managers understand (a) how these systems influence the behavior of their subordinates and (b) what trade-offs occur in each control strategy can they learn to use organizational control systems effectively.

In the balance of this article we shall discuss what managers should consider when they choose a control style. We shall examine the various ways in which control systems influence managerial behavior. Then, we shall discuss two major strategies for using control systems, the various issues that ought to be considered when choosing a particular control style, and the implications of the final decision.

INFLUENCE ON SUBORDINATES

When an area is covered by a control system, organization members concentrate on improving their performance in the measured area. There are three reasons for this direction of energy:

1. Measurement of an area of activity indicates that top management feels the area is important and bears watching.

2. Managers generally use control system measures when they evaluate subordinate performance. Since the subordinate usually feels that the manager's evaluation influences his or her rewards, the subordinate tends to put energy into the measured areas.

3. It is easy for an organization member to see changes in performance measures that are part of the control system. If his performance is improving, this can be a source of personal satisfaction.

Exhibit 1 provides an example of how performance measurement directs subordinate energy. In two different organizations — one a northeastern public utility, the other a midwestern bank — employees

[2]Anthony G. Hopwood's *An Accounting System and Managerial Behavior* (London: Haymarket Publishing, Ltd., 1974) and Geert H. Hofstede's *The Game of Budget Control* (Assen, Netherlands: Van Gorcum, 1967) look systematically at the ways in which accounting information is used and the impact these uses can have.

EXHIBIT 1

Area measurement and effort in two organizations

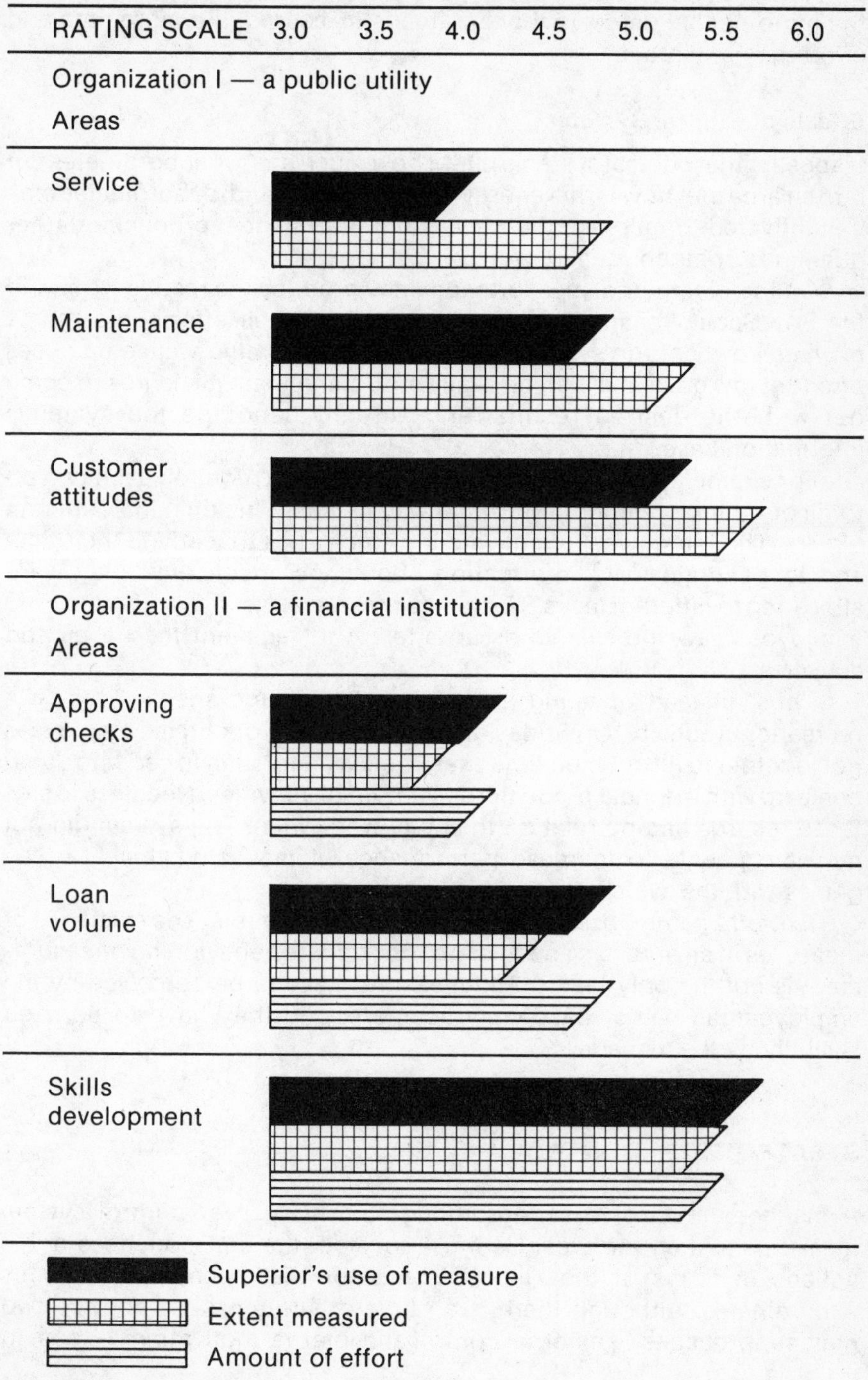

RATING SCALE	3.0	3.5	4.0	4.5	5.0	5.5	6.0

Organization I — a public utility

Areas

Service

Maintenance

Customer attitudes

Organization II — a financial institution

Areas

Approving checks

Loan volume

Skills development

■ Superior's use of measure

▦ Extent measured

▤ Amount of effort

were asked to indicate to what degree different areas of activity were measured. At another point, they were asked how much time and effort they put into each area. As shown in the exhibit, the general pattern is that the more people perceive that an area is measured, the more time and effort they put into it.

Effects of Control Systems

It appears that control systems direct how much energy subordinates put into an area, but how is this energy used? On one hand, subordinates may be motivated to increase their levels of performance, producing larger quantities or higher quality work.

On the other hand, measurement may produce the results we saw in the Boy Scouts' example. Subordinates direct their efforts into "game playing" to "beat the system." Rather than performing well, employees often set low goals that can be easily met, manipulate measures to come out with the desired results, and actually sabotage the system's information base.

For example, a large government organization required each person to fill out a form accounting for the way he spent his time in 20-minute blocks. The intent was to motivate the employees to manage their time and to generate valid information about how much time they were allocating to different tasks. The result, however, was vastly different. The employees saw the system as an attempt to regiment their lives and activities.

Thus, instead of being a useful tool, the time sheets became a recreational activity. On Friday afternoons at the work break, employees got together to fill out their time sheets, each competing to see who could come up with the most preposterous record of activities. Needless to say, these records had no relation to actual work done. The system did not motivate people to increase performance; it motivated them to play games with the system.

Exhibit 2 summarizes the effects of control systems. The existence of measures in an area has an effect on subordinate behavior, but measurement is not the only factor. The measures have to be perceived by the employees as being reasonably accurate, and they have to be used skillfully by the managers.

STRATEGIES OF CONTROL

A manager must give serious thought to his use of control system measures in any one area. He must consider the consequences of his actions in terms of the kinds of behavior that he motivates in his subordinates. Although there is a range of strategies for control, two major approaches — external control and internal motivation — seem to

EXHIBIT 2

How control systems and their use affect behavior

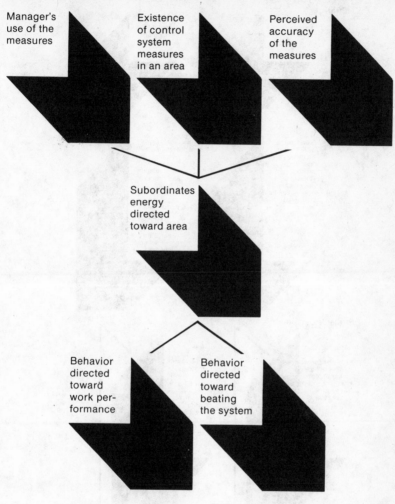

Manager's use of the measures

Existence of control system measures in an area

Perceived accuracy of the measures

Subordinates energy directed toward area

Behavior directed toward work performance

Behavior directed toward beating the system

prove most useful for many managers. *Exhibit 3* shows that each of these strategies requires different behavior on the part of the manager; each can have either desirable or undesirable effects on subordinate behavior.

External Control

This strategy is based on the assumption that subordinates in the particular situation are motivated primarily by external rewards and need to be controlled by their supervisors. To use the control system effectively in this way requires three steps.

EXHIBIT 3

Two different strategies of control

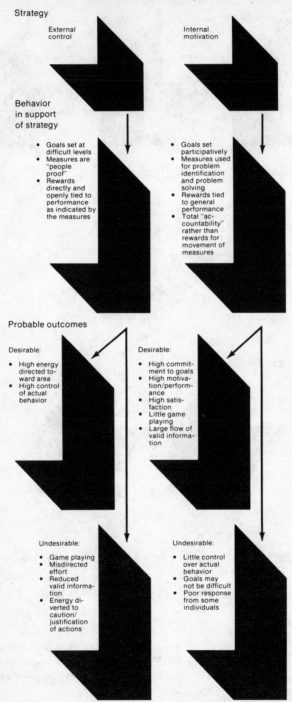

Strategy

External control

Internal motivation

Behavior in support of strategy

- Goals set at difficult levels
- Measures are "people proof"
- Rewards directly and openly tied to performance as indicated by the measures

- Goals set participatively
- Measures used for problem identification and problem solving
- Rewards tied to general performance
- Total "accountability" rather than rewards for movement of measures

Probable outcomes

Desirable:

- High energy directed toward area
- High control of actual behavior

Desirable:

- High commitment to goals
- High motivation/performance
- High satisfaction
- Little game playing
- Large flow of valid information

Undesirable:

- Game playing
- Misdirected effort
- Reduced valid information
- Energy diverted to caution/justification of actions

Undesirable:

- Little control over actual behavior
- Goals may not be difficult
- Poor response from some individuals

EXHIBIT 4
Questions a manager should ask himself when choosing a control strategy

1. In general, what kind of managerial style do I have?

Participative	*Directive*
I frequently consult my subordinates on decisions, encourage them to disagree with my opinion, share information with them, and let them make decisions whenever possible.	I usually take most of the responsibility for and make most of the major decisions, pass on only the most relevant job information, and provide detailed and close direction for my subordinates.

2. In general, what kind of climate, structure, and reward system does my organization have?

Participative	*Nonparticipative*
Employees at all levels of the organization are urged to participate in decisions and influence the course of events. Managers are clearly rewarded for developing employee skills and decision-making capacities.	Most important decisions are made by a few people at the top of the organization. Managers are not rewarded for developing employee competence or for encouraging employees to participate in decision making.

3. How accurate and reliable are the measures of key areas of subordinate performance?

Accurate	*Inaccurate*
All major aspects of performance can be adequately measured; changes in measures accurately reflect changes in performance; and measures cannot be easily sabotaged or faked by subordinates.	Not all critical aspects of performance can be measured; measures often do not pick up on important changes in performance; good performance cannot be adequately defined in measurement terms; and measures can be easily sabotaged.

4. Do my subordinates desire to participate and respond well to opportunities to take responsibility for decision making and performance?

High desire to participate	*Low desire to participate*
Employees are eager to participate in decisions, are involved in the work itself, can make a contribution to decision making, and want to take more responsibility.	Employees do not want to be involved in many decisions, do not want additional responsibility, have little to contribute to decisions being made, and are not very involved in the work itself.

First, the goals and standards associated with the system need to be made relatively difficult in order to "stretch" subordinates and leave little room for slack.

Second, the area measures need to be constructed so that they are "people proof," to prevent individuals from being able to manipulate the measures.

Third, rewards need to be directly and openly tied to performance, as indicated by the measures in the control system, to ensure that the subordinates have an incentive to work hard.

An example of the external control approach would be to evaluate a manager solely on the performance of his profit center, with relatively high levels of profit being budgeted and with his compensation tied primarily and directly to the number of dollars of profit.

This external control strategy can have different effects. On one hand, subordinates may channel a great deal of energy into measured areas and may try hard to make their measures moves, since they can gain rewards by doing so. Where the system is very tightly structured, the result will be a high degree of control of subordinate behavior. On the other hand, several undesirable results may occur.

First, such a strategy may motivate organization members to improve their performance measures but not create any commitment to their doing a better job. The subordinates will begin to develop an attitude toward performance in which "doing well" means doing well on the performance measures, not necessarily performing their jobs more effectively. As a result, if they can increase their "performance" by manipulating the measures, providing false information, intentionally setting low goals and standards, or sabotaging the system, the organization members can be expected to do so.

Second, such a strategy may result in misdirected effort. Subordinates may put all of their energies into the particular behavior that is measured, while forgetting other behavior that, although not measured, is also vital. For example, if all efforts are directed toward increasing sales volume, the amount of effort devoted to ongoing customer service may be decreased. In this case, the result is short-term maximization in the measured area with possible negative long-term effects on unmeasured areas.

Third, such a strategy may tend to reduce the flow of valid information, particularly negative information. If people are directly rewarded for positive movement of measures, they may become motivated to withhold information that would negate the meaning of those measures and to withhold negative information from higher-level managers who need it for decision making.

Finally, such a strategy may bring about excessive caution, directing energy toward justification of all actions. Subordinates may be motivated to ensure that the measures either continue to look good (by not taking any risks), or to assemble "just in case" files filled with information justifying a decrease in measured performance. In either case, energy is directed toward coping with the system, rather than toward the larger goal of making the organization more effective.

Internal Motivation

In this strategy, management assumes that subordinates can be motivated by building their commitments to organizational goals and by their being involved in the necessary tasks. They assume that employees will be motivated by the feelings of accomplishment, achievement, recognition, and self-esteem that come from having performed a job well. The strategy of internal motivation is implemented by using the control system in a very different manner than in the external control strategy.

First, although goals are set, the most important feature of this approach is not the difficulty in achieving the goals but the fact that they are set participatively. Those people who are responsible for achieving goals are given some influence over the nature of those goals.

Second, the measures are used for joint problem identification and solution rather than for punishment or blame. When a performance begins to move in an undesired direction, it is not the time for heads to roll. It is the time for managers and subordinates to meet together (a) to determine the reasons for the change, and (b) to develop solutions to the problems that have come up. Thus the system takes on an "early warning" function of surfacing problems, beginning the resolution process before those problems reach the crisis state.

Finally, although rewards are tied to performance, they are not tied to one or two specific measures. Rather, the reward structure emphasizes accountability for the entire job performance, only part of which may be represented by the measures. In general, the control system becomes problem-based and future-oriented. The system helps the manager exercise control of subordinate behavior by directing future efforts, rather than by punishing each person's past actions.

This internal motivation strategy may have different effects. It may generate high commitment to goals because the organization member participates in setting them and feels responsible for seeing that they are achieved. This may lead to greater energy directed toward task performance. As performance increases and as the individual monitors his progress through the measures of the control system, the strategy may also enhance the employee's satisfaction in performing his job well.

Thus the open nature of the control system and its general, rather than specific, accountability mean that there is little incentive for subordinates to play games or to behave dysfunctionally. More important, it encourages and rewards the flow of valid information, particularly negative information.

At the same time, such a strategy may have some undesirable effects. The comparatively loose nature of this approach means that the manager will have less control over the behavior of his subordinates. Because the manager gives up total control over the specific goals, subordinates may establish less ambitious goals.

In addition, since the information provided by the control system is for problem solving and not for evaluation, it becomes difficult to use it as a basis for giving rewards. Thus the manager has to sacrifice some of the value that is inherent in the external control approach in order to build internal motivation on the part of subordinates.

Finally, some individuals may not respond to the participative process because of differences in working style or personality. These people, therefore, will not be motivated to perform well within this strategy framework.

CHOICE STRATEGIES

Neither of the two strategies just discussed is necessarily the "right" strategy to use in all cases. Since each has certain drawbacks and benefits, a manager must consciously and carefully choose the approach that suits his particular situation. In making that choice, he needs to consider the following four issues:

1. *Consistency between strategy choice and managerial style.*

   In choosing a control strategy, a manager may have to modify either his style or the strategy so that his total approach to managing is consistent. For instance, if a manager generally makes all important decisions without involving subordinates, it would be a mistake for him to use an internal motivation approach. The subordinates would be accustomed to following the manager's lead. They may not be capable of setting realistic goals on their own; or worse, they may use their influence to set easy objectives that they know they can achieve. It is only in the context of a generally participative manager-subordinate relationship that an internal motivation approach to organizational control is likely to be effective.

2. *Organizational climate, structure, and reward system.*

   A control strategy, to be most effective, should be consistent with other factors in the organization that determine employee behavior. For example, a tight control system in an organization that normally provides a great deal of discretion and freedom for employees would soon run into problems.

3. *Reliability of job performance measures.*

   In some cases, control system measures accurately reflect job performance. In others, the measures do not adequately indicate how well the job is being done. When the control system is an unreliable indicator of performance, it is hard to implement a tight external control strategy since the use of inaccurate or unreliable measures as a basis for evaluation and reward could have disastrous consequences. Under such conditions, a looser and more internally oriented organizational control strategy is required.

4. *Individual differences among subordinates.*

Because people are motivated by different needs, they may respond differently to the same organizational structure. The choice of control strategy assumes that the manager knows something about the

EXHIBIT 5
A decision tree for choosing a control strategy

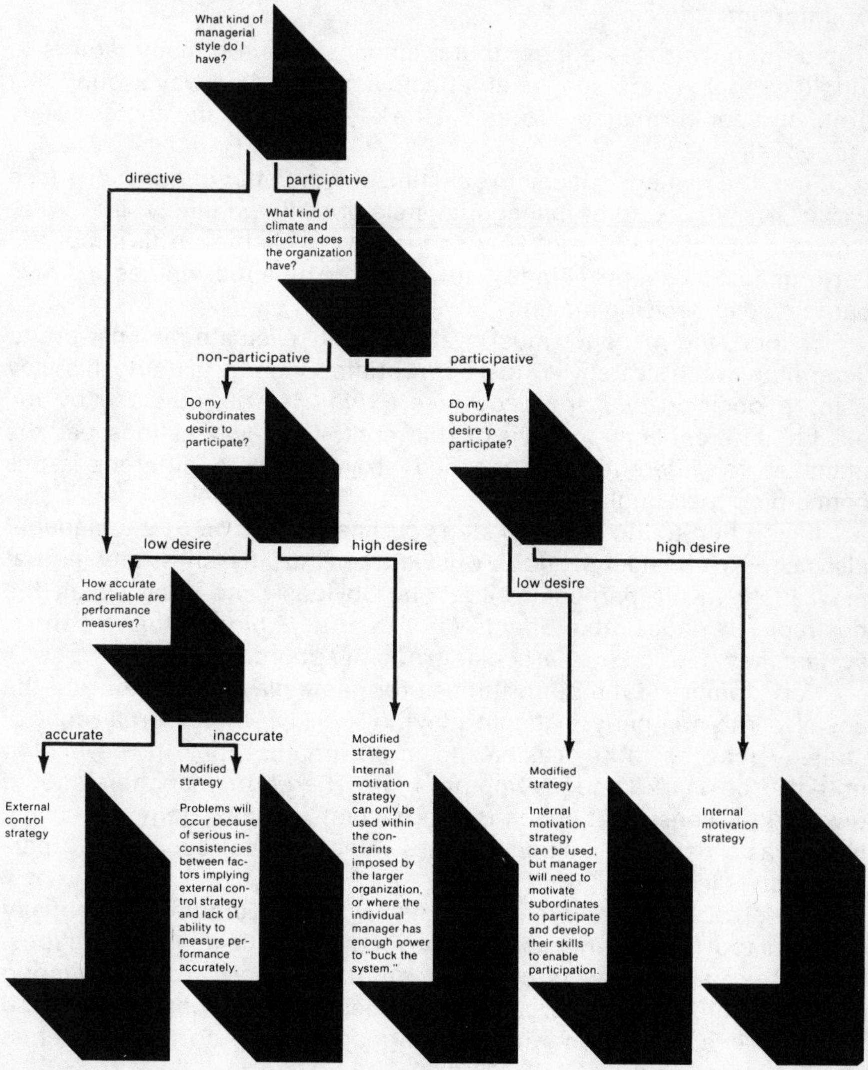

nature of the people who work for him. Individuals who are committed to the work itself (e.g., in many professional occupations) are likely to be less responsive to an external control strategy than those individuals whose primary motivation is financial reward or promotion.

A manager must also consider how much employees desire to participate in decision making. Some people may respond well to the opportunity for participation, while others may not want to become more involved or assume the responsibility. Thus the types of people who work for the manager should be a factor influencing his choice of a control strategy.

An Informed Choice

At first glance, it may appear that a manager has too many factors to juggle to enable him to make an effective choice. One way around this problem is for the manager to lay out the key decisions and choice points sequentially.

First, the manager needs to ask himself a number of questions (see *Exhibit 4*). What kind of managerial style does he generally use? What kind of organization is he in? How accurate and reliable are his important performance measures? Finally, how much do his subordinates desire to participate in decision making?

Second, the manager must systematically evaluate his answers to determine which strategy is most appropriate. One way of doing this is by using a decision-tree approach (see *Exhibit 5*). As indicated by the exhibit, different combinations of answers to the key questions lead the manager to different recommended strategies with different issues concerning their implementation.

In addition to the decision steps outlined in *Exhibit 5*, the manager also needs to consider the trade-offs between the different strategies that may apply to his particular situation. Obviously, he must weigh the desirable or undesirable effects (as listed in *Exhibit 3*) that a control system may have on his particular group of subordinates.

For example, if the opportunities for game playing are few and the costs to the company of game playing are low, the external control strategy may be more feasible. In most organizations, however, the potential costs of game playing are high. Therefore, managers should give serious consideration to the internal motivation strategy, especially if the basic decision-making process indicates that subordinate participation is feasible.

A control system and the way that it is used constitutes a potentially powerful tool for influencing the behavior of individuals in organizations. Just as the manager needs to make a careful and informed choice among control strategies, the organization needs to be conscious of the alternative approaches to designing and using control systems.

Becoming aware of the potential effects of control systems and of the great importance of the process of control — as opposed to the technology of control — is central to making an organization and its people more productive and effective.

DEUTERO-LEARNING IN ORGANIZATIONS: LEARNING FOR INCREASED EFFECTIVENESS

Donald A. Schon

Concern with organizational effectiveness is of long standing. There is nothing new about asking: Are institutions working well? Is government doing its job? How good are universities? Indeed, there is nothing new about asking what is meant by terms such as "working," "effectiveness," and "goodness"; the ancient Greeks were known for this kind of inquiry. But over the centuries, the ways in which these questions have been asked reflect shifting concerns and assumptions about organizational effectiveness.

In the United States, for example, these questions have evolved significantly in the period from World War I to the present. Business firms, in particular, often have been subjected to questions that later were asked of all kinds of organizations. The evolution of questions on organizational effectiveness has gone through four distinct stages.

WORLD WAR I TO WORLD WAR II

"Is the firm well organized? Is its product or service in demand, economical, and of high quality? Are the best techniques employed? Does the firm have good leaders and good workers?"

Relevance, economy, and quality of output are understood to depend on sound organization for performance, while organization is defined in terms of the appropriate functional division of labor. Technique is a subject for inquiry because it is deemed possible to achieve or approximate the best technique for any given purpose.

Individual performance is important to organizational performance and is thought to be different for managers and for workers. Effective performance depends on the proper matching of techniques to organizational position (as in Taylorism or the concepts of good management as defined by Chester Barnard). It also depends on certain character traits — for leaders: determination, courage, and entrepreneurship; for workers: conscientiousness, loyalty, and dependability.

Sound organization, quality of product, good leadership, and best technique — all are conceived as stable models. The problem is to achieve and maintain a level of performance that approximates these models.

WORLD WAR II TO THE LATE 1950s

"Does the organization foster individual creativity, and with it, intervention and discovery?"

This question reflects the emergence of research and development in the wake of World War II, the maturation of the research cycle in the business firm, and the beginnings of the perception that development of new products and services may be a continuing and central function of the firm.

But the focus on novelty is conceptualized in terms of individual performance and tends to be limited to one segment of the firm, the research and development department. If individual scientists and technologists are creative, the organization, in turn, will become creative in developing new products or services.

The nature of business is no longer seen as given and no longer assumed to be permanently fixed. *Best technique* gives way to *creativity*, but creativity remains subject to the general rule of division of labor and is conceived (as is character) as a property of individuals.

In this period, organizations concern themselves with designing a climate for creativity, and universities launch a wave of research on the creative individual and his selection and on the conditions that stimulate creative work.

LATE 1950s TO MID-1960s

"Is the organization innovative?"

This question reflects disillusionment with central and autonomous research and development divisions. These enterprises (based largely on the model of the Manhattan Project) are perceived as questionably effective and unquestionably expensive. Attention shifts to the design and functioning of the organization as a whole. Perhaps the whole organization must be restructured and must change its style of operation in order to employ the creativity of individuals properly. Perhaps the firm has a limited capacity to digest the creative output of individuals.

Guided by this perspective, the structure of the firm and the interactions of production, marketing, finance, and technology are no longer assumed to be stable. There is a shift in attention from individual to organizational performance. But many of the underlying assumptions and values of business remain intact.

MID-1960s TO PRESENT

"Is the organization able to manage change?"

New product or *new service* may no longer be the proper unit of analysis. There is an awareness of broad-scale shifts in the nature of business and the business environment, many of them unanticipated, ambiguous, and poorly understood. These include changes in the ratio of service to manufacturing industries; the rise of multinational and international firms as dominant forms; emergence of quasi-public organizations such as COMSAT and erosion of public/private boundaries; changing assumptions about the workforce and its requirements; the conspicuous emergence of regulatory and environmental issues; and questioning of previously unquestioned business values and assumptions at the instigation of youth, civil rights, antiwar, and environmental movements.

But the familiar rhetoric of the management of change already has begun to appear unsatisfactory. Not all change is good; some is regressive, and some is even moving in the direction of organizational entropy — that is, toward a reduction in order and coherence. When the ends themselves are perceived as ambiguous, conflicting, and shifting, it seems necessary to ask, "Change to what ends?" Technique, character, creativity, and innovativeness no longer seem adequate as descriptions of effective leaders or effective workers.

Further, the present context challenges a model of organizational action, planning, and policy making that has been taken for granted in previous stages — the model of rational purpose.

According to this model, rational action, for organizations as well as for persons, consists in progressive adaption of means to ends. Organizations and their environments are assumed to hold steady for periods of time sufficient for planning, decision, and action. Organizational objectives are assumed to be definable, understandable, and consistent. Decisions are undertaken within a framework of prediction of the likely consequences of alternatives for action, predictions that in turn are based on the experience of the recent past.

None of the accepted ideas on creativity, innovation, and change required a fundamental revision of these assumptions. On the contrary, creativity, innovation, and change were conceived of as occurring within a context of stability sufficient to permit organizational self-identity over time, objectives and alternatives ascertainable in the period required for planning and based on a prediction of future consequences drawn from the experience of the recent past. This model seemed adequate, indeed unquestionable, in a period in which we could believe that our basic institutions and the assumptions on which they rest would hold steady for a lifetime. But the discontinuities and zones of turbulence we used to think about as occasional events in the background — events we had to endure as part of the price of getting to the stable place on the other side — now have become foreground. We no longer can conceive of future action simply as a linear extension of the past. We no longer can assume that there are clear rules for making valid inferences from past experience. In most areas, we know that we cannot make predictions that will be valid for the next 15 years. We cannot compartmentalize problems and their solutions. We lack techniques for understanding or controlling the full complexity of the situations with which we are confronted; hence, any faith in such techniques would be misplaced. And it is no longer possible for one group at the apex of society to plan, to make policy, to decide for the rest of society, and then to diffuse its solutions throughout the society. There is, with all of this, a sense of loss of an antecedent stable state and a growing doubt whether any restabilization will last very long. Under these conditions, the model of rational purpose no longer seems unquestionable.

With the business manager, competence for learning becomes a crucial requirement. If his task environment is continually shifting, and shifting in ways that are only marginally predictable, then he cannot be expected to learn ahead of time the techniques by which he will confront new situations effectively. What becomes crucial is his capacity to learn on-line — to detect the new features of his task environment and to design effective responses to them.

Not only the manager but also the entire organization face a shifting task environment, the future direction of which is only marginally predictable. The effective business firm, thus, is one that has a high capacity for organizational learning. The effective business manager, in turn, is one who has developed the capacity to foster organizational learning.

THE MEANING OF ORGANIZATIONAL LEARNING

Although the term *organizational learning* is difficult to define, we are used to hearing statements such as these:

"We have learned very little from the Vietnam War."

"The United States learned from the experience of the 1930s to take regulatory measures that will prevent another Depression."

"The 3M Corporation has learned to launch new businesses under a corporate umbrella."

"The period from 1960 to 1970 was one in which the federal government failed to learn how to implement new social programs effectively."

"The Student Movement learned, after 1964, to carry out a new style of confrontation politics."

"Our private universities have not learned to become financially self-supporting."

Ordinary discourse is full of such references to learning, and although we may often consider them false, we seldom regard them as devoid of meaning. On the other hand, a closer inspection may convince us that organizations such as the government, the 3M Corporation, or the

Student Movement cannot literally be said to learn. If individuals are the only appropriate subjects for the verb *learn*, then organizational learning is a metaphor.

Yet organizations can act in a sense that is not reducible to individual behavior (although never, of course, without the intervention of individual behavior). Why can't we literally apply the term *learning* to organizations? Organizations are artifacts designed for human purposes. Their effectiveness depends on their continuing redesign in response to changing values and a changing context for action. Organizational learning would then refer to this process of continuing redesign. The terms' vagueness, analogous to the vagueness of *natural force* or *evolution* at earlier stages of intellectual history, merely points out the need for inquiry into a phenomenon that is poorly understood.

Recent histories of learning theory, educational reform, and educational research suggest that individual learning is also poorly understood. But ordinary discussion calls attention to some features of individual learning that distinguish it from mere change, and these may be sufficient to guide an initial inquiry into organizational learning.

For example, in order to say that a person learns:

- There must be a learner who is self-identical over time so that one can say he learns rather than simply that learning happens. The learner must have past experience from which he learns, present experience in which he learns, and prospective experience to which he will apply his learning. Learning, in short, presupposes a learner and his history.

- There must be a content to learning that is expressible, at least in principle, in propositional form. It is paradoxical to say that there has been learning, but nothing has been learned. And if something has been learned, it seems paradoxical to say that the something is not expressible, even in principle, as knowledge.

- Learning must leave a residue in the form of a pattern of behavior, different from the learner's previous behavior, that persists over time.

- Learning must be in response to experience. It would be very strange to say, "I learned something, but experience played no part in my learning," even though it may be difficult to identify the past experience from which a particular instance of learning derived.

Learning, then, is that particular sort of change in which a subject as a result of past experience evidences a pattern of behavior — new for him — that signifies knowledge — also new for him — and that can be expressed — at least in principle — in propositional form.

THEORY-IN-USE

This formulation poses an interesting problem. If what is learned is a new pattern of behavior, then what is the new knowledge associated with that behavior?

In *Theory in Practice*, Chris Argyris and I describe the concept of *theory-in-use*, the theory constructed to account for a person's actions by attributing to him a complex intention consisting of governing variables or values, strategies for action, and assumptions that link the strategies to the governing variables.

Thus for a teacher in a classroom, a partial statement of a theory-in-use might include the following:

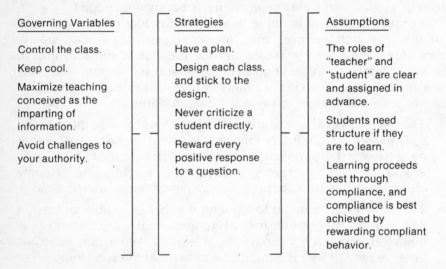

Governing Variables	Strategies	Assumptions
Control the class.	Have a plan.	The roles of "teacher" and "student" are clear and assigned in advance.
Keep cool.	Design each class, and stick to the design.	
Maximize teaching conceived as the imparting of information.	Never criticize a student directly.	Students need structure if they are to learn.
Avoid challenges to your authority.	Reward every positive response to a question.	Learning proceeds best through compliance, and compliance is best achieved by rewarding compliant behavior.

Such a theory-in-use, if it accounts for the teacher's behavior correctly, is assumed to be available to the teacher in the form of knowledge, explicit or tacit. We distinguish theory-in-use from *espoused theory*, which is the individual's explicit version of his theory of action, advanced for public or personal consumption. Theory-in-use and espoused theory need not be, and often are not, congruent.

I would like to advance here the concept of *learning as experience-based change in theory-in-use*. Although any experience-based change in theory-in-use may be called learning, some kinds of change in theory-in-use are more important than others. The most central kinds of learning involve change in the governing variables of the theory. This is called *double-loop learning* and is distinguished from the *single-loop learning* of new strategies for achieving existing governing variables. The teacher in a traditional classroom may learn (single-loop) to ask the students more specific questions in order to control student responses more readily; or the teacher may learn (double-loop) to reduce requirements for control in the classroom.

Given the value placed by the individual on constancy of his theory-in-use and the even greater value placed on constancy of the more central elements of his theory-in-use, a requirement for double-loop learning comes into conflict with the requirement for constancy. It is our hypothesis that given prevailing models of theories-in-use, learning that involves change in the governing variables of a theory-in-use comes about only through dilemmas — that is, through the individual's discovery that he is confronted with a progressively intolerable conflict of central elements in his theory-in-use.

DEUTERO-LEARNING

In *Steps to an Ecology of Mind*, Gregory Bateson introduces the concept of deutero-learning, which is simply learning to learn. Bateson offers as an example a very simple model:

> A female porpoise . . . is trained to accept the sound of the trainer's whistle as a "secondary reinforcement." The whistle is expectably followed by food, and if she later repeats what she was doing when the whistle blew, she will expect again to hear the whistle and receive food.

> This porpoise is now used by the trainers to demonstrate "operant conditioning" to the public. When she enters the exhibition tank, she raises her head above surface, hears the whistle and is fed. . . .

> But this pattern is [suitable] only for a single episode in the exhibition tank. She must break that pattern to deal with the *class* of such episodes. There is a larger *context of contexts* which will put her in the wrong. . . . When the porpoise comes on stage, she again raises her head. But she gets no whistle. The trainer waits for the next piece of conspicuous behavior, likely a tail flap, which is a common expression of annoyance. This behavior is then reinforced and repeated [by giving her food]

> But the tail flap was, of course, not rewarded in the third performance.

> Finally, the porpoise learned to deal with the context of contexts — by offering a different or *new* piece of conspicuous behavior whenever she came on stage.

Each time the porpoise learns to deal with a new and larger class of episodes, she learns *about* the previous contexts for learning. Her *creativity* reflects deutero-learning.

Coming closer to home, a person deutero-learns about the process by which he changes his theory-in-use in response to experience. Examples of his deutero-learning would include learning:

- To make his theory-in-use explicit.

- To seek data that would allow him, for the first time, to test a proposition within his theory-in-use.

- To confront theory-in-use with espoused theory.

- To focus explicitly on dilemmas within the theory-in-use.

- To use unproved maxims for the learning process such as, "Break the problem down into manageable parts," "Name the unknowns," and "Seek simpler problems related to the one you are solving."

On the assumption that theories-in-use are to be tested in part by their effectiveness, theories of deutero-learning are to be tested by their assistance in enabling the individual to develop more effective theories-in-use.

ORGANIZATIONAL DEUTERO-LEARNING

Under this perspective on organizational learning, organizations also have theories of action, the organizational equivalent of the individual's theories-in-use. From this point of view, an organization represents the answer to a set of questions about purposes, functions, activities, and methods. Consider a company engaged in sugar refining. Observations of the company's activities and operations could be used to infer the answers offered by this company to questions such as these:

- How is sugar best grown and harvested?

- What is the most effective means of transporting raw sugar to refineries?

- What is the most effective distribution system from plantations to international sugar markets?

The answers to these questions are the theories of action that account for the company's behavior in production, transportation, and distribution. We can formulate questions and answers for every facet of the company's operations. The same holds for more general aspects of organizational behavior. (As in the case of personal theories of actions, organizational theories-in-use may be, and usually are, more or less incongruent with espoused theory — here, with the formal, announced policies and procedures of a firm.)

- How is accountability of unit supervisors best assured?

- What is the most effective means of organizing functional and regional operations?

- What reward systems are most conducive to effective staff performance?

Answers to these questions consist of theories of action constructed to account for the company's processes of accountability, organization, and reward.

With this view, the concept of an organization's theory-in-use expands to include these four areas:

- Planning and policy — the theory-in-use constructed to account for the behavior of the organization-as-a-whole in relation to its task environment. For example, its changes in marketing and pricing policies, its growth pattern, and its pattern of introduction of new products and services.

- Structure — the theory-in-use constructed to account for the programming of interaction of units and subunits of the firm. For example, the program for interaction of production, marketing, technology, and finance in the development of new products.

- Technique — the theories-in-use constructed to account for the performance of unit operations, such as cane cutting, can storage, accounting, merchandising, and so forth.

- Behavioral world — the theories-in-use constructed to account for the interactions of individuals within the organization of the company. For example, the extent to which individuals, in their interactions within the organization, behave in ways that are confronting, open, manipulative, or protective.

Taken together, these theories-in-use account for the ways in which the organization interacts with its task environment and maintains itself. Organizational learning, then, consists of experience-based change in theories-in-use in any of these domains.

It is immediately apparent that, in this broad sense, organizations have always learned. The experience-based development of new policies, structures, techniques, and approaches to the behavioral world has characterized American business firms throughout the various stages of development described earlier. Indeed, the very stability of organizations, in the face of the centrifugal and entropic forces constantly at work in them, signifies a kind of learning.

The learning model previously described — the model required by loss of the stable state — refers to the organizational capacity to set and solve problems and to design and redesign policies, structures, and techniques in the face of constantly changing assumptions about self and environment. In other words, this is the capacity for deutero-learning.

We must explore the conditions under which organizations can learn to improve their capacity for making experience-based changes in their theories-in-use. In particular, we must ask how increased competence for deutero-learning reflects itself in the interaction of the areas of planning and policy making, structure, and the behavioral world.

It is fruitless to ask which of these domains is most important or which should become a focus for attention. All are intertwined. When we take them up in sequence, it is only to distinguish for purposes of exposition phenomena that are in reality inseparable.

PLANNING AND POLICY MAKING

Competence for deutero-learning consists not of particular plans or policies or even particular techniques, but of a particular stance toward these activities — a stance related to what it is that can be known and to the way in which that knowledge is regarded.

This stance is best understood in its historical context. Starting with the period between the two World Wars, I find four stages in the development of organizational attitudes toward planning and policy making that correspond roughly to those listed earlier.

In the first stage, the dominant question is: What has gone wrong and what policy can make it right? Issues emerge in the form of crises. (They must do so in order to generate enough energy to surmount the dynamic conservatism that prevented their being noticed earlier.) Problems are seen as distortions or deviations from some previous equilibrium. The problem is to get back where we were, to put things right. Problems are discrete and disconnected. There may be a crisis of morale among the workers; there may be a crisis of pollution in the cities. But for all practical purposes, these have nothing to do with each other. Crises are seen as one-shot problems that lend themselves to fixes. In early 1964, for example, a very respected scientist wanted to solve the problem of racial unrest by installing air conditioners in the ghettos. Problems also are seen as external in origin. They are not understandable as consequences of our earlier actions; instead, they have been done to us or have happened to us.

In the second stage, the dominant questions are these: What is the policy we currently have? How have we contributed to what we now see as the problem? How has it become a crisis? How can we develop a better policy? There is the beginning of recognition of personal, governmental, and institutional causality; it is at least partly our fault. With this perception also comes the beginning of a disposition to see problems as recurrent and cyclical, to see that solutions to problems generate new problems. After all, we helped to produce this situation by the actions we took in response to some earlier situation. There is a sense of a need to recognize and diagnose the shortcomings of our earlier policy. There is a new concern with the outcomes of policy together with a belief in rational models for the solutions to problems. I would offer as an example U.S. corporate planning in the middle and late 1950s and, within the federal government, the process by which the Bureau of the Budget became "MacNamarized" in the mid-1960s with the spread of the Planning-Programming-Budgeting System from the Pentagon to other governmental agencies.

In the third stage, issues are seen as a localized symptom of an underlying change in our relationships with our environment. A shift is going on. What we have been doing in the design and management of a system of activities is seen as being mismatched to the environment of these activities. We deal not only with hospitals but with health services, not only with welfare payments but with the social welfare system. It is an issue of large and complex systems. The question is: How can we develop a progressively more effective policy? We recognize the need to create a continual process of response to the changing environment and to change policies in response to the outcomes of earlier policies. Here we perceive a need to formulate clear objectives and measures of performance. There must be an intelligence function that senses the environment. There must be techniques for learning what needs to be worked on. There must be sophisticated methods of cost-benefit analysis and evaluation in order to establish the feedback loops between outcomes and policy. The theory of knowledge underlying this learning process can be described as pragmatism, and it is borrowed directly from experimental science. The view is that we can never know the truth; at best, we can approximate the truth through progressively more adequate hypothesis, prediction, and experiment. As part of the pragmatic approach, there is recognition of the need for a system to permit such learning.

In the fourth stage (which we are now, I think, beginning), we recognize that poverty is not a problem of housing, jobs, welfare, income, finance, health, social welfare, family life, or genetics but is somehow an interacting process involving all of these factors. We separate problems not because they deserve to be separated but in order to accommodate our limited understanding of them and because we cannot act unless we do so. At the same time, we see these interacting systems of activities and institutions as continually shifting, while the shifts are understood to impose new requirements for response. We recognize that our conceptual tools are inadequate to the complexity of these interacting systems. We sense that we are dealing with more information than we can handle. We expect and can live with high uncertainty, and we do not take this as a reason for fatalism. The question is: How shall we design and live with a process for learning in this context? We recognize that organizational learning is an existential process, that is, we learn from the past. But there are no rational means of extrapolating from the past. We direct ourselves toward the future, but there are no valid means of predicting the future. Our processes of learning must permit us to learn about the situation while we are in the situation and to organize so that we learn through the action we undertake. We learn on-line, and the results of our learning we always regard as propositions on which we are prepared to act. We commit ourselves to them in order to act on them, but we are prepared to find them disconfirmed.

There is a willingness to accept, indeed a disposition to seek out, dilemmas. The search for clear operational objectives is bound to be flawed. Objectives are basically conflicting, incorporating as they do the inevitably disparate values of the various parties that take part in formulating them. It is understood that there is no objective diagnosis of the situation. Instead, our commitment is to specific values that enable us to make sense out of any situation.

STRUCTURE

The attitude toward planning and policy making reflected in the fourth stage has its counterpart in the design of organizational structure — that is, in the theory-in-use for the division of labor and for the interaction of organizational elements.

The classic pyramidal form of the business corporation prior to World War II assumed a stable concept of the business built around a product or service and a notion of corporate planning limited to matching the curves of supply and demand. When organizational planning is conceived as being in the fourth stage, organizational structure must become a design capable of continuing restructuring; yet this flexibility must be compatible with organizational survival.

Let us take the 3M Corporation as an example. 3M began as a manufacturer of sandpaper. They ground up a mineral, coated a substrate with it, cut it into pieces, and marketed it in the manner of a traditional product firm. Shortly after World War II, a man named Cook in the 3M laboratories invented Scotch tape — Scotch because it was designed to save money. The idea was to use the tape in order to mend books. However, when they put Scotch tape on the market, they found that people responded to it very differently than 3M thought they would. How do people use Scotch tape? They hang things on the wall, wrap packages, and make decorations with it. Teenage daughters even come down to breakfast with their hair done up in Scotch tape. Therefore, 3M developed a hairsetting Scotch tape. What they did was to conceive of the product as a projective test for the consumer. They did not know what they had made; the consumer told them what they had made, and they entered into a dialogue with the market. The product was a joint invention.

Another 3M invention was a social invention. Once they had marketed Scotch tape, they let Cook run the business, saying to him, "Look, Cook, we don't know how to manage Scotch tape. We know how to manage sandpaper. Take your invention and build a little company all your own. We won't bother you, but we want to see your profit and loss statement every month." Because the consumer turned out to see more in Scotch tape than 3M had seen, and because 3M was smart enough to see that the consumer had seen something in it, Cook did very well.

As he began to do well, Armour Research Corporation in Chicago invented another form of tape, magnetic tape, and people in the 3M laboratory said, "If we can make Scotch tape, we can make magnetic tape, too. It is the same kind of problem — you have a cellulose acetate base, you deposit ferrites on it, and you have made it." And they did. When they marketed it, they repeated the process of social invention, and it worked — consumers once again told them what they had made. Then somebody said, "Look, if we are making magnetic tape, we can make tape recorders; that would be like razors and blades. You sell the recorders to sell the tape, and the tape to sell the recorder." So they did. Then somebody said, "You know, we are really in the music business. We could be making phonographs." And they did. Then someone else said, "You know, what we really have is a kind of system for tapes and machines. We ought to have a business machine division. Because we have tapes and machines, we know a lot about both aspects of that problem." And they did. Then they said, "We have a reputation for consumer products. People know who we are. We could begin to market things in supermarkets. We have all these minerals. We will make abrasive cleaning pads and put them in supermarkets." And they did. Then they said, "Look, we can be making games." And they proceeded to do so. Pretty soon there were 40 semiautonomous companies surrounding a bank and a development facility.

If we ask ourselves the question what business are they in, how shall we answer it? We cannot say they are in the tape business because they also make machines. We cannot say they are in the music business because they also manufacture business equipment. We must say something such as: "They are in the business of making money from development" or "They are in the business of corporate entrepreneurship" or "They are in the business of commercializing new developments." But any suitable definition turns out to be a definition not of a category of products but of a category of processes. 3M is not an Aristotelian company; that is, there is no set of characteristics common to all 3M products that only 3M products possess. Their products share not a set of defining properties but a family resemblance that grew out of the ways in which one product led to another.

Consider the resulting structure of the firm. A bank and a development laboratory are at the center with a collection of little companies connected to it, forming a constellation. If the market for sandpaper deteriorates, it is possible to abolish the sandpaper division without much injury to the center of the constellation. Only one quasi-autonomous company has been removed; another one presumably will sprout to take its place. 3M becomes, then, an organization peculiarly well adapted to changing market conditions. Indeed, in the United States during the 1960s, 3M was the major corporate social invention of its kind. It was a model in corporate learning for responding to change in the business environment.

THE BEHAVIORAL WORLD

What does competence in deutero-learning require of the organization's behavioral world? Principally that members of the organization be effective at shared inquiry. The capacity for learning about learning — at the several levels of policy, structure, technique, and the behavioral world itself — requires that interacting members of the organization continually be able to carry out tasks that cannot be carried out by top management or by organizational planners alone. Five of these tasks are:

- *Integrate scattered perceptions of organizational phenomena.* Such an integration is essential to detect a problem situation affecting the organization as a whole, but before it assumes crisis proportions (at which point it becomes easily detectable from the top or from the outside).

An organization is a peculiar sort of system. Its members naturally have mental constructs of the theories-in-use of the organization to which they belong. Thus a member of the sugar-refining company can describe his picture of the company's theory-in-use for production and transport — indeed, for all four domains of theory-in-use.

Characteristically, however, individual members have partial constructs of the organization's theory-in-use; they *see* it from the perspective of their own positions in the organization. They grasp more fully the theories-in-use of the segments of the organization to which they are closest; one member's construct of the organization's theory-in-use is apt to be inconsistent with the construct of another member (or with his own construct at another time).

Organizations have espoused theories as well as theories-in-use. As with individuals, espoused theories and theories-in-use are often incongruent. For example, the organization may present itself in its public statements as committed to environmental quality, but its production and waste disposal operations may consistently violate environmental standards. Or management's formal statements to staff may subscribe to a theory of open discussion of all issues important to organizational performance, whereas the behavioral world of the organization is actually one in which the most crucial issues are taboo. Typically, again, individual members of the organization can offer their constructs of the organization's espoused theory *and* of its theory-in-use. (This department is supposed to test sugar quality every day, but it usually does it every week.)

A great deal of time and energy of members of the organization is expended in what is essentially a cognitive process — an effort to know the organization's espoused theory and theory-in-use, to reconcile or account for differences in the constructs of individual members, and to maintain or defend one's own construct.

The ability to say, "This is where we are; this is what we see," is an essential starting point for any shared inquiry. Scattered perceptions are the organizational analogy to individual subconsciousness;

380

integration of perceptions, drawn from different reference points throughout the organization, is the analogy to individual consciousness.

- *Generate and test interpretations of the perceived phenomena and make them ideas in good currency — that is, ideas that generate action within the organization.* This is a competence that depends upon the ability to *name* the phenomena so perceived and to bring them into the open for discussion, for confirmation or refutation — a thing particularly difficult to do when they run counter to espoused organizational theories of action. Such countervailing phenomena are often taboo within organizations and are all the more likely to be taboo as their recognition requires central changes in organizational theories of action. Hence their explicit recognition is usually associated with high risk to the persons who undertake the task of exposure.

- *Conjure up new structures and policies designed to remedy dysfunctions and bring these into good currency.* These images must be generated out of a context of uncertainty. They must be drawn from past experience and projected into future behavior at a time when the relevance of past experience and the predictability of future consequences are most in doubt. Hence they require a shared commitment to a point of view beyond what the evidence available strictly would justify.

- *Respond to conflicts in interpretation and prescription through inquiry rather than through bargaining.* Bargaining is not an adequate model because it rests on the assumption that the ingredients of an adequate solution are already present in the known components of the bargain. Often they are not, and bargaining tends, in general, to dilute the existing ingredients. An alternative process can emerge only if there is a commitment (on the part of the several parties involved) to the value of shared learning, which can take its place alongside the substantive values of the participants.

  Moreover, it must be possible to accumulate the perceptions of individuals. The behavioral world must function in such a way that the perceptions of those working on the problem can build on one another rather than being winnowed out in the interests of winning or establishing agreement.

- *Experiment with new structures and policies.* The concept of organizational experiment requires the capacity to generate shared commitment to enterprises that cannot be fully justified ahead of time and then to gain valid information about their results — that is, to bring together scattered perceptions in such a way as to avoid self-fulfillment, both with respect to "success" and "failure."

  It requires, in particular, the ability to draw from experiments that are perceived as failing a more precise and comprehensive representation of the organizational situation. This refusal to bury failures requires that the parties involved attribute their disappointment to shared misconceptions rather than to individual guilt. The behavioral world must permit such shared examination in a context of inquiry rather than in the context of allocating or avoiding praise or blame.

A behavioral world conducive to shared inquiry is by no means typical of present-day organizations. Yet it is a necessary correlate to the existential stance toward planning and policy making described above as the fourth stage and to the flexible organizational designs of which the constellation firm is an instance.

TOWARD ORGANIZATIONAL DEUTERO-LEARNING

Organizational deutero-learning requires that individuals within the organization develop the competence for continuing shared inquiry into the effectiveness of experience-based theories of organizational action and develop it in the face of unplanned ecological changes in the organization's inner and outer environments. This competence means, in the first instance, the development of a behavioral world conducive to effective inquiry on-line and under stress.

Such a behavioral world would be one in which individuals, in their own theories-in-use and therefore in their transactions with one another, create the conditions for the public testing of important assumptions about self and others, for double-loop learning about one's own theory-in-use, and for the discovery, invention, and production of new behavior consistent with this learning. Argyris and I have given the name "Model II" to the model of theories-in-use conducive to this kind of learning. We contrast it with the "Model I" behavioral world of normal organizational life in which control of the task, win-lose dynamics, a form of rationality exclusive of feelings, and protection of self and others combine to prevent shared double-loop learning.

Our experiences in teaching and consulting convince us that movement from such a normal behavioral world toward a Model II world is possible and practical. The process, however, is extraordinarily difficult and time-consuming and requires assistance from persons who have learned to behave more nearly in conformity with Model II and have inquired into the conditions under which others can learn to do so.

In working toward a Model II behavioral world, the learning of new behavioral competences will be at first awkward and demanding of time and energy. The willingness to work in this direction will depend on an awareness of the waste of time and energy already inherent in a behavioral world inimical to shared inquiry. It also will depend on an awareness that creation of a more nearly Model II behavioral world is an essential condition if we wish to achieve organizational deutero-learning in structure, planning, and policy making.

BIBLIOGRAPHY

Chris Argyris and Donald Schon in *Theory in Practice: Increasing Professional Effectiveness* (Jossey-Bass, 1974) present the notions of theory-in-use and espoused theory and of Model I and Model II theories of action and the transition from the first to the second — all of which provide the basis for this article.

In *Beyond the Stable State* (Random House, 1970; in paperback, the Norton Library, 1973), Schon advances the argument for the loss of the stable state and the resulting requirements for learning systems and organizations.

Gregory Bateson's *Steps Toward an Ecology of Mind* (Ballantine Books, 1972) contains the most acute discussion of levels of learning, in individuals and in societies, and of deutero-learning, in particular.

In *Learning from Experience: Toward Consciousness* (Columbia University Press, 1972), William R. Torbert expounds the theory and practice of experimental learning. His ideas on this subject complement and extend those of Argyris and Schon.

Last, Edgar S. Dunn's *Economic and Social Development: A Process of Social Learning* (Johns Hopkins University Press, 1971), develops a learning model of planning and development that draws on theories of biological evolution and individual learning as well as experiences in economic development.

ON THE IMPORTANCE OF FEEDBACK
AND THE RESISTANCES TO IT

Donald N. Michael

Information feedback is the *sine qua non* of cybernetic systems. It is through information feedback that a system evaluates where it is in terms of where it intends to go. It is the means by which error is detected and thereby it provides the basis for learning how to get from here to there through changes in performance that result in successive reductions in error. Of central importance for lrsp,* feedback also provides the information needed for learning what now constitutes "here" and for deciding whether to continue to try to get "there," in the future. That is, it provides the basis for evaluating whether the appreciation of "here" and "there" needs to be revised. In the nature of the situation with which we are dealing, the very process of learning through feedback provides the means for making changes in definitions of "here" and "there," along with the means for linking them through time via programatic actions, and for evaluating those actions (Bauer, 1967, and Webber, 1965).

WHAT CHARACTERIZES FEEDBACK APPROPRIATE FOR LRSP?

Ideally, the feedback process consists of:

1. Putting into the environment "output" signals, that is, symbols, or materials, or events (which are combinations of symbols and materials) intended to produce specific results.

2. Detecting in that environment signals, presumably related to the results, that can be used to assess the effectiveness of the output signals introduced into the environment for the purpose of producing the intended results.[1]

3. Detecting other signals that can provide a context for analyzing the meaning of the gap between intended and actual results.

4. Detecting other signals that can provide a context for revising goals and objectives and hence for revising programs intended to produce specific results.

---

[1]There is a generally unremarked-on subtlety in the feedback process that becomes critical in the societal situation because the matching process is so poor: "the output message must be in such a form that when it acts on the [environment] the [environment] will be able to generate a message which is usable by the feedback system for controlling the output source. [Components of systems] exist as systems because they can generate signals to which they can respond; when they cannot do this they cease to be [parts of] systems" (Michael, 1954, p. 4).

*long-range social planning

Reprinted by permission from Jossey-Bass Publishers, Inc., San Francisco, California.

5. Gathering those signals in forms that can be interpreted.

6. Bringing them into the initiating organization (or other organizations assigned the task of feedback analysis).

7. Evaluating the meaning of the feedback in the light of extant objectives and goals and of the programs intended to meet them.

8. Disseminating that evaluation in such ways that it is *in fact acted on* by the organization so as to change or otherwise influence the output signals intended to produce specific results in the environment.

In spite of the centrality of feedback for system adaptation, most human organizations generally use a very low order of feedback under most conditions — indeed, it is often so poor or misleading as to be worse than no feedback at all. There are many reasons why this is so in organizations that are responsible to complex environments. There are deep technological and conceptual inadequacies in existing schemes for evaluating organizational impact on the environment. There is always the question of whether turbulence, in Emery and Trist's sense, is so great as to block out evidences of relationship between organization output and environmental impact. There are ambiguities in goals and objectives that make it difficult if not impossible to specify what feedback to get. There are also contradictions and ambiguities inherent in the statutes and other directives that determine the mandate of government programs. (This situation is beginning to change, however, with the growing understanding that society is a system, not a collection of recipients for categorically funded programs.) There are time constraints and money limitations and all those other characteristics of the organization's operating context that permit no more than "bounded rationality," in Herbert Simon's phrase.

HOW THE CHARACTERISTICS OF FEEDBACK INFORMATION INTERACT WITH ORGANIZATIONAL STRUCTURES FOR INFORMATION PROCESSING

But other factors weave through and exacerbate these circumstances by sustaining the personal, interpersonal, and structural arrangements that make such familiar constraints more persistent and obstructive than they need to be. These are social psychological factors that revolve around the needs of the organization's members to be protected from turbulence, uncertainty, error, and sentient group instability. Doing what would need to be done to get and use better feedback for the purposes of moving toward lrsp will be resisted to the degree that it removes the social psychological advantages that organizations provide by avoiding feedback.

Even if the social psychological sources of resistance to much better feedback were removed, other sources of feedback enfeeblement would still be there and would still need to be overcome as well. However, the latter sources in some degree operate as they do because the social psychological rewards — or as H. David puts it, the benefits of calculated ignorance — discourage overcoming them. Doubtless the comforts of not knowing, because the feedback is either absent or unrevealing, have contributed to disinclinations to work hard at evaluation technology and to risk trying it in the real world. Similarly, the comforts of ignorance have made it easier to live with the disadvantages of gratuitous sub-unit autonomy and competition. So too with disinclinations to expose internal conflicts, either to resolve them or to make them work more effectively for overall organizational accomplishment vis-a-vis the environment. If attempts are made to change feedback processes in ways appropriate for lrsp, they will not succeed if the benefits of calculated ignorance as sources of resistance to change are not attended to at least as carefully as the other factors presently obstructing effective feedback.

The structural arrangements that exist between the organization and its environment, and the structural arrangements within the organization for dealing with feedback (when it does get through the organization's boundaries), contribute to the resistances to the use of feedback. "An organization is a system of structured relations. But an organization also acts, and such actions imply intellectual, rational, decision-making processes. Both organization structure and the nature of the intellectual phase of organizational life (decision making) limit the modern organization's ability to absorb feedback information, especially data regarding second-order social consequences. Learning how to perceive or detect these consequences is difficult; it is even more difficult to make these perceptions effective within the organization" (Rosenthal and Weiss, 1966, pp. 316-317).

As is true in all these matters, the interdependence of persons and structures makes precise distinctions misleading and awkward. Here the interactional amorphousness is especially pronounced in the interplay between two factors: (1) organizational doctrine and mission definition, which are, so to speak, held in the minds of men and which thereby determine what aspects of the environment men will pay attention to; and (2) the articulation of the organizational structure ("specialization, authority relations, and communication patterns"), which determines how those doctrines and definitions will be processed in transactions with the environment. Doctrine and mission tell the members what to pay attention to, but the organizational structure of expertise, of boundary-spanning, of other environmental scanners, of "receiving terminals" that seek and feed in information from the environment, all determine what in fact will be collected and introduced into the organization. The persons a bureaucrat on the interface between organization and environment chooses to listen to will depend on his definition of mission and his definition of what he can do with what he reads or hears. What he feels he can do is partially determined by how he perceives the way in which the authority system in his organization deals with information from his level and location, and by how he deals with it in view of his perceptions. I need not belabor this fairly obvious generalization.[2] But it will be useful presently to typify several important arrangements that organizations use to avoid feedback from the environment; this will help us appreciate the formidable task of dealing with resistance to feedback and hence with resistance to attempts to introduce feedback-dependent aspects of lrsp.

Within the organization, structural factors, interacting with personal and interpersonal factors, will significantly affect whether or not feedback information once obtained will be shared or encapsulated. Other factors, such as the structure of sub-unit differentiation and integration, will contribute to the capacity or incapacity, the willingness or reluctance, of members to process and distribute information so that it is useful within the time constraints that may ultimately determine its utility. I will not attempt here to show how various internal arrangements and responsibilities might affect the processing of feedback. Research on this would be important for a full understanding of the overall task involved in implementing efforts to change toward lrsp. Here I will conjecture about how organizational structures facilitate resistances to dealing with feedback — how they help people resist using the information itself and resist changing to structures that might facilitate that use.[3]

Ideally, feedback should help reduce uncertainty by clarifying the extent to which an intended result is presently on track and the ways in which it is not; and by clarifying and discriminating between options by feeding back into the present, so to speak, carefully worked out conjectures about the future. Sometimes this does happen, and when it does those espousing a planning perspective will gain support. But far more often feedback about the present and the future will produce irritation, exhaustion, and anxiety because it will increase uncertainty or render worthless that which was held to be certain. On the one hand, if feedback is richly reflective of the environment, it will impose more information on users than they can manage — information rich in cognitive, valuative, and emotional content. If users wish to reject some of it as "irrelevant," "awkward," or "outside their responsibility," then means for sorting it out will have to be invented, and this will call for new screening procedures and new arrangements of subgroups in the organization — and the creation and implementation of these will carry heavy opportunity costs in already overburdened organizations.[4]

[2]Downs (1966) delineates many interrelationships of this kind.

[3]Wilensky (1967) and Webb (1969) offer a number of suggestions about what to do structurally to reduce avoidance or distortion of feedback. But the problem of making the transition to those structures has not been dealt with in social psychological terms, nor is there an adequate empirical base of comparative studies demonstrating what works better than what, and why.

[4]For examples of how these overload burdens are dealt with, see Meier (1963). Also Downs (1966, Chapter 15) and Miller (1960)

In this regard, it seems to me that we will face a growing problem of distinguishing signals from noise. It is generally recommended that more groups in the environment feed back more information to organizations, both as means for informing and influencing organizations and for stimulating members of the environment to participate in planning.

The law of requisite variety suggests that a system of strategic control will only succeed to the extent to which it can develop a similar level of complexity to the system it sets out to influence; it can never, however, be expected to achieve this if it is forced to rely entirely on the scanning abilities of one individual or even a single small group of individuals who occupy a central position in relation to the agencies concerned. It is here, if anywhere, that potential may exist for drawing on the diversity of perspectives which may be provided by a larger body of representatives, particularly where these are directly elected on a ward or constituency basis, and therefore have a direct motivation to keep in touch with events and pressures within defined sectors of the total community system. If the strategic control group can find effective ways of drawing on the existing scanning functions of all elected representatives, it may thereby considerably enhance its own internal capacity to identify areas of relevant connection between agencies [Friend and Jessop, 1969, p. 132].

But as the number of advocates increases and more authorities and experts take more sides, and as we see increases in the amount and variety of feedback that is asserted to be relevant for decision-making, policy formulation, evaluation, and the rest, it will become increasingly difficult to know what to pay attention to. What might be interpreted as signals, if there were enough resources to sort and compare them and enough time to do it, will instead become mere noise. The overwhelming tendency, when faced with such overloads, is to withdraw (as a person or as an organization) into familiar perspectives and styles of performing. In that case, we would be pretty much where we are now, with selected feedback used to reinforce positions rather than to facilitate societal learning. In the second place, the information will seldom be definitive, and this grossly complicates the question of what to do with it and who is responsible for the doing. For a long time to come, such information will for the most part demonstrate to the professionals involved in lrsp — and, if they are open about it, to their organizational and inter-organizational constituencies — how limited is our understanding of what is going on "out there" and how small is our ability to do anything effective about it.

How to live constructively with noisy "non-definitive" information is one of the things to be learned through lrsp efforts. A major task will involve learning what constitutes a signal that can be meaningfully transmitted into the environment; that is, what constitutes a signal that the environment will be able to recode as a function of its responses to that signal, and then transmit across environment-organization boundaries in forms that allow the organization to evaluate its activities.

Many signals into the environment will turn out not to recode in these ways. Only as a result of the development of powerful theory that relates specific kinds of social change to the properties of signals will improvements in signal generation and evaluation occur; and theory development will depend on successive analyses and alterations in what at any time is hopefully referred to as "social indicator" data.

Social indicator designers are not the only ones faced with problems. Adjustments in signals into the environment and in the selection and processing of signals from the environment mean that the programs that produce these signals, and the structured relationships in the organization among programs and the functions that facilitate them, will be subject to change too. This means that personal, intellectual, and emotional commitment to a program may have to be altered or scrapped. So too, with the sentient-group supports that invariably are created by and among people associated with a given program. It means that feedback will expose the failures as well as the successes of programs and projects. This, in turn, confronts program proponents with the task of acknowledging error — indeed, of seeking it out, of embracing it — in the interests of learning how to create better programs. Feedback can raise questions about the sufficiency of original goal choices and planning for action regarding them. This will raise the harrowing question of who is accountable for information about the errors, and who can be trusted with such information. And it raises the difficult task of dealing with interpersonal and intrapersonal conflicts over goals, values, and feelings with regard to their choice and priority. In short, feedback will present all recipients with the likelihood of frequent and deep intellectual and emotional discomfort from information overload — provided they expose themselves to the feedback at all.

The personal and interpersonal burdens of adjusting preconceptions to more information, and the strains of coping with uncertainty and its repercussions in the organization is not our purpose; our concern here is with possible structural consequences. For example, those responsible for initiating administrative-managerial responses to the feedback face the task of reorganizing program activities in response to the feedback implications. This requires dealing with other's errors as well as one's own, with shifting mandates, status, and roles, and with removing people from programs to which they are committed and with which they have an intimate self-identification. The readjustments and rethinking will place heavy social psychological burdens on initiators and receivers. *Typical* bureaucracies are chronically and pervasively overloaded from their struggles with competing and conflicting internal empires and external demands. The idea of having to adjudicate between these *and* additional lrsp-oriented feedback, resulting from the multiple impacts of organizational output, will be too much for most people most of the time; they will tend to respond with avoidance behaviors, unless the circumstances force or reward them to do otherwise.

STRUCTURAL MEANS USED TO AVOID FEEDBACK

It should be no surprise, then, that people have structured organizations (and organizations have structured people) to avoid unfamiliar feedback. It is worth listing these avoidance processes, because their removal will be resisted and these resistances will interfere with changing toward lrsp. Roughly put, organizations arrange to receive a minimum of turbulence-generating feedback, and to use as little as possible of that to generate further turbulence.

In the first category are such devices as structuring the organization so that sub-units are rewarded for using indicators of organizational *input* to the environment as if they represented what was going on in the environment in response to them. Use of this device has been endemic among organizations that do not use profit and related measures as their feedback signal of environmental response. Historically, this approach reflected widespread naïvete about the relationship between "input" and "output" in cybernetic systems. It also reflected the absence of the technology needed for data processing and analysis. But naïvete was sustained by a reluctance to face the consequences of abandoning it. However, this means of avoiding feedback is beginning to be undermined by growing recognition of the need for cost-benefit type analyses as a basis for public welfare program selection. Cost-benefit studies set the stage for defining the feedback needed to check the anticipated relationship between the symbols, materials, or events put into the social system and the results produced by them. Once this stage is set, expectancies and demands grow to get that feedback. But so far very little feedback has been produced because of the technical weaknesses and organizational resistances to effective utilization of PPBS* and related techniques.

Meantime, the perennial argument continues to be made that *some* measure is better than no measure, and that input indicators are the best that can be done in the absence of validated theory that relates input to output. "No measure" has the virtue of signifying ignorance and therefore the need to invent and seek valid feedback. Thus recognition of ignorance is precisely what is avoided if "some" measure has become a reinforcer for the extant organizational structure and its concomitant rewards for its members. What is more, recent environment-initiated feedback in the forms of consumerism, muckraking, and protest, as well as the long-standing awareness of the potential utility of the Swedish invention of the ombudsman, demonstrate that the use of input rather than impact is a rationalization hiding the basic need to minimize personal and organizational turbulence that would be produced by impact-indicating feedback[5].

Feedback which is disrupting because it is unfamiliar is also avoided by structuring the feedback retrieval process so that it selects from the

*Planning, Programming, Budgeting Systems
[5]See Anderson (1968).

environment only those signals that are compatible with the structure and norms of the organization. " 'The tendency of bureaucratic language to create in private the same images presented to the public never should be underrated.' In domestic policy surely such bogies as 'the balanced budget' have worked similar mischief. Doctrines of economic individualism, activated by phrase-making, help explain why America, unique among the rich countries, tolerated an unemployment rate of 4 per cent or more from 1954 until 1966 and has moved so reluctantly toward a humane welfare state. Francis Bacon's warning that man converts his words into idols that darken his understanding is as pertinent today as it was three centuries ago" (Wilensky, 1967, p. 22).

In the past, the environment has been placid enough, or could be treated as placid enough, that learning about highly complex and changing social issues could be minimal or at least slow.[6] Survival of the organization was dependent upon comparatively predictable intra-organizational and inter-organizational bargaining relationships between fund sources, stable constituencies, and formal internal structures — in contrast to the presently changing environment. Hence structures and norms were designed to be responsive to anticipated congressional feedback (or feedback from whatever sources the organization depended on) rather than to new environmental feedback.[7] In corporations, the familiar signals to which they are structured to respond usually have to do with profit or other profit-relevant measures such as corporate growth, market share, or public image, and the signals are sought by sub-units specializing in these preoccupations. Corporations typically have not sought feedback on the extra-market consequences of the production, distribution, or consumption of their products, most notably the external costs to both non-consumers and consumers. As a result, the new consumerism and concern for the natural environment have created new sources of feedback that have been disrupting to corporations and for the most part resisted, advertising to the contrary notwithstanding. Corporate organizational structures have rewarded inattention to these matters, and therefore they are mostly populated by persons who see themselves as competent in part because they successfully fill roles that reward such inattention. Governmental agencies and governmental personnel have similarly restricted their feedback to that which is comfortable because it is compatible with "recognizing" special constituencies and with specifying the conditions for communicating

[6]Schick (1969) gives a most illuminating insight into the historical circumstances of a tranquil domestic environment that encouraged the promulgation of what he calls "process politics," otherwise recognizable as "disjointed incrementalism."

[7]The classic delineation of organizational structures and norms for getting and using feedback useful to the federal budgetary process is Wildavsky (1964). Also see Seidman (1970).

with the organizations through specific organizational sub-units or boundary spanners.[8]

An organizational need was not met by operating officials unless it or the fact that their tasks had become routine disturbed them sufficiently to interest them in making the required innovation. By the same token, external dysfunctions cannot be expected to disappear unless they are transformed into organizational needs, which means that their occurrence is so deleterious for administrators or for all officials that they are compelled to make adjustments. This raises the problem of developing democratic techniques that enable the public or its representatives to hold officials specifically accountable for the various consequences of bureaucratic operations, thus converting external dysfunctions into internal needs of the organization that disturb its personnel. The difficulty of finding solutions to this problem is matched only by the urgency of doing so [Blau, 1963, pp. 263-264].[9]

Put in another relevant perspective, only some environmental sources of support or criticism are deemed legitimate. And "legitimate" generally means those values, behaviors, and environmental auspices that are compatible with the program and information-processing structure, and are thus understandable and approved by the servicing agency. Usually, therefore, much of what an agency ought to be receiving as feedback, if it is to adapt to meet environmental needs, is screened out as unreliable, misguided, irrelevant, not within the agency's mandate, or politically infeasible.[10] At the same time, some feedback is overly responded to because it fits personal and organization biases.

This is not to say that symbols in support of established policy and comfortable prejudice inevitably serve as a substitute for policy deliberations. It is to say that facts, arguments, and propaganda directed at friends and enemies alike, in and out of an organization, can be self-convincing. Executives and politicians often become persuaded that the world of crisis journalism they create and respond to is the real world; many a decision maker is in this way diverted from things which really

[8]"When a business or a government agency is under the administration of scientific management, its clients may feel that they are not getting the service they are entitled to. But service to the client — at least as the client perceives it — is not what keeps scientific management in business. Under modern Taylorism, management's performance is judged not by the clients' perceived welfare, but by their *demonstrable* welfare. And since the managers themselves design the criteria that demonstrate welfare, demonstrable welfare can be counted on to increase" (Thompson, 1968, p. 54).

[9]For related behavior by congressmen, see Bauer, Pool, and Dexter (1963). Also Downs (1966) is illuminating on this.

[10]One way organizations adapt to the unreliability of information is by devising procedures for making decisions that can ignore possibly relevant information: they develop "special coding categories" (Cyert and March, 1963, p. 110). Related observations, though not interpreted in terms of legitimacy, are made under the rubric "coding scheme barrier" to communication in Frohman and Havelock (1971, Chapter 6, p. 7). They also cite several studies demonstrating this phenomenon.

happen or which are not happening but should be. Many a leader becomes captive of the rhetoric he customarily presents or of the media image he projects. Students of modern society have given too little attention to this reverse action of propaganda — the effect on the people who themselves make the news. If supplying the symbols that guide executive action is "window dressing," it is the kind of display that tells what is in the store [Wilensky, 1967, pp. 23-24].[11]

Since legitimacy criteria also function to structure and to justify the structure of organizational activities, they are a powerful means for reducing uncertainty, in Friend and Jessop's terms, about what knowledge will be needed for decision-making, the anticipated state of inter-organizational relations, and about the appropriate values from which to choose actions. This lowered uncertainty encourages a routine perspective which in turn can be transformed into structural arrangements that reinforce the prevailing definitions and screen feedback so as to leave these definitions as little disturbed as possible. But resistances to feedback utilization, rationalized in terms of exclusive obligations to legitimate clientele, will be increasingly vulnerable as uncertainty about organizational legitimacy increases among members of the organization and as parts of the environment continue to challenge organizational legitimacy. Whether this vulnerability can be used to facilitate changing toward lrsp by intruding more effective feedback will depend on the simultaneous availability of other circumstances.

Another way a prevailing definition of legitimacy is used as a feedback-reducing device is to structure the organization so that it only attends to feedback from those parts of the environment that do produce feedback compatible with the organization's output signals of symbols, things, and events. Those in the environment that do not respond to these signals do not increase organizational turbulence. By the criteria of legitimacy subscribed to, they have excluded themselves from organizational responsibility by not responding to the signals offered to them. In this situation the members of the organization convince themselves and others that "they've tried" but that the environment is indifferent, or antagonistic, or unappreciative of their efforts. The fault, then, is in the environment, not in the organization's input to that environment. The fact that the environment doesn't make a corresponding "effort" to respond removes further obligations toward it on the organization's part. Such an approach permits legitimacy distinctions between the "worthy" and the "unworthy" poor, between "self-helping" and "lazy" ethnics, and between "appreciative" and "unappreciative" recipients, and it results in the familiar process of "creaming off" the

---

[11]The most illuminating and devastating analysis and description of this situation is found in Boorstin (1964). Also see Downs (1966).

environment.[12] More generally, it allows the organization to ignore or be ignorant of feedback it ought to be using as inputs to its conjectures about the future, which in turn should be affecting its goal and program choices.

In the extreme, organizations try to avoid undesired feedback by threatening to deny services or by taking punitive action. Examples of such actions are midnight check-ups by social welfare agencies; General Motors' effort to "get something on Ralph Nader"; firing an internal source of threatening feedback, be he a corporate engineer, a Defense Department critic, or a Food and Drug Administration biochemist; cutting off resources, such as funds or legitimating auspices, supplied by research-supporting agencies; or retracting a tax-free status, as the Internal Revenue Service did to the Sierra Club; or sweeping up antiwar protesters without recourse to due process.

Serious and systematic attention to feedback from the future, via future studies, is avoided by using these same devices. Future studies can be written off as illegitimate because they do not meet conventional standards of verifiability (though often they are overly legitimized by their champions, simply because they do meet other conventional professional standards of "in" jargon and logical operationalism). They remain unnoticed or unused because the organization is not structured to take in feedback from this quarter: there is no place established for it. They are ignored because organizational structure rewards management and personnel for the production of inputs that respond to existing opportunities. These, it is presumed, will take care of the future. This presumption often expresses the same kind of avoidance behavior as that which did not look closely at the assumptions that accepted other input measures as if they would correctly project impact in the environment.

Yet vicarious exposure to the future is a necessary part of the organization's feedback if it is to try to change toward lrsp. Otherwise there is no way to evaluate the feedback from the present in terms of anticipated impacts. Two devices serve to resist appropriate future-oriented feedback with its freight of uncertainty and problems. One means is to attend only to future-oriented feedback that is compatible with present activities and expectations. The other is to avoid gathering from the extant environment information that presages future developments which would be upsetting for the organization; that is, to avoid carrying out steps three and four in the feedback sequence (described at the beginning of this article). By concentrating on what is expected and familiar, the organization can overlook precursor signals that might indicate discomforting or even irresponsible incompatibilities between present actions and future outcomes. Also avoided in this way is the requirement to seek and to use continuously other more contextual

---

[12]See Caplan and Nelson (1973). For an incisive summary of the history of American social-work attitudes toward the poor, concerning what it is "proper" to do to improve the lot of the "worthy," see Lubove (1966).

conjectures about the future, which, if combined with precursor information from the present environment, probably would be even more upsetting. If we think of future studies as a form of feedback that is resisted as such, it is easier to understand why such studies are frequently commissioned but seldom used if they are incompatible with present operations and perspectives.

Sometimes feedback that has the potential for increasing uncertainty does get into an organization. Usually, it is forced on it from outside or is introduced by its own boundary spanners or boundary spanners to it (such as consultants). Occasionally it is inadvertently produced, as when new senior personnel bring in a different appreciation of environmental reality. Sometimes it is produced by deliberate efforts undertaken within the organization, such as internally generated program-evaluation studies, or a decision to invite the environment to become part of the organization (for example, adding members of the environment to the organization's advisory boards). Commissioned studies of the future are one kind of effort that may be undertaken deliberately to shake up the organization, or that may inadvertently do so.

Whatever the means by which the turbulence-generating feedback is produced and however it gets into the organization, organizations are structured to attenuate, diffuse, obscure, and otherwise reduce the impact of the feedback, usually to the point of impotence. "The structure of interpersonal relationships that permits the organization to coordinate the actions of its members often blocks, or at least severely limits, communication of information between the feedback system and the rest of the organization" (Rosenthal and Weiss, 1966, p. 317). The means for doing so have been well described and documented.[13] Essentially they consist of three processes:

1. Progressively screening out turbulence-generating information feedback as it moves up through the system.

2. Distributing the task of discovering and coping with the implications of the feedback between contending and competing subgroups who lack intention, mandate, substantive skills, or interpersonal skills to cope with the threats to values, goals, and images of competence, or to cope with the requirements for error acknowledgment and creative reprograming and restructuring.

3. Transforming the feedback into concepts and categories that allow the decision-maker to treat it as if it were familiar and called only for application of familiar approaches and commitments. This reduces anxiety about self-competence and that of others. It also reduces anxiety about purpose. In all, information overload demands are thereby kept from becoming intolerable.

[13]See Wildavsky, Wilensky, Webb, Downs, and Rosenthal and Weiss, as cited in the References.

Over time an organization fabricates an idealized self-image, which becomes a sort of mythological basis for the organizational ideology that explains "what the hell we are doing." The elements of fantasy in the view of the organization involve, usually, some distortions of reality and, therefore, prejudice the evaluation of incoming information. For example, an organization easily develops the fantasy element of essential rectitude, which then leads its members to discount any information that would suggest otherwise. In some degree organizational myths are essential for continuity of purpose. If the myth of 'what the hell we are doing' is overly responsive to signals from the environment, it cannot serve as an organizational balance wheel. Yet at some point there is an optimum balance between the benefits of continuity of purpose and the costs of biased information.

. . . It seems probable that no organization actively seeks feedback information that contradicts such necessary organizational beliefs unless, of course, it is provoked to do so by some kind of crisis [Rosenthal and Weiss, 1966, pp. 321-322].

POSSIBLE WAYS OF REDUCING RESISTANCE TO FEEDBACK

There are, then, many rewards deriving from the structural arrangements that protect the organization's members from the disruption encouraged by feedback, with its concomitant threats of overwhelming uncertainty, exposure of error, questions of legitimacy and purpose, and so on. Two change-over questions are posed by this situation: How can the organization overcome the resistances that protect it and its membership; and how can this be done so that the organization doesn't overrespond or underrespond to feedback from the present and the future? Indeed, this second question contains another: What would characterize an effective balance in a changing and problematic world between, overresponse and underresponse to feedback?

Whatever else is involved in dealing with these questions, certainly two capabilities are critical. First is the capability of the organization to reduce fears and anxieties about competence, purpose, status, and so on, that are elicited by the threat that if there is more feedback there will be more information available to more people about the environmental consequences of one's activities. Reducing such fears would depend on discovering how to replace the present structure and norms with ones that would sustain and reward a learning context. Then the very information that is feared, for what it might reveal about organizational and individual incompetence, would be actively sought out for the opportunity it would provide to improve. Such a shift might reduce the tendency of organizations to overrespond or underrespond to un- expected feedback. Certainly some portion of either response is simply an effort to "cover up," sometimes expressed as panic, other times as withdrawal. This shift to a learning norm of course leaves unresolved other knotty issues about allocations of effort and resources for decision-making. Hopefully, once the social psychological rewards of resisting extensive use of feedback were lowered, restraints on imaginative approaches to weakening other constraints would be reduced as well.

The second needed capability has to do with the capacity of the environment to force greater openness and responsiveness to feedback. (In what follows I am referring to the non-governmental, non-corporation components of the environment, that is, voluntary organizations and ad hoc groups.) Everything we have examined makes it clear that a very large part of the incentives to change, the counterforce to the internal resistances, will have to come from the environment and from those organizational members who, in role identification or function, link themselves to that environment. To be such a counterforce, members of the environment will have to learn what feedback it is useful to supply. This will not always be the same as what they want to supply. That is, members of the environment, organized into information-generating entities, will have to become sophisticated about what constitutes useful and valid information about their conditions and their needs and wants for change, and about how to obtain and provide such information in forms that organizations can effectively recode.[14] And they will have to become sophisticated about the structure and processes of the organizations into which they force-feed information. Elsewhere (Michael, 1971) I have described the role of voluntary organizations as "reality redefiners" and as resources for generating future-responsive policy and program-influencing information to be used as forced feedback for changing those corporate and government organizations whose actions affect various aspects of the general welfare.[15] But in order to meet the requirements for doing so, voluntary organizations will have to overcome the same internal resistances to becoming lrsp organizations as will the government agencies on which we have been focusing.

If voluntary organizations can make such changes, and a few of them are working very hard to try to do so (at least in their national offices), then they may be able to force enough newly salient information into old structures to give leverage to those proponents of lrsp within government organizations who will also be trying to make them more feedback-responsive. There are universities and even high schools that have learned, in the last few years, to respond to a larger range of feedback than they used to. In some situations they are even learning a little about

---

[14]Organizations seeking useful feedback would find it in the interest of frsl to help the environment develop its sophistication and skills regarding these requirements. Before Congress and city political establishments emasculated them, OEO's programs, which funded neighborhood development activities, were in part intended to help poor people develop such skills.

[15]The Center for a Voluntary Society in Washington, D.C., exists to facilitate these developments. Common Cause can be seen as another experiment in this spirit.

how to learn to continue to respond to changes in feedback — though it has taken traumatizing crises to move them that far (Chesler and Guskin, 1970). These schools are not doing Irsp — though a few universities are beginning to begin to try to — which emphasizes that, like the other requirements for Irsp, feedback responsiveness is a necessary but not a sufficient condition. But when its ramifications are recognized, it seems to be nearer than any other requirement to being a sufficient condition as well.

REFERENCES

Anderson, S. (Ed.) *Ombudsmen for American Government?* Englewood Cliffs, N. J.: Prentice-Hall, 1968.

Bauer, R., Pool, I. De Sola, and Dexter, L. *American Business and Public Policy.* New York: Atherton, 1963.

Bauer, R. "Societal Feedback." *The Annals of the American Academy of Political and Social Science,* September 1967, *373.*

Blau, P. *The Dynamics of Bureaucracy: A Study of Interpersonal Relations in Two Government Agencies.* Chicago: University of Chicago Press, 1963.

Boorstin, D. *The Image: A Guide to Pseudo-Events in America.* New York: Harper and Row, 1964.

Caplan, N., and Nelson, S. "On Being Useful: The Nature and Uses of Psychological Research on Social Problems." *American Psychologist,* 1973, *28*(3).

Chesler, M., and Guskin, A. "Intervention in High School Crises: Consultant Roles." Ann Arbor: Educational Change Team, School of Education, University of Michigan, 1970.

Cyert, R., and March, J. *A Behavioral Theory of the Firm.* Englewood Cliffs, N.J.: Prentice-Hall, 1963.

Downs, A. *Inside Bureaucracy.* Boston: Little, Brown, 1966.

Friend, J., and Jessop, W. *Local Government and Strategic Choice.* London: Tavistock Publications; Sage Publications, 1969.

Frohman, M., and Havelock, R. "The Organizational Context of Dissemination and Utilization." In R. Havelock and others, *Planning for Innovation.* Ann Arbor: Institute for Social Research, Center on Utilization of Scientific Knowledge, 1971.

Lubove, R. "Social Work and the Life of the Poor." *The Nation.* May 1966, *202.*

Meier, R. "Information Input Overload." *Libri,* 1963, *13.*

Michael, D. "Cybernetics and Human Behavior." Bethesda, Md.: Army Medical Service Graduate School, Walter Reed Army Medical Center, 1954.

Michael, D. "Influencing Public Policy: The Changing Roles of Voluntary Associations." *Journal of Current Social Issues,* 1971, *9*(6).

Miller, J. "Information Input, Overload, and Psychopathology." *American Journal of Psychiatry,* 1960, *116.*

Rosenthal, R., and Weiss, R. "Problems of Organizational Feedback Processes." In R. Bauer (Ed.), *Social Indicators.* Cambridge: M.I.T. Press, 1966.

Schick, A. "Systems Politics and Systems Budgeting." *Public Administration Review,* 1969, *24*(1).

Seidman, H. *Politics, Position, and Power: The Dynamics of Federal Organization.* New York: Oxford University Press, 1970.

Thompson, V. "How Scientific Management Thwarts Innovation." *Transaction,* 1968, *5*(7).

Webb, E. *Individual and Organizational Forces Influencing the Interpretation of Indicators.* Research Paper P-488. Arlington, Va.: Institute for Defense Analyses, Science and Technology Division, 1969.

Webber, M. "The Roles of Intelligence Systems in Urban-Systems Planning." *Journal of the American Institute of Planners,* 1965, *31*(4).

Wildavsky, A. *The Politics of the Budgetary Process.* Boston: Little, Brown, 1964.

Wilensky, H. *Organizational Intelligence: Knowledge and Policy in Government and Industry.* New York: Basic Books, 1967.

SECTION SEVEN

REWARDS

Overview

"No questions will dominate the workplace in the 1980s more than how to revamp incentives to match the new motivation of workers."

— Daniel Yankelovich

Implicit in Daniel Yankelovich's claim is the recognition of the extent to which the question "What's in it for us?" has changed in character over the past twenty years. The "new" workforce coupled with the changing requirements of business have run havoc over the assumptions and practices that have guided the manager's concept of rewards and how they effectively can be managed to improve both the organization's performance and the welfare of its employees.

Management theory has not kept pace with reality, and the issue today is "How do we begin to think about rewards in a fresh way so that they again can become a relevant motivational tool for the manager?" As Yankelovich observes, this will likely be a problem for the decade. The four articles in this section do not provide a complete answer, but together they begin to point us in the right direction.

In "Why the Work Ethic Isn't Working," Daniel Yankelovich and John Immerwahr are interested in what they call the "discretionary effort" of workers — that portion of the work effort controlled by the people themselves rather than by the employer or the inherent nature of the job. The amount of discretion in the workplace has greatly increased due to changes in technology, the economy, and the educational level of workers. Workers today increasingly choose the degree of effort they will give in their work. Most of the readers of this volume are managing people with very high-discretion jobs.

Yankelovich and Immerwahr report, for example, that particularly among high-discretion job holders:

- Fewer than one out of four workers claim they are performing to their full capacity.

- Nearly half of the workforce say that they do not put a great deal of effort into their jobs over and above what is required.

On the other hand, the authors also found that the work ethic is still strong as a basic belief. At first glance, the decline of worker effort and the sustained strength of the work ethic seem like incompatible findings. Much of the article is an effort to reconcile these results. Yankelovich and Immerwahr conclude that "The trend toward greater discretion on the job

403

is outrunning present management practices." Managers today do not have the tools or sensitivities required to support the work ethic.

In fact, the American workplace is structured in such a way as to effectively undermine the work ethic. The authors claim that there are four basic problems in this regard:

1. *Companies have undercut the linkage between rewards offered people and their performance.* About half the workforce believe that there is no connection between how good a job they do and how much they are paid.

2. *Managers lack the ability or willingness to motivate workers.* Almost three out of four workers believe that the inability of managers to motivate workers is a reason people are working less than they could.

3. *There is a mismatch between people's values and most companies' reward systems.* Approximately half of the workforce report such a mismatch.

4. *Managers continue to confuse job satisfaction and productivity.* Improving job satisfaction as a route to increase productivity has just not been borne out by research.

Until these structural disincentives and managerial shortcomings are corrected, companies will continue to underutilize one of their greatest assets — the overwhelming commitment of the American people to the work ethic.

Steven Kerr, in "On the Folly of Rewarding A, While Hoping For B," explores one of the most pernicious tendencies in all organizations — to profess a desire to accomplish certain objectives while structuring and sustaining a reward system that pays off behavior that is directed somewhere else. This article will hit close to home with managers frustrated by a work unit that seems intent on going in directions other than the ones the manager wants.

Kerr uses a number of examples to make his points — from failures in the Vietnam war, to the propensity of medical doctors to overdiagnose sickness, to performance problems experienced by a manufacturing plant and an insurance firm. Kerr's insights are obvious, but only after he has revealed them. His proposals are straightforward and extremely useful in diagnosing seemingly intractable performance problems.

"One More Time: How Do You Motivate Employees?" by Frederick Herzberg was first published in 1968. This delightful classic article is just as relevant today, if not more so, than it was sixteen years ago.

In this article, Herzberg humorously reviews managers' efforts to motivate workers through negative and positive reinforcement. He argues that not only are these approaches marginally successful, but in fact, they can never produce true motivation. The manager is the one who is motivated; he is merely trying to stimulate his workers to move. This tactic is analogous to having to recharge someone's battery. Only when employees have their own generator and become their own source of energy, can one say they are motivated.

With this in mind, Herzberg proceeds to trace the history of management efforts to build motivational generators in people — attempts to improve pay, benefits, and work schedules; human-relations and communications training; job-participation programs and employee counseling. These efforts have all met with varied success and generally promote only short-term results.

According to Herzberg, the problem underlying all of these attempts is management's failure to understand the difference between factors that serve to reduce the level of worker dissatisfaction and those that serve to promote intrinsic motivation. The former, hygiene factors, are most often the ones managers have attempted to influence. The latter, motivators, such as (a) degree of control and responsibility, (b) opportunity for achievement and recognition, and (c) personal growth and learning, are factors that are imbedded in the content of the work itself.

Consequently, Herzberg proposes the strategy of *job enrichment* —the restructuring of jobs so that they are loaded with intrinsic motivators. As he carefully acknowledges, the process of job enrichment is not a one-time proposition, but rather an ongoing approach to managing rewards productively.

Edward Lawler completes this section with "For A More Effective Organization — Match the Job to the Man." Lawler extends Herzberg's perspective by observing that virtually all approaches to improving employee motivation, including job-enrichment programs, have suffered from a common flaw. They have all assumed the "myth of the average man" and succumbed to the fallacy of standardized approaches to jobs and job holders. Lawler argues that, while job-enrichment programs, such as proposed by Herzberg, do demonstrate that the average person is both happier and more productive, the statistics camouflage the fact that few people are actually average. A significant number of people are less happy and less motivated as a result of these programs.

Lawler recognizes the practical difficulty that attempts to treat people as individuals pose large companies. But he argues that the attempt must be made and that significant strides are beginning to be made in a number of reward-related areas. For example, Lawler refers to programs for workers in a number of companies that: provide workers with choices regarding the design of their jobs, offer "cafeteria" benefits and personalized compensation programs, allow diverse evaluation methods and flexible working hours, and encourage situational perspectives toward management styles.

Herzberg, Lawler, and others have begun to point toward a new direction in the theory of managing rewards — one that places less emphasis on the reinforcement qualities of extrinsic rewards and more on the inherent motivational qualities that the content of the work itself can provide if properly designed. The emerging perspective is one that recognizes the highly personal nature of inherent motivation and the requirement of managers to provide their people with diversity and choice. The external and internal environments of business are, apparently, beginning to mirror each other in important ways. In the language of Alvin Toffler, the demassification of a business's relationship with its customers is coming to be mirrored in the demassification of its relationship with its employees.

WHY THE WORK ETHIC ISN'T WORKING

Daniel Yankelovich
John Immerwahr

A CHANGE IN WORK BEHAVIOR

A great deal of evidence indicates that Americans are not now working at their full capacity and that their work effort has declined in the last several decades.

The Public Agenda research found that most people say that they are giving considerably less to their jobs than they believe they could give and, in principle, are willing to give. A majority feel that under the right conditions they could significantly increase their performance:

- Fewer than one out of four (23%) say that they are performing to their full capacity and are being as effective as they are capable of being. The majority say that they could increase their effectiveness significantly.

- Nearly half of the work force (44%) say that they do not put a great deal of effort into their jobs over and above what is required.

Objective studies of the workplace confirm these findings. Observers who study work behavior have reported that considerable work time is spent on nonproductive activities. D. J. Cherrington, for example, clocked actual work behavior over a two-year period. Cherrington found that only half of the workers' time (51%) was related to the job — the other half (49%) went for coffee breaks, late starts and early quits, personal activities, waiting, and otherwise idle time.[1]

Even more striking than the amount of nonproductive time are the signs that effectiveness has been decreasing. The Public Agenda found that the vast majority of jobholders (62%) believe that other people are not working as hard as they used to. The fact that respondents in surveys say that work effectiveness has decreased does not in itself prove that work behavior has actually changed. But it is difficult to discount such widespread impressions, particularly when they are shared by leaders as well. The Harris/Etzioni study found that business leaders (62%) and even labor union leaders (62%) also believe that people are not working as hard as they did ten years ago.[2]

One direct sign of a decline in work behavior comes from a study conducted in 1965 and 1975 by the University of Michigan's Institute for Social Research. Researchers measured work behavior by asking a sample of workers to keep a detailed diary of their activities on the job.

[1]D. J. Cherrington, *The Work Ethic*, Amacom, 1980, p. 110.

[2]Louis Harris Associates/Amitai Etzioni, *Perspectives on Productivity: a Global View*, Sentry Insurance, 1981, p. 10.

Reprinted by permission of the Public Agenda Foundation.

These diaries were used to compare the nominal number of hours on the job with the amount of time people actually spent working. Not surprisingly, the number of actual hours worked fell considerably below the nominal work time. But the study also showed that between 1965 and 1975 the gap between the actual time worked and the "official" work hours increased by more than 10%. The researchers noted a parallel drop in the rate of productivity increase. Productivity growth rates rose by 3% from 1955 to 1965, but then slowed to an annual average growth rate of 1.9% between 1965 and 1975. The researchers suggest that if their findings were extrapolated to all American workers, this decline in itself, quite apart from such factors as insufficient investments or aging equipment, could account for almost all of the slowed tempo of productivity growth in the decade from 1965 to 1975.[3]

Taken together, these findings suggest that there is a basis of truth in the popular impression that people are not working as hard as they used to and that this decline has contributed to the slowdown in competitive vitality that the U.S. has experienced in the past decades.

THE MANAGERIAL OBSTACLE

So far we have presented two sets of seemingly incompatible facts. On the one hand, working Americans endorse the ideal of giving one's best to the job. At the same time, their actual performance on the job reveals a slackening effort. If Americans have an inner need to give their best to their jobs, and if, increasingly, they have a great deal of control over their level of effort on the job, what is preventing them from giving more?

The answer, in its simplest terms, is that managerial skill and training have not kept pace with the changes that have affected the workplace. The trend towards greater discretion on the job is outrunning present management practices. It is true that the increase in discretion in the workplace reinforces the work ethic, but it also places greater demands on management. Without the built-in external control implicit in managing low-discretion jobs, people have much more opportunity to fritter away their time, or otherwise do less than the best possible job. To use an example from education: going from strictly supervised examinations to an honor system may encourage honesty in the students, but at the same time, it can also increase the level of cheating. The developing sense of integrity will not necessarily keep pace with the increased opportunity for dishonesty. Perhaps jobholders implicitly recognize this problem when they state a preference for demanding managers rather than easy ones.

[3]Frank Stafford and Greg J. Duncan, "The Use of Time and Technology by Households in the United States," Institute for Social Research, Working Paper, June 1979. The same conclusion has been reached by a different set of calculations by Samuel Bowles, David M. Gordon, and Thomas E. Weiskopf in Beyond the Wasteland, Anchor Press, 1983, Chapter 6. They argue that problems in America's productivity have been directly correlated with declining "work intensity."

To put this point another way, given the increase in discretion and the devaluation of existing motivators, it is surprising that U.S. economic competitiveness has not deteriorated even more than it has. If our interpretation is correct, the growing vitality of the work ethic may have saved the nation from an even more serious economic slowdown.

To explain how incentive and managerial systems are failing to take advantage of the work ethic, we need to make a crucial distinction between cultural norms and the social practices that either reinforce or weaken them. Consider, as one example of this interrelationship, the practice of saving money. It is frequently pointed out that the Japanese save a much larger portion of their income than Americans do; this, in turn, contributes to greater investment in Japan. Some observers explain low American savings rates by a deterioration in the norms of thrift in favor of an ethic of consumption. But the fault is not necessarily with the norms alone. In countless ways, American institutions reward consumption and punish savings, while Japanese institutions do the reverse. Interest earned on savings is taxable in the U.S. but not in Japan. U.S. tax law makes interest payments on consumer credit tax deductible; Japan does not. It is generally much more difficult to get consumer credit in Japan — interest rates tend to be higher and larger down payments are required. Thus, in many ways, our institutions undermine the norm of saving rather than strengthening it.

A number of findings suggest that the American workplace is currently structured in ways that undermine the strong work ethic values that people bring to their jobs. Four specific problem areas emerged in our research:

1. **Disincentives.** One of the most startling findings of the national survey of working Americans is the degree to which the American workplace has undercut the link between a jobholder's pay and his or her performance. This situation represents a sharp departure from the traditional American value of individualism. A central theme of our cultural heritage supports the idea that individuals will fail or succeed through their own effort and hard work. When people receive equal rewards regardless of effort or achievement, the implicit message from management is: "We don't care about extra effort, so why should you?"

There is evidence, however, that many managers are gradually undercutting the link between pay and performance. Norma Carlson, a researcher for the Bureau of Labor Statistics, has observed that there has been a steady increase in the percentage of production workers who are paid strictly by time. (The study covered the period from 1960 to 1970.) This "decline in the incidence of incentive systems," she points out, "has coincided with lagging productivity rates in manufacturing."[4]

The Public Agenda found that most jobholders now say that there is little or no connection between how good a job they do and how much

[4]"Time rates tighten their grip on manufacturing industries" in *Monthly Labor Review*, Volume 105, Number 5, 1982, pp. 16-17.

they are paid. Almost half of the work force (45%) believe that there is no relationship, and another 28% say that there is some relationship. But only 22% see a close link. In addition, most Americans do not think that they themselves will be the primary beneficiaries if they work harder and more effectively. Only 13% of the work force believes that they would benefit more from their own hard and effective work. Most people believe that the benefits will go primarily to their employers (48%) or at best will be shared equally by themselves and their employers (29%).

Jobholders also see little connection between their pay and the overall productivity of their companies. In the Gallup/Chamber of Commerce study, only 9% of the jobholders thought that they would be the primary beneficiaries of improvements in productivity. Most assumed that the beneficiaries would be others — consumers, stockholders, management, or society in general — and very few saw any propensity in their employers to reward workers for gains in productivity.[5] By contrast, a 1982 study of Japanese workers, conducted by the Asian Social Problems Institute, found that 93% of Japanese workers believe that they will benefit from improvements in their employers' profitability. Our survey provides evidence that many people in the work force are deeply concerned about the lack of connection between their effort and their pay. More than six out of ten working Americans (61%) identified "pay tied to performance" as a feature they wanted more of on their present job.

The study also allowed us to measure the "fit" between what most people want from their jobs and the qualities that are offered by existing jobs. In some aspects of work, there is a reasonably good fit. Most people say that they want interesting work, for example, and only a small number (12%) say that their jobs are not at all interesting. The area with the greatest lack of fit, however, concerns the relationship between pay and performance. Close to two-thirds of the work force (61%) say that they want a closer connection between pay and performance; only 22% say that a connection between pay and performance exists in their present jobs. Some of the other areas where there is a relatively bad fit are also closely related to traditional American values of individualism and reward for effort.

Lack of good fit:

	Describes Present Job %	Want More of on Job %
Pay tied to performance	22	61
Good pay	39	77
Not too much strain and stress	20	56
Chance for advancement	29	65

[5]Clarke and Morris.

The survey also shows that a close relationship exists between the failure of the workplace to reward effort and the tendency of people to hold back on the effort that they put into their jobs. When we asked people to explain why work effort has declined, close to three-quarters of the work force (73%) concur that work effort has declined because "quite often everyone gets the same raise no matter how hard they work." Fifty-eight percent of those who say that they want a closer link between pay and performance on their own job also say that it would make them work harder.

The concern about a lack of connection between performance and reward is not restricted purely to monetary rewards. More than seven out of ten working Americans (70%) say that they want more recognition for good work on their present job. (Only more pay received as high a rating.) And 58% of these said that they would work harder on their present jobs if they did receive more recognition for their effort.

These findings suggest that most Americans want to work hard and do a good job, but people also see that the workplace does not reward people who put in extra effort. Under these conditions, people who live up to their work ethic norms begin to feel like fools. Thus, the reward system undermines the work ethic.

The work ethic norm, by itself, cannot guarantee high effort without support from the environment and from the reward system. For the most part, this support is missing.

2. **Managers who don't motivate.** A second problem is the failure of managers to motivate people to perform effectively. It is easy to dismiss such complaints as routine grumbling about the boss. But Public Agenda's research shows that jobholders' perceptions of their managers is considerably more sophisticated.

In fact, most jobholders hold a generally positive attitude toward their managers. They like them personally and respect their dedication. Nearly seven out of ten jobholders (69%) say that their own managers care more about getting the job done than they do about bossing people around. Managers also get high marks (73%) for making sure everyone knows what they are supposed to do. Only a quarter of the work force (25%) believe that their managers are overpaid.

Jobholders also have very positive feelings about the treatment that they receive from their managers. Fewer than one out of five complain of unfair criticism (15%) or of being criticized in front of others (16%). The overwhelming majority of jobholders say that their managers are considerate of requests to take time off for urgent reasons (90%) and are careful not to change job responsibilities without consulting the employee (80%). A majority of the work force (61%) say that morale in their place of work is either good (44%) or even excellent (17%).

These favorable attitudes towards management are particularly impressive when we compare them to some of the other countries surveyed in the Public Agenda International Project. The chart below

411

compares German employee attitudes to their managers with their American counterparts, and illustrates that American workers appear to receive much better treatment than German workers.

Incidence of bad experiences with managers:

	U.S. %	Germany %
Transferred against my wishes	13	70
Criticized in front of others	16	53
Unreasonable workload	19	44
Refused time off for urgent reason	8	24

When it comes to the question of whether managers know how to motivate people to perform effectively, jobholders' attitudes shift dramatically. Forty percent say that their own managers do not know how to motivate them to get the best results; 75% say that managers in general do not know how to motivate workers.

American workers also blame managers for the deterioration in work behavior. Three-quarters of the work force (75%) believe that the inability of managers to motivate the work force is a reason why people are working less than they could. Many of the other reasons that people give for declining work effort also reflect poorly on motivation systems.

Reasons that people aren't working as hard as they could:

	Agree %
Management doesn't know how to motivate workers	75
Everyone gets the same raise regardless of how hard they work	73
People don't respect authority in the workplace anymore	70
Today people want more of a challenge on the job	67
People don't see the end result of their work	68
Labor unions don't encourage their members to work hard	64

3. **A mismatch between people's values and the existing reward system.** A gap between what people value and the rewards and incentives that they receive also weakens work behavior and undercuts the work ethic. For much of our recent history, managers have assumed (reasonably enough) that most jobholders sought material success and an improving standard of living.

Our findings show that today's work force brings a remarkably pluralistic set of values to the workplace. This diversity, in turn, puts great strain on the existing, single-value reward system. Jobholders who work primarily for self-development have a very different set of needs and expectations from people who work for material success and for an increasing standard of living.

The Public Agenda survey allowed us to quantify the mismatch between the reward system and the qualities that jobholders consider important. We compared each jobholders' core motive for working with the rewards available on their current jobs. For a person who works primarily for survival, the research assumes that the basic job requirements are job security and acceptable pay. If neither of these conditions is available on the person's present job, we have a mismatch.

For jobholders who work primarily to increase their standard of living, the basic job requirements are: (a) high pay, (b) some relationship between pay and performance, (c) a chance for career advancement and promotion, and (d) some degree of fairness in the rules governing promotions. If a jobholder who primarily works to improve his or her standard of living does not have at least two of these features, we again have a mismatch.

For a person whose primary motive for working is self-development, the research shows that the most important qualities are: (a) a job that enables a person to develop abilities and potentials, (b) an interesting job, (c) a creative job, and (d) a job with a say in important decisions. A mismatch would be a failure to have at least two of these characteristics on one's present job.

Defined in this way, about half (49%) of the American work force experiences a mismatch between their values and their jobs, while the other half (49%) have a good match (2% cannot be measured). Significantly, more than two-thirds of those who work for self-development have a good match between their jobs and their needs. At the other end of the spectrum, a majority of those who work to survive also have a good match. The worst mismatch occurs for those who work to improve their standard of living: Two-thirds of them have a mismatch between their needs and their jobs.

Mismatch between jobs and values:

	Good Match (49%) %	Bad Match (49%) %
Work to survive (38%)	22	16
Work to improve living standard (43%)	15	28
Work for self-development (17%)	12	5

4. **A persistent confusion between job satisfaction and productivity.** There have, of course, been frequent attempts to restructure managerial and incentive systems to provide greater motivation and support for the work ethic. In many cases, however, these attempts have been flawed by a failure to make a crucial distinction between job satisfaction and job effectiveness. Intuitively, it seems plausible that a satisfied jobholder will

also be an effective worker. As a result, some managers have attempted to improve motivation by improving job satisfaction. Research conducted for the National Science Foundation (Katzell and Yankelovich, 1975) has shown that this superficially plausible approach is largely incorrect and at best, tells only part of the story.[6] The Public Agenda findings have confirmed and elaborated this conclusion.

Some work characteristics enhance both motivation and job satisfaction. Our research suggests that this is true of interesting work. But other factors increase job satisfaction without increasing motivation. Most people, for example, state that a convenient location or good fringe benefits or low amounts of rush and stress make their jobs more agreeable. But they also say that these factors do not enhance their motivation to work more effectively. Indeed, some factors that make jobs more satisfying, such as congenial co-workers and supervisors, may be attractive precisely because they do not require greater effort or commitment.

The Public Agenda research revealed a third category of factors, which enhance productiveness without enhancing job satisfaction. Most jobholders make a surprisingly sharp and clear distinction between factors that primarily enhance motivation and those that primarily are satisfiers. The features that enhance motivation center on such work ethic values as responsibility, a chance for advancement, and a challenging job.

Factors that enhance productiveness:

	Would work harder for %	Makes job more agreeable %	Both %
Good chance for advancement	48	22	19
Good pay	45	27	22
Pay tied to performance	43	31	16
Recognition for good work	41	34	17
Job enables me to develop abilities	40	27	21
Challenging job	38	30	15
Job allows me to think for myself	37	33	17
A great deal of responsibility	36	28	14
Interesting work	36	35	18
Job requires creativity	35	31	20

[6]Raymond Katzell, Daniel Yankelovich, et. al., *Work, Productivity and Job Satisfaction,* Harcourt Brace, 1975. Katzell and Yankelovich also review a number of other observers of the workplace, beginning with Hertzberg, who have noted similar phenomena, pp. 140-151.

Factors that enhance job satisfaction:

	Makes job agreeable %	Would work harder for %	Both %
A job without too much rush and stress	61	15	13
Convenient location	56	12	12
Workplace free from dirt, noise, and pollution	56	12	12
Working with people I like	54	17	13
Get along well with supervisor	52	19	12
Being informed about what goes on	49	21	16
Flexible work pace	49	20	12
Flexible working hours	49	18	15
Good fringe benefits	45	27	18
Fair treatment in workload	45	24	18

Jobholders are concerned with both satisfiers and productiveness. When asked what features would improve their jobs, they mention motivators such as "recognition for good work" (70%) and "a good chance for advancement" (65%) as frequently as they mention satisfiers such as "good fringe benefits" (68%) or "job security" (65%). The following chart shows the degree to which people want better motivators in their jobs. The highlighting indicates whether the feature primarily enhances job satisfaction or effectiveness.

Job satisfaction and productiveness:

	Want more of on present job %	Motivator %	Satisfier %
Good pay	77	**45**	28
Recognition for good work	70	**41**	35
Good fringe benefits	68	27	**50**
Chance for advancement	65	**48**	22
Job security	65	29	**43**
Interesting work	62	35	35
Pay tied to performance	61	**43**	31
Job allows me to learn new things	61	34	36

In sum, we conclude that the American economy is failing to utilize one of its most powerful resources — a widespread commitment to the work ethic. Although many people want to work hard and do good work for its own sake, the workplace is structured in ways that discourage rather than support this norm. As a result, people work below their potential and do less than they want to. The demands of jobholders for managers who know how to motivate, for pay tied to performance, and for other changes in the workplace that increase motivation, reflect people's desire to give more to their jobs than they are currently giving.

ON THE FOLLY OF REWARDING A, WHILE HOPING FOR B

Steven Kerr

Illustrations are presented from society in general, and from organizations in particular, of reward systems that "pay off" for one behavior even though the rewarder hopes dearly for another. Portions of the reward systems of a manufacturing company and an insurance firm are examined and the consequences discussed.

Whether dealing with monkeys, rats, or human beings, it is hardly controversial to state that most organisms seek information concerning what activities are rewarded, and then seek to do (or at least pretend to do) those things, often to the virtual exclusion of activities not rewarded. The extent to which this occurs of course will depend on the perceived attractiveness of the rewards offered, but neither operant nor expectancy theorists would quarrel with the essence of this notion.

Nevertheless, numerous examples exist of reward systems that are fouled up in that behaviors which are rewarded are those which the rewarder is trying to *discourage,* while the behavior he desires is not being rewarded at all.

In an effort to understand and explain this phenomenon, this paper presents examples from society, from organizations in general, and from profit making firms in particular. Data from a manufacturing company and information from an insurance firm are examined to demonstrate the consequences of such reward systems for the organizations involved, and possible reasons why such reward systems continue to exist are considered.

SOCIETAL EXAMPLES

Politics

Official goals are "purposely vague and general and do not indicate...the host of decisions that must be made among alternative ways of achieving official goals and the priority of multiple goals..."(8, p. 66). They usually may be relied on to offend absolutely no one, and in this sense can be considered high acceptance, low quality goals. An example might be "build better schools." Operative goals are higher in quality but lower in acceptance, since they specify where the money will come from, what alternative goals will be ignored, etc.

On The Folly of Rewarding A, While Hoping for B by Steven Kerr. Reprinted by permission of Dr. Steven Kerr, Los Angeles, California.

The American citizenry supposedly wants its candidates for public office to set forth operative goals, making their proposed programs "perfectly clear," specifying sources and uses of funds, etc. However, since operative goals are lower in acceptance, and since aspirants to public office need acceptance (from at least 50.1 percent of the people), most politicians prefer to speak only of official goals, at least until after the election. They of course would agree to speak at the operative level if "punished" for not doing so. The electorate could do this by refusing to support candidates who do not speak at the operative level.

Instead, however, the American voter typically punishes (withholds support from) candidates who frankly discuss where the money will come from, rewards politicians who speak only of official goals, but hopes that candidates (despite the reward system) will discuss the issues operatively. It is academic whether it was moral for Nixon, for example, to refuse to discuss his 1968 "secret plan" to end the Vietnam war, his 1972 operative goals concerning the lifting of price controls, the reshuffling of his cabinet, etc. The point is that the reward system made such refusal rational.

It seems worth mentioning that no manuscript can adequately define what is "moral" and what is not. However, examination of costs and benefits, combined with knowledge of what motivates a particular individual, often will suffice to determine what for him is "rational."[1] If the reward system is so designed that it is irrational to be moral, this does not necessarily mean that immorality will result. But is this not asking for trouble?

War

If some oversimplification may be permitted, let it be assumed that the primary goal of the organization (Pentagon, Luftwaffe, or whatever) is to win. Let it be assumed further that the primary goal of most individuals on the front lines is to get home alive. Then there appears to be an important conflict in goals — personally rational behavior by those at the bottom will endanger goal attainment by those at the top.

But not necessarily! It depends on how the reward system is set up. The Vietnam war was indeed a study of disobedience and rebellion, with terms such as "fragging" (killing one's own commanding officer) and "search and evade" becoming part of the military vocabulary. The difference in subordinates' acceptance of authority between World War II and Vietnam is reported to be considerable, and veterans of the Second World War often have been quoted as being outraged at the mutinous actions of many American soldiers in Vietnam.

Consider, however, some critical differences in the reward system in use during the two conflicts. What did the GI in World War II want? To go

[1]In Simon's (10, pp. 76-77) terms, a decision is "subjectively rational" if it maximizes an individual's valued outcomes so far as his knowledge permits. A decision is "personally rational" if it is oriented toward the individual's goals.

home. And when did he get to go home? When the war was won! If he disobeyed the orders to clean out the trenches and take the hills, the war would not be won and he would not go home. Furthermore, what were his chances of attaining his goal (getting home alive) if he obeyed the orders compared to his chances if he did not? What is being suggested is that the rational soldier in World War II, *whether patriotic or not*, probably found it expedient to obey.

Consider the reward system in use in Vietnam. What did the man at the bottom want? To go home. And when did he get to go home? When his tour of duty was over! This was the case *whether or not* the war was won. Furthermore, concerning the relative chance of getting home alive by obeying orders compared to the chance if they were disobeyed, it is worth noting that a mutineer in Vietnam was far more likely to be assigned rest and rehabilitation (on the assumption that fatigue was the cause) than he was to suffer any negative consequence.

In his description of the "zone of indifference," Barnard stated that "a person can and will accept a communication as authoritative only when...at the time of his decision, he believes it to be compatible with his personal interests as a whole" (1, p. 165). In light of the reward system used in Vietnam, would it not have been personally irrational for some orders to have been obeyed? Was not the military implementing a system which *rewarded* disobedience, while *hoping* that soldiers (despite the reward system) would obey orders?

Medicine

Theoretically, a physician can make either of two types of error, and intuitively one seems as bad as the other. A doctor can pronounce a patient sick when he is actually well, thus causing him needless anxiety and expense, curtailment of enjoyable foods and activities, and even physical danger by subjecting him to needless medication and surgery. Alternatively, a doctor can label a sick person well, and thus avoid treating what may be a serious, even fatal ailment. It might be natural to conclude that physicians seek to minimize both types of error.

Such a conclusion would be wrong.[2] It is estimated that numerous Americans are presently afflicted with iatrogenic (physician *caused*) illnesses (9). This occurs when the doctor is approached by someone complaining of a few stray symptoms. The doctor classifies and organizes these symptoms, gives them a name, and obligingly tells the patient what further symptoms may be expected. This information often acts as a self-fulfilling prophecy, with the result that from that day on the patient, for all practical purposes, is sick.

Why does this happen? Why are physicians so reluctant to sustain a type 2 error (pronouncing a sick person well) that they will tolerate many

[2]In one study (4) of 14,867 films for signs of tuberculosis, 1,216 positive readings turned out to be clinically negative; only 24 negative readings proved clinically active, a ratio of 50 to 1.

type 1 errors? Again, a look at the reward system is needed. The punishments for a type 2 error are real: guilt, embarrassment, and the threat of lawsuit and scandal. On the other hand, a type 1 error (labeling a well person sick) "is sometimes seen as sound clinical practice, indicating a healthy conservative approach to medicine" (9, p. 69). Type 1 errors also are likely to generate increased income and a stream of steady customers who, being well in a limited physiological sense, will not embarrass the doctor by dying abruptly.

Fellow physicians and the general public therefore are really *rewarding* type 1 errors and at the same time *hoping* fervently that doctors will try not to make them.

GENERAL ORGANIZATIONAL EXAMPLES

Rehabilitation Centers and Orphanages

In terms of the prime beneficiary classification (2, p.42), organizations such as these are supposed to exist for the "public-in-contact," that is, clients. The orphanage therefore theoretically is interested in placing as many children as possible in good homes. However, often orphanages surround themselves with so many rules concerning adoption that it is nearly impossible to pry a child out of the place. Orphanages may deny adoption unless the applicants are a married couple, both of the same religion as the child, without history of emotional or vocational instability, with a specified minimum income and a private room for the child, etc.

If the primary goal is to place children in good homes, then the rules ought to constitute means toward that goal. Goal displacement results when these "means become ends-in-themselves that displace the original goals" (2, p.229).

To some extent these rules are required by law. But the influence of the reward system on the orphanage's management should not be ignored. Consider, for example, that the:

1. Number of children enrolled often is the most important determinant of the size of the allocated budget.

2. Number of children under the director's care also will affect the size of his staff.

3. Total organizational size will determine largely the director's prestige at the annual conventions, in the community, etc.

Therefore, to the extent that staff size, total budget, and personal prestige are valued by the orphanage's executive personnel, it becomes rational for them to make it difficult for children to be adopted. After all, who wants to be the director of the smallest orphanage in the state?

If the reward system errs in the opposite direction, paying off only for placements, extensive goal displacement again is likely to result. A common example of vocational rehabilitation in many states, for example, consists of placing someone in a job for which he has little interest and few qualifications, for two months or so, and then "rehabilitating" him again in another position. Such behavior is quite consistent with the prevailing reward system, which pays off for the number of individuals placed in any position for 60 days or more. Rehabilitation counselors also confess to competing with one another to place relatively skilled clients, sometimes ignoring persons with few skills who would be harder to place. Extensively disabled clients find that counselors often prefer to work with those whose disabilities are less severe.[3]

Universities

Society *hopes* that teachers will not neglect their teaching responsibilities but *rewards* them almost entirely for research and publications. This is most true at the large and prestigious universities. Cliches such as "good research and good teaching go together" notwithstanding, professors often find that they must choose between teaching and research oriented activities when allocating their time. Rewards for good teaching usually are limited to outstanding teacher awards, which are given to only a small percentage of good teachers and which usually bestow little money and fleeting prestige. Punishments for poor teaching also are rare.

Rewards for research and publications, on the other hand, and punishments for failure to accomplish these, are commonly administered by universities at which teachers are employed. Furthermore, publication oriented resumés usually will be well received at other universities, whereas teaching credentials, harder to document and quantify, are much less transferable. Consequently, it is rational for university teachers to concentrate on research, even if to the detriment of teaching and at the expense of their students.

By the same token, it is rational for students to act based upon the goal displacement which has occurred within universities concerning what they are rewarded for. If it is assumed that a primary goal of a university is to transfer knowledge from teacher to student, then grades become identifiable as a means toward that goal, serving as motivational, control, and feedback devices to expedite the knowledge transfer. Instead, however, the grades themselves have become much more important for entrance to graduate school, successful employment, tuition refunds, parental respect, etc., than the knowledge or lack of knowledge they are supposed to signify.

It therefore should come as no surprise that information has surfaced in recent years concerning fraternity files for examinations, term paper writing services, organized cheating at the service academies, and the like. Such activities constitute a personally rational response to a reward system which pays off for grades rather than knowledge.

[3]Personal interviews conducted during 1972-1973.

BUSINESS RELATED EXAMPLES

Ecology

Assume that the president of XYZ Corporation is confronted with the following alternatives:

1. Spend $11 million for antipollution equipment to keep from poisoning fish in the river adjacent to the plant; or

2. Do nothing, in violation of the law, and assume a one in ten chance of being caught, with a resultant $1 million fine plus the necessity of buying the equipment.

Under this not unrealistic set of choices it requires no linear program to determine that XYZ Corporation can maximize its probabilities by flouting the law. Add the fact that XYZ's president is probably being rewarded (by creditors, stockholders, and other salient parts of his task environment) according to criteria totally unrelated to the number of fish poisoned, and his probable course of action becomes clear.

Evaluation of Training

It is axiomatic that those who care about a firm's well-being should insist that the organization get fair value for its expenditures. Yet it is commonly known that firms seldom bother to evaluate a new GIRD, MBO, job enrichment program, or whatever, to see if the company is getting its money's worth. Why? Certainly it is not because people have not pointed out that this situation exists; numerous practitioner oriented articles are written each year to just this point.

The individuals (whether in personnel, manpower planning, or wherever) who normally would be responsible for conducting such evaluations are the same ones often charged with introducing the change effort in the first place. Having convinced top management to spend the money, they usually are quite animated afterwards in collecting vignettes and anecdotes about how successful the program was. The last thing many desire is a formal, systematic, and revealing evaluation. Although members of top management may actually *hope* for such systematic evaluation, their reward systems continue to *reward* ignorance in this area. And if the personnel department abdicates its responsibility, who is to step into the breach? The change agent himself? Hardly! He is likely to be too busy collecting anecdotal "evidence" of his own, for use with his next client.

Miscellaneous

Many additional examples could be cited of systems which in fact are rewarding behaviors other than those supposedly desired by the rewarder. A few of these are described briefly below.

Most coaches disdain to discuss individual accomplishments, preferring to speak of teamwork, proper attitude, and a one-for-all spirit.

Usually, however, rewards are distributed according to individual performance. The college basketball player who feeds his teammates instead of shooting will not compile impressive scoring statistics and is less likely to be drafted by the pros. The ballplayer who hits to right field to advance the runners will win neither the batting nor home run titles, and will be offered smaller raises. It therefore is rational for players to think of themselves first, and the team second.

In business organizations where rewards are dispensed for unit performance or for individual goals achieved, without regard for overall effectiveness, similar attitudes often are observed. Under most Management by Objectives (MBO) systems, goals in areas where quantification is difficult often go unspecified. The organization therefore often is in a position where it *hopes* for employee effort in the areas of team building, interpersonal relations, creativity, etc., but it formally *rewards* none of these. In cases where promotions and raises are formally tied to MBO, the system itself contains a paradox in that it "asks employees to set challenging, risky goals, only to face smaller paychecks and possibly damaged careers if these goals are not accomplished" (5, p. 40).

It is *hoped* that administrators will pay attention to long run costs and opportunities and will institute programs which will bear fruit later on. However, many organizational reward systems pay off for short run sales and earnings only. Under such circumstances it is personally rational for officials to sacrifice long term growth and profit (by selling off equipment and property, or by stifling research and development) for short term advantages. This probably is most pertinent in the public sector, with the result that many public officials are unwilling to implement programs which will not show benefits by election time.

As a final, clear-cut example of a fouled-up reward system, consider the cost-plus contract or its next of kin, the allocation of next year's budget as a direct function of this year's expenditures. It probably is conceivable that those who award such budgets and contracts really hope for economy and prudence in spending. It is obvious, however, that adopting the proverb "to him who spends shall more be given," rewards not economy, but spending itself.

TWO COMPANIES' EXPERIENCES

A Manufacturing Organization

A midwest manufacturer of industrial goods had been troubled for some time by aspects of its organizational climate it believed dysfunctional. For research purposes, interviews were conducted with many employees and a questionnaire was administered on a companywide basis, including plants and offices in several American and Canadian locations. The company strongly encouraged employee participation in the survey, and made available time and space during the workday for completion of the instrument. All employees in attendance during the day of the survey completed the questionnaire. All instruments were collected directly by the researcher, who personally administered each session. Since no one employed by the firm handled the questionnaires, and since respondent names were not asked for, it seems likely that the pledge of anonymity given was believed.

A modified version of the Expect Approval scale (7) was included as part of the questionnaire. The instrument asked respondents to indicate the degree of approval or disapproval they could expect if they performed each of the described actions. A seven point Likert scale was used, with one indicating that the action would probably bring strong disapproval and seven signifying likely strong approval.

Although normative data for this scale from studies of other organizations are unavailable, it is possible to examine fruitfully the data obtained from this survey in several ways. First, it may be worth noting that the questionnaire data corresponded closely to information gathered through interviews. Furthermore, as can be seen from the results summarized in Exhibit 1, sizable differences between various work units, and between employees at different job levels within the same work unit, were obtained. This suggests that response bias effects (social desirability in particular loomed as a potential concern) are not likely to be severe.

Most importantly, comparisons between scores obtained on the Expect Approval scale and a statement of problems which were the reason for the survey revealed that the same behaviors which managers in each division thought dysfunctional were those which lower level employees claimed were rewarded. As compared to job levels 1 to 8 in Division B (see Exhibit 1), those in Division A claimed a much higher acceptance by management of "conforming" activities. Between 31 and 37 percent of Division A employees at levels 1-8 stated that going along with the majority, agreeing with the boss, and staying on everyone's good side brought approval; only once (level 5-8 responses to one of the three items) did a majority suggest that such actions would generate disapproval.

Furthermore, responses from Division A workers at levels 1-4 indicate that behaviors geared toward risk avoidance were as likely to be rewarded as to be punished. Only at job levels 9 and above was it apparent that the reward system was positively reinforcing behaviors desired by top management. Overall, the same "tendencies toward conservatism and apple-polishing at the lower levels" which divisional management had complained about during the interviews were those claimed by subordinates to be the most rational course of action in light of the existing reward system. Management apparently was not getting the behaviors it was *hoping* for, but it certainly was getting the behaviors it was perceived by subordinates to be *rewarding*.

EXHIBIT 1

Summary of Two Divisions' Data Relevant to Conforming and Risk-Avoidance Behaviors (Extent to Which Subjects Expect Approval)

Dimension	Item	Division and Sample	Total Responses	Percentage of Workers Responding		
				1, 2, or 3 Disapproval	4	5, 6, or 7 Approval
Risk Avoidance	Making a risky decision based on the best information available at the time, but which turns out wrong.	A, levels 1-4 (lowest)	127	61	25	14
		A, levels 5-8	172	46	31	23
		A, levels 9 and above	17	41	30	30
		B, levels 1-4 (lowest)	31	58	26	16
		B, levels 5-8	19	42	42	16
		B, levels 9 and above	10	50	20	30
	Setting extremely high and challenging standards and goals, and then narrowly failing to make them.	A, levels 1-4	122	47	28	25
		A, levels 5-8	168	33	26	41
		A, levels 9+	17	24	6	70
		B, levels 1-4	31	48	23	29
		B, levels 5-8	18	17	33	50
		B, levels 9+	10	30	0	70
	Setting goals which are extremely easy to make and then making them.	A, levels 1-4	124	35	30	35
		A, levels 5-8	171	47	27	26
		A, levels 9+	17	70	24	6
		B, levels 1-4	31	58	26	16
		B, levels 5-8	19	63	16	21
		B, levels 9+	10	80	0	20

EXHIBIT 1 (Continued)

Dimension	Item	Division and Sample	Total Responses	Percentage of Workers Responding		
				1, 2, or 3 Dis-approval	4	5, 6, or 7 Approval
Conformity	Being a "yes man" and always agreeing with the boss.	A, levels 1-4	126	46	17	37
		A, levels 5-8	180	54	14	31
		A, levels 9+	17	88	12	0
		B, levels 1-4	32	53	28	19
		B, levels 5-8	19	68	21	11
		B, levels 9+	10	80	10	10
	Always going along with the majority.	A, levels 1-4	125	40	25	35
		A, levels 5-8	173	47	21	32
		A, levels 9+	17	70	12	18
		B, levels 1-4	31	61	23	16
		B, levels 5-8	19	68	11	21
		B, levels 9+	10	80	10	10
	Being careful to stay on the good side of everyone, so that everyone agrees that you are a great guy.	A, levels 1-4	124	45	18	37
		A, levels 5-8	173	45	22	33
		A, levels 9+	17	64	6	30
		B, levels 1-4	31	54	23	23
		B, levels 5-8	19	73	11	16
		B, levels 9+	10	80	10	10

An Insurance Firm

The Group Health Claims Division of a large eastern insurance company provides another rich illustration of a reward system which reinforces behaviors not desired by top management.

Attempting to measure and reward accuracy in paying surgical claims, the firm systematically keeps track of the number of returned checks and letters of complaint received from policyholders. However, underpayments are likely to provoke cries of outrage from the insured, while overpayments often are accepted in courteous silence. Since it often is impossible to tell from the physician's statement which of two surgical procedures, with different allowable benefits, was performed, and since writing for clarifications will interfere with other standards used by the firm concerning "percentage of claims paid within two days of receipt," the new hire in more than one claims section is soon acquainted with the informal norm: "When in doubt, pay it out!"

The situation would be even worse were it not for the fact that other features of the firm's reward system tend to neutralize those described. For example, annual "merit" increases are given to all employees, in one of the following three amounts:

1. If the worker is "outstanding" (a select category, into which no more than two employees per section may be placed): 5 percent.

2. If the worker is "above average" (normally all workers not "outstanding" are so rated): 4 percent.

3. If the worker commits gross acts of negligence and irresponsibility for which he might be discharged in many other companies: 3 percent.

Now, since (a) the difference between the 5 percent theoretically attainable through hard work and the 4 percent attainable merely by living until the review date is small and (b) since insurance firms seldom dispense much of a salary increase in cash (rather, the worker's insurance benefits increase, causing him to be further overinsured), many employees are rather indifferent to the possibility of obtaining the extra one percent reward and therefore tend to ignore the norm concerning indiscriminate payments.

However, most employees are not indifferent to the rule which states that, should absences or latenesses total three or more in any six-month period, the entire 4 or 5 percent due at the next "merit" review must be forfeited. In this sense the firm may be described as *hoping* for performance, while *rewarding* attendance. What it gets, of course, is attendance. (If the absence-lateness rule appears to the reader to be stringent, it really is not. The company counts "times" rather than "days" absent, and a ten-day absence therefore counts the same as one lasting two days. A worker in danger of accumulating a third absence within six months merely has to remain ill [away from work] during his second absence until his first absence is more than six months old. The limiting factor is that at some point his salary ceases, and his sickness benefits take over. This usually is sufficient to get the younger workers to return, but for those with 20 or more years' service, the company provides sickness benefits of 90 percent of normal salary, tax-free! Therefore . . . .)

CAUSES

Extremely diverse instances of systems which reward behavior A although the rewarder apparently hopes for behavior B have been given. These are useful to illustrate the breadth and magnitude of the phenomenon, but the diversity increases the difficulty of determining commonalities and establishing causes. However, four general factors may be pertinent to an explanation of why fouled-up reward systems seem to be so prevalent.

Fascination with an "Objective" Criterion

It has been mentioned elsewhere that:

> Most "objective" measures of productivity are objective only in that their subjective elements are (a) determined in advance, rather than coming into play at the time of the formal evaluation, and (b) well concealed on the rating instrument itself. Thus industrial firms seeking to devise objective rating systems first decide, in an arbitrary manner, what dimensions are to be rated,...usually including some items having little to do with organizational effectiveness while excluding others that do. Only then does Personnel Division churn out official-looking documents on which all dimensions chosen to be rated are assigned point values, categories, or whatever (6, p. 92).

Nonetheless, many individuals seek to establish simple, quantifiable standards against which to measure and reward performance. Such efforts may be successful in highly predictable areas within an organization, but are likely to cause goal displacement when applied anywhere else. Overconcern with attendance and lateness in the insurance firm and with number of people placed in the vocational rehabilitation division may have been largely responsible for the problems described in those organizations.

Overemphasis on Highly Visible Behavior

Difficulties often stem from the fact that some parts of the task are highly visible while other parts are not. For example, publications are easier to demonstrate than teaching, and scoring baskets and hitting home runs are more readily observable then feeding teammates and advancing base runners. Similarly, the adverse consequences of pronouncing a sick person well are more visible than those sustained by labeling a well person sick. Team-building and creativity are other examples of behaviors which may not be rewarded simply because they are hard to observe.

Hypocrisy

In some of the instances described the rewarder may have been getting the desired behavior, notwithstanding claims that the behavior was not desired. This may be true, for example, of management's attitude toward apple-polishing in the manufacturing firm (a behavior which subordinates felt was rewarded, despite management's avowed dislike of the practice). This also may explain politicians' unwillingness to revise the penalties for disobedience of ecology laws, and the failure of top management to devise reward systems which would cause systematic evaluation of training and development programs.

Emphasis on Morality or Equity Rather Than Efficiency

Sometimes consideration of other factors prevents the establishment of a system which rewards behaviors desired by the rewarder. The felt obligation of many Americans to vote for one candidate or another, for example, may impair their ability to withhold support from politicians who refuse to discuss the issues. Similarly, the concern for spreading the risks and costs of wartime military service may outweigh the advantage to be obtained by committing personnel to combat until the war is over.

It should be noted that only with respect to the first two causes are reward systems really paying off for other than desired behaviors. In the case of the third and fourth causes the system *is* rewarding behaviors desired by the rewarder, and the systems are fouled up only from the standpoints of those who believe the rewarder's public statements (cause 3), or those who seek to maximize efficiency rather than other outcomes (cause 4).

CONCLUSIONS

Modern organization theory requires a recognition that the members of organizations and society possess divergent goals and motives. It therefore is unlikely that managers and their subordinates will seek the same outcomes. Three possible remedies for this potential problem are suggested.

Selection

It is theoretically possible for organizations to employ only those individuals whose goals and motives are wholly consonant with those of management. In such cases the same behaviors judged by subordinates to be rational would be perceived by management as desirable. State-of-the-art reviews of selection techniques, however, provide scant grounds for hope that such an approach would be successful (for example, see 12).

Training

Another theoretical alternative is for the organization to admit those employees whose goals are not consonant with those of management and then, through training, socialization, or whatever, alter employee goals to make them consonant. However, research on the effectiveness of such training programs, though limited, provides further grounds for pessimism (for example, see 3).

Altering the Reward System

What would have been the result if:

1. Nixon had been assured by his advisors that he could not win re-election except by discussing the issues in detail?

2. Physicians' conduct was subjected to regular examination by review boards for type 1 errors (calling healthy people ill) and to penalties (fines, censure, etc.) for errors of either type?

3. The President of XYZ Corporation had to choose between (a) spending $11 million for antipollution equipment, and (b) incurring a fifty-fifty chance of going to jail for five years?

Managers who complain that their workers are not motivated might do well to consider the possibility that they have installed reward systems which are paying off for behaviors other than those they are seeking. This, in part, is what happened in Vietnam, and this is what regularly frustrates societal efforts to bring about honest politicians, civic-minded managers, etc. This certainly is what happened in both the manufacturing and the insurance companies.

A first step for such managers might be to find out what behaviors currently are being rewarded. Perhaps an instrument similar to that used in the manufacturing firm could be useful for this purpose. Chances are excellent that these managers will be surprised by what they find — that their firms are not rewarding what they assume they are. In fact, such undesirable behavior by organizational members as they have observed may be explained largely by the reward systems in use.

This is not to say that all organizational behavior is determined by formal rewards and punishments. Certainly it is true that in the absence of formal reinforcement some soldiers will be patriotic, some presidents will be ecology minded, and some orphanage directors will care about children. The point, however, is that in such cases the rewarder is not *causing* the behaviors desired but is only a fortunate bystander. For an organization to *act* upon its members, the formal reward system should positively reinforce desired behaviors, not constitute an obstacle to be overcome.

It might be wise to underscore the obvious fact that there is nothing really new in what has been said. In both theory and practice these matters have been mentioned before. Thus in many states Good Samaritan laws have been installed to protect doctors who stop to assist a stricken motorist. In states without such laws it is commonplace for doctors to refuse to stop, for fear of involvement in a subsequent lawsuit. In college basketball additional penalties have been instituted against players who foul their opponents deliberately. It has long been argued by

Milton Friedman and others that penalties should be altered so as to make it irrational to disobey the ecology laws, and so on.

By altering the reward system the organization escapes the necessity of selecting only desirable people or of trying to alter undesirable ones. In Skinnerian terms (as described in 11, p. 704), "As for responsibility and goodness — as commonly defined — no one . . . would want or need them. They refer to a man's behaving well despite the absence of positive reinforcement that is obviously sufficient to explain it. Where such reinforcement exists, 'no one needs goodness.'"

REFERENCES

1. Barnard, Chester I. *The Functions of the Executive* (Cambridge, Mass.: Harvard University Press, 1964).

2. Blau, Peter M., and W. Richard Scott. *Formal Organizations* (San Francisco: Chandler, 1962).

3. Fiedler, Fred E. "Predicting the Effects of Leadership Training and Experience from the Contingency Model," *Journal of Applied Psychology*, Vol. 56 (1972), 114-119.

4. Garland, L. H. "Studies of the Accuracy of Diagnostic Procedures," *American Journal Roentgenological, Radium Therapy Nuclear Medicine,* Vol. 82 (1959) 25-38.

5. Kerr, Steven. "Some Modifications in MBO as an OD Strategy," *Academy of Management Proceedings*, 1973, pp. 39-42.

6. Kerr, Steven. "What Price Objectivity?" *American Sociologist*, Vol. 8 (1973), 92-93.

7. Litwin, G. H., and R. A. Stringer, Jr. *Motivation and Organizational Climate* (Boston: Harvard University Press, 1968).

8. Perrow, Charles. "The Analysis of Goals in Complex Organizations," in A. Etzioni (Ed.), *Readings on Modern Organizations* (Englewood Cliffs, N.J.: Prentice-Hall, 1969).

9. Scheff, Thomas J. "Decision Rules, Types of Error, and Their Consequences in Medical Diagnosis," in F. Massarik and P. Ratoosh (Eds.), *Mathematical Explorations in Behavioral Science* (Homewood, Ill.: Irwin, 1965).

10. Simon, Herbert A. *Administrative Behavior* (New York: Free Press, 1957).

11. Swanson, G. E. "Review Symposium: Beyond Freedom and Dignity," *American Journal of Sociology,* Vol. 78 (1972), 702-705.

12. Webster, E. *Decision Making in the Employment Interview* (Montreal: Industrial Relations Center, McGill University, 1964).

ONE MORE TIME: HOW DO YOU MOTIVATE EMPLOYEES?

Frederick Herzberg

How many articles, books, speeches, and workshops have pleaded plaintively, "How do I get an employee to do what I want him to do?"

The psychology of motivation is tremendously complex, and what has been unraveled with any degree of assurance is small indeed. But the dismal ratio of knowledge to speculation has not dampened the enthusiasm for new forms of snake oil that are constantly coming on the market, many of them with academic testimonials. Doubtless this article will have no depressing impact on the market for snake oil, but since the ideas expressed in it have been tested in many corporations and other organizations, it will help — I hope — to redress the imbalance in the aforementioned ratio.

"MOTIVATING" WITH KITA

In lectures to industry on the problem, I have found that the audiences are anxious for quick and practical answers, so I will begin with a straight-forward, practical formula for moving people.

What is the simplest, surest, and most direct way of getting someone to do something? Ask him? But if he responds that he does not want to do it, then that calls for a psychological consultation to determine the reason for his obstinancy. Tell him? His response shows that he does not understand you, and now an expert in communication methods has to be brought in to show you how to get through to him. Give him a monetary incentive? I do not need to remind the reader of the complexity and difficulty involved in setting up and administering an incentive system. Show him? This means a costly training program. We need a simple way.

Every audience contains the "direct action" manager who shouts, "Kick him!" And this type of manager is right. The surest and least circumlocuted way of getting someone to do something is to kick him in the pants — give him what might be called the KITA.

There are various forms of KITA, and here are some of them:

- **Negative physical KITA.** This is a literal application of the term and was frequently used in the past. It has, however, three major drawbacks: (1) it is inelegant; (2) it contradicts the precious image of benevolence that most organizations cherish; and (3) since it is a physical attack, it directly stimulates the autonomic nervous system, and this often results in negative feedback — the employee may just kick you in return. These factors give rise to certain taboos against negative physical KITA.

The psychologist has come to the rescue of those who are no longer permitted to use negative physical KITA. He has uncovered infinite sources of psychological vulnerabilities and the appropriate methods to play tunes on them. "He took my rug away"; "I wonder what he meant by that"; "The boss is always going around me" — these symptomatic expressions of ego sores that have been rubbed raw are the result of application of:

- **Negative psychological KITA.** This has several advantages over negative physical KITA. First, the cruelty is not visible; the bleeding is internal and comes much later. Second, since it affects the higher cortical centers of the brain with its inhibitory powers, it reduces the possibility of physical backlash. Third, since the number of psychological pains that a person can feel is almost infinite, the direction and site possibilities of the KITA are increased many times. Fourth, the person administering the kick can manage to be above it all and let the system accomplish the dirty work. Fifth, those who practice it receive some ego satisfaction (one-upmanship), whereas they would find drawing blood abhorrent. Finally, if the employee does complain, he can always be accused of being paranoid, since there is no tangible evidence of an actual attack.

Now, what does negative KITA accomplish? If I kick you in the rear (physically or psychologically), who is motivated? *I* am motivated; *you* move! Negative KITA does not lead to motivation, but to movement. So:

- **Positive KITA**. Let us consider motivation. If I say to you, "Do this for me or the company, and in return I will give you a reward, an incentive, more status, a promotion, all the quid pro quos that exist in the industrial organization," am I motivating you? The overwhelming opinion I receive from management people is, "Yes, this is motivation."

  I have a year-old Schnauzer. When it was a small puppy and I wanted it to move, I kicked it in the rear and it moved. Now that I have finished its obedience training, I hold up a dog biscuit when I want the Schnauzer to move. In this instance, who is motivated — I or the dog? The dog wants the biscuit, but it is I who want it to move. Again, I am the one who is motivated, and the dog is the one who moves. In this instance all I did was apply KITA frontally; I exerted a pull instead of a push. When industry wishes to use such positive KITAs, it has available an incredible number and variety of dog biscuits (jelly beans for humans) to wave in front of the employee to get him to jump.

Why is it that managerial audiences are quick to see that negative KITA is *not* motivation, while they are almost unanimous in their judgment that positive KITA *is* motivation? It is because negative KITA is rape, and positive KITA is seduction. But it is infinitely worse to be seduced than to be raped; the latter is an unfortunate occurrence, while the former signifies that you were a party to your own downfall. This is why positive KITA is so popular; it is a tradition; it is in the American way. The organization does not have to kick you; you kick yourself.

Myths About Motivation

Why is KITA not motivation? If I kick my dog (from the front or the back), he will move. And when I want him to move again, what must I do? I must kick him again. Similarly, I can charge a man's battery, and then recharge it, and recharge it again. But it is only when he has his own generator that we can talk about motivation. He then needs no outside stimulation. He *wants* to do it.

With this in mind, we can review some positive KITA personnel practices that were developed as attempts to instill "motivation":

1. **Reducing time spent at work**. This represents a marvelous way of motivating people to work — getting them off the job! We have reduced (formally and informally) the time spent on the job over the last 50 or 60 years until we are finally on the way to the "6 1/2-day weekend." An interesting variant of this approach is the development of off-hour recreation programs. The philosophy here seems to be that those who play together, work together. The fact is that motivated people seek more hours of work, not fewer.

2. **Spiraling wages**. Have these motivated people? Yes, to seek the next wage increase. Some medievalists still can be heard to say that a good depression will get employees moving. They feel that if rising wages don't or won't do the job, perhaps reducing them will.

3. **Fringe benefits**. Industry has outdone the most welfare-minded of welfare states in dispensing cradle-to-the-grave succor. One company I know of had an informal "fringe benefit of the month club" going for a while. The cost of fringe benefits in this country has reached approximately 25% of the wage dollar, and we still cry for motivation.

   People spend less time working for more money and more security than ever before, and the trend cannot be reversed. These benefits are no longer rewards; they are rights. A 6-day week is inhuman, a 10-hour day is exploitation, extended medical coverage is a basic decency, and stock options are the salvation of American initiative. Unless the ante is continuously raised, the psychological reaction of employees is that the company is turning back the clock.

   When industry began to realize that both the economic nerve and the lazy nerve of their employees had insatiable appetites, it started to

435

listen to the behavioral scientists who, more out of a humanist tradition than from scientific study, criticized management for not knowing how to deal with people. The next KITA easily followed.

4. **Human relations training**. Over 30 years of teaching and, in many instances, of practicing psychological approaches to handling people have resulted in costly human relations programs and, in the end, the same question: How do you motivate workers? Here, too, escalations have taken place. Thirty years ago it was necessary to request, "Please don't spit on the floor." Today the same admonition requires three "please"s before the employee feels that his superior has demonstrated the psychologically proper attitudes toward him.

   The failure of human relations training to produce motivation led to the conclusion that the supervisor or manager himself was not psychologically true to himself in his practice of interpersonal decency. So an advanced form of human relations KITA, sensitivity training, was unfolded.

5. **Sensitivity training**. Do you really, really understand yourself? Do you really, really, really trust the other man? Do you really, really, really, really cooperate? The failure of sensitivity training is now being explained, by those who have become opportunistic exploiters of the technique, as a failure to really (five times) conduct proper sensitivity training courses.

   With the realization that there are only temporary gains from comfort and economic and interpersonal KITA, personnel managers concluded that the fault lay not in what they were doing, but in the employee's failure to appreciate what they were doing. This opened up the field of communications, a whole new area of "scientifically" sanctioned KITA.

6. **Communications**. The professor of communications was invited to join the faculty of management training programs and help in making employees understand what management was doing for them. House organs, briefing sessions, supervisory instruction on the importance of communication, and all sorts of propaganda have proliferated until today there is even an International Council of Industrial Editors. But no motivation resulted, and the obvious thought occurred that perhaps management was not hearing what the employees were saying. That led to the next KITA.

7. **Two-way communication.** Management ordered morale surveys, suggestion plans, and group participation programs. Then both employees and management were communicating and listening to each other more than ever, but without much improvement in motivation.

   The behavioral scientists began to take another look at their conceptions and their data, and they took human relations one step further. A glimmer of truth was beginning to show through in the writings of the so-called higher-order-need psychologists. People, so they said, want to actualize themselves. Unfortunately, the "actualizing" psychologists got mixed up with the human relations psychologists, and a new KITA emerged.

8. **Job participation**. Though it may not have been the theoretical intention, job participation often became a "give them the big picture" approach. For example, if a man is tightening 10,000 nuts a day on an assembly line with a torque wrench, tell him he is building a Chevrolet. Another approach had the goal of giving the employee a *feeling* that he is determining, in some measure, what he does on his job. The goal was to provide a *sense* of achievement rather than a substantive achievement in his task. Real achievement, of course, requires a task that makes it possible.

But still there was no motivation. This led to the inevitable conclusion that the employees must be sick, and therefore to the next KITA.

9. **Employee counseling**. The initial use of this form of KITA in a systematic fashion can be credited to the Hawthorne experiment of the Western Electric Company during the early 1930's. At that time, it was found that the employees harbored irrational feelings that were interfering with the rational operation of the factory. Counseling in this instance was a means of letting the employees unburden themselves by talking to someone about their problems. Although the counseling techniques were primitive, the program was large indeed.

The counseling approach suffered as a result of experiences during World War II, when the programs themselves were found to be interfering with the operation of the organizations; the counselors had forgotten their role of benevolent listeners and were attempting to do something about the problems that they heard about. Psychological counseling, however, has managed to survive the negative impact of World War II experiences and today is beginning to flourish with renewed sophistication. But, alas, many of these programs, like all the others, do not seem to have lessened the pressure of demands to find out how to motivate workers.

Since KITA results only in short-term movement, it is safe to predict that the cost of these programs will increase steadily and new varieties will be developed as old positive KITAs reach their satiation points.

HYGIENE VS. MOTIVATORS

Let me rephrase the perennial question this way: How do you install a generator in an employee? A brief review of my motivation-hygiene theory of job attitudes is required before theoretical and practical suggestions can be offered. The theory was first drawn from an examination of events in the lives of engineers and accountants. At least 16 other investigations, using a wide variety of populations (including some in the Communist countries), have since been completed, making the original research one of the most replicated studies in the field of job attitudes.

The findings of these studies, along with corroboration from many other investigations using different procedures, suggest that the factors involved in producing job satisfaction (and motivation) are separate and distinct from the factors that lead to job dissatisfaction. Since separate factors need to be considered, depending on whether job satisfaction or job dissatisfaction is being examined, it follows that these two feelings are not opposites of each other. The opposite of job satisfaction is not job dissatisfaction but, rather, *no* job satisfaction; and, similarly, the opposite of job dissatisfaction is not job satisfaction, but *no* job dissatisfaction.

Stating the concept presents a problem in semantics, for we normally think of satisfaction and dissatisfaction as opposites — i.e., what is not satisfying must be dissatisfying, and vice versa. But when it comes to understanding the behavior of people in their jobs, more than a play on words is involved.

Two different needs of man are involved here. One set of needs can be thought of as stemming from his animal nature — the built-in drive to avoid pain from the environment, plus all the learned drives which become conditioned to the basic biological needs. For example, hunger, a basic biological drive, makes it necessary to earn money, and then money becomes a specific drive. The other set of needs relates to that unique human characteristic, the ability to achieve and, through achievement, to experience psychological growth. The stimuli for the growth needs are tasks that induce growth; in the industrial setting, they are the *job content*. Contrariwise, the stimuli inducing pain-avoidance behavior are found in the *job environment*.

The growth or *motivator* factors that are intrinsic to the job are: achievement, recognition for achievement, the work itself, responsibility, and growth or advancement. The dissatisfaction-avoidance or *hygiene* (KITA) factors that are extrinsic to the job include: company policy and administration, supervision, interpersonal relationships, working conditions, salary, status, and security.

A composite of the factors that are involved in causing job satisfaction and job dissatisfaction, drawn from samples of 1,685 employees, is shown in *Exhibit 1*. The results indicate that motivators were the primary cause of satisfaction, and hygiene factors the primary cause of unhappiness on the job. The employees, studied in 12 different investigations, included lower-level supervisors, professional women, agricultural administrators, men about to retire from management positions, hospital maintenance personnel, manufacturing supervisors, nurses, food handlers, military officers, engineers, scientists, housekeepers, teachers, technicians, female assemblers, accountants, Finnish foremen, and Hungarian engineers.

They were asked what job events had occurred in their work that had led to extreme satisfaction or extreme dissatisfaction on their part. Their responses are broken down in the exhibit into percentages of total "positive" job events and of total "negative" job events. (The figures total more than 100% on both the "hygiene" and "motivators" sides because often at least two factors can be attributed to a single event; advancement, for instance, often accompanies assumption of responsibility.)

To illustrate, a typical response involving achievement that had a negative effect for the employee was, "I was unhappy because I didn't do the job successfully." A typical response in the small number of positive job events in the Company Policy and Administration grouping was, "I was happy because the company reorganized the section so that I didn't report any longer to the guy I didn't get along with."

As the lower right-hand part of the exhibit shows, of all the factors contributing to job satisfaction, 81% were motivators. And of all the factors contributing to the employees' dissatisfaction over their work, 69% involved hygiene elements.

EXHIBIT 1
Factors Affecting Job Attitudes, as Reported in 12 Investigations

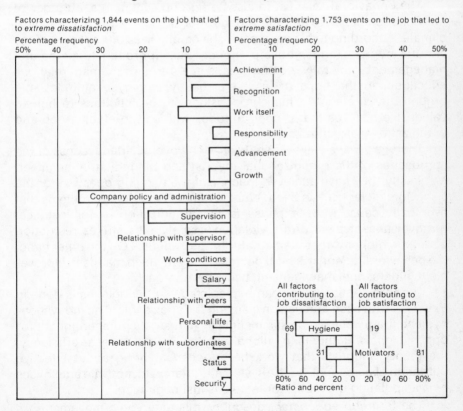

439

Eternal Triangle

There are three general philosophies of personnel management. The first is based on organizational theory, the second on industrial engineering, and the third on behavioral science.

The organizational theorist believes that human needs are either so irrational or so varied and adjustable to specific situations that the major function of personnel management is to be as pragmatic as the occasion demands. If jobs are organized in a proper manner, he reasons, the result will be the most efficient job structure, and the most favorable job attitudes will follow as a matter of course.

The industrial engineer holds that man is mechanistically oriented and economically motivated and his needs are best met by attuning the individual to the most efficient work process. The goal of personnel management therefore should be to concoct the most appropriate incentive system and to design the specific working conditions in a way that facilitates the most efficient use of the human machine. By structuring jobs in a manner that leads to the most efficient operation, the engineer believes that he can obtain the optimal organization of work and the proper work attitudes.

The behavioral scientist focuses on group sentiments, attitudes of individual employees, and the organization's social and psychological climate. According to his persuasion, he emphasizes one or more of the various hygiene and motivator needs. His approach to personnel management generally emphasizes some form of human relations education, in the hope of instilling healthy employee attitudes and organizational climate which he considers to be felicitous to human values. He believes that proper attitudes will lead to efficient job and organizational structure.

There is always a lively debate as to the overall effectiveness of the approaches of the organizational theorist and the industrial engineer. Manifestly they have achieved much. But the nagging question for the behavioral scientist has been: What is the cost in human problems that eventually cause more expense to the organization — for instance, turnover, absenteeism, errors, violation of safety rules, strikes, restriction of output, higher wages, and greater fringe benefits? On the other hand, the behavioral scientist is hard put to document much manifest improvement in personnel management, using his approach.

The three philosophies can be depicted as a triangle, as is done in *Exhibit 2*, with each persuasion claiming the apex angle. The motivation-hygiene theory claims the same angle as industrial engineering, but for opposite goals. Rather than rationalizing the work to increase efficiency, the theory suggests that work be *enriched* to bring about effective utilization of personnel. Such a systematic attempt to motivate employees by manipulating the motivator factors is just beginning.

The term *job enrichment* describes this embryonic movement. An older term, job enlargement, should be avoided because it is associated

EXHIBIT 2
"Triangle" of Philosophies of Personnel Management

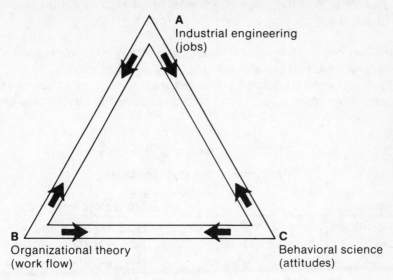

A
Industrial engineering
(jobs)

B
Organizational theory
(work flow)

C
Behavioral science
(attitudes)

with past failures stemming from a misunderstanding of the problem. Job enrichment provides the opportunity for the employee's psychological growth, while job enlargement merely makes a job structurally bigger. Since scientific job enrichment is very new, this article only suggests the principles and practical steps that have recently emerged from several successful experiments in industry.

Job Loading

In attempting to enrich an employee's job, management often succeeds in reducing the man's personal contribution, rather than giving him an opportunity for growth in his accustomed job. Such an endeavor, which I shall call horizontal job loading (as opposed to vertical loading, or providing motivator factors), has been the problem of earlier job enlargement programs. This activity merely enlarges the meaninglessness of the job. Some examples of this approach, and their effect, are:

- Challenging the employee by increasing the amount of production expected of him. If he tightens 10,000 bolts a day, see if he can tighten 20,000 bolts a day. The arithmetic involved shows that multiplying zero by zero still equals zero.

- Adding another meaningless task to the existing one, usually some routine clerical activity. The arithmetic here is adding zero to zero.

- Rotating the assignments of a number of jobs that need to be enriched. This means washing dishes for a while, then washing silverware. The arithmetic is substituting one zero for another zero.

- Removing the most difficult parts of the assignment in order to free the worker to accomplish more of the less challenging assignments. This traditional industrial engineering approach amounts to subtraction in the hope of accomplishing addition.

These are common forms of horizontal loading that frequently come up in preliminary brainstorming sessions on job enrichment. The principles of vertical loading have not all been worked out as yet, and they remain rather general, but I have furnished seven useful starting points for consideration in *Exhibit 3*.

EXHIBIT 3

Principles of vertical job loading

Principle	Motivators Involved
A. Removing some controls while retaining accountability	Responsibility and personal achievement
B. Increasing the accountability of individuals for own work	Responsibility and recognition
C. Giving a person a complete natural unit of work (module, division, area, and so on)	Responsibility, achievement, and recognition
D. Granting additional authority to an employee in his activity; job freedom	Responsibility, achievement, and recognition
E. Making periodic reports directly available to the worker himself rather than to the supervisor	Internal recognition
F. Introducing new and more difficult tasks not previously handled	Growth and learning
G. Assigning individuals specific or specialized tasks, enabling them to become experts	Responsibility, growth, and advancement

A Successful Application

An example from a highly successful job enrichment experiment can illustrate the distinction between horizontal and vertical loading of a job. The subjects of this study were the stockholder correspondents employed by a very large corporation. Seemingly, the task required of these carefully selected and highly trained correspondents was quite complex and challenging. But almost all indexes of performance and job attitudes were low, and exit interviewing confirmed that the challenge of the job existed merely as words.

A job enrichment project was initiated in the form of an experiment with one group, designated as an achieving unit, having its job enriched by the principles described in *Exhibit 3*. A control group continued to do its job in the traditional way. (There were also two "uncommitted" groups of correspondents formed to measure the so-called Hawthorne Effect —that is, to gauge whether productivity and attitudes toward the job changed artificially merely because employees sensed that the company was paying more attention to them in doing something different or novel. The results for these groups were substantially the same as for the control group, and for the sake of simplicity I do not deal with them in this summary.) No changes in hygiene were introduced for either group other than those that would have been made anyway, such as normal pay increases.

The changes for the achieving unit were introduced in the first two months, averaging one per week of the seven motivators listed in *Exhibit 3*. At the end of six months the members of the achieving unit were found to be outperforming their counterparts in the control group, and in addition indicated a marked increase in their liking for their jobs. Other results showed that the achieving group had lower absenteeism and, subsequently, a much higher rate of promotion.

Exhibit 4 illustrates the changes in performance, measured in February and March, before the study period began, and at the end of each month of the study period. The shareholder service index represents quality of letters, including accuracy of information, and speed of response to stockholders' letters of inquiry. The index of a current month was averaged into the average of the two prior months, which means that improvement was harder to obtain if the indexes of the previous months were low. The "achievers" were performing less well before the six-month period started, and their performance service index continued to decline after the introduction of the motivators, evidently because of uncertainty over their newly granted responsibilities. In the third month, however, performance improved, and soon the members of this group had reached a high level of accomplishment.

Exhibit 5 shows the two groups' attitudes toward their job, measured at the end of March, just before the first motivator was introduced, and again at the end of September. The correspondents were asked 16 questions, all involving motivation. A typical one was, "As you see it, how many opportunities do you feel that you have in your job for making worthwhile contributions?" The answers were scaled from 1 to 5, with 80 as the maximum possible score. The achievers became much more positive about their job, while the attitude of the control unit remained about the same (the drop is not statistically significant).

EXHIBIT 4

Shareholder Service Index in Company Experiment
(Three-month, cumulative average)

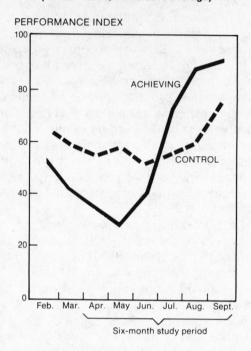

EXHIBIT 5

Changes in Attitudes Toward Tasks in Company Experiment
(Changes in mean scores over six-month period)

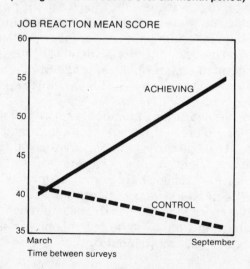

How was the job of these correspondents restructured? *Exhibit 6* lists the suggestions made that were deemed to be horizontal loading, and the actual vertical loading changes that were incorporated in the job of the achieving unit. The capital letters under "Principle" after "Vertical

EXHIBIT 6

Enlargement vs. Enrichment of Correspondents' Tasks in Company Experiment

Horizontal loading suggestions (rejected)	Vertical loading suggestions (adopted)	Principle
Firm quotas could be set for letters to be answered each day, using a rate which would be hard to reach.	Subject matter experts were appointed within each unit for other members of the unit to consult with before seeking supervisory help. (The supervisor had been answering all specialized and difficult questions.)	G
The women could type the letters themselves, as well as compose them, or take on any other clerical functions.	Correspondents signed their own names on letters. (The supervisor had been signing all letters.)	B
All difficult or complex inquiries could be channeled to a few women so that the remainder could achieve high rates of output. These jobs could be exchanged from time to time.	The work of the more experienced correspondents was proofread less frequently by supervisors and was done at the correspondents' desks, dropping verification from 100% to 10%. (Previously, all correspondents' letters had been checked by the supervisor.)	A
The women could be rotated through units handling different customers, and then sent back to their own units.	Production was discussed, but only in terms such as "a full day's work is expected." As time went on, this was no longer mentioned. (Before, the group had been constantly reminded of the number of letters that needed to be answered.)	D
	Outgoing mail went directly to the mailroom without going over supervisors' desks. (The letters had always been routed through the supervisors.)	A
	Correpondents were encouraged to answer letters in a more personalized way. (Reliance on the form-letter approach had been standard practice.)	C
	Each correspondent was held personally responsible for the quality and accuracy of letters. (This responsibility had been the province of the supervisor and the verifier.)	B, E

loading" refer to the corresponding letters in *Exhibit 3*. The reader will note that the rejected forms of horizontal loading correspond closely to the list of common manifestations of the phenomenon.

STEPS TO JOB ENRICHMENT

Now that the motivator idea has been described in practice, here are the steps that managers should take in instituting the principle with their employees:

1. Select those jobs in which (a) the investment in industrial engineering does not make changes too costly, (b) attitudes are poor, (c) hygiene is becoming very costly, and (d) motivation will make a difference in performance.

2. Approach these jobs with the conviction that they can be changed. Years of tradition have led managers to believe that the content of the jobs is sacrosanct and the only scope of action that they have is in ways of stimulating people.

3. Brainstorm a list of changes that may enrich the jobs, without concern for their practicality.

4. Screen the list to eliminate suggestions that involve hygiene, rather than actual motivation.

5. Screen the list for generalities, such as "give them more responsibility," that are rarely followed in practice. This might seem obvious, but the motivator words have never left industry; the substance has just been rationalized and organized out. Words like "responsibility," "growth," "achievement," and "challenge," for example, have been elevated to the lyrics of the patriotic anthem for all organizations. It is the old problem typified by the pledge of allegiance to the flag being more important than contributions to the country — of following the form, rather than the substance.

6. Screen the list to eliminate any *horizontal* loading suggestions.

7. Avoid direct participation by the employees whose jobs are to be enriched. Ideas they have expressed previously certainly constitute a valuable source for recommended changes, but their direct involvement contaminates the process with human relations *hygiene* and, more specifically, gives them only a *sense* of making a contribution. The job is to be changed, and it is the content that will produce the motivation, not attitudes about being involved or the challenge inherent in setting up a job. That process will be over shortly, and it is what the employees will be doing from then on that will determine their motivation. A sense of participation will result only in short-term movement.

8. In the initial attempts at job enrichment, set up a controlled experiment. At least two equivalent groups should be chosen, one an experimental unit in which the motivators are systematically introduced over a period of time, and the other one a control group in which no changes are made. For both groups, hygiene should be allowed to follow its natural course for the duration of the experiment. Pre- and post-installation tests of performance and job attitudes are necessary to evaluate the effectiveness of the job enrichment program. The attitude test must be limited to motivator items in order to divorce the employee's view of the job he is given from all the surrounding hygiene feelings that he might have.

9. Be prepared for a drop in performance in the experimental group the first few weeks. The changeover to a new job may lead to a temporary reduction in efficiency.

10. Expect your first-line supervisors to experience some anxiety and hostility over the changes you are making. The anxiety comes from their fear that the changes will result in poorer performance for their unit. Hostility will arise when the employees start assuming what the supervisors regard as their own responsibility for performance. The supervisor without checking duties to perform may then be left with little to do.

After a successful experiment, however, the supervisor usually discovers the supervisory and managerial functions he has neglected, or which were never his because all his time was given over to checking the work of his subordinates. For example, in the R&D division of one large chemical company I know of, the supervisors of the laboratory assistants were theoretically responsible for their training and evaluation. These functions, however, had come to be performed in a routine, unsubstantial fashion. After the job enrichment program, during which the supervisors were not merely passive observers of the assistants' performance, the supervisors actually were devoting their time to reviewing performance and administering thorough training.

What has been called an employee-centered style of supervision will come about not through education of supervisors, but by changing the jobs that they do.

CONCLUDING NOTE

Job enrichment will not be a one-time proposition, but a continuous management function. The initial changes, however, should last for a very long period of time. There are a number of reasons for this:

- The changes should bring the job up to the level of challenge commensurate with the skill that was hired.

- Those who have still more ability eventually will be able to demonstrate it better and win promotion to higher-level jobs.

- The very nature of motivators, as opposed to hygiene factors, is that they have a much longer-term effect on employees' attitudes. Perhaps the job will have to be enriched again, but this will not occur as frequently as the need for hygiene.

Not all jobs can be enriched, nor do all jobs need to be enriched. If only a small percentage of the time and money that is now devoted to hygiene, however, were given to job enrichment efforts, the return in human satisfaction and economic gain would be one of the largest dividends that industry and society have ever reaped through their efforts at better personnel management.

The argument for job enrichment can be summed up quite simply: If you have someone on a job, use him. If you can't use him on the job, get rid of him, either via automation or by selecting someone with lesser ability. If you can't use him and you can't get rid of him, you will have a motivation problem.

FOR A MORE EFFECTIVE ORGANIZATION — MATCH THE JOB TO THE MAN

Edward E. Lawler III

Of all the ways society serves the individual, few are more meaningful than providing individuals with decent jobs. And it is not likely to be a decent society for any of us until it is for all of us.

— John Gardner, 1968.

Work can be made a more rewarding place to be and organizations can be made more effective if approaches to organizational design treat employees as individuals. This important and optimistic statement is supported by a number of recent studies; however, it is often overlooked in the national debate over employee alienation and job satisfaction, a debate that has been preoccupied with what in many ways is the least important issue: whether job dissatisfaction and alienation are increasing.

Twenty, thirty, even forty years ago, social scientists were pointing out that the way organizations and jobs are designed frequently creates dissatisfying and alienating work experiences. They were also noting such serious social consequences of work alienation and job dissatisfaction as physical illness, mental illness, alcoholism, drug abuse, and shorter life spans. A more recent concern has been that when job dissatisfaction is high, individuals do not grow and develop. And there is no doubt that because work is still dissatisfying for many, everyone in our country is worse off. Thus, we need to concentrate our energies on searching for better ways to design work organizations, rather than on debating whether the situation is worsening.

The research that I have been involved in over the past ten years on organization and job design suggests a number of approaches that organizations can take to make work more satisfying, interesting, involving, and sometimes more motivating. All of these efforts have a common aspect: They all recognize that for the work experience to be a positive, growth-producing one, the work situation must be designed to fit the differences that exist among people in their skills, needs, and abilities.

Unfortunately, many organization theorists have argued for the principle of standardization in the design of organizations. Inherent in the concept of standardization is the view that everyone should be treated the same, but treating everyone the same inevitably leads to treating some people in ways that are dissatisfying, dehumanizing, and ineffective. The reason for this is simple: Because of the differences among people, no

Reprinted, by permission of the publisher, from ORGANIZATIONAL DYNAMICS, Summer; 1974; © 1974; by AMACOM, a division of American Management Associations, New York. All rights reserved.

single way of dealing with individuals is ever the best way to deal with all or even most individuals. Further, the whole concept of treating people in a standardized, homogeneous manner runs counter to the need of many people to be treated as individuals. We know from the research that one of the greatest contributors to alienation is the collective treatment of individuals without regard for their distinctiveness and sense of unique identity. Work organizations are given to this collective treatment because they mass-produce products and frequently handle their employees in a standardized, mass-production way designed to deal with the "average" person. Dissatisfaction is an inevitable result, since very few people are average.

What we need, then, are ways of running organizations that recognize the importance of treating people differently and placing them in environments and work situations that fit their unique needs, skills, and abilities. How can this be done? It isn't easy, because the more people are treated as individuals, the more complex organizations become. But according to the data I and others have collected, there are some approaches that have already been tried and that seem to work well. I should like to share the results of this research and give some examples of how an organization can structure its practices and policies to fit the important differences that exist among individuals.

In considering ways that make work more satisfying, we must not forget that society cannot tolerate approaches that will seriously undermine the economic effectiveness of organizations in order to increase employee satisfaction. Psychologists used to believe that job satisfaction was capable of causing employees to perform better. If this were true, there would be no problem finding new work designs that would increase job satisfaction without harming organizational effectiveness. Unfortunately, my own research and that of many other psychologists show that satisfaction does not cause employees to work harder. In fact, it has a very low relationship to performance and is probably best thought of as a consequence of performance. Despite this, there is evidence that increasing the job satisfaction of employees can increase the effectiveness of organizations. Why is this so? Satisfied employees are absent less, late less, and less likely to quit. Absenteeism, turnover, and tardiness are very expensive — more costly than most realize. Recent research, for example, shows that the loss of an employee usually costs an organization ten times his or her monthly salary. Thus, because increases in employee satisfaction result in decreases in turnover, absenteeism, and tardiness, organization changes that increase job satisfaction can increase the economic effectiveness of organizations even though they do not increase motivation.

Job Design

One of the most commonly suggested cures for worker alienation and job dissatisfaction is job enrichment. It has been suggested that if we enrich people's jobs, the result will be lower absenteeism, lower turnover, less tardiness, higher productivity, higher job satisfaction, and less alienation. We now have a considerable amount of research data on the effect of job enrichment. It does, indeed, show that the average person is both happier and more effective working on an enriched job than he or she is working on the traditional, standardized, specialized, repetitive, routine job. However, as I remarked before, not everyone is average.

There are many people (at this point, we are not sure how many) who are happier working on repetitive, monotonous, boring jobs. In a recent study, for example, I found a number of telephone operators who did not react favorably to enriched jobs. The older employees, in particular, tended to prefer the more repetitive jobs because they had adjusted to them and knew how to do them well. In addition, the new design threatened to disrupt some of the comfortable interpersonal relationships they had established. Thus, any job enrichment effort that enriches the jobs of everyone in a work area or of everyone doing a particular type of work is bound to make some people less happy and less productive. Admittedly, as a rule, performance and satisfaction go up, but can we afford to engage in work redesign practices that make the work experiences of some people more negative? I don't think we can, when there is an alternative available, and in this case there often is an alternative.

The idea of an alternative is nicely illustrated by the job design approach taken in a Motorola plant where the same product is produced in two different ways — on an assembly line and on a bench where one worker puts the entire product together. This particular version of job design allows people to work on the kind of job that they are most comfortable with. Those people who prefer routine, repetitive jobs have them; those people who prefer enriched jobs have them. Originally, only a few employees chose to work on the enriched jobs; eventually, about half of the 60 workers decided to work on them. Individualizing jobs to meet the needs and abilities of the employees seemed to result in both the individuals and the organization being better off, for absenteeism and turnover went down, while product quality went up.

A similar approach has been tried out at Non-Linear Systems with good results. There, however, the employees were allowed to share the work among the members of their teams. Some teams chose to have each member produce the whole product, while others decided to have different people work on different parts of the assembly process. The result was a high degree of individualization.

My own research suggests that the kind of a solution arrived at in Motorola and Non-Linear Systems can be applied in many other situations. Job enrichment can be selectively done and can be limited to only those people who will respond positively to an enriched job. There are, however, many practical problems involved in giving individuals jobs that involve the optimal degree of enrichment for them. For example, there is the problem of who is to decide how much a given job should be enriched. Many social scientists suggest that these decisions should not be made by the individual workers and go on to suggest that individuals should be "coerced" to experience situations where higher-order needs can be satisfied (for example, enriched jobs), because unless they experience them, they won't know what they are missing. I don't think, however, that this position is correct. Our responsibility as social scientists is to provide valid data to individuals about the results of doing certain things. It is not to coerce people into certain actions that we feel are "good" for them. Forcing someone to try an enriched job is somewhat akin to arguing that a virgin should be raped because otherwise he or she cannot know what is being missed. Thus, I don't think that organizations should be defined as providing a high quality of working life only if everyone has his higher-order needs satisfied. Instead, they should be defined as providing a high quality of working life if everyone has a realistic opportunity to satisfy his higher-order needs if he wants to.

The use of work modules represents one approach to giving individuals a greater opportunity to determine the nature of their jobs. As proposed, it would divide up tasks into modules of work, each of which would last for several hours. Employees would then ask to work on a set of modules that together would constitute a day's work. So far this approach has not been tried anywhere, so it is difficult to spell out the details of how it would work. Probably the closest approximation of it that is presently operational is in the airline industry, where pilots and stewardesses request different flights and thus have some control over when and on what they work. To be effective, the use of a work module approach would have to take place in conjunction with some job enrichment activities. Otherwise, employees might be faced with choosing among modules that were all made up of simple, repetitive tasks, so that they would have no real choice. Using work modules has the very distinct advantage of letting individuals pick their work settings, thus taking into account individual needs and preferences. It also recognizes that different individuals prefer different tasks and facilitates the matching of individuals with tasks.

Fringe Benefits and Pay Systems

A clear example of where research suggests organizations can and should treat everyone in a different manner is in the area of fringe benefits. At the present time, regardless of their marital status, age, education, and so on, employees receive the same fringe benefits package — one that is designed for the hypothetical average employee. A considerable amount of research shows that the fringe benefits packages offered by most organizations are favored by only 10 percent of their employees, because, again, there are few "average" employees. To put it in a different way, given the opportunity, 90 percent of the employees would choose different fringe benefits. Despite this, most organizations continue giving everyone the same benefits. Thus, inevitably some employees receive unwanted and inadequate fringe packages, and further, they are denied the opportunity to improve them. Can this situation be changed?

Yes. People can be given the opportunity to choose fringe benefits that fit their own set of needs. Employees can be given the amount of money the organization is presently spending on their pay (salary plus fringes) and they can divide it up themselves among cash and a large number of fringe benefits. This "cafeteria" kind of plan allows the organization to control its costs, so that it ultimately spends the same amount of money as it would in the standardized fringe benefits plan. Both the organization and its employees stand to benefit if the employees receive only those fringe benefits that they desire.

First, the employees will feel that they are being paid more, because they will realize for the first time the value of the benefits they receive and will receive only those that they value. Second, working for the organization should become more attractive, because the employees will be receiving a more highly valued reward package, and this should reduce turnover and make recruiting easier. The systems division of TRW and the Educational Testing Service are among the companies that are experimenting with these flexible benefits.

It would be foolish, however, to overlook the technical problems that are involved in implementing a cafeteria plan. It is not simple to work out a choice system; there are various tax and insurance problems involved. But the experience so far of organizations that have tried it shows that these problems are solvable and worth solving. They are worth solving because this is an area where an organization can design its policies to fit the needs and desires of its employees.

It is also interesting to note that when given the chance, employees do seem to make responsible choices. Older people invest more in retirement, younger people with families get good medical protection, and so on. This finding is in notable contrast to the common but fallacious notion that if employees are given the opportunity for decision making in this area, they will make unwise choices, and therefore, organizations need to protect their employees by choosing the fringe benefits packages that are best for them.

There is another way in which pay systems can be individualized. Most organizations pay people according to the jobs they perform; thus, all people who do the same job receive the same basic pay, regardless of their skills and abilities. In short, the job is paid, rather than the person. On the other hand, several plants, including the General Foods plant at Topeka, Kansas, have successfully experimented with a way of paying people that recognizes differences among individuals in terms of their skills and abilities, that pays the person, not the job. It recognizes that the kind of work an individual may be doing at the moment does not necessarily reflect his abilities and knowledge. Thus, these companies pay people in terms of the number of jobs they are capable of doing, rather than in terms of the job they may be doing at the time. In this system, employees can increase their pay as they become able to do other jobs. An active training and job rotation plan is offered to help individuals learn new jobs and thereby increase their pay.

Although the results are just coming in, they are encouraging. First, it seems that individuals feel more fairly treated because now their individual skills and abilities are recognized and rewarded. Second, the organizations gain employees who are more versatile. The capacity to transfer employees easily allows the organization unprecedented flexibility in adjusting to market demands and to problems of absenteeism, tardiness, and turnover. It also solves some of the difficult problems that are involved when an employee must be shifted from a higher-paying job to a lower-paying job or the reverse.

Even if an organization does not go to a skill-based pay plan, it can depart from the established practice of paying all employees on the basis of the same job evaluation system. As part of a recent study of mine, employees in four work groups were given the opportunity to design their own pay plans. The result: Each group designed slightly different plans, because each had somewhat different needs. All groups decided to operate with a three-pay-grade system, but since the groups differed in skill levels their jobs needed, they set different minimum time periods for reaching the higher pay grades. The impact of this process on the employees was very positive. Satisfaction went up because the employees had a chance to design a plan that fitted their individual needs. Incidentally, the employees behaved very responsibly when given the opportunity to design their pay system. They set pay rates for themselves that were in line with the market and that management felt were fair.

Selection

There is one area in which organizations make a conscious, research-based, and often effective attempt to assure that individuals fit into the jobs and job situations where they are placed: Most organizations conduct lengthy and often well-researched selection and placement programs. They typically measure the employee's ability, background, and so on and then decide whether or not the individual can handle a particular job. This is an important process and one that often does ensure that individuals will fit and perform well in the jobs that they take. Two practices are noticeably missing, however, in the selection programs of most organizations, and as a result, misplacement and/or unsatisfying job placement frequently occurs.

First, most selection procedures ignore the issue of whether the individual will be satisfied in the job. Instead, they emphasize ability assessment in an attempt to determine whether the person can do the job. This is a serious omission in most selection programs and often leads to unsatisfying job placement and high turnover, and it subverts both organizational effectiveness and the quality of individual life.

Second, most selection programs leave out information designed to help the job applicant decide whether he can perform the job and will find it satisfying. Organizations typically place great emphasis on attracting people to apply for job openings, because they realize that only if a large number of applicants appear for a job can their selection program operate effectively. However, in their attempt to attract many applicants, they often fail to give a realistic picture of what the jobs will be like. Because the individuals do not have a good picture of what their jobs are like, they start work with unrealistic expectations and are often quickly disillusioned. The result is rapid turnover.

Several research studies have shown that this is a problem that can be solved to the benefit of all by giving individuals accurate information about the nature of the jobs. For example, one study with life insurance salesmen showed that when the applicants were given an accurate picture of all aspects of prospective jobs, they seemed to make good choices about whether to go to work for the company. They were less likely to quit and more effective than were employees who decided to come to work as life insurance agents without accurate pictures of their jobs. Another study has shown that telephone operators who were given accurate pictures of their prospective jobs were less prone to quit than those who were not and also tended to be more satisfied once they began work.

What kind of information should individuals receive? In addition to simple descriptive information about the nature of the prospective jobs and job situations, my research suggests that applicants should be supplied with: the results of job satisfaction surveys, employee descriptions of prospective supervisors, and data on turnover and grievance problems associated with a particular work setting. In addition, employers could aid the individual's decision process by feeding back the results of any psychological tests that were administered. The results of such tests are typically retained for company use to aid the organization in the selection process, but there is no reason why the results of these tests and an explanation of their implications cannot be shown to the applicant, to give him individualized information about the nature of his fit with the job environment.

Why does a realistic job preview tend to produce more satisfaction and lower turnover? The answer seems quite simple. Given accurate information, people are able to determine with some precision whether particular job situations will fit their needs and abilities. Further, they develop realistic expectations about the nature of the job and disappointment is minimized. This helps both the individual and the organization, since it reduces turnover and increases satisfaction.

Leadership

Most organizations spend considerable amounts of money training managers to use particular leadership styles. Psychologists have been active in this kind of training and have argued that more democratic and participative leadership will increase employee satisfaction and performance. This view has been accepted by many organizations, and they have invested considerable amounts of money in training supervisors to be more democratic in their leadership styles.

The issue of how democratic management affects employees is not a new one, and there is a great deal of data about it. As a rule, participative management is more likely to produce high levels of satisfaction and motivation than is authoritarian management. Thus, when organizations change the leadership styles of their managers from highly authoritarian to move to more democratic, they often improve the performance and motivation of their employees. However, they do not improve the satisfaction and motivation of all their employees. Again, the problem is that not everyone is average.

To put the issue quite simply, our research at Michigan shows clearly that some people prefer to be directed and ordered, while others prefer self-direction and self-control. Young, well-educated employees who work on technical and high-level jobs are particularly likely to want to exercise self-control. The desire of employees to participate in decision making varies according to the type of decision. For example, most employees simply are not interested in participating in decisions that involve corporate finance, such as what kinds of bonds to issue. Individuals also differ in their abilities to participate in decision making. Some lack the mental abilities and education required to understand certain types of problems. Frequently, organizations fail to recognize these facts, and in their leadership training programs and their leadership practices an inordinately high value is placed on leaders who consistently "treat everyone the same." The concept of equal treatment is usually equated with fair and good supervision, but the research evidence suggests just the opposite. It shows that effective leadership involves individual treatment, in which the supervisor recognizes individual differences and alters his behavior accordingly. For this to be done well, supervisors must be able to diagnose situations and individuals and use the resulting information in selecting their leadership styles. Admittedly, it is not easy to do this kind of diagnosis, but it is a skill that can be developed and one that must be developed if leaders are to become more effective.

Hours of Work

One of the traditional assumptions about how organizations are best run is that everyone should come to work at the same time and leave at the same time. This assumption is congruent with the idea that standardization is important and that everyone should be treated in the same way. It is inconsistent, however, with the fact that people have different preferences about when they want to come to work and when they want to leave work. It also ignores the fact that people find themselves in different family situations, that transportation is not equally available for everyone, and that there are a number of disadvantages in having everyone arrive simultaneously, namely, overcrowding, transportation problems, and so on.

Some have suggested the four-day, 40-hour workweek as a way of improving the quality of life in organizations, but in terms of treating people as individuals, it is equally as bad as the five-day, 40-hour workweek. It, too, ignores the differences among individuals. Some people prefer the four-day, 40-hour week to the five-day, 40-hour week, but many do not. Thus, a change from the five-day, 40-hour workweek to the four-day, 40-hour workweek helps some and harms others. Again, we have the fact that many people are not average.

There is now an encouraging trend with respect to hours of work. More and more organizations are adopting flexible work hours that allow some people to come to work early and leave early and others to come late and leave late. Admittedly, there are a number of complexities in getting the approach operational. By and large, however, the companies that have tried it have found that the problems are soluble and have developed practical mechanisms for resolving them.

For example, a number of companies work with a set of core hours, perhaps four a day, when everyone is present, so that necessary meetings, communications, and so on can take place. Others have developed log books in order to tell when people will be at work so that events can be scheduled accordingly. The idea of flexible work hours can also be extended to include having individuals work weeks of different lengths. For example, some employees could work 40-hour weeks while others worked 20- or even 10-hour weeks. This would make it possible for husbands and wives to share a job, and it would recognize that while the 40-hour week is accepted by most, it certainly doesn't fit everyone's needs. Installation of the module concept, incidentally, could make it much easier to vary working hours, since individuals could sign up for as many modules as they wanted.

Flexible work hours and similar experiments will undoubtedly spread, because not only do they cater to individual preferences with regard to hours of work, but they also do much to eliminate tardiness — a continual headache in most organizations. In short, many organizations can individualize their employees' work hours. This is not a panacea for all the problems of job satisfaction and alienation, but it is one more way that organizations can adapt themselves to the needs and desires of individuals.

Summary and Conclusions

Organizations can change their job designs, selection, evaluation, pay, work hours, and leadership styles in order to adapt to the needs of individuals and thereby create working environments that will be more effective, satisfying, motivating, and less alienating. Of course, not all organizations can change all of these aspects in order to create better individual-organization fits. It is also clear that not one of these practices in and of itself is going to solve the problems of alienation, dissatisfaction, and low motivation. Taken together, though, and combined with a real concern for the individuality of each employee, they can make a contribution.

It is to be hoped that the practices suggested here are just the forerunners of other, soon to be articulated, practices that will allow further individualization. In my view, it is crucial that we develop more ways for organizations to adapt to the unique needs of each employee, to provide more acceptable job situations and thereby reduce organizational ineffectiveness. It should also help make work a place where people can grow and develop. If our sense of social responsibility is not sufficient to prompt us to action, simple self-interest should be, for making work better for some can make society better for all.

SELECTED BIBLIOGRAPHY

A book of mine, *Behavior in Organizations* (McGraw-Hill, 1975), with L. W. Porter and J. R. Hackman, extensively considers the role of individual differences in determining behavior in organizations. It is a general text that is written for beginning students and managers.

The best summary of the work on job design that is available is a book by Louis Davis and James Taylor, *The Design of Jobs* (Penguin, 1972). It contains most of the important articles that have been written on job design. Robert Kahn described the work module approach in a *Psychology Today* article ("The Work Module — A Tonic for Lunchpail Lassitude," 1973, Vol. 6, No. 44).

Most of the behavioral research on pay is reviewed in my book *Pay and Organizational Effectiveness* (McGraw-Hill, 1971). This book considers the relevant theory research and practice and can be read by a manager who has a background in either pay administration or behavioral science. A classic book in this area is W. F. Whyte's *Money and Motivation* (Harper, 1955). It does a nice job of highlighting how individuals differ in their reactions to pay.

Marvin Dunnette's book *Personnel Selection and Placement* (Wadsworth, 1966) presents a good discussion of the issues involved in dealing with individual differences in the selection process. An article by J. Wanous, "Effects of a Realistic Job Preview on Job Acceptance, Job Attitudes, and Job Survival" (*Journal of Applied Psychology,* Vol. 58, No. 3), provides a good discussion of the use of realistic job previews.

A recent book by Victor Vroom and P. Yetton, *Leadership and Decision Making* (University of Pittsburgh Press, 1973), deals with how and why leadership styles should be varied according to situations. It is research-oriented but can be read by the nonprofessional.

SECTION EIGHT
SUPPORT
Overview

As with each of the other leader-manager factors discussed in this volume, the very meaning of *support* is being transformed by the needs of the new business environment.

Until recently, managers could reasonably think of their support responsibilities as being limited to providing direct help to their subordinates, when needed. From this point of view, support hardly warranted much attention, since what seemed to be required was common sense personal relations and task assistance. In fact most managers shied away from learning support skills as they appeared "soft" and seemed to ask managers to get involved in the personal or emotional lives of their people. This perspective of benign neglect is reflected in the management literature; very little outside of the area of communications has been written about the nature of support in a business environment.

Today, the changing context of business requires a reexamination of support as a critical management function. The meaning of the question "Where do we go for help?" has taken on important new dimensions. In part, the elevation of support as a central management function is due to such changes as:

1. The issues facing most middle-level work units of an organization today have become so complex that managers can no longer assume that either they or their people know everything they need to know to accomplish their responsibilities with quality. Help is an ongoing need and it must come from diverse sources, both inside and outside the work unit.

2. Companies must learn to encourage creativity and innovation, particularly among their middle-level work units. Experienced managers will increasingly be responsible for managing innovative environments that encourage people to take responsible risks.

3. Continuous change requires the capacity to make increasingly responsive adjustments. Managers must insure that the system of procedures and structures within which their people work is flexible and adaptive.

The source of help today clearly is no longer solely the manager or even necessarily within the work unit — it is wherever it happens to be, inside or outside the unit. The management of support will progressively require the manager to create and sustain organizational conditions

461

which empower people to seek and find the help they need in order to accomplish the changing ends expected of them.

The two articles in this section each focus on an issue central to this emerging support role. In "Managing the Paradox of Organizational Trust," Louis B. Barnes explores the central role of the manager in establishing and sustaining an environment that can deal with increased complexity. Rosabeth Moss Kanter is concerned with the conditions that facilitate innovation and change in organizations in her contribution, "Empowerment."

For Barnes, rigid patterns of behavior are the critical nemeses in an organization's ability to handle complexity. The most important behavior patterns in this regard are those that expose the organization's fundamental stance toward trust.

According to Barnes, the manager is the key factor in determining a work unit's pattern of behavior related to trust. Managers, like everyone else, act on the basis of underlying assumptions, and over time, those actions inevitably establish a self-fulfilling behavior pattern. Barnes explores how the lack of trust in a work unit is generally a function of three interrelated management assumptions about how the world works:

1. That important work-related issues inevitably fall into opposing camps (either/or decisions).

2. That hard data is always better than soft ideas.

3. That the world is dangerous and one must always be on guard.

Together these assumptions, when continually acted upon, serve to limit options, build up negative future expectations, and generally establish a rigid pattern of behavior that is dominated by mistrust.

The author recognizes that the roots of these assumptions are established very early in childhood. However, he argues that whether they are acted upon in an automatic, unconscious way is primarily a matter of self-management. A manager can learn to become aware of these assumptions and begin to treat new situations that confront him or her consciously.

Barnes argues that managers who intend to establish an effective, trustworthy work-unit environment must learn to do several things:

1. Become conscious choosers of their actions in new situations rather than automatically react on the basis of old beliefs.

2. Take a position of tentative trust in facing new situations.

3. Work from "and/also" rather than "either/or" expectations.

4. Be open, inquiring, and caring with respect to interpreting information.

Together, according to Barnes, these skills permit managers to take "paradoxical action" and thereby keep the patterns of behavior in their work unit open and fresh.

Rosabeth Moss Kanter is concerned with the distribution of power in organizations. In particular, she is interested in what makes power more widely accessible in some highly innovative organizations. Kanter thinks of organizational "power tools" as consisting of three basic commodities that can be invested in action. These commodities are:

1. *Information*: data, technical knowledge, political intelligence, expertise.

2. *Resources*: funds, materials, space, time.

3. *Support*: endorsement, backing, approval, legitimacy.

The role of the manager is to assure that there is an active marketplace for these commodities in his or her organization. To do this, the author proposes that the following conditions be established:

1. *Open communications systems* to facilitate face-to-face communications and access across organizational segments.

2. *Network forming arrangements* to provide people with opportunities to build a network of relationships with peers both within and outside the work unit.

3. *Decentralization of resources* that makes it possible for people to access resources locally.

Kanter argues that these conditions are particularly critical to establish at middle-management levels of organizations that desire to become more innovative. These are the conditions that make "help" available today and which provide, at least partially, an operational definition of support in the new business environment.

MANAGING THE PARADOX OF
ORGANIZATIONAL TRUST

Louis B. Barnes

Several years ago, the largest subsidiary in a giant international complex found itself with a new president, a bright young marketing manager named Jones from one of the subsidiary's divisions. Jones soon let it be known that the old days of delegation were over and that he was going to create a strong, centralized head office with himself as its driving force. On more than one occasion, Jones made it clear that he had little respect for either the previous management or some of the managers still in the company. He introduced specific cost, measurement, and reporting procedures; a number of managers and staff members were fired, took early retirement, or resigned. As Jones set his policies in motion, other old-timers were immobilized or by-passed.

Jones spent a good deal of time in the field, and every three months he took a team of headquarters staff with him to area plan-and-review sessions that cynics labeled "jump for Jonesie" shows, "rock 'em, sock 'em" binges, and "point the finger" days. Along with his periodic outbursts about the shortcomings of certain subordinates or reports, Jones's tough-spoken demands for tight budgets, detailed action plans, and short-term goals set the tone for management meetings.

As time went on, opposition to Jones appeared within both the company and the parent organization, but it remained underground because his company's measurable benefits seemed to outweigh the obvious costs of his behavior. The performance figures looked good. With increased inflation, cost cutting, and rising demand, the so-called bottom line showed the company to be very successful. Balanced against these positive indicators, high dissatisfaction, high turnover, postponed investments, and little evidence of succession planning all seemed negligible.

After several long, serious strikes in three of the subsidiary's key plants, however, top management finally became concerned with Jones's hard-line approach. Shortly after the last strike, senior managers in the parent company began to review their options — and about a year later replaced Jones with a senior manager from the parent company. No one within the subsidiary appeared capable of taking the job at that time.

This story may sound dramatic, but I suggest that the Manager Joneses of the world are legion. Sometimes the battle lines are more subtly drawn than in this case; sometimes managers are the masters and sometimes the victims, but almost invariably at one time or another managers fall into Jones-like situations.

Like all people, managers behave according to their assumptions of how the world works — whether, for instance, it is a kind or a cruel place. Disastrous behavior such as Jones's follows when a manager's assumptions about the world establish a dangerous and self-defeating pattern.

The pattern develops, I believe, when managers hold three simple assumptions that, in combination, prevent trust from forming. Even though managers like Jones will state that it is trust more than either power or hierarchy that really makes an organization function effectively, these same managers all too often find themselves operating in and sometimes creating an atmosphere of pervasive *mis*trust in their companies.

Using Manager Jones as representative of all of us at times, I want to explore this mistrust — so subtle, so prevalent, and yet so unproductive — and then to describe how the three assumptions people make daily can create this destructive atmosphere.

I will briefly describe the three "harmless" assumptions, show how they appear in a managerial context, and then explore some alternative approaches and assumptions. In presenting these alternatives, I argue in favor of two fragile but important concepts — namely, tentative trust and paradoxical action.

Too often we fail to go beyond our initial reactions in order to look at an issue's deeper levels and thus avoid the time and the tension that such work entails. Then, as Manager Jones did, later on we pay the price. To see how this happens, let's begin with the assumptions as Manager Jones might have experienced them.

THREE HARMLESS ASSUMPTIONS

The three assumptions are, first, that important issues naturally fall into two opposing camps, exemplified by either/or thinking; second, that hard data and facts are better than what appear to be soft ideas and speculation, exemplified in the "hard drives out soft" rule; and finally, that the world in general is an unsafe place, exemplified by a person's having a pervasive mistrust of the universe around him or her. These assumptions can often be useful and necessary. Separately, they seem so natural that we don't see them as harmful. As a matter of fact, we often see them as healthy; in certain situations, for instance, we think only a fool would *not* be mistrustful.

Nevertheless, when managers combine all three assumptions at the same time, which we do very naturally as well, the assumptions may benefit us in the short run — but be very destructive in the long. Now let's look at them in turn.

Do or Die

A person holds assumption 1 when *either/or* thinking dominates choices and decision making. Like the rest of us, Manager Jones had to turn complex sets of alternatives into useful prime choices. Under conditions of uncertainty, Jones relied on experience and instinct to help him limit the alternatives, make choices, and then implement them. Using analysis and discussion, managers typically narrow their alternatives into such options as make or buy, act or react, centralize or decentralize, expand or retrench, and reward or punish.

But the problem with this way of thinking is more serious than that it limits options. People often become emotionally attached to a symbol or choice and see it as either good or bad. We set up the alternatives as adversaries and turn them into unions *versus* management, blacks *versus* whites, government *versus* business, theory *versus* practice, and us *versus* them (whoever they are). Despite Lincoln's reminder that a house divided against itself cannot stand, American tradition and history have taught us to separate issues into their two most obvious alternatives —and then to pronounce one of them "good" and the other "bad." It seems that part of what Manager Jones created in those around him was this either/or mentality. By his own definition, his choices were good. Others were to be criticized and attacked.

Even when it occurs, however, either/or thinking by itself is not destined for disaster. The real problem is that the assumption builds certain future expectations. For Manager Jones, these expectations prevented him from stepping outside of each either/or dichotomy to look again at the ingredients — to find an unseen paradoxical alternative or ingenious recombination. In Jones's case, for instance, he never sought to reintegrate the old-timers into his new management scheme. Because he saw them as having caused the problems, that would have seemed absurd at the time. Yet, paradoxically, they might have helped Jones overcome his subsequent turnover, morale, and strike problems.

Other examples of either/or ingredients illustrate the problem as well as a resolution. For example:

- For several generations now, people have viewed the management versus union dichotomy as a fact of life. One is good while the other is bad, depending on your perspective. If not enemies, the two have been at least antagonistic adversaries bound mainly by a legal contract. In many companies, this view leads to daily frictions between workers and supervisors. These can escalate into formal grievances. Under such conditions, even honest cooperative gestures are seen as dishonest or hostile. In one company, management tried to start some "improvement meetings" with workers. But because of past union-management experiences, the meetings were doomed before they started.

  Yet in other companies, workers and managers have bargained hard on some issues and achieved shop floor cooperation on others, beyond the legalities of the contract. They were both bound to but not always limited by the contract.

Are these latter situations an exception to the rule? Probably they are, simply because the rule in most companies seems based on the more prevalent either/or assumption and its traditions. It is easier to take a firm position and act as if us or them, right or wrong, and good or bad were the major real-life options. But again, the villain here is not the either/or assumption itself. It is the distortion that occurs when people assume they need to defend their positions while also adopting the other two assumptions.

A Bird in the Hand . . .

Assumption 2 is the principle that *hard is better than soft*, which means that hard drives out soft. We saw it in Jones; we see it in ourselves. The idea goes as follows. Once Jones began to make either/or choices, he almost "had to" show their superiority and defend them; at least, that's the way he saw it. And to defend his position, he needed hard facts rather than soft feelings, hard numbers rather than soft words, and hard data and concrete steps rather than abstract possibilities. It meant short-term action taking rather than long-term planning, "tell it like it is" statements rather than speculative explorations.

Consequently, Jones became a tough wheeler-dealer manager who needed to win out over the other side. As "they" became the opposition, having the best defense meant having a good offense. In Jones's case, as in many of our own situations, it is easy to see how the dangerous link between the first and second assumptions gets fused.

Holding this second assumption easily leads a person to a hard-nosed, buccaneer management style that turns doubt into action and stirs the hearts of those who idolize such uncompromising figureheads as General George S. Patton, Harold Geneen of ITT, the Ayatollah Khomeini, or the late John Wayne's macho cowboy roles. Such leaders at least *act* as if they know what they're doing. And the shoot-from-the-hip style is not restricted to management; the hard/soft assumption shows up in the hard-nosed skepticism of science and in the lawyer's quest for hard evidence. In the best competitive tradition, people who hold this assumption "get things done," despite later consequences.

Yet both proponents and opponents of hard-is-better-than-soft can make profound mistakes in its name. Both can propel an either/or position a long way toward a disaster of the extremes, as the following example shows:

- When John F. Kennedy took office in 1961, he was confronted with the CIA's plans for the Bay of Pigs invasion. Although Kennedy seemed to have early doubts about the invasion and even though a few advisers like Arthur Schlesinger, Jr., and Chester Bowles expressed reservations, Kennedy went along with the arguments for an attack as presented by Allan Dulles of the CIA, some joint chief of staff members, and other highly qualified advisers.

Schlesinger later wrote about the hard-drives-out-soft mood of those meetings in his book *A Thousand Days:* "Moreover, the advocates of the adventure had a rhetorical advantage. They could strike virile poses and talk of tangible things — fire power, air strikes, landing craft, and so on. To oppose this plan, one had to invoke intangibles — the moral position of the United States, the response of the United Nations, 'world public opinion,' and other such odious concepts.

"But just as the members of the White House Staff who sat in the Cabinet Room failed in their job of protecting the President, so the representatives of the State Department failed in protecting the diplomatic interests of the nation. I could not help feeling that the desire to prove to the CIA and the Joint Chiefs that they were not soft-headed idealists but were really tough guys too influenced State's representatives at the Cabinet table."[1]

The Bay of Pigs example illustrates the power of the hard-is-better-than-soft assumption in combination with its either/or companion. When opposing sides are formed, people feel almost compelled to choose one or the other — and to find tangible ways of defending their choices. The side that usually seems most convincing is the one that is supported by hard evidence and defended by hard tactics, which have both an intellectual and an emotional appeal for the tough-minded and the would-be tough-minded, like Jones.

The danger with people's tendencies to make hard-nosed choices is that, as in the Bay of Pigs discussions, such choices quickly acquire their own momentum. To stop the snowball — to try to reexamine the options — means violating the either/or and hard/soft assumptions, while seeming, as Schlesinger says, to be a "soft-headed idealist." As many managers know, in most tough-guy contexts it can be very hard to appear soft.

Pitting himself and his hard-line approach against both old-line practices and old-time managers, Jones exemplified the tough-guy manager. However, he personified a third assumption as well.

Nice Guys Finish Last

The third harmless assumption forms a basis for and helps contaminate the other two. It holds that the world is a dangerous place requiring that a person adopt a position of *pervasive mistrust* to survive. When held, this assumption dominates the atmosphere and blots out situational factors. Like the other two assumptions, mistrust can be very useful when our safety or well-being is at stake. On other occasions, however, our own mistrust helps set the stage for either/or thinking and hard-drives-out-soft behavior.

---

[1]Arthur W. Schlesinger, Jr., *A Thousand Days: John F. Kennedy in the White House* (Boston: Houghton Mifflin Co., 1965), p. 255.

According to those who had known him in earlier years, Manager Jones had been taunted in childhood for being weak. To avoid the appearance of weakness, he adopted an aggressive posture and an air of superskepticism, which fit his view of the world. He was bright enough to be a rising star in a company where mutual trust among managers was considered important. Jones, himself, was considered trustworthy by his superiors in the sense of being a predictable producer.

As Jones set one subordinate faction against another, however, and as hard began to drive out soft, the parent company managers saw how destructive Jones's sense of mistrust was and how absent and important the softer, more caring side of trust had become. Not surprisingly, key subordinates reciprocated Jones's lack of caring, which led them to indulge in inconsistent and unpredictable behavior. As a result, any earlier bases for organizational trust disappeared.

Jones's assumption of pervasive mistrust was reinforced by his either/or and hard-drives-out-soft viewpoints. The situation deteriorated even more as Jones's subordinates took sides and added fuel to the fires of mistrust. It took the company more than five years to move out of what was by then commonly acknowledged to be a very difficult situation. This experience suggests how much harder it is to drive out hard with soft than vice versa, even though it can be done over time. It also suggests that we should examine the tenacious roots of trust and mistrust more closely. For this, the work of Erik H. Erikson is instructive.

Although Erikson's work rests on rich clinical evidence, it seems reasonable to ask, "What do early trust-mistrust patterns have to do with managers like Jones?" In response, researchers would generally agree that we never fully conquer old anxieties or doubts; when we encounter difficult new situations, we often reexperience old tensions. Thus the early major dilemmas of the human life cycle can often return in later years when we meet new tension-filled settings and experiences.

In addition — and most important for managers — even though our earliest and most basic assumptions about trust and mistrust are formed in early infancy, they are affected by new situations and by how a person feels about the immediate situation. Consequently, the trust versus mistrust dilemma constantly confronts us as we face new situations, new people, new adversities, and even new successes.

In this fashion, much of our initial behavior in these new situations is an effort to search for, test out, and initiate a tentative sense of trust or mistrust. When other people see this initial behavior as *both* predictable and caring, they develop an expectation of future hope, which accompanies trust. Such early search behavior also invites similar responses from others.

This exchange creates the giving and getting-in-return behavior that Erikson pictures and which pervades all cultures in what sociologists call the norm of reciprocity. Its universal pattern gives us (and Jones) a way to check out and test for the presence of trust. When we try to give something, we have a chance to see what we get in return. If the exchange is unsuccessful, for whatever reason, we usually assume it is a situation in which mistrust prevails.

To further show how the trust/mistrust assumption works, though, let me briefly describe three studies by other behavioral scientists.

The first, by James Driscoll, shows how satisfaction in organizations is determined more by the degree of trust present than by either levels of participation or people's inherent trust. In other words, Driscoll suggests that with trust, the immediate environment is more important than either one's background or one's participation in decisions.[2]

The second study of trust and mistrust is Dale Zand's simulation of managerial problem solving, and the third is R. Wayne Boss's replication of Zand's study done some years later.[3] Both studies examine how high-trust and low-trust conditions affect the quality of managerial problem solving involving a company president and three vice presidents. Each study set up teams with sets of instructions; some teams' instructions were filled with high-trust assumptions, others' had low-trust assumptions. The surprising thing in these studies is how easily the simple instructions given to each set created these trust differences. Zand's instructions for the high-trust teams, all of whom were managers attending a course, read as follows (note the words I have italicized):

> You have learned *from your experience* during the past two years that *you can trust* the other members of the top management team. You and the other top managers *openly express your differences and your feelings of encouragement or of disappointment.* You and the others *share all relevant information and freely explore ideas and feelings that may be in or out of your defined responsibility.* The result has been a *high level of give and take and mutual confidence in each other's support and ability.*[4]

According to Zand, the instructions given to the low-trust groups were "worded to induce a decrease in trust." This was epitomized by the president perceiving the vice presidents as potentially competitive.

The key difference in the two sets may be the specific cues about the give-and-take reciprocity among managers. In the high-trust teams, the norms of reciprocity included expressing differences of opinion, stating feelings of encouragement and disappointment, sharing information, exploring ideas outside of one's own function, providing high give and take, and giving support. For the low-trust teams the opposite was implied.

[2]James W. Driscoll, "Trust and Participation in Organizational Decision Making as Predictors of Satisfaction," *Academy of Management Journal*, 1973, vol. 21, no. 1, p. 44.

[3]Dale Zand, "Trust and Managerial Problem Solving," *Administrative Science Quarterly*, June 1972, p. 229; and R. Wayne Boss, "Trust and Managerial Problem Solving Revisited," *Group and Organizational Studies*, September 1978, p. 331.

[4]Zand, "Trust and Managerial Problem Solving," p. 234.

Both the Zand and the Boss studies indicate that high trust was the key factor in problem-solving effectiveness. Moreover, in his replication study, Boss reports a surprising finding (italics mine):

> *The fact that trust was the overriding variable was not initially apparent to the subjects.* When participants were asked to explain the reasons for the obvious differences in team effectiveness, they offered a number of plausible explanations . . . . When told of the different instructions, the group members reacted with amazement and relief. *They were amazed that they had not perceived what seemed to them after the fact to be obvious.*[5]

What does all this tell us about the soft assumption of trust?

1. Our concerns about trust apparently begin very early and recur throughout our lives.

2. Trust seems important for both effective performance and high satisfaction.

3. Trust may be easier both to create and to destroy, under some conditions, than we have assumed (it depends on how norms of reciprocity develop and take hold).

4. Managers may gloss over the crucial role of trust and mistrust assumptions and fall back on more convenient explanations for behavior in their companies, such as personality differences and the boss's actions.

5. Perhaps most important, our assumptions of trust and mistrust come at us from both past and present situations.

We may not be able to do much about the past, but we do have some control over present and future actions. In new situations, once we question the inevitability of pervasive mistrust, then the either/or and hard/soft assumptions also stand on shakier ground. Indeed, if we question all three assumptions enough, it becomes apparent that they no longer need to combine to our detriment. But what can we use to replace them?

ALTERNATIVE APPROACHES

So far I've discussed how — even though separately each may be very useful — long-term problems arise when managers combine the three harmless assumptions. The same is true when we combine their most obvious alternatives, which, in good either/or fashion, happen to come from their exact opposites. Manager Jones would most likely reject the idea that pervasive trust (the obvious alternative to pervasive mistrust) could possibly replace his assumption. His experience has taught him otherwise. And he would surely (and with reason) reject the idea that a

[5]Boss, "Trust and Managerial Problem Solving Revisited," p. 338.

prolonged-tolerance-for-ambiguity or a soft-is-better-than-hard viewpoint is a suitable replacement for any more rigorous stance.

Even though Jones might reject these obvious alternatives, others do not. For some people, the concepts of pervasive trust, prolonged ambiguity, and soft-overwhelming-hard fit together and have great appeal. With almost religious fervor, like flower children or sensitivity training converts, they promote their causes to proclaim the new utopias. Typically, that fervor is all it takes for their more mistrustful adversaries to draw new lines and define new battlegrounds.

Ultimately, holders of opposing viewpoints emerge and throw loaded overstatements at the other side, as both parties get drawn into defending fixed positions.

Over the years the management pendulum swings back and forth from liberal to conservative, from centralization to decentralization, from harsh layoff periods to expensive benefit programs, and from severe survival controls to expanded product development and cries for creativity. A major problem is that early dialogue between the opposing viewpoints often triggers defensive thinking within each position, as happened in Jonestown, Watergate, and Iran. In each case, typically — and tragically — either/or, mistrust, and hard-drives-out-soft prevail in the short term.

At the same time, people in organizations can and do learn. What appears to be pendulum behavior isn't merely that. Opposites sometimes converge or change as they develop. Sometimes new managers and new situations phase new assumptions into old issues. Sometimes a wise, experienced manager can rise above a repeated false dichotomy and furnish the impetus for finding new approaches. Such approaches, however, require people adept at a third path, not just a middle way, as well as specific steps toward organizational trust and constructive reciprocities. To do this, managers need to abandon the three assumptions and their opposites in favor of less rigid, more creative combinations.

Things Aren't Always as They Seem

Another example, as follows, might help to illustrate how this third way can work:

- The faculty and administration of a small college were torn by argument and dissension. The veteran president had recently resigned, and a search committee had chosen a woman with a distinguished academic record as the new president. Not long after the new president arrived, the dean of faculty also resigned.

  After conferring with the executive committee of the faculty, the new president appointed a young, recently tenured faculty member as the acting dean of faculty. She also announced three short-term goals: improving the enrollment picture, improving the financial situation, and building new trust. She resisted strong pressures to produce a specific "mission" statement, saying that as soon as she did, it would polarize the college community into those who agreed with the statement and those who didn't. She also chose to keep the new dean of faculty as an acting dean so that he could be tested in his new role while she and the faculty learned to work with him and with each other.

During their first year of working together, the new president and the acting dean took supportive but active roles in faculty discussions, helped to pass legislation that greatly simplified the cumbersome committee structure, improved the enrollment and financial pictures, and tried to strengthen faculty work relationships.

Specifically, the new dean worked hard to reinvolve a number of senior faculty members who were described by others as "burned out" and "losers" of earlier faculty battles. He did this by going to them for advice on important matters, frequently seeking them out in their offices, refusing to let them withdraw, helping them to get money for such mundane tasks as manuscript typing and library research, sending them to conferences on innovative practices in their own fields, asking them to chair short-term task forces, and seeking and finding financial help for them to start new research.

At the start of the second year of the acting dean's appointment, the president still refused to appoint him as the permanent dean until the official search committee was set up and made its own report and recommendation. The acting dean agreed: "I have everything to gain by not having the official title and authority. This way I can still get help from everyone and don't have to act like an official dean." Nevertheless, within a few months a search committee did recommend that his title be made official.

A number of knowledgeable sources have since reported that the college is progressing excellently.

As managers, the new president and her acting dean posed a puzzle to most of their constituents. She was new, an outsider, and wouldn't take a firm position on educational policy; he was young and had little administrative experience. In an institution where protocol, tradition, and gestures of strong leadership had been important, neither administrator leaned on them. Where mistrust had been rampant, she set out to assume and to build trust. In an effort to demonstrate that there was still leadership in the faculty ranks as well, he set out to revitalize burned-out faculty members.

In effect, the president and the dean refused to adopt either set of simple hard or soft assumptions. Instead they assumed a condition of tentative trust and worked toward a set of *and/also* rather than either/or expectations. They did this by behaving in ways that explored, listened, and confronted while exemplifying care for the school and its people. In effect they began reciprocities that could lead to organizational trust.

In doing so, the president and dean created a sense of shared hope for the future. Both gave ample evidence of caring for the school and its individual members. After identifying a set of crucial problems — enrollment, finances, trust, a demoralized faculty, little support for faculty projects, and low student and faculty initiative — both confronted them. As new leaders, they worked on old issues in new ways and surprised some people. They did not initially set forth a master plan or mission. She chose a relatively inexperienced person as dean. They both tried to build and rebuild faculty leadership instead of drawing attention to their own. And even after the acting dean had convinced the faculty of his competence, the president refused to push for his permanent appointment until the faculty also took responsibility for it.

As a result, the either/or power struggles that had existed between the previous administration and the faculty moved toward a set of and/also expectations. The new administration, the senior faculty, the junior faculty, the students, and the subfactions built a new leadership network where the quality of students rose, student turnover and attrition declined, programs expanded, and finances improved. Paradoxically, the president and dean accomplished the expected, or hoped-for, results by creatively pursuing the unexpected — at least in the eyes of many constituents.

These seemingly inappropriate about-faces are what I call paradoxical actions. In using the word *paradox* in this way, I'm borrowing from philosopher W. V. Quine's notion that paradox is "any conclusion that at first sounds absurd but that has an argument to sustain it," although these arguments are often buried, ignored, or brushed over quickly.[6] Paradoxical actions are the "absurd" steps, such as listening hard to the other person when one is trying to win an argument, that break up and bridge false dichotomies. They create working links toward trust where there were few or none before.

Paradoxical Actions . . .

The mysteriousness of paradox has fascinated poets, scientists, philosophers, and laymen for thousands of years. Paradoxical puzzles can both pose unanswerable questions and lead to insightful creative answers; Kierkegaard called paradox the "source of the thinker's passion." The reconciliation of apparent contradictions underlies some of the most truly creative discoveries of science, not to mention most religions, while the suggested unity of opposites permeates the works of great writers, like O'Neill and Conrad. Most important, partly because it is

[6]W. V. Quine, *The Ways of Paradox* (Cambridge: Harvard University Press, 1976), p. 1.

based on an unfamiliar logic or rationale, a paradox's true workings always seem to be just beyond our understanding.

Once we see these same paradoxical situations as and/also propositions rather than either/or contradictions, the reconciliations seem relatively obvious. That awareness, though, doesn't always help us find the underlying unities the next time we face a set of apparent opposites. Manager Jones is not the only one who finds it difficult to break old reciprocities or the patterns that reinforce them. Sometimes, however, change requires the very opposite of what appears to be logically appropriate behavior.

At the same time, paradoxical actions are not foreign to many a modern manager. To buy when others are selling, to ask questions when others expect answers, or to give new autonomy when subordinates expect tighter controls are all actions that make sense under certain conditions.

In a sense, these real and theoretical examples highlight the almost unnoticed role of paradox in organizational behavior. In similar fashion, I suspect, most readers overlook the crucial role that paradox plays in their own more creative actions. And yet, acting paradoxically constitutes one way to get beyond tentative trust rather than adopting the extremes of pervasive trust or pervasive mistrust.

Likewise, a manager who avoids either/or thinking or its mushy opposite, prolonged ambiguity, must consciously adopt an and/also viewpoint whereby ingredients are kept separate but are not assumed to be in conflict. Finally, and most difficult, managers need to replace the hard versus soft behavior with paradoxical actions that *cope* with new information, *confront* important discrepancies, and *care* for individual people and issues. The goal is not to do one or the other; it is to weave them into a pattern of separate behaviors that sets the basis for new reciprocal patterns.

. . . and Norms of Reciprocity

Earlier, I suggested that the fragile toughness of trust is a crucial factor in blending extremist hard- and soft-line assumptions into an organizational bonding that holds a company's disparate parts together. Trust that is too tentative, emotional, and fragile will fall back into pervasive mistrust. Trust that is too tenacious, impervious, and tough becomes inflexibly shaped into a pattern of pervasive trust. Organizations with too much mistrust become overly differentiated, with people succumbing to either/or expectations and hard-drives-out-soft behavior. Organizations with too much trust become overly integrated, with people lapsing into prolonged ambiguity and soft-is-better-than-hard behavior. Both extremist patterns depend on emotions more than on data and self-awareness. Both also build up ineffective reciprocity patterns.

The three-path diagram in Exhibit 1 displays the points I've made so far plus another path that is based on the more modest assumption of

EXHIBIT 1

The Assumptions and the Patterns They Create

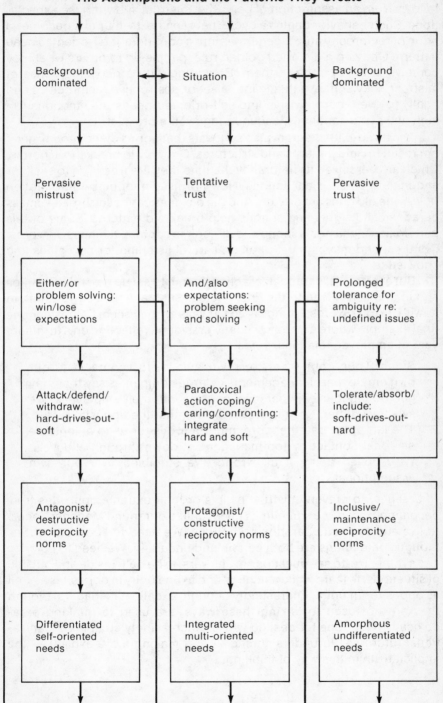

Background dominated	Situation	Background dominated
Pervasive mistrust	Tentative trust	Pervasive trust
Either/or problem solving: win/lose expectations	And/also expectations: problem seeking and solving	Prolonged tolerance for ambiguity re: undefined issues
Attack/defend/withdraw: hard-drives-out-soft	Paradoxical action coping/caring/confronting: integrate hard and soft	Tolerate/absorb/include: soft-drives-out-hard
Antagonist/destructive reciprocity norms	Protagonist/constructive reciprocity norms	Inclusive/maintenance reciprocity norms
Differentiated self-oriented needs	Integrated multi-oriented needs	Amorphous undifferentiated needs

tentative trust. The diagram also suggests that the patterns persist because people reinforce them: that is, attack/defend/withdraw behavior follows from an assumption of pervasive mistrust and win/lose expectations. Such behavior begins a cycle that repeats itself until it becomes a norm of reciprocity and degenerates into a continuing self-oriented need pattern. Obeying a distorted golden rule, people do to others what they perceive is being done to them. Beginning with a pervasive sense of mistrust, they shift eventually into a set of destructive reciprocities and finally to even more divisive and self-oriented needs. As emotions run high, the cycle continues, engendering even more mistrust.

The three-path diagram also suggests that norms of reciprocity need not result in rigid patterns and structures. One way to break those norms, which are perceived as natural by the time they are frozen, is to seek for and initiate paradoxical actions. New norms cannot be set into motion unless the old ones are broken. And the old ones cannot be broken unless paradoxical insights and actions help break old patterns. Some of this paradoxical behavior is subtle and difficult to capture. It hinges on words, gestures, and maybe most of all on careful listening for new clues and knowledge.

But even more, paradoxical actions begin to set up new relationships and in that sense lead to the unexpected. Such actions suggest that, in Lewis Carroll's words, "things aren't always as they seem." Consider one final example where a major company president, reflecting on a turbulent year of employee relations, notes:

> Some of our problems are our own fault. We lost contact with our own employees. Managements in large companies say that they get too big to stay in personal contact with their employees. We swallowed that. Now, however, I think that the opposite is true. The larger we get, the *more* important it is for us to emphasize personal contact by top management down through all levels. We've been doing it all wrong. We stumbled over our own assumptions.

In essence, to prevent mistrust beliefs or their extreme opposites from becoming frozen, we sometimes need, unlike our friend Manager Jones, to live and to create paradoxical actions. We need to know and act as though some things are both certain and uncertain. We need to polarize and synthesize, to see questions in answers, to be both inside and outside of situations, to learn while teaching, and to find unity in opposites as well as opposites in unity. Interestingly enough, excellent managers, though they are not used to talking these ways, *are* used to thinking paradoxically. Our hope for dealing with an increasingly complex organizational future lies in understanding — and making more explicit — the implicit truth in this way of thinking.

EMPOWERMENT

Rosabeth Moss Kanter

*I think it's impossible to really innovate unless you
can deal with all aspects of a problem. If you can
only deal with yolks or whites, it's pretty hard to
make an omelette.*

— Gene Amdahl,
founder of Amdahl Corporation
and Acsys, Ltd.

In organizations that support a culture of pride and change, people are
more innovative when they are not told exactly what to do and they do not
have full authority to do it anyway.

This hardly seems like a prescription for corporate success. Among
other things, it contradicts every orthodox principle about job clarity. So
clearly we have to add a second set of conditions for successful
managerial innovation: the factors which ensure that people can indeed
get the power they need to innovate.

I showed in *Men and Women of the Corporation* that people
performing tasks involving discretion, visibility, and relevance to "critical
contingencies" (pressing organizational problems) find it easier to attract
the credibility that brings power.[1] My interest then was in demonstrating
how differences in where *individuals* stood in the organization, by virtue
of their job design and location, affected their access to power. I was not
particularly concerned with how available power was in general. Here the
problem is slightly different: *What is it about some organizations that
makes power more widely accessible?* What conditions help information,
support, and resources to circulate rapidly, so that managers can "grab"
and use them?

Even to speak of "grabbing" power conjures up the wrong image, I
should hasten to say. In innovative companies, entrepreneurial managers
use a process of bargaining and negotiation to accumulate enough
information, support, and resources to proceed with an innovation. This
is not a matter of domination of others — winning over them and cutting
them out — or of monopolization of resources, but rather of coalition
building to persuade others to contribute what they can to the
innovation's launching.

At "Chipco," managers gave this process a name — "buy-in" — and
showed how it served as a control against abuses of power. The very
possibility that managers could attract power tools from peers served as a

check on their use of the power. Several Chipco managers offered these details about buy-in at a training program where the subject came up:

A working compromise is better than an optimal solution poorly implemented — this is the spirit of the buy-in . . . . The process itself, which gives access to ideas and knowledge, is beneficial . . . . Do your homework . . . . You must estimate the proper level of effort needed to get buy-in, and must get key groups and key individuals to buy in . . . . Use dual-authored memos . . . . Be clear on goals and objectives . . . . Buy-in is not a barrier . . . . It's okay to refuse to buy in, as long as your criticism is constructive. You don't need buy-in on everything . . . . It's hard to tell when you have buy-in, but it's easy to tell when you don't . . . . If you can't get buy-in of a missing actor, proceed, and be sure to get his agreement later . . . . Buy-in reduces some risk, but managers must act at some point; time matters.[2]

Buy-in was an unofficial, informal, but well-known pattern at Chipco, part of the folklore.[3] The need to get buy-in was itself a check that was designed to screen out chancy or unneeded ideas. One manager was sanguine about his inability to get others to buy in to a pet idea, explaining that if he couldn't get their agreement, it showed that he didn't deserve to proceed. Elaborations on the buy-in process involved several steps, which could be independent or part of the same power search: "preselling," "tin-cupping," "sanity checks," and "push-back." Each of these steps, as elaborated by my researcher, Ken Farbstein, reveals the checks and balances involved in the circulation of power.

From talks with others the middle manager has learned who fits into his network, who is competent, and who should be bypassed. "Preselling" the appeal of an idea to one or two key people in one-on-one meetings was done by managers in every department. Once the idea is bought into in this stage, the manager widens the coalition with further one-on-one talks with managers whose support is deemed necessary. Then a meeting is held, ostensibly to gather support, but in fact to demonstrate it and test the competence of new players. One manager explained:

After you've been around here, you know people's track records. But with new players it's harder to determine their abilities. So there are a helluva lot of meetings, probing in areas you understand to see if their understanding is the same as yours . . . we live in meetings.

The step after preselling is a "sanity check" with someone older and wiser, and possibly outside the department. The sanity check is a highly legitimate test of the reasonableness and relevance of an idea whose enactment is in progress. The next step, "tin-cupping," is the process of knocking on the doors of managers' offices and seeking money to fund a pet idea. In its purest form, a manager solicits a product-group organization for money — e.g., from manufacturing to enable a manager in engineering to build prototypes; money can also be obtained from clients or customers. (Farbstein commented in his report to me, "As any beggar can attest, tin-cuppers have cash-flow problems.") One manager explained:

> Tin-cupping from users brings in money too late to help. Tin-cupping is hard with long-range projects. You have to get the right people in, and get enough money up front . . . . It makes you susceptible to a fire elsewhere . . . . You have to expect change, ups and downs. It's like living with variable interest rates — payments may change with the prime rate . . . . You have to be optimistic . . . . You can go out of business if no one needs your product right away. The more centralized you are, the harder it is to appeal through tin-cupping . . . .

The difficulty in tin-cupping is aggravated by the combination of the oral nature of almost all agreements and the constant change in the players as they are hired and promoted. New managers must be persuaded to honor the monetary commitments of their predecessors and must be taught to tin-cup for themselves. We were told it takes six months to a year to learn tin-cupping. Since folk wisdom at Chipco says managers should move on to a new job after two years, this provides a small window of competence. Managers using buy-in did not necessarily need more money to proceed than did other managers; buy-in is therefore used more to gather support than to gather money.

"Push-back," another check on the power-acquisition process, is a generic term for an expression of disagreement, often by a manager needed on the team. Examples of push-back include telling a manager he's not the right one to bring about a given task, or giving someone a small amount of seed money and telling him to try to sell the idea. Another form of push-back, exercised at meetings, is to say "The CEO says — " or "A senior vice-president thinks — " which really means, "This group is about to do something I don't want them to, and by claiming I know that top management thinks they shouldn't, I hope to stop them."

The buy-in cycle at Chipco elaborates an informal, peer-oriented process of power gathering that would be recognizable by any corporate entrepreneur. The climate that makes this work — reaching outside of and beyond the authority of position to develop an idea for a change — is one in which power tools are locally available and those who control them can be persuaded to invest them in an innovative effort.

POWER TOOLS

Organizational power tools consist of supplies of three "basic commodities" that can be invested in action: *information* (data, technical knowledge, political intelligence, expertise); *resources* (funds, materials, space, time); and *support* (endorsement, backing, approval, legitimacy).

To use an economic analogy, it is as though there were three kinds of "markets" in which the individual initiating innovation must compete: a "knowledge market" or "marketplace of ideas" for information; an "economic market" for resources; and a "political market" for support or legitimacy.[4] Each of the "markets" is shaped in different ways by organizational structure and rules (e.g., how openly information is exchanged, how freely executives render support), and each gives the person a different kind of "capital" to invest in a "new venture."

We can hardly speak of "markets" at all, of course, where the formal hierarchy fully defines the allocation of all three commodities — for example, when money and staff time are available *only* through a predetermined budget and specified assignments, when information flows *only* through identified communication channels, and when legitimacy is available *only* through the formal authority vested in specific areas with no support available for stepping beyond official mandates. In companies where there is really no "market" for exchanging or re-arranging resources and data, for acquiring support to do something outside the formal structure — because it is tightly controlled either by the hierarchy or by a few people with "monopoly" power — then little innovative behavior is likely, as we shall see later. On the other hand, the "market" for information, resources, and support is not totally free and open in a corporation either, and even corporate entrepreneurs can find some portion of the power tools already attached to their positions, available for investing in an innovative project.

Indeed, managers who believe in their projects eagerly leverage their own staff and budget or even bootleg resources from their subordinates' budgets. But typically, innovations require a search for additional supplies, for additional "capital," elsewhere in the organization — and innovations thus are ultimately integrative, requiring connections beyond predefined categories.

Three broad aspects of the operation of innovating companies aid power circulation and power access. *Open communication systems* help potential entrepreneurs locate information that can be used to shape and sell a project. *Network-forming arrangements* help them be in a position to build a coalition of supporters. And *decentralization of resources* helps them get the resources to use to mobilize for action. These three clusters of structures and processes together create an empowering, integrative environment.

OPEN COMMUNICATION: AIRWAVES FOR INNOVATION

The innovative managers agreed that the most common roadblock they had to overcome in their accomplishment, if they faced any at all, was poor communication with other departments on whom they depended for information; at the same time, more than a quarter of them were directly aided by cooperation from departments other than their own as a critical part of their innovation. Therefore, a communication system, depending on the kind adopted by a given corporation, can either constrain or empower the effort to innovate.

The most entrepreneurial companies I looked at — the Chipco/Wang rather than the GE/Honeywell end of the innovation continuum — generally encouraged face-to-face information sharing in "real time" — that is, at the moment the issue comes up. Chipco thought this so important that it developed its own transportation system to move people between facilities, on the theory that in-person meetings work best. In other, similar companies, lack of reliance on support staffs for message taking and typing also facilitated live communication. There were departments with only one secretary for the entire twelve-person staff —cutting down on bureaucratic paper generating, if nothing else.

Examples of "open communication" systems from innovating companies stress access across segments. "Open door" policies mean that all levels can, theoretically, have access to anyone to ask questions, even to criticize. At Wang Labs I was told that there is even a policy that all meetings are open, that anyone may attend any meeting. Such norms acknowledge the extent of interdependence — that people in all areas need information from each other. Furthermore, parties and other social events, like Tandem Computer's beer parties by the company pool or Chipco's baseball games, ensure that people become known to each other outside of their job roles, facilitating contact back on the job. And sometimes the desire for keeping communication live gets absurd. For a while at a division of one of these companies, there was a paging system rather than intercoms on phones, so that people who needed to could reach one another instantly; but this caused so many distractions for "innocent bystanders" that it was finally replaced by a telephone system, which was quieter but also made instant communication less possible.

"Open communication" may mean that problems as well as successes cannot be kept secret and that public punishments occur — often of people who themselves *failed* to communicate. One marketing manager created brochures for a new division and went off to produce them without consultation with other department members. The brochure was beautiful, but "out of sync" with company standards. The division general manager called him to account for this in front of peers and upper-level managers, and his resources were frozen. The penalties for secrecy or hoarding of information serve as a warning to others.[5]

"Openness" at such companies is reflected in physical arrangements as well. There may be few "private" offices, and those that do exist are not very private. One manager had a "real" office enclosed by chest-high panels with opaque glass, but people dropped by casually, hung over the walls, talked about anything — and looked over his desk when he was not there. In general, people walk around freely and talk to each other; meetings and other work are easily interrupted, and it is hard to define "private" space. They often go to the library or conference room to "hide" to get things done, especially on "sensitive" matters like budgets.

There are two problems with "open communication" that middle managers frequently encountered, however: "underload" and overload. The "underload" problem is when people do not keep information circulating out of ignorance. The existence of such an informal system encourages people to think that everyone knows everything, and so they either fail to pass something on (on the assumption that it is known already) or take authoritative-sounding misinformation passed on through informal channels as the "truth," and do not bother to check out rumors. At Chipco, people who received unwarranted "bad press" for a supposed mistake sometimes found that the incorrect information kept moving through the system, with others rarely bothering to seek to add the other side of the story. At a facility that was visited just before an impending move of part of the staff to a new location, practically all employees seemed to have information about when and how this would happen and claimed that their information was confirmed; the only flaw was that their stories contradicted each other.

But perhaps people did not seek to correct "underload" because of information overload. Managers and professionals felt burdened by inessential communications that were simply cast upon the organization rather than targeted only to the people who should get it. "We hold a meeting where a memo would do," a manager complained, in a lament echoed frequently at the more innovating companies. (But complaints about this should be weighed against the better performance that can result from fewer filters eliminating useful data that might be viewed as "noise" for the filterer.)

Still, for all the drawbacks of open communication, from lack of privacy to slippages in its very informality, it served a very important function for the potential entrepreneur. Information and ideas flowed freely and were accessible; technical data and alternative points of view could be gathered with greater ease than in companies without these norms and systems. And thus both the "creative" and the "political" sides of innovation were facilitated.

NETWORK-FORMING DEVICES:
ENSURING A SET OF SUPPORTIVE PEERS

Corporate entrepreneurs often have to pull in what they need for their innovation from other departments or areas, from peers over whom they have no authority and who have the choice about whether or not to ante up their knowledge, support, or resources, to invest in and help the innovator.

The frequency with which peers in other areas cooperate readily, in the highly innovating companies, contrasts sharply with the absence of horizontal cooperation at "Southern Insurance" and other segmentalist organizations. For many innovators, relationships with people in other areas are essential to their success.

This was certainly true for "Bill Golden's" dramatic achievements. Working within severely constrained budgets, Golden, a marketing manager at Honeywell, met the company's sales goal in his first year and tripled it in his third year, achieving the year's goal by March. He did this by restructuring personnel and reorganizing work to separate marketing and sales, while instituting weekly staff meetings to tie the functions together. Not only were the numbers impressive, so was Golden's endurance. Four managers he characterized as "exceptionally talented" had held this job before him, and none had lasted more than a year; Golden was now in this third year.

When Golden took over, the sales people were all expected to do marketing chores, including generating new product lines, taking care of market planning, and handling constant paperwork. As a result, he said, "the operation was on its knees. Sales were off by fifty percent, and the competition was eating us alive." Golden had to manage the initial turnaround with the same people and fewer dollars, because of the financial constraints stemming from the recession; and in midyear, his budget was cut further. But he did it. And in his second year, because of the credibility of Golden's unit, he got additional resources and had the best year ever. But he never could have done it without unusual amounts of support.

Topping Golden's list of supporters was his boss, the officer who had recommended him for the job. Golden's boss backed him when he asked for it, gave him latitude, and, perhaps most important, wanted him to succeed. Golden also needed the support of the product line managers, which he got because of long-standing relationships. "They knew I would never end-run them; they had respect for me, knew I was a team player." The product line managers were initially critical of Golden's efforts. They "all wanted to get into the sales game and have client contact. Two of the three felt they knew how to sell better than I." But Golden kept stressing the fact that all of them had common problems and common goals, and he won them over. He wrote a memo defining responsibilities, establishing sales people as the first line of client contact and product line managers as the second, to which they "bought in."

Many innovators besides Golden draw on long-standing relationships with people in other areas to aid their accomplishment. One long-service GE manager turned around a production area using a new team approach that reduced both the production time and costs for his product by 50 percent. But to do this, he needed both capital funding for the introduction of modernized equipment and the freedom to move poor performers to areas where their skills could be better used without jeopardizing the project. Securing the funds turned out to be easier than getting good people as replacements, and so he used his extensive contacts with peers in other production facilities and the personnel department to speed up the process — and speed up his results.

There are four principal kinds of integrative devices that aid network formation in innovating companies: frequent mobility, including lateral moves; employment security; extensive use of formal team mechanisms; and complex ties permitting crosscutting access.

Mobility Across Jobs

Mobility — circulation of people across jobs — is a first network-facilitating condition.[6] In the more entrepreneurial companies, managers change jobs frequently, even if the moves are lateral rather than vertical. At Chipco, about two years is an average job tenure, and managers often begin to get ready for another move after eighteen months. At GE Med Systems "unusual" career moves across functions are not uncommon: e.g., from headquarters staff to district sales manager, from finance to manufacturing, from personnel to operations manager for a key product — without a technical background.

Too rapid mobility has some negative consequences for accomplishment completion, as I will demonstrate shortly, but a reasonable pace is one of the keys to the circulation of information and support. The constant moving around of parts of Chipco, for example, meant that people rather than formal mechanisms were the principal carriers of information and integrative links between parts of the system. Communication networks were facilitated, and people came to rely on a strong information flow from peers. As people moved around, they took with them the potential to establish another information node and support base for a particular network in a different corner of the organization. Knowledge about the operations of neighboring functions was often conveyed through the movements of people into and out of the jobs in those functions. As a set of managers or professionals dispersed, these people took with them to different parts of the organization their "intelligence," as well as the potential for the members to draw on each other for support in a variety of new roles.

It does not take very many series of moves for a group that has worked together to be spread around in such a way that each person in it now has a close colleague in any part of the organization to call on for information or backing. The more frequent the moves and the more widely dispersed the original group, the more widely information and support can potentially circulate.

Several things are noteworthy about mobility as a network-forming vehicle and thus an admission ticket to the power centers. Those who move clearly have an advantage in terms of network breadth over those who don't. The moving have both previous and current ties; those who remain in one place while others flow in and out may begin with the same number of direct personal ties, but they soon fall behind unless everyone in their area turns over frequently. Thus, the organization's *opportunity* structure — who moves, out of what jobs, and how often — has a direct bearing on its *power* structure because of the impact on networks.[7] Those who lack the opportunity to move at all or are confined to moving within a narrow space (as are those with nontechnical backgrounds at Chipco) or enter later, when others at their level have already made several moves, pile up handicaps with respect to network access. I am thinking particularly of women in this regard, but the condition could hold true for anyone.

If one thinks of each co-worker or colleague group as a "graduating class" spreading itself over many sectors of the organization and picking up new connections along the way, it is easy to see how the links between people created by moving people through jobs over a variety of areas can be a valuable tool in organizational communication, integration, and empowerment.* Points of view are likely to be more cosmopolitan; segmentalism is less possible. But this kind of change can also create instabilities. It is thus an opportunity, rather than a threat, to people only if it is coupled with basic overall security. And so long-term employment is the second part of the network-building apparatus that keeps power circulating in innovating organizations.

Employment Security

There is both a past and a future dimension to the employment-security issue. Looking back, one can see that over time, relationships form among mobile employees which facilitate the exchange of favors, the willingness to back one another, the agreement to commit to one another's projects. Many entrepreneurial managers are aware of the ways in which their long-standing relationships, and perhaps cashing in on a favor done in the dim past, eased communication, melted opposition, or gave them unusual access for someone in their position.

But this phenomenon is true of less innovating companies as well as the enterprising ones. It is in looking forward that the differences become apparent. The security that comes from an expectation of *continued* "place" in the organization is what creates not only an innovation-embracing outlook — higher flexibility and lower resistance to change[8] — but also a willingness to invest in the future.

Furthermore, it is not only one's own continued employment that seems certain but also that of others. If people fear tackling innovative projects that do not guarantee short-term results because they might not last, they also fear investing their support in projects of their colleagues for the same reason.

Thus, Med Systems' and Hewlett-Packard's variants on "permanent employment" helped promote cooperation; providing individual security, we can see, also fosters teamwork. At Polaroid, a company which, until recent setbacks, had made employment security a centerpiece of its

---

*This is useful, however, only if the people are moving across parts of the organization that have to work together or that have useful intelligence for each other, as generally occurred at Chipco. At GE, some of the moves took people outside, to other divisions, or brought them in from other sectors, with wide variation in net gain in information for Med Systems itself.

people-centered policies and which was small enough for mobility to occur within a narrow geographic area, middle-manager projects generally had the longest time orientation of any of the companies I examined. Those in the middle as well as at the top could afford to take a long view.

Teams

A third network-forming device is more explicit: the frequent use of integrative team mechanisms at middle and upper levels. These both encourage the immediate exchange of support and information and create contacts to be drawn on in the future. The organizational chart with its hierarchy of reporting relationships and accountabilities reflects only one reality; the "other structure," not generally shown on the charts, is an overlay of flexible, ad hoc problem-solving teams, task forces, joint planning groups, and information-spreading councils.

It is common at innovating, entrepreneurial companies to make the assignments with the most critical change implications to teams across areas rather than to individuals or segmented units: e.g., a team of mixed functional managers creating a five-year production and marketing plan for a new product. Such formal teams, not incidentally, served as models of the method that top management endorsed for carrying out major tasks and projects. Indeed, one of the managerial accomplishments at GE Med Systems involved developing a system to measure team performance and to make comparisons across teams. At Chipco, the establishment of formal interdepartmental or cross-functional committees was a common way managers sought to improve the performance of their own unit.

Collaborative and consultative rather than unilateral decisions were the expressed norm. It was expected that all managers — even those not tied into a matrixed situation — would not generally reach decisions alone, without consulting others, and company philosophies explicitly encouraged teamwork. Furthermore, because of an unexpressed but strong "norm of modesty," it seemed easier to get credit and recognition for others than for oneself. Thus, the implication was that it was beneficial to get onto other people's teams as well as getting them onto yours.

Teamwork is not just a high-tech touch. In older industries as well, practice in the use of integrative team mechanisms may account for successful problem solving and innovation. In 1981, for example, a terrible year for retailing, J.C. Penney stood out for its superior financial performance (an earnings rise of 44 percent on a mere 4.5-percent increase in sales). Success was attributed by top executives to a "new management style involving teamwork" and "creating developmental opportunities by helping people understand what happens at different levels of the organization," as the chairman put it. The mechanisms for teamwork involved a set of overlapping permanent and ad hoc committees, the groundwork for which dates at least back to the early

1970s, but which flowered fully a decade later: a management committee of the fourteen top officers; seven permanent subcommittees on key issues such as strategic planning, transitional planning, personnel, and economic affairs; and task forces on operating problems composed so that diverse points of view would be available. The leaders appeared aware that such team vehicles not only paid off in immediate problem solving but laid the foundation for a more informed, versatile, and integrated management.[9]

Note that it is not just *any* team that aids innovation but a tradition of drawing members from a diversity of sources, a variety of areas. Innovating companies seem to deliberately create a "marketplace of ideas," recognizing that a multiplicity of points of view need to be brought to bear on a problem.[10] It is not the "caution of committees" that is sought —reducing risk by spreading responsibility — but the better idea that comes from a clash and an integration of perspectives.

A General Electric Med Systems manager, for example, told me some of the reasons for this diversity on teams in his slightly rueful comment that "It is now impossible to know everything about one of our products, or to have someone work for me who does." So he accepted — he supposed — the need for so many teams and task forces. It was not clear whether specialists or generalists dominated at Med Systems — one self-described generalist said there were "too many Ph.D.s and engineers running around" and another felt like a maverick for being a generalist, but some top executives said that broad-based managers rather than technical experts were the wave of the future. Regardless, both groups were pulled together on teams to solve complex problems or make changes.

Complex Ties and Crosscutting Access

A formal structure acknowledging complex ties also forces a great deal of interunit contact between managers. Although managers nearly everywhere complained about excessive meetings, such occasions provided them with opportunities to develop formal and informal working relationships with persons from many other functions or disciplines. This encouraged coalition formation, helping managers to mobilize support or resources to complete an accomplishment. And it discouraged segmentalist overidentification with one area or divisive, polarizing politics.[11]

"Matrixed" managers at GE Med Systems typically reported to both the function where the manager had traditionally worked (generally the stronger and more direct tie) and a connected department, or the office where tasks would be integrated for a particular product (often a less direct "dotted line" tie). Although the "dotted line" relationship was often ill-defined, it benefited the manager by providing him or her with access to another powerful upper-level manager (generally a department head). Managers were thus able to use their dotted-line reports to secure support, resources, or information, gaining an additional route to vital organizational commodities. There were also important implications for sponsorship; if a manager was unable to obtain sufficient backing from his direct superior, then there was an alternative in the dotted-line boss.

Finally, the legitimacy of crosscutting access promoted the circulation of all three power commodities: resources, information, and support. By this I mean managers could go across formal lines and levels in the organization to find what they needed — vertically, horizontally, or diagonally — without feeling that they were violating protocol. They could skip a level or two without penalty. Indeed, at Chipco managers were frequently counseled that direct access was better than going through channels. At Honeywell's Defense and Marine Group, upper management was viewed by middle managers as "very open, looking for and encouraging innovating approaches," so that "anything that makes sense will be listened to by them," providing the sponsorship to bypass the usual formal channels to make an unusual move. (Six of Honeywell's twenty-seven innovators benefited from a clear, explicit top-management sponsor's making it possible for them to open needed doors quickly.)

Matrix designs, though not essential for crosscutting access, can be helpful in legitimizing it, for the organization chart shows a number of links from each position to others. There is no "one boss" to be angered if a subordinate manager goes over his head or around to another area; it is taken for granted that people move across the organization in many directions; and there are alternative sources of power. Similarly, formal cross-area and cross-hierarchy teams, as in Honeywell's parallel organization, may provide the occasion and the legitimacy for reaching across the organization chart for direct access.

DECENTRALIZATION OF RESOURCES

The last broad condition for power circulation is local access to resources.

The existence of multiple sources of loosely committed funds at local levels makes it easier for managers in innovating companies to find the money, the staff, the materials, or the space to proceed with an entrepreneurial idea. Because no one center has a monopoly on resources, there is little incentive to hoard them as a weapon; instead, a resource holder can have more influence by being one of those to *fund* an innovative accomplishment than by being a nay-sayer. Thus, managers at Chipco could go "tin-cupping" to the heads of the various product lines in their facility who had big budgets, collecting a promise of a little bit of funding from many people. This process reduced the risk on the part of all "donors" at the same time that it helped maintain the "donee's" independence.

Sheer availability of resources helps, of course. Typical organizational characteristics in other research on innovation match those of Med

Systems and Chipco: rapid growth, resource abundance, absence of "distress." Richer and more successful organizations innovate more than poorer and less successful ones, especially in technology.[12] At Chipco, for example, money never seemed to be tight; only one manager — in a financial area, to be sure — commented that there was not enough money to fund every good idea.

There are a variety of ways that innovating companies make resources accessible locally or give middle-level people alternatives to tap when seeking money or materials for projects. One is to have formal mechanisms for distributing funds outside the hierarchy. Chipco had a corporate research-and-development committee which heard proposals from any part of the company; at the time I started to meet with Chipco people, the committee had just decided to seek proposals for organizational and work process innovations as well as technical innovations. 3M has put in place "innovation banks" to make "venture capital" available internally for development projects. Honeywell's DMSG divisions have top-management steering committees guiding their organizational-change activities. The original steering committee solicited proposals quarterly from any employee for the formation of a problem-solving task team; the teams may receive a small working budget as needed.

Decentralization itself keeps operating units small and ensures that they have the resources with which to act — and thus makes it more likely that managers can find the extra they need for an innovation locally. Business analysts have commented that Chipco has avoided the problems of large companies despite its large size because it has operated as an aggregate of many small groups. Hewlett-Packard and 3M are among the companies that find a wide variety of virtues in small-scale divisions, creating new ones when existing ones get too large. 3M's gains from this strategy are impressive: in the 1970s sales and earnings rose by almost 44 percent, with a much smaller increase in employment. An emphasis on small size showed up at every level. In 1982, the company's manufacturing plants had a mean size of 270 people and a median of 115; only five had more than 1,000 employees. This enabled, in turn, a variety of other integrative mechanisms to work well: problem-solving quality circles, regular work-crew and management-group meetings, task flexibility, and lots of informal communication. It was also said that work at 3M was thought of in terms of "projects" with a usual size limit of a dozen managers and professionals.[13]

Despite employment of about 60,000, Hewlett-Packard managers often say: "We feel like a small company" and "We are responsible for our own destiny." Corporate philosophy holds that about 2,000 people and/or $100 million reaches the limit of manageability for a division, after that becoming impersonal and procedure-bound, limiting personal growth and innovation. In response, as a division reaches this ceiling, an elaborate "cloning" process takes place. A division will split along some subdivision of product lines (sometimes into two, sometimes into three divisions), moving employees into new plants, each self-contained, each more in line with company guidelines for size. This ensures the existence of small-scale, decentralized, but also highly integrated units as well as the continuity and coherence of the corporate management style and philosophy. And it keeps resources available locally.

Of course, a number of the issues with which managers deal can be handled without money at all. Only about half of the 234 accomplishments in the six-company study required new financial resources. Instead, the most common resource sought was staff time. This was also decentralized in the form of "slack" and local control: people locally available with uncommitted time, or with time that they could decide to withdraw from other endeavors to be attached to an appealing project. Because mid-level personnel, professionals, and staff experts had more control over the use of their time in the more frequently innovating companies, it was easier to find people to assist in a project, or to mobilize subordinates for a particular activity without needing constant clearances from higher-level, non-local bosses.

Most innovating managers at Chipco and Med Systems perceived a great deal of "running room" (freedom) in the course of completing their accomplishments. Of course, it is possible that these were individuals viewed by their superiors as extremely competent managers and sub-sequently given autonomy by virtue of some outstanding personal characteristics. But the extent of the pattern suggests instead that the structure of these companies diffused the authority of superiors; bosses had to understand that their managerial subordinates must also work actively with other functions, must rely on the participation and contributions of others, and hence were not entirely in control of the outcomes of their own tasks. Knowing this, bosses seemed more likely to grant those under them more autonomy, realizing that their subordinates must have more freedom to take any action that will translate into significant accomplishment because of their connections to other managers and other areas. We can call this a system of "passive sponsorship": superiors may be less likely to take direct action to assist in a manager's accomplishment, but they may offer a general mandate such as "Do what has to be done." Thus, time as a resource is also decentralized and under local control.

In innovating companies, then, a number of aspects of the organization's culture and structure make the potential for power — for the acquisition of information, support, and resources — available to middle-level managers and professionals.

THE CIRCULATION VERSUS THE FOCUSING OF POWER: A QUESTION OF BALANCE

Unlimited circulation of power in an organization without focus would mean that no one would ever get anything done beyond a small range of actions that people can carry out by themselves.[14] Besides, the very idea of infinite power circulation sounds to some of us like a system out of control, unguided, in which anybody can start nearly anything. (And probably finish almost nothing.)

Thus, the last key to successful middle-management innovation is to see how power gets pulled out of circulation and focused long enough to permit project completion. But here we find an organizational dilemma. Some of the focusing conditions are contrary to the circulating conditions, almost by definition. This is what makes organizational innovation so tricky; an organization has to constantly balance the circulation and the concentration of power.

While measures of complexity and diversity in an organization are positively related to initial *development* of innovations, they are often negatively related to eventual *adoption* of the innovation by the organization. Diversity gives the individual more latitude for discovery, but may make it difficult to get agreement on which of many proposals or demonstration projects should be implemented on a wider scale. Similarly, innovation is aided by *low* formalization at the initiation stage, when freedom to pursue untried possibilities is required, and by *high* formalization at the implementation stage, when singleness of organizational purpose is required.[15]

What all this means in practice is something else again. A corporation cannot shift from "decentralization" to "centralization" at a moment's notice. Even if it could, different projects would be at different stages, requiring opposite conditions. The issue is balance: never to disperse power fully but merely to temporarily loosen it, to allow units autonomy and single-minded focus when they need it while preventing segmentalism from setting in.*

General Electric Medical Systems is a good example of a balanced system, in which centralized planning mechanisms ensure sufficient focus for innovations to be developed which can and will be implemented.

First, Med Systems' headquarters retained control of large expenditures and remained central in giving guidance to the company by setting overall strategic direction. "Headquarters" often seemed to managers to speak with one voice, unlike the sense of temporary-but-detachable coalition one gets at the top of a looser system like Chipco. Some areas within the organization attracted more attention than others. A "hot" new product line had received considerable attention for three to four years and was still a focal point. One reason for this, at least initially, was that the division vice-president put most of the organization's resources into this product in order to develop it more quickly and capture a share of the market. This generated a tremendous amount of

*This is my answer to a question raised by a colleague about whether there could ever be "creative segmentalism," as when an R&D unit in the throes of an invention has to wall itself off. My answer is no. Temporary protection of activity boundaries or projects is not the same as segmentation, which implies the erection of permanent walls.

enthusiasm within this product-line organization but also jealousy in other departments. Diagnostics, for instance, the mainstay and oldest product line in Med Systems, seemed to have suffered the most from the attention given to the new area, and there was vocal resentment from several diagnostics managers.

The issue of product quality was another one on which top management focused attention. For a while there was high turnover of managers of this area until a handpicked "star" took over and remained in the position for about a year to a year and a half. Since then there had been more emphasis upon quality, not simply in the manufacturing stage but in design and engineering as well.

Second, Med Systems emphasized both short- and long-range planning at the middle-manager level as well as higher. Planning was done both for the immediate year ahead and for a five-year period, modified every year. Although several managers complained that Med Systems does not think well for the long run, middle managers' participation in creating a five-year plan enabled them to conceptualize accomplishments and changes that would benefit the organization for many years and might take years to consummate. Vertical communication around these plans served to guide the choice of projects in organizationally useful and connected directions.

Third, a clear financial "results orientation" limited requests for major projects. The ability to obtain essential resources or information was basically contingent upon the manager's promise, generally implicit, to produce something of benefit to the organization or the unit or person for whom one had negotiated. Sometimes this was a formal process — particularly when a manager used a routine approach for requesting large-scale financial backing for a significant task, and in such cases would invariably be asked to guarantee a 20-percent return on the money that was provided to him. There were two different kinds of time frames around which managers organized their tasks and planning. Some projects were linked to the long-term planning process or had a long time orientation. But many managers were also assigned "fast-track projects," with a great deal of attention from top management and easy access to vital resources to complete their tasks. These projects were often described with images conveying intensely high pressure and risk.

Fourth, higher-level managers did not abdicate in the face of all the delegation and teamwork emphasis in the company. They used their power to bend rules, to isolate a project from the matrix to give it sufficient autonomy to pursue an important task to completion. This was most likely to happen in connection with new-product development.

Fifth, there was stability and more formality in lower-level assignments. The company had a set of "permanent" subordinates over whom middle managers had legitimate authority; they were mobilizable for the managers' projects. In short, labor did not float freely; labor was clearly attached, in relatively fixed proportions, to different areas. The matrix stopped just below middle-manager level, and so did other power-circulating conditions such as crosscutting access. This may seem like an obvious point, but it is worth remembering. While the hierarchy was loosened at middle-manager levels by the matrix, it remained in full force below — perhaps why middle managers mentioned that some of their managerial reports behaved more "dictatorially" then they did. Most managerial projects were accomplished because the manager had a pool of clearly subordinate subordinates, even if he or she behaved toward them in participatory fashion.

Chipco, in contrast, had somewhat less overall concentration and focus, which showed up in a certain air of creative disorder, duplication, and waste accompanying the entrepreneurial spirit there. This relative "chaos" was both cause and effect of Chipco's innovativeness on my measures. One of the reasons for the large amount of structure/method innovation at Chipco was simply the need to invent mechanisms to cope with the lack of rationalization and routinization in the corporation.

Because so much power, or potential power, circulated so freely at Chipco, it was hard for some people to accumulate enough to sustain a significant project. Since nearly everyone at managerial levels seem to have the potential to start something, there was often an air of many people running off in all directions. What was the inducement for all of these potential entrepreneurs to join someone else's team — in the sense of real work, not just verbal support? Or if they did sign on, what would actually get them to meetings if they had other investments in other directions? (Chipco-ers were notorious for arriving at meetings late or missing as many as they attended.) Teamwork, despite its value, was sometimes hard at Chipco because of the "entrepreneurial," not the "bureaucratic" trap; as an observer put it, "The motivation and drive are to seek individual stardom. Besides, people are confident; they feel they *can* do it themselves if let alone." If bureaucrats isolate themselves to protect territory, entrepreneurs may do it to prove their worth.

High-level sponsorship or support for a project counted for *something* at Chipco, in terms of focusing people's attention, but much less than at Med Systems. Similarly, Chipco had a hierarchy, with levels of subordinates fanning out below middle managers, but it did not instill the same automatic respect as at Med Systems, and besides, there were more staff managers without assigned subordinates at Chipco. Furthermore, it was more difficult to isolate projects at Chipco than at Med Systems (perhaps because their issue *was* the organization), harder to buffer them against the effects of external changes.

The need for peer collaboration at Chipco and the infrequency of top-down authorization, compared with Med systems, made the selling process — "buy-in" — a lengthy, frustrating effort that was hard to sustain over time, as many managers complained. Because agreement in this complex, rapidly changing environment was usually oral, ill-defined, and situation-specific, a "yes — I'll support you" was often not a "yes" a few months later when new players and circumstances entered. Indeed, a safe way to say no was to say "yes" and not mean it. Everything took longer than expected. One manager groused, "Previously, it took me an hour to write a memo. Now it takes a hundred and twenty people-hours —thirty people in a meeting for four hours!"

In such cases, schedules slipped by several months, so that "buy-in" sometimes meant only, "you hang in there so long that there's agreement by default." (Twenty-one months for an average accomplishment involving peers may be too much for a company in the electronics industry; Med Systems, in contrast, often "fast-tracked" important projects.) A variant of the process, which Ken Farbstein called "railroad buy-in," was described by several managers in different departments as a way to speed things up. An idea and a "departure date" (sometimes an obligatory first meeting) would be proposed. Supposedly the train was leaving on that date, with one passenger or a full load. (But the initiating managers deemed it prudent in those cases to wait for the "boarding" of "important passengers.") In each of these cases, well over half the needed supporters got on board early enough, and each of the accomplishments was significant and successful.

Impatience with the process may be the reason one manager enlisted the support of a vice-president who could order people (his subordinates several levels lower) to help the manager search for information; but he still felt the need to define this as "buy-in," calling it "top-down buy-in."[16] Frequent jokes were told about the need to get "buy-in" even to go get coffee, go to the bathroom, or empty the wastebasket, reflecting impatience with the process.

The strong interpersonal communication networks and reliance on peer approval at Chipco sometimes caused competent people to be ignored or humbled. New on the job, one manager asked, "Whom should I talk to about X?" and was told, "Don't talk to Jim: talk to Bob Anderson instead." The manager did so and then explained, "You bypass someone you never met, and assume he's incompetent. People get slaughtered by innuendo . . . . If you're associated with a failing product, you're not to be spoken to." The need to maintain face explains the norm of never surprising, and hence embarrassing, another manager in a meeting. One manager commented, "A person may have some good ideas, but if he's not a good advocate who can present his case persuasively in a meeting with lots of critics, he won't succeed."

Newcomers, especially those from hierarchical firms, typically needed six months to a year to become comfortable with this, and often left in frustration. One manager, who had joined Chipco after years in a more traditional and hierarchical company, was given an award by co-workers for finally learning to master the lateral-communication process, years after arriving at Chipco. Meanwhile, he occasionally longed for the good old days, when life was simpler, even if less exciting and more constrained.

Decentralization at Chipco seemed both cause and effect of what some managers saw as an inability to make long-range plans. Where there is a sense of vast opportunity, there may be little perceived need for planning. The large number of people bargaining for resources and attention in a rapidly growing company made plans little more than goals, and long-range planning science fiction. Planners sometimes said they felt like "voices in the wilderness" with their plans a "necessary evil, subject to change at a moment's notice." This explained the high number of assigned tasks at Chipco which, despite their authorization by a boss, were still not strongly supported by top management. Occasionally, when higher-level management saw a problem but had no time to develop a solution, it would announce a problem and a haphazard solution which would be put into effect unless someone came up with a better one.

Not everything at Chipco worked this loosely, of course. Some areas were more structured than others: finance, manufacturing, and lower-level, nonexempt jobs in general. Still, Chipco had fewer focusing mechanisms than Med Systems. Except for product innovations that were likely to require a top-determined concentration of resources, many Chipco management innovations were vulnerable to replacement later. Despite a large number of innovations, most involved technological or work methods that often did not outlast the innovating manager.

Thus, a company can stimulate a great deal of initiative and enterprise without necessarily getting maximum payoff from managers' projects; power must be *focused* as well as available. In the ideal situation, there is a "marketplace" in which power circulates at middle levels of the organization, guided by a hierarchy above and serviced by a hierarchy below. The innovating organization, in effect, has a kind of quasi-free "market" sandwiched between two "hierarchies."

A CULTURE FOR ENTERPRISE AND INNOVATION

Some of the innovating companies, such as Chipco, GE Med Systems, and others in high-tech industries, have an automatic advantage in the innovation game: they are younger, growing faster, in more "modern" industries, in highly competitive markets, and have cultures of change. These are features associated with greater enterprise and innovativeness across a wide variety of organizations and societies. But I can also find examples of the same kinds of innovation-enhancing practices in older firms in more traditional industries characterized by integrative practices and cultures; Procter and Gamble is a frequently cited illustration.

Innovating companies in high-technology fields have also clearly benefited from the impact of location in certain geographic areas where they are surrounded by company-spawning institutions that both keep inventions flowing and also create competitive pressures on companies to offer the kinds of opportunities that attract and hold talent. The connections between companies because of common origins and exchange of personnel also serve to keep their practices current and ensure that they remain innovative.

In Boston, for example, three organization-creating organizations were particularly important to the growth of high-technology companies in the area: the Massachusetts Institute of Technology; Arthur D. Little, the world's largest technical consulting firm; and ARD, a publicly held venture-capital firm established in 1946. Lincoln Laboratories at MIT, established in 1951 to develop an air defense system for the United States, had spawned about fifty companies by 1966, according to Edward Roberts of MIT, who sat on the boards of a number of them; MIT's Research Laboratory for Electronics led to about fourteen companies; and its Instrumentation Lab, about thirty. In 1972, MIT even incorporated a development foundation to launch new companies that would use MIT technologies.[17] The companies "spun off" from others, as ex-employees formed their own. Sylvania's electronics division in Boston was the "parent" of perhaps thirty-nine companies; Data General was one of a number of companies founded by former Digital Equipment managers; and high-level executives carried expertise from one to another, like the vice-president of manufacturing at Wang Labs, who came from Digital. In Silicon Valley (Santa Clara County, California), Hewlett-Packard set the style, and Fairchild was the company spawner.

In other, smaller high-tech centers, there were similar patterns: Control Data was founded by an engineer from Sperry Univac; Cray Research by a former Control Data employee. Entrepreneurs often left one firm to start another in a chain still replicated today; for example, James Treybig was a marketing manager at Hewlett-Packard just before he founded Tandem Computers in 1976, and recently a new company, Stratus, was started by former Tandem employees.

It is thus the whole context, the whole system at the more innovating companies — and indeed, norms within their industries — that generates the enabling conditions for managerial enterprise, rather than a set of discretely separable features. Out of the design and structure of the organization arises a set of patterns of behavior and cultural expectations that guide what people in the system consider appropriate modes of operating. At Chipco, managers feel compelled to demonstrate their entrepreneurial spirit and to look for it in others, resisting "stifling" it with too much "bureaucracy." They know they are expected to invent or develop or plan something; this is the cultural image of success. At Med Systems, managers need to haul out their teamwork credentials and show how they use a team to get something done that improves on an already smooth-running operation. Such expectations or cultural "norms" guide behavior in a holistic sense; managers are not responding to a specific set of incentives or a concrete "program to stimulate innovation." This is perhaps why the matrix form of organization has not worked well in companies that do not support it with other culture changes.

The highest proportion of entrepreneurial accomplishments is found in the companies that are least segmented and segmentalist, companies that instead have integrative structures and cultures emphasizing pride, commitment, collaboration, and teamwork. The companies producing more managerial entrepreneurs have more complex structures that link people in multiple ways and encourage them to "do what needs to be done," within strategically guided limits, rather than confining themselves to the letter of their job. They are encouraged to take initiative and to behave cooperatively.

Ironically, though power seeking is a necessity for managers in innovation-producing companies, raw "power politics" seems much more common in the heavily segmented and bureaucratic companies like Southern and Meridian than in more entrepreneurial settings which encourage managerial innovation. The specific, delimited authority characteristic of more bureaucratized organizations not only creates an incentive for territorial protection and fighting across groups, but also creates the illusion that managers can, indeed, act alone, maximizing the value of their own areas without having to take the needs and concerns of others into account. In the more entrepreneurial settings, the very ambiguity surrounding the managers' areas and the absence of clear possession of all the resources, coupled with the nature of the issues that are being tackled, means that managers are impelled to behave more cooperatively in order to survive.

Thus, even though the system in innovating companies is more "politicized" in one sense — with managers having to capture power that they are not directly given in order to get anything done — it is also more "civil," at least on the surface. "Opponents" are won over by persistent, persuasive arguments; open communication is used to resolve debates, not back-stabbing. Perhaps the very publicness and openness of the battlegrounds — if that word even seems appropriate — makes "reason" prevail. It is hard for back-room bargaining or displays of unilateral power to occur when issues are debated in group settings. Public meetings require that concerns be translated into *specific* criticisms, each of which can then be countered with data or well-mounted arguments. And the heavy reliance on informal communication networks as a source of reputation places a check on dirty dealing. "Bad press" would ensure that such a person gets frozen out. An innovating company, then, begins to substitute a control system based on debate among peers for one based on top-down authority.

Life is by no means perfect in the innovating companies. Certainly not all managers have the same access to power; and systems promoting innovativeness also bring with them a new set of problems of managing participation, ambiguity, and complexity. But if life is not perfect, at least the tools exist for individuals to use to make corrective changes.

REFERENCES

1. Rosabeth Moss Kanter, *Men and Women of the Corporation,* New York: Basic Books, 1977, Chapter 7.

2. Ken Farbstein, "Achieving at Chipco: Supporting Managerial Enterprise in a High Technology Firm," in *Stimulating Innovation in Middle Management,* Cambridge, Mass.: Goodmeasure, Inc., 1982.

3. I am indebted to Ken Farbstein for much of the discussion of "buy-in" at "Chipco," as indicated in the text.

4. The overall determination of how much power anybody has in the organization is twofold: first, how much he or she gets of the three basic commodities (information, resources, and support), and second, what he or she manages to use of them. Organizational power is in this sense *transactional:* power exists as potential until someone makes a bid for it and then invests it in activities and people that will produce results. Three variables on both the acquisition and the investment side further determine relative power: the amount of each of these commodities, the number of suppliers of investments, and the certainty of transactions.

5. This has echoes of the practice of "mortification," or public display of weakness, that serves to build commitment in strong communities; see Rosabeth Moss Kanter, *Commitment and Community,* Cambridge, Mass.: Harvard University Press, 1972.

6. Organizations with more career opportunity appear to be more innovative in general; J. Victor Baldridge and Robert A. Burnham, "Organizational Innovation: Individual, Organizational, and Environmental Impacts," *Administrative Science Quarterly,* 20 (1975): 165-76. This is perhaps because of the motivational aspects of opportunity; Kanter, *Men and Women of the Corporation,* Chapter 6. Furthermore, those with upward-mobility aspirations are likely to be more innovative; Floyd Rogers and Everett Shoemaker, *Communication of Innovations,* New York: Free Press, 1971. But mobility patterns have more than an incentive value; a major contribution to innovation may lie in the information and support networks they create. The research literature is very clear on this point: there is more innovation where there is more "communication integration" — closer interpersonal contact or interconnections via interpersonal-communication channels. And innovators are more likely to have more exposure to such channels. Innovation may be facilitated, furthermore, to the extent that frequent mobility breaks up project groups and adds new blood. Ralph Katz's studies of R&D teams show that increasing group longevity (especially beyond five years) may lead to innovation-stifling outcomes (more behavioral stability, more selective exposure to information, greater group homogeneity, and reduced communication within and outside the project group — all

forms of what I call "segmentalism"). Katz, "Project Communication and Performance: An Investigation into the Effects of Group Longevity," *Administrative Science Quarterly,* in press.

7. In this present analysis, I am viewing mobility in terms of its organizational structure-forming impacts and not in terms of its effect on people — as it is usually considered, and as I did in *Men and Women of the Corporation,* Chapter 6.

8. Melvin L. Kohn, "Bureaucratic Man: A Portrait and an Interpretation," *American Sociological Review,* 38 (February 1973): 461-474.

9. "Teamwork Pays Off at Penney's," *Business Week,* April 12, 1982. See also Charles Burck, "The Intricate 'Politics' of the Corporation," *Fortune,* April 1975.

10. There is a great deal of agreement among researchers that specialization and functional differentiation in organizations aids innovation, even though specialization is a phenomenon we usually associate with bureaucracy. It is not so much that specialists themselves innovate — they may, indeed, be subject to a narrowness of focus — but that the existence of many different kinds of internal experts and professionals enlarges, in my terms, the marketplace of ideas. Some of the related characteristics that researchers claim are innovation-enhancing include: a larger number of professional specialties, greater specialization in jobs, and more administrative components. These coalesce into multiple demands, pushing for new ideas and practices to suit their professional interests, and in general, pushing for change. See Rogers and Shoemaker, *Communication of Innovations;* Baldridge and Burnham, "Organizational Innovation"; John R. Kimberly, "Managerial Innovations," in W. Starbuck, ed., *Handbook of Organization Design,* New York: Oxford, 1981; Gerald Zaltman, Robert Duncan, and Jonny Holbek, *Innovations and Organizations,* New York: Wiley, 1973. By placing a high value on knowledge, these groups also ensure that there is a diversity of sources of information to bring to bear on problems. Potential innovators are thus likely to scan more of the internal environment for ideas, and benefit, in turn, from the diversity of approaches which ensures that more of the external environment will have been scanned, with better ideas resulting.

"Chipco," Polaroid, Honeywell, and GE fit this model. There are large numbers of scientists and professionals, working on a range of distinctive products and technologies, divided into decentralized local units with their own administrative apparatus.

11. In political theory, the crosscutting ties of a pluralist system have long been held to prevent strong ideological divisions in electoral politics in the United States and to reinforce a consensus-seeking centrist orientation. If crosscutting ties aid political democracy, then perhaps they may aid "organizational democracy" too.

12. John Kimberly has argued that organization structure and process innovations are more likely when an organization is in distress, cutting back or looking for ways to improve internal operations. This gets weak support from the pattern at "Meridian Telephone," in Chapter 3; a high proportion of its innovations concerned the reorganization and reduction-in-force. But still, overall my findings indicate that even structure/method innovations are more common in the richer, less-distressed companies. Kimberly, "Managerial Innovations."

13. Frederick C. Klein, "Some Firms Fight Ills of Bigness by Keeping Employee Units Small," *Wall Street Journal,* February 5, 1982.

14. In my emerging theory of power-in-use, there are limits on how much power can be expanded, on how widely it can circulate. These limits include:

- *The size of the resource pool.* Several scholars argue that jockeying for advantage in organizations occurs when the resource pool is rather small to begin with, but when it is rather large and looks expandable, there is more cooperative and less oppositional activity.

- *The transformability or transferability of power commodities.* There are certain things that cannot really be passed on to other people, that cannot be transformed and used beyond the original intent residing in the object. The commodity can be spent in only certain places and certain ways: like a gift certificate. Investment of certain kinds of highly technical information in nontechnical parts of the organization, for example, could be wasted.

- *Too much counterproductive circulation of some of the commodities.* Organizational structure is one way we have of channeling the circulation of resources, information, and support so that organizational purposes are served. Not all directions are equally possible, and there is not equal access to these commodities from all parts of the system.

- *The capacity of components of an organization to process, or act upon, supplies.* Information overload, too much noise in the system, can also be dysfunctional. Attempting to expand power by circulating all information to everybody can make the system break down.

- *Differential time span involved in acquiring certain kinds of supplies.* Resources, information, and support come in a variety of forms, some of which take longer to produce than others. Technical knowledge as a kind of information, for example, often takes a great deal of time to acquire, and the replacement costs of producing it again can be very high. Experts can often gain more power in organizations from the fact that they have already spent the time to get the knowledge, and for other people to get equivalent amounts would take much too long. So acquisition time for cumulative knowlege — professional expertise — places a limit on power expansion.

- *The capacity of the organization to handle new activities.* Even the largest organization cannot do everything at once, and this places limits on the expansion of power via the circulation of such commodities as support. The boundary condition for legitimacy of support seems to be the capacity of the organization to handle all the things people would do with the support they get. Each of us may have a proposal for a project we want our function to carry out, but the ultimate limit on how many people can get legitimate authority to do theirs may have more to do with organizational capacity than with the desires of the individuals involved to limit power. (The implication for entrepreneurial activity is clear; an organization has limits on the amount of such enterprise it can realistically incorporate.)

15. Zaltman, Duncan, Holbek, *Innovations.* Decentralization/centralization measures show some of the same kind of fluctuation with phase, but the findings are less clear-cut. There seems to be more initiation of innovation in decentralized systems, but much less adoption; John L. Pierce and André Delbecq, "Organization Structure, Individual Attitude, and Innovation," *Academy of Management Review* (January 1977): 27-37. There is evidence that more "participation" favors innovation — a positive relationship between participation in decision making and rate of organizational change in core activities, and a negative relationship between power concentration in a hierarchy and change rate; Hage and Aiken, "Program Change." Kimberly argued that formalization and centralization in a company reduce the probabilities of adoption of innovation, holding that there is greater receptivity to innovation in organic organizations with minimum procedural specification, minimum routinization of behavior, and widespread internal communication — just the conditions that fit my integrative model; Kimberly, "Managerial Innovations." But more decentralization can also raise the rate of conflict and disagreement, which interferes with implementation; Zaltman, Duncan, Holbek, *Innovations.* This is perhaps why one study finds more innovativeness in organizations with conflict-prevention committees; Baldridge and Burnham, "Organizational Innovation." By and large, then, the evidence for the effects of decentralization versus centralization is mixed — if we can even make the distinction between two ends of the same process anyway. Centralized power concentration seems to help in the adoption of innovations that require the organization, as opposed to individual units only, to change, as I am arguing here.

16. This is an interesting example of the institutionalization process: persistent use of a label with important symbolic meaning even where it clearly does not apply.

17. Gene Bylinsky, *The Innovation Millionaires,* New York: Scribner's, 1976. For a theoretical account of this process, see Jack W. Brittain and John H. Freeman, "Organizational Proliferation and Entity Dependent Selection," in J. R. Kimberly and R. H. Miles, eds., *The Organizational Life Cycle,* San Francisco: Jossey-Bass, 1980, pp. 291-338.

The Leader~Manager
BIBLIOGRAPHY

BIBLIOGRAPHY

Ainsworth-Land, George. "New Rules for Growth and Change." Eden Prairie, MN.: Wilson Learning Corporation, 1984.

Baird, Lloyd, and Kathy Kram. "Career Dynamics: Managing the Superior/Subordinate Relationship." *Organizational Dynamics* (Spring 1983).

Barnes, Louis B. "Managing the Paradox of Organizational Trust." *Harvard Business Review* (March-April 1981).

Bennis, Warren. "Four Traits of Leadership." *The Hay Group Lecture*, October, 1983.

Berlew, David E. "Leadership and Organizational Excitement." *California Management Review*, vol. XVII, no. 2, pp. 21-30, 1974.

Bradford, David, and Allan Cohen. "Overarching Goals." In *Managing for Excellence*. New York: John Wiley and Sons, Inc., 1984.

Cammann, Cortlandt, and David A. Nadler. "Fit Control Systems To Your Management Style." *Harvard Business Review* (January-February 1976).

Davis, Stanley M. "Transforming Organizations: The Key to Strategy Is Context." *Organizational Dynamics* (Winter 1982).

Enright, John. "Change and Resilience." Eden Prairie, MN.: Wilson Learning Corporation, 1984.

Fairbank, John A., and Donald M. Prue. "Developing Performance Feedback Systems." In *Handbook of Organizational Behavior Management*. New York: Wiley, 1982.

Greiner, Larry E. "Evolution and Revolution As Organizations Grow." *Harvard Business Review* (July-August 1972).

Grove, Andrew S. "Task-Relevant Maturity." In *High Output Management*. United Kingdom: Random House and Souvenir Press, 1983.

Harrison, Roger. "Strategies for a New Age." *Human Resources Management* (Fall 1983).

Herzberg, Frederick. "One More Time: How Do You Motivate Employees?" *Harvard Business Review* (January-February 1968).

Kanter, Rosabeth Moss. "Empowerment." In *The Change Masters*. New York: Simon & Schuster, 1983.

Kanter, Rosabeth Moss. "Transformations in the American Corporate Environment, 1960s-1980s." In *The Change Masters*. New York: Simon & Schuster, 1983.

Kerr, Steven. "On the Folly of Rewarding A, While Hoping for B." *Academy of Management Journal*. Vol. 18, No. 4, December, 1975.

Lashbrook, William B. "Management As a Performance System." Eden Prairie, MN.: Wilson Learning Corporation, 1984.

Lawler, Edward E. "For a More Effective Organization — Match the Job to the Man." *Organizational Dynamics* (Summer 1974).

Levinson, Harry. "Appraisal of What Performance?" *Harvard Business Review* (July-August 1976).

Likert, Rensis, and Jane Gibson Likert. "Integrative Goals and Consensus in Problem Solving." In *New Ways of Managing Conflict*. New York: McGraw-Hill, 1976.

Lippitt, Gordon L., and Warren H. Schmidt. "Crises in a Developing Organization." *Harvard Business Review* (November-December 1967).

Michael, Donald N. "On the Importance of Feedback and the Resistances to It." In *On Learning to Plan — And Planning to Learn*. San Francisco: Jossey-Bass, 1976.

Pascale, Richard Tanner, and Anthony G. Athos. "Great Companies Make Meaning." In *The Art of Japanese Management*. New York: Simon & Schuster, 1981.

Phillips, Julien R. and Allan A. Kennedy. "Shaping and Managing Shared Values." San Francisco, CA.: McKinsey & Company, 1980.

Schon, Donald A. "Deutero-Learning in Organizations: Learning for Increased Effectiveness." *Organizational Dynamics* (Summer 1975).

Thomas, Roosevelt. "Managing Work Relationships Through the Psychological Contract." Decatur, GA.: R. Thomas and Associates, 1978.

Toffler, Alvin. "Beyond The Break-Up Of Industrial Society: Political And Economic Strategies In The Context Of Upheaval." New York: New York, 1980.

Yankelovich, Daniel, and John Immerwahr. "Why the Work Ethic Isn't Working." New York: Public Agenda Foundation, 1983.

ACKNOWLEDGMENTS

The preparation and production of *The Leader-Manager* was possible only because of the dedication of several outstanding people. Joan Poritsky was an invaluable colleague helping to identify potential contributions to the collection, negotiating permissions, and directing the entire preparation effort. Ellie Winninghoff contributed essential research and writing assistance. Ken Kylie's preliminary literature search was invaluable, as was Brad Bradley's graphics' contribution. Nickie Dillon, Kathy Pruno, and Joan Torkildson edited the volume, and Catherine Zimba coordinated the graphics design and printing.

John N. Williamson, Ed. D.
September, 1984

About the Editor:

John Williamson's expertise and professional capabilities cover a broad range of related fields.

He earned his B.A. degree in mathematics/economics at Duke University, studied at the Carnegie-Mellon Graduate School of Industrial Administration, and then attended Harvard University where he secured an M.A.T. in education/mathematics and an Ed.D. in education/organizational development. His academic honors include acceptance into Phi Beta Kappa and the Order of Red Friars at Duke University and a Citation for the Outstanding Doctoral Thesis of the Graduating Class at Harvard.

Dr. Williamson is currently Vice-President, Strategic Business Services, with Wilson Learning Corporation, Eden Prairie, Minnesota. He is responsible for the design of new generic programs that focus principally on assisting corporations and their leadership to deal strategically and adaptively with change.

Previously, he was President of Manifest Learning Systems, Tiburon, California; Director of Planning and Policy Development for the National Institute of Education, Washington, D.C.; on the faculties of the University of Southern California and the Oregon College of Education; and Policy Analyst for the Rand Corporation.

Dr. Williamson has also been a member of the Editorial Boards for the *Harvard Education Review* and the *Educational Forum.* His articles have appeared in a number of professional journals, and he has spoken at several national conferences on organization development, corporate wellness programs, school reform, adult learning, and national educational policy.